African
Oral Literature

African
Oral Literature

Backgrounds, Character, and Continuity

Isidore Okpewho

Indiana University Press
Bloomington and Indianapolis

The paper used in this publication meets the minimum requirements of American
National Standard for Information Sciences—Permanence of Paper for Printed
Library Materials, ANSI Z39.48-1984.

Manufactured in the United States of America

Library of Congress Cataloging-in-Publication Data
Okpewho, Isidore.
    African oral literature : backgrounds, character, and continuity /
Isidore Okpewho.
        p. cm.
    Includes bibliographical references (p.   ) and index.
    ISBN 0-253-34167-1 (cloth : alk. paper). — ISBN 0-253-20710-X
(paper : alk. paper)
    1. Folk literature—Africa—History and criticism.   2. Oral
tradition—Africa.   I. Title.
GR350.037   1992   91-25671
398.2'096—dc20

2 3 4 5

In cherished and grateful memory
of my mother

REGINA NWANYIMGBO ATTOH OKPEWHO

Contents

Preface

So much work has been done on African oral literature in the two decades since the publication of Ruth Finnegan's epoch-making and immensely useful *Oral Literature in Africa* that there is need for a more up-to-date critical introduction such as I have tried to provide in this book. In addition to the insights I have gained from the extensive fieldwork and analyses undertaken by my students (graduate and undergraduate) and myself over the years, I have benefited from the light shed on various aspects of the subject by colleagues both inside and outside Africa, at conferences and seminars and in publications. Unlike my two earlier studies (1979, 1983), which were intended to correct certain misapprehensions about two key concepts (epic and myth) in African oral literature, the present book is an attempt to crystalize the benefits gained from years of intellectual dialogue and to put the central issues of the subject in much clearer focus.

The contributions of this book are, I hope, clear enough from the contents. Although chapters 1 and 4–8 revisit issues explored by earlier discussions of African oral literature, I have tried to provide a more systematic schematization of the salient topics and to incorporate critical insights derived from publications that have appeared in the past two decades. But I consider the greater contributions to be contained in chapters 2, 3, and 9–12. Chapters 2 and 3 attempt a detailed examination of the creative genius and personality of the oral artist and the circumstances within which that genius works. The discussions in those chapters are useful because they try to provide a proper understanding of the ways and nature of oral creativity and so give us clearer guidelines for an assessment of the continuities and discontinuities between oral and literate culture. These relationships are explored at considerable length in chapter 9, which deals mainly with oral-dramatic productions in both rural and urban settings, and chapter 10. These chapters examine the vibrancy of modern African literature (acknowledged by the recent awarding of the Nobel Prize for Literature to two African writers) against the backgrounds of the oral literature.

Chapters 11 and 12 try to suggest what we should do if we are to avoid the mistakes made by earlier students of this subject and to advance the frontiers of its study. Since most of those recording African oral literature are native Africans or non-Africans who have lived long enough in African communities to acquire an adequate competence in the host language and culture, the fieldwork guides in chapter 11 especially are intended as a clear departure from the approach of those who treated the cultures and traditions they studied as alien if not inferior.

Perhaps I should expatiate on the terms *critical* and *literature*. This study has concentrated its focus on evidence provided mainly from sub-Saharan Africa and the Horn. But even within this manageable zone, any effort to cover every culture or society seems to me an unfortunate ambition given the ever-present risk of being repetitive and diffuse. Besides, most of the texts of African oral literature published so far are heavily flawed by disciplinary and other biases and so offer very limited analytical insights. I have therefore opted for a selective use of the more dependable texts from a realistically broad cultural geography and for a sufficiently detailed critical analysis.

The bias toward literary analysis is no doubt supported by the general consensus that this aspect of African folklore belongs squarely in the province of literature. Indeed, those scholars from disciplines as varied as history and social anthropology who have been concerned primarily with the elements of personal (stylistic) bias and of symbolism in the oral texts—such as Vansina (1965 and even more, 1985) and Beidelman (1961)—have been honest enough to recognize that these elements are of a fundamentally literary character. The analyses given to various texts in this book, which show clearly enough my recognition of the various contexts (historical, sociological, and so forth) of their provenance, can be no more than exploratory in a study of this nature; for more detailed insights I refer readers to monographs devoted to specific traditions, such as Seitel 1980 and Jackson 1982. The pursuit of "total analysis" is, however, an ungainful illusion. I have shown a bias for performatory and other literary insights because I believe that an understanding of art is the surest key to an understanding of culture.

In a study of this scope, my indebtedness is understandably incalculable. My numerous references in the book to colleagues both personal and professional will no doubt indicate how much credit is due to whom, while the shortcomings remain mine alone. I must, however, salute my colleagues and students, especially at Ibadan, whose works have both qualified and advanced my insights on this subject. I also acknowledge with awe the stamina and good disposition of Israel Akiode, who typed every word of the original manuscript of this book. But my warmest salute goes to my beloved wife, Obi, and our four adorable children—Ediru, Ugo, Afigo, and Onome—in whose company even the most formidable task becomes a labor of love.

I gratefully acknowledge the following permissions for the use of extracts:

From *Horn of My Love,* by Okot p'Bitek, published by Heinemann Publishers, Ltd., 1974.

From *Arrow of God,* by Chinua Achebe, published by Octopus Library, 1964.

From *Oral Literature of the Maasai,* by N. Kipury, and *Myths and Legends of the Swahili,* by Jan Knappert, both published by Heinemann Kenya, Ltd., 1983 and 1970, respectively.

The Kipsigis lament ("Send a message") and the Mozambique song "I suffer, I do" appear in *Oral Poetry from Africa,* published by Longman Group UK, 1983, and are reprinted here by permission.

From *Drumming in Akan Communities of Ghana,* by J. H. Kwabena Nketia, published by the Publishing House, University of Ghana, 1963.

From *See So That We May See,* by Peter Seitel, and *The Epic of Son-Jara,* by John William Johnson, both published by Indiana University Press, 1980 and 1986, respectively.

"The Battle of Tumu Tumu Hill" is reprinted courtesy of Granada Publishing, Ltd.

The Moshoeshoe poem is reprinted by permission of Oxford University Press.

From *Popular Culture of East Africa,* by Taban lo Liyong, published by Longman Kenya, 1972.

From *The Palm-Wine Drinkard,* by Amos Tutuola, published by Faber and Faber, 1952. Reprinted by permission of Faber and Faber.

From *Myth in Africa,* by Isidore Okpewho, published by Cambridge University Press, 1983.

From *Ogun Abibiman,* by Wole Soyinka, published by Rex Collings, Ltd., 1976.

Extracts from *Content and Form of Yoruba Ijala* (1966), by S. A. Babalola; *Limba Stories and Storytelling* (1967), by Ruth Finnegan; *The Heroic Recitations* (1964), by H. F. Morris; *The Xhosa Ntsomi* (1975), by Harold Scheub; and *The Dinka and Their Songs* (1973) all appear by permission of Oxford University Press.

From *Spirit Mediumship and Society in Africa,* edited by J. Beattie and J. Middleton, published by Routledge, 1969.

From *Sunjata: Three Mandinka Versions,* by Gordon Innes, published by the School of Oriental and African Studies, University of London, 1974.

From "African Puppets," by J. Chesnais, in *World Theatre,* a publication of the International Theatre Institute, Paris, and UNESCO.

Part One

Backgrounds and Resources

1. The Study of African Oral Literature

Before getting down to the main topic of this chapter, it will be useful to settle a few issues relating to terms used in our subject.

What Is "Oral Literature"?

The subject of our study is identified by various scholars by such terms as *oral literature, orature, traditional literature, folk literature,* and *folklore.* Perhaps the most predominant element in these terms is the word *literature,* and we may as well tackle that element first. It is true that nowadays the word is generally used to cover any volume of written or printed text. When I say to a student, for instance, "Let me have the available literature on bribery," I mean that the student should bring everything that can be found written on that subject, including newspaper articles and tribunal judgments. But of course the word *literature* is more commonly used in a restricted sense to refer to creative texts that appeal to our imagination or to our emotions (such as stories, plays, and poems), not to factual texts such as newspaper reports or historical records, however attractively written these may be. Chinua Achebe's *Things Fall Apart* and Okot p'Bitek's *Song of Lawino* would qualify to be called works of literature, but E. J. Alagoa's *History of the Niger Delta,* being mainly a record of facts, would not.

If we accept the idea of literature as a creative text, we will find that the other words used for qualifying it are simply attempts to emphasize one aspect or other of the subject. *Oral literature* is now the most commonly used term for the subject. It simply means "literature delivered by word of mouth" and has turned out to be a very useful concept for those scholars interested in examining the cultural relationships between those who can read and write and those who cannot—or, in a more professional language, between orality and literacy. The idea is that there are certain techniques which may be used to good effect in oral literature but which may not work in written literature; on the other hand, there are certain techniques and elements in written literature which may be seen as borrowings or survivals from oral literature. These various techniques and elements have emerged as an interesting subject of comparative study, and in chapter 10 we shall look into this subject to some extent.

Orature is a recent but seldom used term that again emphasizes the oral character of the literature. *Traditional literature* puts emphasis on the fact that this form of literature comes from the past and is handed down (Latin *trado*) from one generation to another. Sometimes a prejudice is implied, in the sense that the material is simply passed on from mouth to mouth and nothing really new is ever added to it. Some earlier scholars actually felt this way, but the idea has since been dismissed by more recent study. *Folk literature* identifies the creators of this literature as the folk, by which was frequently meant the common, uneducated people mostly in villages or rural communities. Nowadays we collect some of our most exciting pieces of oral literature from performers who live in cities and some not-so-rustic towns who have at least a primary school education and have traveled far and wide (even outside Africa) with their performances.

The word *folklore* implies much more than just literature and in some quarters underplays the literary aspect of what the folk do. It was first used by the Englishman William John Thoms in a letter he wrote to the *Athenaeum* at a time when the study of traditional culture was attracting a lot of attention in Britain and Europe. Let me quote the first part of this letter to show Thoms's and his generation's understanding of the word.

> Your pages have so often given evidence of the interest which you take in what we in England designate as Popular Antiquities, or Popular Literature (though by-the-bye it is more a Lore than a Literature, and would be most aptly described by a good Saxon compound, Folklore,—*the Lore of the People*)—that I am not without hopes of enlisting your aid in garnering the few ears which are remaining, scattered over that field from which our forefathers might have gathered a goodly crop.
>
> No one who has made the manners, customs, observances, superstitions, ballads, proverbs, etc., of the olden time his study, but must have arrived at two conclusions:—the first, how much that is curious and interesting in these matters is now entirely lost—the second, how much may yet be rescued by timely exertion. (Quoted in Dundes 1965: 4)

Two important insights may be gathered from this classic statement. First, because of the simplicity of the lives of the folk from whom the materials were gathered— because of their level of education and sophistication—they were considered incapable of producing anything that may be considered "literature" in the same sense that one would see the works of Shakespeare. For a long time the study of oral literature was governed by the sort of prejudice which Thoms shows here in his description of "Popular Literature" as being "more a Lore than a Literature," i.e., more of an ordinary body of information than an artistic text. This prejudice has, of course, since been modified if not altogether abandoned.

The second point made by Thoms establishes the concept of folklore: "manners, customs, observances, superstitions, ballads, proverbs, etc." are roughly its constituents. Oral literature—which comprises riddles, puns, tongue-twisters, proverbs, recitations, chants, songs, and stories—represents only the verbal aspect of folklore, and I am happy to quote this definition by two East African scholars:

> Oral literature may be defined as those utterances, whether spoken, recited or sung, whose composition and performance exhibit to an appreciable degree the artistic charac-

teristics of accurate observation, vivid imagination and ingenious expression. (Nandwa and Bukenya 1983: 1)

Other aspects of folklore include traditional methods of cooking, architecture, medicine, and dressmaking as well as religion or ritual, art, instrumental music, and dance. The total body of information which a community possesses about all these things is its folklore.[1]

Sometimes the use of the term *oral literature* and *folklore* is a little confusing. In many cases the latter is used when only the former is meant, i.e., a scholar may praise a Yoruba or Kikuyu proverb as an example of the poetic quality of the people's folklore. This is something of a generalization, for if we examined various aspects of the material culture of the same people (e.g., their traditional architecture and weaving) there might be nothing quite so "poetic" about them. Such generalizations, whereby a part is made to represent the whole, are quite frequent in literature and are perhaps excusable. Whatever errors may have been made by scholars in the early history of this subject, however, it is important to note that the folklore of a people consists essentially of two kinds of activity: what these people traditionally say (e.g., songs, proverbs, tales) and what they traditionally do (weaving, dance, rituals).

Having examined the issue of definition, we may now trace some of the history of our subject. It was necessary to cite the classic statement by Thoms because it gave us an insight into the problems encountered in the collection and study of African oral literature for over a century, from the generation of Thoms to the 1960s. Let us now see how these problems have arisen and been tackled by examining the three major interests that have so far governed the study of African oral literature.

An Interest in Culture

The serious study of what has come to be known as oral literature began in nineteenth-century Europe. This study was part of a general concern which European intellectuals showed in the whole question of human culture: what are its origins and characteristics, and what steps are to be taken to teach the best examples of culture to those members of the human race who show the least awareness of it? This general study of human culture is known as ethnology.

One group of scholars who set themselves the task of answering questions about the origins of human culture are the evolutionists. The concept of evolution is rooted in the belief that all biological species have over a long period been undergoing various changes until they have reached the form in which we find them today. The pioneer in this study was Charles Darwin (1809–1882), and his arguments had a great influence on students of culture such as his fellow Englishmen Edward Burnet Tylor (1832–1917) and James George Frazer (1854–1941). Following Darwin, these students of culture believed in certain fundamental principles regarding the development of human culture: there is one human race and one human mind spread out across the face of the earth; if we examine two societies at the same stage of cultural development, we will find that their folklore (folktales, folk songs, rituals, etc.) will reveal very much the same qualities; and consequently, to understand any aspect of the traditional literature or culture in any society it will help to compare it with a similar aspect in another society.

Frazer pursued the comparative study of folklore as far as it could go, and his work has had a deep impact on the growth of interest in African oral literature. His classic work *The Golden Bough* began as a narrow research into the origins of magical and religious rituals among a small tribe in Italy. But this modest project grew steadily until it covered thirteen volumes because Frazer went on to record bits of evidence from numerous "primitive" communities throughout the world to prove the point he was making about his Italian case: that the origin of religion would be found in the magical rites of "primitive" man.

Frazer gathered a great deal of his evidence from Africa. By the turn of the century, many British scholars were going out to newly created British colonies on the African continent as administrators. Some of these scholar-administrators had been students or colleagues of Frazer's, and he encouraged them to collect pieces of evidence of traditional customs and oral literature from the communities which they governed. Consequently, *The Golden Bough* and other writings by Frazer are filled with references to the traditional literature of numerous African ethnic groups, such as the Egyptians, the Nubians, the Bantu, the Akan, and the Yoruba. Of the numerous colonial scholars who collected African oral literature under the encouragement of Frazer, perhaps the most notable were John Roscoe among the Baganda (Uganda), Edwin Smith and Andrew Dale among the Ila (Zambia), the Reverend Henri Junod among the Tonga (South Africa), Robert Rattray among the Akan (Ghana) and Hausa (Nigeria), and P. Amaury Talbot among the Ekoi (Nigeria).

In their own books these scholars examined various texts of tales, songs, riddles, proverbs, and other forms of oral literature, as well as the people who performed them, as part of a general program of studying "primitive" societies. The ultimate aim of that program was to study the early forms out of which aspects of modern culture developed and the stages through which they passed in this development. These scholars frequently came to the conclusion that people in Africa were essentially like people anywhere else in the world. H. Chatelain, who studied folktales from Angola, was convinced, for instance, that African folklore generally is a "branch of one universal tree." But certain fundamental problems of approach in this ethnological study led to an unfortunate conclusion and consequently prevented the scholars from recognizing as literature the texts that they collected.

First, their evolutionist way of looking at culture convinced them that whatever texts they found were simply survivals of earlier ones; as these texts were passed down from one generation to another they must have lost certain qualities which appealed to their original owners, and whatever survived must have been weakened versions of the original texts. Since the scholars were mainly interested in collecting details and ideas in these texts that gave them an insight into the nature of man and the history of human culture, they paid little attention to whatever stylistic merits the texts had; in many cases, indeed, they simply contented themselves with bare summaries of the contents.

The second problem of approach is closely connected with the first. The evolutionists believed that since the texts of the oral tradition had passed from one mouth to another and from one generation to another, we could no longer speak of one author or creator for any one of them. We could only see each text as the common property of the community and as a product of joint or communal authorship. As a story passed from one narrator to another, each narrator added his or her own touch to it; and since the tales bore no signatures, there was frequently no way of distinguishing one person's touches from another's.

These errors of judgment arose primarily because of the improper method of collecting and especially of recording the texts. If a tale is presented only in summary, many of the stylistic touches which the narrator put into it to please an audience will obviously be missed. And unless one version of a story is compared carefully with another version of it, a scholar will not be able to discover that each version bears the stamps of character and technique peculiar to its narrator. Such stamps are among the qualities which identify any text as literature. But the evolutionists were so obsessed with the concept of the development of culture and the history of cultural ideas that they lost the opportunity for appreciating them.

Another group of scholars interested in the history of culture who have had some influence on the study of African oral literature are the diffusionists. This group was opposed to the evolutionists in a fundamental way. The evolutionists believed that if two tales from two societies showed similar elements and a similar pattern, it was because human beings all over the world thought alike and the tales reflected the same stage of cultural development in both societies. The diffusionists, on the contrary, believed that where such similarities occured it could only be because at some time in the distant past the two societies had some contact with one another which caused the borrowing of certain cultural ideas by one of them from the other. To make it easy to trace the paths of movement of these ideas from one society to another, diffusionists mapped out the world into "culture areas," grouping peoples on the basis of the kinds of similarities that they showed in language, belief systems, customs, climate, and other aspects of existence.

Diffusionist studies of folklore grew as a result of the interest shown by European scholars in finding the origins and the paths of movement of European languages, customs, and other forms of culture. It became widely accepted by many of these scholars that these origins were to be found in India, and they wanted to find out how far across the world this large "Indo-European" culture had spread. Like Frazer and other evolutionist scholars, these diffusionists engaged in comparative studies of folklore throughout the world. Much of this work was done under the encouragement of the German brothers Jacob and Wilhelm Grimm, who themselves collected and published many folktales from India as well as from their own country.

The Grimm brothers also had a few things to say about tales from other parts of the world. In the introduction to their classic work *Household Tales,* for instance, they expressed the view that if any similarities were found between tales told in Africa and those told in Europe, the former should be seen as offshoots of the parent Indo-European culture. The Grimm brothers made such a statement because they were working under the prejudice that culture can only spread from a superior to an inferior people, not the other way round—and Africa was of course considered racially inferior to Europe. The position of the Grimms was echoed by the American diffusionist scholar Stith Thompson. In his authoritative book *The Folktale* he suggested that where similarities existed between European and African folktales, they could be explained by the probability that the Europeans brought the tales with them to Africa during the period of the slave trade (Thompson 1946: 438).

Diffusionist research into African folktales still goes on, though not with the same zeal as in the days of the Grimms and Thompson; happily, too, the prejudice which guided the earlier generations of scholars has been mostly abandoned. These days diffusionist scholars occupy themselves with studying the distribution of tale units within the various "culture areas" of Africa or with earnest debate on the African origins of tales told among the blacks of the northern and southern United States. Whatever the stage or shade of research we are dealing with, however, diffusionist scholarship shows a fundamental disregard for the literary qualities of the folktale. Unlike the evolutionists, the diffusionists look closely at versions of a tale and have a better opportunity of discovering the interesting differences between one version and another. But instead, they concentrate on the similarities in constituent units (motifs) which these tales employ. For them, the stylistic differences between tales do not matter. Consequently, like the evolutionists, they content themselves quite often with the bare summaries of tales so long as these summaries show the motifs that constitute the tales. Although their methods of research differ somewhat from those employed by the evolutionists, the diffusionists are nevertheless equally obsessed with the idea of the origins of culture. Such an obsession has left them little room to consider the literary qualities of oral literature.

One final concern with culture may be considered here. The high period of ethnological research in Africa coincided with the period of European colonial activity, and some of the great ethnologists of that generation were colonial administrators: Roscoe in Uganda, Rattray in the Gold Coast (Ghana), Talbot in Nigeria. It is well known that the colonial powers that came to Africa were primarily interested in seeking raw materials (cocoa, palm oil, groundnuts, copper) for their growing industries and outside markets for their finished products. But these powers pretended that they were bringing culture (in the sense of European civilization) to a "primitive" race of people. Africa was then seen as a "dark continent" which must be opened up with the light of European culture, considered at that time to be the highest mark of human achievement. The two arms of that culture were technology and Christianity. To spread ideas of Christian conduct, the colonial administrators worked closely with the Christian missions in Africa. The colonial scholars also directed their efforts along lines which in many ways coincided with the objectives of the Christian missions. The linguists among them studied the grammatical systems of the African languages closely and proceeded to translate some of the major texts of Christian doctrine such as the Bible and the hymn books into the indigenous languages. But a more interesting effort may be seen in what the scholars did with the texts of oral literature. Not only were they quick to give credit to those texts which uphold good conduct, such as the morality tales which abound in the continent. It would seem that in addition they did not particularly encourage the study of texts which showed some evidence of moral laxity. In his introduction to a collection of Ekoi (southeastern Nigerian) folktales, Talbot, for instance, remarks on the "cleanliness of tone" of the tales while pointing out that "only one sentence . . . has been expurgated" from the texts recorded (1921: 337).

We can see clearly from this latter point how much the oral literature of Africa suffered at the hands of these early scholars. Apart from reducing the texts to bare summaries which contained mainly what were considered the essential points, the scholars also took the liberty to edit the texts so as to get rid of material they considered "unclean" by European standards. It is quite possible that the narrators from whom Talbot collected his stories, knowing full well how much these colonial educators frowned on "unclean" material, made every effort to restrain themselves from using the kind of language they would have used under normal circumstances to attract an audience. In chapter 4 we shall see to what extent oral performers could indulge their language to please the audience. At the time that Talbot was writing, however, the peculiar nature of African oral literature could not be fully recognized because the colonial government felt it had a mission to "civilize" the African peoples away from their "crude," "primitive" habits of life and expression.

An Interest in Society

By the end of the first thirty years of the twentieth century, scholarly study had moved from a more general interest in culture to a more specific interest in society. As more and more scholars visited and lived in various traditional societies throughout the world, they became increasingly aware of the danger in making general statements about human nature and human culture. They felt that these general statements often ignored certain specific details of life such as language and other habits which make one society different from another; for them, these differences were more interesting than the similarities. They therefore preferred to study every society in its own right and to record as much of the various aspects of the people's folklore as possible.

Among the founding fathers of this approach were Bronislaw Malinowski, a Polish-born British anthropologist; A. R. Radcliffe-Brown, also a British anthropologist; and the American Franz Boas. Malinowski and Radcliffe-Brown studied communities in the Pacific—in the Trobriand Islands and Andaman Islands, respectively—and wrote extensively about these peoples. Boas studied and wrote on Native American communities, especially the Kwakiutl of the Northwest. Other scholars studied and discussed African societies: E. E. Evans-Pritchard on the Nuer and Geoffrey Lienhardt on the Dinka, both communities in the Sudan; the American William Bascom on the Yoruba and S. F. Nadel on the Nupe, both in Nigeria; the Frenchman Marcel Griaule on the Dogon of Burkina Faso; and so on.

Earlier scholars had also lived among individual societies and written extensively on them: Rattray on the Akan (Ghana), Talbot on the Ekoi (Nigeria), Roscoe on the Baganda (Uganda), and so on. But these scholars were guided by evolutionist ideas, whereas the scholars inspired by Malinowski were hardly interested at all in the histories of the cultures they studied. They concentrated on the things—including the oral literature—each community did here and now. For them, the usefulness of these things helped to preserve the community as a social unit. Of the various differences of approach between these groups of scholars, this one is particularly worth noting:

whereas the evolutionists saw the folklore of a present society as a survival from the past (mostly misunderstood by the users) and tried to speculate on what the 'original form might have been, Malinowski's generation saw it in terms of its usefulness for the society—its functions. This newer approach is much more dependable than that of Frazer's generation. Its advantage is in putting emphasis on the known rather than on the unknown.

Of the various societal functions which the sociologically inclined scholars of African oral literature have identified, we may mention a few. In his study of the poetry of divination *(ifa)* among the Yoruba of Nigeria, Bascom emphasizes the usefulness of this vast body of chants as an encyclopedia of the people's wisdom and their relevance for present-day needs and problems among the Yoruba (Bascom 1959). In examining tales of origin among the Kimbu of Tanzania, Aylward Shorter is convinced that these "historical charters" are particularly useful in helping the people keep a record of the various stages of their formation as a social group (Shorter 1969). Proverbs have been studied among various African societies—for instance, by J. C. Messenger among the Anang of Nigeria (1958: 229–307) and J. B. Christensen among the Fante of Ghana (1958: 232–43)—for the several ways in which they help to establish the authority of a statement or a custom in situations like court cases or contests for a chieftaincy. Numerous other publications give similar emphasis to the function of oral literature in the contemporary lives of various African societies.

The sociological interest has also helped in the emergence of oral literature from the vast body of information generally known as folklore. The area covered by the ethnologists was too wide—they had at the back of their minds human nature in general—and their conclusions were often not based on a close examination of the materials they studied. But the sociologists, by confining their interest to single societies, have inevitably been forced to recognize not just the content of the folk literature but certain features of its form and technique. This recognition of the artistic quality of oral texts has led to the use of such terms as *verbal art* and *oral art* in describing the literature.[2]

It was Malinowski who first encouraged this recognition by urging ethnographers to record everything related to the "social context" of the folklore texts that they collected during their fieldwork. Bascom spelled out the important details of such a record.

> The first point I wish to discuss is that of the social context of folklore, its place in the daily round of life of those who tell it. This is not a "problem" in the strict sense, but rather a series of related facts which must be recorded, along with the texts, if the problems of the relation between folklore and culture or the functions of folklore, or even the creative role of the narrators, are to be analyzed. These facts include: (1) when and where the various forms of folklore are told; (2) who tells them, whether or not they are privately owned, and who composes the audience; (3) dramatic devices employed by the narrator, such as gestures, facial expression, pantomime, impersonation, or mimicry; (4) audience participation in the form of laughter, assent or other responses, running criticism or encouragement of the narrator, singing or dancing, or acting out parts in a tale; (5) categories of folklore recognized by the people themselves; and (6) attitudes of the people toward these categories. (1965: 281)

Such recommendations have proved influential in getting ethnographers to focus their attention on the practice of oral art in traditional African communities. The call was heeded by quite a few scholars, who took it upon themselves to provide fairly detailed information about the lives and careers of African folk artists and about situations in which they practice their art. One such effort has been made by the Dutch scholar Daniel Biebuyck in his studies of traditions of the heroic narrative among the Banyanga of Zaire. In a number of publications he has given us insight into the lives of the narrators, their careers as oral artists, and how their work fits into the overall culture of their people (Biebuyck 1978, Biebuyck and Mateene 1969). A similar job has been done by Dan Ben-Amos (1971, 1972) in his studies of story-telling traditions among the Bini of Nigeria.

The value of these scholars' contributions will be seen when we compare them with the views of earlier scholars, especially the evolutionists. The evolutionists were not interested in studying the performers of the oral tradition, mainly because they believed that these performers were simply passing on material that came from the distant past, most of which the performers did not understand. They in fact believed that these performers were too primitive to make any truly creative additions to the texts. The sociologists, on the other hand, by focusing attention on the performers, have demonstrated a considerable faith in their creative skill and taken us one step forward in the understanding of the traditional art.

But there are some problems even in the sociological approach that have prevented the scholars from reaching a full understanding of the artistic quality of oral literature. Although they have done a good job in highlighting the "social context" of this literature and in stressing its functional or practical values within the society, they have given far less time to illuminating and analyzing its artistic properties; we can see that clearly from Bascom's recommendations. As a result, they have published tales, for instance, in flat, unimpressive prose, eliminating features of the oral style such as repetitions and exclamations; they have done few careful analyses of techniques in the original language that appealed to the audience of the tale in the first place; and even when they have cared (and this was not often) to report the circumstances surrounding the performance of the tale (audience participation, use of musical instruments, and so on), they have failed to tell what bearing these circumstances had on the success or otherwise of the tale. It was therefore not easy to see, from the work of these sociologists, how such a tale could be appreciated as literature.

Again, in accordance with their interest in the place of folklore in the culture of a people, scholars such as Bascom and Ben-Amos have constantly stressed that any judgment of a folk text must be based on the views of the society from which the text comes. To a large extent this is right and proper. But surely, if these texts of African folklore appeal to non-Africans like Bascom and Ben-Amos, it must be because they contain certain qualities which go beyond an indigenous African sense of beauty. It is therefore the duty of scholars, if they truly understand the language and culture from which a piece of oral literature comes, to explain its literary qualities so that an outsider can appreciate it. This basic job of literary criticism was not made easy by the narrow interest in "social context" which the sociological approach encouraged.

An Interest in Literature

The champions of the sociological interest (mostly Europeans and Americans) were unable to get down to a proper analysis of the literary merits of African oral literature chiefly because they lacked a sufficiently deep understanding of and feeling for the indigenous languages in which that literature was performed. Many foreign scholars went to the African communities they wished to study, spent about six months at a time, and had lived among the people for no more than two years by the time they completed the study. In many cases their understanding of the indigenous language was at best disjointed. The result was that when they came to record the texts of the oral literature they had collected, they were frequently unwilling to publish the original language versions of these texts, partly for fear of revealing their shortcomings. They contented themselves and their readers with translations in which gaps in the original texts were carefully and skillfully concealed.

In some cases, it is true, these scholars secured the services of indigenous assistants who were either villagers based in the community under study or, as in more recent times, university research students under the scholars' supervision. In such cases, efforts were made to publish the indigenous text as well as the translation. Nevertheless, the literary qualities of such a text still suffered both from the inadequate understanding of the language by the foreign scholar and from the sociological bias of the whole research project.

A major advance in the study of African oral literature as literature came when native African scholars began to undertake research into the oral traditions of their own people. Here were scholars who spoke the African languages before they went out to be schooled in foreign languages and who understood perfectly well what constitutes a beautiful expression in their own tongues before being exposed to the same sense of beauty in other tongues. The differences between such scholars and their European counterparts were inevitably strong. Whereas many Europeans treated African culture and everything that came from it as "primitive" or inferior to their own, the African scholars approached this culture with a feeling of understanding and pride. And whereas the foreigners saved much trouble by eliminating from the texts whatever they did not understand, the native scholars took the trouble to explain the meaning and effectiveness of various techniques in the original texts which give them their artistic qualities.

One of the first African scholars to revolutionize the study of African oral literature was S. Adeboye Babalola of Nigeria. His book, *The Content and Form of Yoruba Ijala* (1966), has shown how much better the insider could do in presenting this sort of literature than the outsider. He tells us in the preface that he undertook to do the study from "the need to give not merely the English translation of the texts but also the original texts themselves and the need to give an account of both the inner form and the outer form of this particular type of poetry." The book appeared at a time when European scholars themselves had come to the conclusion that despite a hundred years or so of collecting and studying African oral literature, not much of an advance had been made and that there was need for African scholars to come to the aid of their colleagues by doing careful stylistic analyses of the literature of their mother tongues (Berry 1961).

This is precisely what Babalola has done in his book. *Ijala* is the poetry of Yoruba hunters, chanted with a high tremulous voice and in a way which allows the performer to use changes in tone to manipulate the meanings of words. The subject of *ijala* is mainly aspects of the hunting life, such as descriptions of various kinds of animals and birds, glorification of distinguished hunters, homage to divinities that protect hunters, and so forth. But the poets also concern themselves with other subjects, such as exploits in war and issues relating to moral conduct.

The book is divided into two main parts, part 1 being titled "A Critical Introduction to Ijala." In the introductory chapters, Babalola gives us the kind of information that is contained in standard ethnographies: the cultural background to the performance of *ijala*, in terms of its being attached to a cult of hunters devoted to Ogun, the god of iron and protector of all who make use of metals (e.g., hunters with their guns and cutlasses); the festive and other occasions during which this kind of poetry is performed; and the subject matter of *ijala*, being essentially a glorification of distinguished animals and men as well as a poetry of social comment. After this Babalola gives us a detailed account of the training of the poets, the nature of their performances, and the criteria by which these performances are judged by the Yoruba. This very enlightening portrait is followed by a chapter titled "The Language of Ijala." Here Babalola treats us to an insider's view of the various stylistic techniques, characteristic of the Yoruba language, which lend *ijala* its poetic flavor, such as the complex structure of imagery and allusion, the manipulation of sounds and of the voice to achieve specific effects of beauty and meaning, and (more interesting) those linguistic devices which are not common in everyday speech but are part of the "poetic diction" of *ijala*. This is clearly the kind of contribution that could have been made only by someone steeped in the language and culture of the people, a contribution which has raised the study of African oral literature to the level of sophistication that had been achieved in the study of modern (written) literature.

Part 2 consists mainly of a selection of some fifty chants of various kinds in corresponding Yoruba and English versions, with accompanying footnotes carefully explaining details of content and style. At this point students of *ijala* poetry have been so carefully introduced to the characteristic features of this form of expression that even if they were not Yoruba, they could hardly resist the temptation of reading the corresponding Yoruba and English texts line by line and looking out for those peculiar stylistic touches.

Another significant landmark in the study of African oral literature by an African came with the publication of Daniel P. Kunene's *Heroic Poetry of the Basotho* (1971). Two things had happened by this time which encouraged Kunene in his work. First, inspired by the efforts of American scholars Milman Parry and Albert Lord, many scholars were beginning to study the nature of oral heroic poetry of various cultures around the world; in his preface, Kunene acknowledges "Professor Albert Lord of Harvard University, whose *The Singer of Tales* inspired me to seek him out and solicit his advice, which he readily gave me." Second, as more and more African nations gained independence from colonial rule, there was a growing feeling of nationalism among the scholars, who resented the inferior position in which their cultures had been put by several generations of imperialist scholars. In his introduction, Kunene strongly condemns the prejudices not only of the imperialists but also of those "de-culturated" Africans who joined the imperialists in underestimating the merits of African oral poetry.

Kunene's book is more of a literary study than Babalola's, giving somewhat less room to an explanation of the cultural background of Sotho heroic poetry than Baba-lola does to the Yoruba *ijala*. Kunene first devotes himself to a careful analysis of the structure of the Sotho language, then goes on to explain the Sotho concept of a hero and the techniques used in choosing appropriate praise names for the hero. He then analyzes these praise names (or "eulogues") so as to identify the various categories into which they fall. Next, following the work of Parry and Lord, Kunene examines the pattern of repetition ("formula") on which these praises are built and the ways in which the formula is manipulated. He moves on to examine the ways in which the poet builds imagery out of various elements taken from the surrounding culture and environment (e.g., cattle, storms), and the various kinds of objects praised. He concludes by examining the relationship between the heroic style in the oral tradition and its influence on Western-educated Sotho poets.

We should perhaps point out that this was not the first time an African language had been so carefully studied. As we saw earlier, European linguists had analyzed various African languages as a way of helping the colonial administrators and the missionaries cope with the strange cultures that they had come to control or convert, or else as a way of satisfying their academic curiosity about the unfamiliar and the "uncivilized." Kunene's study, on the contrary, was the work of a man proud of his culture and determined to reveal the complex and highly sophisticated ways in which the language shapes the oral literature.

Useful work in projecting the literary beauties of African oral literature has in more recent times been done by African writers who were determined to show the world that though they have been educated in the white man's language and are using it effectively in expressing their literary thoughts, they nevertheless come from a rich cultural heritage. One of the really interesting collections of traditional African poetry published from this perspective is the Ghanaian poet Kofi Awoonor's *Guardians of the Sacred Word* (1974). Awoonor studies three living experts of Ewe (Ghanaian) poetry, giving us an insight into their lives and careers as performers; presents selections of their poetry; and provides notes which use facts from his portraits of their lives to explain the effectiveness of their poetic styles. But the real beauty of the book is in the translations. European translations of traditional African poetry were often quite flat and tasteless, partly because the scholars did not understand the original languages sufficiently but even more because they considered the people too "primitive" to have anything truly "poetic" in their languages or literatures. In Awoonor's book, a distinguished Ewe poet uses the benefit of his creative experience to reveal the poetic beauties contained in the literature of his people.

One of the most valuable contributions made to the study of African oral literature may be seen in *The Ozidi Saga*, edited by J. P. Clark (1977). The story, recorded by

Clark in 1963, comes from the editor's Ijo homeland in the southernmost part of Nigeria. Told traditionally over a period of seven festival days, it narrates the fighting exploits of the culture hero Ozidi and is accompanied throughout with music, song, dance, and dramatization of significant episodes.

Earlier editors of folklore texts took little trouble to record the conditions under which an oral performer told a tale or sang a song, despite the plea by Malinowski and Bascom that this should be done. But Clark, himself a poet and a playwright, has used his understanding of the creative process to give us a text that represents as vividly as possible the various things that happened both to and around the narrator as the story of Ozidi was performed; he has set down for us whatever his tape recorder has been able to catch from the performance. At certain points of the story, for instance, the narrator says or does something that amuses the audience and they burst out laughing; at such points in the text, Clark indicates *"Laughter"* to show us the effect of the performance on the audience. At other points of the story we get the notation *"Exclamation,"* and we at once realize that the narrator must have said or done something that made the audience shout. At yet other points of the story, Clark indicates statements made by spectators in the audience, whether in the form of questions or of comments on aspects of the performance, and the narrator's responses to these statements. In addition to all these, Clark indicates those points of the performance where music is played and where certain tunes are sung by the narrator's musical group. The whole text is preceded by a detailed introduction in which Clark not only gives us the cultural background to the performance of the Ozidi story by the Ijo but also explains the role of music, song, and dance in the whole business. There are also useful notes at the end of each of the seven sections representing the seven days of the performance of the story.

The contribution of Clark's book is that it highlights the element of performance in the oral narrative event. Many European scholars had considered African oral narratives as primitive and unsophisticated because they judged them on the same standards as the written literature. The usefulness of Clark's work is that it draws attention to the fact that oral narratives are produced in circumstances different from those in which, say, novels are written and must therefore be judged in different terms. If a statement in the tale is repeated several times, for instance, it could be because it drew a favorable response (e.g., laughter) from the audience the first time it was made, so the narrator wanted to please his audience by making that statement a few times more. In written literature, such a repetition might be considered boring; but in oral literature, where the audience plays a major role in the creative process, the repetition would be seen to be very much justified. In chapter 3 we shall examine other ways in which the audience influences the production of the text in an oral performance.

It would be wrong, of course, to form the impression that non-African scholars have made no contribution to recent trends in the study of African oral literature. During the 1970s it became clear that the emphasis in the study of the oral traditions had shifted considerably toward an examination of their artistic or literary merits, and one of the scholars who helped this move was Ruth Finnegan. In fact, in a book that she published toward the end of the 1960s, *Limba Stories and Storytelling* (1967), she stood firmly against the prevailing trend in folklore studies. Although earlier scholars had been inclined to ignore the element of individual artistic skill in the oral traditions, she says quite firmly:

> The storytellers [among the Limba of Sierra Leone] are all *individuals,* individuals who perform on specific individual occasions. There is no joint common "folk" authorship or set form of performance dictated by blind tradition. The stories are, naturally, composed and enacted within the limits of the social background of Limba life and literary conventions; but each individual performer has his own idiosyncracies and unique fund of experience, interests and skills. (1967: 17)

But it is in her survey study *Oral Literature in Africa* (1970) that Finnegan reveals her full appreciation of the literary qualities of African oral literature. Although she commits a few errors of judgment—for instance, in declaring that Africa does not possess certain types of oral literature such as epic and myth—she gives the subject as a whole the sort of detailed treatment that we might find in any survey of modern literature.

Another useful contribution from European scholars has been made by Gordon Innes. Part of what Finnegan means when she considers the traditional storytellers as "individuals who perform on specific individual occasions" is that in a community where two or more storytellers tell the same stories, one version of a tale is bound to differ from another version, depending not only on the narrator's personal skill and experience but also on the context (e.g., type of audience) within which the tale is told. This is the sort of issue that Innes has tried to examine. In his collection of heroic and historical narratives among the Mandinka of the Gambia—*Sunjata: Three Mandinka Versions* (1974), *Kaabu and Fuladu: Historical Narratives of the Gambian Mandinka* (1976), and *Kelefa Saane: His Career Recounted by Two Mandinka Bards* (1978), he has in each case presented the same story as told by two or three narrators. We are given a brief but useful biography of each narrator and the circumstances of his performance of the tale (e.g., use of musical instruments). This practice of presenting the same theme from a variety of perspectives helps us a great deal in understanding the relationship between what may be considered a "tradition" (in the sense of a generally accepted body of information) and the individual creative skill of narrators who undertake to reshape that body of information to suit their own contexts. Each story is presented by Innes in both the original Mandinka and an English translation. There are also detailed notes at the end which explain, among other things, how skillfully each narrator bends the Mandinka language to suit his own artistic purposes.

We have constantly talked about performance in our discussion so far, and indeed this is one aspect of the study of African oral literature that is gaining increasing attention. By the term *performance* is implied the total act as well as the context or environment involved in the delivery of oral literature—issues relating not only to the role of the audience (as we saw in Clark's *Ozidi Saga*) or of music but also to the narrator's use of the movement of the face, hands, and other parts of the body in giving life to the narration. This aspect of oral literary study has received great emphasis in the work of Harold Scheub, most notably in *The Xhosa Ntsomi* (1975). In this study of a South African oral narrative tradition, Scheub devotes considerable time to explaining the various ways in which the oral narrator manipulates symbols and images within the tale, showing how one small image develops in scope as the tale progresses. But even more interesting, he introduces us to the fascinating ways in which the storyteller dramatizes various actions described in the tale so that even though it is set in a fantastic world, it assumes the proportions of real life. In this book and in other publications on this subject, Scheub provides, as no scholar before him ever did, a variety of photographs capturing the dramatic movements of his narrators (mostly women) as they portray the various emotions and attitudes underlying their tales.[3] Such a study is clearly useful in giving insight into the warmth and life that is involved in the production of the oral art.

Benefits of the New Trends

In giving greater recognition to the literary qualities of African oral literature, we have no doubt freed African culture to a considerable extent from the prejudices of the earlier European scholars. One outcome relates to the use of notions such as "primitive" and "savage," which occurred frequently and unapologetically in the works not only of the evolutionists but even of the sociologists—take the subtitle, for example, of Rattray's *Ashanti Proverbs: The Primitive Ethics of a Savage People* (1916). This book was published in the heyday of imperial arrogance in Africa by a colonial administrator who had little understanding of or feeling for the Ashanti language. In more recent times, these witticisms—proverbs, riddles, tongue-twisters—have been found by numerous scholars (African and non-African) to reveal not only a depth of wisdom but especially a high level of artistry or poetry in the way their tellers manipulate sound and meaning. The literary interest taken in these aspects of African oral literature has helped to show that the culture form which they come is far more complex and sophisticated than words such as *primitive* and *savage* would seem to suggest.

Another interesting offshoot of the literary interest in African oral literature has to do with the growth of modern African literature as well as its study. This literature was studied as an aspect of anthropology—that is, by scholars who were primarily interested in understanding the nature of human culture and society at the fundamental level, in small rural communities, for instance. It was in such an environment that the use of words such as *primitive* inevitably grew. However, as scholars became increasingly aware of the high level of cultural sophistication contained in African oral literature, it was equally inevitable that the study of this literature should move out of its old environment. In most African universities and other institutions where the subject is taught, it is located within departments devoted mainly to the study of language and literature. In these departments, oral literature is studied not only for its own sake but also in the context of its relationship to modern African literature. The justification for this is twofold.

First, as we have observed, African writers have been in the forefront of the continuing efforts to collect and translate texts from their people's oral traditions, and they have done this as a way of advertising the greatness of their indigenous cultures. From Francophone Africa we may mention the Malian novelist A. Hampate Ba, who has translated (with Lilyan Kesteloot) some of the heroic tales, or epics, from the Bambara; the Senegalese Birago Diop, who has done the same for Wolof folktales; and the Guinean Djibril T. Niane, who was the first to provide a classic French translation of the famous Mandinka (Mandingo) epic of Sundiata (Sunjata). In Ghana we have had the poets Kofi Awoonor and G. Adali-Mortty translating pieces of the traditional poetry of their people into sensitive English. In Nigeria the poet-dramatist Clark has given us the epoch-making edition of *The Ozidi Saga,* and even the novelist Chinua Achebe has become involved in translating Igbo folktales especially for young readers (Achebe and Iroaganachi 1972). In East Africa Okot p'Bitek of Uganda led the way in the collection and translation of texts of African oral literature; an example is his translation of folktales *Hare and Hornbill* (1978). In South Africa the pioneering work of Thomas Mofolo in presenting the story of Shaka has inspired the poet Mazisi Kunene to publish the texts of greater epic narratives about the war leader in a notable edition, *Emperor Shaka the Great* (1979). There are numerous other such efforts across Africa.

Second, African oral literature is studied side by side with modern African literature because many modern African writers consciously borrow techniques and ideas from their oral traditions in constructing works dealing essentially with modern life. These writers would like to feel that even though their societies have changed drastically from what they were several generations ago and even though they communicate with the world in a language that is not their own, there must be certain fundamental elements in their oral traditions that they can bring into their portraits of contemporary life. In *Weep Not Child,* for instance, Ngugi wa Thiong'o has evoked the image of the ancestor of the Kikuyu race (Mumbi) in his portrait of the struggle of the Kenyan people against foreign oppression. Wole Soyinka, in many of his writings, has used the image of the Yoruba god Ogun as a symbol for the revolutionary spirit needed to combat the social evils that plague both his country, Nigeria, and the black race as a whole. In poetry, both Okot p'Bitek and Kofi Awoonor have borrowed heavily from the techniques of folk expression in writing about present-day situations. In chapter 10 we shall explore more fully the relationships between the oral and written literatures of Africa.

Perhaps the more lasting benefit of the latest trends in the study of African oral literature may be in helping us answer some very fundamental questions about the nature of literature and of culture. In the final analysis, it seems, all knowledge aims at helping us understand who we are, the value of what we do, how we have reached the stage of civilization we have achieved, and what steps we can take to improve our condition. From our discussion so far, it is clear that the earlier students of culture tackled very much the same problems. But their error was in starting from rather sweeping assumptions about the direction of human evolution (from "primitive" to "civilized") and treating the evidence at their disposal somewhat carelessly. Consequently they showed no interest in oral artists because they believed that at the "primitive" stage of culture at which oral literature developed, it would be premature to talk about individual artists.

Happily, recent studies in African oral literature are helping us look more closely at the nature of the creative process in both Africa and the rest of the world and at the relationship between one type of culture and another. For instance, how is oral poetry composed both in societies without writing and in those that have had contact with writing, and what is the place of this poetry in the society in which it exists? What are the components, in terms of content and form, of the oral narrative, and in what ways does the audience before whom the narrator performs such a tale influence these components? What are the similarities and the differences between the psychological outlook that gives rise to oral literature and the one that produces written literature, and what happens when a society moves from an oral medium of expression to a written one? On the evidence of both the oral and the written literature, what are the essential differences between European and black African cultures? These and various other questions can now be tackled because of the increasing interest in the study of African oral literature as a subject in its own right.

2. The Oral Artist

If there is anything of artistic or literary merit in African oral literature, then it should be possible to examine those who perform this literature and see in what sense they could be given the same sort of recognition that we give to novelists, playwrights, and poets in the culture of writing. As we saw in chapter 1, this interest in the oral performer as an individual artist is a more or less recent development. The evolutionists who studied human cultures believed that a piece of oral literature (especially the folktale) had passed through so many generations of transmission that it was no longer possible to speak of one single "author" and that in any case these oral performers were too primitive to be considered artists in any regular sense of the word. But a closer look at the careers of these performers in specific social situations soon opened the eyes of scholars to the level of creative and imaginative skill that went into an oral performance.

And yet, in spite of the sociological interest in the careers of individual artists, the impression continued to hold among many people that oral art was a skill generally possessed by members of a community. One would often hear a statement such as "Anybody in the village can tell you a story." To some extent, such a view was encouraged by the sociological interest in folklore. If, as was commonly believed by the early generation of social anthropologists, society was generally held together by a shared understanding and acceptance of its customs and beliefs, then it is easy to see how the impression would be formed that the members of that society shared various skills to a fairly equal degree. That may be the reason why these scholars, even when they gave attention to the career of an individual oral artist, put more emphasis on how the social environment influenced or shaped the artist's work—the "social context"—than on evidence of individual skill.

In a sense, the statement that anybody in the village could tell a story is right, but it makes no more sense than to say that any educated person can write a poem or a novel. Although the artist is exposed to the various forms of cultural and other education available to every member of the society, what generally separates the artist from the nonartist is a more than average sense of what is beautiful and exciting, a high capacity for expressing oneself with effective idioms and images, and a deep interest in practicing a particular type of art. To all this must be added the opportunity for training. This training does not always happen in a conscious or formal way, but in many cases a well-organized training will lead to art of truly professional excellence. Let us devote the next few pages to examining ways in which African oral artists achieve their competence.

Training and Preparation

To be an accomplished oral artist, some form of apprenticeship or training is necessary. Essentially two kinds of training are involved in the development of the African oral artist: informal and formal. Informal training entails a kind of loose attachment whereby the future artist happens to live or move in an environment in which a particular kind of oral art is practiced and simply absorbs the skill in it as time goes on. It is possible, of course, for a person to live forever in such an environment and not develop the skill; one's mind or nature has to be predisposed toward art before the skill can successfully take root.

I will illustrate what I mean by informal training with examples from two pieces of research. The first is from a narrator I have been recording since 1980, Charles Simayi from Ubulu-Uno in the southwestern part of Nigeria. When I asked Simayi how he learned the tales he had told me, he replied:

> The events of which I tell, as concerning Ezemu or the border wars—I wasn't eyewitness to these events. It's as it is with you and your father: we were the homegrown ones who served our fathers at home and in the farm. I never went to the city, for they didn't let us go to school in the old days. . . . They said we might get lost if we were taken to school. So, when you sat in the farmhouse with your father and it was raining, they (i.e., father and fellow farmers) would lay aside their whisks and ask you to go and fetch firewood. He and his friends would tell tales of war, and you would listen to them as they told these tales. So that was how I learned those tales about events I was not eyewitness of.

This is one case in which the future artist simply listened to the elders and absorbed the stories he was to tell later on. It is easy to see from Simayi's life why he never needed any kind of formal training to be an accomplished storyteller (acknowledged by his village to be the most outstanding). At the time I met him, he was in his late fifties but had already attained a considerable level of skill in several occupations. He was first and foremost a traditional doctor (medicine man), but in addition he was a farmer, a barber, a builder, a handicrafts maker, and various other forms of artisan. He participated in building the first secondary school in his village, which he helped persuade the local government authorities to locate there. He also built drums, which he hired out to others at very low rates ("simply for publicity, not for money," he told me). He was a member of his village council of elders, one whose advice was highly valued. Although unschooled in Western education, he participated in some of the most delicate missions sent by the ruler of his village to communities far and near. He had therefore shown himself to be a man of many skills, blessed with a sharp natural intelligence. Although he never formally attached himself to anyone to learn the art of storytelling, his "education" in village life more than made up for whatever he may have lost by loose attachment.

From research among the Xhosa of southern Africa, Harold Scheub (1975) reports on similar kinds of preparation. Informal training seems to be the rule among oral artists in this area. "When I specifically asked artists where they had acquired their stylistic tools," Scheub reports, "they said that they were unable to tell. They learned the art, they insisted, by watching others, then making certain elements of performances that they witnessed a part of their own equipment" (p. 17). What Scheub tells us about two kinds of oral performer among the Xhosa is illuminating. The first is a female narrator of folktales (*iintsomi*), who told him:

> I learned from my grandmother. I used to sit and listen to her every night. To my aunt, too. Then I told little *iintsomi*. Very short. About the jackal and the wolf. About the *amaZimu* (man-eating creatures). And then my *iintsomi* got longer and longer. I heard a new *intsomi*, and wanted to tell that. I added from this *intsomi* and from that one, and then I was telling longer ones. (Ibid.)

The second informant is an *imbongi*, or singer of praise poetry (*izibongo*), who spoke along the same lines.

> There's no place to learn *izibongo* except to hear someone saying *izibongo*, and then you learn one word there, and then you hear somebody again at a certain place saying *izibongo*, and you . . . become a *mbongi* because of your interest when hearing the people saying these things. And then you begin to wish to do as they do. . . . Just as in all things, you have to think—I mean to say, when you are interested in anything, then you begin to think, to think, to think, and then . . . the first time you try to start it, then when you start on the next time you will say more. On the next day you will say more. . . . You notice the events that are happening during the time of that chief when he is ruling, or you begin to think about events that happened long ago. And then you just begin to join these things. . . . (p. 22)

From the above statements made by three different oral artists it is reasonably clear what goes on in the informal kind of training. First, the future artist must be a person blessed with a considerable amount of natural genius who possesses an interest in the kind of oral literature that is practiced around him or her. Second, since no formal coaching is involved, these novices must look and listen closely and in this way absorb the ideas, the idioms, and the techniques peculiar to the art. "They must," as Nketia says, "rely on their own eyes, ears, and memory. They must acquire their own technique of learning" (1973: 88). And finally, the process of learning entails that the novices use their imagination to select the relevant materials from the large amount they may have acquired and to increase their store of knowledge as time goes on.

Very much the same things happen in the formal kind of training, except that the process is better organized and the relationship between the trainee and the teacher properly established. In some cases, the type of oral literature involved is a rather special and complex one. The novice may be understudying his or her father or other close relative, and it may be understood that the novice will take over from the senior person at a later stage (e.g., at the death of the latter). In cases where the novice leaves the family house to live with the teacher, it is frequently understood that the novice will perform various kinds of duties (e.g., domestic) not necessarily related to the training. In yet other cases, the novice is trained in a "school" or association established to bring up young persons in a particular form of oral art. Whatever the situation may be, the main difference between the formal and informal kinds of training is that the process is somewhat shorter in the former case. "The lack of systematic formal instruction," as Nketia tells us, "protracts the learning process, which depends too heavily on favourable social conditions" (1973: 89). Formal training is particularly useful for the more complex kinds of oral literature—e.g., some forms of ritual poetry and performances involving the accompaniment of music—on which the future artist could depend as a major source of livelihood. Let us examine briefly some instances of formal training in African oral literature.

Two examples come from the Yoruba of western Nigeria. The first relates to the training in *ijala*, or hunter's poetry, and we may best cite the description of the process by the authority in the subject, Adeboye Babalola. We are first told that for the training to be successful the pupil has to show a deep interest in the chanting of *ijala* poetry, even if he is going to be taught by his own father. This apprenticeship begins, in most cases, in early youth (about the age of six) and lasts about a dozen years. Babalola describes the major stages of this training.

> The first stage of pupillage is a period of merely listening to the ijala chants performed by the teacher in his own house as well as at every social gathering where he entertains people with ijala. The pupil first imitates his teacher when he, the pupil, is on his own and thus he practises ijala-chanting. Subsequently, when he is at a social gathering as the *asomogbe* or *elegbe* (pupil) of his master, he is able to repeat the words of his master's chant almost simultaneously and the sound of the ijala performance then resembles that of choral chanting. The third stage is when the master orders his pupil to give solo performances of ijala chants at social gatherings to which he has taken him. This is obviously a sort of promotion, for the pupil ceases to provide merely an accompaniment to his master's chanting voice. (1966: 41–42).

After he has gained confidence as a performer, the *ijala* poet ultimately sets up on his own, parting ways with his master either with the latter's consent or without notice (fearing that his master may not voluntarily release him).

Babalola concludes his discussion of the training of the *ijala* poet with a question: how is the poet able to retain so much text in memory and perform steadily without faltering? To this question there is usually a twofold reply. First, practice makes perfect: constant repetition helps the artist to master the text so well that the chances of error are drastically reduced. Second, the chanters admit that they make use of various kinds of medicinal charms (called *isoye*) which aid in the retention of memory. These charms come in the form of magical chants, which are said to instill retention, or of powder taken with food and drink or incised into the poet's bloodstream with a barber's knife. Through these various forms of preparation—i.e., the more practical steps of careful apprenticeship and the less obvious powers of traditional magic—the future *ijala* poet is equipped with the skills he needs for the rather complex demands of a public performance.

The second instance of formal training among the Yoruba relates to *ifa*. This divination poetry is practiced mainly by traditional priests, healers, fortune-tellers, and general counselors on various problems of life. Wande Abimbola, the best authority on this form of oral literature, has carefully sketched the various stages of the training of the *babalawo*, the term generally used for the *ifa* expert (Abimbola 1976: 18–25). To start with, the pupil must in most cases live with the expert and, while training, help in the performance of various domestic chores. Since the art is an extremely complex and demanding one, the training starts at about the age of seven and lasts for about a dozen years. According to Abimbola, the process of becoming a full-fledged *babalawo* is divided into two segments. The first segment entails the actual period of training of the pupil, while the second relates to the ceremonies of initiation of the fully trained *babalawo* into the rites and the secrets of the profession.

The *ifa* divination system may be described briefly. When a client brings a problem to a *babalawo*, the latter listens carefully, then throws either a divining chain (a string of half-nuts) or "sacred palm-nuts" on a divining board. The nuts fall into a combination which signifies one of the 256 *odu* in the divination corpus. Each *odu* is a body of narrative verse, subdivided into a number of chapters known as *ese*. The number of *ese* in each *odu* is limitless, but as a group they embody (from various angles) the answer to the specific problem brought by the client. After the relevant *ese* has been recited, the *babalawo* spells out for the client the sacrifice he or she must perform to obtain a successful solution to the problem.

The first stage of the training of the *babalawo* involves the use of the divining chain. It is followed by training in the use of the sacred palmnuts—though, since this tool is used less frequently now than the chain, the period of training is considerably shorter. Toward the end of the training period, the pupil learns the various sacrifices (e.g., money, food, clothes) that the client is asked to offer should the *ese* chosen provide the right solution to the problem. But by far the most important part of the training of the *babalawo* is to learn (especially during the first and second stages) the *ese* pertaining to the various *odu*. These narrative verses are committed to memory at a rate commensurate with the capacity of the pupil—one a day, one every other day, and so on. The trainee learns the *ese* independently at his own pace; otherwise, the trainee imitates a master *babalawo* reciting the verses to consulting clients or at appropriate ceremonies. Learning these poems is such a rigorous task that many trainees soon drop out of the program. For trainees in both *ijala* poetry and *ifa* divination, the task of retaining the texts in memory is helped by taking the medicinal *isoye* during meals.

The second and closing stage of the formal training of the *babalawo* is initiation into the profession. This involves a series of ceremonies lasting many days during which sacrifices are offered to the deities of *ifa* and time is spent in entertainment of practicing *babalawo* from far and wide. Secrets of the *ifa* cult are revealed to the initiate, and the entire ceremony is accompanied by dancing and the chanting of various *ese ifa*.

The formal training in the practice and transmission of various forms of the oral tradition shows how seriously this aspect of culture is taken in the traditional society. Such formal training is so strictly organized that we may see the system very much in the same sense as we see schools in modern society. A school of oral literature may be run on a small scale, as in the case of a *babalawo* who has a handful of trainees living in his house and understudying him. But there are schools organized at the larger level of an association or guild of poets with a president at the head of the body. Among the Ruanda of central Africa, for instance, there was until recent times an association of court poets known as the *umutwe w'abasizi,* made up of families officially recognized for the singing of court poetry, i.e., poetry sung for praising kings and recording the history of the royal line. Headed by an *intebe* (president), this association was set up for training young men from those families in the skills of court poetry. In other cases, the state may recognize both the cultural value and the popularity (especially with foreigners) of a category of oral traditions and so set up a "school" where young men can be taught the skills of that art—not only to preserve the culture but also to promote the tourist economy. Such a facility is the school for the training of *griots* (singers) in the island of St. Louis in Senegal.

Modes of training and preparation differ from one society to another and from one type of oral literature to another. But the very fact that some training is involved, whatever its duration, does indicate that oral literature requires a certain level of competence for which the intending artist must be specially prepared.

Artists and Patrons

The issues of training and patronage are closely connected because, in many ways, the type of oral literature that the artist trains for depends on the kinds of people who will listen to him. It is important to understand this clearly if we are to appreciate the content and qualities of certain texts of oral literature that we come across today. For instance, with the disappearance of the old kingdoms of Africa or the decline of their influence, the poets who sang in praise of the kings are now forced to practice their art before not so royal audiences; some references in their songs can only be understood if we know something about the backgrounds from which they derive. Let us look at the different kinds of patronage and the ways in which they influence the nature of oral literature.

We may best discuss patronage under two broad subheads, private and public. Perhaps the best example of private patronage is to be sought in the royal courts, although we must stress yet again that the situation is not always what it used to be. Traditional African communities used to be governed mostly by kings and chiefs who had absolute authority over all matters, even of the life and death of their citizens. One principal way in which these rulers tried to secure their positions of preeminence in the society was through the services of court poets. Although once in a while these court singers enjoyed the liberty to advise the ruler on a course of action or suggest caution (however mildly) when the ruler seemed to be doing something improper, their major role was to swell the image of the ruler.

On ceremonial occasions such as the installation of a new chief, the king of the community would come out in all his pomp and circumstance, preceded by his court singer or singers. The main duty of the poet on such an occasion would be to recite, in praises, the family background of the king and the greatness of that family, the personal attributes and achievements of the present king, and various other positive statements. All these would be proclaimed with a loud voice and designed to impress the merits of the king in the minds of the audience even as their attention was engaged by the person who was about to be installed chief. Besides this ceremonial role, it was the duty of the court poet to record in his mind the occasional successes of the king during his reign—e.g., in war, government, acts of generosity, etc.—so that these might be woven into the body of praises that the poet sang from day to day; the king's failures or weaknesses would be either completely left out or twisted to sound mild, if not positive.

In these various ways the court poet established the king's claims to authority over his people and secured him a lasting place in the people's memory. For these services the court poet was rewarded in a variety of ways. In some cases the poet was given residence in the palace or its immediate environs. If not paid a regular salary, the poet was at least given handsome gifts and occasional allowances, sometimes even a portion of land on which to farm. And the poet enjoyed the protection as well as the privilege of being the official mouthpiece of the ruler of the land.

A few examples of court poets in some African communities will do. Among the Mandinka-speaking peoples of the western Sudan in countries such as Mali, Guinea, Senegal, and Gambia, the *griot* was traditionally a poet attached to the royal family. The job was apparently hereditary in the sense that it was understood that a son would succeed his father as *griot* to a particular line of kings. So at least we learn from one famous singer of the legend of Sunjata, the founder of the empire of Mali.

> I am a griot. It is I, Djeli Mamoudou Kouyate, son of Bintou Kouyate and Djeli Kedian Kouyate, master in the art of eloquence. Since time immemorial the Kouyates have been in the service of the Keita princes of Mali; we are vehicles of speech, we are the repositories which harbour secrets many centuries old. . . . I derive my knowledge from my father Djeli Kedian, who also got it from his father. . . . I teach kings the history of their ancestors so that the lives of the ancients might serve them as an example. . . . My word is pure and free of all untruth; it is the word of my father; it is the word of my father's father. (Niane 1965: 1)

In the story of Sunjata which Djeli Mamoudou Kouyate proceeds to tell, the hero's father, Maghan Kon Fatta, the king of Mali, had as his *griot* a certain Gnankouman Doua; when the king died and Sunjata succeeded to the throne, he inherited as *griot* the son of Doua, Balla Fasseke Kouyate. Djeli Mamoudou was therefore descended from a long line of court poets who served the traditional rulers of the Malian Mandinka.

From other versions of the Sunjata story we get various other facts about court patronage and what it entails. In one version recorded by Innes (1974) we are told that the relationship between Sunjata and his *griot* Balla Fasseke was so close that when during his exile from Mali he had no food to give to Balla, he proceeded to cut off a portion of his calf and to cook it as meat for Balla to eat (p. 61). A *griot* who enjoyed such generous treatment had no qualms about glorifying the image of his lord even when there was no justification for it. That was why when, during his war with Sumanguru, Sunjata showed a sign of fear by evading his enemy, his *griots* were forced to bend the truth and say that "Sunjata knows not fright" (p. 301).

Other examples of court patronage have been recorded in various communities across Africa. Among the Akan of Ghana the *kwadwumfo* was a court poet whose duty was to recount the family history and achievements of the king whenever the latter appeared in public. In the emir's or royal palace of northern Nigeria, there is still the court *maroka* (singer), who has no other business but to sing the praises of the ruler and to herald distinguished visitors to his presence. Among the Nguni peoples of southern Africa (the Xhosa, Zulu, etc.), the *imbongi* did such service in the king's palace. So did the *umusizi* in the royal courts of the Ruanda of central Africa, and in their case we can see how strict the poet's loyalty to his patronage could be. With the decline of the old kingdoms, these poets have been forced to perform their chants more or less professionally. But as Coupez and Kamanzi tell us, if at any point in a poet's recitation of a royal genealogy the audience applauds, the poet will suspend the recitation until the applause has stopped (1970: 77), apparently because he recognizes that he is beholden more to the account he is giving than to the audience that has paid to watch him.

Besides this private patronage offered by the royal court, there is what may be seen as the semi-private patronage offered by distinguished individuals in a community, like a warrior, a hunter, or a politician. In the traditional society and even in our own day, such individuals often hire the services of acknowledged performers to inspire them to action and to proclaim their merits to the public so as to swell their image. Unlike their counterparts in the royal courts, these semi-private artists perform for their patrons for specific or limited periods though they take their loyalty nearly as seriously as the court poets. The well-known performer from Mali, Seydou Camara, did such service for hunters, as may be seen from a salute contained in one of his stories. It is a highly poetic tribute to his generous patron, a hunter who normally went to his hunt bare-bodied.

Naked Buttock Battler and Naked Chest Battler.
Look to the Green Head Smasher for the Green Eye Gouger.
You who have offered me a skull
As a face-washing bowl,
And offered me a skin
As a covering cloth.
You have given me a great tongue
So that I may speak to the world.
The brave offered me fresh blood
As face-washing water,
And gave me a tail
As a hut-sweeping broom
And offered me a thigh bone
To use as a toothpick.
It is the hunter who has done this for me. (Bird 1974: 3)[1]

Semi-private patronage is also a feature of the political life in many African societies. Ambitious politicians frequently hire the services of oral poets—especially in rural areas—during campaigns for election; it is the duty of such a poet to introduce

the politician to campaign audiences in the most fitting phrases so as to ensure maximum attention, to project the politician's image in and out of the campaign scene,
and even to reduce the image of the opponent. In the tumultuous political life of
countries such as Nigeria and Ghana, the latter function has frequently got the oral
artist into trouble, indeed cost him his freedom if not his life. But the importance of
the artist as a hired spokesperson for such purposes can hardly be overestimated.
Statements by a Xhosa *imbongi*, Nelson Mabunu, from an interview are quite enlightening.

> You see, an imbongi could be useful in delivering a message. Say you are perhaps a
> candidate, you want to be elected for a seat in Parliament. Then you have your imbongi.
> That imbongi before you speak he can sort of, I don't want to use this English word, to
> "hypnotise" people, he could . . . *inspire* the people so that when you stand up and
> deliver your address they are already having confidence in what you are going to say. An
> imbongi could be dangerous: He could incite people. He can incite people, because in the
> olden days when there's going to be a war or I would say a battle between two sides, you
> would always find an imbongi. . . . That's the same thing. This imbongi, if there's a
> meeting here, take for instance the Transkei National Independence Party and the Dem-
> ocratic Party, now perhaps the man who is for or pro-government is going to address a
> meeting where there are people in opposition, then the imbongi gets up. He inspires, in
> so much that if anyone of those dare stand up he could be assaulted. (Opland 1983: 87)

We have used the word *private* in our discussion of various kinds of oral artists
because their performances are "owned," so to speak, by specific individuals and their
freedom of opinion considerably restricted. However, the large majority of oral artists
in most African communities could be said to enjoy a public patronage, in the sense
that they are free to perform to anyone who is willing to pay. The question of opinion
may not matter much here; it could be bent either way, especially since artists never
know who their audiences might be. The performance is offered either as pure entertainment or to satisfy a specific need; the patronage can come from any sector of the
society, not solely from the leadership as in the case of private patronage.

A few examples will show how the art of the free-lance performer is geared to a
variety of occasions and purposes. One such type of performer is the *nyatiti* (harp)
singer among the Luo of Kenya. This musician is generally paid to perform whenever
there is a ceremony or celebration where drinks flow and the company is warm. He
or she is to be seen mostly at funeral ceremonies but performs also at merry-making
ceremonies. At funerals he or she may or may not be specifically invited but goes
nevertheless to sing well-chosen songs of sorrow and of praise of the deceased and
generally receives gifts of money and drinks from the impressed observers. The *nyatiti*
could indeed move from a funeral ceremony to a lighthearted celebration, depending
on the strength of the demand: his or her art is available to all and sundry.

Another interesting example is the Hausa *maroka* (singer) in northern Nigeria.
Besides those *maroka* who hire out their services to the distinguished leaders in a
community, there are numerous wandering *maroka* who accost passersby on the street
and offer to sing and play for them. *Maroka* may stop strangers and begin to sing

their praises, pointing out their outstanding beauty even when this is not true, all because they expect a gift; when that gift does not come and the stranger walks away in disregard, the *maroka* may change their tune and tell the truth! Many *maroka* are known to have been banned by the political authorities because they caused offense to innocent citizens.

A further example of public patronage may be seen in the *griots* of present-day western Sudan. With the decline of the old kingdoms and empires, these performers have moved from the royal courts to the general public. These days they can be seen performing for scholars who are interested in collecting specimens of the heroic tales of bygone days, at wedding celebrations, or even on the street.

The purpose of discussing the patronage of the oral artist is not to draw any firm lines of distinction between types. It may be possible to argue, as some scholars have done, that oral artists performing in certain restricted kinds of environment (e.g., the palace) do a more specialized job than those who make themselves available to all and sundry. One reason given for this is that while the former are assured of a livelihood and so have a lot of time to devote to perfecting one category of oral art (e.g., praise or heroic poetry), the latter are jacks of all trades and masters of none. This may well be true in some instances, but it would be useful to recall that the position of the oral artist has not always been stable. In the past, in fact, many African praise poets were received into royal patronage only after they had been practicing as free-lance poets and had shown themselves to be outstanding. This was certainly the case with the royal *imbongi* of southern Africa and the court *maroka* of northern Nigeria. Now, of course, the court singer of yesterday has moved down to the general public. Whatever the environment in which artists find themselves, all of them are trained in fundamentally the same skills: the sensitive use of words and images, the delicate balance between music and words, the art of holding the attention or interest of an audience, and so on.

We have discussed patronage in the foregoing pages primarily to establish that oral literature is performed on demand or to suit specific types of interests. In that sense, the oral artist is less of a free agent than the modern writer. There was a time, of course, when writers had to seek the support of rich and powerful patrons in order to survive—for example, in eighteenth- and early nineteenth-century England. Now, with a vast population of readers most of whom the writers have never thought of, writers can afford to address themselves to any issue no matter who gets hurt. But oral artists are somewhat more restricted. To be able to make ends meet, they must attach themselves to specific interests or bend their art to suit anyone willing to pay.

Consequently, we should not expect to find much objectivity or stability in the texts of oral literature. We noted above how the free-lance Hausa *maroka* can change from praise to abuse simply because he or she fails to get the expected gift. A similar shift could be seen even within the patronage of the royal court. We learn from the legend of Sunjata how Sumanguru, in usurping the kingship of Mali from Sunjata, also took the latter's *griot* (Balla Fasseke) from him; to ensure the favor of his new master, the *griot* had to change his tune from singing the greatness of Sunjata to extolling the supremacy of Sumanguru (Niane 1965). In later pages we shall find other reasons why changes occur in the content of oral literature, but it is useful to bear in mind meanwhile that patronage is an important cause of this instability or fluidity.

The Artist as Maker

Most earlier studies of African oral literature put undue emphasis on the fact that a proverb, a song, or a tale was the common property of the society in which it was found. Since these texts were handed down from person to person and from one generation to the next, the question of individual authorship was considered superfluous. We should, of course, be honest enough to admit that the material of a large portion of the oral literature available in any community comes from the distant past and that the original authors cannot be accounted for. This is due partly to the passage of time and partly to the circumstances (which we shall consider later) whereby certain texts are deliberately made to abdicate the identity of their composers. However, if we are to continue to look upon oral literature as art, we must be prepared to examine the conditions under which it is made.

Some of the more recent scholars of oral literature who have managed to draw attention to individual oral artists have described the nature of their art at the stage of completion but have not, unfortunately, been patient enough to examine individual pieces and see how they arise or how they grow either independently or from the general body of tradition. Albert Lord, in *The Singer of Tales*, which brings together the results of several years' study of oral narrative traditions of Yugoslav *guslari* (performers), laid the foundations for the developmental study of oral literature by comparing a text collected in 1935 with another collected fifteen years earlier from the same singer (see Lord 1956). We do not all have to wait as long as Lord did, but he has at least shown that questions about the nature of composition are as valid in the study of oral literature as they have always been in the study of written literature.

One of the few studies done roughly along such lines is contained in Finnegan's research among the Limba of Sierra Leone. In a visit to this ethnic group, Finnegan told the story of the temptation and fall of Adam and Eve to a notable Limba narrator, Karanke Dema. More than two years later, she returned to the same community and Karanke, who had meanwhile been telling that story to his Limba audiences, volunteered to retell it to Finnegan. The old Judaic story had undergone considerable metamorphosis and now looked every bit like a normal Limba story in terms of form and content. For instance, it was given a conventional Limba opening—"Suri, reply to me"—whereby a storyteller appoints a member of the audience to be an "answerer," repeating various statements made by the narrator and confirming the truthfulness of what the latter tells. In the body of the story itself, several changes had been made to reflect the conception of human relations among the Limba. For instance, Eve (Ifu) was portrayed as a woman thoroughly subservient to her husband, Adam (Adamu), very much as in a traditional African household; and the relationship between the serpent (given the name of a local species, *bankiboro*) and Eve in the old story was portrayed in the Limba concept of an illicit affair between a married woman and her lover. Finally, the storyteller indulged the practice of assigning causes and explanations to present-day phenomena. Of the action of God (Kanu) in cursing the snake and banishing it from human company, Finnegan was told: "Since the *bankiboro* snake went off into the bush—if you see a *bankiboro* snake now with human beings, whenever they see each other, they kill him. That is why they hate each other." The story ended with God banishing man from a life of ease and condemning him forever to hard work:

> If you see now—we Limba, we live now to work; the sun burns us; the rain soaks us; ha! we endure that suffering; if you want to get something to eat you have to struggle for long—that began from the serpent, the bankiboro snake. . . . If you see how we live, we Limba, working—that was where it began. That is it, it is finished. (Finnegan 1967: 270)

It is interesting how a Judaic story has been given a thoroughly African home, and this does indeed tell us something about the genesis of stories in the African oral tradition. New stories *are* created, and if it happens that the material for them comes from outside the culture, that material has to be reshaped so as to look familiar. It is frequently assumed that because many stories are unaccompanied by their tellers' names (though this may be the fault of their collectors), the stories are simply considered as part of a larger tradition and the individual creativity of the storyteller does not count. We shall discuss this issue in the next section of this chapter. Meanwhile, when in future any other Limba narrator tells the story of Adamu and Ifu to a group of listeners, we can at least explain how that story got into the Limba oral tradition and hopefully trace how it has developed.

It is true, of course, that in some situations the identity of the artist is deliberately suppressed. In a fascinating study of the *udje* poetry of the Urhobo (southwestern Nigeria), G. G. Darah (1982) has given a clear picture of how oral poetry arises as the product of an individual's imagination but ends up losing the imprint of the original composer. *Udje* among the Urhobo generally is the poetry of social comment. Such comment is fundamentally of a topical nature, and many songs have therefore had a rather short life. But depending on the beauty of the composition and the depth of its sentiment, a topical song may enjoy a lasting popularity and be seen as a transcending comment on life.

The real strength of *udje*, however, is in its comment on social morality, done with sharp satirical wit. So old is this art and so developed its techniques that it came to be organized on a larger, community-versus-community scale, especially among the Udu and Ughievben clans of central Urhoboland. Among these clans, group festivals were until very recent times held periodically with the satirical rivalry—or what Darah aptly calls the "battle of songs"—forming a principal ingredient of the occasion. In some songs the community as a whole would be attacked, but in many others the objects of attack were individual citizens and especially those among them known for their skill in composing *udje* songs. In fact, the better known the citizen and the cleaner his moral reputation, the more was the effort made to destroy him and so the more successful the song was considered to be. *Udje* satire was principally an art of poetic exaggeration aimed more at destroying character than at exposing evil. A community attacked in one festival would wait for the next festival to reply accordingly.

The description which Darah gives of the genesis of *udje* songs establishes clearly the progression from individual authorship or composition to communal ownership. To start with there was a careful division of labor, in any song group, between the composers *(irorile)* and the lead singers *(ebuole)*, as indicated by this statement from a song:

Ororile ta vberen phrun
Sieyen ǫbuole o ki yovb'urhuru

The song-maker must first compose beautifully
Before the vocalist can sing melodiously. (P. 84)

Well before the festival commenced, the orchestra would meet to identify the individuals in the rival community to be attacked and to assign the duty of composing the prospective songs—whether long *(ile-eshan)* or short *(ibro-ile)*—to a committee of composers, persons of recognized skill. In fact, any of these people would already have composed a song or two for the purpose. Later, at an appointed time and in a place sufficiently removed from the living quarters of their town (so as to keep their strategy closely guarded from their rivals, who might have posted spies within the community), the composing committee would meet to review and edit the songs composed by various individuals.

The actual process of composition shows what a delicate and painstaking job is involved in the making of African oral poetry. The lives of the individuals to be attacked are carefully reviewed so as to highlight the negative aspects and to distort as skillfully as possible the positive ones. The principal stylistic tools of this job are metaphor, allusion, analogy, and other kinds of oblique imagery designed to make it reasonably clear who the subjects are even when fake names are used. One of Darah's informants tells him of this process.

> The accomplished *ororile* does not have to wait for incidents to occur before creating a song. All of us in the neighbourhood know ourselves *(sic)*. If I want to accuse you in a song as a drunkard, I can do so without minding whether the allegation is true or not. Already I know you. Meanwhile it is someone else who is a drunkard that I have in mind, but since it is you I intend to humiliate I can mention your name in his place. That is why many people tend to think that a particular song refers to them simultaneously. A gifted *ororile* creates by deft use of allusions and analogy. As the song progresses metaphors are introduced. Once a metaphorical remark or proverbial allusion is made and explained logically later in the song, then that piece is acclaimed a successful one. (P. 91)

Although in most cases a song is initially the product of an individual imagination, there are situations in which a single song is the sum of various contributions, as another informant points out.

Two or three *irorile* can combine to produce a song. Even after one person has completed a new song, he can sing it to his colleague for possible refinement. It is this method that makes some songs to be profound *(muuririn)*. Sometimes, as many as three short songs can be combined into one. That is why we have songs with a lot of variety in tune. The number of such tunes in a particular song is often indicative of the number of artists involved in its creation. (P. 93)

These various compositions are then submitted to the composing committee for editing. Phrases and references here and there are refined or sharpened as the case may be; a word is added to one place or removed from another place to achieve the proper effect; and each line of song is appropriately regulated to achieve the maximum harmony with the musical beat and the dance movement that accompany the song.

One major reason why all this business of composition and editing is done in secret is to protect the identity of the individual composer. There is always the fear among every group that if the rival group can spy out the composers of these dangerous songs, medicinal charms can be prepared against them or some physical harm visited upon them. Over time, of course, the identity of a composer will emerge from recurring phrases, styles, and inadvertent personal references; but this is something that each group tries hard in these editing sessions to avoid. When the editing has been completed, the song is performed first to the rest of the orchestra who did not participate in the composition (including the lead singers) and, after the accompaniment of music and dance has been refined, finally to the public. The song at this stage is now the property of the orchestra as a whole, and the name of the composer is not advertised; but this is more because the composer's life or reputation must be protected than because his or her skill is not recognized.

The examples which we have examined so far are of oral literary compositions which have taken some time to shape. Perhaps one fundamental point about the nature of the oral composition should be grasped: it always involves some amount of compromise between tried and tested techniques and new elements invented or substituted for a specific occasion or purpose. In other words, artists have at their disposal a ready stock of phrases and devices which they have adopted from older artists and which are available for use in a variety of situations; it may be the technique for opening a story, as in the case we saw above of Karanke Dema introducing his Limba version of the story of Adam and Eve, or it may be the *udje* lead singer's standard method of introducing the subject of the satire for the group to pick up and elaborate. The ready-made phrase or pattern of procedure (called formula in discussions of oral composition) is now combined with new elements (names, situations, etc.), and a new song or tale is born.

Sometimes composition and performance happen simultaneously, especially in cases where an oral poet is moved to chant a piece of poetry on the spur of the moment. In *The Singer of Tales,* Lord made the classic statement that "an oral poem is not composed *for* but *in* performance," meaning that whatever the text of the poem artists have in mind before they come to perform, they necessarily make certain adjustments to suit the type of audience they face. In some cases, the question of a premeditated text does not arise, and the artist simply summons his or her skill to address an immediate subject.

A situation of this kind was reported by Archie Mafeje about the *imbongi* Melikaya Mbutuma. The poet had accompanied his patron, the Thembu Chief Mtikrakra Matanzirua, from their home in the Transkei to raise funds in Langa, a black township in Cape Town. During the reception held for the chief, there was a commotion when some of the guests tried to show their resentment of the presence of Mtikrakra and the other traditional leaders. One of those who tried to cool tempers at this point was a chief from the Joyi clan. He welcomed Mtikrakra with a speech that touched everyone but made a particular impact on the *imbongi* Mbutuma, who rose up and burst forth in an instant praise poem.

> I have been wondering what is happening to everybody else,
> That up to now nobody has made any reference to Joyi,
> The dark bull that is visible by its shiny horns,
> Horns that today are besmeared with streaks of blood.
> It is for that reason that today he is not amongst us,
> As I am talking to you now, he is far away in a
> Lonely desert. But, to me, it seems that even that
> Loneliness will not stop his bellowing. (Mafeje 1963: 92)

The atmosphere surrounding the reception was a politically charged one. The Transkei was one of those black South African homelands that the apartheid government had granted a sham independence. Many of the African youths in townships such as Langa (and Soweto) deeply resented this insult to black people's intelligence and were equally resentful of traditional rulers such as Mtikrakra for cooperating with a shameful political arrangement. The "Joyi" referred to in Mbutuma's instant chant had also been opposed to the policies of the government in respect of black rule, and for that had been banished from his homeland. In his chant Mbutuma would seem to be lamenting the absence of this great black leader; he may also have used the lament as a subtle attack on these urban youths for showing such little regard for their traditional leaders who (like the "Joyi") were the true heroes of the race.

But even more significant is the skill with which the poet delivered an impromptu composition. In the Xhosa tradition of praise poetry, human beings are eulogized with attributes of beauty, greatness, and nobility borrowed from the surrounding animal life. Here the heroic Joyi is pictured as a "dark bull," his eminence is portrayed with the metaphor of "shiny horns," and his bold and irrepressible protests portrayed by his incessant "bellowing." The oral poet has done an outstanding job here of bestowing, totally unrehearsed, a traditional pattern of imagery and diction on a brand-new subject, showing rather impressively how in African oral poetry the acts of composition and performance can take place simultaneously.

The Personality of the Artist

I have indicated some situations in which artists are forced to compromise themselves or suppress their personalities in the interests of their work. For instance, in our discussion of patronage we have seen how artists, in an effort to make a living, would not hesitate to bend the truth a little bit, especially if it might offend their patrons. And in tracing how a song is born in the *udje* satiric tradition of the Urhobo, we saw how composers gradually lose their identity for reasons beyond their control. But we also discovered that, despite all efforts to efface that identity, it was still possible to recognize certain peculiar techniques and references in a group of *udje* songs that would point to a particular composer in a community. Perhaps we should now give a little more attention to ways in which the personality of the artist continues to emerge and is sometimes forcefully asserted against the pressure or tyranny of the tradition.

A brief mention of my own experience in collecting oral literature in Nigeria may indicate how much artists' personalities and life-styles can influence the character of their work. Most of the performances I have recorded from Charles Simayi are stories of great men of the past, such as Meeme Odogwu and Ezemu, and of historic wars, such as the Ekumeku war. I pointed out above that Simayi is a highly respected man in his village, a man of considerable diplomatic wisdom and tremendous self-assurance; by occupation he is, among other things, a traditional doctor who deals in potent charms and medicines. Now, whatever may be the background for it, I have observed that these are fundamentally the same qualities and powers possessed by the principal heroes in Simayi's tales. At one point during my recordings I asked him if he had any tales in which he himself featured as a character. Thereupon he and his group struck up their instruments, and he told me a story about a rivalry for a chieftaincy title between the brothers Azujionye and Odobukwu in the palace of Obi (King) Izediuno of Ogwashi-Uku. In that encounter, Simayi features as a close counselor who helps the *obi* to resolve the contending claims of two men who exploit to the full the atmosphere of intrigue characteristic of court circles.

At the end I asked him if this was the only tale in his collection that he featured in. He then cleared his throat and, without any musical accompaniment and with a deep personal feeling, told me the story of his people's misfortunes during the Nigerian Civil War (1967–70) and the role he played. Part of that role involved going across to Ogwashi-Uku (about five kilometers away), where the victorious federal troops had a garrison, and rescuing cattle that had been salted away in the turmoil of war. In this story Simayi acts much like the major figures of his heroic tales, men blessed with considerable shrewdness but above all daredevil men who venture single-handed, armed as much with magic as with wit, into hostile territory. Whether we argue that Simayi is simply projecting his own personality on the characters of his tales or that he is trying to see himself in the light of these powerful men of bygone days, we will at least acknowledge that this form of art succeeds largely because the personal interests of the artist are involved in one way or another.

This is not to say that in every instance there is a close correspondence between the life of the artist and the subject of his or her song or tale. Finnegan tells us that one of her Limba storytellers, a blind man, "frequently added to the vividness of his narration by adding in an aside that he had been there at that point, standing silently by and observing with his own eyes—blind though his listeners knew them to be in actuality—the fantastic doings of animals or of Kanu (God)" (1967: 74). If the blind man's claim proves nothing else, it at least indicates that however distant the world of the tale is from him and whatever its origin, the artist is anxious to weave his personality into it.

Sometimes the presence of the artist's personality is not so obvious as it may seem in the case of Simayi, nor so deliberate as it clearly is in the case of the blind Limba narrator. To be able to determine in what way the artist impresses his or her personality upon the content of the work, we may have to compare versions of one tale or song by various artists and examine the differences in treatment of a particular detail, episode, or subject. Whatever may be the facts of a story as it exists in tradition, all storytellers treat the story in their own way and in accordance with their energies, temperament, and overall personality. Let us take, as an example, one fairly significant episode in the Sunjata legend as told by two of the artists recorded in Innes's *Sunjata: Three Mandinka Versions* (1974). In this episode Sunjata's mother dies in exile and Sunjata asks his host, the king Farang Tunkara of Mema, to give him a plot of land in which to bury his mother. Strangely enough, the king tells Sunjata that he will have to purchase the plot; Sunjata, hurt by what he considers an act of bad faith on the part of his host and friend, sends the king a few objects which are meant to show him how much he will suffer for his act.

This episode appears in the versions of the story by Bamba Suso and Dembo Kanute. At the time the story was recorded, Bamba was over seventy years old, while Dembo was in his fifties. Bamba could no longer sing very well nor play the traditional harp *(kora)* with which he once accompanied his tales; this was now done by his accompanist Amadu Jebate. Dembo, by contrast, was a rather energetic performer, and though he left the playing of the *kora* to his accompanist, the music accompanying his version of the story was varied (unlike Bamba's) eight times.

Now the treatment of the above episode by either of these men tells us something about the influence of his temperament and his personality on it. In his version Bamba tells us that Sunjata offered Tunkara a piece of gold (as money for the purchase) as well as a broken pot, a bush fowl's eggs, and some old thatching grass. One of Tunkara's soothsayers was present and interprets the meaning of these symbols to him.

> He said, "What Sunjata has said here
> Is that a day will come
> When he will smash this town of yours just like this broken pot;
> A day will come
> When old thatch will not be seen in this town of yours
> Because he will burn it all;
> A day will come
> When bush fowls will lay their eggs on the site of your deserted town.
> He says here is your gold." (P. 59)

There is a slight but significant difference in the objects which Dembo enumerates in his version, as well as in their interpretation. Dembo tells us that Sunjata gave Tunkara some red thread, a piece of old bamboo, a length of old rope, a piece of charcoal, a broken pot, and some old thatching grass. A *griot* named Bee Domo was there and proceeds to tell Tunkara the meaning of all this:

> Bee Domo said, "Makhang Sunjata says
> That if you accept this money,
> He will tie you up with this old rope;
> He will cut your throat with this old knife;
> This red cotton thread is your blood;
> This old bone is a broken arm and a smashed skull;
> This broken pot is strongholds razed to the ground
> And ruined compounds;
> This piece of charcoal is fire
> Set to the town;
> This old thatching grass is a deserted village." (P. 289)

Bamba enumerates three objects (that is, besides the piece of gold meant to pay for the plot of land) in the list of ominous symbols by which Sunjata threatened Tunkara, while Dembo has six objects. It is quite possible that the older artist is inclined to be rather economical in his use of details and to keep his performance under control, whereas the younger artist is a little more lavish in his use of details. The impression of the difference in temperament between the two artists is perhaps stronger in the interpretation of the symbols. In Bamba's reading we get a fairly ordinary picture of destruction or of a fallen city. But in Dembo's version the picture is a little more frightening because, in addition to the images of destruction, there is a considerable touch of horror in the references to blood and fire, to slashed throats, broken arms, and smashed skulls. All this points to an artist with a vivid sense of color and action but especially with a certain exuberance which may be a mark of relative youth. It is entirely possible, of course, that these two artists have told their versions of the story almost exactly as they have learned them. But performance depends to a large extent on personality, and what survives in a story, especially after the artist has been telling it for so many years, is what his temperament and his personality can accommodate.

A comparison of versions of the same subject by different artists could also reveal differences which point to the upbringing and personal lives of the artists. We shall see in chapter 6 that this kind of investigation has been the hallmark of the psychoanalytic branch of scholarship. In the meantime, let us examine briefly the possibilities of this approach as revealed by the fieldwork done by my former student Babatunde Ipinmisho as his bachelor's degree project (1980).

Ipinmisho selected two well-known narrators in his village of Ogidi-Ijumu in Kwara State, studied their lives as carefully as possible, and got each of them to tell his version of a popular folktale, "Idawa Erekefo." The story is about a hunter who goes to the bush to hunt specifically for a buffalo calf that he and his wife will serve to guests at a ceremony for the naming of their newborn child. The hunter kills the buffalo and carves the carcass on the spot but is unable to take all the meat home. His three dogs offer to turn into humans and help him so long as he keeps it secret; he gives them his promise. At home, his wife hardly believes his story that he was able to get all this meat with the help of three mere youngsters; in her persistence she consults a seer, who recommends that she feed her husband with such food and drink that he is forced to reveal the secret. She later taunts the dogs with this knowledge, and the disappointed animals run off to sea to transform themselves into marine life, driving their master into frustration and desperation.

One narrator, Ajayi Okoh, was in his mid-forties. He had lost his father quite early and was raised by an uncle whose name (Olora) was frequently cited as Ajayi's surname. Ajayi grew up to be a somewhat deprived man; deeply attached to traditional religion but rather diffident, he formed the habit (evident even in his tale) of invoking God's providence. He was notorious as an alcoholic and perhaps on account of this, had severe problems in his domestic life. His marriage was far from happy; quarrels with his wife (known to be a hard, domineering woman) virtually turned into a daily entertainment for their neighbors. Ajayi did not enjoy good relations with other members of his family, three brothers and a sister, who despised his alcoholism. On the whole Ajayi revealed the outlook of a man with a fairly troubled life, marked by frequent moments of depression which he sought to relieve with alcohol.

Ajayi had been drinking before he came to narrate his version of the tale to Ipinmisho, and the narration was occasionally interrupted by moments of lost coordination. But the alcohol had an even more intrinsic role to play in his story. We are told of the hunter in the story that he "likes drinks very much," and perhaps it is a reflection of the narrator's dominant habit that the hunter is lured into revealing his secret only with alcohol. Even more significant is the dominant role of women in this version, considering that Ajayi had an oppressive and quarrelsome wife. According to him, the hunter's wife is a woman who "could give orders and commands more than the man"; it is remarkable that the idea to procure a buffalo calf for the child-naming ceremony came from the hunter's wife in a language that is far from pleasant. The narrator also tells us that of the three dogs who transformed themselves into humans to help the hunter carry his meat home, one chose a female form; later the hunter produces three girls from the neighborhood to vouch to the hunter's wife that they helped the hunter carry the meat home. It seems likely that the image of woman dominates the events in this story mainly because of the menacing influence of Ajayi's wife on his life.

Thaddeus Medupin, Ipinmisho's second narrator, is a thoroughly different personality from Ajayi Okoh. Aged thirty-eight at the time of the recording, he was born into a reasonably prosperous and harmonious family. The discipline in his family was stern, but there was a great deal of love and security as well. His father was a well-to-do farmer with a large household, and his brothers, who had done well in various callings (law, teaching, politics), treated him with the same cordiality that they shared in their early youth. Even as a married man, he still lived with his parents in a household full of children. His wife, Adeboro, was born into a similarly comfortable family, and he had a happy, trouble-free marriage. Thaddeus was an agile, flamboyant, vivacious man with an expansive heart; he loved the company of children and was ever willing to tell a story and share a joke. His stories were frequently long and vivid; in Ipinmisho's words, "He can narrate a scene or an event you witnessed together in a manner that would make it more interesting and leave you with the feeling that you had actually never watched the event. In addition; he is a great lover of food and expects to be asked to join if he encounters anyone having a meal!"

The first thing that strikes us about Thaddeus's version is that it is much longer than Ajayi's. The dialogues are extended and fuller; there are three songs to Ajayi's none; there are frequently elaborate descriptions of scenes and objects, especially a lavish portrait of a beautiful woman into which the mother of the buffalo calf had turned; the idioms of the narration are quite poetic; and on the whole the plot of the story is larger and more complex than Ajayi's. These touches reveal Thaddeus's expansiveness and fullness of life. There are other significant pointers to Thaddeus's personality. There are a few references to food in this version, and perhaps it is remarkable that while Ajayi's hunter is lured to reveal his secret only with drink, Thaddeus's hunter is lured with food as well as drink. But perhaps the most telling element in Thaddeus's version has to do with the image of the man in it, as against the imposing presence of the female figure in Ajayi's version. Here it is the hunter, not his wife, who decides a buffalo calf should be procured for the ceremony; the three dogs all change into males to help the hunter carry the buffalo meat; and when the hunter's wife exposes the action of the dogs and thus drives them to escape in disappointment, the hunter cuts her down with a matchet (machete) rather than tolerate her impertinence. It may seem an intemperate thing to do, but the imposing image of the male in Thaddeus's version reveals a narrator who comes from a background of stern discipline and tremendous self-assurance, qualities traditionally associated with a masculine personality.

The above examples demonstrate, I think, that in the final analysis the merits of any piece of oral literature rest primarily on the peculiarities of the artist's personality. Those who sing chants or tell stories have a deep respect for the material they are handling because they realize, more than anyone else does, that that material is part of the cherished heritage of their people. But however sacred that material is, there is always room enough in it to accommodate the personal interests and outlook of the individual artists, even unconsciously. In fact, for all their respect for the tradition, artists are hardly inclined to compromise their personalities—which is why the Yoruba hunter-poet, when accused of deviating from the generally accepted facts of a chant, immediately demands that his personal views on the matter be respected:

> Let not the civet-cat trespass on the cane-rat's track.
> Let the cane-rat avoid trespassing on the civet-cat's path.
> Let each animal follow the smooth stretch of its own road. (Babalola 1966: 62)

The Artist's Place in Society

Whatever the degree of importance attached to the work of the oral artist in the past, there is no doubt that the passage of time has reduced it considerably in at least two ways. First, modern education and modern technology have relegated the artist to the background; in fact, many people who would have achieved prominence in their communities as oral artists are now finding their way into school and seeking employment in urban centers that removes them from opportunities for practicing their art. Second, even those oral artists who practice the art now are not always sure what the situation was like in the past; their styles as well as their roles have changed with time, and their memory of the tradition must be affected by the passage of time and the change in circumstances.

Still, there is enough consistency in the claims made by informants to give us an idea of the picture of things. First let us consider the image of the African oral artist in society. It would appear to be the pattern across the continent that court singers and chroniclers enjoyed a considerable amount of privilege and respect. In the highly sophisticated kingdom of Rwanda, for instance, the court poets and their families were not only given some income by the royalty but were also held to be outside the jurisdiction of the civil authorities and were exempted from performing communal labor. Even ordinary poets could have some of these privileges extended to them so long as they could recite the royal genealogies. In the old days, the Mandinka *griots* enjoyed a similar regard. Although historically they belonged to the lower castes of Mandinka society, they were given such special protection by the royalty that, as one of them tells us today,

> In Sunjata's day a griot did not have to fetch water,
> To say nothing of farming and collecting firewood.
> Father, world has changed, changed. (Innes 1974: 159)

It is also known today the royal *imbongi* of southern Africa enjoyed such a high regard that he could even swear at his chief if the latter went amiss.

The image of oral artists not attached to the royal court is not, unfortunately, quite so uniform. Since they are not protected by the prestige and the wealth of the ruler, these free-lance artists earn their regard mostly from the manner in which they comport themselves but partly also on the basis of their economic status. I will illustrate with two examples from my field experience. As I have mentioned, Simayi of Ubulu-Uno combines his skill as oral artist with a number of trades. Although he would not be considered a rich man, he has been able to put his children through school; his eldest son occupies a high government position in Lagos, the federal capital. A self-assured man, he once told me in an interview that modern civilization held no more mysteries for him, presumably because he had mastered these by securing education for his family. Although he takes a few drinks when he performs, he has no reputation as a drunkard. He is well respected in his town both by the ordinary citizens and by the *obi* (paramount chief).

A second artist in a nearby village is not that well regarded. He is recognized as an outstanding performer of stories but is rather notorious as a beer drinker; in a three-hour recording session, he and his supporting group of four musicians will consume about two cartons of beer. He is a farmer, but he has not done a very good job of it (partly because of poor health) and is known to be supported mainly by his younger sister in their father's house. He is notorious also as a follower of women. On the whole, he enjoys far less respect in his community than Simayi does in his.

Many oral artists across Africa have earned themselves a similar disrepute, and in most of these cases it would appear that reputation is closely tied to economic standing. It seems to be the case that in many traditional African communities no one sees oral art as a regular occupation; artists are expected to have respectable jobs as an economic base. Presumably the absence of such jobs would force the artists to put themselves perpetually at the mercy of all and sundry and thus compromise their personalities. The situation can be so bad that in some communities free-lance musicians have a somewhat low ranking in the eyes of the general public. Thus we are told by Hugo Zemp, for example, that among the Dan of the Ivory Coast the *griots* are considered so inferior socially that no father would let his daughter marry one of them (1964: 376). It does happen, of course, that some popular oral performers, especially in the urban centers, do so well that they do not need any other jobs to survive. But they are catering to cosmopolitan audiences who can pay handsomely for their entertainment.

Perhaps we should dwell a little longer on the difference in image and status between traditional (rural) African oral artists and their urban counterparts so as to highlight the changes which have occurred over time. In contrast to the rural artists, many urban performers can sustain themselves solely on their art. Not only do they perform frequently for the media and at crowded social occasions; they can also manage to be the main act in urban nightclubs and may indeed own these clubs themselves. They therefore make a reasonable amount of money on a regular basis; and although some of them may not have an enviable life-style, a large number of them are men living comfortably and married to women from respectable households. Others (such as the *waka* artist Salawa Abeni of Nigeria) are women whose fortunes make them the envy of other women whether married or single. The urban centers today offer the oral artist greater opportunities for economic independence than the traditional villages do, and the chances of social respectability are consequently increased.

But there is another significant difference. The modern city is a melting pot of people from various communities and ethnic groups, so that whereas in the village the artist and his fellow citizens are known to one another, in the city fewer people know the artist personally or relate to him or her outside the arena of performance. The role of the urban oral artist is therefore reduced almost entirely to entertainment for people who simply want to be relieved after a hard day's or week's work and who care somewhat less for what the artists say in their songs than for the music which accompanies them.

In the traditional setting of the village or small town, the artist does more. This brings us to a consideration of the artists' role in their society. But we shall save this for chapter 5, where we shall discuss in some detail the social functions which oral literature performs in African society.

3. The Oral Performance

The preceding chapter was intended to give us an insight into the background, the personality, and the status of the oral artist. It now remains for us to see the artist in action and consider the various factors that determine the success or the failure of the art. Here we shall be examining the circumstances surrounding the performance of African oral literature so as to understand how its literary character is realized within the only context where it is meaningful: before an audience.

The study of performance has become one of the most exciting and rewarding developments in the study of oral literature in recent years. In chapter 1 we saw how Malinowski and Bascom, pursuing their interest in the social context of folklore, urged scholars to record as much as possible the physical as well as the cultural circumstances in which tales and songs are performed. The interest in performance was an offshoot of this project, and in that chapter we saw the significant contributions made especially by literary scholars such as J. P. Clark and Harold Scheub in emphasizing the physical elements of performance—comments and questions by members of the audience (and the performer's reactions to these) as well as the performer's dramatization of the various moods and actions described in the text of a story. It is therefore in the study of performance that we are able to see the essential character of oral literature as distinct from written literature, that is, as an art form created in the warm presence of an audience as against the cold privacy of the written work. In this chapter we shall examine the various physical factors that influence the creativity of the oral artist.

Performances differ one from the other, depending on such factors as the age and energy of the performer, the nature of the occasion (death or merriment), the type of setting (cult enclave or open square), whether or not any musical accompaniments are used especially by the performer, and whether it is a solo or a group act. Let us therefore attempt a few brief sketches to get a feeling of the varied nature of the performance of African oral literature.

Varieties of Performance

To begin with, let us get clear what is involved in the oral performance. Oral literature is fundamentally literature delivered by word of mouth. This implies that there must be a certain appeal not only in what the performer is saying but in the way it is said (whether in the manner of plain speech or of chanting or singing). Even in some categories of oral literature where a more or less fixed body of text is recognized and the speaker-performer is expected to recite it (as in divination poetry), much of the appeal lies in the quality of the voice used and the skill with which the speaker manipulates the tones of the words involved. Other more elaborate forms of oral performance involve the use of musical instruments and dancing as accompanying devices.

Some of the simpler kinds of performance have to do with games played at times of relaxation. An example is the practice of telling proverbs and riddles in competition when the evening meal is over and the immediate or extended family is gathered in the compound to relax before going to bed. The group may be small or large; the primary objective in such sessions is the fun and excitement derived from the success or failure with which one person responds to the verbal challenge posed by another. John Kaemmer (1977) has reported such a tradition of riddle telling among the Tshwa of southern Mozambique. In these riddling sessions, someone tells a riddle and the challenge is for someone else to reply to that riddle with the appropriate statement. The first aim of the response is to demonstrate wisdom by giving the right response, but other objectives include giving a response that matches the challenge exactly in number of syllables and balancing the tones of the response with those of the challenge to achieve similarity or contrast. The Tshwa language, being highly tonal, makes this sort of tradition possible. No musical instruments are played, and contestants get no help from the audience; they are left to depend entirely on the skill with which they can match the wisdom stored in their memories with the subtleness of their voices.

We may now move on to discuss the more complex kinds of oral performance involving extended texts of oral literature, such as songs and chants. There seems to be a strong general feeling among scholars that some kinds of chants have a rather fixed text from which the performers are not expected to deviate. Evidence suggests, for instance, that the dynastic chants performed by the royal poets of Rwanda were rather rigidly presented and that reactions from the audience were not particularly encouraged.

> Unlike the amateur, who makes gestures with the body as well as the voice, the professional reciter adopts an impervious attitude, with a rapid and unaccented style of delivery. If his audience reacts with admiration, the reciter holds back his voice with detachment, until silence is restored. (Coupez and Kamanzi 1970: 77)

This may be largely because such a reciter saw himself more as a chronicler than as a performer. Besides, considering the sensitive political nature of these royal histories, it is possible that the reciter here wanted to be sure that the facts of his account were not corrupted by the distracting influence of the audience. Still, the "rapid and unaccented style" that he employed was a skill which he developed in training and which was considered the most effective style for performing such a text in public.

In ritual divination poetry such as that used in the Yoruba *ifa* system, it is true, the diviner endeavors to recite faithfully some parts of the text, though the difference between one diviner and another may lie in the skill with which the voice and the face are manipulated in the process of the chanting. But in other parts of the system the diviner is expected to use his own resourcefulness to improvise the text of the chant so long as the essential message of the *ese* is conveyed. "The language of *ese ifa* is therefore not static at all," Abimbola tells us. "The Ifa priest has some freedom to innovate" (1976: 63).

In other performances of songs and chants there may be a fixed basic text but portions of the performance are adjusted to suit the interests of the audience. This is particularly the case with song and dance groups. As a rule, the portions sung by the chorus (e.g, refrains) may not change; the chorus is simply expected to follow rigidly the basic rhythm of the performance. But the leader of the group may vary the solo sections, for instance, to salute a familiar person coming into the scene of performance, to pay tribute to a patron, or even to make a comment. Take the story told me by Charles Simayi about the struggle for chieftaincy in Ogwashi-Uku. Here is one of the many songs accompanying the story.

Bard:	Mm, let's go to the palace. Oh——	
Chorus:	Let's go to the palace	
Bard:	Nwadobe, my son ⎫	*seven times*
Chorus:	Let's go to the palace ⎭	
Bard:	5 Just look at you!	
Chorus:	Let's go to the palace	
Bard:	Let's go to the palace	
Chorus:	Let's go to the palace	
Bard:	You're sleeping off!	
Chorus:	10 Let's go to the palace	
Bard:	Let's go to the palace	
Chorus:	Let's go to the palace	
Bard:	Let's go to the palace	
Chorus:	Let's go to the palace	
Bard:	15 Music man, save your pay	
Chorus:	Let's go to the palace	
Bard:	Save your pay	
Chorus:	Let's go to the palace	
Bard:	Mm—	
Chorus:	20 Let's go to the palace!	

This song is sung by the group at a rather fast pace, underlining the feverish haste with which each contestant carries gifts to the king to influence the award of chieftaincy. If the words did not change, the pace of the singing would still be enough to carry the force of the event. But the bard's digressive comments enhance the effectiveness of both the song and the story. One of the musicians accompanying the bard has become sleepy and his music has slowed a bit. The bard calls his attention to this on lines 5 and 9, and warns him on lines 15 and 17 that he may lose his reward or payment as a result of a poor job. It is all a joke, of course, and everyone laughs at the end of the song. The variation of the song certainly improves its effectiveness with the audience.

One could even go further and say that variation or manipulation of the material is a standard ingredient in the performance of oral literature and that the audience is more likely to be impressed by a performer who shows some resourcefulness with the text of a chant or song than by one who simply recites his lines mechanically.

It is in storytelling performances that we see the maximum use of innovation and manipulation. In most narrative traditions across the African continent, the storyteller simply has the bare outlines of the story and is expected to make the appropriate adjustments to the details in accordance with the interests of the audience. But the storyteller often does more. To make the narration more vivid and convincing the performer must accompany the words of the tale with the appropriate face and body movements to illustrate such things as fear, anxiety, delight, and the behaviors of various characters in the tale. An early report by two British scholars, Smith and Dale, about narrative performances among the Ila of Zambia bears witness to the picturesque nature of the event.

> It would need a combination of phonograph and cinematograph to reproduce a tale as it is told. One listens to a clever story-teller, as was our old friend Mungalo, from whom we derived many of these tales. Speak of eloquence! Here was no lip mumbling, but every muscle of face and body spoke, a swift gesture often supplying the place of a whole sentence. He would have made a fortune as a raconteur on the English stage. The animals spoke each in its own tone: the deep rumbling voice of Momba, the ground hornbill, for example, contrasting vividly with the piping accents of Sulwe, the hare. It was all good to listen to—impossible to put on paper. (Smith and Dale 1920: 336)

Some narrators perform alone and are able to make a deep impression on their audience. But others perform with a group of backers with music and other resources. Perhaps the best available record so far of an African narrative performance in which the various resources and techniques are put to effective use is *The Ozidi Saga*, collected and edited by Clark from the Ijo of the Nigerian delta. The story of Ozidi—the posthumously born child who avenges his fathers' killers, destroys all the other evil forces in his community, and ultimately reigns supreme—is known and told by several storytellers in the Ijo area. It is also performed in appropriate sequences over the seven days of a ritual festival among the Tarakiri-Orua subgroup of the Ijo, where the story originated in the first place. The entire performance is accompanied by music, dancing, and dramatic actions aimed at illuminating various moments and episodes of the story. The version of the story published by Clark was tape recorded from a narrator operating outside the traditional festival circumstances. But a reading of the book reveals that the storyteller and his group of accompanists lost little in not performing in that kind of environment. Numerous instances of dramatic action are evident in the text, and songs frequently accompany the story; but the most exciting aspect of this particular performance is the countless intrusions of members of the audience into the narrative—asking questions, exclaiming, laughing, and making comments—and the responses of the narrator to the challenges. Later in this chapter we shall look in detail at the ways in which this narrator's audience influences his work.

I have tried in this section to give a general picture of the various kinds of oral performance that may be encountered. It now remains for us to examine how factors operating within and around a performance affect the quality of the oral literature produced at the scene.

Paralinguistic Resources

In *Oral Literature in Africa*, Finnegan makes the important point that in oral literature "the bare words can *not* be left to speak for themselves." Part of what she means is that so many factors are involved in the delivery of the words that to understand the meaning or impact of the words themselves in their proper context, we have to take these factors into consideration. In appreciating the literary effectiveness of a written work, all we may need to concern ourselves with is the text we have before us. But oral artists use more than their mouths to express their words; to consider the effectiveness of the words, therefore, we should examine the usefulness of those accompanying resources where such information is available or can be deduced. These accompanying resources are variously described as nonverbal, extraverbal, paraverbal, paratextual, or paralinguistic, in the sense that they occur side by side with the text or the words of the literature.

One of these resources is the histrionics of the performance, that is, movements made with the face, hands, or any other part of the body as a way of dramatically demonstrating an action contained in the text. These movements may or may not be specifically named in an account of the performance. What Smith and Dale tell us about the narrative performance of the Ila storyteller Mungalo—"every muscle of the face and body spoke, a swift gesture often supplying the place of a whole sentence"— is clearly a description of the man's histrionic skill. Scheub paints an equally impressive picture of the movements made by a Xhosa storyteller, Nongenile Zenani, in her production of folktales.

> She is not given to broad outward dramatic gesticulation, and one is apt to miss the extraverbal elements of her production if one does not watch her carefully. . . . Her art is subtle, and understated even when it is most bombastic. Her face and body are constantly in harmony with the developing production: a slight grimace, a flash of fear, anger, joy. Her hands work softly, calmly, deftly, moulding the performance, giving a nuance to this character, adding depth to that one, her red blanket shimmering slightly and continually as her body moves rhythmically to the poetry of her narrative. (1972: 116)

So important are these dramatic movements considered for the effectiveness of the story that in many traditions of narrative performance across Africa, a story is told in convenient movements or episodes, in such a way that each episode is preceded by a miming of its basic details. Without these subtle dramatic efforts, the story in the oral tradition is often considered to have been ineffectively told. Not every storyteller, of course, goes into all this elaborate histrionic or dramatic activity. But it is frequently considered a measurement of good narrative skill on the part of a storyteller.

During my fieldwork at the village of Onicha-Ugbo, I asked some people why they considered Odogwu Okwuashi to be the best storyteller in the village. They replied that he was unequaled in the way he used his body for miming and dancing.

Dancing is indeed closely related to dramatization in the oral performance; it is a way of making the performance a thoroughly attractive spectacle. Dancing has an appeal of its own, of course, and no doubt every African community has a number of traditional dance groups who sing and dance on a variety of occasions purely as entertainment. But certain dance movements are specifically aimed at giving vivid emphasis to actions expressed in a song and may indeed suggest those actions without any need for words. Enoch Mvula has described a song and dance performance among the Chewa of Malawi. Called *gule wamkulu*, it is "an art form in which music, dance and drama are totally integrated." During the *gule wamkulu* performance—done originally at initiation ceremonies but nowadays at other occasions, such as commemorative rites for the dead and even independence celebrations—various persons dressed in animal masks to conceal their identities are engaged to sing and dance about various social ills and problems. In one of these episodes, a masked dancer called a *kapoli* appears with a song about a mistreated wife urging her husband to set her free from her miserable marriage. Mvula describes how the dance and dramatic movements of the *kapoli* lend much effectiveness to the message of the song, with the full participation of both the orchestra and the audience.

> Kapoli begins to dance by paddling with the left leg then the right one. The dancing builds up slowly and warms up to the required climax. The drummers play the drums with their palms but you see from their head and body movements and facial expressions that they are part of the song and the performance too. The audience-participants wear beaming faces; and they imitate the continuously elastic and plastic body movements of the kapoli as they take up the chorus and clap their hands. Some of them talk to each other indicating that the song refers to so and so who is among the crowd. They point at him and laugh as the performance goes on. The kapoli acts the role of the woman complaining in the song. He moves towards the audience-participants, slightly bends towards them, clasps his arms and puts them behind on his back as the women jubilantly join him, melodiously singing the song. He shakes his head as the woman's gesture of making a plea to the husband to leave her free. He dances with a lot of elasticity and plasticity, and a crowd of dust rises up. The dancing, clapping of hands, singing, drumming and acting humorously mix to reach the climax of the situation. (Mvula 1990: 91–92)

Donatus Nwoga gives an equally interesting description of the performance of satirical poetry among the Igbo of Nigeria by women dance groups. These groups, which perform on a variety of occasions, are particularly versed in the composition and performance of songs dealing with aspects of social morality, especially the sexual laxity of young boys and girls. One of these poems, beginning with the line *O di la gbakisima ukwu umu anyi e* ("Opening the waist is not the problem, our children"), makes a subtle but (to that particular village) obvious attack on "a young girl who found no problem with having sex, but was screaming in pain when it came to delivering the baby." According to Nwoga, the point about the girl's immorality was driven home by the performers not simply through the constant repetition of that first line (four times more in a ten-line poem) "but also by their dance movement," which obviously emphasized swift and lewd gyrations of the waist (1982: 235).

Even in the performance of extensive heroic tales and chants, dance movements are frequently included. Eno Belinga, who has done research into traditions of the heroic narrative *(mvet)* among various communities in Cameroon, draws attention to the fact that the performers (called *mbomo-mvet*) dance a good deal in the course of telling their stories to musical accompaniment (1965). In performing the extensive episodes of the Ozidi story among the Ijo of Nigeria, as Clark tells us, the performer and group often dance several movements to give vivid account of the significant events of the story (1977: xxxi). And the narrator of the heroic tale of Mwindo among the Banyanga of Zaire dances to good measure and compares his skill in dancing to that of *kasengeri* (an animal) as he wags his tail (Biebuyck 1969: 71).

In fact, to enhance this image of the dancer-performer, many narrators adorn themselves with clothes and implements which are either associated with the story being told or at any rate are intended to make the narrators more spectacular than ordinary storytellers. This picture is evident among the Cameroonian and Zairean performers just mentioned. In many instances the *mbomo-mvet* is decked out not only with leaves and frills but also with animal skins and amulets; clearly the purpose of the latter two articles is to symbolize the strength and magical power of the great hunter-warriors immortalized in the stories. The narrator of the Mwindo story also adorns himself both with the "conga-scepter," the magical instrument that the hero constantly uses in the story, and with an arm band. As Biebuyck points out in his note on the reference to *kasengeri:* "The narrator, who dances while singing this song, wears around the upper arm an armlet made of fibers cut from dried banana leaves. He praises himself as a good dancer and asks the onlookers to observe the movements of his arms adorned with the fiber armlets." The performer of the Ozidi story among the Ijo often holds a fan, a magical implement associated with the hero Ozidi's grandmother-witch, Oriame, who protects him throughout his numerous encounters. These examples may also be compared to the habit of the South African *imbongi* of holding up a spear as he chants his *izibongo* (heroic praises) and does some manly movements in the process.

The significance of these instances of dance and dramatic movements to the text of oral literature is sufficiently clear. In many an oral performance, the words spoken are only part of a general spectacle designed to please both the ears and the eyes. In written literature, however much the adjectives and the descriptions employed by a novelist or a poet appeal to our imagination, they are at least two steps removed from the object or the event that the writer is trying to capture. Besides, since the novelist usually has no personal contact with the audience (the readers) and often has no idea who is going to read the work anyway, the phrases, being devoid of physical demonstration, must be explicit. But in the oral performance the words are frequently given this physical demonstration and in many cases depend on this demonstration for their effectiveness. For instance, in describing a fight between two combatants, an oral narrator is apt to tell us of the action of one or the other: "He stabbed him, and stabbed him, and stabbed him." Part of the background to the repetitiveness of that statement comes from the fact that the narrator repeatedly jabbed his or her own hand (or perhaps head) while making the statement. Writers are not likely to write in that fashion because, since they do not do their work in the presence of a physical audience, they do not engage in any physical demonstration which would support a repetition of words; so they simply write something like "He stabbed him many times."

Or let us take that repetition of "Opening the waist is not the problem, our children" in the Igbo dance satire. By itself that line may be understood as a sober warning to youths to consider the larger consequences of sexual laxity. But when we realize that that statement was accompanied by lewd gyrations of the waist among the dancers, then it will be clear to us that this seemingly sober statement drew a laugh from the audience and that the dancers repeated it so many times partly because they expected laughs and partly because of the musical appeal of repetition. When we see repetitions in the text of an oral performance, we may wish to ask questions about the manner in which the text was performed in the first place (including the nonverbal techniques used); when we encounter repetitions in a writer's work, such questions hardly arise.

Let us dwell a little longer on the use of implements that create a visual impact during performances. In the cases referred to above—the "conga-scepter" held by the performer of the Mwindo story, the fan held by the performer of the Ozidi story, the spear held by the *imbongi*—the implements play a symbolic role in relation to the text of the performance as well as enhance the dance and dramatic roles of the performer (in the case of the *imbongi*, for instance, the person being praised with the spear may never have been a warrior). There are cases, however, in which a visual image is used as a sign rather than a symbol, in the sense that it provides a direct illustration of the text being performed and so impresses the message of the text far more deeply in the minds of the audience. When I performed burial rites for my mother in April 1984, one of the dance groups attending the ceremony held an enlarged portrait of her aloft as they sang and danced in her honor round our town.

Daniel Avorgbedor reports an experience from Ghana.

> During one of the *xatsevu* (rattle music) performances in an Ewe village called Seva, a sculptural piece depicting an eagle hovering over a turtle was displayed. At one stage during the singing of songs, both the performers and the audience turned to look in the direction of the sculpture. The words being sung at that stage . . . are directly related to the images:
>
> > We are the turtle that does not lie down as a prey for eagle,
> > The eagle will prey on us and its claws will be ruined;
> > The eagle tried but found nothing to eat,
> > That is why they are angry. . . .
>
> This visual memory of the sculpture will help concretize the text into a more permanent and effective whole. With the visual illustration the words are less likely to be forgotten, and permanence is consequently achieved. (1990: 223)

Darah reports an even more amazing tradition of the use of physical effects during performances of *udje* satirical poetry among the Urhobo of Nigeria.

One of such is the bearing of an effigy of the satirized person into the arena. The effigy scene preceeds the performance of the song in which the character is attacked. Messrs Omoko and Djekota of Egbo-Ide told me of how their ward (Uduvbepian) used this device to create sensation in one year of public performance. The effigy was that of one Mr Obophien who had crooked legs. These features were faithfully represented by the carver. The figure was made more grotesque by painting it with charcoal. A few moments before Obophien's song was started, some men rushed into the dance ring with the effigy and stood it in the centre amidst thunderous ovation. Soon after, the performers danced round it singing:

> Obophien has come out
> Crooked, crooked legs!
> Obophien's song is on
> Crooked, crooked legs!

It is further reported that Obophien's ward stole the effigy the night after the performance because, as my informants put it, it was feared that the object could have adverse magical effect on Obophien's life. (1982: 121–22)

In these various performances the text has, of course, a self-contained message, but the use of visual imagery enhances it. Such a device has its relevance only in an oral performance.

One final paralinguistic resource which has a deep impact on the performance of oral literature is music. The *griot* who narrated to Djibril Niane the story of Sunjata told him, "Music is the griot's soul" (Niane 1965: 15). This statement should no doubt be taken to imply that music provides the basic inspiration for whatever these artists say in their performances. There are, of course, oral performances in which music in the normal sense of the term is not prominent. For instance, riddles and proverbs are mostly unaccompanied by any kind of instrumentation or even the clapping of hands. Tales told in the moonlight are also not generally accompanied by instrumental music, although there is singing and clapping of hands. Such simpler forms of performance do not pose grave challenges to the oral art; errors could always be corrected with the artist beginning the riddle or the story afresh. And since the performance is not being held on a grand scale before a large audience, there is little need for instrumental accompaniment to provide a stable rhythm on which the words could be sustained without any awkward breaks.

The element of stability is important, for there has to be the right balance between the music and the words in the oral performance; this at any rate has been discovered by many collectors of oral literature in the field. In tales that I have collected, the narrator and his musical accompanists have often started by making sure that the music is properly tuned to the right key and speed. Other scholars have made even more radical discoveries. Bruno Nettl found from his numerous recordings across Africa that traditional singers give either text or music alone of their songs only with difficulty (1956: 21). And Daniel Biebuyck told me in a personal letter (March 10, 1975) about his own experience in collecting stories in Zaire: "Without the right rhythm, the narrator simply seems to lose the thread of his inspiration."

Let us look at a few examples which reveal the close relationship between music and words in an oral performance. *The Ozidi Saga* is made up essentially of the numerous fights which the hero Ozidi has with one figure after another. In one of these terrible fights, between Ozidi and a monstrous figure known as the Scrotum King, the hero's hornblower goes into a feverish act of hornblowing to warn the hero that it is time to suspend the fight; at this point, the narrator feels that a corresponding act on the part of the supporting musicians is needed to drive home the message, so the narrator tells the orchestra, "Now let the things speak up" (p. 220). Later on, the hero is confronted by another monster, the seven-headed Tebesonoma whose seven heads issue loud, confused noises as he moves; again, to portray the monster's approach effectively, the narrator instructs the orchestra, "Time the drum was touched a little" (p. 236).

These examples show the musical accompaniment playing a role similar to that of dance and dramatic movements as discussed above, i.e., supporting the oral text in such a way as not only to drive home a point but also to make the overall performance a more impressive spectacle. But an even more revealing role of the music can be seen in the fact (which, as I said, Biebuyck mentioned in his letter to me) that if the music is not right the oral performer tends to be distracted and even disorganized. An amusing incident took place during my recording of the story "Meeme Odogwu" from Simayi in 1980. When, at a certain point of the narration, Simayi observed that the younger of his two percussionists had lost his musical timing, he snatched the bottle from him and struck it at the right rhythm, saying, "We are not doing the samba!"

A similar experience had been recorded earlier in the performance of the Malian epic *Kambili*. From the various instructions which the narrator gave to his harp players, it would seem that the narrator expected a fairly quick rhythm to back some of the songs occurring in the story and so warned them with such words as "Hurry up on the strings, harpists," and "Ah! Harpist, you're slowing down my words!" For the regular narrative section of the tale, the narrator did not need a particularly fast beat and so cautioned, "If you speed up the strings, I am not able to speak," and "Ah! Rhythm man, rhythm man! Slow down a little!"[1] It seems clear, therefore, that the oral text is at the mercy of the musical accompaniment in such a situation and, for the whole performance to be a successful event, there has to be a just balance between the two.

Music is not the only element in the oral performance from which the artist faces the risk of a disorientation, or which at any rate exerts a certain amount of influence on the performer. Let us consider a few other factors.

Performer and Accompanist

Many oral artists in Africa perform alone, but many are accompanied by one or more persons who provide support for the artist. Some of these accompanists may be artists in their own right, who have decided to join the leader either because they have not been particularly successful in organizing their own groups, have no interest in leading a group, or wish to do the leader a good turn. One instrumentalist accompanying my narrator Simayi is a young elementary schoolteacher, Dennis Amamfueme; he has won prizes in state-organized storytelling contests, but being a full-time teacher he has not bothered to organize a group and frequently accompanies Simayi both out of respect for the man and as a way of keeping his narrative talent alive. The older accompanist, Okondu Enyi, is a farmer like Simayi, has known him since youth, and accompanies him regularly purely out of respect and goodwill. Simayi is also sometimes accompanied by a man named Osadebe, who does not play any instruments but makes comments now and then as the narration progresses. In other groups, especially song and dance groups, the artist may have, in addition to musicians, accompanists who appear in uniform dresses and dance to the rhythm of the music, as a way of enhancing the spectacle.

Besides attending to the music and spectacle of a performance, accompanists play the significant role of influencing the oral artist in the delivery of the words. There are a number of ways in which we could consider the influence of accompanists on the text of the oral performance, and perhaps we should begin by looking at instances in which their participation is most welcome and least likely to cause distraction. One of these may be seen in storytelling sessions in the moonlit village, when the narrator appoints someone from the audience—or perhaps someone volunteers—to aid by offering brief statements now and then, confirming the truth or the wisdom of what the narrator says in the story. Finnegan discovered such a situation among the Limba of Sierra Leone.

> The narrator sometimes chooses a special friend and designates him as the "answerer" *(bame)* to reply *(me)* to the narration. . . . Once appointed, this "answerer" must then interject phrases like "yes" *(ndo)*, "mmm," "fancy that" *(woi)*, "really!" *(ee)* at appropriate moments, and react quickly with laughter, exaggerated amusement, or dismay at the events related in the story. He often repeats the important points or proper names of the characters in an undertone to emphasize them, or interpolates clarifying words such as the name of the character speaking or acting at the time, especially if the audience seems at all confused, with reiterations of key phrases at dramatic moments, brief questions when the point is a little obscure, or prompting if the teller appears to hesitate for a name or sequence. This formal practice of "replying" often gives an extra impression of speed and intensity to the telling of a story, and, though by no means universal, is one way in which a member of the audience can formally take part in the actual narration. (1967: 62–68)[2]

This device, whereby an accompanist corroborates the statements of the performer, also occurs in poetic chants. A Yoruba masquerade chant *(ewi egungun)* contains comments of the accompanist or fellow-masquerade (First Oje) on the supreme power of death.

Second Oje:	Offspring of Abilodesu, listen to my words.
	One with disordered head-pad
	Offspring of one whom the drums hail with rebellious strains.
	But for death.
5	Adisa, listen to my sermon
	But for death, three persons would have designated themselves, God the King.
	Now ask me, say, who are they?

First Oje:		Who are they?
		However it may be, explain it
	10	Because a woman will always open wide the door of the feared one.
Second Oje:		A rich man would have designated himself, God the King.
		What of the medicine man (the Doctor)?
		He would have designated himself, God the King.
		The great priest, would have designated himself, God the King.
	15	On the day death would kill the rich man
		Money would be of no avail
		On the day death would kill the medicine man
		The charm that locks up man's intentions,
		The one that stupefies one
	20	The one that makes one look like a fool
		The one that arrests one's movements,
		Indeed, everything will perish.
		On the day death will kill the great priest,
		Gentle winds will carry off all his papers.
First Oje:	25	It is true, it is perfectly so.
		Death kills a herbalist
		As if he learnt no Ifa. . . . (Olajubu 1977b: 170)

In the preceding example of performer-accompanist exchanges, it is clear that the accompanist makes a great deal of impact on the work of the main artist. The element of "speed" which Finnegan has observed in such a dialogue may not be immediately obvious on the printed page; but anyone who has observed such sessions, especially of the *ewi egungun* kind, will know that the lines are chanted at considerable speed and that these exchanges are consequently marked by a high level of excitement. Added to all this is the fact that the accompanist's remarks not only expand the scope of the main performance but also underscore it by highlighting certain aspects that may not be immediately apparent. For instance, in line 8 the masquerade's companion complies with the invitation from the main performer to ask a question but then goes on to add, in the next two proverbial lines, that however closely guarded it is, the secret is bound to be revealed. That statement is likely to cause laughter among the audience, thereby giving the whole performance added effect. From line 25 onward the accompanist not only concurs with the masquerade poet but goes on to elaborate on the poet's statements.

Finnegan, in her description of the situation among the Limba, cites "prompting" as one of the jobs done by an accompanist in a narrative performance. It may happen that in the course of the narration a storyteller forgets a character's name or the next event in the story's sequence. Some narrators save themselves embarrassment by filling in the interval with music until they can remember the missing detail. But often it is the job of the accompanist to correct such lapses of memory. More than that, the accompanist may feel that certain details (e.g., archaic words, ancient customs, and other references) may not be clear to members of the audience; the accompanist may then come in and ask the artist to clarify these points. At other times, the accompanist may throw in comments to induce the artist either to curtail or to expand the

performance. Innes (1974) has been sensible enough to record such interruptions as
they occurred in the performance of *Sunjata,* and we may take a look at a few of these
from the first version of the story by the *griot* Bamba Suso.

The story tells essentially how a Susu king, Sumanguru, overran the Mandinka of
Mali (Manding) and usurped the kingdom there, forcing the young heir to the throne,
Sunjata, and his mother and sister (or sisters) into exile. Sunjata grows from strength
to strength, and when the time comes for him to fight back and reclaim his kingdom,
he summons a number of powerful allies to his aid. As Bamba Suso reports the arrival
of each ally, he spends considerable time in showering praises on him and recounting
some of his deeds of valor. After he has introduced and glorified Sunjata's maternal
grandfather, Sankarang Madiba Konte, at great length, Bamba goes off into a digressive chant recalling heroes of bygone days and lamenting that the days of heroism are
no more. At this point Bamba's musical accompanist Amadu Jebate cuts in.

> *Amadu asks:*   At that time was he preparing to wage war against Susu Sumanguru?
> *Bamba:*   He declared that he would not become king of Manding
>   Until he and Susu Sumanguru had first joined battle.
>   They were at that point
>   5   When Sora Musa came—(P. 67)

It is not clear why Amadu thought it necessary to cut in. It may be that he felt his
master had gone into the digressive chant because he had lost the trend of the story,
or he may have thought the digression had gone on too long. In any case, his interruption has the effect of forcing Bamba back into the story proper and introducing
the next ally, Sora Musa (the great Faa Koli).

Amadu was to engage Bamba shortly after this in a series of interruptions. Although he has been receiving some very powerful allies (like Madiba Konte and Sora
Musa) to his side, Sunjata persistently says he will not join battle with Sumanguru
until a particular leader, Tira Makhang, whom he describes as a trusted and untiring
warrior, has arrived. Bamba narrates this time and again until Amadu again inter-
rupts.

> *(Amadu:*   Make clear to us which families, with which surnames
>   Trace their descent from Tira Makhang.
> *Bamba:*   When you hear the name Sora Musa,
>   If someone is called by the surname Dumbuya, that is Suuso.
>   5   If someone is called by the surname Kuruma, that is Suuso.
>   If someone is called by the surname Danjo, that is Suuso.
>   If someone is called by the surname Geyi, that is Suuso.
>   All of those are descended from Sora Musa.
>   If someone is called by the surname Njai, that is Konte.
>   10   If someone is called by the surname Jara, that is Konte.)
>   When Tira Makhang rose up—
>   That Tira Makhang is the great Taraware.
>   *Amadu asks inaudible questions.*

Bamba:	The Tarawares' surname is Tira Makhang.
15	The surname Dambele is Tira Makhang.
	The surname Jebate is Tira Makhang.
	The surname Job is Tira Makhang.
	The surname Juf is Tira Makhang.
	The surname Saane is Tira Makhang.
20	The surname Maane is Tira Makhang.
	The descendants of Tira Makhang are all scattered,
	Their surnames are all changed in this way.
	But the original surname of all of them was Taraware.
	Tira Makhang was descended from Siisi,
25	Siisi fathered Taamana,
	Taamana fathered Kembu,
	Kembu fathered Kembu and Teneng,
	And the latter fathered Tarakoto Bullai Taraware.
	From that the griots say,
30	"Kirikisa the man who accompanies the king,
	The man who rides horses to death and kills anyone who gainsays him."
(Amadu:	Then the warriors arrived.)
	When Tira Makhang was coming,
	He said, "Wrap me in a shroud,
35	Because when I see Susu Sumanguru, either I put him in a shroud or he puts me in a shroud.
	That is my declaration."
	He called his wives,
	And he put them in mourning,
	And he declared, "When I see Susu Sumanguru,
40	If he does not do this to my wives, then this is what I will do to his wives."
	He lay down upon a bier,
	And they carried it on their heads and came and laid it at Sunjata's feet,
	And Tira Makhang said to him, "There is no need to make a speech;
	As you see me,
45	Either he will kill me and wrap me in a shroud and lay me upon a bier
	Or else I will kill him and they will wrap him in a shroud and lay him upon a bier."
(Amadu:	At that time they were preparing for battle, but they had not yet set out.
Bamba:	War had not yet broken out.
	At that time they were preparing for battle.)
50	When the leading men had responded,
	The army rose up
	And battle was joined at Taumbaara. (P. 69–70)

It is clear that in the first two lines of this passage, Amadu wishes Bamba to expand his narration, and for a good reason. These heroic narratives told about the great leaders of the past usually give the *griots* a chance to perform their traditional role of imparting lessons of social and political history. As Innes tells us in his introduction, the story was performed in a school hall with students (and neighbors of the school) attending; such a lesson could not have been given in a better place. Besides, since Tira Makhang is reputed to have been an ancestor of many families of the western Mandinka (especially in Gambia and Guinea-Bissau), certain members of the audience there would feel extremely proud to have their families mentioned in the distinguished ancestry here glorified by the narrator.

But Bamba would seem to have got Amadu's request wrong at first; instead of tracing the descendants of Tira Makhang, he has gone on (from line 3) to trace the descendants of Sora Musa. Hence, in line 13, although his words did not register clearly in the tape recorder, he seems to have corrected Bamba, who then goes on to trace the descendants of Tira Makhang. Incidentally, on line 16 we may find a personal reason why Amadu Jebate felt the need to correct Bamba: his own family is part of this glorious roll call!

Bamba goes on about Tira Makhang's family and would seem to be overdoing it, until Amadu comes in again on line 32 to bring him back to the main story, which now introduces the long-awaited warrior Tira Makhang. Here is a warrior who is not only powerful but exceedingly self-confident (as heroes of the oral tradition generally are). And again Amadu may have felt that Bamba was overdoing the bragging act of Tira Makhang, and would seem to have cut him short on line 47 by stressing that, despite the fierce battle readiness of these allies of Sunjata, the fighting had not yet quite begun; or Amadu may simply have wished to help Bamba emphasize that, whatever the tension and fierceness shown by the warriors at this stage, we have not seen the real action yet. Whatever the case may be, these various interruptions by Amadu show clearly that although in general terms the accompanist helps the performer to realize the full scope of his presentation and brings some needed control to an act that might get out of hand, in certain respects his comments may (if not properly understood or handled) drive the performer into an unnecessary digression, as lines 3–10 in the above passage would seem to do.

Still, when a performer and his accompanist have worked long enough with each other, their instincts may be expected to fit well together. The performer comes to know what sorts of prompting to expect from the accompanist and in general would be well equipped to handle whatever distractions he may experience as a result. Some artists, however, would rather not be bothered; they would prefer that the accompanist stick to his principal job of providing musical accompaniment and leave the narration itself to the master. In my recording of the story "Meeme Odogwu," we can see how the artist Simayi swiftly but politely stops his accompanist Okondu Enyi from anticipating him. (The transcription style used here will be discussed later in chapter 11).

Narrator:	SHORTLY AFTER, BEHOLD OUR FRIEND rushed out, driving the goats into the goat-pen.
	TOLD THEM (i.e., the Council), "CHIE! CHIE! CHIE! CHIE! CHIE!
	I am Meeme the Scourge,
	Okeeme my kinsman is on his way here.

5 It's been long since I arrived Abba today, and I am hungry.
I have come looking for articles
For the rites of the king, *and haven't found them yet.*
COME, MY FRIEND (Odogwu), haven't you been told
That I am after Onukwu's wife?
What has kept you since morning? Do you want me to to starve
to death, or Ogwashi to come after me?"
(Laughter)

First Percussionist: 10 Pardon me
Pardon me, sir.
Er . . . that article the king . . . uses . . . for . . . his rites,
Isn't it . . . a human head?

Narrator: We are still on our way, aren't we?

Audience: 15 Right! (Okpewho 1990: 131)

The story, briefly, is about a strongman, Meeme Odogwu, a member of the king's war council at the village of Ogwashi-Uku (southwestern Nigeria), who volunteers to rescue the wife of a fellow councillor, Onukwu Agbada, from abduction by another strongman, Odogwu of Abba. In this scene, Meeme storms into the council of Abba where Odogwu and the others are meeting. He is later to take Odogwu away and kill him before the latter's own shrine; Odogwu's head is to be taken along with other articles such as cattle and goats for sacrifice at the king of Ogwashi-Uku's annual rites. The "first percussionist" (Okondu Enyi) apparently asked his question about the human head for the benefit of me and my recording team (who might not understand such cultural references). The storyteller had obviously intended to make the revelation at the appropriate time; he had his performance rather carefully worked out and had no wish to be distracted by his accompanist. A very self-assured man, Simayi on a number of occasions during his performances frowned at his accompanist's efforts to "disturb" his work. Simayi certainly knows what are the attendant risks in an oral performance.

Performer and Audience

We have remarked that an audience is the only context within which an oral performance makes any sense. There are, of course, performance situations in which an audience is either not present or is not significant. For instance, shepherds and cattle herders often entertain themselves with flute music and songs as a way of relieving the boredom of their long hours of work; quite often no one but their animals is listening. Some forms of ritual chanting are done solely by the priest or officiant and addressed to the divinity in a shrine. These examples can hardly be seen as oral performances in the normal sense of the word, especially when there is no one to attest to the activity. An oral performance truly exists where there is an audience that compels the respect of the performer and puts the performance on record (whether of memory or of tape).

The question of respect is important, because what is good for the goose may not always be good for the gander. Certain details in a song or story may pass unnoticed by one audience but give considerable offense to another group of listeners. Innes brought this fact to light with his edition (1978) of two separate performances in the Gambia of the story of the nineteenth-century Mandinka warlord Kelefa Saane, who was to lose his life in a war between the two neighboring communities of Niumi and Jokadu (in Guinea-Bissau).

The war stemmed from a dispute that had arisen between cattlemen from the two communities. King Demba of Niumi sent a messenger to the king of Jokadu in an effort to settle the dispute, but the messenger played a treacherous role by not only delivering an offensive message but also deliberately injuring himself on his return and letting the king of Niumi understand that the people of Jokadu had caused him that harm. The *griot* Bamba Suso, performing his version of this story before an audience of mostly schoolchildren in the village of Brikama, had no hesitation whatsoever in mentioning the name of the messenger who played that treacherous role: Hajji Darbo. Another *griot*, Shirif Jebate, also refers to this incident in his recording of *Kelefa Saane*. But his recording was done on Radio Gambia in the capital, Banjul; as a broadcast, the story would be heard by everyone in the Gambia, and so Shirif tells us why he has decided to be reticent on the name of that messenger.

> As you know,
> King Demba sent a man to Jokadu
> To try to settle the dispute;
> I know the name of the man who was sent,
> 5 But I have not mentioned it.
> The past and the present are not the same,
> And it is for that reason that I am not answering that question.
> If one were to hear the name
> On some occasion when a relative of the man in question were present, his relative
>   might ask, "Oh,
> 10 Who was it who said that?"
> And the answer would be, "It was Shirif who made that statement."
> That is why the past and the present are not the same;
> But the name of the messenger who was sent
> Is certainly known to me. (Innes 1978: 93–95)

The past and the present are different here in the sense that whereas in the olden days a storyteller or singer could say anything and get away with it, nowadays he could be taken to court on a charge of libel or defamation of character. If Bamba Suso had told his story on Radio Gambia, he probably would have had reason to exercise the same caution shown here by Shirif Jebate for a larger audience and in an urban setting where issues of the law are taken more seriously.

A good storyteller is also expected to exercise discretion in the structuring of his stories before a variety of audiences. From his observation and recording of storytelling performances among the Xhosa of South Africa, Scheub has reported that although the central ideas ("core-cliches") on which a tale *(ntsomi)* is built are not necessarily altered, narrators guide the images of the tale in a somewhat different direction for an audience of children from the way they would for an audience of adults.

> If the audience is composed primarily of children, the artist will concentrate on techniques and devices which will give the image a vividness and an animation that will delight the children. Details will be used sparingly, the attention of the performer being diverted to action and moving the narration along with dispatch. If the audience is made up primarily of adults, and if the performer feels comfortable with them, the image will be altered, largely through the introduction of details which will deepen certain aspects of the narrative, the artist turning her attention from bold action to nuance and motivation—but without changing the basic core-cliches which are the structural key-notes of the performance. This is not to say that the stylistic devices used to create *ntsomi*-images for the children will be ignored in the company of adults. They will be utilized, but they too will be altered somewhat; they will be sophisticated, and emphases will be placed elsewhere. If the audience is composed of both adults and children (which is usually the case), the artist will decide the direction in which she will take the narrative and those aspects of the core-image which she will give prominence. . . . Children are not asked to leave if the performer decides to create a more serious, more complex image, but often they will become bored because they are unable to follow the narrative and will leave of their own accord. Some bawdy narratives will probably not be performed in the presence of children, but this is a matter of discretion. (Scheub 1977: 39)

These are delicate choices; and although not every performer will care or be able to exercise such discretion, the truth remains that in the oral performance the nature of the audience is an important consideration in the choice of subject and sometimes of style.

Besides assessing the nature of the members of the audience, the oral performer sometimes actively acknowledges their presence by paying a courteous salute either to particular persons or to the gathering at large. In a heroic narrative recorded by a former student of mine, John Edemode, the narrator, on seeing another notable storyteller of the village entering the scene of performance, stops to salute him with a little song before continuing his narrative (Edemode 1979: 35).[3] Before starting to narrate the story of the hunters' hero Kambili, the Malian storyteller Seydou Camara pays tribute to his apprentice, Sacko, and everyone else.

> Gaoussou Sacko, I salute you!
>> I say, my apprentices, I greet you.
>> Guests, I greet you.
>> Respected guests, I greet you, Allah! (Bird 1974: 2–3)

It also behooves performers to ensure that they hold the attention and interest of the audience throughout the show. When members of the audience begin to leave or to show displeasure or boredom on their faces, the artist may take this as a sign of disapproval of the performance. If the artist is accomplished, experienced, and even-tempered, he or she may ignore the rudeness and carry on as if nothing had happened.

But some artists may be driven to curtail the song or the tale or even react with impatience, as one performer of *Sunjata* recorded by Innes did.

> Kibili Demba, thank you.
> Salimata Dembo,
> Husband of a Jebate woman, Demba, thank you.
> If you take it from here,
> You must join it to Karata.
> You come from
> Jallo and Jagite,
> Great Sidibe and Sankare.
> Dembo, who used to live with the people of the Island,
> Dembo, son of a Sanyang woman, thank you.
> But the griots have a complaint, Demba;
> Don't you know
> That an ordinary narrator and an expert singer are not the same? (Innes 1974: 201).

It would seem that the host of the performance, Bakari Sidibe, is showing his boredom with the performance at this point; the narrator, Banna Kanute, greets the host courteously enough with references to his family connections but observes that the host does not give him sufficient recognition as an artist.

None of these distractions from the audience is, of course, anything compared with those instances in which members of the audience actually interrupt the performer with statements or questions which put a certain stress on his imagination. In a truly traditional setting of an oral performance, it is highly unusual for members of the audience to watch passively and not make any sort of comment whatsoever as the performer sings or narrates. Melville Herskovits made this discovery while collecting oral narratives in Dahomey (present-day Republic of Benin).

> One usage that is as common to discursive speech as to narrative is the interpolated explanation from the listener, or listeners. So important is it for narrative tempo that in the absence of an audience, or where the interjection is too long delayed, the narrator himself pauses to exclaim "Good." While this pause serves stylistic ends in narration—to introduce a transition, as a memory aid, or to heighten suspense, among others—it is but part of a traditional complex of patterned responses from the listener, demanded by the canons of taste. A Dahomean views the silent European listener as either boorish, or incapable of participating adequately because of lack of feeling or understanding. (Herskovits 1958: 52)

Clark's recording of *The Ozidi Saga* gives us a remarkable opportunity to observe the various ways, positive and negative, in which remarks made by members of the audience or "spectators" affect both the tempo and the direction of a story. The important fact to bear in mind about *The Ozidi Saga* is that it is a fight story. The hero, Ozidi, first engages his father's assassins—Agbogidi, Azezabife, Ofe, etc.—and destroys them all; then he takes on various other hideous monsters such as the Scrotum King, the headwalking Tebekawene, and the seven-headed Tebesonoma, again destroying all of them right to the very last opponent, Engradon the Smallpox King, with his retinue of diseases. Every one of these combatants, including Ozidi, is heavily supported by magical powers, so each contest is protracted as the combatants deal blow for blow, die and revive, and use every means at their disposal to gain the upper hand. The story is performed, as tradition dictates, over seven days; and we can well imagine the strain as well as the excitement that audience members experience as they are treated day after day to a charade of fights and deaths. Let us examine carefully some of the ways in which the audience participates intimately in the performance as it unfolds.

In the first place, the audience shows its approval of the creative act of the narrator and gives him full encouragement as he builds his scenes. There is abundant laughter as the narrator describes and dramatizes Ogueren's collapse under the magical blows of Ozidi.

> Ogueren remained there anchored—
>> (Laughter)
> His eyes rolled—
>> (Laughter)
> and rolled. (P. 124)

The interesting thing about the editor's notations on the laughter is that without them we could never have guessed what dramatic effort the narrator added to his description of the event. We can also see that the laughter of the audience has helped in no small way to encourage the artist to give fuller life to his description.

The audience also participates effectively in dramatizing predicaments in which the characters find themselves. At one point, for instance, Ozidi and his witch-grandmother, Oreame, who aids him throughout with magic, are about to kill the sister of the monster Tebesonoma and her little baby. Despite his bloodthirsty tendencies, the hero has no desire to kill defenseless people who have caused him no offense, so he hesitates to do the deed. But his grandmother interprets his tenderness here as weakness and tries to force him out of it. In the dialogue between Oreame and Ozidi, a member of the audience helps the narrator to portray effectively the hero's hesitation or disinclination toward the act, to the delight of all.

> "When the real fight we sought is waiting there to be finished, are you dilly-dallying here? I say do the job quickly."
> "Oh mother, I'm horrified."
> When he spoke in this strain Oreame darted away.
> "So this boy has eyes running with tears like this! Come on, come out quick!
>> Spectator II: I won't come out
>> (General laughter)
> Come out! Come out!" (Pp. 266–67)

And when the narrator is at a loss for words or for the right detail for describing an event, the audience is there to try to supply it. In one passage, Oreame is putting together various articles to be used as magic against one of Ozidi's difficult opponents.

The young of a toad, she also brought with her a tadpole.
Next, (you give me your ears there). That bird, what do we Ijo call it now—this bird
. . .
    Spectator: Is it somewhat red?
Quite red. That one too, she added to the lot. (P. 368)

    A second influence exercised by the audience is similar to what we saw above in the relationship between the Gambian *griot* Bamba Suso and his musical accompanist Amadu Jebate—that is, in controlling the scope of the narrative performance. Many observations and comments made by members of the audience have the tendency to force the narrator to expand the text of the story by incorporating their ideas and even their phrases; the story told under such circumstances is a sum total of the narrator's descriptions and the audience's observations, in the sense that the entire performance is a collaborative activity. If we look, for instance, at a passage that describes the old witch Oreame turned into a young woman with the aim of attracting Ozidi's enemies to a fatal fight, we will see that the narrator is pushed to stretch the picture under the audience's encouragement, even borrowing words from the spectators.

Indeed with those breasts . . .
    Spectator I: She was like a young woman.
    Spectator II: A young woman.
If you saw her Lagos blouse, or her headtie, you'd seen a spectacle!
    Caller: O STORY!
    Group: Yes!
Or if it was the wrapper she tied about her waist you saw, it flowed right to the ground.
Indeed she looked like a young woman of Accra.
    Spectator I: Most graceful.
    Spectator II: And charming.
If you saw her figure, it really was graceful. (P. 343)

On the other hand, when audience members feel that the narrator is going too far, they do not hesitate to cut him short. In his effort to impress the audience the narrator has obviously stretched their patience a bit, especially in a story taking as many as seven days. One spectator is so overwhelmed by the interminable fighting between Ozidi and another of his opponents (Azemaroti) that he asks, "When two men fight, is there no running away?" The audience's desire to see that particular episode curtailed and concluded is clear.

With the sound of each blow . . .
    Spectator I: Why not rest?
The blows! How could he pause for breath, when he was in the field of battle? However hard he hacked at him, he danced away.
    Spectator II: Leave off when he hasn't killed! (P. 367)

It would appear that the narrator misunderstands the question by Spectator I to refer to the fighters, when in actual fact the spectator is suggesting that the narrator should take his leave of that endless episode. The suggestion is made clearer in the statement by Spectator II: cut everything short and get to the actual point where Ozidi kills his opponent.

The greatest challenge faced by this particular narrator comes, however, from statements in which spectators actively contradict his choice of words and details. The story was told by an artist who had been exposed in some degree to Western culture, and the setting of the performance was not the traditional Ijo homeland but the university town of Ibadan, about five hundred kilometers away. The performance was recorded with modern equipment by Clark, a university scholar and writer, and the audience was made up of both Ijo citizens in the town and non-Ijo people, including some expatriate teachers from Ibadan University. Under these circumstances, there was a constant temptation on the narrator to use words and ideas that were not particularly native to Ijo culture but might appeal to the rather sophisticated environment in which the story was being performed. But every once in a while when he steps out of the idioms of Ijo culture, the narrator is briskly confronted by Ijo members of the audience. "Don't speak English!" is a warning that we find here and there in the text. When he uses loan words such as *taim* (time), *kulude* (cooled), and *bede* (bed), he is at once reminded of the Ijo words he should have used. Quite often the narrator takes all this nagging in good spirits and corrects himself, but on a few occasions he gets impatient with his critics and sticks to his borrowed idioms.

Clearly, these various instances that we have considered suggest that the audience *in a truly traditional setting of the oral performance* is a force to be reckoned with. I emphasize these words because I am aware that the texts we find published today may not all have been performed in such a setting. In the traditional setting, most public performances of songs and tales are done in such a way that there is no physical separation between performer and audience members. The artist is practically surrounded by them and in some cases moves through their midst in the course of the performance. This intimate contact inevitably encourages them to express their feelings directly in sounds and gestures which the performer can hardly miss or ignore. This is clearly the best atmosphere for recording the oral performance. But many collectors do not exploit such an opportunity; instead, they isolate the artist in a recording studio or a room with a limited number of people in the audience who, out of courtesy and deference, would not wish to "upset" the recording by interjecting questions and comments. Such a courtesy is usually shown when the recording scholar is a foreigner. But *The Ozidi Saga* was recorded by Clark, himself an Ijo, before whom the largely Ijo audience felt at ease. Although not every recorded performance can attain the full excitement that we find in the Ozidi text, we can see there what a performance is like if it enjoys the unrestrained involvement of the audience.

Performer and Recorder

We might as well address ourselves to the recording itself and see in what ways it influences the text of the performance. There are principally three methods of recording the oral performance. The first and traditional method is handcopying, which is in many respects a very inadequate way of representing the event. The second and most common method is tape recording, which ensures that the various sounds (mainly vocal and instrumental) made during the performance are captured as faithfully as possible. The third and by far the most expensive method is filmed recording, a more recent development that has not come into general use; by this method everything (words, music, and movement) is recorded, and we have a total picture of what goes on in a performance. In chapter 11, we shall examine the advantages of, as well as the problems posed by, each of these methods. For the moment, let us see how the oral performer manages to deal with the presence of the scholar and the recording equipment and what impact this presence has on the text of the performance.

For all practical purposes, the recording apparatus is a foreign body in a scene of performance, in many ways a distraction to the job at hand. To some extent we could see it in the same light as we saw the notable storyteller who came into the scene of the performance recorded by John Edemode, or even as we viewed the comments made by this spectator or that in *The Ozidi Saga*. It challenges the skill, the sense of coordination, and sometimes the ego of the performer, and the texts that we have today show performers coping with the problem in various ways. Let us take an example from a masquerade chant recorded by Romanus Egudu from the Igbo of eastern Nigeria. In this performance marking a title-taking ceremony, the masquerade poet chants a whole variety of claims to greatness intended to put him (and by extension the title-taker in whose honor the masquerade poet is performing) in a glorious light. This chanting is done at some speed and in a falsetto voice while the scholar is busy copying the statements of the masquerade poet, who concludes the chant with a reference to the struggling copyist.

> My *uturu*-voice
> Is singing in the *Odo*-fashion;
> I've come, I've come, I've come,
> Son of the Almighty *Odo:*
> The copyist cannot pick up
> All that flows from my voice, what I am singing,
> I, the *Uturu*. (Egudu and Nwoga 1971: 43)

There are two ways of seeing the comment made on the copyist by the masquerade poet. Singing in the high, sonorous voice of a nightingale *(uturu)* but especially at considerable speed, he seems to imply that the copyist is too slow to keep up with him and is thus slowing down the pace of his performance. On the other hand, observing the feverish haste with which the copyist is laboring to keep up with him, the masquerade poet may have meant his comment as a playful challenge to a contest for speed between the two of them.

A similar situation occurs during the performance of *The Mwindo Epic,* which was recorded by Daniel Biebuyck and two research assistants copying down the narrator's words in the heat of performance. In the course of his narration of the gruesome fight between the hero, Mwindo, and his father, Shemwindo, the narrator sings this chant:

> I shall fight over there at Shemwindo's.
> The cattle that Shemwindo possesses,

May they join Mwindo.
Oh! scribe, march! (Biebuyck and Mateene 1969: 142)

Again, this episode of the fight is marked by a certain anxiety, which is underlined by the speed of the chant. The last line may be seen either as the performer's impatient warning to the copyist ("scribe") not to slow him down or as an invitation to the copyist to join in the advance on Shemwindo's territory.

In whatever way we choose to see the statements addressed to the recording scholar, there is no doubt that his effort puts pressure on the performer. The performer has simply tried to exorcise the presence of the recorder by co-opting him into the text of his performance in a statement that, whatever the degree of impatience felt by the artist, is nevertheless intended to be taken in good humor.

The spirit of the comment may not, however, always be a cheerful one, especially if the performer has sufficient understanding of the implications of the recorder's work. Let us take the accounts by *griots* of the heroic feats of the founders of their race. Today as in the past, these performers see themselves as chroniclers or custodians of the achievements of these great Mandinka leaders and of the secrets of that greatness. It was from one of these custodians that the historian Djibril Niane recorded (in writing) the story of the legendary Mandinka leader Sunjata. Although the *griot* consented to the enterprise, it was not without reservation (not to say jealousy) that he watched the scholar appropriate his ancient role. A comment by the *griot* in the middle of the story is enlightening.

> Griots know the history of kings and kingdoms and that is why they are the best counselors of kings. Every king wants to have a singer to perpetuate his memory, for it is the griot who rescues the memories of kings from oblivion, as men have short memories.
>
> Kings have prescribed destinies just like men, and seers who probe the future know it. They have knowledge of the future, whereas we griots are depositories of the knowledge of the past. But whoever knows the history of a country can read its future.
>
> Other peoples use writing to record the past, but this invention has killed the faculty of memory among them. With them everybody thinks he knows, whereas learning should be a secret. The prophets did not write, and their words have been all the more vivid as a result. What paltry learning is that which is congealed in dumb books!
>
> I, Djeli Mamoudou Kouyate, am the result of long tradition. For generations we have passed on the history of kings from father to son. The narrative was passed on to me without alteration and I deliver it without alteration, for I received it free from all untruth. (Niane 1965: 40–41).

There are essentially two contexts within which we may try to understand this extended comment credited to the *griot*. The first is the sense of rivalry with which the *griot* obviously views the activities of those whom he considers a threat both to his traditional role and to his source of livelihood. In the oral tradition, soothsayers and chroniclers may safely be seen as arch-competitors for authority in the relation of experiences in the past as a guide for future conduct; this role can be seen, for instance, in divination poetry discussed in chapter 2. The presence of the modern scholar now poses an added threat, to which the *griot* feels constrained to react. The second constraint felt by the *griot* here is the need to establish the authenticity of his account. He is no doubt aware of the power of the written word in achieving a permanent and perhaps incontrovertible record of an event. He must therefore justify his own activity in this light, so he comes to the defense of the oral tradition by invoking, among other evidence, the timeless message of prophets delivered solely by word of mouth.

It is not clear how this diversion has affected the essential text of the Sunjata story as told by the *griot*, especially because Niane may not have set the story down exactly as it was told to him. But some of the things which the *griot* says toward the end of the story seem to bear out the pressure which he must have felt in the presence of the recording scholar. As a way of establishing the authenticity of his account in the context of the past and the future, he continually stresses that the nation (Mali) founded by Sunjata is "eternal" and urges anyone who doubts this to go to the scenes of Sunjata's victories and check out the monuments—including, curiously enough, "the bird that foretold the end" of Sunjata's arch-enemy Soumaoro, or Sumanguru (p. 83). And he is so convinced that "learning should be a secret"—so distrustful of the role of writing in openly advertising information—that he seems to have withheld from Niane certain more intimate facts about Sunjata's career (presumably, facts about Sunjata's later disgrace and downfall, as known from other accounts). He only tells him, "But never try, wretch, to pierce the mystery which Mali hides from you. . . . Do not seek to know what is not to be known" (p. 84).

The tape recorder presents a slightly different set of problems. For most tape recorders—the more accessible ones, in terms of price—the tape would need to be turned over or rewound before the end of an hour, and the interruption would have to be handled carefully. Some oral performers are a little more experienced than others in coping with this delicate moment. Odogwu Okwuashi, who told me stories at Onicha-Ugbo, has been taped so many times that he is familiar with the intricacies of the tape. He would cast a quick glance at the recorder every once in a while during our sessions; if he noticed that the tape was about to run out, he would motion his musical group to step up their singing of the background tune to provide a smooth transition from one segment of the tale to the next and so save the tale from being interrupted. In many ways, such an interlude of transitional singing is very much in order. Since the narrative performance is often a total act involving song and dance as well as story, the audience may welcome an interlude of songs as a refreshing break from the intellectual demands of the story itself.

That such an interlude could nonetheless be overdone can be seen in a few places in *The Ozidi Saga*. On the fourth night of his performance of the story, the narrator concludes the rather long episode of the fight between the hero Ozidi and Ofe (chief assassin of Ozidi's father) with the slaughter of Ofe. It is clear from the transcription that the narrator intended to go no further that night: "I am cutting it, the story is finished," he tells us on page 203. The rest of the transcription for that night is taken up with singing; in fact, from the end of the Ofe episode (p. 202) to the "end of night four" (p. 205) there are nine different songs, each "repeated several times" by the choral group, with the sole aim of filling out the tape. The fact is particularly obvious in instructions given first by Madam Yabuku, the hostess of the performance, and then by the narrator himself (Okabou Ojobolo).

Yabuku: Anybody who knows a song should name it for us to sing and fill this thing (i.e., the tape).

(Okabou:)   The thing, well, let's finish with it at once. Now what is it? Is it not song! Bring out the songs and fill up the place before we rise. Night has now grown very big. But it isn't time yet for palmwine tapping. (P. 202)

We probably cannot go so far as to charge this particular performance with what scholars have called an "empty fullness" (Parry 1971: 446). But it seems clear that the narrator and his group have been pressed to "fill up" the tape beyond their visible needs. The implication of Okabou's statement seems to be that if the performance had gone on into the early hours of morning, when palmwine tappers are about, they would probably have abandoned it for their daily business. This may indeed lead us to ask questions about the tale itself: is it not possible that its great size (nearly four hundred pages of printed text) is due more to the self-consciousness of the narrator before the tape recorder than to the needs of the story?

The self-consciousness or uneasiness is perhaps nowhere so evident as on the final (seventh) night of performance, which presents the fight between Ozidi and Azemaroti, easily one of the longest episodes of the story. In the midst of this episode, someone from the audience makes an observation which catches the attention of the narrator.

Spectator I: Has the thing (i.e., the tape) been changed?

Spectator II: Go on!

Okabou: If it's been changed say so for in truth I feel like stooling right now . . .
                (Laughter)

(P. 362)

The editor does not tell us whether or not Okabou does go to the toilet at this point. The next three pages are taken up with songs and commentary in which our narrator does not appear to have participated, and it is possible that in the interval he has relieved himself; for when he does resume the story (pp. 365–66) he locks Ozidi and Azemaroti once again in a protracted fight which draws uneasy comments from spectators urging curtailment of the episode. Whether we see the influence of the tape recorder here as positive or negative, we can at least observe that it does have a role to play in determining the size of the text at various points of the performance.

Composition and Performance

It seems clear, in light of the above considerations, that oral literature is in a fundamental sense dependent on the very context within which it is created. A piece of oral poetry or narrative may appeal to us in the same way as a similar piece of written literature would. But that oral piece was performed for one particular audience and, if properly recorded and examined, is likely to reveal some of the effort made by the performer to please that audience or some of the ways in which the audience tried to influence the performance. Although in written literature different readers (or generations of readers) react to a piece of work (say a poem by Milton or Eliot) in different ways, the text nevertheless remains the same, with all the original punctuation marks intact. In oral literature, on the contrary, a text performed for one audience may be altered considerably when the oral artist performs it for another audience. Here, the contact between creator and consumer is more immediate and there is much greater need of caution or courtesy.

That is no doubt the motivation behind the statement Lord made in *The Singer of Tales,* that "an oral poem is not composed *for* but *in* performance." It is true, of course, that there are situations in which composition and performance may be seen initially as two distinct efforts. For instance, in chapter 2 we discovered that in the *udje* poetry of the Urhobo the *ororile* (composer) and the *obuole* (singer) are normally different people. And among the Somali oral poets would take care to point out that the poem they were about to recite was composed by someone else (Andrzjewski and Lewis 1964: 46). But when the piece of oral literature is actually performed, there are frequently a few departures from what the performer may have borne in mind or perhaps committed to memory.

Some of these departures may be attributed to the limitations of human memory. If the oral text is a rather long one, it would be difficult for the performer to remember all the details faithfully or the order which they follow. Until scholars understood better the fluid nature of oral literature, it was assumed that the "oral tradition" was handed down from one source (or generation) to another in "word-perfect" form. But there is simply no way in which an oral artist, however skilled, can recall every word of the extensive texts of, say, Ifa divination poetry or tales like those of Sunjata or Ozidi. Hence it is expected that the artist use his imagination to fill in the gaps or make whatever adjustments are necessary. In the case of the Ozidi story, one would expect that so long as the performer recognizes that the fight with the Smallpox King is the final confrontation or test of the hero Ozidi, every other episode in between could be juggled around as the performer sees fit or as his memory can recall. Each of these performances is a new creation or composition done at the particular moment, however it may have been done on a previous occasion.

The departures may also be due to the courtesy or discretion that the performer feels like observing in the presence of a particular audience. Take the episode about the treacherous messenger (already referred to) in the Gambian story of Kelefa Saane as told separately by Bamba Suso and Shirif Jebate. If there was a "standard text" of that story (though the idea is highly questionable in oral literature), it might have contained the name of the messenger, Hajji Darbo. But when Shirif came to perform the story for radio, he knew it would not be safe for him to mention Darbo's name. In addition, therefore, to the various other adjustments dictated by the conditions under which he did that performance—limitations of memory, recording in a radio studio rather than before a large audience of people, etc.—he extemporizes a witty excuse for not mentioning the messenger's name at the appropriate point. Is the story told on such an occasion a new composition? In a sense, yes. To the extent that relevant changes are made to suit the new circumstances, the text of the story has a life of its own that is in many senses independent of the text performed previously and under a different set of circumstances, however close the essential details of the two performances may be.

The departures may be more radical, and may be a matter more of caprice than of discretion. In an earlier book I mentioned a story that a narrator told me off the record about the origin of the musical instrument that he used for accompanying his tales (Okpewho 1983: 58–59). According to him, some spirits had given the original of the box-harp to a friend of his, and it was from that original that he constructed his own. When I later turned on the tape recorder and asked him to repeat the story, the details about the first owner being a friend of his and about his actually seeing that first box-harp dropped out. Although in the narrator's terms the two versions are essentially the same, the second one is a new composition dictated by the caution which he chose to exercise before the recording equipment.

These and the other points discussed earlier in this chapter would seem to lend proof to Lord's statement about composition in performance. The statement does not deny that a piece of oral literature may be initially composed by one person but presented by a different person; nor does it deny that two versions of the same piece by the same performer may be strikingly similar in details. It simply suggests that, considering that the circumstances under which oral literature is performed are hardly ever similar in all respects, the body or order of words put together (Latin *compono*) in one performance is likely to differ in some respects from whatever may have been in the artist's mind prior to that performance or from the way in which it was presented by the same artist on an earlier occasion. For one thing, audience members may make comments which encourage the artist to extend a passage or to make other changes to suit their interests. For another thing, the artist may be subject to certain distractions—e.g., inadequate musical backing, the presence of recording equipment—which either unsettle the presentation or inspire a certain self-consciousness in the artist's statements. Oral literature is by its nature a fluid form of art. Factors operating at the scene of performance provide one more explanation of the fluidity or variability of its text.

4. Stylistic Qualities

In the last chapter, we examined the conditions or circumstances in which the words of oral literature are delivered and the effect of these circumstances on the text that is produced. In this chapter, we are going to look at the text itself to see some of the ways in which the words are organized and the resources within the words that ensure the effectiveness of the oral performance. In other words, we shall be concerning ourselves with questions of style and techniques of presentation, especially those aspects that make oral literature as an art form somewhat distinct from written literature.

To appreciate the basis for this distinctness it is necessary to remind ourselves again and again that oral literature is literature delivered by word of mouth before an audience. This word-of-mouth medium of presentation implies that oral literature makes its appeal first through the sound of the words that reach the ears of the audience and only secondarily through the meaning or logic contained in those words. The importance of this sound may be seen in the fact that even in the more intimate or limited types of oral performance such as divination poetry, the listener-client at least expects to hear the texts being recited by the diviner and to know thereby the ways in which he or she is supposed to participate in the whole process. In the more public types of performance such as singing or storytelling, of course, the performers gain little credit or popularity if their voices are not strong enough and their words are barely audible to the audience.

The appeal of sound can indeed be so strong, the premium placed on it so high, that performers can at times indulge in certain "nonsense" words or other kinds of sound either for sheer entertainment effect or perhaps to fill in a gap when they forget what to say next. Herein, then, lie two of the principal factors motivating the delivery of the text of oral literature: one, the performers are anxious to say things that will please the ears of their audiences, that will be "good music" to their ears, so to speak; and two, realizing that they are under some pressure to be seen as good performers, they hang on to certain devices that will ensure the steady flow of their presentation and save them the embarrassment of awkward breaks in that presentation. Writers, since they do not face a physical audience, are considerably freer from some of these obligations and pressures. And although writers are as anxious as oral performers to give good accounts of themselves as artists, they can take as much time as they want in the quiet of their studies to order their thoughts and presentations in a somewhat different way from that of oral performers.

Since African languages are numerous and diverse, it is hardly possible to outline the stylistic qualities of every one of them or to account for more than a few elements of style and structure that can be treated on a general scale. The problem is compounded by the fact that few publications available today represent these elements faithfully enough for us to rely on them for our discussion. We shall therefore content ourselves with a handful of examples of texts mostly in translation and, where the discussion warrants, with the accompanying indigenous text.

Repetition

Repetition is no doubt one of the most fundamental characteristic features of oral literature. It has both an aesthetic and a utilitarian value: in other words, it is a device that not only gives a touch of beauty or attractiveness to a piece of oral expression (whether song or narrative or other kind of statement) but also serves certain practical purposes in the overall organization of the oral performance.

The relevance of repetition to oral literature was not sufficiently appreciated by earlier scholars. Most early collectors and editors of folk songs and folktales had the unfortunate habit of cutting what they considered the "wearisome repetition" of phrases and whole passages. Even today some editors, either out of sheer impatience or under advice from a publisher aiming to keep the size and so the price of the publication under control, are forced to eliminate repetitions from their texts. In so doing, they have tampered with the very heart of these texts; in the case of the earlier generations of scholars, the texts were so severely drained of their essential "oral" qualities that they were invariably judged to be inferior to written literature. But many texts collected and transcribed in more recent years have respected these qualities, and we are now in a better position to understand the roles played by devices such as repetition.

It is necessary to grasp first the aesthetic value of repetition in a piece of oral performance. In a fundamental way, the repetition of a phrase, a line, or a passage does have a certain sing-song quality to it; if the repetition occurs between intervals in, say, a song or a tale, the audience is often delighted to identify with it and to accompany the performer in going over a passage that has now become familiar. Besides this general aesthetic impact, repetition does have more specific stylistic values within the text, and perhaps we should look at some of these. One is in giving a certain amount of emphasis to a point that needs to be stressed, as may be observed in a rainmaking chant from the Lango of Uganda.

We overcome this wind.	*We overcome.*
We desire the rain to fall, that it	
be poured in showers quickly.	*Be poured.*
Ah! thou rain, I adjure thee fall. If	
thou rainest, it will be well.	*It is well.*
A drizzling confusion.	*Confusion.*
If it rains and our food ripens,	
it is well.	*It is well.*
If the children rejoice, it is well.	*It is well.*
If it rains, it is well. If our	
women rejoice, it is well.	*It is well.*

> If the young men sing, it is well.   *It is well.*
> A drizzling confusion.   *Confusion.*
> If our grain ripens, it is well.   *It is well.*

(See Okpewho 1985: 122)

Part of the poetic effect of this chant comes from the tremendous force of urgency with which these lines are chanted. In 1984 a visiting German musicologist, Arthur Simon, gave a lecture at Ibadan during which he played a tape-recorded prayer-chant from the Sudan structured very much along the same lines of call-and-response as in the above piece. The speed and force of the heavy tenor voices of the performers (all men) was quite captivating. Equally striking was the device whereby the responding voices picked up and repeated the last word of the statement from the lead voice; we can see from the repetitions in the above chant how significant and pressing the ideas of abundance *(poured, confusion)* and prosperity *(it is well)* must have been in the minds of the performers.

Repetition is also employed, sometimes profusely, to mark a feeling of excitement or agitation, whether in the sense of utmost delight or deepest anxiety and fear. We may borrow one of the numerous instances we have of this in *The Ozidi Saga*. In one episode Ozidi has tried to provoke a fight with one of his opponents, Odogu the Ugly, by making love to Odogu's wife in Odogu's house. In the course of this apparently suicidal act, the two lovers are surprised by Odogu.

> After they had played for some time, Odogu suddenly flung open a door and looking round, there was Ozidi ensconced on the lap of his wife.
>   *Spectator:*   Hey, hey!
> "Hey, Odogu! Hey, Odogu! Hey, Odogu! Odogu! I have seen what's not seen, what's not seen. Hey, Odogu! Hey, Odogu! Hey, Odogu! Hey, Odogu! Hey, Odogu! Hey, Odogu!"
> (P. 277)

There is clearly agitation in Odogu's exclamation of his own name many times over in this passage. It comes partly from his consternation at the audacity with which someone else here assaults his wife in his very bed. But it indicates even more the delight with which Odogu contemplates the punishment he will deal out to this bold intruder, for shortly afterward Odogu remarks, "how sweet that an animal has walked of its own into my house today for me to kill and eat!"

In many oral performances in which the artists make a determined effort to impress their audiences with the diversity of their wisdom, there is an abundance of information which bestows upon the texts a certain sense of fullness. Much of this fullness of effect is achieved through the repetition of a key word or phrase in a variety of settings, as in this Yoruba praise-chant, "Salute to the Onikoyi Lineage," from Babalola's collection of hunters' poetry (1966).

> When you were surprised by the enemy in an open forest tract,
> You changed yourselves into forest trees.
> When you were surprised by the enemy in a savannah tract,
> You changed yourselves into savannah grass.

And when you were surprised by the enemy in a tract full of disused ant-hills,
You transformed yourselves into ant-hill mushrooms.
You are known as people who sometimes stay at home,
Sometimes live in the open forest,
Sometimes live in "transition woodland" tracts,
Sometimes live in the streets,
Sometimes live on the farm,
Sometimes live at Aawe,
Sometimes live at Aagba,
Sometimes at Kobai,
Sometimes at Ogbomoso,
Sometimes at Ile Ifon,
And sometimes at Kuta.
Men of war carrying sheaves of arrows. (Pp. 124ff.)

The Onikoyi was a legendary Yoruba warrior noted for his ruthless campaigns and his restless belligerence, which took him and his men from one place to another, constantly in search of action. The first six lines above underline the variety of settings in which these warriors risked their lives, while the remaining lines portray effectively the wide coverage of territory in Yorubaland where their campaigns took them. On the whole we get a picture of men constantly on the move, of daredevils ever anxious to test themselves in one theater of action after another, and of a fullness of military life. This sense of fullness and variety is achieved in no small measure by the frequent repetition of verbal particles (e.g., *gbe*, live). It is possible, of course, that the fame of the Onikoyi did not spread as far as the poet here implies in so many locations; from what is known of praise poetry generally, this poet may simply be glorifying the Onikoyi with exaggerated references as well as trying to impress us with his wide grasp of Yoruba geography. That, in itself, is part of that sense of fullness and variety which the repetitions aim to achieve.

In these various instances of repetition there is either a sense of urgency, of vividness, or a certain musical feeling which lends a touch of effectiveness to the passage. Other instances of repetition do not, however, succeed quite as much, especially when it is clear that the passage has been used purely for filling a gap or for marking time. The audience may not necessarily find such repetition offensive and may indeed have actively called for it or encouraged it. This is particularly true in the performance of songs. Mvula tells us of songs accompanying Chewa narratives: "The audience enthusiastically joins in singing refrains of songs within the folk narrative. . . . When [the narrator] observes that the excited audience finds the song interesting, he continues singing it with profuse repetition so that the audience enjoys taking up the chorus of the song" (1982: 35). But sometimes the device of repetition can be abused by less skilled performers who, exploiting the appreciativeness of their audiences, spin out their references endlessly with simple, unimaginative changes. Babalola quotes an example of such an unimaginative use of repetition:

Olukoyi offspring of the leopard at Kaba-on-the-hill.
Olukoyi offspring of the leopard at Kaba-in-the-valley.

Olukoyi offspring of the leopard at Kaba-on-the-right.
Olukoyi offspring of the leopard at Kaba-in-the-middle.
Olukoyi offspring of the leopard at Kaba-on-the-left.
Olukoyi offspring of the leopard at Kaba-on-all-sides. (1966: 52)

This is obviously a case of an "empty fullness" which the chanter would hope to pass off as a variation or an improvisation on a single image. But anyone with a keen ear for traditional poetry would hardly be impressed. "Such improvisation," Babalola tells us, "is regarded as the great noise of an empty barrel, the effusion of a shallow-minded ijala artist who makes light of the adage that quality is more important than quantity and who erroneously thinks that the merit of his ijala consists solely in its length" (ibid.).

The idea of marking time is seen here as a weakness, but it also suggests that repetition can serve certain purposes within the structure of an oral performance. One such use is to help to maintain the rhythmic beat on which the lines of a song are based, as in this war song from the Kipsigis of Kenya.

Child's mother *oo wo ho*
Child's mother *oo wo ho*
Put the pot on the fire *oo wo ho*
The one which can hold a head *oo wo ho*
The army is going to war *oo wo ho*
The army is going to war *oo wo ho*
You don't know where *oo wo ho*
The army is going to war *oo wo ho*
The army is going to war *oo wo ho*
To Mangorori *oo wo ho*
Oye leiyo oo wo ho
Oye leiyo oo wo ho (Okpewho 1985: 137)

Various lines of this chant are repeated for sheer aesthetic effect, but it is clear that the phrase *oo wo ho* (which means nothing) has mainly a functional value. As the soldiers sing this song, they are stomping their feet to the rhythm of it; the repetition of *oo wo ho* helps to ensure the regularity of that rhythm.

The function performed here by *oo wo ho* on a single-line basis is performed on a larger basis by the refrain (i.e., repeated chorus) that helps to mark off the stanzas of a song. Such refrains may be one line or several lines long. As the lead singer in the group or orchestra introduces a new idea in a line or portion of lines, the other singers sing the refrain before the lead singer comes in again with a fresh idea. Again, the refrain here carries with it the charm or the appeal of familiarity, but it also serves the technical purpose of separating one element of the message of the song from the other and giving each an emphasis and integrity of its own. An example is found in an Ngoni (Malawi) song about death.

The earth does not get fat. It makes an end of the chiefs.
Shall we die on the earth?

The earth does not get fat. It makes an end of the women chiefs.
Shall we die on the earth?
Listen O earth. We shall mourn because of you.
Listen O earth. Shall we all die on the earth?

The earth does not get fat. It makes an end of the nobles.
Shall we die on the earth?
The earth does not get fat. It makes an end of the royal women.
Shall we die on the earth?
Listen O earth. We shall mourn because of you.
Listen O earth. Shall we all die on the earth? (Okpewho 1985: 162)

Presumably the first four lines of each stanza are sung by the lead singer, who indulges in repetitions even of whole lines or statements. The essential points in each stanza are made on the first and the third lines, while the last two lines, sung by the chorus or the group as a whole, complete the stanza and mark off the ideas contained in it from those of the next stanza.

Refrains of songs also help to mark off segments or episodes of folktales one from the other. There are numerous examples of this phenomenon in the oral narrative traditions of communities across Africa; we need only cite one tale from the Igbo of southeastern Nigeria, a tale which seeks to explain why the tortoise's shell looks cracked. Briefly, there was once a famine in the animal world, and while all the animals jointly resolved to kill and eat their mothers, the squirrel and his brother secretly hid their mother up in heaven. Whenever they felt hungry, they would go to an appointed spot and sing to her.

Mother, let down the rope
Let down the rope
Mother, let down the rope
Let down the rope
The animals killed off their mothers
Let down the rope
Only the squirrels saved their mothers
Let down the rope.

The brothers would climb to heaven and eat their fill before coming back to earth. This happened again and again until the animals, led (as usual) by the tortoise, caught the squirrels in the act. One day, unknown to the latter, the tortoise sang the song at the usual spot and began to climb the rope along with the others. Unfortunately for them, the squirrels got to the spot before they could get very far, and sang a countersong.

Mother, cut the rope
Cut the rope
Mother, cut the rope
Cut the rope
The animals killed off their mothers

Cut the rope
Only the squirrels saved their mothers
Cut the rope.

Their mother recognized their voices as authentic and cut the rope. The animals all fell down and sustained severe injuries, the tortoise having his shell badly cracked.

The request to "let down the rope" is sung no less than three times during the story and helps to mark off successive stages in its development. The italicized lines in these songs are sung by members of the storytelling audience, and provide them an opportunity to participate in the narrative activity. The participation adds some cheerfulness and warmth to the whole event, but it is clear that the repetition of the main song (given only a slight but significant twist in the "cut the rope" version) serves a practical purpose in the construction of the story.

This technical role of repetition in the oral narrative has been the subject of considerable research. It is not only refrains like the above that aid in the development of the plot; it has been found that even in the regular portions of story in which the narrator does not alter or raise his voice in a song mode, certain phrases or lines—even a whole framework of details—are used over and over again for constructing successive stages in the story. This technique has been found to be particularly useful in the performance of longer narratives, especially the heroic kind known as epics. In oral literary scholarship, such a stock phrase or statement repeatedly used has been called the *formula,* while the framework of details (e.g., description of an event or scene) has been called a *theme,* which is simply an extended formula. This "formulaic" device in storytelling—this technical use of repeated phrases and passages—is the subject of Lord's *Singer of Tales* (1960), which has influenced numerous studies especially of the oral narrative art in various communities across the world, including Africa.

The understanding of the formula is roughly as follows. As narrators develop their stories before an audience, they endeavor to hang their imagination on certain key phrases and sets of details which they use again and again especially in situations which are roughly similar; since they are doing their performance under a certain pressure, there is not much time or even need for them to think up a new phrase or set of details each time they narrate a situation similar to one they have done before. So they find it convenient to use those phrases and details as often as possible whether in the same story or between stories. Over time, these repeated statements come to acquire a certain musical charm, though it is clear that they were first developed under pressure.

Let us examine briefly the use of these repeated phrases called formulas. In an *mvet* epic from the Fang of Cameroon narrating the exploits of the war hero Abo Mama (Awona 1966), whenever any character has to make a frantic run (whether on an errand or from sheer fright), we are told that he

dashed like the branch of a broken tree,
Like the furious racing of a young antelope,
Like a bird that takes off without saying goodbye to the branch.

This formula is used no less than seven times in the story. Obviously, since every character is different we would expect that he would make a run in his own individual way. But the narrator already has an effective enough style for describing the idea of a quick dash and does not need to rack his brains (especially there before the gazing audience) for a new style; so he simply uses the one he used before. Repeated so many times, the description sounds like a sweet refrain in the ears of the audience; but we can see that the technique served first of all a technical purpose.

Or take the version of the Sunjata story as narrated by Bamba Suso (Innes 1974). When Sunjata finally prepares to raise an army to fight Sumanguru and recover the kingship of Mali from him, he summons a number of powerful allies to his side: Kama Fofana, Sankarang Madiba Konte, Faa Koli, and finally his most valued ally, Tira Makhang. Of the appearance of the first three (before the flamboyant entry of the last), Bamba tells us that each of them answered Sunjata's call with "one thousand four hundred and forty-four bowmen." Now, the narrator does not tell us that Sunjata specifically asked for that number of soldiers from each of these allies, and there seems no logical reason why leaders from three different communities should come along with exactly the same number of soldiers. But all Bamba wishes to do in these scenes is to convey the idea that each of them came to Sunjata's aid with a substantial number of soldiers; the number itself does not count. The formula of 1,444 bowmen, repeated over and over, rings like a sweet refrain, but we can at least appreciate its practical value within the organization of the plot of the story.

In fact, this structural or formulaic use of repetition can go beyond the building of independent scenes to cover the broad pattern on which most if not all of a story is organized. This situation may be seen on close examination in *The Ozidi Saga*. As we have remarked, it is essentially a fight story built on the basis of the hero Ozidi's engaging and destroying one opponent after another—from the assassins of his father (Ofe, Agbogidi, etc.), through various monster figures in the community (Odogu the Ugly, the Scrotum King, Tebesonoma the seven-headed ogre, etc.), to the final rival the Smallpox King with his retinue. Virtually every one of these numerous contests follows basically five stages. First, the opponent makes light of Ozidi's powers and goes out determined to kill him and put an end to his "empty" reputation. Second, the two rivals lock in a deadly fight, only to discover that each has grossly underestimated the strength of the other; the earlier part of the struggle goes in fact against Ozidi. Third, Ozidi, aided by his witch-grandmother Oreame, procures certain medicinal antidotes that have the power to neutralize his enemy's magical strength. Fourth, now thoroughly invincible, the hero moves in and destroys his enemy and dumps him or his head into his shrine-house, which goes into an ear-splitting commotion from the spirits of the numerous victims now harbored within it. And fifth, the power-drunk Ozidi rages all over the place, bragging about his invincibility. Of course, the constituent details of these fight episodes vary somewhat one from the other, considering that each opponent has his distinct powers and characteristics. But the pattern on which the struggles are built remains essentially the same from the beginning to the end of the story.

If the oral performance (whether song or story) relies so heavily on these repeated devices not only to achieve a musical effect that appeals to the audience as well as the performer but also to support the overall framework on which the performance is built, then repetition can justly be said to be a distinguishing feature of oral literature. This does not mean that we cannot find instances of repetition in written literature—essay, novel, poem, or play—either in the simplest or most complex forms. But whereas the writer generally makes every effort to avoid repetition (whether in phrase or in logic) and carefully eliminates any noticeable instances of repetition in the fear that they might cause the composition to drag and so bore its readers, the oral performer cultivates repetition both as a means of achieving auditory delight in listeners and as a convenient framework for holding the distinct elements of the composition together. This device of repetition does not by any means make the oral artist any less skilled or sophisticated than the writer; it is simply a tool of pleasure and of convenience determined largely by the circumstances of performance before an audience that stares the artist in the face.

Parallelism

Those who see oral literature as the product of a "primitive" culture are amazed to find that it reveals, on closer examination, a tremendous degree of balance. It is certainly not easy for performers, no matter how long they have practiced the art, to hold themselves together before audiences that are liable to ask embarrassing questions or make upsetting remarks. For a performance (say, of a story) to succeed, the imagination of the artist will need to do a delicate job of selecting details that may seem to be independent of one another but at bottom have a common affinity, and of bringing these together to present a convincing picture or image.

The similarity may be quite strong; the details may echo one another so closely that the device is little more than a simple repetition. But they may be so distinct that it takes a certain amount of intelligence to identify the closeness between them. Whatever the case may be, this device, whereby the oral artist brings together in a balanced relationship ideas and images that may seem independent of one another, is called parallelism. There are various kinds of parallelism, and I think we should examine a few examples to see how this device reflects the purposes as well as the pressures of the artist in performance.

Let us begin by examining those cases of parallelism in song or chant in which the same words or phrases are used but simply transposed in consecutive lines. The first may be called lexical parallelism or chiasmus, as beautifully illustrated by the first two lines of a well-known portrait of the Yoruba god Ogun.

> He kills on the right and destroys on the left.
> He kills on the left and destroys on the right. (Beier 1966: 45)

Kunene gives us two interesting examples from Sotho praise poetry.

> *Tau ya Bolokwe le Marajaneng,*
> *ya Bolokwe Tau dinala di ntsho*
> The Lion of Bolokwe and Marajaneng

of Bolokwe, the Lion, his claws are black.

Tawananyane, so llele bohale,
Bohale ke ba ditau tsa ditona.
Little young lion, cry not for warrior fame,
Warrior-fame is for the great big lions. (Kunene 1970: 75)

The indigenous texts make it possible for us to see the fundamental principle of lexical parallelism, which simply consists in the transposition or criss-crossing, between adjacent lines, of identical units of speech *(lexis)*, in this case identical words. In the first example the order of words in the first line *(Tau . . . Bolokwe)* is reversed in the second line *(Bolokwe Tau)* to achieve a certain musical or poetic balance. The second example contains a little more than lexical parallelism. The position of *bohale* (warrior-fame) in the first line is reversed in the second line, but there is also a slight change to the other part of the lexical balance. Although the basic idea is that of lion, we are here speaking of a difference between little lions and big lions or young lions and adult, experienced lions.

Parallelism indeed becomes more exciting, or at least more striking, when two elements are brought together in a decisive contrast within the same or similar structures of statement. Let us take a simple example from Dembo Kaunte's version of the Sunjata story (Innes 1974). During the earlier part of the fighting between Sunjata and his arch-enemy Sumanguru, Faa Koli (on Sunjata's side) engages Jibrila (on Sumanguru's side) in a single contest to show which of them has more physical and magical strength. Faa Koli is of course superior, and as a proof he goes on to break Jibrila's arms and legs one after the other, in cold-blooded horror and in full view of soldiers from both sides, Mali (Manding) and Susu. At this point, as Dembo narrates,

Jelo dunta Manding, kaso dunta Susu
Laughter came to Manding, weeping came to Susu (P. 303)

The parallelism here consists purely in describing the reaction (laughter/weeping) that the fate of Jibrila brings upon the group (Manding/Susu). This type of parallelism, where the change is not in the positions of words within the structure but in the senses or meanings assigned to them, may be properly called semantic parallelism.

The device is perhaps more common in songs and chants than in stories. A beautiful example may be seen in a praise of Ndaba, the Zulu chief, which Trevor Cope considers a case of "perfect" parallelism.

Obeyalala wangangeminfula,
Obeyavuka wangangezintaba.
Who when he lay down was the size of rivers,
Who when he got up was the size of mountains. (Cope 1968: 84)

The beauty of these examples from the Mandinka and the Zulu is evident in the balance not only of the sense or ideas but even more of the number of syllables in the two halves of the parallel structure: six in each half of the Mandinka text, eleven in each half of the Zulu.

For an excellent piece in which lexical and semantic parallelism are blended together in true poetic harmony, let me cite in full a praise salute to a legendary Yoruba warrior.

> Onikoyi, the warrior who never received an arrow in his back.
> Child of the water-lily, child of the squirrel.
> The bird's foot shall never touch the water,
> The river shall never be at rest.
> 5 Onikoyi, the warrior
> Who frightens death himself.
> Child of the vulture perching on the baobab tree;
> Child of the eagle sitting on the silk-cotton tree:
> Child of the hawk waiting on the camwood tree.
> 10 When the vulture flaps down
> He will eat the intestines of a brave warrior;
> When the eagle glides down
> He will eat the liver of a brave warrior;
> When the hawk pounces down
> 15 He will eat the eyes of a brave warrior.
> Onikoyi loves nothing but war:
> When others drink wine, he drinks blood;
> When others plant yams, he is planting heads;
> When others reap fruit, he is reaping dead warriors.
> 20 One day Onikoyi went out to rob.
> Then a thief broke into his own house.
> Onikoyi met the thief on the road.
> The thief said, "Ha—is that not Onikoyi?"
> Onikoyi said, "Ha—is that not the thief?"
> 25 They pounce on each other:
> Onikoyi cuts off the thief's head.
> The thief cries, "Oshun, Sonponna, help me!"
> Onikoyi replies, "Whether you call Oshun or whether you call Sonponna,
> I am the one who cuts off the head; for every warrior is a bit of a thief."
>   (Beier and Gbadamosi 1959: 54)

The first instance of parallelism in this chant is in line 2, where the ubiquitous presence of the Onikoyi is represented first by the water-lily and then by the squirrel. This is a simple case of semantic parallelism, developed into a more complex form in lines 3 and 4, which portray the restless energy of the Onikoyi, first by the image of a bird constantly hovering above water and next by the endlessly flowing river. Lines 7–9 are three semantically parallel lines whose ideas are developed in the three corresponding pairs of 10–11, 12–13, and 14–15. Lines 17–19 are built somewhat along the same pattern as lines 7–9. The short but dramatic narrative illustrating the parallel relationship between the warrior and the thief (lines 20–30) contains both lexical and semantic parallelisms. To start with, the quiet implication in lines 20 and

21 is that Onikoyi and the thief are robbing each other; while Onikoyi goes *out* to rob the thief, the thief comes *in* to rob Onikoyi, an example of both lexical and semantic parallelism. Lines 23 and 24 are purely a case of lexical parallelism, or chiasmus, while lines 27 and 28 continue the semantic exchange between Onikoyi and the thief on which the narrative is fundamentally built.

A more advanced form of semantic parallelism may be seen in those instances in which various images within a chant are developed independently and the relationship between them is not apparent on the surface. To some extent this is illustrated in the relationship between lines 5–9 and lines 16–19 in the chant to Onikoyi. Although both sets of images illuminate the personality of Onikoyi, they do so from different angles: while lines 5–9 portray the lurking terror of the man, lines 16–19 portray his bloodthirsty zeal for war. In other African traditions of praise poetry, this form is somewhat more fully developed in such a way that distinct attributes or episodes from the person's career are strung together in parallel bundles of lines. In the study of southern African praise poetry these consecutive bundles are called stanzas by Cope and paragraphs by Daniel Kunene.

Examples are found in a long praise salute (*izibongo*) to Shaka the Zulu.

> The joke of the women at Nomgabhi,
> Joking as they sat in a sheltered spot,
> Saying that Shaka would not rule, he would not become chief,
> Whereas it was the year in which Shaka was about to prosper.
> The beast that lowed at Mthonjaneni,
> And all the tribes heard its wailing,
> It was heard by Dunjwa of the Yangweni kraal,
> It was heard by Mangcengeza of Khali's kraal.
> Fire of the long dry grass, son of Mjokwane;
> Fire of the long grass of scorching force,
> That burned the owls on the Dlebe hill,
> And eventually those of Mabedlana also burned. (Cope 1968: 90)

In these three consecutive bundles of lines, Shaka is portrayed as a "joke," a "beast," and a "fire." These are obviously three distinct images, and each bundle contains references to different events in the long glorious career of Shaka. Interestingly, Cope tells us in a footnote to the first "stanza" that it "is out of place chronologically" from the previous stanzas, and it is clear from the references in each of the next two stanzas that the poet has brought together various military encounters under one controlling image. Yet, despite their distinctness, these three images are unified in illustrating the ferocity of the leader Shaka. The "joke" played by the women in stanza one is intended as a tragic irony, for the prosperity referred to in the last line of that stanza is the bloody defeat of one of Shaka's principal rivals, Phakathwayo. The "beast" lowing in the kraals in stanza two is the image of the lion in all its ferocious temper, showing Shaka devouring tribe after tribe in his military campaigns. The "fire" in the third stanza continues the idea of ferocity and again shows Shaka on a variety of military exploits. We can see therefore that although he has his hands full of incidents in the life of Shaka which he has to commemorate, this *izibongo* poet or *imbongi* has evolved one neat central idea (ferocity) around which he ranges them in a parallel arrangement.

By now the principle involved in the device of parallelism should be sufficiently clear. Essentially, the device is a form of repetition in which a single idea is restated or reaffirmed in a variety of ways. It is, in other words, a repetitive device that puts more emphasis on diversity and contrast than on similarity between details. In its simplest form (i.e., the chiasmus), parallelism consists in the transposition of identical words or details within the same or adjacent statements, as in the examples from the Mandinka and the Yoruba. In its more developed form (semantic parallelism) it involves the substitution of words or details between statements though the central idea remains the same; the extreme example of this can be seen in the salute to Shaka in which the similarity between the details is extremely faint while the central idea persists.

The examples which we have used in our discussion of this topic would seem to indicate that there is much greater incidence of parallelism in songs and chants than in, say, narratives. If this is true, it may well be because there is more self-conscious play with words and ideas in songs and chants than in narratives. But if we look closely enough at the structure of narratives, especially of the longer kind which tax the imagination of the narrator, we will find that we have much less reason to make the assumption than we thought we had and that parallelism is a device quite as basic to the needs of narrative as of song and chant.

If we compare the structure of the salute to Shaka with what we saw of the "formulaic" structure of episodes in *The Ozidi Saga*, we will find that the principle is really the same. In other words, parallelism is a formulaic device which allows the oral performer to bring a diversity of ideas within a convenient structural identity. For just as the narrator of the Ozidi story organizes the numerous fight episodes in parallel sequences along the central theme of Ozidi's invincibility, so the Zulu *imbongi* organizes the diverse attributes and achievements of Shaka in a parallel order built around the central theme of his ferocity.

In fact, this device of parallelism may be employed not just for one narrative but between a whole body of narratives. In studies of the narrative traditions of various African communities, various scholars—e.g., Michael Jackson among the Kuranko (Mende) of Sierra Leone (1982), Peter Seitel among the Haya of Tanzania (1980), Ronald Rassner among the Agiryama of Kenya (1989), and Harold Scheub among the Xhosa of southern Africa (1975)—have been able to identify certain central themes around which bundles of tales told by the narrators have been organized. Scheub in particular has argued in one publication after another that the Xhosa folktale *(ntsomi)*, both individually and collectively, is built on a foundation of "core-images" around which the narrator hangs a variety of incidents and whole tales. In *The Xhosa Ntsomi* (1975), Scheub has carefully examined the use of the repetitive structure in those narratives and presented a chart showing "the use of parallel images to create a *ntsomi* production" (p. 164). Obviously, this parallel structuring of tales helps the narrator to achieve a sense of order and harmony in the large amount of folktale material swimming around in his or her head at any given time.

As a repetitive device, therefore, parallelism is a tool of pleasure and of convenience. On one hand, there is a touch of beauty in the skill with which the performer plays one set of words or images against another without altering either the structure of statement or the central message. On the other hand, there is a real need for a balanced framework which will order the vast amount of information harbored into a set of harmonious relationships. To that extent, then, parallelism is, like repetition, the soul of the oral performance.

Piling and Association

The reader will have observed that in our discussion of the literary techniques employed in the performance of oral literature, we have constantly seen pleasure and convenience as the two basic factors motivating this performance, sometimes jointly. It should be borne in mind, however, that these factors are not found to the same degree in all performers. Take the device of repetition, for instance. Some performers are so experienced and skillful at their job that in their hands the repeated line or "stanza" is a tool deliberately used for the delight of the audience; other performers, however, may be so inexperienced and lacking in self-confidence that they desperately need to hang on to a line or a stanza longer than is necessary. Whatever the level of skill or experience possessed by an oral artist, the principal aim of most performances is to give satisfaction to the audience.

Now, in these performances it will not be enough for the performer to sing the basic tune or lines of a song or to tell the bare outlines of a tale. Even in the shorter forms of oral literature such as riddles and proverbs, the aim or the challenge is for the teller to tell as many of them as possible to impress the listeners with the depth and variety of his or her wisdom. The more fully he or she performs, the better the impression the artist will have left on the audience. In African oral literature, it is perhaps true to say that fullness, not economy, of expression is a fundamental virtue. Although this fullness can sometimes be abused, as we have already seen, the oral performer who keeps the audience's attention through the night is more likely to be fully rewarded than the one who sends them home after only a very short performance.

Once this principle is grasped, we can easily see that various devices used in oral literature are designed to achieve this sense of fullness as well as impress the audience. One way in which this fullness can be achieved is by piling or coupling one detail or idea to another so that the whole performance builds up to a climax. This device is particularly common in songs and chants. In its simplest form, piling or linking can take the form of the last detail in one line of song becoming the first detail in the next, as in two lines from a praise salute to Shaka the Zulu.

> He who armed in the forest, who is like a madman,
> The madman who is in full view of men. (Cope 1968: 72)

We can see from this example that repetition is a basic ingredient in the device of piling. In the more extended forms, we see successive lines of a song built up in such a way that each line borrows an element from the last; the result is a mounting effect which ends in an ironic twist, as in an Igbo song recorded by Romanus Egudu.

> Give me pear
> Parrot's pear
> Give me parrot
> Wren's parrot
> Give me wren
> Moth's wren
> Give me moth
> Palm's moth
> Give me palm
> Earth's palm
> Give me earth
> Wealthy earth
> Give me wealth
> Wealth is hatred! (Egudu 1975: 207)

This song is a sample of the sort of word games played especially by youngsters in an African night's entertainment. An alternative to the climactic effect seen in this song is a circular effect: one line is linked to the next by the repeated detail, but the song works its way back to the detail from which it started, as in this example from the Chewa of Malawi.

Iri ni derere.	This is okra.
Derere la njani?	Whose okra?
Derere la muwana.	Child's okra.
Mwana wa njani?	Whose child?
Mwana walira amjina.	The child cries for its mother.
Anyina bayankha?	Where's the mother gone?
Baya kumunda	She's gone to the garden
Bamutola ngoma.	To collect maize.
Ngoma za skobo	Green maize
Derere ni dee—	Okra it is—
	(Mvula 1982: 63)

The device of piling or linking is also used in oral narratives for the development of episodes. In many cases a song is employed to underline the repetitive structure of the plot, but we can see that the real interest of the narrator is in the additional detail that moves the story forward toward the intended climax. Take the story which I collected from a maternal aunt in 1976 but which is common among the Igbo of Nigeria.

Once upon a time, there was a woman with an only child whom she named "Nwaka-dimkpolo." They lived alone in a hut—she had nobody to help her, and she was very poor. She had a little cassava farm a long distance from her home. One day, before she went to the farm, this cassava farm, she put Nwakadimkpolo in a fence of sticks. (*Listener:*

She was afraid someone would steal her child away). Yes, so she put him in that fence. Then she went to the farm. She returned in the evening with a basket full of cassava tubers. She put it down and went to Nwakadimkpolo in the fence. On looking in, she found that Nwakadimkpolo had been killed by a fallen breadfruit. (*Audience exclamation:* E-oh!). The woman cried, cried, cried. She was filled with hatred for the breadfruit, and sang:

Narrator:	What will happen to this breadfruit?
Audience:	Eh, Nwakadimkpolo!
Narrator:	Breadfruit that killed my Nwakadimkpolo.
Audience:	Eh, Nwakadimkpolo!

In sympathy for her, a stake fell on the breadfruit and crushed it to pieces. (*Listener:* Good!). The woman hated the stake, and sang again:

Narrator:	What will happen to this stake?
Audience:	Eh, Nwakadimkpolo!
Narrator:	Stake that crushed my breadfruit.
Audience:	Eh, Nwakadimkpolo!
Narrator:	Breadfruit that killed my Nwakadimkpolo.
Audience:	Eh, Nwakadimkpolo!

Some ants heard her song and came out from the ground and ate up the stake. (*Laughter*). The woman hated the ants, and sang:

Narrator:	What will happen to these ants?
Audience:	Eh, Nwakadimkpolo!
Narrator:	Ants that ate my stake.
Audience:	Eh, Nwakadimkpolo!
Narrator:	Stake that crushed my breadfruit.
Audience:	Eh, Nwakadimkpolo!
Narrator:	Breadfruit that killed my Nwakadimkpolo.
Audience:	Eh, Nwakadimkpolo!

A fowl heard the song, and rushed over and ate up all the ants. (*Chuckles*). The woman hated the fowl, and sang:

Narrator:	What will happen to this fowl?
Audience:	Eh, Nwakadimkpolo!
Narrator:	Fowl that ate my ants.
Audience:	Eh, Nwakadimkpolo!
Narrator:	Ants that ate my stick.
Audience:	Eh, Nwakadimkpolo!
Narrator:	Stick that crushed my breadfruit.
Audience:	Eh, Nwakadimkpolo!
Narrator:	Breadfruit that killed my Nwakadimkpolo.
Audience:	Eh, Nwakadimkpolo!

So it went on and on—oh! (*Narrator's hand points aloft to indicate continuity*). The woman kept on crying and crying. (*Discussion follows*). (Okpewho 1983: 79–80)

The discussion that followed was really a way of getting the audience involved in the continuing narrative. First my aunt asked us (me and the neighborhood children listening to her) what killed the fowl, and so on and so forth. We can see, however, that much of the interest in this story comes from the way in which the story grows by one element being linked to another in a progressive chain of episodes building up to a climax.

The examples of linking which we have considered so far have something well-ordered and deliberate about them: the punning song quoted from Egudu and the sung episodes of the story just discussed follow exactly the pattern or sequence known to the narrator. When linking becomes less predetermined, it is known as association. In other words, when a storyteller must compose the text on the spur of the moment rather than simply recall a ready-made sequence of events, then the ideas and details that follow one another are linked together not by an exact similarity between them (as in pear-parrot/parrot-wren/wren-moth/moth-palm, etc. in Egudu's song above) but by some kind of approximate relationship, i.e., association, between them.

It may happen, for instance, that a member of a storytelling audience is suddenly invited to tell a story as a way of filling in the time while the main performer takes a rest. Not being particularly prepared for storytelling, our narrator is slightly at a loss how to begin. Another member of the audience, trying to help out, sings a tune from a well-known story about the tortoise. Our narrator recalls the tune and the image of the tortoise, but the exact sequence of the story in which that tune occurs is not recalled. However, rather than give up in disgrace, our narrator quickly substitutes another story about the tortoise in which the tune could be used defensibly enough. What our narrator has done is to provide details of a story that are plausibly associated with the tune.

It is important to bear this in mind, because much of what goes on in an oral performance, especially a storytelling performance, happens on the spur of the moment. The narrator is not reading a ready-made script and so must rely on imagination most of the time. It may be, as we have just seen, that the narrator has forgotten the exact details of the story and simply looks around for other details that may be used in their place. Alternatively, the narrator may wish to demonstrate what an expert storyteller he or she is by using a tune or an image to recall or narrate any number of stories in one sitting. Scheub, in his treatment of Xhosa oral narratives (*ntsomi*), calls such a key song or image a core cliché and tells us:

> The cliché contains an emotion or an action which is in itself sufficient to call up the necessary associated details. The images [of the cliché] suggest, if they do not actually contain, the kernel of conflict and resolution in the performance. . . . The song is enough to recall the details necessary to the full embodiment of the *ntsomi*. . . . These details need not be memorized. They come to mind immediately when the song is recalled. (1975: 96).

Enoch Mvula also tells us about some selfish narrators among the Chewa of Malawi:

> Sometimes, the good storyteller strings two or three narratives together during one rendition when she [wants] to monopolize a tale-telling session. . . . The storyteller selects stories which have common characters or a common picaresque hero, for example, Kalulu

the hare. However, it is not only characters who make it easier for a narrator to successfully string tales together. A common theme does in some cases contribute to this particular device. (1982: 64)

What these statements and examples tell us is sufficiently clear. The mind of the oral artist works more conveniently in an associative way; in other words, the oral literary imagination is easily inclined—much more so than the mind of a writer—to seek ways of linking or yoking ideas together either as a way of displaying its skill (as in Egudu's punning song) or for its own convenience. But perhaps a more revealing use of association can be seen in situations when artists are at pains to hold their imagination together in the heat of narrative performance, especially of extensive tales. Let us consider two examples briefly.

The first example comes from *The Mwindo Epic* from the Banyanga of Zaire, edited by Biebuyck and Mateene (1969). Toward the end of this story, in a section dealing with the destructive fight between the hero, Mwindo, and his father, it is obvious that the narrator has become rather worn out by the performance. In a song accompanying the tale at this point, the hero is denouncing the evil schemes of his father:

My little father threw me into palavers.
Substitute, replace me now!
My father believed that I would faint away.
He threw me into palavers. (P. 140)

The real quarrel ("palavers") between Mwindo and his father started when the latter, unwilling to have a male child succeed him on the throne, threw the newborn Mwindo into a drum, sealed it up, and threw it into a river so that the child would be choked to death. But the child was aided by supernatural forces and survived to overcome his father. We can see the immediate connection between the narrator and the child at this point: just as the child, in the course of his struggle with his father, is in danger of "fainting away" (especially in the air-tight drum), so is the narrator, in the course of his struggle with this rather long story, in danger of fainting. The second line, in which the narrator calls on one of his accompanists to take over the performance from him and save him from losing his breath, applies just as much to the struggling hero as to the narrator. Here in this song, the narrator shows his brilliant creative imagination by associating his plight with that of the main character of his story.

Our second example comes from *Kambili*, a heroic tale from Mali edited by Charles Bird with some Malian colleagues (1974). In the earlier part of this story, several soothsayers are invited to foretell which of nine wives is going to bear the hero-child (Kambili) who will do great deeds for his community. After some traditional medicine men have failed in the task and been executed, it is now the turn of an *imam*, a Muslim divine, to try his luck. Here is how the narrator introduces the *imam* into the story.

Ah! The holyman has come. . . .
The man of the Koran has come, Kambili!

Man, the hero is only welcome on troubled days.
It is not good to put aside tradition for one day's pain.
Death may put an end to a man, it does not end his name.
There is no other source of pity beyond Allah.
Hearing the wretched out is better than mine-is-at-home.
        Ah! The holyman has come!
        The holyman of the Koran has come! (P. 27)

In his performance of the entire Kambili story, the narrator constantly used lines of proverbs as a way both of displaying his traditional wisdom and of giving some variety or respite to the performance. The challenge, however, is to find a convenient way of engaging in these proverbs without losing control of the sequence of the story. In this passage, the narrator has done this by choosing a group of proverbs (the italicized lines) whose ideas are linked or associated, from one line to the next, until he is able to pick up the story from where he digressed into the proverbs. In this passage, "Kambili" in the second line suggests "hero" in the third; "trouble" in the third line suggests "pain" in the fourth; "pain" itself gives rise to "Death" in the fifth line; it is to "Allah" (sixth line) that men go when they die; "Hearing the wretched out" (seventh line) is a work of God (Allah) and an act of "pity" (sixth line), ostensibly best performed by the servant of Allah, the Muslim "holyman" (eighth line)—and this brings the narrator back to the line from which he originally digressed.

Let us recall once again that performers of oral literature are not working with a prepared script. As they narrate or chant their oral texts before an audience, they have to depend both on their memory (which is sometimes unreliable) and on their imagination to be able to do a successful job. One way of ensuring the success of that job is by organizing the material of their texts in convenient groups or patterns that will make it possible for their imagination to keep the sequence or the logic of the texts intact. Very much like repetition and parallelism, linking and association provide artists with patterns of pleasure as well as of convenience.

Tonality

Because the text of African oral literature is performed by the human voice, it benefits greatly from the flexibility of the voice, which is not easily represented on the printed page. Earlier in this chapter, we made the point that oral literature makes its appeal first through the sound of the words and that the oral performer whose voice is not strong enough gains little popularity. Let us now look at a few ways in which oral artists can put the tone of their voice and the tonal qualities of their language to good use in their performance.

Those who are not quite familiar with performances of African oral literature may, as a way of understanding the role of the voice in this regard, consider the chanting of hymns or litanies in Christian churches, especially among Roman Catholics. In the antiphonal singing between the officiating priest and the congregation, words and lines are frequently stretched out to unusual lengths by giving individual syllables a variety of tones so as to produce a lyrical effect. Anyone familiar with Muslim worship may also recall the manner in which the *imam* leads the congregation in prayer by chanting, at a rather high pitch, relevant lines from the Koran in such a way as to prolong and vary the tones of some syllables.

Although the style of traditional African worship is not exactly the same as these, there is abundant evidence of the manipulation of vocal sounds in the call-and-response of African ritual chants. In discussing repetition, I made reference to a tape of a Sudanese chant played by the German musicologist Arthur Simon during his lecture at Ibadan on African music. As the leading officiant chanted each line, the others repeated the last word of the line in a tone different from that used by the leader: invariably, the leader's last word was toned high, while his followers' repetition was given a middle tone throughout the chant. A lyrical effect was clearly intended, whatever other purposes were served by the tonal counterpoint.

Such tonal counterpoint is also used for less serious, recreational performances such as the telling of riddles. In these riddling sessions, the idea is to display both cultural wisdom and linguistic skill. One person poses a question, and someone else responds with a statement that matches it not only in terms of content but also of beauty of expression; in many cases, this beauty is achieved by matching the tones of the answer almost exactly with the tones of the question. This practice of tone riddles has been observed among various African communities, and we may just cite a couple of examples to demonstrate this skillful use of the human voice.

Donald Simmons (1958) has done some notable studies of tone riddles among Efik-Ibibio speakers in southeastern Nigeria. Like all riddles, according to him, the tone riddle "poses a question, the answer to which is culturally accepted as correct," but it also has a peculiar character: both query and response differ in meaning but possess similar tone patterns for the most part. Often, in fact, the points made by the query and the response are so difficult to reconcile that the only recognizable relationship between them is in tonal pattern. How does this similarity of tonal pattern happen? "In the majority of instances," says Simmons, "in order to achieve tonal similarity, the Efik have used noun and verb roots in the response which possess the same inherent tone as the noun and verb roots used in the query, and morphological tone mutations which change the inherent tones of the noun and verb root according to regular patterns."

One of the numerous examples given by Simmons demonstrates the point.

> *Query:*   *éyén íkanke eka*
> Child does not conquer mother
> *Response:*   *ídáp ífi kke ukut*
> Sleep does not know suffering.

This riddle—which simply means "one must give precedence to important things"—is analyzed by Simmons: "The subject of the query and the subject of the response (*éyén* child and *ídáp* sleep) . . . belong to the same group of disyllabic nouns possessing high tones; the direct objects (*eka* mother and *ukut* suffering) belong to the same group of disyllabic low toned nouns; and the two verb roots (*kan* conquer and *fik* know) have inherent low tone. Moreover, both verbs have the same pronominal prefix (*í-*) and the same negative suffix (*-ke*)."

A majority of the other examples given by Simmons follow this scheme; and although there seems to be a reasonably large number of cases in which there is tonal dissimilarity, the incidence of similarity is high enough to convince us that tonal counterpoint is a deliberate feature in Efik-Ibibio riddles. Here we have a solid demonstration of the skillful use of the tonal element of an African language in the oral literature mainly for purposes of entertainment. "Any example," as Simmons tells us from a survey of his collection, "illustrates the usage of the tone riddle as a form of amusement."

Our second example, coming from the Tshwa of Mozambique, would seem to indicate that tone riddles are widespread on the continent. John Kaemmer has done some work in this area, and the report (1977) which he has given is in most respects similar to what Simmons has told us about Efik-Ibibio tone riddles. The Tshwa, like the Efik, hold riddling competitions in the evening mainly for entertainment, and in a large proportion of these riddles tonal counterpoint is a predominant feature. Although there are many instances of tonal dissimilarity between the query and the response, there are equally many in which there is a deliberate effort to match not only the tones of the one with the tones of the other, especially in the final syllables of the statement (which Kaemmer calls "resultant tones"), but even the phrase structures of both statements. Here are two examples of tone riddles cited by Kaemmer (the second has the form of a proverb, as do many of the riddles collected by Simmons).

> *Query:*   Xìkhàtò xáchùtí
>   bottom of mortar
> *Response:* likùlù lámànzá
>   large amount of eggs

> *Query:*   à kílí wáxímángà lòkù wángákhótsà wùkhótsílè
>   the tail of a cat, if it is curled, it is curled
> *Response:* à nwínyí wámútì lòkù ángásùkà ísùkílè
>   the headman of a hamlet, if he has gone, he has gone.

It seems clear therefore that tonality is well represented in languages across the continent and is a notable feature of the oral literature as well. One language in which considerable research has been done is Yoruba, and here we can see how effectively this stylistic element is used to manipulate meaning in the oral literature. The earliest notable study of tonality in Yoruba oral literature was done by E. L. Lasebikan (1955), and in it he has demonstrated how chanters make effective use of tonal changes, especially in the last syllables of their lines, to achieve a variety of cadences. To show how the Yoruba oral poet uses tones to good musical and semantic effect, we may cite the first two lines of an example he has given.

> *Ìjà kan, ìjà kàn ti nwọn jà l'Ọfà nkọ́ -*
> *Ojú tal' ó tó diẹ ṁbẹ?*

What about a great fight that was fought at Ofa—
Is there anyone here who witnessed a bit of it? (P. 36)

To start with, we can see the counterpoint between the predominantly low tones (`)
in the first line and the predominantly high tones (´) in the second line; there is
deliberate music in that balance. But an even more interesting manipulation of tones
occurs in the first line. The phrase *ìjà kan* (a certain fight) is repeated, but the tone
of the word *kan* (one, a certain) is altered from mid or unaccented in the first occurrence to low tone in the second occurrence; the effect of this is to give the repeated
phrase a forceful meaning like "A certain fight, oh what *a* fight!" which Lasebikan
has loosely rendered "a great fight." Here, clearly, is a skillful way of using accentual
or tonal changes to good semantic effect, i.e., to achieve a forceful meaning.

Other studies of tonality in Yoruba oral poetry have been done by Adeboye Babalola in his work on *ijala* (hunters' poetry), Wande Abimbola in his researches into *ifa*
divination poetry, and other Yoruba scholars. In fact, Yoruba is such a highly tonal
language that the use of tonal modulation easily strikes a listener as one of the most
prominent features of any form of poetic performance.

Let us take an example from one of the *ijala* pieces recorded by Babalola in *The
Content and Form of Yoruba Ijala* (1966). Titled "Salute to Fabunmi," the chant is a
dirge devoted to the praise of a departed hunter noted both for his skill at shooting
down monkeys and for his generosity with the game he kills. The chant is performed
as a duet by two hunter-poets, members of the guild of hunters to which Fabunmi
belonged and which was now mourning him. Here is how the second poet describes
the generosity of Fabunmi.

> Ó pa fún Akintólá torítorí.
> Ó pa fún Oníròkò tọlẹ̀tọlẹ̀.
> He once killed a game animal and gave it, head and all, as a gift to Akintola.
> He once killed a game animal and gave it, foetus and all, as a gift to Oniroko. (Pp. 212–
> 13)

The parallelism in structure and detail between the two lines is no doubt obvious,
and accounts for much of their beauty. But the more significant stylistic achievement
of these lines is in the tonal counterpoint between *torítorí* and *tọlẹ̀tọlẹ̀*. To start with,
it may be observed that the choice of tones or accents in each word is determined by
the accents immediately before it: thus, the high tones in *torítorí* have been influenced
by the high tones in *Akintola,* while the low tones of *toletole* have been influenced by
the final low tone of *Oniroko.*

In addition to the musical appeal of this counterpoint, however, the tones play a
more intrinsic role within their respective contexts. As Babalola tells us in his notes
to these two lines, Akintola was the Balogun of Ibadan from 1893 to 1899, when he
died. Oniroko is a reference to the Baale of Iroko. Now, in the Yoruba traditional
hierarchy the rulership of Ibadan would be ranked higher than that of Iroko (which
is really a village); the use of high tones for Ibadan and low for Iroko thus aptly
reflects this hierarchical order between the two communities. In addition to this, the

use of high tones for head *(ori)* and low for foetus *(ọlẹ)* skillfully reflects the relative positions of these elements in the human body. Finally, the distribution of high tones in the one word and low tones in the other serves to indicate that Fabunmi extended his generosity to a wide range of people, as the "Salute to Fabunmi" in fact goes on to show in its closing lines.

These diverse uses of tonal changes in song and chant—to enhance meaning and to indicate extent or variety—have been observed by other scholars. From their findings it is clear that tonality is an important feature of African oral literature (especially songs and chants) and marks an important distinction between the stylistic resources available to the oral artist and those available to the writer.

Ideophones

Like the vocal and tonal devices that we have just discussed, the ideophone is a stylistic technique that relies on sound. Simply defined, it means "idea-in-sound," in the sense that from the sound of the word one can get an idea of the nature of the event or the object referred to. Ideophones are not like normal words to which meanings are readily assigned. They are simply sounds used in conveying a vivid impression. From the examples we looked at in our discussion of tonality, we could see that it is a device that is more frequently used in songs and chants (as well as tighter forms such as riddles) for achieving lyrical and other effects. Ideophones, however, are more frequently used in narratives for achieving a stronger sensual or dramatic impact than any words available in the language could have done.

The usefulness of ideophones in storytelling is well outlined by Enoch Mvula in his discussion of narrative performances among the Chewa of Malawi.

> Chichewa as the language of storytelling is rich in ideophones. The storyteller exploits this advantage and employs ideophones which vivify his speech, lend him eloquence, complete his thought and help him to create a fresh picture of an event, and to convey contrasting images. . . . You can hear the sound of a person walking on dry leaves *(tswatsuratsura)*, a child walking in water *(chuwachuwa)*, the frying of maize *(weyeweye ndi thethethe)*, the hunter chasing an antelope *(suyosuyo)*, and the thunder storming and flashing *(gulugulu* and *ng'aning'ani)*. The images created by using ideophones help the audience to see, hear, feel, smell, touch and enjoy the narrative. (1982: 62)

We can therefore see that the ideophone has a wide range of applications as a device for achieving vividness in narrative performances. Charles Simayi, from whom I have collected many tales, makes frequent use of ideophones in his tales, and perhaps I should cite some of them to demonstrate the range of uses. One of these tales is particularly widespread throughout Africa. It tells how, of the many wives of a king, only one—the mistreated one who is consigned to live near the rubbish heap of the palace—is able to bear him a male child to succeed him. The other wives conspire and throw the baby into a river, but he is rescued from the currents and cared for by an old woman, who endows him with all kinds of supernatural skills with which he overcomes other youths. As his reputation grows, he is eventually summoned to the king's palace where, to find out who his mother might be, he is invited to taste the meal cooked by each of the king's wives. While he treats with contempt the sumptuous meals cooked by the treacherous wives, he settles down with gusto to eat up the wretched broth made by the equally wretched woman whom natural instincts have now identified as his mother. The boy is thereupon recognized as heir apparent.

Simayi's use of ideophones in this tale shows the scope of application of this device. For instance, it can be used to portray the sound made by an object or action. When the old women who rescued the child from the river proceeds to build him up with superhuman powers, she invites a hunter to fire his gun at the child; the hunter levels his gun and fires a blast which resounds *dakwalalalam*. The child remains standing as the gunpowder scatters in vain. The old woman challenges the hunter to load the gun more sturdily with powder and ball; the second blast fired resounds *gbawalalalalalam*. The gun itself disintegrates, while the boy remains untouched. The effectiveness of these ideophones lies in the root verbs from which they have been formed. *Dakwaa* in Igbo connotes "to fall about"; the ideophone aptly captures the futility of the gunpowder as it scatters and falls to the ground. *Gbawaa* in the second ideophone is a much stronger word, and perhaps its superiority can be seen in the fact that the plosive sound of *gb* is stronger than the dental *d* of *dakwaa*. *Gbawaa* means "to shoot to pieces," and although the hunter fails to do this to the boy, it aptly indicates the added effort in the second gun blast; even the difference in length between the two ideophones points to this added effort.[1]

Another use of the ideophone is for indicating length, size, or distance covered in a movement. As the child tastes the meal of one wife after another of the king, we are told that he

Jegidezię tiii, luę nke last, nk' ikpaazu
Walked on *tiii*, got to the last, the final one.

The narrator does not tell us at the beginning of the tale how many wives the king has. But the ideophone *tiii*, which indicates a long distance covered, makes clear both that the king has a rather extensive harem and that it has taken the child a long time to get to the last wife—his mother at the rubbish heap. Sometimes the distance covered is not so much indicated as implied by an ideophone which points to the abruptness of the movement. For instance, on the day that the boy is appointed to taste the meals of the king's wives, the old witch who raised him simply places her hand on a charmed pot and, as we are told,

O kunię nwata a—na b' Ǫba shojim!
She lifted this boy—right to the king's
    [palace] *shojim!*

The ideophone *shojim* portrays the suddenness with which the boy is transported over a long distance and lands at the palace.

There are also ideophones for indicating sensations, such as taste, smell, and so on. These ideophones are very much like those Mvula has pointed out from Malawi.

When the boy finally comes to taste the broth prepared by his mother, concocted mostly from the vegetable okro and a dead bush-rat she found in the garbage heap, we are told that

> Ǫkwụlụ ne-esigẹẹ wanị wanị wanị, o yen' eye
> The okro was by now smelling *wani wani wani*, it was not done.

This ideophone has in fact succeeded not only in suggesting the raw smell of the okro, but the shoddy and insecure manner in which the poor, maltreated woman has put the meal together.

One final example from this story will show how skillfully the ideophone can be employed in vivid description. Here, Simayi has used it to portray activity. In describing the feverish and lavish efforts made by the other (favored) wives of the king to prepare meals that would charm the boy, the narrator uses a concatenation of vivid ideophones:

> Ǫlǫkǫtǫ kpam kpam kpalala kpam kpam
> kpalala ǫlǫkǫtǫ pụụ pụụ yǫǫ yǫǫ,
> o liẹ k'ǫ sị na mmụ mụ a
>
> Ǫlǫkǫtǫ kpam kpam kpalala kpam kpam
> kpalala ǫlǫkǫtǫ pụụ pụụ yǫǫ yǫǫ,
> when he eats let him say that I am his mother.

Various components of this extensive ideophone reflect the respective efforts of the women in this regard. *Ǫlǫkǫtǫ* connotes abundance, and cleverly suggests that while the maltreated woman has little at her disposal, these other wives have everything they want for the cooking. *Kpam kpam kpalala* aptly describes the sound of the utensils and crockery used in this overzealous effort to cook the best meal possible. *Pụụ pụụ yǫǫ yǫǫ*, on the other hand, carries a note of contempt with it; the narrator uses those sounds to imply that although there is an abundance of ingredients in such a meal, it is really little more than a worthless and messy hotchpotch. In fact, taken together the long ideophonic statement may be construed as an incomprehensible magical formula intended to charm the boy. This impression is certainly emphasized by the last part of the sentence. But the narrator has effectively used the ideophones to suggest the worthlessness of the effort mounted by the favored wives.

The ideophone has various other possibilities, for instance for describing physical appearance. In one *ntsomi* (tale) from South Africa the narrator tells us of a character, "when she was far off, she saw a fire glimmering—*lozi, lozi*" (Scheub 1975: 79), no doubt from the brightness of the flames. And in *The Ozidi Saga*, Clark (1977) has preserved in the original Ijo language as well as English translation the very vivid and exhilarating ways in which his storyteller describes forms of beauty and ugliness. For instance, when the witch Oreame transforms herself into a young girl to attract one of Ozidi's opponents and thus provoke a fight with the hero, the narrator tells us of the smashing, sexy look of the lady's breasts.

Endoubo wo wo wo . . . kene yereke yereke
Her bosom was full and large, all yearning and yielding. (P. 372)

Another of Ozidi's opponents, the Scrotum King, has enormous testicles, and the heavy, awkward movements of the fellow are effectively captured in the following description:

Kene kpiridi, engbe kiri kpon pake tekie tekie tekie tekie
Rolling, his balls trundled along. (P. 211)

From the examples that we have examined so far, we will have observed a few basic features of ideophones. First, the ideophone can sometimes come in the form of a single word that makes an adequate impact: *shojim*, for example. More frequently, however, the ideophone is found in the form of a sound multiplied several times over, like the examples we have just seen from *The Ozidi Saga*. The repeated or multiple ideophone not only achieves the effect of vivid description but often has the capacity to affect us emotionally—as in the gross image of the rolling scrotum—partly because the artist may accompany the words with certain dramatic movements. Second, many ideophones can be related or traced to recognizable root verbs and can therefore be described as onomatopoeic ideophones; useful examples already cited are *dakwalalalam* and *gbawalalalalam*. And yet there are many others which cannot be so identified but whose descriptive value is recognized by native speakers of the language: *wani wani wani* is a good example, though I would not be surprised if *lozi lozi* also belongs in this class.

Difficulty of identification of the kind I just demonstrated has often led to one prejudice or the other among certain scholars. For instance, the phrase *nonsense syllables* has been used for describing any indigenous sounds in a song or tale that defy translation. Take the example in this folk song which I recall from my childhood.

Little bird, little bird
    Tuluzamzam tulunzam
What are you doing up there?
    Tuluzamzam tulunzam
I'm up there fetching wood
    Tuluzamzam tulunzam
After fetching what will you do?
    Tuluzamzam tulunzam
After fetching I'll light a fire
    Tuluzamzam tulunzam

Such sounds are usually left untranslated—rightly, perhaps—because there is no obvious meaning or function to them other than to complete the rhythmic beat of the song. But it is equally possible that those sounds have been derived from a close observation of the habits of little birds and are employed as a vivid phonological way of representing the "personality" of the bird in this particular dialogue.[2]

On a more serious level, it has been charged that these ideophones or "nonsense sounds" are frequently found in "primitive" languages in their infancy of development. Again, it could be argued that some of these sounds have long lost their currency and that we no longer know their exact meanings because the language has developed well beyond them. On the whole, however, it is safer to see ideophones and similar sounds as proof of their users' sensitive feeling for language, a deep sensitive attachment to sounds and their power of vivid suggestion or representation. In many cases, a speaker or an oral artist can avoid an ideophone by simply duplicating a word of action: for *jegidezie tiii*, for instance, the narrator could have said *jegide jegide,* which would translate into something like "walked on and on." But *tiii* has a special appeal both as a sound and as a more dramatic way of capturing the idea of extent.

There are a few other characteristic features of African oral literature that we need not discuss at length, either because they could be conveniently seen in the light of topics treated earlier or because they are found in one form or another in written literature and are not necessarily peculiar to oral literature. Three in particular are worth mentioning.

Digression

This is a device whereby the oral performer departs for a moment from the main line of the subject of a story or song either to address an object (or person) at the scene of performance or to comment on an issue which may be closely or remotely connected with the main subject. In chapter 3, we gave detailed attention to the various factors operating within the context of the oral performance—the accompanist, the audience, and the recorder—and how they influence the text of the performance. A review of the examples which we discussed under those subheadings would help the reader to appreciate the role of digression as a characteristic, and in some cases inevitable, element in the performance of oral literature. This kind of digression may be called external digression, being prompted by an element outside the subject of performance.

A more internal kind of digression occurs when the oral artist feels the need to comment briefly on an issue that arises within the song or story. Those who have watched great performers such as the South African Miriam Makeba and the Nigerian Fela Anikulapo-Kuti (whose songs usually deal with the social and political problems of Africa) on the stage will recall that every once in a while they would stop to lecture the audience on one issue or another related to the theme of the song being performed. This kind of digression also happens in storytelling. Babalola sees it as a characteristic feature of Yoruba hunters' performances *(ijala).*

> In performing ijala chants, ijala artists continually wander at will from their themes, apparently in order to provide the spice of variety, especially relief from a tragic theme, to create suspense, and/or to teach a moral. For example, in an ijala chant which tells a long story about a hunter's tragic experience on an elephant hunt, the chanter abandons the thread of his story, after following it up to the point of the hunter's safe return home from the first trip and before he set out again on the second trip, which took him to his

death. The digression takes the form of a commentary on women's fickleness, linked with a character sketch of a barn-yard fowl, and with a moral that men should never reveal all their secrets to their wives. The listener's attention is temporarily distracted from the hunter's fate until the chanter picks up the thread of the story again with:

Listen now to the rest of the story. (1966: 64–65)

Let us take one more concrete example of internal digression to drive home the point just made by Babalola. The final version of the Sunjata story contained in Innes's *Sunjata: Three Mandinka Versions* was performed by Dembo Kanute. According to Dembo, envoys were sent from Manding (Mali) to Sunjata in his exile, urging him to return home and recover the kingdom from the tyrant-usurper Sumanguru. Since these envoys were not sure where exactly Sunjata (with his mother and sister) was, they simply picked some neighboring foreign land and spread out a few peculiarly Mandinka vegetables in the market for sale, believing that this food would automatically attract any Mandinka resident in that community who might give them information about Sunjata. Here is how Dembo describes this show of good judgment on the part of the envoys.

They said, "Let us take as provisions groundnuts,
And bitter tomatoes and okra and maize."
That is what made these four things so loved by the Mandinka.
Before you cook oily food for a Mandinka elder,
Cook groundnuts for him—that is what he likes.
When a Mandinka man grows old, he likes to grow a patch of bitter tomatoes;
When a Mandinka woman grows old, she likes to grow a patch of okra.
In any Mandinka town you go to,
You will find in it a garden growing maize.
They came and put down the three little piles of goods in the market.
Markets have been in existence for a very long time.
You know yourself, Seni Darbo, that even if you are in Europe,
When you see something from your own country in the market
That is the first thing you will buy. (Innes 1974: 281–82)

Internal digressions are generally useful for expatiating on a detail that the performer feels may not be immediately clear to the audience, or for throwing light on aspects of morality or social history. In this passage, we can see Dembo Kanute using this little episode within the Sunjata story to educate his audience (specifically Seni Darbo, the host of this performance) on aspects of Mandinka culture.

How can we defend digression as a characteristic feature of oral literature? It is true that unless properly controlled, digression is likely to disorganize the logic of a text and perhaps cause it to lose its point. But we must realize that unlike the writer, who can set out his or her ideas in a straightforward order and eliminate anything that may seem irrelevant to the logic of a work, the oral artist is frequently at the mercy of various forms of distraction which may threaten the neatness (so to speak) of the presentation. Also, unlike the writer, who does not usually know who the actual audience (readers) will be and can therefore ignore their reactions, the oral artist is directly facing the people who have paid (or will pay) for the performance and whose patronage he or she hopes to maintain. It is in the effort to steady the mind through those distractions, or to say things designed to please these patrons and ensure that they keep coming, that the artist sometimes goes into digressions.

Imagery

While it is true that oral literature and written literature differ fundamentally from one another in their methods of presentation—the one by word of mouth and the other through the printed word—they are both united, fundamentally also, in the use of words and in the ways in which they employ words to paint mental pictures that appeal to our feeling and our understanding. These mental pictures are what we know as images.

Images may be expressed directly. A narrator or a singer may describe a scene or an event with little reference to anything else but with such a powerful choice of words that we are deeply touched either with admiration or with shock. Take for example the description of the fierce war between the Mandinka leader Janke Waali of Kaabu and the Fulani invader, the Almani of Timbo, as narrated by the Gambian *griot* Amadu Jebate. In the final encounter between the opposing armies, so heavy was the toll of slaughter that

> You would plunge into human blood up to your knees:
> Blood was soaking the walls and they were collapsing.
> They fought on;
> The swords stuck to their hands;
> Human blood was gushing forth like a spring. (Innes 1976: 55)

The narrator has presented the horror of the fighting in straightforward terms until the last line, where he has employed a simile, that is, an image whereby one thing is compared to another, very often with the conjunction *like* or *as*.

For a more forceful use of the simile, let us consider the first part of "Poet's Lament on the Death of his Wife."

> Like the *yu'ub* wood bell tied to gelded camels that are running away,
> Or like camels which are being separated from their young,
> Or like people journeying while moving camp,
> Or like a well which has broken its sides or a river which has overflowed its banks,
> Or like an old woman whose only son was killed,
> Or like the poor, dividing the scraps for their frugal meal,
> Or like the bees entering their hive, or food crackling in the frying,
> Yesterday my lamentations drove sleep from all the camps. (Andrzjewski and Lewis 1964:
>   64)

Composed by the Somali poet Raage Ugaas, the song conveys through its crowded imagery the very deep sense of loss suffered by the mourner. There is a mounting effect in the succession of similes, and no doubt the repetition of the opening con-

junction *or like* (*ama* in the original Somali) bestows on the piece the musical flavor
of oral poetry.

A simile is a comparison achieved by indirect reference (*a* is like *b*); a comparison
achieved by direct reference (*a* is *b*) is called a metaphor. This technique is particularly
common in praise songs and chants in which the artist is so carried away with admiration of objects or persons that he or she conceives of them in exaggerated terms.

Take this chant from Botswana in praise of the eighteenth-century leader Masellane.

> Masellane is a self-spreading rock,
> spreading itself out from the start.
>   A pestle that rattles and jars,
> he spoils other people's rhythm,
> 5 he stamps though he was not invited. (Schapera 1965: 45)

A chief of the Kgatla clan, Masellane was well known for his extensive military
campaigns and victories during which he not only appropriated large territories (lines
1–2) and caused great commotion among his enemies (lines 3–4) but also usurped
their belongings: line 5 is an allusioin to Masellane's act in taking over the cattle
earmark (stamp) peculiar to the Mabodisa, the clan he is best known for subjugating.
The force of metaphor in this chant can be seen in the fact that, after its first mention
in line 1, the name of Masellane practically disappears and his personality is hence-
forth directly represented by objects of ferocity like the rock and the pestle: he is not
just like those objects, he is those objects.

Or take these verses from a Dinka (Sudan) song in praise of cattle.

> The old man of the leopard world
> Gives his will the day he dies,
> "My children, the forest of Ameth
> Never leave it
> 5 It is your home.
> That is where to hunt.
> That is where to steal the goats."
> The big leopard of the son of Mijok,
> When he finds a goat of the Falata,
> 10 He eats it;
> When he finds a goat of divinity,
> He eats it. (Deng 1973: 120)

The basic metaphors of this piece are contained in the first line: "old man" and
"leopard." So dominant are these metaphors that they have completely overshadowed
the object that they are supposed to refer to; anyone unfamiliar with Dinka pastoral
life and culture would hardly imagine that this song had anything to do with cattle.
Here the image of the poet's ox is represented first by an old man. The ox is probably
not old, but the idea of age is used for giving an air of dignity and grandeur to the
animal. The act of leaving a will, usually done by an old man for his descendants and

relatives before he dies, reinforces that air of dignity and grandeur. The ox is also seen as a leopard, partly because it is spotted (*Mijok* in line 8 is the name that the Dinka give to the black-and-white pattern in their cattle) and partly as a way of giving the ox a further image of grandeur and especially ferocity; hence the animal is portrayed as living in the forest and hunting all kinds of goats. The way in which the real subject of this song has been completely obscured by its metaphors shows to what extent this stylistic device can be exploited in African oral literature.

Allusion

This technique shows how a people's language grows by borrowing images and ideas from real experience or from imaginative literature such as folktales. Found as much in oral as in written literature, allusion is a device whereby such an idea or image is used in a tightly compressed form; the origin or source of the allusion is hardly apparent from the context in which it occurs, but the user has assumed that the speakers of the language already know that source.

Allusions come frequently in the form of compressed metaphors which are more commonly called proverbs. For instance, among the Asaba Igbo (in south-western Nigeria) the expression *Mkpi akwolu Mbe onwu* (The billy goat has taken over the tortoise's burden of death) is commonly used to describe a generous act which lands the doer in trouble; it alludes to a folktale in which such a goat ends up as a victim of the tortoise's villainy. This sort of allusion is somewhat similar to certain proverbial allusions in English, such as "curiosity killed the cat," which is from a familiar European folktale.

Allusions also occur as standardized phrases of identification or epithets, again with an origin in folktales. In Asaba folktales the tortoise is frequently referred to as *Mbekwu Nw'Aniga* (Tortoise, child of Aniga), or in Yoruba folktales as *Ijapa 'Tiroko, Oko Yannibo* (Ijapa being Tortoise, *'Tiroko* or *Atiroko* the surname, and the rest meaning "husband of Yannibo"). These relatives of Tortoise have their full roles in some of the folktales involving him. In others, although the Tortoise appears without them, the epithet has simply stuck with him and the relatives' names occur without any explanation; only someone familiar with the culture can understand the allusion.

One area in which allusions enjoy truly fertile usage is in songs and chants. This is probably because while in storytelling there is ample room for elaborate description and expansion, songs and chants concentrate on select ideas and sentiments neatly expressed. Such allusions are found frequently in praise songs where, because there are so many things to say about the subject of the praise, a few of them are inevitably couched in abbreviated references left to the imagination of the audience. In Babalola's collection of Yoruba hunters' poetry *(ijala)* there are numerous uses of allusion. Babalola tells us about one particular category.

> Especially in *oriki orile* (the verbal salutes to particular lineages and distinguished persons) allusions and epigrams figure recurrently in ijala chants. A short sentence or nominal phrase is used as a covert reference; the identification of what the words are really aimed

at, usually a long story, is left for the listener to make. Consequently, the style of such ijala chants becomes terse and epigrammatic. (1966: 71).[3]

A good example of this kind of allusion can be seen in a chant in Babalola's collection, which is a salute or appeal to the god Ogun (patron of hunters and other users of metal).

> Ogun, don't fight against me.
> Don't play with me.
> O Belligerent One, you are not cruel.
> The Ejemu, foremost chief of Iwonran Town,
> He who smartly accoutres himself and goes to the fight.
> A butterfly chances upon a civet-cat's excrement and flies high up into the air. (Pp. 172–
> 73)

The last line of this extract is a highly condensed allusion to an incident in the career of Ogun which Babalola explains:

> One day, during his wanderings in his lifetime, Ogun reached a town that he had never visited before. At the town gate the tall gatekeeper on duty, denied him entry. Ogun was immediately infuriated and he decided to teach the gatekeeper a lesson. So he walked back a little and then executed a magnificent high jump, landing on the shoulders of the standing gatekeeper. There Ogun sat astride the man's neck and pressed down vigorously on him. The manner in which Ogun almost literally flew up to sit on the gatekeeper's shoulders resembled the manner in which butterflies, on finding a civet-cat's faeces, are said to fly up for joy, first of all, before they settle down for a feast. (P. 72)

Allusions of this nature are evidently employed in praise songs in many African communities; notable examples may be found in the praises of great figures such as Shaka and Moshoeshoe in southern Africa (see especially Cope 1968).

Symbolism

This is another device which occurs as much in oral as in written literature. A symbol is a concrete or familiar object that is used in reference to, or as an explanation of, an abstract idea or a less familiar object or event. It is a particularly useful means of conveying certain important truths or lessons about human life and the problems of existence.

Symbols are often used in wisdom literature such as riddles and proverbs. An example may be seen in a riddle from the Lamba of Zambia: "That which digs about in the deserted village." The answer is "the heart," seen in its constantly turning "to think of the past" (Beuchat 1965: 200). An even more profound symbolism may be seen in a proverbial riddle from the Lingala of Zaire: "Seven years, fat ox; the gardener with the wife of the chief." The meaning is that "the fat cow lasts only seven years, the gardener will one day marry the wife of the chief." The answer usually assigned to this statement comes in the form of advice: "Think [of the future] when you eat" (p. 202).

Symbols are also frequently used in ritual and divination chants, which deal mostly with deep spiritual matters and concepts. The issues involved are usually weighty, but the people who chant these texts must reduce them to familiar objects to bring them closer to their understanding.

Let us take as our example the Bagre "myth" performed by the LoDagaa of northern Ghana during the Bagre initiation rituals. A person is initiated into Bagre when he or she is troubled by sickness or other problems, and the ceremony is said to have originated from the "first men" (an elder and younger brother fabled to be the original ancestors of the LoDagaa) who were similarly troubled. By various acts of trial and error they were able to receive from the divinities and certain "beings of the wild" the secrets of the Bagre ceremony which were to help their descendants overcome their problems the way their first ancestors overcame theirs. The Bagre initiation is in two parts, the White Bagre (done by fresh initiates) and the Black Bagre (performed much later by those who have first done the White). The beginning lines of the White Bagre, which tells the story of the first brothers, give a good indication of the highly symbolic level on which the language of the chant operates throughout.

> Gods,
> ancestors,
> guardians,
> beings of the wild,
> 5 the leather bottles
> say we should perform,
> because of the scorpion's sting,
> because of suicide,
> aches in the belly,
> 10 pains in the head.
> The elder brother
> slept badly.
> He took out some guinea corn
> and hurried along
> 15 to the diviner
> who poured out his bag
> and then said,
> let's grasp the stick.
> They did so
> 20 and he picked up "deity"
> and he picked up "the wild"
> and he picked up "sacrifice."
> He picked up "deity,"
> that was what
> 25 he picked up first.
> He picked out "deity"
> and began to ask,
> What "deity"?

Deity of childbirth?
30 Deity of farming?
Deity of daughters?
Deity of grandfathers?
Deity of grandmothers?
35 Deity of chicken breeding?
You reject them all.
Deity of meetings?
The cowries fell favourably:
it was so. (Goody 1972: 121)

In this passage, the visit of the elder of the first men to a diviner provides the setting for an appeal to the gods through divination. The "leather bottles" (line 5) contain cowries that will be used during the divination, and the "guinea corn" (line 13) was traditionally used for paying for the consultation. The consultation begins with the diviner and his client holding on together to a forked stick; the diviner then empties his bag on the ground, throwing out various objects such as stones and shells, one of which the client picks. In this case, the elder brother picked out an object symbolizing "deity," and the next step is to verify what deity this is. The client then empties out the cowries from his leather bottle; after several false arrangements formed by these cowries, the right one emerges which spells out the kind of deity required; in this case, the deity dictates that a meeting should be held.

A meeting is later held with the children of the elder brother, who are advised how to conduct themselves to prepare for the coming of a divinity that will bring good fortune and save the family from its troubles.

For when he comes
back to this place,
he comes
with food.
5 He does not come empty-handed.
He points
with the right hand,
never with the left.
He comes
10 with the truth
and does not bring
falsehood;
so that our Bagre
will flourish. (P. 123)

The symbolism of the right hand for truth and the left hand for falsehood, as well as food for contentment and well-being, further reveals the highly figurative language of the chant. Such language is used throughout this extensive story, which details the processes observed in the performance of the Bagre initiation ritual, lasting many days.

Other ritual chants throughout Africa, such as *ifa* divination poetry among the

Yoruba, employ very much the same pattern of symbolic references for analyzing the issues brought for consultation by various clients. Like the Bagre "myth," *ifa* divination employs stories (called *ẹsẹ*) as parables, using highly symbolic language to explain problems of existence.

Indeed, many folktales in Africa perform this specialized function: the characters and events contained in them are fundamentally symbols illustrating various moral and philosophical issues relating to people. In many cases a specific message is given at the end of the story, which confirms that the various elements operating in the tale have simply been used as symbols to illustrate that message. For instance, a Kikuyu (Kenya) story tells how a pregnant woman cracks the eggs in a bird's nest, killing all the children the bird would have had in them; when later the woman delivers her baby, the bird (disguised as a woman) succeeds in reaching the baby and pecking it to death. The story ends with the message *Njika na njika ndiri maruru,* meaning "what is done in retaliation should bring no bitterness," thus advising caution in human conduct (Liyong 1972: 111).

Other tales do not necessarily spell out their messages, but the audience is expected to derive meaning from the events narrated. Since most of these tales are set in the fantasy world of animals and spirits, the events contained in them can only have meanings for us if we treat them as symbols illustrating certain aspects of the problems and issues surrounding life in the real world of human beings.

As in written literature, therefore, symbols are widely employed in various forms of African oral literature for probing deep philosophical, moral, and spiritual matters. They are a mark of high artistic sophistication in oral culture.

5. Social Relevance

So far we have examined, in some detail, two major contexts in which African oral literature operates. In chapter 2, we put considerable emphasis on the oral artist and the artist's personal circumstances as a principal factor in the achievement of any level of excellence in the art: oral literature may be communal property, but without the individual recreation given it by one artist after another its appeal or its permanence can hardly be guaranteed. In chapter 3, we gave full attention to factors operating at the scene of performance and the visible effects of these factors on the verbal text of the performance. In the present chapter, we shall examine the wider social or cultural milieu within which oral literature is set so as to understand that usefulness or relevance of it that partly explains its continued appeal.

The issue of context is an important one in the study of oral literature. To help us get a vivid picture of this concept, perhaps we should set down a scheme.

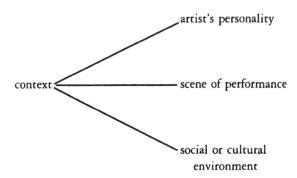

The artist's personality implies everything that the artist brings as an individual to the performance of the literature: personal artistic inclinations, family background, and personal experiences as well as training received and the circumstances in which the artist has frequently worked that may be said to have contributed to the formation of a personal style. These elements of the artist's total personality provide a context for the oral literature in the sense that together they shape the material that ultimately emerges in performance.

By the scene of performance is meant the totality of factors surrounding the text that comes from the mouth of the artist: the resources of movement and music and the effigies used for enhancing the text; the presence and actual impact of the various persons surrounding the performer (accompanist, audience, and recorder); and other factors which immediately influence the success or failure of each performance. The word *each* must be emphasized; each performance differs from others precisely because these physical factors are never quite the same in all cases of performance even of the same material. The audience may be hostile one time but absolutely cooperative the next time; the musicians may be inspired on one occasion but drowsy on another; the performer may be working at one time with a scholar who handles the tape recorder expertly and at another time with an amateurish scribe who proves a thorough nuisance. No two performances are ever quite the same because these physical conditioins are never really duplicated.

Let us now turn to the social or cultural context of African oral literature. Specifically, we are going to examine some of the principal purposes or functions served by this literature for the society with which it enjoys an interdependence. In chapter 1, we observed that the idea of functions was an overriding concern among certain social scientists who studied African oral literature in the late nineteenth and earlier twentieth centuries—social anthropologists, mainly. We pointed out that despite their contributions to the growth of this study, they promoted an obsession which underplayed the literary or aesthetic merits of oral literature. It would be wrong, of course, to assume that an interest in the functions of oral literature is totally misplaced. Having established the grounds on which the material of our study qualifies to be treated as literature, we may now conclude these introductory chapters by giving our attention to the principal ways in which this literature defines and sustains the African world within which it is set.[1]

Entertainment and Relaxation

One major usefulness of any form of literature is that it offers delight and so relieves us of various pressures and tensions both physically and mentally.

Under the physical conditions of work, oral literature, mostly in the form of songs, helps to keep up the spirits and relieve the worker of boredom. This hunting song from Zimbabwe is obviously intended to make the job of hunting a lighthearted one and perhaps suppress the fear of whatever dangers may lie ahead.

> Come on, men, let's go hunting with the dogs,
> Our dogs of Murewa, it's their lucky day!
> For today we'll hunt kudu,
> Hunt kudu down to Usamba,
> 5 Down to Usamba to hunt the wild pig.
> For today, let's go to the porcupines,
> And leaving the porcupines let's go to the buck,
> And leaving the buck to Mtanargwa,
> To Mtanargwa and Mutendahombe,
> 10 And away beyond Zumba,
> *He-i! He-i! He-i!* (Mapanje and White 1983: 60)

This is clearly a high-spirited song as revealed not only by the exclamations of the last line but also by the linking arrangement of the ideas in lines 1–2, 3–5, and 6–9.

Still under work, we may cite the widespread tradition of cattle songs in several pastoral communities across the continent. Among the Dinka of Sudan, for instance, this is recognized as a distinctive category of the oral literature. Francis Deng tells us that these songs in admiration of cattle, especially the ox, "are often sung in cattle-camps" (obviously after a hard day's work with the animals in the field) and even "when the singer is accompanying his ox" and "the clanging of [its] bell and the bellowing of the ox" provide accompanying music for the words of the song. In one of these "ox songs," the composer heaps a variety of attributes and names on his beautiful animal.

> How grow the horns spreading!
> How grow the horns sweeping the earth!
> The horns of Mangar are straying
> The horns of Mangar are straying like a lost man
> 5 The horns go to greet the things in the sky.
> The rafter-horned Jok, I call him "The Breaker of Ropes,"
> The breaking ropes of the Flour-White one thunder-clap like shots on the rifle range.
> The trotting Curve-Horned One has a voice like trumpets
> And like the gourd of the wind.
> 10 Why my Mangar roars in the evening
> Why my Mangar roars in the evening when the cattle are tethered
> I do not know whether this will be a permanent way of bellowing
> Or whether it is being gorged which rings the head of my father's Ngar
> Like a man drunk with *aregi*. (Deng 1973: 99)

Besides the exaggerative tone of this piece (especially in lines 5, 7, and 8), notice the expansion of ideas from one line to the next (e.g., 1–2, 3–4, and 10–11) as well as the linking in 6–7. Notice also the considerable use of similes (lines 4, 7, 8, 9, and 14) within a rather short space of fourteen lines.

Much more frequently, oral literature provides relief after the day's work is over. In many African communities, it is common to find families (whether immediate or extended) gathered together in the open compound at night, especially during periods of moonlight. Young ones are even fond of straying far from their own homesteads to congregate at convenient or familiar spots in the village with their friends. In these random gatherings, various types of oral literature are practiced in a more or less lighthearted vein. For a portrait of one of such occasions, we may cite a description of the prelude to a narrative session in a typical Nigerian setting.

> For the evening storytelling session, we go to a compound in a ward of Ibadan where we find an extended family that has not been wholly caught up by creeping modernization. Apart from such concessions to progress as the use of electricity, pipe-borne water, and the Rediffusion box that brings a fixed radio program by wire from a local transmitting station, the household remains a redoubt of tradition. After the evening meal, the mem-

bers of the family gather on a porch and if there is moonlight, the younger members
gather in the courtyard to play games like hide and seek.

On the porch, the entertainment begins with riddles. What dines with an *oba* (paramount chief of a community) and leaves him to clear the dishes? A fly. What passes before
the *oba's* palace without making obeisance? Rain flood. On its way to Oyo its face is
towards Oyo, on its way from Oyo its face is still towards Oyo. What is it? A double-
faced drum.

After a few riddles, the tales begin. (Owomoyela 1977: 264–65)

The ensuing narratives engage the attention of both the narrators and the audience.
As the narrator tells the story, he accompanies it with various paralinguistic devices
such as gesticulations and facial movements. The audience for its part identifies with
the plights of the characters or at least adopts a critical attitude toward their behaviors. Audience members also frequently laugh, exclaim, make comments, and do
various other things to participate fully in the narrative experience.

A comment by Scheub on the situation among the Xhosa of South Africa is, I
think, sufficiently representative of the atmosphere of relaxation and entertainment
that surrounds an evening's narrative performance in many an African community.

Entertainment is one of the chief aims of both storyteller and performer. The storyteller
seeks to entertain mainly by producing little more than an objectification of the core-
image, allied with relatively unsophisticated stylistic devices. The performer goes beyond
that, but in her efforts to do more than merely entertain the members of her audience,
the fact remains that she still entertains them. She seeks to externalize the core-image, to
evoke it, to give it a pleasing form. We can deduce certain structural patterns of the
tradition from the productions of both storyteller and performer, but aesthetic principles,
while they do exist in rudimentary form in the works of the storytellers, can be found
fully realized only in the works of the performers. (1975: 165)

Scheub stresses a distinction between an ordinary storyteller who lacks artistic sophistication in the narration of a tale and a "performer" who shows a certain professional
expertise in the control of the central ideas and images around which the tale is built.
For Scheub, however, entertainment of the audience remains a principal objective
whatever the level of skill or sophistication of the artist. It is also pertinent to mention that, as they watch and listen to the performance, the members of the audience—
especially the younger ones among them—rather unconsciously absorb the skills revealed by the artist. As we observed in chapter 2, these are the first steps in the
informal training of the future artist. Whatever the case may be, the audience on the
whole is being exposed to an aesthetic experience, in the sense that the stories thus
performed not only give them pleasure and relaxation but also implant certain artistic
skills in them.

At these performances, members of the audience have the much-needed opportunity of relaxing not only their bodies after a hard day of work but even more important their minds. Psychological relief is not the least of the functions performed by
oral literature for members of the society. The minds of both performer and audience
are relieved of various problems that have been pressing on them throughout the day.
Some problems are of course stubborn and will not easily go away, but the entertain-

ment at least provides a temporary respite. In the case of storytelling, the fact that the tales are set in a fantastic, nonhuman world helps to lift the minds of both performer and audience away from the limitations of human life to a world of blissful wish fulfillment. Some narrators are particularly fond of telling stories of bygone days. Such stories give the society a chance of feeling good about itself: we may not be worth much today as a people, but in the past our forefathers did great things, and we have a history we can be proud of.

Perhaps nobody enjoys this psychological release quite as much as the artists themselves; for a start, these tales of fantasy are products of their own creation or recreation. But the more interesting thing about these stories is that somewhere between the lines we see aspects of the artists' own lives reflected either directly or indirectly. In our examination of the oral artist's personality in chapter 2, I made reference to the fieldwork done by a former student of mine, Tunde Ipinmisho, in which he analyzed versions of a tale told by two narrators from his village, against the background of their personal lives and experiences. It was reasonably clear that each version reflected the deep-seated feelings and outlook on life of its narrator. While one narrator revealed himself through his characters as a self-assured man in full control of his affairs and the world around him, the other narrator showed himself as an internally disturbed person in whose life woman loomed large as a dominant figure, evidently because he himself had a rather unhappy marriage with a wife who wrested the control of affairs from him. It is clear that this second narrator had, rather unconsciously, used his story as a way of unburdening himself of his problems. In such ways, oral literature serves as a vehicle for the psychological release of the tensions harbored by the artist.

In other cases, the release is more openly demonstrated as the artist pours out his or her grievances directly in song. A song from the Kikuyu (Kenya) is perhaps characteristic of the pressures of contemporary working life on the traditional African marriage.

On Friday as I was coming from work,
I was thinking I was being waited for to go and eat
Buy my heart was deceiving me—listen and you will hear.

When I got home there was nobody,
At her parents' home there was nobody.
I ran very, very fast to a nearby river—
And there my wife was talking to her lover.

I had thought getting married was good.
I sat and thought and tears came out.
Girls will never be trusted ever,
Men are always to be trusted, always. (Liyong 1972: 132)

The singer has obviously poured his heart out in song; speaking about his problems openly would no doubt make them a little easier to bear. By thus providing an avenue for emotional and psychological release in day-to-day relations between members of the society, oral literature helps to promote the bases for social harmony and an emotionally balanced citizenry.

Asserting Interests and Outlooks

We have seen oral literature in the service of members of the society, whether individually or in relation to one another, making it possible for them to come to terms
with the world in which they live. A much wider service provided by oral literature
is to give the society—whether isolated groups within it or the citizenry as a whole—
a collective sense of who they are and to help them define or comprehend the world
at large in terms both familiar and positive to them. The justification for this kind
of service is essentially that as society develops and becomes increasingly complex, a
variety of interest groups inevitably emerge, each united either by similar professional
concerns or by the knowledge that its members derive from a common stock. To
protect these common interests, they often tend to develop and circulate pieces of oral
information (whether in songs or in stories) that will help them feel a certain sense of
security in the face of other contending groups within the society.

Furthermore, every society or community of people makes an effort to explain
certain aspects of nature or the universe in which they live. Such an explanation
frequently comes in the form of a story that sounds reasonably original to the society
and its natural environment; but should the ideas for the explanation come from the
outside by some process of diffusion, the society will reformulate them in a manner
and with idioms that are native to their language and their culture. These are all
ways in which a society seeks to safeguard its outlooks and interests and thus to
establish securely an identity which they can cherish for as long as possible, in the
face of the vicissitudes of history.

Take this chant from the Akan of Ghana.

> Is the chief greater than the hunter?
>   Arrogance! Hunter? Arrogance!
> The pair of beautiful things on your feet,
> The sandals that you wear,
> How did it all happen?
> It is the hunter that killed the duyker:
> The sandals are made of the hide of the duyker.
>
> Does the chief say he is greater than the hunter?
>   Arrogance! Hunter? Arrogance!
> The noisy train that leads you away,
> The drums that precede you,
> The hunter killed the elephant,
> The drum head is the ear of the elephant.
> Does the chief say he is greater than the hunter?
>   Arrogance! Hunter? Arrogance! (Nketia 1963b: 43)

Or this one, also from the Akan.

> When the creator created things,
> When the manifold creator created things;
> What did he create?

He created the court crier,
He created the Drummer,
He created the Principal State Executioner. (Daaku 1971: 120)

Each of these songs clearly reveals some spirit of competion. Despite what we have been told by many writers about the close communalistic style of life in traditional African society, the available oral literature would seem to indicate that there has always existed within each community a variety of interest groups struggling to assert themselves against one another. The development of any society has usually been accompanied by the so-called division of labor or the emergence of distinct occupations, each striving to establish its importance vis-à-vis the others. This is no doubt the spirit that underlies the hunter's comparison of himself to the chief in the first of these two chants, or the court (palace) musician's assertion of his precedence over the other court functionaries in the second chant. Here we can see oral literature being used for the assertion of group interests within a single community.

The sense of rivalry is even keener between communities. Here oral literature serves the purpose of asserting patriotic or nationalistic feelings. For all the love that it implies for one's native land, nationalism often entails a blind disregard or underestimation of the qualities or merits of other lands or peoples. In a tale of origin told by a chief from the Idoma of Nigeria's Benue State, we find an attempt to trace the order in which God created the various races on earth. In this piece, the Creator has just created the earth and the entire environment except man.

After leaving that, then the child which he begot first this is what has made us to be the senior (creatures) on the earth. The child that he begot first, he begot Ofukwo, then he begot Ajuma after him, then he begot Akpanaaja, then he begot Igwume and this Otada here. These are the five brothers, the children that he begot at one time, whom he begot at the same time. Then he was about to beget another child. Regarding the other child he was to beget, then he begot Agbaduma. Then he begot Igede, he begot Edumoga: he begot those three children. Then he also begot another child again, he begot Agatu. Regarding the Agatu whom he begot, he begot women, women, seven women in Agatu. That is what makes Agatu more numerous than we are. Having left Agatu like that, as he left Agatu, he also went to beget Adoka, he begot Adoka, begot Adoka alone.

Regarding Adoka whom he begot alone, then he went to beget Ugbooju. He begot Ugbooju alone. Then he also went and begot Ogilewu. He begot six Ogilewu (people). After also begetting Ogilewu, then he went and begot Akpa. Onyilo, Onyilo Ikilede, that Onyilo Ikilede became the name of Akpa. Then he came back again, and then he said that he had finished making Idoma. As he had finished making Idoma, (he said something) still remains, and he was still coming and I said I would sit waiting for you. Then he went again. Having gone like that, then he went to beget the Europeans. The Europeans whom he begot all at once to the ground, the Europeans whom he begot, he begot Europeans, seventeen Europeans: males, males are what he begot at the same time. As he had begotten like this, then he said, "In this situation, what shall they eat so that they may grow?" . . .

Having left the Europeans, then he went to beget the Abakpa (Hausa), after the Europeans. Then Abakpa, the thing that they will do, since they cannot farm. . . . (Armstrong 1983)

The Creator goes on to create other peoples adjacent to the Idoma—the Tiv, the Igbo, the Igala—"then he said that he had finished making people."

Any community with some pride in itself would naturally see itself as the first and the best in creation, so it is not surprising that this Idoma chief makes God create the various Idoma clans before going on to create the rest of mankind. It is a cardinal aspect of a people's cultural outlook that they should seek to justify their place in the universe, and that is what the Idoma have done here.

But notice what happens after God has created the Idoma. It does not seem to matter very much to this narrator who comes next. There is some hesitation in the narrator's account before he finally mentions the Europeans. This story happens to have been collected by an American, Robert G. Armstrong, who had lived among and studied the Idoma for a long time; so warmly was he accepted by them that he was in fact made a chief there. The Idoma chief had little hesitation therefore in extending the recognition given to Armstrong to his European race, in preference to the Idoma's next-door neighbors. The devaluation of these neighbors is itself based, no doubt, on the background of historical relations with them. The Hausa are traditionally an agricultural people; but here they are portrayed as agriculturally incompetent, a prejudice inspired by the history of religious conflicts between Islam (to which the Hausa were early converted and in which they have played a prominent role alongside the Fulani) and traditional communities like the Idoma. In this story, therefore, we can see oral literature helping a community to assert its historical claims against its rivals and to project thereby its view of the universal order: God created us first; the rest of the world, especially our neighbors, was simply an afterthought.

Such accounts of origin are inevitably open to question. I doubt that any Hausa narrator, if he has any pride whatsoever in his race, would agree that God created the Idoma before his own people. This conflict of outlooks or world views was brought home to me in my fieldwork. A tale I collected from my friend Simayi in 1980 deals with the historical relations between his people (Ubulu) and the great kingdom of Benin. The story goes that the kings *(Obas)* of Benin used to die as soon as they were installed ("Crowned today, dead tomorrow"). One of them finally proclaimed an invitation to medicine men throughout the empire; anyone of them who passed an appointed test would get a chance to cure the Oba, while the failures would be beheaded. In the end a powerful medicine man from Ubulu named Ezemu passed the test; he eventually set about curing the king of his malady and ensured for him a long life. As a reward the king gave him a princess in marriage as well as a page. The king's high priest and executioner *(Ezomo)* could not stand to see a mere medicine man from the outbacks of the empire marrying a whole princess of Benin, so he accosted Ezemu on his way home and took the princess and page from him. Unperturbed, Ezemu went back to Ubulu; but no sooner did he get there than he cast a spell, and the princess and page suddenly landed at his house.

The result of this affront was war between the two nations in which a handful of Ubulu hunters, led by Ezemu and equipped with charms, wiped out successive expeditions—of soldiers as well as "witches"—sent from Benin. In the end the great King of Benin was forced to beg for peace. It was agreed that the opposing parties should set out and meet each other anywhere along the way between the two peoples.

It took Ezemu and his men (fortified with magic, of course) just a twinkle of the eye to cover a distance equivalent to what the trekking Benin party achieved in about three days. By the undisputed order of Ezemu, the point of meeting of the two parties was established as the boundary between Ezemu's people and the land of Benin, which was warned in its own interest never to wage war on Ubulu again.

But the story of Ezemu is also told among the people of Benin. According to a Benin version, this powerful chief from "Obolo" (for Ubulu) had visited Benin as a guest of the Oba and stayed with the Ezomo. During his stay he was strongly attracted to one of the princesses, but she rebuffed his advances. When he returned to his land he cast a spell on the princess, and she was suddenly transported to Obolo. She still rebuffed him, whereupon he dug a pit, caused it to be filled with boiling water, and threatened to throw the princess into it if she still wouldn't yield; on her own the princess jumped into the boiling pool rather than be violated, and died. To punish the impudent chief, an imperial army was sent to Obolo but was completely wiped out by the chief and his men, with the aid of magical powers. Two more such expeditions followed and suffered a similar fate. In the end the Obolo chief was overcome by a power that he himself had raised. On a much earlier occasion, he had been summoned to cure a certain Agboghidi, a child whose sickness had overcome all medicinal skills available to the Benin people. Having cured the child, the Obolo chief had proceeded to make him impregnable to any charm whatsoever and even taught him his own magical skills. It was Agboghidi who eventually went to Obolo, after much hesitation, to destroy his old benefactor and end the war.[2]

The similarities between these two versions show that the story is most likely based on a historical experience. But each version has been presented in a way that projects each people's sense of themselves. On one hand, the Ubulu version portrays their nation as blessed with magical and medicinal skills, strong enough to frustrate and overcome the dreaded might of Benin. On the other hand, the Benin version presents the kingdom in all its pride and superior self-esteem, a power well equipped to tame the impudence of any upstart community within its control. Like the Idoma tale of origin, this story of the encounter between Ubulu and Benin shows how oral literature can serve as an instrument of national pride, helping a people to form and maintain a positive outlook on themselves and thus justify their place within the universe of nations near and far.

Beyond rivalry, oral literature also helps a people to explain the mysteries of nature and the universe in a way that makes sense to them and reflects their peculiar culture. Take the story of creation. The Jewish account of the creation of man, as we know it from the Old Testament of the Bible, states that God—presented in a male image—first created a male from sand, breathed into him, and called him Adam; later he created a female called Eve out of a rib from Adam's side. He put them in a Garden of Eden containing trees, including the apple, warning them not to eat the apple of all the fruits in the orchard. Under temptation by a serpent, they disobeyed God's command; as a punishment he banished them from Eden and cursed them and future generations of mankind to a destiny of suffering.

But consider a story of creation from the central Ijo in Nigeria's delta region. There was once a large field in which stood an enormous iroko tree with large buttresses.

Pairs of men and women appeared, each woman with a broom and each man with a bag, to sweep the field clean of dirt. As the women swept the field, the men collected the dirt into their bags. And the dirt was manillas (copper rings used long ago as money). Some collected ten or more manillas, others none, and when the field was swept clean they disappeared back into the edges of the field, two by two. The sky darkened, and there descended on the field a large table, a large chair, and an immense Creation Stone, and on the table was a large quantity of sand. Then there was lightning and thunder, and Woyengi ("our Mother") descended. She seated herself on the chair and placed her feet on the Creation Stone, and out of the sand on the table she molded human beings. But they had no life and were neither man nor woman; only by embracing each in turn and breathing into them did Woyengi make human beings out of them, and then asked them to choose their sexes. Woyengi further asked them to make the following choices: what kind of life they would lead on earth; what kind of blessings they wanted (children, powers, riches, and so on); and by what kind of death they would return to her. They all got what they asked for.[3]

There are many notable differences between the biblical story and its Ijo counterpart. To start with, the former presents an image of male dominance in the culture; not only is God male, but the first human created is a male, and the female is only an afterthought. The Ijo story, on the contrary, puts the woman first. The Creator is female: notice that in place of the phrase "Our Father" used for God in Christian worship, the Ijo has "Our Mother." Also in the Ijo story, although the male's role as a worker is acknowledged, the female is by no means subordinated to him. If anything, perhaps the fact that the woman sweeps the field while the man is left to collect the dirt puts the woman in a somewhat superior light. Nevertheless, it seems clear in this story that woman is given considerable prominence. Traditional Ijo society traces descent mainly from the female line, so it is no wonder that the image of woman looms large even in that aspect of their oral tradition where they try to explain the origins of life.

Other elements of the Ijo story also identify it as belonging in an environment visibly different from that of the Jewish story. Apple trees in the latter belong very much in the temperate climate of the Middle East. The Ijo story, however, speaks of the iroko tree, which is a prominent feature of the mangrove vegetation of the Atlantic seaboard in Nigeria; here, too, manillas (horseshoe-shaped metal rings) had been brought by British and Dutch merchants as far back as the seventeenth century and used as currency. The Ijo story therefore projects a peculiarly African environment and historical experience. One more significant difference between the two stories concerns the idea of destiny. We can see that as a result of Adam and Eve's abuse of the comfort given them, mankind has been condemned by God to a destiny of hard work and suffering. In many traditional African societies, however, destiny is seen not as imposed by the supreme deity but as a choice freely made by man prior to birth. While therefore we can say of the Jewish story of creation that it projects a God-centered theology, I believe we can safely say that the Ijo version is very much an African one in reflecting a man-centered theology.

Although there are a few striking similarities between the two stories—the idea of a supreme deity, creation from sand and breath—it is safe to assume that neither borrowed consciously from the other. But many stories in Africa, as elsewhere, are demonstrably indebted to non-African sources, having made their way into the continent by some process of diffusion. Some of these stories have to do indeed with fundamental issues of life and the universe. But here likewise the peculiar environment in which the foreign story finds a new home asserts itself upon its content and even on the pattern of the narration. A good example is seen in the story of Adam and Eve. In chapter 2 we saw how Finnegan had told this story to a notable storyteller among the Limba of Sierra Leone and what changes the story had undergone in two years at the hands of that narrator: Eve treated as a subservient African housewife; the tempting serpent seen as her lover; the snake itself given the name of a local species; the condemnation of Adam and Eve to a life of toil seen as the reason why the Limba toil in their farms under sun and rain; the story set not in a garden of ease but in a peculiarly African agrarian economy; and even the narration itself dressed in the peculiarly African pattern of call-and-response.

Teaching Ideals and Conduct

Today we have educational institutions at various levels where young men and women are taught lessons on life and conduct as well as skills which will help them to earn a living. In traditional African society, there were no such schools organized for general instruction; as we saw in chapter 2, certain individuals could have a handful of youths under them for the purpose of understudying a specialized form of art, like divination and the poetry that goes with it. So how is it possible for the citizens of a society to acquire, on a general or collective basis, information concerning themselves: who they are, their origins and connections, and the peculiar ways of living and behaving that identify them as a people and that must be preserved for the sake of cultural continuity? Obviously, such information is contained in the various forms of oral literature practiced in the society—songs, narratives, proverbs, riddles, and so on—which are delivered either privately (e.g., mother to child, artist to apprentice) or publicly (e.g., in moonlight entertainment or in open performances by skilled artists). Through these media the younger members of the society absorb the ideas that will guide them through life and the older ones are constantly reminded of the rules and ideals that must be kept alive for the benefit of those coming behind them. Let us look at a few of these areas of cultural education.

As society changes or grows, some of the old ways of life inevitably give way to new ones. Much of the oral literature that is performed today, or that we see preserved in books, reflects a life-style that may have served the earlier generations well but would be considered outmoded or even dangerous today. Although both performer and audience may respond to the contents of the material with nostalgia and perhaps pride, it is clear to everyone that things are no longer what they used to be.

Let us take the Mandinka legend of Sunjata as an example. It is essentially the story of a powerful and fearless warrior who rescued his people from the tyranny of a "foreign" usurper (Sumanguru) and went on to consolidate the kingdom of Mali and build it up into an empire. In the course of his conquests Sunjata did, of course, practice the same kind of tyranny and high-handedness that the citizens of Mali had previously denounced in Sumamguru. But he had the privilege of being a winner; his acts of courage and daredevilry tended to outweigh his acts of injustice, precisely because he was living in an age when a man won whatever he had largely on the basis of physical courage. People certainly abhorred injustice as much then as they do now, but society had an even greater regard for those who took great risks to achieve whatever they had in a world where might was regarded as right, a world filled with the sheer physical danger of war. We can therefore understand why, in the various versions of the Sunjata story, courage (especially in war) is upheld as a praiseworthy ideal and the most fearsome warriors are set up as the standards to be emulated.

Consider a chant in praise of Sunjata (here called "Maabirama Konnate") by the Gambian *griot* Bamba Suso in his version of the story.

Ah, mighty war king,
A man who likes making deserted villages.
Many great matters have passed from the world.
Ah, you have an army.
You seize, you slay.
Maabirama Konnate, fighting goes well with you. (Innes 1974: 63)

Or the *griot* Banna Kanute's chant in honor of Sunjata in his version of the story.

Others run away from Sunjata,
Sunjata does not run from anyone. . . .
Death is better than disgrace, Sumanguru. (P. 231)

It is clear that in their different versions these performers are giving their audiences, especially present-day Gambians, the sort of ideals that were admired or upheld in the old days: fierceness and excellence in war, no matter how much damage was done; the courage to stand one's ground to the last and refuse (even at the cost of death) to suffer disgrace.

Some of these ideals may have much relevance today—disgrace is no less unattractive now than it was in the days of Sunjata—and perhaps the listeners to these stories are expected to take as much from them as is relevant to their own present-day situations. But times have changed, and even these *griots* know it. There is little room now for men to practice the kind of reckless military action that made men like Sunjata heroes and standards of excellence in their time; for a start, both the army and the police are there to deal with anyone who tries to set himself up as a law unto himself. So even in stories in which they recall the "glorious" careers of the likes of Sunjata, these Gambian *griots* occasionally take the opportunity to drop some lessons meant to guide their present-day listeners in the kind of world in which they now live. As Banna Kanute says in one of his interludes in the Sunjata story,

Let the whole of The Gambia take up work,
Oh, workers.
Let the whole of The Gambia take up work,
For that is what profits a man. (P. 161)

War is no longer an ideal to be looked up to in present-day society. The true ideal of action today is excellence in whatever work or profession one practices. Indeed, if one does it well, one is assured of a fulfilled existence; hence Dembo Kanute tells his host in his own version of the story:

> Seni Daabo, do something sir;
> Life consists of doing something,
> Not of doing everything,
> For there is no end to that, and failure wins no support. (P. 269)

In these ways oral literature, even when it deals with events of history, presents constantly to members of contemporary society the standards of excellence that they should practice in their own interests and for the survival of the society.

Stories like the Sunjata legend are performed on a more or less professional scale these days, and deal mostly with lofty ideals. For lessons of conduct on a day-to-day basis—the kind of education that the citizens of a society need to get along in their ordinary lives—we have to turn to proverbs and to fables that are exchanged in the moonlit family compound. Proverbs are in themselves told in all sorts of situations—during conversation, within stories, etc.—and serve a variety of purposes. In chapter 8 we shall give detailed attention to proverbs. For the moment it is useful to make the point that they are part of that system of informal education available to traditional society, designed to equip especially the younger citizens with the fundamental lessons of conduct. A Ganda (Uganda) proverb advises us, "You don't judge the affairs of a place where you do not sleep" (Liyong 1969: 151), implying that until we achieve reasonable familiarity with a situation or with the facts of a case, we should not consider ourselves as being in a position to offer an opinion. My friend Simayi had this statement in some of the tales he told me: "He who has a yam roasting does not stray far." It is similar to the Kikuyu (Kenya) saying that "He who is going on a journey does not leave a banana roasting" (Liyong 1969: 154)—obviously advising that we concentrate on one business at a time.

Perhaps it is in the folktales or fables—stories centered on animals and other beings and not related to any historical events—that we have the clearest example of oral literature designed to teach specific lessons of behavior. Little animals such as hare dupe the big ones such as elephant, demonstrating that everything should be given its due respect or recognition, however small it is. The overambitious tortoise frequently lands himself in trouble, sometimes even in death, revealing to us that there must be limits to our ambitions. In Simayi's story already cited, the despised wife of a king turns out in the end to be the mother of the heir to the throne—pointing out that patient suffering and justice will ultimately triumph over oppression and exploitation. Although many of these tales end with an explicit moral, the portraiture of the characters and their behaviors is invariably so explicit that no moral need be stated specifically. And one principal appeal of these tales is that they reflect so closely the fundamental ways of life of the average citizen. Rose Mwangi tells of the situation among her people: "Kikuyu folktales are based primarily on day to day happenings and for this reason they bear such a close relationship to life that their educational and, therefore, social significance derive from it" (Mwangi 1982: 32).

Are there any lessons contained in these pieces of oral literature on the consequences of breaking the accepted rules of conduct? Certainly, if a tale assures us that patience will triumph over oppression, or that the small can overcome the mighty, it also implies that both the oppressor and the mighty should beware, for their unjust ways can only lead them to disgrace if not death. But it would be foolish to expect that everyone in the society would heed these lessons. It would also be unsafe for society to leave its moral health solely in the hands of tales and proverbs which in many cases tell how to conduct oneself only by implication. Society therefore has more direct methods of enforcing conduct and punishing actions that violate the established codes of behavior. Although there are more formal instruments of punishment, such as fines, banishment, or even execution, a large number of the moral lapses committed in society are usually denounced by satirical songs or lampoons which are meant to bring shame on the culprits and so discourage future misconduct. Nwoga makes the point quite clearly in his discussion of the function of satirical songs as an instrument of punishment among the Igbo of Nigeria.

> Homogeneous, kindred societies depended on the sense of full human dignity being shared by all members. To find oneself regarded as in any way below the standard, to become the object of ridicule, or of children pointing fingers at one and sniggering, was punishment of a great dimension. Satire was the verbal equivalent of actions like tying a stolen object round the neck of the thief and parading him through the village. . . . Everybody is brought into full knowledge of what the person did so that his spirit would fight an internal battle with him and he would spend sleepless nights worrying about himself. Shame and the scorn and amusement of others would prevent his free movement in the town for some time. This is punishment that would stop others from following the same line of action, just as most judicial punishment of an offender is a preventative of other similar action; satire therefore served as a means of social control. (1981: 162)

By his use of the past tense, Nwoga would seem to be leaving the impression that this situation no longer exists among the Igbo people. It is true that modern judicial authority has taken control of many of the roles played by these satirical songs in traditional society and that the law of libel now discourages to some extent the practice of composing songs denouncing people. But such songs are still in vogue today, especially among dance groups which perform on a variety of occasions, condemning the lapses not only of individuals from socially accepted norms of conduct, but even of institutions such as governments which frustrate the aspirations of their citizens and make life intolerable for the common man. In chapter 6 we shall examine some of these songs.

Recording Life

One of the most acknowledged uses of oral literature is in recording the historical experiences of a people, both the rulers and the ruled. The careers of leaders such as

Sunjata and Chaka, narrated by professional or appointed bards (*griot, imbongi*, etc.) have been the subject of much recording and study; but, as is clear from the varying accounts of the war between Benin and Ubulu presented above, we now know the basic motivations of such accounts. In chapter 7 we shall see something of the historical record of a private citizen's experience. Here we shall be concerned simply with examining the cycle of life which the average citizen is recognized by society to cover as he moves from birth to death. Each of the five basic stages in this journey through life—birth, initiation, marriage, title-taking, and death—is traditionally marked by a ritualized observance (professionally called a rite of passage) which is itself captured in oral literature of some kind or other. Let us see how these stages are reflected in oral literature.

Birth is generally considered a significant moment because it provides an entry into life itself. Among the Igbo of Nigeria, birth songs are traditionally sung by women upon the birth of a child. In many cases nowadays, women from the immediate kin of the baby's mother, as well as friends and clubmates, accompany her from the clinic singing these songs. In other cases, the songs are performed on a traditionally appointed "outing" day several days after the birth of the baby. On this occasion, the women (who may come with their children) are entertained with food and drinks as they sing and dance to celebrate the arrival of the new baby.

Welcome, child, into the world!
May good fortune attend us.
Be wide awake in the morning
May good fortune attend us.
Be wide awake in the afternoon
May good fortune attend us.
But go to sleep in the evening
May good fortune attend us. (Ogbalu 1974: 31; translation mine)

The repeated wish for good fortune shows clearly that, for the Igbo, the major emphasis is on success in life: even as the baby is being welcomed into the world, it is reminded that the only time of day when it may be excused from struggling for success is the night, when all human beings must go to sleep. In other Igbo birth songs, this materialistic interest is not so loudly proclaimed. The child is welcomed as a thing of joy and a blessing from God to its lucky parents. Perhaps no African song expresses more vividly a joy in children that surpasses all material wealth than this one from the Akan:

Someone would like to have you for her child
but you are mine.
Someone would like to rear you on a costly mat
but you are mine.
Someone would like to place you on a camel blanket
but you are mine.
I have you to rear on a torn old mat

Someone would like to have you as her child
But you are mine. (Beier 1966a: 63)

Initiation ceremonies are designed to introduce the young African male into adolescence. They correspond roughly with girls' puberty rites, except that for reasons mainly of modesty the latter are not always as boldly advertised as the boys' rites and are consequently not always accompanied by the sort of oral literature that the boys perform. The boldness of the boys' songs is explained by the aims and nature of the ceremony. In these initiation rites, young boys of the same age-set or age-group are periodically isolated from the community in a camp or some chosen site, where they are circumcised amid certain rituals. Since this is the first major test of a youth's qualification for manhood, he is not expected to show any sign of fear during circumcision; trembling or crying would earn the initiate considerable disgrace, and many circumcision songs are characterized not only by the initiate's exaggerated sense of his claims to manhood but especially by the pride that, during the circumcision, he never uttered a sound in pain. Initiation songs are mostly songs of self-proclamation, bristling with the young man's feelings of reaching the threshold of a significant stage of his life.

An initiation song from the Dinka of the Sudan is typical.

> I hate being a boy
> And I shall not remain (a boy)
> The Great Vulture flew to Puduonythiek
> We met, and the place turned red like a firefly
> 5 The ram is tethered for the invocation.
> The ram is tethered for the invocation in the home of Dorjok
> Kwol of clan Pajok
> I will not bring shame on you.
> The knife turned red with blood
> 10 Jipur, have we said a word?
> The thrust of the spear of the tribe of Majuan
> The age-set of Deng, the Dancing Head, came like locusts.
> If pain is not endured
> A man is not a man
> 15 Veins bled like a stormy rain
> The head of the bull is torn apart. (Deng 1973: 192)

First of all, perhaps, this song is significant for the information it gives about the initiation process. Every age-set about to be circumcised is ushered into the ceremony by its "father" or patron: the "father" in this case is praise-named the Dancing Head, i.e., the Crested Crane (line 12). Also, before the ceremony a ram (line 5) is sacrificed to ensure the success of the entire business. And finally, we are reminded of the shame involved in not bearing the cut of the knife like a man (lines 13–14).

But even more striking in this song is the exaggerated self-esteem of the initiate. The whole encounter between him and the initiator (i.e., the circumciser) is portrayed as a war or some such violent experience. The knife used in the circumcision is seen as a spear thrust at an enemy (line 11), and the effusion of blood is described with the most frightening images (lines 4, 9, 15). The age-set of the initiate is also portrayed with images which show them as equal to the danger facing them on the occasion (lines 3, 12), and at the end of the circumcision the initiate sees himself as a sacrificed bull—the bull being, of course, a symbol of courage. All this exaggerated, heroic language is employed because the young boy, here being initiated into early manhood, already imagines himself as a future warrior performing deeds of honor and courage.

Marriage is no doubt the next significant stage in the life of the male. At this stage he is considered sufficiently responsible to start a family of his own and raise the next generation. Apart from the exchange of items like drinks, cola nuts, and other agricultural products, traditional African weddings are frequently accompanied by a good deal of singing and dancing. On the night of the wedding, the groom is surrounded by his peers and relatives, waiting for the bride to be led over to his house. Shortly after, she is accompanied by her friends and relatives with singing and dancing and the numerous gifts given to her for her new station. Wedding songs in many African communities are directed mostly at the bride as she goes into her new life. Some are framed as a congratulation of the girl or her family for picking a fine young man to marry; others are addressed as an advice to the young woman on how to conduct herself in her new circumstance. Yet others are put in the form of a mild joke, mocking the girl for losing her freedom to someone else, as in a song from the Gisu of East Africa (the chorus *Oho, sister, oho* is repeated after every line).

>   Oho, sister, oho,
>   You may dance for the last (time),
>   You kick the shoe for the last (time),
>   So that you'll tell your man that
>   5   I danced like this.
>   Then you'll tell another
>   I danced like that.
>
>   A man said in Busamali
>   "I left the key at Bunamwamba,"
>   10 But a woman said in Busamali
>   "If you have no child sleep while the lamp is lit,
>   If you have no husband,
>   You spend the night awake." (Liyong 1972: 128)

The differences in position between a man and a woman are particularly highlighted in the last six lines of this song. A man can forget his keys anywhere (even if he slept with a woman in another town, as perhaps in line 9), and nothing will come of it. But a woman cannot claim such liberties; in fact, her only security in life comes from having a husband and bearing him children. Traditional African culture, like most others, is quite often male-chauvinistic in character, and some of these wedding songs are designed to affirm the superior position of the male over the female.

Having achieved full manhood, the male must now have something to show for it in real terms besides simply marrying a wife and having children. The major areas in which the traditional African male proved his manhood were agriculture (land farming), cattle raising, hunting, and war. War was not seen as an occupation as such; but in certain places, especially the pastoral communities of eastern and southern Africa, raids were frequently organized against populations for the prime purpose of rounding up their cattle. Victory in such a "war" not only ensured the growth of the winners' pastoral economy but also established their supremacy over the losers. Songs composed after such a war often emphasized the warriors' bravery and heroism. In one such song from the Bahima of Ankole (Uganda), the composer tells of the reward he won for his heroic role: "Thereafter was I never excluded from the counsels of princes" (Morris 1964: 44).

This, then, is the sort of reward or recognition often accorded a man in traditional African society when he has distinguished himself in the eyes of his people: he is given (or takes) a chieftaincy title and thus made a member of the inner council of the rulership of the community. During the ceremonies marking the installation of the new chief, there is much singing and dancing. Among the Igbo of Nigeria, for instance, in these chieftaincy *(ozo)* ceremonies the celebrant often stands forth to declaim his own praises; alternatively, he employs a masquerade to extol his achievements, in most cases with highly exaggerative idioms and images designed to put the celebrant in an even better light than he deserves. Earlier we observed that traditional Igbo society puts special emphasis on achievement in the climate of competition; it is therefore understandable why in these title-taking chants the sense of competition drives the celebrant to claim some rather unbelievable merits for himself. As one such chant recorded by Romanus Egudu declares,

> I am:
> Tiger that defends neighbours
> King that is liked by public
> Fame that never wanes
> Flood that can't be impeded
> Ocean that can't be exhausted
> Wealth that gives wisdom
> Child with washed hands. . . .
> Child that accomplished a difficult journey quickly. (Egudu and Nwoga 1971: 37)

The various images used here are simply metaphors conveying the celebrant's heightened sense of his accomplishments. The last two lines in particular are intended to impress us that the man won these accomplishments early in life. The Igbo have a proverb which says that a child who has washed his hands may sit at the table with elders; the celebrant here is therefore telling us that he has achieved rather early ("quickly") what most other men achieve later in life.

The last state in the journey of life is death. The occasion is generally accompanied by a sense of loss and sadness. In many communities, the traditional observances range from the laying out of the body and the lamentation of the relatives (especially the women, around the laid-out corpse) to the final obsequies preceding the deposition of the body into the earth. The obsequies vary, depending very much on factors such as the age of the deceased, his status in the society, his professional or cult affiliation, and so on. Children and adolescents are usually buried without more ado than the sorrowing of their parents and immediate relatives; in a sense, the mourners are thankful that God has seen fit to take the young one away before he or she showed any promise and meant anything to relatives. Titled men and women are usually mourned with fanfare and extensive ceremonies lasting several days; the ceremonies are a celebration of a life well and fully lived and an ushering (with appropriate implements and paraphernalia) into life in the world beyond. In the case of a cult member, his fellows conduct a peculiar ceremony around his duly dressed-up body, while certain chants are performed.

In chapter 6 we shall examine the theme of death from various angles. Meanwhile, let us conclude our discussion with a chant performed at an aged Yoruba dignitary's funeral by a hunter-poet *(onijala);* it contains random observations on the experience of death.

> The chameleon is dead, he has died a royal natural death.
> The cat is dead, he has put an end to his mewing.
> I thought I would see him, I no longer see him.
> Ha! Hey!
> 5 When the Gaboon viper is dead, its young one inherits its poison.
> And when the *adi*-maker dies, to her daughters must go her legacy of *adi* manufactory.
> When you are dead, your children shall inherit your property.
> My offspring shall inherit the gun that now belongs to me, Bisaje, the sweet-voiced man.
> Peevishness makes us reluctant to voice our complaints against someone else.
> 10 Hunger makes us unable to keep a shilling unspent, here I am with my songs.
> Death doesn't let us bid our friends goodbye.
> The skin covering the skull peels off easily.
> The neck rots messily.
> The thumbs receive a hank of cotton thread, the head right down to the mouth receives a white cloth bandage.
> 15 The dead man's occiput is squarely rested on the floor.
> One's inferiors talk freely about one after one's demise.
> Death renders us controllable for our inferiors. Death makes a fish curl up, User of a mighty net.
> When death kills a man, it renders his penis permanently much contracted.
> When death kills a woman, it renders her private parts soggy.
> 20 It's death that disarranges the Ifa divination paraphernalia including the divining chain.
> It mixes the pigeons with the domestic fowls, it mixes the domestic fowls with the pigeons.
> Death shall not mistakenly carry you away with anybody at all, O my comrades here.
> (Babalola 1966: 238)

Part of the beauty of this passage comes from the poet's celebration of his role as a performer, especially in lines 8, 10, and 22. Part also comes from the parallel structure of various lines, e.g., 1–2, 5–7, 9–10, 18–19. But the passage is equally striking in its portraits and comments on the experience of death and the treatment of the dead: the various effects of death on the physiognomy of the human body (12–13, 18–19), the disorganizing or humiliating effects of death (16–17, 20–21), and various customs sanctioned by the culture to follow the death of a person (5–8, 14–15). Together these comments not only give us a valuable insight into the people's philosophical attitudes toward death but preserve for future generations certain procedures that have served the culture well at this point in the life of a person.

Part Two

Types and Themes

6. Songs and Chants

In the first section of this book, we addressed ourselves to certain basic theoretical principles necessary for an understanding of the phenomenon of African oral literature in its varied contexts. In this section, we shall try to examine the major kinds of oral literature to be found in Africa and the subjects they treat. As we shall soon discover, there are problems in identifying these various categories.

Problems of Classification

Many European and American scholars—Malinowski, Bascom, and Ben-Amos being perhaps the most notable—have suggested that whatever systems of classification we apply to the folklore (including oral literature) of a people must be based on the systems traditionally recognized by the people themselves. On the face of it, this looks like a very good idea. The citizens of a community are perhaps better qualified than outsiders to determine into what aspect of their lives a particular song or story fits. There will be no point, for instance, in grouping a song under a category such as "praise poetry" when the people who sing it would prefer to group it under "funeral poetry," or in considering a story an "explanatory" tale when the people themselves treat it as a "historical" account. But the trouble with relying solely on the judgment of the indigenes is that we will be unable to see each society in relation to another. Even though we recognize that there are numerous ethnic and linguistic groups within Africa, there are nevertheless several common features and customs that unite these groups as an African people.

Indeed, even if we were to get down to the job of classifying the various forms of oral literature practiced within one African community or ethnic group, it would be just as frustrating to depend solely on the categories recognized by the people there. To start with, the kind of neat differentiation which we frequently try to make in our scholarly work between one category of things and another—in such a way that the categories are mutually exclusive—has very little place in traditional culture, where there is a great deal of interdependence between one aspect of life and another. Within any one community, various criteria are used in identifying the different kinds of songs and chants performed there—by subject matter, by the kinds of instruments used, by the style of vocalization, by the association to which the performers belong, by the occasion during which the performance is done, and by several other criteria. But when we look closely at the content of the songs and chants we find that there is little point in separating one from the other on the basis of, say, performer or vocalization.

Let us look briefly at one ethnic group to see some of this difficulty of classification. The Yoruba of Nigeria have various kinds of "oral poetry" performed on a variety of occasions. But the lines between these forms are so loose that those scholars who have devoted themselves to the study of this art have not always agreed on how to draw the lines. For instance, Babalola, in his authoritative *Content and Form of Yoruba Ijala* (1966), is firmly convinced that "Yoruba traditional poetry in general is best classified not so much by the themes as by the stylistic devices employed in recitals"—by which he means styles of vocalization—although he also identifies the major types with the respective performers (p. 23). Earlier in the book he spells out what the basic distinctions are.

> Although Yoruba scholars have recently selected the word *"ewi"* to connote "poetry in general," the vocabulary of the Yoruba language has always contained specific words for the different types of Yoruba oral poetry classified according to the manner of voice production employed for a particular poetic utterance. *Esa* or *ewi* is a type of Yoruba oral poetry in which a falsetto voice is employed. *Ijala* is another; this is chanted in a high-pitched voice. *Rara* is yet another, recognized by its slow wailing, long-drawn-out chanting style. *Ofo* or *Ogede* is another type and this is distinguished by its being entirely a stock of centuries-old magic formula sentences uttered very fast with the normal voice of ordinary speech. (P. vi)

Olatunji, in his useful *Features of Yoruba Oral Poetry*, agrees that style of vocalization (the "musical mode of performance") is a valid criterion for differentiation but thinks that the songs and chants could just as validly be grouped in accordance with their traditionally recognized performers.

> Rara is chanted by men and women, old or young, for entertainment on social occasions . . . , and Ijala is performed by hunters or devotees of Ogun, the Yoruba divinity of iron. . . . Esa is chanted by masquerades, while ekun iyawo is sung by brides on the eve of their marriage. . . . Iyere ifa is chanted by devotees of Orunmila when they come together on festive occasions. . . . Each of these poetic forms has its characteristic musical style. There are still other musically identifiable forms which can be added to the list. They include Sango-pipe, Esu-pipe and Oya-pipe which are associated with their particular divinities and devotees. (1984: 7).

The bulk of Olatunji's book is devoted to a discussion of what he calls the "feature types" of Yoruba oral poetry. The first feature is the *oriki*, or praise, which indicates a theme; the second is *ese ifa*, or divination poetry, which identifies the context of the poetry; the third is *ofo*, or incantation, which identifies the form; and the fourth feature embraces the *owe* and *alo apamo*, which are gnomic forms representing proverbs and riddles respectively. The most significant aspect of Olatunji's study is that it expresses the fluidity of these categories of Yoruba oral poetry. The features, as we can see from the above summary, are not uniformly identified—theme is different from context or form—and in his first appendix (pp. 201–8) Olatunji shows how each feature (e.g., *oriki*, *ofo*) is represented in the various "chanting modes" (e.g., *ijala*, *rara*, *esa*) recognized by the Yoruba. Of these the most common is the *oriki* or praise theme, which Olatunji identifies as featuring in *ijala*, *rara*, *ekun iyawo*, *esa*, and *iyere ifa*. No wonder that another Yoruba scholar, Oludare Olajubu, has recognized *oriki* as the centerpiece or "essence" of Yoruba oral poetry generally (Olajubu 1977a).

Although Olatunji's differentiations are quite illuminating and well-informed, a look at some sample passages from his "feature types" in relation both to one another and to similar types from outside the Yoruba ethnic group soon reveals the problems in relying on indigenous systems of categorization for our understanding of the nature of African oral poetry. Take these lines from his discussion of the *ofo* (incantation) feature type.

> It is on the day that pepper gets into the eye that it spoils the beauty of the eye.
> It is on the day that pepper gets into the eye that it spoils the beauty of the eye.
> It is on the day that fire meets gunpowder that it bursts out.
> It is on the day that fire meets gunpowder that it bursts out.
> Immediacy (of action) belongs to the *ina* stinging twiner
> The nettle makes a man run helter-skelter.

Compare this passage with lines from the discussion of the *owe* (proverb) feature type.

> It is in the elder's mouth that the kola nut sounds ripe. (P. 171)

> Twenty years since the grilled maize pudding has been using clothes,
> It is in nakedness that the fried bean ball has been. (P. 174)

> It is towards someone by whom one sleeps that one rolls. (P. 176)

It is true, as Olatunji tells us, that while *ofo* is marked by a certain personal and impromptu quality, *owe* is distinguished by its being a piece of communal wisdom tested by time and traditional usage. It is also obvious that while *ofo* has a certain repetitive looseness, there is in *owe* a certain dignified economy of expression. But it is equally clear that the two features are similar in revealing the Yoruba's colorful use of language for reflecting philosophically on various aspects of Yoruba social life and environment.

Now compare the above passages and statements with a segment of a heroic narrative performance from Mali.

> Look to the cat for the thing not easy for all.
> Look to the sitting-stool for seizing all the smells.
> Look to the loin-cloth for all-smells-catching cloth.
> A man's totem is not the woman's loincloth.
> Neither is the woman's totem the woman's loincloth.
> It's the loincloth that is the smell-catching cloth. (Bird 1974: 3)

Whether we see these proverbial lines as impromptu or tried and tested, it is clear that the Malian performer shares with his Yoruba counterpart the same love of language as an instrument for philosophical comment on social life. If we are to make sense, therefore, of the nature and qualities of African poetry, it will no longer be useful for us to be tied to local criteria of classification. Although we should have an adequate understanding of the social and other backgrounds of a piece of text from any ethnic community, it is only by crossing these ethnic and geographical boundaries that we can usefully appreciate the essentially African as well as human message in such pieces of literature. It is for this reason that, in the latter part of this chapter, we shall adopt a thematic approach in the discussion of African songs and chants— i.e., by examining the basic themes or concerns of these pieces of oral literature— rather than make a futile effort to reconcile the numerous local systems of classification across the continent.

The Nature of Songs and Chants

Before we get into a discussion of the physical form of African songs and chants, we must settle one more problem of classification, concerning the manner in which the texts of oral literature are presented on paper. We have spoken rather loosely of "poetry," especially in our examination of Yoruba chants as classified by Babalola and Olatunji. We must be careful how we construe that word if we are to understand the true nature of African oral literature. It used to be fashionable to draw a clear line between "poetry" and "prose" in this subject: the former was seen as a category under which songs and chants could be discussed, while the latter was considered to be the form in which oral narratives ("folktales") and public speeches come.[1] The reason frequently given for this differentiation is that whereas songs and chants are usually accompanied by some form of musical regulation (instruments beaten or plucked at regular intervals) or rhythmic background (such as humming or a clear division of statements by breath-groups), the other forms such as folktales are generally loosely presented in normal everyday speech.

More recent study has rendered this easy differentiation problematic. To start with, it has been found that the earlier collections of African oral literature were not properly made. Many traditional tales were, and still are, told with musical accompaniment. But collectors of these tales, as we saw in chapter 1, often discarded the musical and other backgrounds of performance and set down the bare texts of the tales and indeed sometimes contented themselves with rough summaries of their plots; surely a differentiation based on such improper methods of representation has little justification.

Furthermore, some scholars have tried to look closely even at pieces of oral literature performed without musical accompaniment and have come to wonder if there aren't other kinds of "rhythm" holding the statements in much the same sort of balance that instrumental music is meant to do. They have looked, for instance, at tales told without music and have found various factors operating within the statements of the narrator: the narrator pauses both within and between statements not only to catch a breath but also to create certain kinds of tension in the events being narrated; certain statements and certain patterns of events are repeated a number of times within the compass of the story, thus gaining some of that musical quality that generally attaches to repetition;[2] the narrator is conscious of the audience members and not only must anticipate their reactions but frequently engages in actual dialogue with them when they ask questions or make comments. These and other factors provide a subtle regulation within the story which may not be quite the same thing as instrumental music but certainly gives the performance an adequate internal balance and the sort of emotional intensity we often associate with "poetry." It is on these grounds that the American scholar Dennis Tedlock has argued that oral narratives should be treated not as the sort of "prose" we find in written fiction but as some sort of "dramatic poetry." We shall discuss these issues more fully in chapters 7 and 11.

It would be much safer for us, then, to distinguish these various forms of oral literature in accordance with the levels of musical regulation contained in them. This method assumes that every piece of oral literature is supported in the first place by the musical quality of the human voice (as well as the other regulating factors just discussed), and that we shall arrange the various forms in an order representing the levels of musicality in them. If we do that, we shall discover that oral narratives occupy perhaps the lowest level of this musical ladder, because for the most part they are told in the style of normal speech and only occasionally do the narrators break into passages in which they consciously alter their tone of voice in the course of the story.[3] The next levels of the musical ladder are occupied by those kinds of oral literature in which there is some conscious twist to the voice all through the performance: these are the chants and songs.

The chant, which is sometimes called recitation, is a widespread form of performance in several African communities. There is a clearly marked difference between the speech voice and the chanting voice. The latter is marked by a higher degree of stress in such a way as to achieve greater emotional intensity than in normal conversational speech. There are a few forms of African chanting in which the voice is stressed predominantly low: examples may be seen in ritual chants or in certain forms of cult utterances, which are marked by a good degree of secrecy as the words are not really intended to be audible to anyone but the very limited circle of cult members gathered in their enclave. Otherwise, the tone of chanting is frequently quite high, the chanter's aim being to impress the audience of the open performance not only with the strength and sonority of the voice but also with the importance of the ideas.

A few examples will do. Nketia tells of a type of "spoken poetry" among the Akan of Ghana "which is recited and not sung." Some of it is used in praising chiefs during their installation or other ceremonies and is usually spoken at high speed, at a high pitch of voice, and with dramatic gestures. Other kinds of recited or chanted poetry there include hunters' dirges, "half spoken and half sung." Again the voice is pitched high. Nketia further explains: "The delivery is usually fast, the emphasis being on the continual flow of utterances which need not be linked by any apparent intellectual thread, but which are united by their cumulative emotional effect" (1979: 23–25).

Among the Yoruba of Nigeria, *ijala* recitation by hunter-poets is one of the best-known forms of chanting. It is done in a regularly high-pitched voice in which "tonal assonance" and "tonal contrast," two of the most characteristic features of Yoruba oral poetry, are employed with great relish. As Babalola tells us,

In ijala chants, both these features are clearly noticeable. A great deal of the musical effect produced is intuitively employed, *inter alia,* by the ijala composers for achieving their desire to please the ears of their audience. . . . The effect of the tonal contrast seems to be to increase the richness of the music of the ijala lines by adding to the element of variety in successive rhythm-segments. (1966: 388–89)

We can see here that in ijala chanting there is a sustained manipulation of the voice to achieve a musical effect and delight the audience.

Another interesting example has been recorded among the Bahima of Ankole (Uganda), sometimes called the Banyankore. This is the tradition of self-praise *(ekyevugo)* in which the poet *(omyevugi)* recites, "without pause for breath" and at high voice, one verse *(enkome)* after another extolling his heroism in war or in cattle-raiding. Henry Morris tells us about the manner of these recitations: "Each *enkome* must be recited at an abnormal speed without pause either between words or between lines and the *omyevugi* must not, of course, falter in so doing. The speed of recitation is such that only those Banyankore who are accustomed to this art can attain to it. . . ." Of the vocal manipulation done in this tradition of chanting, Morris says:

In listening to an *ekyevugo* one is struck by the sharp high tones which, at first . . . appear to be stresses. It soon becomes evident, however, that stress and high tone do not necessarily fall on the same syllable. . . . The pitch of an *omyevugi's* voice tails off during the recitation of an *enkome*. The opening of an *enkome* is extremely forceful and the first high tone of the *enkome* is easily the highest in pitch. The high tones appear to be devices for preventing the level of the voice from falling appreciably until the final line of the *enkome*. There is, however, a fall in pitch in each line and although the high tones of the next line will lift the pitch of the voice again the recovery is not complete. In the latter part of the last line, the voice is allowed to tail off completely. (1964: 21, 37–38)

The tradition of *izibongo,* or praise-chant, among the Zulu of southern Africa is similar, not only in the use of high-pitched voice and speed of recital but also in the division of ideas into verses or stanzas each marked off by a falling tone. Trevor Cope describes the manner of recitation of the *imbongi* (praise-poet).

The praiser recites the praises at the top of his voice and as fast as possible. These conventions of praise-poem recitation, which is high in pitch, loud in volume, fast in speech, create an emotional excitement in the audience as well as in the praiser himself, whose voice often rises in pitch, volume, and speed as he progresses, and whose movements become more and more exaggerated, for it is also a convention of praise-poem recitation that the praiser never stands still. (1968: 27)

From these examples it seems clear that chanting, or recitation, is a technique of oral performance that stands halfway between normal speech and song—hence Nketia refers to it as "half spoken and half sung." Its closeness to normal speech (whether of conversation or of public address) is evident in the reciter's effort to speak in fairly audible tones so as to impress a message on the audience. Its kinship with song can be seen in the reciter's striving after musical effect in the balance between stresses (high and low) at various points in the performance.

Two more characteristics of the chant, or recitation, are worth noting, for they help us to see in what ways it differs from the song. First, because the chanter or reciter is anxious to give prominence to the beauty of his or her vocal style and to impress the words on hearers as audibly as possible, the music is often either severely subdued or totally absent. In such cases the musical accompaniment—whether of instruments or of the human hand—is emphasized only at the end of a line or of a stanza, at the end of the entire vocal performance, or at whatever point the chanter feels a convenient break can be made. Morris tells us (1964: 19) of the heroic recitations of the Bahima: "At the end of each *enkome* the reciter snaps his finger and thumb, a gesture known as *enkome* from which the verse gets its name, and his companions provide the chorus of 'Eeee.' " In *ijala* performances among the Yoruba, the drum is played first before the chanter begins his chanting "in order to urge him on or to inspire him to give unrivalled ijala entertainment," and then "at intervals during the ijala artist's chanting turn" so as to give the audience an opportunity to enjoy and participate in brief interludes of song and dance (Babalola 1966: 55). This is similar to the Akan praise chant as described by Nketia: "When each such poem is being recited, there is always a tense atmosphere which is relieved at the end of each poem by drums and horns which play an interlude while the minstrels get ready to recite the next" (1979: 24).

The other characteristic of chanting, or recitation, is the control of audience participation. All attention is focused on the performer who spins out the lines either alone or with minimal encouragement from a chorus of accompanists; such an encouragement may come by way of the accompanists reciting the last or most important word of each line recited by the chanter, as in the Lango rainmaking chant already quoted. Otherwise the audience must wait until the end of the entire performance or at any such convenient break before it can say anything or participate in any way. This is what happens at the end of a stanza in the Zulu praise chant (*izibongo*), as Cope tells us: "At this point the audience sometimes participates with shouts of approval and cries of *musho, musho* (literally "say him, say him") to encourage the praiser to greater efforts. The degree of audience participation depends upon the nature of the occasion, whether serious, joyful, or sorrowful" (1968: 30).

In comparison with the oral narrative and the chant, the song is characterized by the highest degree of musicality (both vocal and instrumental) and of other aspects of performance (e.g., audience participation). Let us take first the manipulation of the voice by the performer. In the oral narrative, the voice of the narrator is that of everyday speech, although at specific but infrequent moments the narrator may introduce vocal twists to create feelings of tension or expectation in the listeners. In the chant, the vocal manipulation is more pronounced; still, the performer does no more than exploit the balance between the tones of everyday speech (i.e., high, middle, and low tones) to achieve an effective tonal harmony or tonal contrast, as Babalola has pointed out. In the song, however, we reach the highest level of vocal manipulation: the singer exploits the high and low tones of speech at several levels to achieve an even higher degree of affecting melody than is possible in the chant.

But it is in the areas of instrumental accompaniment and audience participation that the song demonstrates its superiority to the other modes of performance. Anthony King has been able to show, in his analysis of the Gambian performances of the Sunjata story (1974: 17–24), the role that music plays in the three modes (speech, recitation, and song) employed by the narrators *(griots).* Of the music played in the speech mode, he tells us that "in passages of vocalization it is subdued and subordinate to the voice," precisely because the emphasis is on the content of the story being narrated. Although the language of King's analysis becomes increasingly technical, what he says of the relationship between the words and the music in the other two modes is particularly enlightening. In the recitation mode, he says, "the voice is used at a much higher pitch level than in the Speech mode, it in fact at times appears to be close to its upper limits. . . . The general characteristics of the (musical) accompaniment in this mode are similar to those of the Speech mode. However the absence of extensive breath pauses arising from phrases of uneven length confines the instrument to a more purely accompanimental role and permits little or no virtuosic display."

King says that the song mode "is however distinguished from the Recitation mode by its much slower syllabic rate (i.e., speed of vocalization), by the ryhthmic variety brought to the realisation of its text, by the occurence of long held syllables especially in line final position, and by the use of contrasted melodic phrases and motion, ascending and descending. In addition vocalisation is frequently by a unison chorus, a practice only possible with lines of fixed form and in contrast to the solo-vocalisation in the other two modes." Of the musical accompaniment King tells us that "the treatment of the instrumental phrase in both the Recitation and Song modes is often much more elaborate than it is in the Speech mode. When a chorus is singing (i.e., in the Song mode) it is yet more elaborate again, and this probably results from the need to balance the increased vocal sonority with a greater instrumental sound."

What King says of choral singing brings us to that element of audience participation in which, as we observed earlier, the song differs considerably from the narrative and the chant. In telling a story, the narrator is completely unlimited in choice of words; since the words are not fixed, there is nothing the audience can do but listen attentively or else make the occasional comment in an independent set of words. In a recitation or chant, there are certain fixed phrases, such as the epithets (called *oriki* in Yoruba, for instance) used in praise of particular individuals, families, clans, or even ordinary creatures such as the tortoise and the spider; certain proverbial chants also come in fixed phrases, as in the examples from the Yoruba and from Mali already cited. But since these are recited in no regular order or sequence and the audience often cannot anticipate this, their participation in the recitation is severely limited, although we may find one or two people mouthing a few words here and there along with the performer. With the song, however, the audience is much freer. The lines and the sequence of a song are on the whole fixed; in many cases the song is generally known to the members of the community where it is performed, so everybody sings along with the performer. The performance of a song is also usually accompanied by music and dance in accordance with steps that are either culturally familiar or else related to the particular style dictated by the song. Whatever the case may be, the audience is delighted to seize the opportunity offered them to sing the words of the song, dance to the tune of the accompanying music, and generally participate in a relaxed way in the unfolding performance.

There are roughly two patterns of performance in songs and chants: the solo performance and the group performance. Certain forms of chanting are particularly suited to the solo performance, such as divination poetry (*ifa*) among the Yoruba of Nigeria and the self-praises (*ebyevugo*) among the Bahima of Uganda. Some of the hunters' praises (*ijala*) among the Yoruba are also done by solo artists. But however interesting such a performance might be, audiences generally prefer performances in which they have a chance to participate in music and dance; as Babalola points out (1966: 55), "ordinary members of the audience tend to prefer the ijala performance of an ijala artist who is assisted by a drummer and his band rather than that of a chanter who has no drummer." Solo singing by virtuoso performers such as the distinguished Hausa poet Dan Maraya of Jos (Nigeria) can also be quite impressive, but the spectacle of Hausa group singing and dancing especially as seen in cultural festivals in Nigeria is far more affecting than anything Maraya can do.

Group performance may in turn be broken into two types: monochoral and antiphonal. Monochoral performance implies that a chorus sings or chants the text together all the way from the beginning to the end of the performance. Such a performance is somewhat rare in chanting, as this is usually done by one performer at a time. Even in singing it is not common in traditional oral performances (as against the modern type represented by the famous Ipitombi troupe from South Africa) for a group to sing a song through without initial or periodic prompting lines from a lead singer.

The most popular style of group oral performance is thus the antiphonal. The group may comprise two or more persons, but the important element in antiphony is that one party provides a "call" and the other a "response." This may sometimes take the form of "question" and "answer," but more frequently it is a device that allows the performers to take turns in bringing out various sides and aspects of the same subject. This is particularly so in Yoruba *ijala* chants, where two artists perform in an alternating sequence, as in this "Salute to Ogunmodede."

    First Hunter: Ogunmodede, offspring of Osunbunmi.
           Modeniyi, a man who fights to grab a concubine.
           Pookomo, offspring of Osunbunmi.
           Ajailapa, offspring of Osunbunmi, there's a special *oriki* for every part of
               his body, Modede, offspring of Osunbunmi.
           Akinlade, offspring of Osunbunmi.
           The Tormentor, father of Obilowo.
           Member of the Owu royal lineage, offspring of Asolagbore. . . .
    Second Hunter: Hey! Thank you! Ha! Ogunmodede.
           The goat is not bald on its head, but its knees are bald.
           Behold an extraordinary animal!
           The sheep is not bald on its head, but its knees are bald.
           Behold an extraordinary animal!
           Modede is not bald on his head, but his knees are bald.
           Behold an extraordinary child! . . . (Babalola 1966: 206ff.)[4]

So too with songs, and here the possibilities are wider. We may have a series of alternating exchanges between one voice and a second, as in this Acholi (Uganda) love song.

> *Girl:* Father, if you are stupid,
>   They will take me without paying the bridewealth.
> *Man:* The daughter of the chief
>   Is like a lake bird.
> *Girl:* Age-mate of my brother,
>   We shall die together.
>   Friend of my brother
>   Has spoken the truth.
> *Man:* If the matter becomes bad
>   I shall elope with you. . . . (p'Bitek 1974: 51)

Or we may have a full orchestral score in which a soloist prompts the responses of a larger chorus, as in a piece of *udje* lampoon from the Urhobo of Nigeria.

> *Leader:*   Oloya who leads a wretched life
>   Boasts his talent in song.
>   Oloya remember, there is always something to pick in fish.
>   You know me well and I know you well
>   5   There is always something to pick in fish
>   I don't brook a tie when I wrestle with a child
>   A duel of songs that is!
> *Group:*   Oloya married a wife called Poverty-is-a-scandal
>   Your type of poverty
>   10   Is a notorious one *(Repeat lines 1–10)*
> *Leader:*   Here comes a song
> *Group:*   Oloya quarrelled with wife, alias Oghoro, stopped eating her food
>   A pauper refusing a wife's food, oh the disease of foolishness has afflicted
>   Oloya
>   Any modern wife whose husband rejects her food
>   15   Rejoices and mocks him saying, "He will regret it." . . . (Darah 1982:
>   293)

There are a variety of antiphonal arrangements in African songs and chants. In one of these which may be identified by the scheme A^1/B^1, A^2/B^2, A^3/B^3, etc., both "call" and "response" are different throughout the performance, as in the three examples just quoted; in fact, as in the case of *udje* poetry, we may have as many as three different soloists drawing alternate and equally distinct responses from the choral group,[5] while in some cases two soloists can engage each other in a series of exchanges before the choral group rounds off the performance in a final clinching statement.

A second arrangement is one in which one part of the group does not change its text throughout the series of exchanges, while the other does. In this lighthearted narrative song from Zimbabwe, which may be represented A^1/B, A^2/B, A^3/B, etc., the solo changes while the chorus is stable.

> There were once some girls,
> There were once some girls,
>   *Let's go to Zinjanja;*
>
> Who went to fetch firewood,
> Who went to fetch firewood,
>   *Let's go to Zinjanja;*
>
> They discovered some eggs,
> They discovered some eggs,
>   *Let's go to Zinjanja. . . .* (Mapanje and White 1983: 40)

Other arrangements, which may be no more than variations of the above, are entirely possible. One final point, however, that needs to be observed is the repetitive structure of these songs and chants. In chapter 4 we described repetition as essentially a musical quality, an evidence of a musical feeling. From the ladder which we recognized earlier in the present chapter, we saw that while this musical element is present in oral narratives told in normal speech voice, there is a higher level of it in chants and in songs. This is why there is a much higher incidence of repetition of actual words and phrases in these songs and chants than in the normal-speech narrative. In the *ijala* "Salute to Ogunmodede" quoted above, it is clear that the repetition of attributive phrases is due far more to the musical impetus generated by the tonal counterpoint in the performance than to the need to stress the qualities of the hunter Ogunmodede. In the various songs quoted, it is equally clear that the repetitions are a token of the lyrical pleasure which the performers feel and wish to transmit to the audience. This is particularly true of the repetition of the first ten lines of the Urhobo *udje* song of abuse and of the Zimbabwean narrative song.

Major Themes

In chapter 5 we discussed important moments of life in Africa that are recorded in the oral literature. Since we used mostly songs and chants in illustrating these instances, it is not necessary here to go into a detailed discussion of the usefulness of songs and chants in African society.

It is, however, important to bear in mind that there is hardly any occasion or activity in traditional African life that is not accompanied by songs and chants. When a child is born, songs accompany the moments of rejoicing and merry-making at the good fortune; when the child is crying or about to sleep, lullabies are sung by the mother or a nurse, intended to "lull" the child to rest. During the ceremonies marking entry into adolescence—initiation ceremonies for boys and puberty rites for girls—songs are performed to mark this important stage in traditional African life.

When the adult gets married, songs mark the occasion—ranging from good-humored taunts at the young man or woman surrendering a long-cherished freedom for the "prison" of the marital home to sincere advice to the young wife on how to ensure a happy home for herself and her new family. Songs and chants also accompany the various honest occupations of men and women: work songs to relieve the hours on the farm, in the fields, at the fishing traps, or at the weaver's loom; the various chants that contain formulae for healing ailments or foretelling the future; or the inspired chants and songs aimed at firing the courage of hunters and warriors before an encounter or to praise them for their feats. As with work, so with play: a variety of moonlight songs are intended to relax young men and women as well as children after a hard day's work in many areas of life.

As the adult man or woman achieves various successes in life, he or she is rewarded by the community with a chieftaincy title, during which occasion yet more praise chants as well as songs of rejoicing are performed. At the death of the individual, some songs lament the loss of the physical life while other songs give consolation for a life well lived and usher the deceased into the glorious company of the ancestors. "Oral poetry," as Babalola has said, "is part of everyday life among the Yoruba" (1966: vi); the same can safely be said of the pervasive role of songs and chants in traditional African life generally.

The themes or concerns of these songs and chants are numerous, just as they are in modern (written) poetry. However, as we saw earlier in this chapter, many of these songs and chants share similar concerns; for instance, the element of praise can be found in chants performed at title-taking ceremonies, in those recited to a warrior before or after he goes to battle, and even at the funeral rites of a notable chief or hunter. It is for this reason that in this chapter we shall concentrate our attention on a few of these themes with examples illustrating the variety of contexts in which they occur. Our themes are love, praise, criticism, war, and death. The examples given here only suggest the rich variety of perspectives from which each theme may be seen and the spread of poetic skill across the African continent.

Love

Love, the feeling of affection or tenderness toward a person or a thing, is expressed in traditional African songs in several ways. We may perhaps begin with what may be called nationalistic or patriotic love, that is, love of one's race or nation, however narrowly defined the area concerned may be. Traditional African songs of this nature often imply a certain amount of prejudice; in showing a sentimental attachment to their land, composers cannot help betraying some comparison of themselves with other peoples. This song from the Somali is, however, little more than a simple celebration of the virtues of the native land.

> The best dance is the dance of the Eastern clans,
> The best people are ourselves,
> Of this I have always been sure.
> The best wealth is camels,
> The *duur* grass is the best fresh grazing,
> The *dareemo* grass is the best hay,
> Of this I have always been sure. (Andrzjewski and Lewis 1964: 144)

The poet is admirably assertive about the qualities with which his people have been blessed and self-assured in his claims; we find this kind of spirit in national anthems across the world.

From patriotic love we may move on to consider love of family. Again, numerous pieces of African oral poetry are devoted to an expression of love or admiration of father, mother, or child. Let us first take a lullaby from the Akan of Ghana, sung by a mother to her child in the cradle.

> Someone would like to have you for her child
> But you are my own.
> Someone wished she had you to nurse on a good mat;
> Someone wished you were hers: she would put you on a camel blanket;
> But I have you to rear on a torn mat.
> Someone wished she had you, but I have you. (Nketia 1979: 27)

In this touching expression of maternal love, the mother, obviously a poor woman, wishes that her child could have the benefit of all those comforts that a child in a rich household enjoys. But she is proud to have the child in spite of her poverty. A feeling of loving possessiveness in the first two lines is echoed in the last line in the idea of a poor mother holding on to a valuable possession that some rich mothers are unable to have. There is also a musical quality in the repeated wish: "Someone . . ."

The more common type of love expressed in traditional African song is the love between a man and a woman. Quite often this comes in the form of an intense admiration of the physical beauty of the woman by the man, or vice versa, in such a way as to indicate feelings of sexual desire or lust. Some of these traditional songs of sex are quite explicit and unabashed in their language, but this one is considered "safe."

> When I see the beauty on my beloved's face,
> I throw away the food in my hand;
> Oh, sister of the young man, listen;
> The beauty on my beloved's face.
>
> Her neck is long, when I see it
> I cannot sleep one wink;
> Oh, the daughter of my mother-in-law,
> Her neck is like the shaft of the spear.
>
> When I touch the tattoos on her back,
> I die;
> Oh, sister of the young man, listen;
> The tattoos on my beloved's back.
>
> When I see the gap in my beloved's teeth,
> Her teeth are white like dry season simsim;
> Oh, daughter of my father-in-law listen,
> The gap in my beloved's teeth.

The daughter of the bull confuses my head,
I have to marry her;
True, sister of the young man, listen;
The suppleness of my beloved's waist. (p'Bitek 1974: 41)

This song, collected by the poet Okot p'Bitek from his native Acholi community in Uganda, is an example of the songs performed at the *orak*, an informal love dance of these people. According to the information put together by Okot, *orak* is the short form of *larakaraka*, named after the man who introduced one of the new styles and movements into this traditional dance. The dance is done mostly in the moonlight by young men and women from neighboring clan groups as a way of getting to know one another and either meeting future spouses or cementing existing love relationships—hence it has also been called the *myel cuna* (dance for wooing). The men form an outer ring while the women form an inner ring for the dance; rhythm was provided originally by sticks struck by the dancers, although these have been replaced by rattles worn on the ankles and gourds struck by independent musicians. The rhythm of the *orak* dance provides the basic background for a variety of love songs which reflect either the excitement of an existing relationship, hopes for a future union in love between boy and girl, or disappointment and bitterness at a lover's dashed hopes.

The song clearly reveals a young man's excited admiration for his girl friend, moving him to a determination to marry her. The specific points of beauty in the girl are identified as the face, the neck, the tattooed back, the teeth, and the waist; the final position given to the waist here is somewhat emphatic and gives only a faint suggestion of the pornographic character of many of these *orak* songs. Yet in spite of this the young man has no intention of behaving improperly and violating accepted social rules, e.g., by eloping with the girl. The references to the young girl's brother (line 3, etc.) and parents (lines 7, 15) are perhaps intended as a declaration of the boy's wishes or at least an appeal that they recognize his interest in the girl.

There is admirable poetic beauty in the structure and language of this song. It is organized into a balanced system of "stanzas" with four statements to each stanza. Within this repetitive pattern there is a recognizable progression of ideas throughout, except for a significant variation in the final stanza. In the first line, the poet identifies the part of the body he admires; in the second he tells us the effect or impression it has on him; and in the third he addresses the girl in reference to a member of her family. The fourth line rounds off the stanza by referring back to the part of the body mentioned in the first line. This repeated structure endows the song with the twin qualities of lyricism and emphasis. But the variations are just as attractive. First, the alternations between sister *(lamin)* and daughter *(latin)* in the third lines enhance the sense of balance between the stanzas. In stanza two, the neck is not simply introduced but given an affecting description. The real twist comes, however, in the last stanza, which is no doubt intended to clinch the message of the poem: although the intentions of the young man (i.e., marriage) are noble, the final part of the girl's body which he mentions (for the first time in the last line) adds a greater touch of sexuality than any of the parts previously mentioned.

This element of sexuality is indeed contained in some of the imagery in the poem.

Among the Acholi, as Okot tells us elsewhere (1974), the "bull" (line 17) is a symbolic title that connotes virility or male potency; the "spear" (line 8) also conveys the image of male sexuality; and gap-toothedness (line 13) in a woman is generally regarded as a mark of sexual appeal. There is no doubt that in the permissive atmosphere of the *orak* dance these references to sexuality would be readily appreciated and enjoyed. The poet uses language in other ways that are equally effective. Likening the girl's teeth to the whiteness of *simsim* (line 14), a grain, brings out its contrast with the dark background of the gap in the teeth. Finally, the progressively strong emotions which the girl arouses in the young man (lines 2, 6, 10) underline not only his excitement about their relationship but even more his confidence in his sexual potency.

But alas, all is not fair in love. The opposite side to excitement in love songs of the sexual kind is disappointment or frustration. In such songs a man or a woman is frustrated that his or her attentions have not been appreciated or returned, or disappointed that the high expectations of union have been dashed by infidelity. A song from the Kikuyu (Kenya) paints just such a picture.

> After a brief struggle I got myself a job;
> My food was meat and banana flour,
> A hundred cents a month and soon I had some money.
>
> Soon afterwards I bought myself a beautiful girl;
> My heart was telling me this was a fortune,
> So, heart, you were deceiving me and I believed you.
>
> On a Saturday morning I was leaving work;
> I was thinking I was being awaited at home,
> But on arrival I couldn't find my bride,
>
> Nor was she at her parent's home.
> I ran fast to a river valley;
> What I saw gave me a shock -
> There my wife was conversing with her lover.
>
> I sat and silently wept;
> I realised there was no luck in this world,
> People are not trustworthy and will never be,
> Girls are not trustworthy and will never be! (Liyong 1972: 133)

Taban lo Liyong, who edited this song, does not give its social and other backgrounds, but it seems much like the kind of lyrics accompanied by a guitar in a drinking bar. The narrative form of the song is, perhaps, the one best suited for drawing attention to the singer in such a context of merrymaking among poor workers in an East African township. The song certainly addresses its sentiments to such urban poor: the first three lines are no doubt aimed at eliciting the sympathy of the suffering workers to the plight of one of their kind. Notice also the progression of the stanzas. The first three contain a certain amount of hope and excitement on the young man's part. Although his disappointment is hinted at as early as line 6, the last two stanzas are longer than the earlier three and thus convey the heaviness of heart felt by the young man whose hopes have been dashed.

The philosophical message of this love tragedy is driven home by the repetitive structure of the last two lines; but the narrative form of the song helps to personalize the experience and bring some vividness to the general idea of infidelity. The narrative form also suggests that the song is likely a solo performance: the absence of frequently repeated lines of the type found in choral refrains does indicate that the song was not originally intended for a group performance, although some members of the audience may on occasions sing along with the singer or contribute some illuminating asides.

Praise

The theme of praise is to a certain extent similar to that of love, for both sentiments are fundamentally based in a feeling of admiration for a person or an object. A poet who praises the manly looks of a warrior is perhaps moved by as much admiration as the young Acholi lover who praises the face and the neck of his girl friend. In discussing praise poetry, however, we are inclined to look at those songs which highlight the achievements of the subject of praise or at least those sterling qualities that make a person superior to everyone else and a leader of his or her kind.

Praise poetry is performed in a variety of circumstances, either by the subject of the praise or by someone else attached to the subject who may enjoy some patronage or employment by the subject. As we have seen, self-praise is practiced by young boys at a traditional circumcision ceremony, where they are anxious to prove that they feel no pain from the cut of the circumcision knife and are proud to be stepping onto the threshold of manhood. In some communities, as among the Bahima of Ankole (Uganda), a man composes and performs praises of himself after a successful battle with an enemy, especially in a cattle raid. In title-taking ceremonies among the Igbo of eastern Nigeria, self-praises are chanted by the celebrant or by a masquerade performing on the celebrant's behalf.

The more common type of praise is praise of others, especially distinguished members of a society. In the traditional society of the Mandinka of the western Sudan—in Mali, Guinea, Senegal, and Gambia—kings kept skilled singers *(griots)* in their courts to sing their praises, offer words of advice as the need arose, and keep a record of events within the context of their songs of praise. Although many African kingdoms crumbled during the era of colonialism, these praise-singers may still be seen in traditional courts such as the *oba*'s palaces in western Nigeria and within the courts of the *emir* in the north of the country. Otherwise, free-lance singer-musicians offer their services to the rich men and politicians in today's West African states. In return for these praises the singer is rewarded either with steady livelihood (as in the palaces) or cash in the case of free-lance performers.

The language of praise is usually lofty and exaggerated. No doubt the background to this is that the praisers are doing their best to please their patrons so as to get as much reward as possible. But it seems also that if the oral poet considers the subject worthy of celebration in song, the poet must show in what way that subject qualifies for the attention above anyone else. Consequently, in praise poetry we often find the subject given attributes and characteristics that are either not possible within the laws of nature or at least go somewhat beyond the truth.

We have already examined an Igbo title-taking chant that is a fairly good example of the lofty idiom of self-praise, but for sheer lack of modesty it hardly compares with this chant from the Bahima of Uganda.

> I Who Give Courage To My Companions!
> I Who Am Not Reluctant In Battle made a vow!
> I Who Am Not Reluctant In Battle made a vow at the time of the preventing of the elephants and with me was The Tamer of Recruits;
> I Who Am Not Loved By the Foe was full of anger when the enemy were reported.
> 5 I Who Am Vigilant called up the men at speed together with the Pain Bringer;
> I found The Giver Of Courage in secret conference.
> I Whose Decisions Are Wise, at me they took their aim and with me was Rwamisooro;
> I Who Overthrow The Foe returned to the fight as they attacked us.
> I Who Am Nimble withstood the bullets together with The Lover Of Battle;
> 10 I Who Am Invincible appeared with The Infallible One.
> I Who Grasp My Weapons Firmly was sent in advance to Ruyanja together with The Overthrower;
> I Who Seek No Avoidance Of Difficulties drew my bow.
> I Who Do Not Tremble prepared to shoot together with The One Who Draws Tight His Bow;
> I Who Crouch For the Attack, they brought me back for my sandals together with The Tall One;
> 15 I Who Do Not Disclose My Plans fought furiously and with me was The Brave One;
> I Who Do Not Miss The Mark crossed over noiselessly together with The Spear Thrower.
> I Who Am Not Reluctant in Battle was with The One Eager for Plunder;
> I Who Attack On All Sides appeared with The One Who Exhausts The Foe.
> I Who Move Forward To The Attack took the track of the Ekirimbi together with The Bringer of Sorrow;
> 20 I Who Am In The Forefront Of The Battle tracked them down at Migyera together with The One Who
> Depends Not On The Advice of Others.
> At Kashaka, my rattle bell rang out and with me was Rwamisooro;
> At Rubumba, I found their courage deserting them.
> I Whose Aid Is Sought was assailed by bullets which left me unscathed and with me was The Fortunate One;
> I Who Stand Firm In Battle defeated them utterly and so did The One Who Needs No Protection. (Morris 1964: 52–54)[6]

This is an example of an *ekyevugo*, or heroic recitation. According to Henry Morris, who recorded it, the passage refers to an incident during the First World War when a group of Bahima decided to migrate from territory occupied by the Germans back to their ancestral home in the Ankole region of Uganda. The interesting point about this particular chant is that although no actual fighting accompanied the emigration of these men, the hero-reciter of this piece makes it look like a bloody battle in which he routed the emigrants with the aid of a handful of his hardy friends. The hero dresses himself in the image of an invincible, tireless, and utterly fearless fighter and the "enemy" as ineffective though daring. This is clearly a superb example of self-praise in which an individual wishes to prove what a special and unique person he or she is in the community. It should be noted that far from encouraging lying or dishonestly, this is basically a tradition of poetry in which individuals cultivate personal pride in the most elevated idiom possible; native Bahima would of course know that no actual fighting took place.

A good majority of praise poetry deals, however, with the praise of others by more or less professional praise-singers, sometimes accompanied with musical instruments such as drums (as among the Yoruba). Many of the people thus praised have distinguished themselves in various endeavors such as war, hunting, and farming. The Yoruba salute to Onikoyi already presented is an excellent example of praises sung to a distinguished warrior in the most elevated idioms possible. One of the many praises of the Sotho leader Moshoeshoe highlights his achievements both as a warrior and as a statesman.

> You who are fond of praising the ancestors,
> Your praises are poor when you leave out the warrior,
> When you leave out Thesele, the son of Mokhachane;
> For it is he who is the warrior of the wars:
> 5 Thesele is brave and strong,
> That is Moshoeshoe-Moshaila.
> When Moshoeshoe started to govern the Sotho,
> He started at Botha-Bothe:
> Thesele, the cloud, departed from the east,
> 10 It left a trail and alighted in the west
> At Thaba Bosiu, at the hut that is a court:
> Every nation heard,
> And the Pedi heard him too.
> Moshoeshoe, clear the road of rubbish
> 15 That the Maaooa may travel with pleasure,
> And travel with ease.
> The Ndebele from Zulu's heard too.
> Lay down the stick, son of Mokhachane,
> Sit down:
> 20 The village of the stick is not built.
> "What can you do to me?" does not build a village:
> The village that is built is the suppliant's, Thesele,
> Great ancestor, child of Napo Motlomelo,
> Protective charm of the Beoana's land.
> 25 The cave of the poor and of the chiefs,
> Peete's descendant, the brave warrior,
> He is loved when the shields have been grasped,
> When the young men's sticks have been grasped. (Mapanje and White 1983: 11–12)

This *lithoko*, or Sotho praise chant, has several qualities worth noting. In glorifying subjects, most African praise poetry endeavors to put them within the larger context of the past and the present: their ancestors as well as their present families or descendants. We are given the names of Moshoeshoe's parents and predecessors (lines 3, 23, 26) to establish that he hails from a distinguished line; in other praises of Moshoeshoe we are also given the names of his children and his wives,[7] but the poet here contents himself with the names of the clans who came under his rule: the Pedi, the Ndebele, and the Beoana. The emphasis of this poem, however, is on Moshoeshoe's power as a warrior, a conqueror and subjugator of other peoples. It is true that most of it (lines 7–25) deals with his techniques as a ruler: building a new capital (Thaba Bosiu) and connecting roads (lines 7–16), establishing the principle that compromise is a better method of government than confrontation (lines 18–22), and offering his protection in equal measure to all classes of his people (line 25). But the poem begins and ends with the portrait of Moshoeshoe as a warrior: a fighter above all fighters (line 4), one who is at his best in the clash of shield and spear-stick (lines 27–28).

Although the tone of this poem is tame in comparison with the loud hyperbole of the Bahima self-praise, the poem is no less vivid and dramatic in its portraiture of Moshoeshoe. The first three lines address themselves directly to Sotho praise-singers generally in an arresting fashion, and even the readers are made to feel the challenge as though it were being thrown at them too. The metaphor of a cloud in the second stanza forcefully captures the historic movement of Moshoeshoe, with large droves of men and cattle leaving an awesome trail, toward the new capital of Thaba Bosiu. In lines 18–19 the poet prompts Moshoeshoe into the idiomatic pronouncement (lines 20–22) that a true and lasting settlement of the people ("village") is achieved not with weapons ("the stick," i.e., spears) but with conciliation ("suppliant"). However, in the repetitive music of the last two lines the poet rubs in rather forcefully the military image of Moshoeshoe.

Praise poetry is also addressed to nonhuman figures and entities. "Salute to the Colobus Monkey" is a specimen of Yoruba hunters' poetry (ijala) from Babalola's collection.

> O Colobus Monkey, whose young are born as twins, hailing from Isokun.
> Twin-born monkey, dweller on the tree-tops.
> An extraordinary animal who shakes the lagbao tree, swaying the branches this way and that.
> Day breaks, every housewife sweeps some floor or some ground; The Colobus Monkey sweeps his tree-top,
> 5 Like the wind which sweeps clean the firmanent.
> "Leave my tail alone; I am touchy about my beetling brows."
> If one intends to pursue a young Colobus to his home, one must perforce speed over a really long distance.
> Look at a young Colobus's occiput.
> Look at the bottom of an esuru yam; aren't both alike?
> 10 Colobus twins, numerous on the highest twigs, numerous in Igbo Odo at Ajagaase.
> Dwellers at Deure,
> Creatures having well-set teeth. (1966: 106)

Yoruba ijala poetry abounds in salutes like this one addressed to animals, birds, trees, and even vegetables. Various explanations have been proposed for this phenomenon. Some scholars believe that such chants are simply occasional poetry devoted to an observation or appreciation of the natural environment; just as cattlemen in northern Nigeria and the cattle kraals of eastern and southern Africa compose and sing praises of their herds partly in honest admiration and partly to accompany the hours of toil, so Yoruba hunters, as they pass through the bush, reflect and comment on the elements of that environment in appreciative verses. Other scholars believe that these environmental chants really have a magical intent behind them, that perhaps in the same way as nurses sing lullabies to pacify difficult children, so hunters chant these verses as a kind of magical formula or spell to enable them to exercise control over the objects that they are after, especially difficult beasts such as monkeys, buffaloes, and elephants.

The latter explanation is no doubt less convincing, for so much effort seems to go into the choice of idiom and imagery in these chants that the magical purpose becomes entirely subordinate if it exists at all. In "Salute to the Colobus Monkey" the poet admires the large population of this species, their "love of great heights on the forest trees" (as Babalola tells us in a footnote), the speed of their movement, the smoothness of their skull, the beauty of their teeth. The double comparisons of the monkey with a housewife and the wind (lines 4–5) poetically capture the intermediate position that this tree-dwelling creature occupies between the earth and the sky. The dramatic statement in line 6 aims, with a touch of humor, to portray the monkey's almost effeminate consciousness of the beauty of its body. And the list of locales with which the monkey is associated—Isokun, Ajagaase, and Deure—glorifies the animal as controlling a large area of habitation or movement. Surely, this is praise poetry that celebrates the beauty of nature with combined sensitivity and wit.

Praise poetry, can, however, be set within a mystical or ritual context, especially in connection with the worship of divinities. In many African communities, for instance, people seek to co-opt the aid of a god by acknowledging its power and attributes in chants of praise. The Yoruba god of inexplicable fate, Eshu, is known to be so mischievous and unpredictable that one can do little more with him than acknowledge these rather delicate attributes.

> Eshu turns right into wrong, wrong into right.
> When he is angry, he hits a stone until it bleeds.
> When he is angry, he sits on the skin of an ant.
> When he is angry, he weeps tears of blood.
> 5 Eshu slept in the house—
> But the house was too small for him:
> Eshu slept on the verandah—
> But the verandah was too small for him:
> Eshu slept in a nut—
> 10 At last he could stretch himself!
> Eshu walked through the groundnut farm.
> The tuft of his hair was just visible:
> If it had not been for his huge size,
> He would not be visible at all.

15 Lying down, his head hits the roof:
    Standing up, he cannot look into the cooking pot.
    He throws a stone today
    And kills a bird yesterday! (Beier and Gbadamosi 1959: 23–24)

Eshu is clearly unique, a deity in a class by himself. The chant is composed throughout on a structure of parallelisms (see chapter 5), and the statements are full of irony and paradox. For instance, how can an action taking place in the present have an effect in the past, as the last two lines indicate? Nothing can be more ironical. And how can a figure who cannot be contained by a whole house feel at ease inside a nut? This is the height of paradox. The mischievous and temperamental nature of the god is also brought out vividly in the first four lines of the chant. This piece of praise poetry is on the whole intended to give us a portrait of the most capricious and unpredictable of all Yoruba divinities; by acknowledging the power of inexorable fate, the poet hopes to appease the god and perhaps stand in his favor.

Criticism

A great deal of critical spirit is embodied in African oral literature. Some of it is to be found even within what generally passes as praise poetry. As we saw in chapter 2 and in the section just concluded, praise-singers attached to traditional rulers and other leaders have often allowed themselves the freedom of advising them on important matters, and their advice would include criticism of unwise conduct even if the harshness of the statement is somewhat controlled. In some societies, in fact, the harshness could be slightly more pronounced; it is known, for instance, that court poets in traditional Akan and Zulu communities frequently told the ruler, in no uncertain terms, where he had gone wrong. This is all in the spirit that society must be guided by certain standards of conduct from which not even the rulers are exempt. An example is found in the concluding part of another long praise chant in honor of the Sotho leader Moshoeshoe, commemorating his victory over the Thembu.

    Black white-spotted ox, though you've come with gladness,
    Yet you have come with grief,
    You have come with cries of lamentation,
    You have come as the women hold their heads
5 And continually tear their cheeks.
        Keep it from entering my herds:
    Even in calving, let it calve in the veld,
    Let it calve at Qoaling and Korokoro.
    To these cattle of our village it brings distress,
    It has come with a dirge, a cause of sadness.
    Thesele, the other one, where have you left him? (Damane and Sanders 1974: 49)

Moshoeshoe made raids on the neighboring Thembu, and in the final one (in 1935) he was so intent on rounding up all their herds of cattle that he was unaware of the death of his brother Makhabane in the fighting. In this passage the poet, while congratulating him on his victory against the enemy, nevertheless points out that this victory has been tainted by death—not only of several young Sotho warriors lost in the reckless campaign (thus bringing sorrow and grief to their mothers and wives) but especially of the king's brother. The cattle won from the Thembu is therefore seen as an unwholesome prize that should be isolated rather than be allowed to taint those of the village. Notice particularly the final line of this passage: the abruptness of the question and the final position given to it lends the criticism of Moshoeshoe's recklessness a certain bite.

Outside the ruling circles, oral poetry is also used for seeking personal redress. These songs of personal abuse, or "lampoons," may or may not have a firm basis in truth—the facts are often twisted in the composer's favor—but they provide the individual an outlet for relieving his injured feelings. Lampoons are widespread across Africa; so well-established were they in the past as a tradition of song that in some communities, notably among the Urhobo of southwestern Nigeria, contests were held during periodic festivals in which villages or wards vilified each other or specific individuals among them in vicious songs skillfully composed and performed by orchestras commissioned for the purpose. This is *udje* poetry, which we discussed briefly in chapter 2. In these contests, because the leaders of the song groups—or the prominent composers of songs—are usually considered the most dangerous members of their community, their rivals choose to concentrate their attacks on them. As with most lampoons, there may be very little support for the charges made in the songs, and the whole attack may be an outright lie; the essential aim is to use the resources of words, coupled with music, dance, and spectacle, in the most poetically effective way to do the utmost harm to the object of the attack. Here is part of an *udje* lampoon directed against Oloya, the song leader of one of the competing orchestras.

Leader:	Let whoever talks of foul-mouthedness
Group:	Know we are masters in the art of satirical song
	We have a masterly control of the song on Oloya
	Oloya the drifter extraordinary! Where has he not been to?
5	He had sex with Ovien's wife and palm wine was demanded
	To appease the ancestors but Oloya had no money for it
	The woman first denied the charge and Oloya was jubilant
	He again invited Ovien's wife
	And Oloya defiled her once more
10	Aruotughwaran had sex in the bush
	It was Umudjo who caught them
	The fear of the ancestors made them confess
	When the matter came to court the woman admitted
	That Oloya seduced her in Etepha forest
15	All you lechers know another's wife is a dreadful charm
	Which on the day of a challenge shows its worth. (Darah 1982: 297)

Such vicious lampoons are no longer widely practiced. Among other reasons, they have been discouraged by libel laws. In the past, lampoon poets got away with their accusations, but these days the fear of being taken to court by the aggrieved person and possibly ending up with a heavy fine (if not a jail sentence) has imposed severe constraints on the practice of wild critical assaults on people.

Although the lampoon tradition was frequently abused by individuals who used it for unjust personal vendettas, it was also a useful instrument for discouraging social evils such as theft, adultery, truancy, and general irresponsibility among young and old alike. This indeed is the real usefulness of these songs in the oral tradition: they encourage the citizens of a society to observe proper conduct, cultivate a sense of purpose and responsibility, and issue a warning whenever anyone or any group indulges in habits that are detrimental to the moral health and general survival of the society. This song from the Igbo of eastern Nigeria deplores the decline in educational standards among the youth.

> We know how to speak English
> We know how to speak Igbo
> Why are school boys of today so ignorant?
> You test them in Igbo they fail
> 5 You test them in English they fail
> The school fees we pay are wasted
> "Bongo" trousers have ruined them
> "Bongo" trousers have ruined them. (Nwoga 1981: 237)

Floppy, bell-bottomed "bongo" trousers were in vogue among young men in Nigeria in the 1960s and 1970s; an indulgence in this mode of fashion, says the song, has turned the heads of the youths away from the pursuit of education. An interesting element of performance of this song has been recorded by Donatus Nwoga, who collected the song from his village: "The singer-dancers leave no doubts as to what they mean by bongo trousers as they throw their ankles wide out as they dance to represent the flopping around of the wide-bottom trousers" (p. 237).

African songs and chants have also taken a critical view of political developments and political leadership. For instance, among the songs that Nwoga collected from eastern Nigeria after the Nigerian civil war (1967–70), there are some that protest the slow pace of reconstruction in areas severely damaged by the war and the high-handedness of government officials at both state and local levels. But perhaps the most documented area of political protest in African oral poetry is in those songs that have fueled the nationalist struggles in eastern and southern Africa: the Mau Mau songs from Kenya, the liberation songs from Zimbabwe, and various songs from Mozambique and South Africa protesting the oppressive conditions in which people live and work under the white minority governments and their law-enforcement officials. Here is one such song from Mozambique.

> I suffer, I do,
>   *Oyi-ya-e-e*
> I suffer, I do,
>   *I suffer, my heart is weeping.*

5 What's to be done?
 I suffer, my heart is weeping.
I cultivate my cotton,
 I suffer, my heart is weeping.
Picking, picking a whole basketful,
10 *I suffer, my heart is weeping.*
I've taken it to the Boma there,
 I suffer, my heart is weeping.
They've given me five escudos!
 I suffer, my heart is weeping.
15 When I reflect on all this,
 Oyi-ya-e-e
I suffer, I do,
 I suffer, my heart is weeping.
My husband, that man,
20 *I suffer, my heart is weeping.*
He went there to Luabo,
 I suffer, my heart is weeping.
He went to work, work hard,
 I suffer, my heart is weeping.
25 He broke off some sugar cane for himself,
 I suffer, my heart is weeping.
Leaving work, he was arrested,
 I suffer, my heart is weeping.
He was taken to the police,
30 *I suffer, my heart is weeping.*
He was beaten on the hand!
 I suffer, my heart is weeping.
When I reflect on all this
 Oyi-ya-e-e
35 I suffer, I do,
 I suffer, my heart is weeping. (Mapanje and White 1983: 139–40)

This song was documented as a specimen of what is generally called a work song. In this case, it is a song sung by Chilomwe women in Mozambique as they pound corn; the refrain sung after every line of this narrative lament shows clearly that the women employ the song to lighten the burden of work. The content of the song is, however, a condemnation of the highhandedness of the Portuguese colonial authorities. Between 1936 and 1961, the government operated a scheme whereby women were compelled, under threat of being beaten, to grow one half-hectare of cotton for sale to the owners of the huge farm lands on which the growing was done. They then took the cotton yield to the local administrative centers (called Bomas, line 11), only to be paid ridiculously low prices (line 13). Sugar was also grown on large estates, but any African caught eating any of it was liable to be punished, as was the case with the poet's husband (lines 19–31). This is basically a song about injustice and brutality under white colonial rule.

It will be obvious from this and the *udje* lampoon song that many traditional songs of the critical, or "protest," category have a narrative structure to them. This is no doubt because the composer is making every effort to portray the cause as a just one or present the other party as guilty or damnable. To do so, the matter is frequently presented in some kind of story even though in many cases the facts are carefully tilted to one side. The language of these songs is also on the whole less figurative than that of praise poetry, since the case needs to be presented as clearly as possible for all to judge. Notice the basic $A^1B/A^2B/A^3B$ pattern of call and response in this Mozambique song.

War

Human relationships are often marred by conflict, which is usually the result of a breakdown in communication or of an attempt by one party to violate the rights of the other. This situation is frequently reflected in African oral poetry, and in many cases the conflict portrayed has to do with fighting or war. War songs or songs depicting the fighting spirit feature prominently in the oral tradition mainly because in traditional African society war provided men with the opportunity to put their manhood to the test and establish for themselves a pride of place in the society. It is also to be expected that since, in the early stages of their development, many of these traditional communities were constantly fighting one another over territory, property (especially cattle), and various matters of honor (e.g., to punish an insult to a chief or the abduction of a girl), songs of war would occupy a prominent place in their imagination.

The consciousness of war comes quite early in the life of average citizens—especially the males—in traditional African society. In many communities, initiation ceremonies organized for teenage boys on the basis of their respective age-sets are designed to usher these youths into early manhood and to prepare them for the task of protecting the land. The Dinka of the Sudan provide an interesting example. According to Francis Deng, the foremost authority on this Sudanese group, Dinka youths enter into initiation between the ages of sixteen and eighteen. In the essential ceremony of initiation, an initiator (who is older than the initiates) cuts knife marks on the heads of the boys; the victims are not supposed to show any signs of pain, and their relatives and friends rejoice as they endure the pain courageously. These boys are conscious of their role as future defenders of the land and this, coupled with their confrontation with the "armed" initiator, provides the inspiration for many of their initiation songs in which they see the experience of initiation as a war and the initiator as the enemy.

> Coward, run away, people are killed
> People are killed by Malek
> People are killed by Ajang
> People are killed by Ador
> 5 Initiators have attacked Magak
> I ask the Big Chief
> Why was I not told of the attack

O Deng, the Saddle-bill Stork?
The junior Magak lie in the morning
10 Bol sat on the right flank
And Marial on the left flank
They met in the centre *Tum!*
The war begins! (Deng 1973: 193–94)

The initiate in this song belongs to the age-set called Magak (line 5). He sees himself and his fellows as being ambushed in a surprise attack by a number of initiators—Malek (also called Bol), Marial (also called Ador), and Ajang—hedging them on both the left and right flanks and killing them off one by one. The initiates finally meet their initiators in a head-on clash (line 12). Although war here is simply a metaphor for the bloody experience of the initiation cuts, we can see how vividly these young men already conceive of their future role as warriors fighting to defend their nation against its enemies.

For the full-grown warrior, the task of defending the nation in a war is embraced with considerable enthusiasm and pride. Many traditional songs of war are imbued with this spirit. There is not the least fear of danger or death; the enemy is treated with scorn, and the victorious celebrate their triumph with unlimited arrogance. A song from the Akan-Ashanti of Ghana celebrates such a triumph by Osee, leader of a royal brigade (Apente) in the Ashanti wars.

Osee, man of Apente.
Osee, man of Apente,
We shall fight battles for our nation,
There was a battle brewing, Osee,
5 But the army of the enemy never arrived.
We did not feel their presence.
You are children of ghosts, and nocturnal fighters.
Night fighters,
You have laid them low.
10 Osee has laid you low.
The night fighter has laid you low. (Nketia 1963a: 108)

This enthusiasm for war as reflected in the oral poetry frequently transcends rational considerations. Once a people have determined to go to war against another people, it is considered cowardly and foolhardy for anyone among them to argue the wisdom of the decision or even attempt to justify it. The warriors are simply glad of an opportunity to show their heroic spirit and have no patience for any form of argument. A war song from the Acholi of Uganda reveals this spirit.

Coward, crawl back into your mother's womb
We are sons of the brave,
Sons of stubborn people.
The coward has blocked my path completely.
Who is that calling my name

And arguing stupidly?
We are sons of the brave, sons of stubborn people,
The coward has blocked my path completely;
Coward, crawl back into your mother's womb. (p'Bitek 1974: 103)

The brave man—the warrior—is nothing less than a stubborn man, who plunges straight into the battle without being deterred by arguments. Those who engage in arguments are stupid and cowardly and should never have been born; they should crawl back into their mothers' wombs and get out of the way of the brave. In calling themselves "sons of the brave," etc., the warriors wish to press the point that they have the warlike spirit in their blood. It is also possible to take "coward" in this song as referring to the enemy; in that case, the Acholi song would be showing the same kind of scorn that we saw in the Ashanti war song.

The songs from the Acholi and the Dinka paint a picture of traditional African warfare, fought by black people on either side. There are also many songs in Africa which have to do with wars of resistance and of liberation fought by Africans against imperialist troops. The Ashanti song refers to the famous Ashanti wars fought against the British in the nineteenth century. More recently, in this century, there have been wars in eastern and southern Africa against white colonial forces and minority governments, notably the guerrilla wars in Kenya (by the Mau Mau) and in Zimbabwe. These wars were fought with modern weapons as against the less sophisticated ones used in traditional warfare. This song, from the Mau Mau fight for Kenya's liberation from British rule in the 1950s, is titled "The Battle of Tumu Tumu Hill."[8]

Listen and hear this story
Of the Tumu Tumu Hill!
So that you may realise that God is with us
And will never abandon us.

It was on a Wednesday:
We were in a village down the valley:
The enemy decided to climb
In order to see Kikuyuland.

When it struck two in the afternoon
Waruanja was sent down the valley
Dressed like a woman
In order to spy.

He brought back a valuable message
That Kirimukuyu was guarded by security forces:
Down in the valley were 400 fighters
Whom the government intended to surround.

Good fortune came our way
In the form of a girl
Named Kanjunio
Who saved a thousand lives.

When it struck two,
A thunderous noise was heard from atop the hill:
Bren guns were firing from every direction,
But God helped us and we descended safely.

Gakuru gave his own life
To save the lives of his friends:
He threw a grenade
And the machine guns ceased their firing.

When we reached the valley
We found parents in tears,
Coming down the hill
To witness the death of their sons. (Mapanje and White 1983: 78)

This folk song is clearly more "modern" than the pieces discussed earlier. To start with, the expression of faith in and gratitude to God reveals the influence of Christianity. Most traditional African war songs show so much confidence in the might of the warrior, so much self-assurance, that there is seldom room for dependence on divine providence; where there is recourse to supernatural power, this is more in terms of magical devices (amulets and other kinds of charms) than of an appeal for divine help. The traditional warlike hero has little faith in anything but himself and the resources he commands into action; God and "good fortune" have no real place in his plans. Other aspects of the modern outlook in this song may be seen in time measurements such as "two in the afternoon" (lines 9, 21) and "Wednesday" (line 5), in the use of guns (lines 23, 28) and hand grenades (line 27). However, the song is no less traditional in celebrating the heroism and self-sacrifice of those who worked for the guerrilla forces—Waruanja, Kanjunio, and Gakuru. The narrative form of the song helps to highlight the glory of the fighters by painting a vivid and dramatic picture of the dangers they faced and the skill with which they overcame those dangers.

Although the overriding spirit in traditional war songs is heroism and glory, there are nevertheless some songs in which the warriors are honest about the problems they face and even the outcome of the encounter. In this song, the Acholi have no illusions about who is superior in their fight against the Lango.

The army of Agoro has filled the valley of Langwen,
People of Gem, come, help me fight them.
Behold, fighting the Lango is not easy;
My brother flees from the spear of the Lango;
Walamoi, take me home
Fighting the Lango is so difficult,
We flee towards Nyamukina;
The army of Agoro has filled the valley of Langwen. (p'Bitek 1974: 114)

Okot p'Bitek, who collected this song, does not tell us in what manner it is performed. But in discussing the *otole* dance of the Acholi at which war songs are performed, Okot describes it as a very lively and moving spectacle during which war gear (spears, shields, etc.) is donned by men; warlike movements are made, as men and women advance in spectacular formations through the community, shouting and singing to the accompaniment of drum music. "The poems sung during the dance," says Okot, "are expressions of the people of the [Acholi] chiefdom about the past glories of the chiefdom, its might, its victories and its future. There is no better occasion, no better atmosphere for the expression of chiefdom 'nationalism.' " This particular song, however, sounds more like the kind sung in a retreat from a powerful enemy and may not go well with the sort of nationalistic spirit that Okot talks about.

Interclan wars are now largely a thing of the past. Okot goes on to tell us that some of these war songs (obviously, the ones that threaten the enemy or celebrate victory over him) are sung today at football matches between one clan or chiefdom and another, as well as during *otole* dance sessions held during annual festivals (in the dry season). We may perhaps assume that on such occasions even a song of retreat may be performed with a certain liveliness by the Acholi if only as an echo of the old warlike days. Everyone would laugh away the underlying message of the song as a thing of the past.

Total defeat in war is, of course, a different matter. In the Acholi song of retreat, we can at least feel that the process is not quite ended and all is not lost. The warriors may be fleeing homeward from an enemy that proves "difficult," but they are only waiting for an opportune time to strike him again; indeed, the Acholi and the Lango were so often at each other's throats, as Okot p'Bitek brings us to believe, that the occasional song of retreat hardly takes anything away from so many songs of victory. But the song of total defeat and destruction has a quite solemn ring to it.

A good example may be taken from the days of Shaka the Zulu. He made so many wars in his time, destroyed so many lives and ruined so many communities, that the effects of his fearsome career could not but be recorded in traditional song. This one was recorded from the Ngoni of Malawi.

> It is because of Zide, chief of the Soshangane people
> That though I lie down I cannot sleep.
> O Zide, chief of the Soshangane people,
> Though I lie down I cannot sleep,
> Shaka scatters us among the forests of Soshangane land. (Read 1937: 9)

This mournful song is said to be performed nowadays during girls' initiation (puberty) ceremonies among the Ngoni-(or Nguni-) speaking people of Malawi. The poet "cannot sleep," no doubt because she and her people are constantly on the run from Shaka's forces and have had to live rather unsettled lives. Margaret Read, the collector of this song, has also recorded other songs from this ethnic group in which they yearn to return to their original home (Swaziland). Zide (or Zwide), son of Ntombazi, was chief of the Ndwandwe clan; he was defeated by Shaka in 1818 and consequently driven into exile along with his people. Soshangane was originally one of Zwide's generals but later became king of a domain covering parts of present-day southern Mozambique.

We may assume that because this song is performed at ceremonies initiating girls into full womanhood, it would be done with some cheerfulness and perhaps none of that sadness which inspired it when it was first composed in the nineteenth century. Nevertheless, we can hardly miss the sense of frustration which it conveys regarding the death and destruction that several communities in southern Africa suffered in the war-mongering days of Shaka the Zulu.

Death

Few subjects are as pervasive in the poetry of any race of people as death, perhaps because of the crucial position that death occupies in the cycle of human life. The idea or experience of death of a relative or friend inspires a variety of reactions ranging from despair to resignation and even courage. In African as in many other traditional societies, elaborate ceremonies surround the occasion of death, and in these a variety of funeral songs and chants—or dirges, as they are commonly called—are performed that convey these different sentiments.

Part of the elaborateness and formality of funeral rites in many African communities comes from the fact that the dirges are often performed by skilled and more or less professional performers; sometimes they attend uninvited, but in many cases they are actually invited by the bereaved family to lend a certain grandeur or fullness to the occasion. One notable example are the *nyatiti* performers among the Luo of Kenya, who are frequently invited to funeral ceremonies and, for a fee, tune their harp (*nyatiti*) to songs in which they celebrate the life or career of the deceased and lament the death. In many African communities, funeral ceremonies are all the more elaborate if the deceased is an aged man or woman, a titled person, or a member of a guild or cult.

Among the Yoruba of Nigeria, certain rites are performed by the guild of hunters when one of them dies. As Babalola tells us in *Content and Form of Yoruba Ijala*, the funeral celebration usually lasts seven days, and on the last day the colleagues of the deceased pay their last respects. These are essentially in two parts, the *ikopa* and the *isipa*, i.e., the collection and the disposal of the various items or paraphernalia connected with the hunting life in one way or another. While the mourners are gathered together, an acknowledged *ijala* poet performs chants throughout the night (the poet might be relieved by another if the first betrays serious deficiencies in chanting), during which these items are assembled one by one in a basket. At cockcrow, the entire gathering rises and the collected items are borne in the basket and disposed of on the outskirts of the town.

One of these night-long chanting performances contains not only comments on the deceased hunter (Ogundiji) but especially details of some of the items collected in the *ikopa* ceremony.

> Hey! Hey! Hey!
> It is a forked branch
> That is suitable for making a hoe-haft
> A forkless branch is of no use for hoeing activities.
> 5 Wake up, you performers, assembled hunters, do wake up, you performers.

The hunter's hoe-haft.
This is it, isn't it?
Assembled hunters, do wake up, you performers.
Ogundiji has entirely disappeared, I see him not, father of Gbadegesin.
10 On the day Ogundiji died, Oyanniyi, he who like rain thrashes a lazy man.
Oyanniyi, killer of a leopard for a feast.
A man of fitting average height, husband of Shade, whose gun was very long, he was
    neither tall nor short.
Ogundiji's hand could reach the ceiling of his father's house, his father was the
    hunters' President.
If a needle drops into the mire, it is lost forever.
15 No needle would drop down and make a resounding noise.
It can't be smithed into a shaft or into a spear, can it?
The hunter's needle.
This is it, isn't it?
Assembled hunters, do wake up, you performers.
20 Black thread,
White thread,
Never appear on a person's neck for fun; they appear on a troubled person's neck.
    Assembled hunters, do wake up, you performers.
The hunter's black thread and his white thread, here they are.
Assembled hunters, do wake up, you performers.
25 I will chant a salute to my father,
Oyanniyi who like rain thrashes a lazy man. (Babalola 1966: 260ff.)

This was no doubt a rousing performance, no less so for the effort constantly made
by the chanting poet to keep the audience alert (lines 1, 5, 19, 22, 24). Perhaps
most notable is the way that the poet builds up ideas gradually to each item in the
ceremonial paraphernalia that the poet is about to mention. The social and philosophical reflections that introduce these items are a mark of the poet's worldly wisdom as
well as skill in the use of language. They serve the combined purpose of not only
entertaining the guests but also sustaining the seriousness of the funeral occasion.

What are the major attitudes to death as revealed in African oral poetry? Without
doubt the first reaction of the bereaved is a certain sense of loss. This may show itself
in the form of moving but dignified grief, as in a lament from the Kipsigis of Kenya
by a man whose son has been murdered and cattle taken in a raid.

Send a message to the Kapmorosek,
Tell them I am not as in past years:
Come and take back these cattle:
My big son has been murdered.
5 I have been torn like a piece of cloth,
I feel helpless as a pond.
I am not as in past years
When we were harvesting the fields,
When I was killing elephants:
10 Now the hyena of the tall grass devours me
Because I have no son living. (Mapanje and White 1983: 99)[9]

Note particularly the touching contrast between the past glory of the man, when he excelled in farming and in hunting skills, and the present state of helplessness. The image of the pond is that of a facility—lower than ground level—that is open to all and sundry and can thus be easily abused, a sharp contrast to the farming and hunting giant of past years. The grief also reveals itself in the structure of this song. It would seem as if the man wishes to tell us, after line 2, what he was like "in past years"; but he is too grieved to do so, and it is only from line 8 that he collects himself to recall his past glory. Whatever the case may be, there is a quiet dignity to the grief of the old man in this song.

On the contrary, the grieving done by women is often marked by a high degree of agitation—weeping and wailing, tearing of hair, etc. Here is a specimen of such a dirge by a woman from the Akan of Ghana.

> Mother! Mother!
> Aba Yaa!
> You know our plight!
>
> Mother! you know our plight.
> 5 You know that no one has your wisdom.
> Mother, you have been away too long.
> What of the little ones left behind?
>
> Alas!
> Who would come and restore our breath,
> 10 Unless my father Adom himself comes?
> Alas! Alas! Alas!
>
> Quite often it is a struggle for us!
> It is a long time since our people left.
> Amba, descendant of the Parrot that eats palm nuts,
> hails from the Ancestral Chamber.
>
> 15 I cannot find refuge anywhere.
> I, Amba Adoma,
> It was my grandfather that weighed gold
> And the scales broke under his weight.
>
> I am a member of Grandsire Kese's household:
> 20 We are at a loss where to go:
> Let our people come, for we are in deep distress.
> When someone is coming, let them send us something.
> Yes, I am the grandchild of the Parrot that eats palm nuts. (Nketia 1955: 69–70)

The mourner is certainly "in deep distress" and shows it clearly. There are numerous exclamations here, especially in the first three stanzas, and the mourner several times points to a deep feeling of helplessness and loss (lines 9, 15, 20). One particularly striking element in this dirge is what it tells us about the Akan concept of death, which may be found in several communities across Africa. When a person dies, he is simply assumed to have departed physically from this world but to have joined the company of ancestors who have gone before. Between these ancestors and the living there is an unbroken line of communication and contact. The living continue to address them and to appeal to them for protection and support; so vivid is the sense of connection in the above poem that the mourner seems to expect someone to actually come from the dead bringing her "something." For the purpose of this communication with the dead, an inner room may be isolated in a family's household; this is the "ancestral chamber" from which the mourner in this poem calls ("hails," line 14) on the departed. In some communities (e.g., among the Asaba Igbo of Nigeria) a shrine may be erected here and sacrifices of food and drinks periodically offered on it for the ancestors to enjoy.

Among the Akan of Ghana, the chanting of dirges is such an established art form that there is a recognized body of conventional usages, and there are quite a few standard phrases and ideas in this particular dirge. Take the word *mother*. Although this chant was addressed to a deceased woman, the word has wider cultural connotations. The Akan are a matrilineal people, for whom there is a much deeper feeling of attachment to mother than to father. Mother is seen as the source and the seat of all sympathy and support; so strong is this feeling, in fact, that in one Akan dirge addressed to a deceased man the mourner says, "Although a man, you are a mother to children" (Nketia 1955: 195). We may therefore understand the added significance of the word *mother* for the chanter of the above dirge.

A second convention here is the idea of total dependence on the deceased, which is suggested throughout but especially in the second, third, and final stanzas. Other conventions are an evocation of the ancestry of the bereaved, as in the last three stanzas, and formula statements as in lines 17, 18, and 22.

These statements and ideas occur in a wide variety of dirges recorded among the Akan and manifest themselves as a stock of usages available for manipulation by individual poets. Now, we should not assume that, because these usages crop up in one dirge after another, the sentiments contained in them are any less sincere. Despite their wide and age-long exploitation, they are, as Kwabena Nketia has pointed out, "traditional forms of expression still pregnant with emotion to the Akan, expressions which are not considered outworn in spite of frequent use" (1955: 49).

The theme of death is not always viewed with a sense of loss, however dignified. In some texts there is a spirit of acceptance of death as something we all simply have to face. This "pagan" song from the Maragoli of Kenya, despite its satirical tone, is just such a reflection of death as the inevitable fate of everyone.

> Christians used to deceive us
> That we would climb the thread on the way to heaven,
> But now the thread is broken;
> We shall all pass to the grave.
> 5   *We shall all die,*
> *We shall all die,*
> *And we shall be buried,*
> *We shall all disappear under the ground.* (Liyong 1972: 142)

The idea of a thread-way to heaven is probably a reference to a folktale motif. The Maragoli probably have variants of the story in which, while all other animals kill and eat their mothers in an effort to survive famine, the squirrel and his brother hide their mother in heaven and periodically climb up there by a rope to feed sumptuously. In an attempt to usurp this benefit, the other animals steal their way up the rope. But they are caught in the act and the rope is cut by the squirrels' mother; the animals all crash to the ground and sustain severe injuries. By reducing the rope to a mere "thread," this Maragoli song seems to reveal a certain imaginative sense of critical purpose; the contrast between the heaven up above and the grave "under the ground" is also satirically effective. The essential message of the song, however, is philosophical: death is the unavoidable lot of mankind.

The liveliness of spirit—the sheer absence of gloom—which we find in this Maragoli song is emphasized rather strongly in song traditions elsewhere in Africa. Most oral poetry in Africa that has to do with death sees it as the end of life and as bringing very deep loss to the bereaved. Not so this song from the Acholi of Uganda.

> If death were not there,
> Where would the inheritor get things?
> The cattle have been left for the inheritor;
> Ee, how would the inheritor get things?
> 5 The iron-roofed house has been left for the inheritor;
> Ee, if death were not there,
> How would the inheritor get rich?
> The bicycle has been left for the inheritor;
> This inheritor is most lucky;
> 10 Ee, brother, tell me,
> If death were not there,
> Ugly one, whose daughter would have married you?
> A wife has been left for the inheritor;
> Ee, inheritor, how would you have lived?
> 15 The house has been left for the inheritor;
> If death were not there,
> How would the inheritor get things? (p'Bitek 1974: 143)

The background to this song is a familiar one in many traditional societies across Africa. When a man dies, his belongings pass on to one or a number of his close relatives. His wife or wives are apportioned to these relatives, principally for protection since it is understood this is one thing a man owes his wife. In many cases, no sentimental or romantic relationship is expected to exist between the inheritor and the "wife" who thus comes under his care; it is even known that in some communities, a responsible adult son may, on the death of his father, inherit his mother as "wife" purely on this symbolic level. If, however, a man dies leaving behind a woman very much in her prime of life, his brother may inherit her as actual wife and she would bear him children. The "ugly" man in this song seems to have had the good fortune of inheriting not only a wife but also a house (the "iron" roof of line 5 indicates the deceased was a man of substance) and various other kinds of valuable property.

The poem certainly bubbles with high spirits which the questions and exclamations in many ways help to sustain: the "brother" in line 10 is obviously said with tongue in cheek. Such a song would perhaps be inconceivable in European or other traditions where the inheritance of a wife is unknown. But perhaps the poem is as remarkable for the point it makes about death as for the sociological information that it provides: death may well be celebrated, not lamented, for the benefits that it sometimes brings to men.

In many traditional African societies, death is conceived as a powerful god, one to be feared and avoided or else appealed to and pleaded with. But even among these peoples there are moments when the death god, persisting in his career of destruction despite several appeals, ceases to inspire any fear and is indeed treated with a certain defiance born of frustration. For instance, the Igbo of southeastern Nigeria have names such as Onwudike (Death is Powerful) and Onwuka (Death is Supreme); they also give names such as Onwubiko (Death, Please) and Onwuyali (Death, Leave Alone) to children born after previous ones have died. In a mood of frustration, however, they are inclined to give names such as Onwuma (Death May Do as He Pleases) or Onwudinjo (Death Is Unkind) when they can no longer bear the unbending will of the death god with patience. The same spirit is evidently present among the Acholi, as revealed by a song in which the young man is so overcome by the death of someone dear to him that he is willing to do battle with death in the latter's own homestead.

> Fire rages at Layima, oh,
> Fire rages in the valley of River Cumu,
> Everything is utterly utterly destroyed,
> If I could reach the homestead of death's mother,
> 5 My daughter, I would make a long grass torch;
> If I could reach the homestead of death's mother,
> I would destroy everything utterly utterly,
> Like the fire that rages in the valley of River Cumu.
> It rages at Layima, oh,
> 10 Fire rages in the valley of River Cumu,
> Everything is utterly utterly destroyed;
> If I could reach the homestead of death's mother,
> My clansmen, we would fight ruthlessly
> If I could reach the homestead of death's mother,
> 15 I would destroy everything utterly utterly
> Like the fire that rages in the valley of River Cumu. (p'Bitek 1974: 126)

Okot p'Bitek tells us, in *Horn of My Love* (pp. 22–23), that this song was performed at the funeral rites *(guru lyel)* for a notable Acholi man in 1946. After the widow and other relatives of the deceased have been shaved and much beer and food have been consumed in this ceremony lasting several weeks, the mourners fall into a spirited performance, which Okot describes.

About fifty or so yards from the homestead the mourners, who up to now were in a single file, form up in battle formation and storm the homestead in a mock attack. The women running behind them, armed with battle-axes, make ululation and shout the praise-name of the clan. On regrouping, the soloist leaps up and stamps the ground rhythmically singing the first line of the dirge, the rest take up the chorus. . . . The dancing is accompanied by drumming and the scrubbing of large half-gourds on planks of wood. The dancers may dance three to five songs before another group replaces them. Later on in the night there are joint sessions. As in all other Acholi dances there is much competition, not only between individuals, but also between the various groups taking part in the *guru lyel.* There is ample scope for self-display in the costumes, singing, performing the mock fight and so on. There is room for both individual exhibition and group performance.

Although the mourners miss the bereaved man, the violence with which they threaten death is a way of saying that death had no right to take him away; if they had their way they would destroy death's home utterly so as to bring back the dead man. The vigorous stamping movement of the dancers aptly underscores the challenge they throw at death. The reference to "death's mother" is very effective: if death were to attempt to escape his attackers, his mother's homestead would perhaps be his last place of refuge. The "daughter" in line 5 is no doubt a tender, sympathetic address to the widow of the deceased; the shift of attention to the clan at large (line 13) has both a social appeal and a poetic effect. There is a deliberate tone of irreverence in this challenge to death, but it simply goes to confirm the point that in African culture the concept of death does not always inspire fear, gloom, or a sense of loss and helplessness. Clearly, the mourners are asking death defiantly, "Is this the worst you can do?"

7. Oral Narratives

In this chapter we are going to discuss what are generally referred to as folktales. So long as we disabuse our minds of the sort of prejudice which earlier generations of scholars had about the concept of folk as the "uneducated" and therefore irrational and unimaginative dwellers of small communities, then there may be situations in which we can excuse the use of the term *folktale* for purposes of convenience. The term *oral narrative* is, however, preferred not only because it leaves little room for that prejudice but also because—perhaps like the term *oral literature*—it gives primary emphasis to the medium of expression of this form of art, which is word of mouth.

The subject of this chapter has also frequently been called prose narratives, but the word *prose* is in some ways misleading. For instance, what about the numerous performances of tales to the background of music, in which the storytellers take care to fit their statements within the regulated or timed beats of their instruments? Would we not be justified in setting down those statements in the "verse" lines defined by the successive segments of regulated music? Certain narratives are told entirely in "song" voice, like the Mau Mau guerrilla war song discussed in the preceding chapter, performed to regulated music. But other tales, although narrated in "normal speech" voice, are situated within a background of regulated instrumental music; it would be wrong to set them down in passages of the kind used in writing fiction and essays.

Even when the words of a story are not performed against a musical background, "prose" may not be the proper form in which to set them down. The American scholar Dennis Tedlock has since 1971 been in the forefront of those opposing the use of prose in recording oral narratives. In chapter 11 we will be examining his arguments further. For the moment, we may just mention his principal reasons for taking that stand: (1) in telling a story, a person observes various breath gaps not only because he or she wishes to catch a breath between one statement and another but also because certain dramatic tensions within the story force those breaks upon the person's statement; and (2) in any storytelling performance, various levels of vocalization are used—high, medium, low; loud, soft; etc. None of these techniques can be adequately represented by the normal prose form which, as Tedlock says, "has no existence outside the written page" (1977: 513).

On the whole I am a supporter of Tedlock's position on this issue, although I do not find it convenient to adopt all his recommendations. As far as I am concerned, the distinction traditionally observed between prose and verse does not make much sense in the study of oral narratives. There is much truth in a statement made by Lestrade in connection with Bantu oral literature:

> The distinction between prose and verse is a small one. . . . . the border-line between them is extremely difficult to ascertain and define, while the verse-technique, in so far as verse can be separated from prose, is extremely free and unmechanical. Broadly speaking, it may be said that the difference between prose and verse in Bantu literature is one of spirit rather than of form, and that such formal distinction as there is is one of degree of use rather than of quality of formal elements. Prose tends to be less emotionally charged, less moving in content and full-throated in expression than verse; and also—but only in the second place—less formal in structure, less rhythmical in movement, less metrically balanced. (1937: 306)

It is true that Lestrade remains relatively tied to the old distinction between prose and verse encouraged by the print culture. But he recognizes the looseness of this distinction, and he even more identifies the role of performance in the relationship between one kind of oral text and another. In chapter 6 we saw this relationship in terms of the level of musical manipulation of the voice. Most oral narratives are told in ordinary speech voice, whereas chants and songs are distinguished by being performed in progressively modulated tones of voice, with songs representing the highest level. However, in many performances of oral narratives in Africa the artist moves quite freely between speech, chant, and song modes—so freely sometimes that it is difficult to determine where one ends and the other begins. But most earlier (especially European) editors of these tales put them uniformly into prose because it was for them the most convenient way of representing this rather troublesome art form. In the process, they did considerable damage to the oral-literary qualities of the tales.

Let us now turn to a brief survey of the work of these scholars to see in what ways they tampered with those qualities.

Schools of Thought

Of all the branches of African oral literature, oral narratives have received the widest attention in terms of collection and study. Work in this connection by both amateur and professional scholars goes back as far as 1828, when the Frenchman Jean-François Roger published (in Paris) a collection of Wolof tales from Senegal. In chapter 1 we discussed the various stages of development of the study of African oral literature generally; some of the issues raised there will echo here as we trace the arguments of the various groups of scholars who have made significant statements about the nature of African oral narratives.

Evolutionism

The nineteenth-century English biologist Charles Darwin was struck by the fossils of various biological species that he encountered in his studies, especially by the ways in which many plants and animals that lived thousands and sometimes millions of years ago (as revealed by their fossils embedded in rocks scattered over various regions of the earth) have been reduced from their gigantic sizes to the manageable proportions in which we find them today. One of the major conclusions which he reached in his studies of the changes was that these species, where they have survived (for some of them have disappeared completely), have been able to do so by (a) fighting off and even destroying other species, as well as some of their own kind, in order to secure the available food resources, thus proving themselves the fittest in the struggle for survival, and (b) having their enormous sizes reduced and their features altered considerably not only to fit them better for the struggle but to accommodate them to the respective environments to which they have been forced to move in search of better conditions for life. Other biologists working along the same lines have essentially confirmed Darwin's conclusions as being valid for biological species across the world.

Darwin's views had a great impact on scholars of his time working in the area of human culture. In their efforts to trace the origins of human civilization and ideas—very much as Darwin researched the origins of biological species—these cultural historians set about trying to find out what were the earliest forms of various aspects of human achievement in religion, technology, government, etc.; for instance, what were the beginnings of the religious life (ritual, worship, and so on) and the manufacture of various implements (fire, houses, etc.)? They found that the best way to answer these questions was to go to various "primitive" societies existing today in Africa, the Far East, and America as well as rural communities in Europe and to record stories from them about these things. A comparison of such stories from around the world would enable them to achieve a synthesis, which would answer these great questions about origins. They were encouraged to make their cross-cultural comparisons by an idea enunciated by a contemporary German thinker, Adolf Bastian, and widely accepted, that since all human beings were created alike, there must be a uniform body of "elementary ideas" (German *Elementargedanken*) shared by all human cultures at similar stages of development. Consequently, when they discovered that there were striking similarities in themes and ideas contained in stories from cultures as far apart as the African and the American Indian, they saw these as sure proof of the "psychological unity" of mankind.

One other belief held by these cultural evolutionists colored their attitudes toward the stories they collected as well as the people who told them. Darwin proposed that the characteristic features of the biological species that have survived today were determined by the environment and other natural conditions; the species themselves had no hand in shaping the evolution. Similarly, the cultural evolutionists held that the stories found among present-day "primitive" peoples have simply survived in their memories through several generations of transmission and that these peoples have not made any conscious changes or contributions to the body of ideas contained in the stories.

The outstanding figures in this branch of learning were the British scholars Edward Burnet Tylor, James George Frazer, and Andrew Lang. Frazer made perhaps the deepest impact on the scholars who came to Africa in the first third of this century either as colonial administrators or as missionaries. From these observations of life and culture among "primitive" peoples, anthropology was taking shape, in the early twentieth century, as a new branch of learning. Frazer was one of those who gave it its shape. He never himself visited any of these so-called primitive societies, but he provided certain documentary guides which the outward-bound scholars took along with them, requiring them to investigate various aspects of "primitive" life and culture, from ritual or magical practices to stories told. Out of these data, pieced together from various areas of the world, Frazer composed several monumental works, most notable of which was *The Golden Bough* (in thirteen volumes).

Of the scholars who came to Africa under the inspiration of Frazer and his colleagues we may mention a few. John Roscoe, a colonial officer in Uganda, published various works about the area, most notable of which is *The Baganda: An Account of Their Native Customs and Beliefs* (1911). Of the origin of Baganda oral narrative traditions he gives this as the primary explanation:

> There were many things which were beyond the understanding of the people, and they wished in some way to account for them; with this object in view they seem to have made a history which would explain the origin of their race, their kings and their gods. As they were recounted, these stories were added to in a variety of ways, and thus there were different versions of what must have been the same story in the first instance; many of these legends have for years been handed down to successive generations as true accounts, and have passed from the legendary stage into history and are believed by the people to be a trustworthy account of the origin of man and beast. (p. 460)

The Reverend Henri Junod, a missionary in the Transvaal region of South Africa, published (among other things) a two-volume study of the Thonga, *The Life of a South African Tribe* (1912–13). On the authorship of the stories told by the people he studied, he tells us:

> This production is essentially collective: tales are not created, on all sides, by individual authors; but they are modified, altered and enriched, as they are transmitted from one person to another, to such an extent that new types, new combinations are adopted and a true development takes place. (1913: 202)

Edwin Smith and Andrew Dale worked among the Ila of present-day Zambia, the subject of their two-volume study *The Ila-speaking Peoples of Northern Rhodesia* (1920). Of the attitudes of the narrators to the tales they told, Smith and Dale have this to say:

> But, however it may be with present-day retailers of the stories we are confident that the tales arose in the stage of culture when the vital differences between men and animals were not yet recognized. . . . it was not unnatural for the makers of these tales to ascribe human characteristics to the lower animals, for they did not recognize any psychic difference between them and us. (p. 338).

Roger Dennet studied the Congolese, and in his categorization of their tale traditions he includes the following type:

Then, we have tales which begin, "A long, long time ago, before even our ancestors knew the use of fire, when they ate grass like the animals," etc., which then go on to tell how a river-spirit first pointed out to them the mandioca root and the banana. These I think go a long way to prove that the agricultural age was prior to the pastoral and hunting age. (1898: 18)

We can see from these statements various shades of the one overriding interest in evolutionist scholarship: change. Roscoe sees the tales in terms of the changes they undergo in their movement from one generation of tellers to another; in true evolutionist search for origins, he deduces that what the Baganda regard as true history today had its beginnings in fanciful tales told in the past as a way of explaining abstract ideas or complex phenomena. For Smith and Dale the roots of the human drama in animal tales lie in the early stage of human psychology when people saw themselves and the animals around them as essentially one. And Dennet sees the tales as providing clues about the origins and history of human economic activity.

This overriding interest in change and in the history of culture had consequences which were somewhat detrimental to the literary quality of the tales. Some of these scholars were often struck by the artistry displayed by African narrators in the performance of the tales and even in the manipulation of the text. The passage from Junod is notable for the credit it gives to the artistic growth of the oral narrative tradition. But even Junod was subject to the narrow-minded interest in the history of civilization shown by his contemporaries. His statement about the collective nature of the authorship of the tales reflects the belief widely held at the time that African tribes were still living "in the collective stage of human society" (1913: 205) which precedes the emergence of the individual creative personality. Since no one artist could be credited with the original composition of a tale and the tales were constantly being altered anyway, the interest of the scholar was therefore concentrated not so much on the artistic beauty revealed by the text as on those essential ideas that have survived several generations of performance and provide clues about human cultural history. The texts of African oral narratives published by this generation of scholars were thus heavily edited—indeed were in many cases presented in summary form—in such a way as to eliminate several of those oral literary qualities that we discussed in chapter 4.

Diffusionism

In order of time, diffusionism as an organized line of research precedes evolutionism. But while the arguments of the evolutionists, especially in the area of oral literature, have been mostly discredited and abandoned, some of the methods if not quite the aims of diffusionist scholarship have continued to appeal to students to this day. The two groups of scholars are basically interested in the same issues of change and the history of culture but take rather different views and approaches. For instance, while evolutionists believe that cultural change takes place vertically, i.e., from one stage or step to the next, diffusionists hold that this change takes place horizontally as a result of contact between peoples. Both groups of scholars engage in a comparison of tales from various distinct societies and find striking similarities in many cases. But whereas evolutionists explain these similarities on the grounds that human beings everywhere have the same psychological makeup, diffusionists think rather that there must have been a historical line of contact between the societies concerned, though this may not be immediately apparent.

Diffusionist research into oral narratives began seriously in the early nineteenth century, spearheaded by two separate groups which may be referred to as the Indianist school and the Finnish school. The Indianist branch was founded by the brothers Jacob and Wilhelm Grimm. Having collected a large number of tales from living informants in their native Germany and elsewhere, they were struck by the similarities in the material of several European tales and decided to trace the original source of these tales. By a careful analysis of the linguistic components of the tales and an observation of the patterns of change undergone by them from one language area to another, the Grimms came to a major conclusion: European tales, like European languages, were descended from a so-called Aryan race that once inhabited a region in north central Asia.

The theory was expanded by subsequent scholars. Max Muller, a German who settled in England, saw "Aryan" not as a race but rather as a language family to which all European languages belonged. In his own linguistic analysis of numerous European and Oriental tales, he proposed that as the tales traveled with various groups of migrants moving from east to west, the words and names in them were corrupted or severely distorted by what he called a "disease of language." He was sure that by a comparative analysis of variants of any tale from several language areas and a careful application of recognized laws of linguistic change (the most notable being "Grimm's Law"), he could reconstruct the original Aryan tale. He did this analysis on a large number of tales and reached the curious conclusion that in every case the story revolved around the figure of the sun in one form of struggle or another.

Two more scholars of the Indianist school should be mentioned. The German Theodor Benfey, who worked mostly on Indian tales, proposed that India was the original homeland of all tales in the Indo-European world and that the tales moved from India to the West by diffusion, especially by oral transmission from one community to another. The French Emmanuel Cosquin agreed largely with Benfey but came upon the evidence of various tales which convinced him that Egypt was an even older homeland than India. On the whole, however, scholars accepted the theory that India was the original source from which most traditional tales dispersed to various parts of the world.

The Finnish school was born even in the generation of Grimm. From 1828 Elias Lonnrot started collecting heroic tales from all over Finland, ultimately weaving them into a composite story which he published in 1835 as *The Kalevala,* the national epic of the Finnish people. This encouraged many Finnish scholars not only in the collection of tales and songs but especially in the systematic classification of their component units into indexed categories. The most notable work in this regard was done by Antti Aarne, who compiled an index grouping a large body of tales across the world into so-called types: a tale type is a kind or class of tale that makes a particular point or deals with a specific issue (e.g., a tale of "magic flight" or a "werewolf" tale). Aarne's tale-type index was later expanded and translated from Finnish into English by the American scholar Stith Thompson as *The Types of the Folktale*. The idea of the tale type was to reduce all known tales of the world into the smallest units of composition. But Thompson felt that the type was too large as a unit; instead of a whole tale, he felt that the smallest unit was really the motif, this being any of the many components that make up the tale, e.g., the seduction of a woman in stories about a werewolf or help rendered by a little animal (such as a rat or rabbit) in stories about miraculous escape. He therefore went on to compile a massive, six-volume *Motif-Index of Folk Literature* (1955–58) covering all the motifs recorded in oral narratives around the world, including Africa.

The program of diffusionist analysis looked quite scientific, but the aims were too ambitious. First, having assumed that tales moved from one group of people to another, the scholars set about dividing the world into "culture areas," or geographic regions inhabited by people who share related social traditions and are therefore bound by a certain psychological unity. In this way the diffusionists hoped to follow narrative units (types and motifs) from one geographical area of the globe to another. In analyzing a tale, therefore, the idea was both to list the various tale units that make up the tale and the origins and routes of diffusion or travel of the units. This would be done for as many variants of that tale as the scholar could lay hands on. When all these variants have been brought together and their components matched and compared, the scholar could then go ahead to the final stage of diffusionist scholarship— constructing what would be considered the original, or "archetypal," version of the tale from which the numerous variants may have grown.

The search for such origins and archetypes turned out to be a futile effort, since abandoned by diffusionist scholars around the world. But they have continued to have recourse to the monumental indexes by Aarne and Thompson, and other indexes have in fact been compiled. For Africa, these works are the most notable, all of them originally presented as doctoral theses at American universities:

1. May A. Klipple, "African Folktales with Foreign Analogues," Indiana University, Bloomington, 1938
2. Kenneth W. Clarke, "A Motif-Index of the Folktales of Culture Area V: West Africa," Indiana University, Bloomington, 1957
3. E. Ojo Arewa, "A Classification of Folktales of the Northern East African Cattle Area by Types," University of California, Berkeley, 1966
4. Winifred Lambrecht, "A Tale Type Index for Central Africa," University of California, Berkeley, 1967

Although some scholars have cited these indexes in their references to tale types and motifs, their practical value has remained highly questionable; the pursuit of types and motifs has itself become a futile academic exercise. Just how futile was revealed by a controversy among American scholars over whether the tales told by African Americans originated in Africa or Europe. The articles in which they made their views known have been collected in a volume edited by D. J. Crowley, *African Folklore in the New World* (1977). The controversy started with the claim by Richard

Dorson in *American Negro Folktales* (1975) that Africa has contributed no more than 10 percent of the body of Afro-American tales he had studied. Many of his colleagues—notably William Bascom and Alan Dundes—reacted by publishing evidence to prove Dorson wrong. Dorson countered with other arguments, and the whole controversy has remained—despite the harsh words used—largely unresolved.

A far more interesting aspect of this debate lies in the origins which the scholars try to propose for certain tale types. In an earlier publication (1972), Dorson cites a Vai (Liberia) trickster tale "about how Turtle made Leopard his Riding Horse" and gives it a European origin. In his contribution to *African Folklore in the New World,* Dundes on the contrary cites references within the African indexes of Kenneth Clarke and Ojo Arewa to demonstrate that the Vai tale is of an indigenous African origin. Such futile academic arguments are inevitable in the pursuit of the mirage of origins. In many ways diffusionist scholarship has proved itself little more useful in the study of African oral narratives than the evolutionist.

Psychoanalysis

Psychoanalysis is a method of investigating the mental background of any human activity. It has been used in the study of various aspects of literature—poetry, drama, and narrative. This approach had its origins in the study of mental health, and its founding fathers were Sigmund Freud and Carl Gustav Jung, the Austrian and Swiss psychiatrists.

Freud tried to treat his mentally disturbed patients by listening to them as they retold their past experiences, from which the doctor could then reconstruct the roots of the mental problem. But rather than lead these patients through their reminiscences by "suggesting" words and images around which their accounts were to be built—as his often impatient predecessors and teachers did as a rule—Freud preferred to allow them to engage in "free association" between words and images as they occurred to the patients during their reminiscences. Freud interrupted them only minimally and afterward undertook the careful job of linking together and interpreting the somewhat disordered images in the accounts that they gave and thus identifying the source of the mental derangement.

The patients were encouraged to go as far back in their reminiscences as they possibly could, even into childhood and the family background; the accounts they gave also included dreams they had had. From his numerous sessions with these patients Freud came to some quite radical conclusions. For instance, the images or symbols contained in the disordered accounts, even those going back to childhood experiences, had a sexual basis. Freud pressed this sexual element into his reading not only of the accounts by mental patients (of their real-life experiences and their dreams) but also of the dreams of apparently sane people and, finally, of myths or folktales of ancient and "primitive" peoples. Why did he link mental illness with dreams and myths? His explanation was that the images found in dreams and tales are as distorted and disorderly as those operating in the mind of a mental patient. This can be further explained by the fact that in these three areas the mind is operating at an "unconscious" level. When we are awake and in our right senses, there are certain shameful and irrational desires that we entertain but which are "repressed" by certain reflexes within us that control civilized social conduct. But the moment we are no longer subject to such controls—when we are asleep or when we are mentally disturbed—our minds lose their consciousness and are driven to indulge those immoral impulses in a search for "wish-fulfilment." In such an uncontrolled exercise, images simply run riot and defy all laws of reason—as, for instance, when in dreams and in folktales, human beings walk on their heads or make love in the most unimaginable circumstances.

Freud made various interpretations of myths or folktales in which these ideas of sexuality, wish-fulfilment, etc. are united. But by far the most famous analysis he made was of the ancient Greek tale of King Oedipus. "King Oedipus," he tells us, "who slew his father Laius and wedded his mother Jocasta, is nothing more or less than a wish-fulfilment—the fulfilment of the wish of our childhood" (Brill 1938: 306). This statement may be taken as a significant watershed in the growth of Freudian psychoanalysis in at least one respect. In encouraging his patients to go back to their childhood experiences Freud preferred to see mental problems from the limited point of view of the individual's family history; but by identifying the Oedipus complex—i.e., the urge for incest—as a universal human problem, he was taking his vision beyond the limited circumstances of the individual.

This universalizing element in psychoanalysis, whereby the symbols contained in dreams and folktales as well as in mental illness are thought to have a larger human rather than an individualist meaning, was pursued by Freud's students and followers, some of whom, like Jung, departed fundamentally from Freud's views. Freud's argument that the sexual impulse (not to mention an incest wish) can be found in everybody's early childhood shocked the world, and Jung, the son of a minister, was determined to remove this disrepute attaching to the psychoanalytic movement. Contrary to Freud, he proposed that sexual impulses have no place in the first few years of the life of a human being; rather, he saw this as the period of utmost purity and innocence and the source of that civilized conduct which human beings ultimately attain. When he analyzed mental patients he allowed them to narrate childhood experiences just as much as Freud did, but his interpretations frequently tried to show that these patients were, in their various aberrations, simply struggling to wander back to that natural purity and those seeds of culture of early childhood from which they had deviated in their adult experiences. These seeds of culture were represented in Jungian analysis as "archetypal images," the universal symbols by which Jung sought to unravel the message behind a variety of accounts.

Jung, who delved into the "science of mythology" more deeply than Freud did, analyzed folktales across the cultures of the world—from the myths of the Greeks and Asiatic Indians to those of American Indians—in terms of these universal symbols rather than in terms of the limited circumstances of the narrator or even of his culture. Some of the archetypes recognized by Jung in various folktales are: the mother image, a symbol of tenderness and all-nourishing goodness; the child-hero, as in various heroic tales, representing the urge to return to the purity and innocence of childhood; the animus (in woman) and the anima (in man) as the spirit drive which helps the human being to assert a "superordinate personality," or the self towering above all obstacles and threats to it; and so on. Various personalities and figures occurring in folktales were interpreted by Jung along such lines with the aim of stressing not the perversity which Freud recognized as inborn in man but the innate goodness which Jung was convinced man came into the world with.

There has been little discussion of African folktales along psychoanalytic lines. On the whole this approach has been viewed with suspicion especially by anthropologists (about whom we shall speak in the next section), who prefer to study societies and their concerns from their own peculiar perspectives rather than in the light of universal or cross-cultural symbols. The American scholar Paul Radin has briefly discussed African folktales along the archetypal lines plotted by Jung. But many of his contemporaries (and he himself) generally recognized that there was very little demonstrable basis in social life for the so-called archetypes; in other words, those archetypal symbols are of questionable value in interpreting the peculiar problems and interests of a society as revealed in its folktales.

The Freudian approach, with some modifications, would seem to hold greater possibilities for analysis of these tales. Another American scholar, Melville Herskovits, once tested the Oedipus theory on a number of tales he collected from Dahomey (present Republic of Benin). He found the element of contest with the father present but not that of marrying the mother or even the least indication of an incest wish. Even in those tales in which father and son fight, the son never kills his father as Oedipus does Laius; there is always some settlement which prevents a horror that is clearly un-African (1958: 94).

The Freudian approach is also useful in probing the differences between one version of a tale and another, as a reflection of the personal backgrounds as well as the peculiar styles of the respective narrators. This approach is particularly necessary in our efforts to explore the literary qualities in the imaginative act of storytelling. In their various psychoanalytic studies of the folktale both Freud and Jung, and their followers, were convinced that the tales, like dreams and mental aberrations, are a product of the mind operating at an unconscious level and have nothing at all to do with the personal interests or skill of the narrators. In chapter 2 we saw how the investigation by Tunde Ipinmisho of two independent storytellers in his hometown telling the same story has revealed differences in detail which have basically to do with the different personal backgrounds and experiences, as well as talents of the two men.

Functionalism

With the growth of the discipline of anthropology in the first half of this century, serious questions began to be asked about the guiding premises of the schools of thought that we have examined so far. All three schools take a somewhat universal view of human cultural activity: evolutionists trace the "elementary ideas" in folktales in their search for the origins and development of culture and civilization across mankind; diffusionists evolve a system for tracing the movement of cultural units (e.g., tale motifs) from one area of the world to another; and psychoanalysts, especially of the line of Jung, analyze tales on the basis of universal (archetypal) symbols revealed in them irrespective of the human or cultural backgrounds of the tales. Perhaps the fundamental objection to these styles of analysis could be stated as follows. Why must we assume from the start that these various traits (motifs, archetypes, etc.) occur always in the same or easily recognizable forms, or that the different cultures around the world are similarly predisposed to harbor them? How much do we know, anyway, about these various cultures to lump them so carelessly together in comparative analyses?

These are very much the sort of questions asked by the Polish-born British scholar Bronislaw Malinowski. The discipline of anthropology grew out of the largely armchair work of scholars such as Frazer in putting together a wide variety of reports and accounts of the folklore (tales, customs, etc.) of numerous communities outside European culture into ambitious studies arrogantly labeled "primitive culture" or "primitive society." But it was Malinowski and his contemporaries, notably A. R. Radcliffe-Brown and Franz Boas, who firmly established the discipline by promoting detailed "scientific" investigations of those communities from which the rather "theoretical" syntheses of Frazer and his group were fed. Malinowski disagreed with this group in a fundamental way. There is no scientific logic, he argued, in first assuming that human beings everywhere think and behave alike before undertaking the study of any aspect of the life of a society (e.g., its oral literature, art, customs, etc.); it would be more rewarding to study these areas of culture by looking closely at the functions which they perform in the life of the society, for every society may be said to have a body of functions or needs that characterizes it and marks it apart from any other society. Functionalism thus emerged as a method of studying the life and culture of a society by examining the functions or roles performed by anything practiced in the society (e.g., the tales told by its members) as well as the ways in which these functions help to ensure the survival of the society.

Malinowski's functionalist views on oral narratives are adequately stated in two of his numerous publications, *Argonauts of the Western Pacific* (1922) and *Myth in Primitive Psychology* (1926). The first is a full-scale report of his field researches into the life and culture of the Trobriands, a group of islands in the Pacific Ocean off the coast of Australia. It helped to establish his brand of anthropology—ethnography, or a systematic record arising from detailed eyewitness investigation of a well-defined community of people—as a fashionable alternative to the more theoretical armchair analysis of the type practiced by Frazer. In this book Malinowski examines the traditional system of commerce carried on in these islands and the tales and rituals that support this system. His analysis brings him to conclude that the tales are a true record of the customs and traditions of the past. Such tales, performed under ritual conditions on a repetitive basis, he calls myths, in the sense that everybody knows and tells them; they are treated with a high degree of respect because they contain all that is sacred to the people, particularly the place or role of their divinities in the people's traditional history; and they serve as a "charter" or reference for proper conduct because they preserve the ways in which the society has always behaved since its early beginnings.

Myth in Primitive Psychology distinguishes the various types of stories told by the Trobriand Islanders, emphasizing the role of their myths as charters of conduct and as authoritative accounts of the people's traditions. So authoritative, indeed, did Malinowski consider these tales that he was unwilling to see them as operating on any symbolic level but took their meanings at surface level. The book is also notable for its classic recommendation, already cited, that ethnographers, in recording texts of oral literature (especially tales), should give as detailed attention as possible to the "context of situation" in which this literature is performed.

The followers of Malinowski, notably Edmund Leach and Raymond Firth, adhered largely to his functionalist approach to social traditions but made a few significant departures which put certain labels on their brand of anthropology. For instance, whereas Malinowski believed that the body of functions or needs recognized by any society—otherwise known as its "functional unity"—invariably worked in the interests and toward the preservation of society, these later scholars did not believe that society remained unchanged in every case; there are, they argued, frequently conflicts (e.g., disputes over kingship) and contingencies (e.g., the colonial or missionary presence) within society that ultimately cause it to disintegrate or undergo certain fundamental changes (e.g., the migration of certain elements in the society or a change in its pattern of beliefs). Consequently, while in his analysis of cultural data (e.g., tales) Malinowski usually looked for factors that brought stabilization to a society, in their analyses Leach and his colleagues looked more closely at the pattern or structure of interests within their evidence that held the potential for conflict. This tendency won them the label "structural-functionalists," for although they agreed that whatever is done by members of a society has a basically utilitarian or practical function, they were more inclined to identify a pattern of disagreements within society that moved it toward change.

A second departure from Malinowski brought about by these later scholars had to do with their mode of analysis of tales. Influenced partly by the growing fashion of symbolic analysis of narratives encouraged by psychoanalysis and partly by their deeper look at the pattern of interests within a social structure, these scholars were no longer prepared to accept Malinowski's superficial interpretation of the elements within their data but indulged freely in symbolic readings. For this they were also called "symbolic anthropologists."

Both brands of functionalism—Malinowskian and post-Malinowskian—have been used in the study of African oral narratives. William Bascom, in his analysis of the story of "Oba's Ear" as told both among the Yoruba of Nigeria and the descendants of Yoruba slaves in Brazil, finds that the tale "explains and validates various religious beliefs and ritual practices" among the Yoruba and that in its various versions the tale helps to ensure the survival of the ethnic solidarity of the two branches of the Yoruba race, those of the homeland and those of the diaspora (1977a: 24). And Jan Vansina, in his discussion of tales of royal descent among the Rwanda of Central Africa, thinks that the tales reflect the hereditary system of rulership which ensures the permanent stability of Rwanda social structure; the tales provide a rule, or charter, for the system of royal succession in Rwanda (1965: 73).

Structural-functional interpretations of African oral narratives are perhaps the ones more in evidence, especially because most of the anthropologists who have worked in Africa have met the continent at the point of transition from a traditional system of values to a culture heavily influenced by the European presence. The ideas of conflict and change have therefore been more prominent in their analyses of the tales. For instance, R. G. Willis, in his analysis of the historical tales of the Ufipa of Tanzania, uses symbolic interpretation to discover two distinct attitudes or foci of interest reflecting the dual lines of development of the society (1964). Aylward Shorter's study of Kimbu (Tanzania) historical narratives, also done on the model of symbolic analysis, reveals a similar structure of social conflicts in the people's accounts of their origins (1969). And even in an analysis of animal tales from the Kaguru, again of Tanzania, Thomas Beidelman is able to discover, through symbolic interpretation, a conflict of interests between social and antisocial forces (1961).

Functionalist studies of African oral narratives have been useful in discovering the various ways in which literature reflects the ways of life, the outlooks, and the interests of the societies that practice it. The symbolic analyses done by the later generation of functionalists have also helped to erase the false impression of earlier scholars that African oral literature reveals a low, primitive level of imaginative thinking of the people; the symbolists have clearly shown the complex level of symbolic thought contained in the tales. But on the whole these anthropologists did not follow the advice of Malinowski that in recording the texts of oral narratives and other forms of literature they should give close attention to the context of situation (e.g., participation by members of the audience) in which the texts were performed. The anthropologists were more interested in seeing oral narratives as records of a people's way of life than as works of imaginative literature. Consequently, many of the texts they collected and published are not very useful for a literary study of the subject.

Formalism

To a large extent, formalism came into existence as a reaction against diffusionism. These two approaches to the study of narratives are devoted primarily to breaking down the tale to discover the constituent units from which it has been formed. But the aim of the diffusionists was both too ambitious and too diffuse. The tale was picked to pieces to isolate the motifs it used, to determine the tale type to which it belonged, to trace the tale progressively so as to discover its original home, and finally to construct the possible original version of the tale. Formalists felt that all this was a waste of effort because it led to needless hairsplitting controversy. It is far more important, they argued, to observe how the units of a tale are arranged progressively to make up the tale than to hunt for motifs and types and then begin to speculate about origins and originals.

The champion of this new approach was the Russian scholar Vladimir Propp. In his epoch-making book, *The Morphology of the Folktale* (Russian edition 1928, English translation 1968), he begins by giving credit to diffusionists such as Antti Aarne who reduced all the available folk tales of the world into a manageable (tale-type) index for easy reference and thus saved scholars of the folktale a lot of confusion. But he thinks that the usefulness of their work does not go beyond that. For instance, Aarne tries to reduce folktales to three basic categories—animal tales, tales proper (i.e., human tales), and anecdotes (i.e., jokes)—and Propp wonders how we can trust such a classification when we have not yet done a detailed enough study of the characteristic features of each category. The study of the characteristic form of a tale, he argues, is the first real step in understanding what category or kind of tale it is; when we have done that, then we can begin to pursue the origins of the tale and other such questions that the diffusionists have busied themselves with. Propp then sets about to do a morphological study of a particular kind of tale that will show its constituent motifs (which he calls functions) and their relationships in the plot of the tale.

Propp chooses his examples from a collection of one hundred tales made by a fellow Russian scholar (Afanas'ev) and which he classifies as fairy tales. These are mostly tales of fantastic events such as magic flights, and the abduction of maidens and their rescue by heroes aided by witches. Propp is able to fit the various functions of these tales into a standard scheme and to conclude that in a fairy tale there are no more than thirty-one such functions. In this way, he hopes, he has been able not only to eliminate the confusion created by having an extraordinary number of motifs and types but to lead the way in the proper classification of tales.

Whatever Propp's contribution, one major shortcoming seems to have marred his program: its sheer impersonality. To start with, he states categorically that the personality or skill of a storyteller has no bearing whatsoever on the nature or structure of the fairy tale; he is not interested at all in considering the artistic quality of a tale. Second, he emphasizes that the functions of the tale remain constant irrespective of the persons or characters that perform them. This abstract, depersonalized approach made formalism rather unpopular after the 1930s, and later scholars have sought to revise it somewhat. Some of these revisions came from within Russia. For instance, Eleazer Meletinsky, while generally following Propp's pattern of analysis of a tale into motifs and their relationships in the plot scheme of the tale, shows how this tale pattern reflects the norms and traditions of society. This interest in social life and social conventions certainly restores to formalism that humane outlook which Propp may seem to have denied it.

Such improvements are also evident in formalist studies of African oral narratives, and we may mention just two of these. Much work has been done on a characteristic African tale type known as the trickster tale; Alan Dundes's study (1971) is surely one of the most enlightening. This category of tales—mostly of animal but also of human characters—has to do with trickery and breach of faith. In his analysis of two of these tales from East Africa, Dundes finds there are basically five functions, or what he calls motifemes, in the following order.

1. Friendship: The tale often assumes or specifies a situation of friendship or solidarity between the characters involved.
2. Contract: Next, there is frequently an agreement reached or some kind of appointment made, which has the value or aim of testing the friendship.
3. Violation: One of the parties in the contract invariably does something that amounts to a breach of faith, e.g., by deceiving or cheating the other.
4. Discovery: The deceived or cheated party frequently discovers the trick played on it or the violation of the agreement reached. In many cases this is followed by a countertrick or counterviolation from the offended party.
5. End of Friendship: The final situation in this sequence is generally the termi-

nation of the cordial relationship between the parties, sometimes with the punishment or disgrace of the original culprit.

A random sampling of African tales, especially those involving trickster characters such as the tortoise, the hare, the rabbit, or the spider, does bear out this neat sequence of moves in the tale.

There are two principal merits in Dundes's formalist essay. The first is that it reduces Propp's rather uwieldy number of functions. Although Propp and Dundes are not really dealing with the same type of tale, it has been clear to scholars for some time that a good number of the functions identified by Propp are really quite similar and the number thirty-one could be scaled down. Dundes's plot scheme is both tidy and clear. A second merit in the essay comes when Dundes compares African trickster tales with American Indian trickster tales. He finds that whereas in the African folktale tradition there is considerable evidence of social cohesion and a communalistic life-style, the American Indian tradition reveals rather a certain individualism and self-centeredness. For instance, whereas in African tales of deceit and trickery there is the picture of a close bond of friendship bringing characters together, the characters in the Indian tales act very much on their own terms and in their own interests. And whereas some African tales end with a question which is meant to be debated and resolved by the audience, the American Indian narrator does not allow his audience any such participatory role. These are clearly sociological insights which have somewhat broadened the narrow outlook of Propp's formalism.

Similar improvements have been made by Marion Kilson in her study (1976) of Mende (Sierra Leone) trickster tales. She is very much a disciple of Propp in looking carefully at the sequence of events that make up the plot of a tale. But she goes beyond both Propp and Dundes by reducing the structure of the tale to three broad stages of development, which she calls the "triadic-sequential" scheme: (1) the initial phase, in which the main characters and the situation or setting of the story are introduced; (2) the medial phase, during which the task or problem posed in the initial phase is tackled and resolved; (3) the final phase, involving the outcome of this resolution, e.g., the award of penalties or gifts. The medial phase, in particular, compresses about twenty-five intermediate functions in Propp's morphology. Finally, Kilson follows earlier social scientists such as Dundes in situating her study of the tales within the context of the society. Hers is not just an abstract morphology; she tries her best to show not only how the structure is borne out by the tales but also how it is a reflection of the social life and the world view of the Mende of Sierra Leone.

These later formalist studies of African oral narratives are perhaps not as guilty as those of Propp and his generation in underestimating the personal element in the tale. But not much improvement has been made in recognizing the literary qualities of the tale. Dundes, in distinguishing between African and American Indian styles of performance, has shown only a token interest in the subtle literary or artistic issues; he is looking at a general stylistic trait shown by the society at large rather than at the peculiar qualities or twists of an individual artist. While detailed attention is given to the content and structure of a tale, little is said about the manner of its telling and the bearing of the context on the performance.

Structuralism

This is perhaps the most complex school of thought to have emerged in the study of various aspects of traditional culture. The complexity stems largely from the fact that this school tries to bring together a variety of approaches under a unified program in the study of any cultural activity. These approaches include an examination of the social background from which a product (e.g., a tale) comes, just as we have seen the anthropologists do; an anatomy of the tale to work out the abstract structure of relationships between the various units of its composition (especially the symbols), somewhat in the spirit of the formalists; and most important of all, an effort to demonstrate the psychological problem within the culture which the tale is trying to resolve by way of a confrontation between these constituent symbols. This last effort would put structuralism squarely within the camp of the psychoanalysts. But the distinguishing quality of structuralism remains its interest in the structure (whether social, compositional, or psychological) of any cultural phenomenon.

This school of thought has its roots in sociological studies. Although problems of a structural nature had been occupying European scholars for several centuries, Claude Lévi-Strauss, the real doyen of structuralism, was influenced in the first instance by the French sociology of his time. This sociology, championed by Emile Durkheim and Marcel Mauss, differed from the British social anthropology of Malinowski in the sense that, while the latter (as we have seen) viewed the various units of a society as continually working toward harmony and stability, the former saw society instead as being constituted of a variety of elements and interests constantly in conflict with one another and held in some kind of delicate balance by certain institutions; it was, indeed, this thinking that influenced the post-Malinowskian generation of British social anthropologists (Leach, Willis, etc.).

This conflict-oriented view of social and cultural life had a major influence on Lévi-Strauss's approach to the analysis of oral narratives. But perhaps even more influential was his exposure to the arguments of the so-called Prague School of structural linguistics. This school, headed by Roman Jakobson and Nikolai Trubetzkoy, held certain revolutionary views about the phenomenon of language which was to guide Lévi-Strauss in his interpretation of the linguistic activity that is narrative. First, in the process of acquiring competence in any language, the human mind organizes the various concepts of that language into a scheme of oppositions so as to grasp them better, e.g., hot/cold, good/bad, etc.; in other words, the human mind naturally operates in a binary fashion. Second, for two people to be able to communicate effectively (whether or not they speak the same language), there must be some kind of code through which the symbols of their communication (words, hand signals, facial expressions, etc.) are processed. Third, all these phenomena happen at an unconscious level. Language and communication occur on the basis of some abstract grammar of relations between symbols; this grammar is beyond conscious human control, and to be able to clearly understand the real meaning of any linguistic activity we have to construct an abstract model which seeks to demonstrate how the symbols relate to one another and thus attain that compromise which is communication.

Lévi-Strauss was so attracted by these arguments that in his anthropological studies he was to apply them to his interpretation of various social and cultural phenomena: kinship relations, traditional thought process, art, but above all mythology (especially tales relating to the origins of various customs and outlooks). The first notable analysis of traditional mythology done by Lévi-Strauss was on the story of Oedipus, which Freud had analyzed as a reflection of the incest wish inherent in man. Unlike Freud, and following the model of structural linguistics—which urges that the analyst should take into account as many available data as possible—Lévi-Strauss combines various tales relating to the Oedipus tradition to construct a grammar or model of relations between their symbols and thus to achieve his interpretation of the essential psychological problem within the Greek culture from which the Oedipus story comes. "The myth," he concludes, "has to do with the inability, for a culture which holds the belief that mankind is autochthonous . . . to find a satisfactory transition between this theory and the knowledge that human beings are actually born from the union of man and woman" (1958: 67). This interpretation, which is surely a far cry from Freud's, has often been denounced as far-fetched and fanciful if not exactly as shocking as Freud's.

Lévi-Strauss later did some interesting analyses of American Indian myths, one of them entitled "The Story of Asdiwal" (1977). On the surface, this adventure story (from the Tsimshian Indians of northwestern America) deals with the hunting and fishing life of the people; but Lévi-Strauss tries to argue that the real interest of the story is in exploring the conflict within this culture between ideas concerning how a man should trace his descent and where he should live.

Indeed, as Lévi-Strauss publishes more and more of these analyses of American Indian tales, his technique and his idiom become increasingly complicated, though they never cease to be challenging. Much of the complication comes from his bringing into the discussion of a basically literary subject certain tools derived from other disciplines. For instance, practically every analysis contains some kind of mathematical formula or calculus, as Lévi-Strauss tries to demonstrate that the story has an internal logic of relations between its symbols. As if this were not enough, in his four-volume study of American Indian mythology entitled *Mythologiques*, Lévi-Strauss introduces idioms and ideas from music in the belief that myth is like music in having a certain harmony within its structure. In all, he discusses 813 "myths" in these four volumes, in the understanding that they all reflect, in one form or the other, the conflict within the culture of these American Indians between ideas about "nature" and about "culture"—as revealed, for example, by the confrontation between symbols representing the "raw" on one hand and the "cooked" on the other, between "sacred" and "profane," "silent" and "noisy," and so on.

Lévi-Strauss's program is extremely complex, but it has given rise to several structuralist analyses of traditional narratives, most notably Edmund Leach's discussions of Biblical myths in *Genesis as Myth* (1969). There have also been a few such analyses of African tales. One of the most notable is Dominique Zahan's treatment of the theme of "the origin of death" (1969), which is widespread in the folklore of numerous communities across the continent. The basic plot of these tales is as follows. God sends one animal (chameleon) with a message to mankind that man can live again after death, thus enjoying immortality; but this animal, being slow, dillydallies on the way. So God in anger sends a faster-moving animal, lizard, to men with the message that when they die, there will be no rising, i.e., death is final. The latter animal gets to mankind first, and consequently men have forever lived with the finality of death.

Zahan analyzes this tale in the standard structuralist fashion. He identifies the "binary structure," or structure of oppositions, on which the tale rests, namely, opposition between the divine and human worlds, between the concepts of speed and slowness, and between life and death. He also identifies a kind of "black box," or zone of transformation, between one element in the oppositions and the other, a stage which facilitates the change. For instance, the insects or herbs which the slow animal stops to eat on the way facilitate the transformation of the message as well as the images in the story from one state to the other: divine to human, slow to fast, life to death. He cites a number of variants of this story of the "failed message" from communities across the continent of Africa and even probes the culture of some of them to discover the symbolic value of the images used in the story (chameleon, lizard, herbs, etc.). Taking all these things into consideration—and not without some of those diagrammatic sketches of the type that Lévi-Strauss indulges in—Zahan is able to derive a message from these tales of the origin of death that shakes the casual reader or listener almost as vigorously as Lévi-Strauss does in his interpretation of the Oedipus story.

> As can be seen, all these myths—like the "failed message" stories—are not intended, despite their appearances, to inform us of the origin of death. Rather, by means of the problem which they set out to resolve, they make known their possessor's conception of the human condition. Life (the original "immortality") constitutes the fundamental principles of man's nature, from which all others derive. It can only be grasped by endowing it with all the attributes opposite to those which characterize mortality. This goes without saying since, on the one hand, death is the opposite of life, while on the other death furnishes men with an experience far more realistic and convincing than life. . . . these stories constitute the human being's first attempt to apprehend himself diachronically. They are man's attempts to find the elements of his own history, or even rough outlines for the first history of human destiny. This means that death and the myths of its origin lead the mind directly toward the problem of social time, of time lived and of duration. (Pp. 44–45)

There have been other structuralist analyses of African oral narratives whose conclusions are just as startling. Structuralists claim that because they are looking far more deeply at the internal problems raised by a tale than other scholars are inclined to do, their conclusions are bound to be out of the ordinary and certainly to differ from the rather superficial meaning that the storyteller tries to ascribe to the tale. Some people think the structuralists are simply playing fanciful games with language. Perhaps the major problem with the structuralist approach lies in the fundamental premises on which it rests, which is that myth or storytelling—like other forms of communication in language—operates at an unconscious level. Lévi-Strauss states categorically at the beginning of the first volume of *Mythologiques* that he will try to prove, "not how men think in myths, but how myths operate in men's minds without their being aware of the fact" (1970: 14). It is quite true that structural analysis has presented us with some rather challenging ways of examining the deep and fundamental human issues raised by oral literature. But any approach that underestimates the level of conscious skill at work in the narrative performance has missed the basic point about that art. Some of the more recent analyses along these lines have endeavored to show that Lévi-Strauss and his followers could have done better by taking into account the element of artistic organization in the oral narrative.[1]

Categories of the Oral Narrative

The classification of the oral narrative is an old problem. We started this chapter by pointing to the term *folktale* as a generally accepted way of describing tales of the oral tradition but preferring the phrase *oral narrative* as being both relatively devoid of prejudice and adequately representative of the nature of the art. There have, however, been several subclasses recognized for this genre, several words and phrases thrown about, highlighting one kind of tale or the other. Let us quickly run through a few of these terms.

There are roughly four ways in which the majority of tales have so far been classified. One is on the basis of the obvious protagonists of the tales. In this sense, it has long been fashionable to draw a distinction between *animal tales, human tales* and *fairy tales*. There are basically two problems with this style of classification. The first is that the one class of beings often behaves so much like the other that it hardly means anything, in the world of the folktale, to separate one from the other. For instance, the animals in the so-called animal tales are made to think, talk, and behave like human beings. Even though skilled performers are inclined, for the sake of vivid realism, to represent every animal as much as possible in its peculiar mannerisms, the tendency is still to ascribe to them language and attitudes (love, jealousy, hate, etc.) peculiar to human beings. These human characteristics are introduced partly to entertain us and partly also because the experiences of these animals are meant to have some relevance or message for us. The second problem with this classification by protagonist is that it ignores the numerous instances of tales in which fairies, humans, and animals interact with one another. An example of a human–animal story—told among the Yoruba and other groups in Nigeria—is the one about how the Tortoise thievishly eats a meal prepared by a human medicine man and designed to make the Tortoise's wife pregnant; Mr. Tortoise ends up being pregnant himself.

The word *myth* has also frequently been used for describing a tale in which gods, or divinities recognized by a community of people (not just fairies or ordinary spirits), are the protagonists and which is therefore thought to have a sacred, serious, and authoritative character. Unfortunately, tales with divine protagonists do not always have such a character. A Yoruba tale from the body of divination texts known as *ese ifa* narrates how the god Orunmila has an amorous affair with a human called Iyewa and impregnates her (Abimbola 1976: 134–35); the story is told with such sensual flavor that the element of delight would seem to have superseded that of the sacred and the authoritative.

A second way of classifying tales has been in terms of the purpose revealed in the content, whether implicitly or explicitly. A large group of such tales, for instance, are seen to have a fundamentally moralistic or didactic purpose. In nearly all of them a moral is drawn by the storyteller at the end, which either encourages good or discourages evil as revealed within the story.

A third method of classification, closely linked with the second, is on the basis of the characteristic quality of the tale. This is perhaps the largest category, as here we have the largest number of terms used. For instance, *trickster tales* are tales involving trickery and deceit, a breach of faith leading perhaps to the end of a relationship between the parties involved, mostly animals. *Dilemma tales* are those that end with a question or a problem to be debated and resolved between the narrator and his audience. For instance, a man ferries his wife and his mother across a river. On the way a storm arises, and the boat capsizes. Since he can only rescue one of the two women, which of them shall it be—his mother or his wife? We also hear of a large category of *historical tales*, with several subclasses. Among these is the genealogy, which narrates the line of descent from one ruler or ancestor to the next; the war story, which describes a military encounter; and so on. The legend is also put within this group, being used in connection with the experiences of historical figures or events of a notable or memorable character. The epic is equally among this group, being the story of extraordinary personalities (i.e., heroes) achieving unbelievable feats under equally extraordinary circumstances.

Origin tales are also a recognized group, in some ways related to the historical tales; they narrate the origins of peoples or else of cultural elements (fire, worship, etc.) and natural phenomena (lightning, death, etc.). When they relate the origins of people they are equally called legends, because they deal with memorable events and personalities. When they relate the origins of elements of nature or culture, they are frequently also called myths, no doubt because in such tales divinities usually play a significant role.

Yet another way of classifying tales has been on the basis of context or occasion. For instance, we often hear of *moonlight tales*, simply on the ground that the tales—which may be any one of the kinds discussed above—are told in the moonlight. One sometimes also hears of *divination tales*, as for instance, those that form the large body of *ifa* divination texts among the Yoruba; of *hunter's tales*, told during breaks from hunting, relating encounters between hunters and beings of the wild (beasts, monsters and spirits); and other groups along these lines.

These are only some of the terms used for classifying various kinds of oral narratives. The confusion caused by the variety of criteria will be obvious by now. For instance, an epic could well be a human tale mostly, or else it may embrace (as more often than not) humans and animals as well as divinities. Besides, there may be such a considerable number of trickster elements in the so-called myth or legend that the one term is just as good as the other for classifying the tale. Such problems are no doubt inevitable in a large number of cases, and scholars who have tried to resolve them have frequently run into difficulties.[2] Perhaps the following method will help to clear some of the confusion.

Legends

This is a fairly broad category of tales. We are retaining the word *legend* because here we are dealing with accounts of personalities and events that are considered so memorable that they deserve to be talked about or recounted (Latin *legenda*) again and again. The events may be as recent as this morning, perhaps just an hour ago, or they may be so far back in the past that the memory of them is now very vague and the details are subject to all kinds of manipulation. This is why we may safely talk about two kinds of legend: the *historic* legend, and the *romantic* (or *mythic*[3]) legend. The historic legend occurs mostly within memorable time—the visible present or the recent past. But its essential quality is that the narrator sticks as closely as possible to details of real life; perhaps because many people know the personalities concerned and can recall the events rather vividly (even with written records), the narrator is careful not to engage in careless flights of imagination, especially if he or she fears being contradicted by listeners. The romantic, or mythic, legend is, on the contrary, not subject to any such restrictions. Because the events are so far back in the past, storytellers indulge their imaginations in the most fantastic details and, when questioned, frequently hide behind the excuse that "things are no longer what they used to be."

This difference in outlook between the historic and the mythic legend is brought out rather clearly by two of the stories I recorded from Charles Simayi, and I will set them down in full. The first is an account of the experiences of Simayi and his people (of Ubulu-Uno) during the Nigerian civil war. Federal troops had routed secessionist Biafran forces out of the state (then called Midwest State), and set up military stations at strategic points in the state. One of these was at Ogwashi-Uku, about five kilometers north of Ubulo-Uno. Then something happened. A prominent matron of the village was about to be installed with the highest female honor there, and one of the articles required for the ritual was a cow. But for some reason, all the cows in Ubulu-Uno had run off to Ogwashi-Uku and were seen grazing in a field at the school compound where the federal troops had set up camp. Simayi, recognized by his people for his skill in dealing with such delicate matters, was delegated to go and rescue the cows. His account captures vividly the trying circumstances under which he did the job.

Narrator:	OKAY. ER—[4]
	My story came and captured my very self, captured my land,
	Our land here, of the town of Ubulu-Uno.
	And captured a certain woman called Egbo.
Mr. Enyi:	5 The Ada, Omu Okolo.
Narrator:	Captured a certain woman called Omu, our Omu.
	Captured the men of our land, the Idi.[5]
	Shortly after, on that day,
	Behold the Idi.

10 THEY SAID THEY HAD CAST EIGHT
At the oracle,
And that the oracle . . . had picked on myself.
Whether I knew or I didn't know how to make charms, I was to save
    Ubulu-Uno
So that corpses may not drop
15 During the Biafra-Nigeria war.
It's a chilling tale!
    (Five-second pause)
What! I took a look at my guests,
None of them was my father's age. I asked them, "How could I make
    charms for the town?
Er. . . . If I am going to save our land, it's our lives we shall all be
    saving.
20 You tell . . . our women to come over here,
I don't want these Idi men."
    (Three-second pause)
They left, and went home.
Day breaking, the Omu delegated four people—
We have four quarters—and they came to my house, pleading my
    grace.
25 Then I incised them with charms.
To save time,
I went ahead and incised them with charms.
    (Three-second pause)
On the day I made the charms,
They caught one buzzard alive.

Mr. Enyi: 30 The buzzard wages an empty war!
Narrator: The buzzard prepares for a fight but never fights it,
He turns from the fight and retreats into his nest.
    (Suppressed laughter)
Charmed them with a fowl, a laying fowl, we mixed her up in the
    charm,
Her with her eggs, she was uncooped with her eggs.

Mr. Enyi: 35 When a fowl lays, she squats![6]
Narrator: I used that in mixing the charm.
So . . . after that,
ER—
ON THAT DAY
40 Beyond reckoning,
Our cows broke loose
RAN OFF to Ogwashi.
Was the female ever known to run?
The cows gave fight, ran off.
45 What!
    (Suppressed laughter)
Before I could bat an eye, behold the Omu
Had sent someone, saying there was an abomination,

That this fellow had come complaining that the cows had all gone off
to Ogwashi, that all our cows were said to have herded off to
Ogwashi,
Mine included.
50 I said, "All right."
THEN I FETCHED ONE TUBER OF YAM, FOR I AM A MER-
CIFUL MAN.
Mine I would grab with my own hands,
And bring her home.
Those others that had escaped,
55 The eye never sees the ear!
"Omu, we shall . . . the fight for our cows shall be our first strug-
gle!"
BEFORE LONG, our quarter made a proclamation,
That the approaches to the square be cleared,
For . . . our Mother was going to take a title.
60 "What! In this bounty . . . of bullets?" I said.
"All right."
Our Mother said to me,
"Go and serve up our things."[7]
When all was quiet and calm: "All right," I said to her.
65 "Hm. But the pot is boiling terribly.
Something will happen,
But there will be terror to it."
Terror prevents a woman from confronting her husband.
A woman never slaps her husband first.

Mr. Osadebe: 70 Certainly not, my man!
Narrator: ER—
We left for Ogwashi.
Got to a check-point,
A soldier called Adamu
    (Suppressed laughter)
75 CHASED BACK THE WHOLE LOT, saying "Get the . . . what's
cows?"
Blocked us with his gun.
    (Laughter)

Okpewho: What! When you hadn't any?
Narrator: ONE OF OUR TOWNSMEN, A VETERAN OF THE EARLIER
WAR,[8] approached him. He told him, "Go away, you . . . this
isn't . . . you were in the British army, not this one.
If you move an inch, I'll—"

Audience: 80 Shoot!
Narrator: Our man retreated.
    {This line is not clear}
The yam I brought in my handbag, with which to catch my cow,
What! Refuge never kills a spell!
85 "Isn't it a gun?" I said. "Well, if he kills me I'll be on my way."
Walked right up to where Adamu was.

He said, "Who are you?" I said, "Don't worry, take it easy.
Let me get close to you.
Take it easy. What's the matter, man, a-ah?"

Mr. Enyi: 90 A cow could take a man—*{The rest of this line is not clear}*

Narrator: Walked right close to his body.

"Our cows," I said to him, "had run off and gone.
The Odafe of Ogwashi had written inviting us
To come and catch our cows, and we have received the permission of
    your commander.

95 So it's good that you and I should go together and meet the Odafe."
"Okay," he said, "let's go."
He picked some of his men, and led me away.
Don't you see I've found myself an escort?

Okpewho: You see!

(Laughter)

Narrator: 100 Walked right up to Odafe's house. "Yes," he said to him,
"I asked them to come,
Lest they (i.e., the cows) should scatter about in the bush or be shot
    up,
Let each man take his own. We are one maternal kin, we are one
    extended family."
I took off,

105 In search of my cow.
Getting to St. Rose's, I was told she was grazing there,
And had been seen around.
On getting there,
No cooking, no eating[9]—I didn't realize that whole quarter had been
    evacuated.

110 I went and sat down.
Looking there, I could see netted helmets, netted helmets[10] out in
    the open.
I didn't know there was not one single civilian there at all.
(Side comments)
When, "HOI! STOP THERE!" *Aha-ah.*

Okpewho: This was addressed to you?

Narrator: 115 Yes, Er—
Shortly after, I was told, "Come."
When I came, he told me to stand in the sun to be shot.
    (Low exclamations)
Just like that!
"What's in your bag?"

120 I didn't know what to say. They said I must have emerged from the
    bush,
That the yam I had on me was for roasting.
I didn't know what to say.
They said it was a stolen article, or a charm.
And I said, "*Mm?*

125 Er . . . I am on my way to Onukwusi's, and I didn't know that you
    . . . I am not from Ogwashi here, but from Ubulu-Uno.

My cow . . . had run off to this place, and this was where I'd bought
   her,
Hence I've come looking for her.
The yam she eats,
Is what I feed her, and I rub her on the head.
   (Laughter)
130 If I see her now, I'll recognize her." Don't you see your man was
   giving answers?

Okpewho: You see!
Mr. Osadebe: Man surpasses man!
Narrator: "I've come to visit Onukwusi."
   ER . . . the one whose name I'd given,
135 He was the only one they were holding, for he was a brewer,
Fetching them brews to drink.
They were at his place, having set up a check-point there; he lived on
   the outskirts of town.
They told him he couldn't leave,
Placing him under house arrest,
140 So he could be with them.
Onukwusi said to me, "Oh, where have you been, my friend?" telling
   them I was his brother.
(The soldiers) said, "Okay, sit down here."
I sat down comfortably.
   (Laughter)
WHEN I LOOKED CLOSELY, behold those—
145 Nobody's-Business, the camp followers,
The big-bosom gang, their friends.
Behold one of our kinswomen there:
You see, a long journey has to be taken in its stride; if you are too
   outspoken about your friends, your enemies will get wiser.
They stuck out their heads, *what!*
150 "Daughter, where have you been?"
"Ah, I see," she said, "father, I see, was it you they were talking to?"
Told the sergeant, "He's my father."
"Is that so?" he said.

Mr. Ajidoe: "Na my father."
Narrator: 155 Well, that's the English that came from her mouth.
THEY SET ABOUT bringing out what the Ogwashi people had do-
   nated to them:
Palm wine, sweet palm,[11] even spirits
Were brought to my feet.
"Papa don't worry, papa don't worry."

Mr. Osadebe: 160 A feast!
   (Exclamations and laughter)
Narrator: We fell to feasting, I tell you!
Er, you know the chameleon is never beset by ants.[12]
   (Laughter)
When we had cut into the wine—two draws, two rounds—behold
   Mr. Two-fisted Mouth, Nwachukwu son of Enuagbana,

Coming to tell me, "They say you've been taken away to be shot:
165 Well, they might as well kill both of us."
He's Mr. Ugly, making his arms like this *(demonstrates)*.
He said he was walking about as he pleased.
He took me with him
Saying, "How is it going?" "Don't worry," I said, "there's nothing at
all."
170 He gave some money to our man (i.e., the sergeant),
Saying I was his father.
HAVING SAT A SHORT SPELL—one should never wear oneself out
sitting—
Told them I had to go . . . in search of my cow.
They said I should leave the searching to them, but I said no,
175 Lest in helping me search they shoot her dead.
"Er . . . I'm coming," for it takes some sense to kill a wasp perching
on the testicles.
(Laughter)

Mr. Enyi: Lest they be smashed!
Okpewho: Lest the poor things be smashed!
Narrator: ER *(laughs)* . . . *tough business!* . . . I TOOK OFF.
180 Getting to the grass, I looked up and saw my cow.
I offered it the yam,
Saying, "A fowl never refuses corn, a goat never refuses palm fronds."
Behold, ketekete,[13] Akuamaka ran up
And I rubbed her on the head.
185 A chick cries after its mother—we went home.
Went right into this house.

Mr. Enyi: She (i.e., the cow) was following him.
Narrator: "Good," I said.
GETTING HOME, WENT TO OMU'S HOUSE and told her, "I've
brought back my own, and the rest have been rounded up.
190 We have been allowed to pass,
And they will soon return."
THE GONG SOUNDED,
Proclaiming that Ada would be installed Omu tomorrow.

Mr. Enyi: Be installed Ada.
Narrator: 195 We said it was all right—
Be installed . . . installed . . . installed Ada.
Ada would take . . . carry the staff of office—
We said it was all right.

Mr. Enyi: That's the tradition.
Narrator: 200 That's the staff.
(Five-second pause)
WE WENT INTO COUNCIL.
(Side comments)
The senior citizens . . . senior citizens came in, the elders, the staff
holders came in.
The pipe-smoking elder is ever led home from council!
They held on to their crutches, all bent with age,

205 *Coming into council.*

WHEN THE SUN WAS ABOVE THE HEAD, when the rites were
 to begin,

The goats were slaughtered.

The officiants carved them up, the drinking went on.

WELL INTO THE DRINKING, AT ABOUT—

210 Well, Let's call it three o'clock like you English speakers,

In double-solid afternoon.

 (Five-second pause)

The goats all carved up, the oil-beans were cooked: we use oil-beans
 in the installation rites,

Whether of women, or of men.

When the elder citizens, under the headman, had performed the rites,

215 Told the Ada—

This is the day on which they both—

Mr. Enyi: Take a joint oath.

Narrator: Perform joint rites.

Said . . . this would cook for that, that would cook for this,

220 And they would eat.

TAKING UP SOME BROTH, some stew,

Er . . . they called me over.

When I came, they put the broth in my two hands,

Asking me to go over to where those people [14] were.

225 One of the officiants, called Okolie Moemeke,

He carried the wine, taking some glasses along.

I was asked to meet the sergeant.

 (Six-second pause)

SUDDENLY SUDDENLY—

We didn't know when they came—

230 They had circled us like ants.

 (Low murmurs)

I COLLECTED the broth and showed it to the sergeant, saying,
 "Here—"

It was in the plate, I mean.

Okpewho: Yes.

Narrator: Put it in a plate, took up the plate and brought it before him, saying,
 "Here's the broth our people are offering you,

235 Here's the wine they've brought you, here's the kola to go with it."

HE SAID TO ME, "GO CHOP DIRTY THING,

 (Laughter and exclamations)

Chop shit.

What have you brought it before me for?

COME, KNOW YOUR WAY COMMOT!" [15]

240 Meaning I should go back where I came from.

Aha-ah.

 (Exclamations)

WHAT SUDDENLY CAME FROM MY MOUTH!—

Was it my fault?

Your man set both hands to eating!

245 Someone from your town Igbuzo[16] told his friend

Saying, "Look, on the day you visit me, you're going to eat with both hands."

Upon his visit, (his host) fried some corn,

Broke a coconut to it.

The Ogwashi man bit off a piece of coconut, took a handful of the corn.

250 He (i.e., host) told him, "Well, don't you see you are eating with both hands?"

(Loud laughter)

MAN, I WAS EATING THE BROTH WITH MY TWO HANDS— me, a whole manchild!

Was it my fault, at the mouth of the gun?

Mr. Ajidoe: The gun is a terrible thing!

Narrator: 255 I had the broth in my mouth,

When I heard, "MOLEST THEM!"

Meaning they should molest them (our people).

(Low exclamations)

They grabbed a young woman from our place, stuck a hand in her . . . armpit,

Led her away.

260 A certain man called Oyibo Carpenter

Dashed off . . . a stalwart of a man he was,

A very daring fellow,

And one called Boy Abasiba.

DASHED OFF, GRABBED THE GIRL, CLASPED HER,

265 Saying they might as well kill him along with her—

Mr. Enyi: She being the wife . . . the wife—

Narrator: She being the wife of his brother.

"DON'T! DON'T! DON'T!" No—

There was a sudden stampede,

270 Behold those at the check-point, they had blown a whistle in the open,

Asking them to come over.

KOI! upwards, KOI![17] upwards.

Behold, war was really looming!

I took a dive i-i-i-into a thornbush, landing tiwai!

(Laughter)

275 At that point, did . . . did I know whether the thorns pierced me?

Crawling was now my way home—the tortoise will always find his way home!

(Laughter)

IT WAS THROUGH THE BUSH THAT I RETURNED.

(Laughter and side comments. Narrator hushes commentators)

WHAT THEY NOW DID WAS, THEY LEVELED A GUN AT THE POST,

BLASTED THE MOUND . . . mound that was padded with earth,[18]

(Laughter)

280 IN THE MIDST . . . midst of the men.
Brought a van, and collected them to Ubulu.[19]
(Side comments)
Beat them up, through and through.
(Exclamations)

Mr. Enyi: There were some who died from it.
Narrator: Yes, but that's . . . another story.
285 It was after the war ended that those ones died.
The welts they received was what gave some of them trouble.
Some are alive as of now.
We then stoked fire to the pot, was it our fault?
When ants have trooped their fill, they settle down.
290 SHORTLY AFTER,
Our king went to Ogwashi
Accompanied by the leading men of Ubulu.
Having gone to Ogwashi—

Mr. Ajidoe: In Captain John's command.
Narrator: 295 HAVING GONE TO OGWASHI,
They returned with the commander to Ubulu.

Mr. Ajidoe: We were the ones who suffered all this!
Narrator: *(To Mr. Ajidoe) It's all right.*
They returned with the commander to Ubulu.
300 Got to Ubulu,
SHOUTED,
Saying, "Who were those that went to the Mound at Ubulu-
Uno?
What have they done, did they go to the war-front?"
(Five-second pause)
They couldn't give a proper reply.
305 He told all of them to get into the . . . the van,
Sent for a good . . . large tipper,
Collected them,
Took them to the war-front.
CALLED THE REST TO AN INTERVIEW.
310 RECOGNIZING THE GOOD-NATURED ONES, he told them to
settle down in this town.
"THIS IS WHERE WE SEND THOSE WHO PREFER TO REST
(i.e., peace),
THIS IS NOT THE WAR-FRONT.
It's not necessary for you to bring the war to the rear, since we have
already left this place behind.
So, you don't know what you're taking on.
315 Go to the war-front, if you love fighting, go over there and fight.
And stop making war on . . . civilians."
That was the order given, and we thus saved our heads.
The Ada was installed,
And that was where I took my leave of them, and returned.

Audience: 320 WELCOME!

We will observe that this account has been introduced and concluded with statements or remarks that are typical of storytelling performances. In some of the tales I recorded from him, Simayi begins by presenting himself as being "captured" by his story; this is perhaps his way of allowing himself to be transported into the world of extraordinary events that his stories generally contain. In the same vein, his last line above (319) is his standard way of stepping off this extraordinary world of the tale and returning to the land of "real" events. It seems clear, therefore, that for Simayi this story of a civil war experience is only one of a repertoire of accounts of extraordinary happenings that he narrates.

Despite the conventional form into which the narrative has been put, there is nothing out of the ordinary about the events. They were still quite recent and fresh in the minds of the citizens of Ubulu-Uno; the occasional interpolations by some members of the audience, especially Enyi and Ajidoe, indicates that they identify with and vouch for the account which Simayi here gives.

It is a story told with considerable skill and charm. Note particularly the description of Simayi's grave encounter with the hoary *Idi* elders (lines 8–22), with the Ubulu women of easy virtue who have made themselves available to the federal soldiers (144–55), and with the loud-mouthed braggart, Nwachukwu (163–71). Note also the skillful contrast between two kinds of military officers, the one cruel and menacing (236–40), the other humane but firm (296–316). And note, above all, the well-chosen turns of phrase that draw frequent reactions (*laughter, exclamation,* etc.) from the audience. These are all marks of Simayi's narrative competence and artistic skill, which have earned him the deep respect of his people. But the story is squarely a historic legend because it deals all through with events of real life.

For an example of the mythic legend, we may now present in full Simayi's account of the war between the Ubulu and the kingdom of Benin, a war which Egharevba records (1960)[20] as having taken place during the reign of Oba Ekengbuda, in the eighteenth century. In this story, Enyi and a younger man, Dennis Amamfueme, supported Simayi with musical accompaniments; the two men struck bottles with sticks at different speeds and pitches as a way of providing a steady rhythmic background to the narration. The story was performed on the same night that Simayi gave the preceding account of the civil war experience.

Narrator:	*(to Mr. Enyi)*	
	Kokom, kokom *(cueing him on the right rhythm)*	
Mr. Enyi:	*(to Mr. Amamfueme)*	
	Put the bottle on your lap,	
	And leave the mouth open,	
	So it would resound.	
Narrator:	5 My tale captures the Oba of Benin,	
	Captures our Ezemu,	
	Captures Aniobodo his brother,	
	That is, our Aniobodo,	
	Of Ubulu-Uno.[21]	

Mr. Enyi:	10	That is of—
Narrator:		Etiti Omamma, descendant of Aniobodo.

        (Four-second pause)
        Er . . . then Ezemu—
        Obas of Benin were dying day after day:
        Crowned today, dead tomorrow.

Mr. Enyi: 15 Then he said that—
Mr. Enyi: Be careful!
Narrator: Sought for a medicine man.
Mr. Enyi: My brother, I'm begging you.
Narrator: Keep to your striking![22]

      20 Looked for a medicine man.
        ALREADY UP TO A HUNDRED MEDICINE MEN
        Had assembled at the Oba's palace
        To cure him.
        (Four-second pause)
        Er . . . Ezemu told his brother Aniobodo,
      25 "I have been summoned
        For . . . healing, and I'm going on a mission.
        So, please help me."
        (Five-second pause)
        THEN HE WENT INDOORS,
        Plucked some herbs—

Mr. Enyi: 30 Aniobodo was the elder.
        (Narrator frowns at him, and hisses; five-second pause)
Narrator: HE WENT INDOORS, I MEAN ANIOBODO
        Into his shrine-house.
        Plucked some herbs, *set off.*
        Ground them in his pot,
      35 Then gave them to him (Ezemu).
        Rubbed them on his eyes, told him to put them in a bag, FOR THE
           YOUNG PARTRIDGE IS THE FIRST TO SEE THE OWNER
           OF THE FARM.[23]
        Ezemu set off to Benin.
        Entered the Oba's palace—Hey!
        What I said before about Ikoma,[24] was full to the brim.
      40 *Ezemu entered.* The Oba had—
        Gravels had been collected,
        Slabs of stone this wide,
        Were buried in . . . the courtyard.
        They had collected sand, white sand, dug up some sand, red sand,
           and covered up (the stones).
      45 Made a proclamation,
        That whoever . . . to the assembled medicine men, (the Oba) said
           that whoever came with an osuu,
        Let him plant it there in the courtyard,
        AND IF IT COULD PIERCE THE GROUND, THEN HE HAD
           WON THE CHANCE TO CURE HIM.

Mr. Osadebe:		Osuu means sword.
Mr. Enyi:	50	Or a dagger.
Narrator:		SO AS ANY ONE OF THOSE MEDICINE MEN WENT CHAKOM! the thing curved, and bent.

(The Oba) ordered them to execute the man, for he had come on a false mission.

(Exclamations)

Heads began to roll—*What! Ezemu—*

(Laughter)[25]

Ezemu came out and said that he—

55 HIS BODY WAS SHAKING KPA-KPA-KPA-KPA, HE DARTED UP FROM WHERE HE SAT, TURNED AROUND, LAID HIS HAND ON THE OBA,[26] GRABBED IT, HURLED IT INTO THE COURTYARD,

AND IT WENT ZUYAM! THAT THING PIERCED THE GROUND TO ITS FULL LENGTH!

Okpewho:		Hear hear!
Narrator:		*The Oba told him to sit down,* the rest to go.
Okpewho:		What! For he had found the man he wanted.
Narrator	60	*That was the end of that.*

Dry corn never eludes the prey![27]

THE SWORD WAS SHAKING KPAKA-KPAKA-KPAKA-KPA, the remaining part of it.

(Ezemu) Told them to go and fetch some tinder,

Seven bundles.

65 They fetched some wood.

He told them to go and pluck

A calabashful of little peppers

and scoop up some ashes.

They scooped up some ashes.

Mr. Enyi:	70	THE OBA WAS REGALED.
Narrator:		Brought the calabashful of little peppers,

Fetched an old-time blade, a shaving blade, made incisions on (the Oba's) body,

Ground the peppers with chalk, and smeared him over.

The smearing done, he brought the wood,

75 Set fire to it,

Spread out a mat, told (the Oba) to bask in the heat.

He sat down carefully beside him.

HARDLY FIFTEEN MINUTES LATER,

The Oba called out—he had not eaten for a year—he said he was starving.

Okpewho:	80	Hear, hear!
Narrator:		They should bring him some food.

They brought . . . brought food, served the Oba. *What!*

At break of dawn, they set out water, and the Oba had his bath.

Sat on his throne.

(Four-second pause)

85 EZEMU TOLD HIM, "I never stay out the third day.

     I will be leaving, for I came yesterday."

     (The Oba) said to him, "Please, stay out the third day,

     So that I may find something to fete you with it."

         (Three-second pause)

     Called out his eldest daughter,

90 *Told her to go with him, and be his wife.*

     Gave her a young man, for going to the market.

     "Farewell," (said the Oba). *"All right,"* said he.

         (Four-second pause)

     Ezemu set off for home.

     He traveled on tiiii, and on getting to the outskirts, BEHOLD THE OBA'S EZOMO.

95 Told Ezemu to wait a while.

     He was the one that executed people.

Okpewho:	I see. He killed all those victims?
Narrator:	Eh?
Mr. Enyi:	Ezomo.
Narrator:	100 Ezomo. That's the Oba's Ezomo.
	He's like the Ozoma.[28]
Okpewho:	Ah, I see, I see.
Narrator:	Thank you. That . . . that was a title.
Okpewho:	Of course, I see.
Narrator:	105 If anyone was to be executed, he carried it out.
Okpewho:	That title is held even today.
	(Other side comments)
Narrator:	Thank you. Are you understanding?
Okpewho:	Yes, I am understanding.
Narrator:	BAWLED AT EZEMU,
	110 Ezemu told him, "No! THE EYE DOES NOT SEE THE EAR."
	DOES THE EYE SEE THE EAR?
Okpewho:	Certainly not.
	(A baby whimpers. Mr. Enyi cautions its mother)
Narrator:	SAID (the Ezomo) . . . "How come you are traveling with the Oba's daughter, the head princess?"
	He (Ezemu) said, "I went to cure the Oba, and he gave her to me as a parting gift,
	115 To be my wife, and gave her this boy for going to the market."
	"Impossible," said (the Ezomo).
	"The Oba could never have offered you his head princess as a wife."
	"Is that so?" said (Ezemu). *"Yes,"* said (the Ezomo).
	Headed for the Oba's (palace), saying "Impossible,"
	120 And taking her along with him.
	"All right," said (Ezemu).
	Shortly after,
	Did he know that the man with whom . . . the man with whom the tiger . . . the man who dines with the tiger must be left-handed?

Okpewho:	Certainly! *(Laughing)*
Narrator:	125 GETTING HOME, walked into his shrine house.

HE HAD ALREADY CAST A SPELL on the girl,

TELLING HER TO COME AND ANSWER HIS CALL, for one never strays far from the yam he's roasting![29]

The girl darted off,

Running lelelelele

130 Right up to Ubulu.

Mr. Enyi: FOR SHE HAD BEEN SUMMONED BY AN EXPERT HAND!

(Exclamations)

Narrator: Dashed into Ezemu's house.

(Laughter)

Our man said to her, "Aha,

Have you arrived?" "Yes," she said.

135 "What about your brother? We must go and fetch him too."

(Laughter)

CAME OUT TO THE OPEN SQUARE,

Asked her to tell him her brother's name. She told him her brother's name, and he grabbed his sword.

Walked on tiiiiii to the open square,

Mixed up some charms, asked that boy to answer the call. At the twinkle of an eye, behold the boy came running in.

140 Led him right up to his house.

Asked him to sit down, for it was all over.

"What! How could—how could—where is the princess? And they have also taken this other one! Impossible!

Your Highness, this is all your fault.

This calls for war! We must go and fetch back those two children."

145 The Benin nation . . . got ready!

Well, it doesn't take time—

Okpewho: Of course not.

Narrator: For the goatskin to make the bag!

War! Behold war!

150 MAN, WAR WAS RAGING, I TELL YOU.

Ezemu grabbed

Seven men, hunters,

Sewed up some girdles

And fitted them all with these.

155 Took a good look at them, then had them loosened.

While they were being loosened—

Mr. Enyi: THE HAND WAS LAID ON EKUMEKU![30]

Narrator: He set a pot on the fire,

Pressed the girdles into it,

160 Stoked fire to it.

Do girdles burn to ashes?

With no water in the pot, he stoked fire to it, it became red hot, and the girdles burnt out bilii (i.e., completely).

Those seven men going to war,

He strung out a piece of thread like this,

	165	Released his charm, right on top of the pot gai (i.e., squarely)!
		Those seven men already standing at attention, the girdles flew to their waists tai (i.e., right on target)!
Okpewho:		Without being tied on?
		(Laughter; three-second pause)
Narrator:		WHO WOULD DARE? The girdles flew out and landed letem (i.e., lightly)!
		Those stalwarts shook their heads.
Mr. Enyi:	170	Which shows there are roots in the ground!
Narrator:		He told them to stand on that thread.
		This man would jump, land on the thread, and slide down sam (i.e., effortlessly)!
		That single thread did not snap.
		(Exclamations)
		That man would fly up, fall on . . . land on the thread.
	175	Just one single thread, but it never snapped, and he would jump down over there sam!
Mr. Enyi:		PRESSURE NEVER BURST THE NERVE!
Narrator:		That was how all seven of them jumped over,
		Easily!
		Along with their guns.
	180	One had a pestle
		One had a rough-hewn hook
Mr. Enyi:		The river never drowns that hook!
Narrator:		One had an arrow that had never been stretched on a bow—
Mr. Enyi:		Not for killing animals!
Narrator:	185	Man, they set off on the road to Benin.
		On their way to Benin, they heard that Benin had sent word asking them to look out for them,
		For they were coming to take home their child.
		MARCHED ON YIIIII (i.e., for a long distance).
		(Three-second pause)
		If you saw them . . . IF YOU SAW THE ROAD TO ABOUT THREE MILES,
	190	The Binis were as black as if they had smeared charcoal on their faces, so that they . . . they (i.e., the Ubulu) could not pass that way.
		BEHOLD CLUBS, MACHETES, GUNS, and whatnot.
		BEFORE THEY COULD GET AS FAR AS THAT DOORPOST—
		OUR MEN WERE ABOUT AS FAR AS THIS BACK DOOR—
		BEHOLD A GOURDLET,
	195	THE GOURDLET ROLLED OFF FILI-FILI-FILI: NO! NO! THEY HAD . . . THE BINIS
		HAD CRUSHED FIVE HUNDRED (i.e., of their own) MEN TO DEATH.
		(Laughter)
Mr. Enyi:		The war was over for them!
Narrator:		The ground was littered with corpses.
Mr. Enyi:		THEY DIED OF THEIR OWN . . . THEIR OWN HANDS.
		(Side comments)

200 NOBODY CUT THEM DOWN.

Narrator: Er . . . the matter . . . had gone past play.

Those (Ubulu) men said they had found no war,

Turned around, and went back

Right on to their home,

205 Saying they had waited for Benin, but Benin never turned up.

(*Laughter*)

SHORTLY AFTER, BEHOLD ANOTHER MISSION.

Ah! They said that these envoys

Now coming would no longer return since war had already begun.

Grabbed those envoys and gave them to their queen—the Oba's princess.

210 Took them to the courtyard, shaved their heads,

And got the men married off.

(The Bini) awaited the return of these men, but they never returned.

No!

The grand matrons got ready,

215 Turned into egrets,

Others turned into vultures—

The grand matrons of Benin.

Some turned into ravens,

Those who took . . . that is, those called witches,

220 Saying they were going there,

(*Side comments*)

For the matter had gone past play.

WENT ON TIIIII, nyima nyima.[31] Before they reached the spot where

their men had met their doom, our men had arrived,

And planted their charm.

They had set out at a time like this, so they could arrive on the same

night.

Mr. Enyi: 225 TETEKITE![32]

Narrator: They had it planted.

At daybreak, you would see a bird with a beak this long (*gesturing*),

All fast asleep.

(*Laughter*)

Mr. Enyi: They could no longer see!

Narrator: 230 AFTER TWO DAYS, they had all rotted to their bones.

That whole gang of powerful figures now lay sprawling.

Mr. Osadebe: Trouble! Trouble!

Spectator: Who else remained?

Mr. Enyi: HAVE PATIENCE—

Narrator: 235 Benin consulted the oracle,

Asking what could be done.

Mr. Enyi: For the story is still going on.

Narrator: To have captured their kinsmen at Ubulu, and captured these others

(i.e., matrons) at Ubulu too,

And killed them all off, hm!

240 *Impossible!*
Somewhat later, the diviner said to the Oba,
"Come,
A corpse never kills the undertaker."[33]

Audience: No!

Narrator: 245 "You must go and settle . . . this war.
Tell him to go over to the boundary,
And you go over to the boundary, and plead with him.
For since you (kings) never fulfilled your days,
And he prepared for you an antidote

250 *Which has helped you to survive*
And taught you how to live,
So that you now enjoy the warmth of fire as never before,
And you understand what your problem was,
You should not now turn an evil back on him.

255 For, having given him your daughter, and made it known that she
    was your gift to him,
You should not then make war on him.
See how best to settle the matter."
At that time, no boundary had been fixed there, nothing whatever
    had been fixed.
"All right," said the Oba, "but how can I send the message?"
(Three-second pause)

Mr. Enyi: 260 To avoid trouble!

Narrator: COME THAT DAY—
(Laughter; four-second pause)
Told his child
To take an eagle's feather,
And hold it firmly in his hand,

265 And place it in a pod of kolanuts,
And tell Ezemu that this feather was a gift from him.
The wisdom of the ancients:
For they never killed a man with an eagle's feather.

Okpewho: Certainly not!

Narrator: 270 Once you saw a man with an eagle's feather on his head, you would
    not so much as insult him.

Okpewho: No.

Narrator: Man, he placed an eagle's feather in a pod of kolanuts and gave it to
    a . . . young boy,
And said, "Go, give this to Ezemu,
And tell him to please come over to the boundary,

275 That I have sent you with . . . this eagle's feather, so that he may
    know the message is from me.
Let him abandon the dispute."
The child took the eagle's feather
And went on his way. On entering, he showed it to Ezemu.
Ezemu took a good look at him—

Mr. Enyi: 280 FROM ONE FEATHER TO ANOTHER, A WHITE CHALK (i.e.,
    of peace)!

Narrator: *Said, "All right."*
                    Took . . . took the feather,
                    And put it in his shrine house.
                    Then called (the people of) Ubulu,
      285 Told them they would go to the boundary.
                    "YOU TELL HIM TO START OUT,
                    FOR WHEREVER WE MEET BECOMES THE BOUNDARY,
                    Since he wants the war to end."
                        (Mr. Enyi groans wistfully)
                    The child departed, gave the Oba the news, and the Oba said, "All right."
      290 Called a meeting.
                    THEY SET OFF THAT NIGHT.
                    From where he sat at home, Ezemu could see them coming.
                    Going into his shrine house,
                    He had long since passed Abudu!
      295 Was nearly reaching the Oba's compound.

Mr. Enyi: UGONOBA.[34]
Narrator: A little past Abudu, he released his sword,
                    One pole—it went gei (i.e., stood firmly in the ground)!
                    He waited for the Oba.
      300 They (i.e., the Benin party) had set out two days earlier,
                    And on finally reaching there, behold—
                        (Laughter)
                    Our man was sitting there!
                    He told them this was now the boundary, and they should stop there.
                    The Bini sat down too,
      305 Saying they did not want any more trouble.

Okpewho: Of course not! *(Laughing)*
Narrator: Pleading—
Mr. Enyi: That they had come begging.
Narrator: That they had come begging.
      310 They began to plead,
                    And . . . bringing out two men,
                    Gave them to Ezemu, saying, "We beg you, for your charms,
                    The princess, and everything—take them, take them,
                    We have abandoned the war.
      315 Please." This was how they fixed the boundary at Abudu.

Mr. Enyi: "We shall no longer kill the Ubulu."
Narrator: "We shall no longer kill the Ubulu."
                    That was how they fixed the boundary at Abudu.

Okpewho: The boundary between the Bini and—
Narrator: 320 And . . . and the Ubulu.
Okpewho: I see.
Narrator: It's at Abudu, which is what entitles us to claim Abudu, we of these parts.
                    That's where Ezemu fixed the boundary.

Mr. Enyi: It's the white man that changed it as it is now.

Narrator:	325	They didn't change it—it remains in the same place till tomorrow.[35]
		Benin dare not overstep it, and pledged never to kill the Ubulu again.
Okpewho:		I see.
Narrator:		So . . . when that recent war came,
		And they killed Ubulu people, their kings began to die.[36]
	330	They no longer fulfill their days, and they have continued to send emissaries to settle matters.
		That was where I took my leave of them, and returned.
Audience:		WELCOME!
		(Laughter)

This story is clearly not of the same character as the story of the civil war experience recorded earlier. Of course, the two stories share the same formulae or frames for opening and closing. In line 2 of the civil war account, Simayi speaks of his story capturing him and his town, and in line 5 of the Benin story we are told of the Oba and Ezemu being similarly captured. In both stories also the storyteller employs the same formula for concluding his narration: "That was where I took my leave of them, and returned." Other similarities between the two stories have to do with the sheer technical and stylistic beauties in Simayi's storytelling. For instance, he has a very sharp sense of the dramatic or the arresting event. Compare, for instance, that shocking scene in the civil war story where the sergeant bawls at Simayi, forcing him to eat the broth that the latter had brought to him as an act of hospitality, and proceeds to brutalize the citizens of Ubulu-Uno (lines 232–74), with that scene where Ezemu pierces his sword into the stone slab with a dash of magical genius (lines 54–60). Although the latter scene is much shorter, we see in both descriptions Simayi's skill in narrating dramatic events with vividness and color. Also in both stories, the narrator uses proverbs at the right moments to drive home his point with pith and force.

In the Ezemu story, however, we are dealing with a different kind of legend. The historical event and personalities around which the story is built are so far back in time that the artist is a little freer in his treatment of fact. We will notice that in the civil war story there is hardly any detail that will arouse anybody's doubt or disbelief, in the sense that it cannot possibly happen in real life. But in the Ezemu story a number of details are clearly open to question, at least from the point of view of the "educated" or "modern" (i.e., nontraditional) audience. That a sword could be pierced into a slab of stone (lines 55–56); that the princess could be transported from Benin to Ubulu in a flash with a spell (126–30); that the girdles could fly to the hunters' waists without being tied on (166); that the grand matrons of Benin could turn into birds of sorcery (214–19); that Ezemu, by simply walking into his shrine house, could cover a distance roughly equivalent to what it took the Oba and his men three days to accomplish (292–95)—all these incidents and events are acceptable only if we are prepared to stretch the imagination beyond the bounds of objective or scientific truth.

There are then roughly two factors which encourage the telling of a mythic legend such as the Ezemu story. In the first place, as I mentioned earlier, the events of such a story are usually so far back in time that the storyteller could defend their seeming incredibility by claiming—as Simayi and the other storytellers I have recorded have frequently done—that the world has changed and that the men of today have lost the skills and powers that their ancestors proudly possessed. Besides, with the passage of time, many of the real historical details of the story may have been lost in oblivion and the narrators simply fill in the gaps with their imagination. In the second place, stories of this kind are told when the events are intimately bound up with the people's interests (political and otherwise) and values, especially when these need to be defended or promoted; when this happens, the people usually exercise their imagination in such a way as to project themselves in the most positive light possible. This is why it is possible to get from the opponents two completely divergent accounts of the outcome of a war. While the Benin version of this story (given in chapter 5) records that the Ubulu were ultimately crushed and their king beheaded, the Ubulu version reports instead that the Benin army was thoroughly overpowered by a handful of hunters and the king brought to his knees. Each of these two peoples is simply trying to protect its national pride, and so employs the imagination to twist the details of its historical records in the appropriate way.

We have identified time and interest as the two principal factors in the composition of the mythic legend. The role played by interest may be so strong, however, that it overrides the element of time. An interesting illustration of this point is provided by the events of the Nigerian civil war. Some of the generals on the federal side were so popular that their successes against the forces of secessionist Biafra were frequently exaggerated, and even their failures twisted to look like successes. During the war, General Benjamin Adekunle (the "Black Scorpion") was often fabled to be using all kinds of magical devices, including the power to weather enemy bullets without sustaining a wound, to frustrate the Biafrans. General Murtala Mohammed (later Head of State) also enjoyed this sort of exaggeration. At one time during the famous battle of Abagana, he and his troops were thoroughly encircled by the Biafrans. Although newspapers at the time reported that Mohammed escaped the encirclement only when the air force and infantry reinforcements from another division of the federal army came to his rescue, those who sought to promote his image spoke instead of Mohammed "disappearing" into the air to elude the Biafrans. Interest could indeed play a major role even on events of a narrator's own day.

One final issue needs to be treated in our discussion of legends. The term *epic* has often been used to describe tales in which human characters, endowed with somewhat superhuman qualities and powers, undertake and execute tasks which would be beyond men with normal human capabilities. These outstanding or extraordinary men are referred to as heroes and, in performing their tasks, are invariably aided by extra-human resources such as magic (as in Ezemu's case), divinities, or spirits, or even certain animals prompted by supernatural forces. Epics are usually broad in their scope (e.g., in the scale of action, the time taken, or the political or cultural geography covered), are mostly set in some historical experience, and in any case reflect some significant stage in the political or cultural history of the communities that tell them. The Ezemu story is clearly an epic on these grounds, while the civil war narrative may simply be called a heroic narrative. Among notable African epics, tales about certain heroes are worth particular mention: Sunjata, the leader of the Mandinka (West Africa), Chaka the Zulu (South Africa), Mwindo among the Banyanga (Zaire), Lianja among the Nkundo (Zaire), Kambili among the Mande hunters of Mali (West Africa), Ozidi of the western Ijo (Nigeria), Da Monzon among the Bambara (West Africa), and the friendly pair of Silamaka and Puluru (or Puluri) among the Fulani (West Africa).

Explanatory Tales

In discussing categories of the oral narrative, it is important to observe how sometimes the boundary between one kind of tale and another becomes somewhat blurry. This is because stories are told for so many reasons and before such a variety of audiences that their characters and interests often vary. A tale will, however, usually be classified on the basis either of its major thrust or its obvious intent; this is a decision that we have to make not so much on the declared wish of the narrator (who may have a partisan interest in the matter) as on our own objective judgment of the facts of a story.

Take for instance the Ezemu story just presented. Toward the end of the story, the narrator offers two explanations: that the peace meeting between the Ubulu and the Bini at Abudu automatically makes the town the territorial boundary between the two peoples, and that the reason the Obas of Benin have started dying again is that the Bini have broken the old peace between them and the Ubulu by killing the latter during the recent civil war. Considering the general historical basis and thrust of the story (and even of the explanations), we have no choice but to classify the story as some form of legend.

In some stories, however, the real historical basis is either so thin or absent that the explanation offered emerges as a paramount interest or intent and has to be taken more seriously. An *explanatory tale* is thus a story that sets out primarily to explain the origin of one of a whole range of things or ideas within a community's environment and experience. Let us consider a few tales of this kind. The first is a Fulani tale expounding the origin of the creation of the world and various aspects of the human experience.

> At the beginning there was a huge drop of milk.
> Then Doondari came and he created the stone.
> Then the stone created iron;
> And iron created fire;
> 5 And fire created water;
> And water created air.
> Then Doondari descended the second time. And he took the five elements
> And he shaped them into man.
> But man was proud.
> 10 Then Doondari created blindness and blindness defeated man.
> But when blindness became too proud,
> Doondari created sleep, and sleep defeated blindness;
> But when sleep became too proud,
> Doondari created worry, and worry defeated sleep;

15 But when worry became too proud,
   Doondari created death, and death defeated worry.
   But when death became too proud,
   Doondari descended for the third time,
   And he came as Gueno, the eternal one,
20 And Gueno defeated death. (Beier 1966b: 1–2).

Perhaps we should begin by remarking the literary beauty of this piece, which may be seen essentially in two respects. First, it appeals to us through the sheer dramatic counterpoint of the series of actions described. By personifying the various elements both concrete (e.g., water) and abstract (e.g., death), the narrator is able to endow them with the force of agency on which the balance between creation and destruction—the basic theme of the story—is conveyed. The second appeal of the piece is in its spiral or chiasmic development and the mounting suspense created thereby, until the ultimate climax.

Like all tales of creation, this story is set in some indeterminate past ("at the beginning") which denies it any dependable historical basis. Most tales of the explanatory kind assume a large prehistoric time scale within which the images can range more freely than may be allowed even in mythic legends. In this way, they are able to deal with the larger philosophical themes of human existence, as against the more limited facts of the experiences of historical figures. As we noted above, this story probes the eternal counterpoint between creation and destruction, between life and death, ending with a hopeful picture of eternity as represented by the figure of the supreme divinity Gueno. There is also a moral message in the denunciation of pride with the successive destruction of the figures that indulge in it.

Despite the general human problems which it explores, this story is remarkable for the way it evokes its local universe. We glimpse some of this in the hierarchical relationship within the Fulani pantheon: Doondari would seem to be a culture hero raised to the level of divinity, while Gueno would be a supreme deity. But even more striking is the image of milk as the beginning of the entire Fulani universe. In chapter 5 we observed the value of oral literature in helping a people comprehend the world through the combined lenses of the familiar ecology and customs. For the Fulani, a pastoral people, nothing perhaps could be more fundamental to life than the milk of their cattle.

Other creation stories abound in Africa—stories about the origin of sun and moon, of rivers and fishes, and so on. The fundamental aim in each of them is to ask larger philosophical questions about human existence, using aspects of the local ecology as dramatic symbols on which the rationalization and explanation are built.

A second type of explanatory tale seeks to reflect on the characteristics and the behavior of various elements of the surrounding environment. Why does the mosquito always haunt the ear? Why do the tortoise and the snail carry their houses (i.e., shells) around with them? Why is the neck of the giraffe so long? Why does the palmwine tapper never reveal what he sees from the top of the palm tree? Why do some animals live at home and others in the forest? How did the leopard acquire its dangerous claws? This story from Sierra Leone is an interesting example of an explanatory tale of (animal) behavior:

A long, long time ago, a leading commercial firm employed a dog as storekeeper in its tyre section. After 25 years of service it happened for once that an auditor's report showed four missing tyres. It looked as if the guilty party was the dog. But Dog (Storekeeper) had had a clean record of 25 years of devoted and meritorious service. So the employers decided that his services would continue with full benefits if he could bring back the four missing tyres (no time limit). From that day to date, all dogs have made concerted efforts to recover the tyres. So each time a dog sees a car passing by, it barks as it chases it (in an effort to remove the four tyres and take them to the General Manager of the firm). (Grenfell-Williams n.d.: 49)

No doubt the first striking thing about this story is the contemporary idiom in which it is told, giving clear evidence that the material of the oral tradition can be adapted from the old rural environment to the more modern setting of industrial life; those who fear that African oral literature is fast dying away have not always considered this potential for adaptation. Equally noticeable is the philosophic or rationalistic tendency of the tale. These tales explaining ecological behavior may sound rather like play, but this is play of solid imaginative texture and should not be carelessly dismissed. One standard "scientific" explanation for the length of the giraffe's neck is that it enables it to reach the nutritious leaves on the taller trees of its environment, that such a length of neck derives from the animal species from which the giraffe has evolved over time. But is there any reason why such a neck could not have adjusted to cope with shorter vegetation? A similar question may be raised for the tendency of dogs to pursue cars. Are we to be content with the explanation—facile as it is—that in pursuing a passing car the dog, as protector of its owner's well-being, is protesting or challenging the commotion emanating from the car's engine? Tales like the above, then, provide imaginative alternatives to the scientific explanation of natural phenomena.

A third subtype of the explanatory tales probes the backgrounds to a community's code of conduct, of values, or of beliefs. This story recorded by Peter Seitel from the Haya of Tanzania is a good example.

> There was once a man
> one.
> O
> That man
> had gone on a journey
> O
> 5 WITH HIS BROTHERS.
> O
> So when he journeyed with his brothers . . .
> O
> IN THE WILDERNESS
> O
> now, they go and stay the night at a certain man's.
> (The traveler's) brothers
> were two in number.
> O

10 So they were two . . .
    He was the third.
    So while they were in the wilderness . . .
                                    they stop and stay
        the night in a man's house.
    Now . . .
            they scheme
                        at night.
    The man was rich.
15 Now they conspire to steal this many thousands . . .
                                    (*holds up three fingers*)
            O

    three.
    O

    Now they travel on and trade their things at the place where they were going.
    O

    Now when they arrived (back) there (at the rich man's place)
    the people had gone to sleep . . .
20 They go and steal the three thousand.
    O

    THEY ARISE IN THE NIGHT
    and go.
    O

    Now when they had gone . . .
    O

    IN THE WILDERNESS THEY SPEND ALL DAY
            G-O-I-N-G
                                    and when it
            got to be about this time of day (late afternoon),
25 now they make camp.
    O

    They remember THEY HAVE NOT EATEN.
    O

    When they remembered they had not eaten,
    now two of them leave . . .
    and go to get food.
    O

30 Something to eat.
    So when they had left to get something to eat . . .
    one remained behind.
    So he remained there
    to bring water and to cut firewood.
    O

35 Now when the two had gotten some distance away . . .
    they said,
            "Now, that one, shall we kill him?
    Won't one take a thousand-five and the other a thousand-five?"
    O

Now when they left . . .
the other one SCHEMES.
40 "If I kill them,
won't those three thousands be mine?"
O
Now he runs.
He goes to someone's house.
He finds them preparing . . .
         sweet juice for banana beer.
45 Now they give him some. He drinks.
He takes some with him
saying, "I'll take it to my brothers."
Now he puts in POISON.
O
After he puts the poison in . . .
50 he comes and sits with it at the camp.
Now THEY COME BACK.
O
Now all peel (plantains) and cook.
(Softly) Now they seize and throttle him.
O
When they had seized and throttled him and wrung his neck . . .
55 now, they throw him out (like trash).
O
AFTER THEY THREW HIM OUT,
AFTER THEY KILLED HIM,
now they seize that unfermented juice and drink.
(softly) They share with each other
60 AND THEY DIE
O
just as the other one died.
O
NOW THAT RICH MAN . . .
WHEN HE GOT UP IN THE MORNING . . .
O
he sees that his money is gone.
65 He takes to the road
O
on his horse.
Now he's coming to spend the night at Kyabagenzi
It's here they have fallen dead.
O
Now dawn comes.
70 He's about to arrive right about there . . .
"Look, someone has died!"
O
"Eh? Let me go look around."
He sees they are dead when he comes to find his money.

    O
    He returns.
    O
75 Now this story
    is to make it known:
    three people CANNOT DO ONE THING.
    (Seitel 1980: 88–91)

In chapter 11 we shall be discussing the effectiveness of the tone changes and other techniques of storytelling which Seitel has preserved above in his peculiar style of transcription. It will be useful, however, to observe how the various breaks represented in the text give us a feeling of the dramatic tension with which the storyteller records the tragic events of the story. As far as the content of the story goes, we can see the message of the story squarely located at the end: it will be hard for three (or more) people to successfully execute a plan, because there is always the danger that one or the other party among them will break the faith for his or her own selfish ends. The entire story has been used in a symbolic way to explain or rationalize this moral issue, which is no less a major concern in Haya culture than in other cultures of the world.

A final type of explanatory tale is used for the purpose of accounting for certain aspects of a people's customs and habits. In such stories we find narrated the origins, causes, or roots of, for instance, rites performed at particular times of the year, or of certain ritual or religious systems, or of various aspects of dance, dress, or even language. A story recorded from the Swahili-speaking peoples of the east African coast tells us how a certain idiomatic expression came to be.

A sultan lived with his wife in his palace, but the wife was unhappy. She grew leaner and more listless every day. In the same town there lived a poor man whose wife was healthy and fat and happy. When the sultan heard about this, he summoned the poor man to his court, and asked him what his secret was. The poor man said, "Very simple. I feed her meat of the tongue." The sultan at once called the butcher and ordered him to sell all the tongues of all the animals that were slaughtered in town to him, the sultan, exclusively. The butcher bowed and went. Every day he sent the tongues of all the beasts in his shop to the palace. The sultan had his cook bake and fry, roast and salt these tongues in every known manner, and prepare every tongue dish in the book. This the queen had to eat, three or four times a day—but it did not work. She grew even more thin and poorly. The sultan now ordered the poor man to exchange wives—to which the poor man reluctantly agreed. He took the lean queen home with him and sent his own wife to the palace. Alas, there she grew thinner and thinner, in spite of the good food the sultan offered her. It was clear that she could not thrive in a palace.

The poor man, after coming home at night, would greet his new (royal) wife, tell her about the things he had seen, especially the funny things, and then told her stories which made her shriek with laughter. Next he would take his banjo and sing her songs, of which he knew a great many. Until late at night he would play with her and amuse her. And lo! The queen grew fat in a few weeks, beautiful to look at, and her skin was shining and taut, like a young girl's skin. And she was smiling all day, remembering the many funny things her new husband had told her. When the sultan called her back she refused to come. So the sultan came to fetch her, and found her all changed and happy. He asked her what the poor man had done to her, and she told him. Then he understood the meaning of meat of the tongue. (Knappert 1970: 132).

Like a true explanatory tale, this story uses the experiences of various characters to explore the backgrounds of an expression that is current among the Swahili-speaking people. Although the explanation is seen through the eyes of a sultan, the message is really meant for the benefit of all and sundry as the story passes from generation to generation.

But other issues in the story are perhaps more interesting than the obvious message relayed at the end of it, and these emerge clearly enough in the class conflict in which the narrator puts the sultan and the poor man: the conflict between ruler and subject or commoner, between rich and poor. These tales of the oral tradition are invariably narrated by the lower or less privileged members of the society, and in the tales they frequently try to set their own simple values and life-styles against the arrogant or superior manners of the rulers. Here the sultan has all the material wealth he needs to buy himself happiness but not the essential wisdom to achieve it. The poor commoner, on the other hand, is not credited in this story with a single article of wealth, but he uses his imagination to achieve a success that eludes the high and mighty sultan. The sultan's aloofness and arrogance prove a bane to the life and well-being of his wife, but the humane warmth and good humor of the commoner are presented as the essential qualities that will sustain life far more than material wealth would. In the end, the story seems to suggest, the poor man with his wisdom is richer than the sultan with his wealth.

It is possible that such tales were traditionally used by the court entertainers to convey words of advice and guidance to their lords. These entertainers would, of course, rather use devices of irony, such as those we see in the tale, than the direct language of instruction or reprimand to drive home their message. Whatever the intentions of the narrator, there is in the above story a touch of humor which reduces the image of the mighty ruler in favor of the less privileged subject.

Fables

These other issues relating to class conflict that we have discovered in the above tale tell us something important about the category of explanatory tales. Although there are other more relevant issues within such a tale, the narrator frequently chooses one obvious line of explanation or message and may seem to force us to accept it as the prominent one if not the only one. A large proportion of tales in Africa are, however, freer and more open-ended than the ones we have so far discussed. They are not designed to record historical or pseudo-historical events as the legend does; nor do they explore the origins of a natural phenomenon or a social habit as the explanatory tale does. Their interest is simply in telling a story, presenting an imaginative drama of experiences involving human beings, animals, or spiritual figures either within or outside the familiar human world. Such tales are more profitably called *fables*, because there is in them a primary emphasis on a story (Latin *fabula*) delightfully presented, whatever the place or period in which they are set. And perhaps we should also stress that because the storyteller does not give us a specific explanation or guide as to how we should interpret the tale, the avenues of rationalization are open and varied. The characters and events of such a story are given any number of symbolic values; the philosophical quality of it is perhaps greater than in an explanatory tale such as that of the sultan and the poor commoner.

Let us begin our examination of fables with a story set firmly in the human world. This story belongs to a group often referred to as dilemma tales, in that the storyteller poses a dilemma or problem at the end which the audience is to tackle. Ruth Finnegan recorded this story from the Limba of Sierra Leone.

> You see now—a girl was bound in love with four men. They got up to come and sleep. She stood up, she put on meat. She stood up, she put on leaves. She stood up, she put on beans. She stood up, she put on ochra. The time came closer for her to cook. She mixed them all up in cooking. The maize and the rice and the guinea corn and the millet—she cooked them together.
>
> She stood up to help it out. She helped out the cooked rice, what had been cooked together! When she had helped it out, the scrapings of the rice, they came out, from a shilling pot. She stood up, she helped out the maize; in one pot, there it had all been cooked! When she had helped it out, she took, she scraped out the scrapings. She took, she helped out the guinea corn, she scraped out the scrapings. She took, she helped out the millet. She took out the scrapings.
>
> The lovers came. She took the millet, she brought it to one. "Here is what I have kept for you today." She was thanked. She took the maize. She brought it to another. "Here is what I have kept for you today." She was thanked. She said, "I will first rest a bit now"—for she knew that she would bring food for the one she loved very much. Then she said, "I will rest." When she had rested, she took the rice, she brought it. "Here is what I have kept for you today." "Thank you."
>
> The men—they had brought wine. The one who had had millet cooked for him, he came first. "You, by your grace, I have come here to sleep today. That is the word." They passed the word between them, saying, "That pleases us." They took, they drank it. The one who had had guinea-corn cooked for him came. "You, by your grace, I have come here to sleep today. That is why I have come." They passed the word between them, saying that that pleased them. They drank. The one who had had maize cooked for him took wine. "You, by your grace, I have come here to sleep today. That is the word." They said, "That pleases us." They passed the word between them. They drank the wine. The one who had had rice cooked for him, because he knew that he was the most favoured in the love, he took wine and added a dress to it as well; for they loved each other. He came. "You, by your grace, I have come here to sleep today. That is it. Here is a dress. Here is wine." They passed the word between them, saying, "We accept." They drank.
>
> The woman got up, she went to the one she had cooked millet for. She went and spent time there, for long. She got up from there, she went to the one she had cooked the guinea corn for. She went and spent time there, for long. She got up. She went to the one she had cooked the maize for. She went and spent time there. She got up. She came and sat down a little first. For she knew that she would go to the one she loved. After some time, she went. She went and slept there.
>
> The sun rose. Each one of them, he set out to go. Each one of them, he went and left her something. They began to go. They came to a river, a big river. "How will we cross

here?" The smoker, he smoked. The smoke which came out, by it they crossed the river. They went.

Now, of them and the girl, who is the greater? (Finnegan 1967: 166–67).

The dilemma in this tale is simply this. The woman has four lovers at the same time, and even though she seems to love one of them the most (having cooked him rice, the most preferred food among the Limba), she gives each one of them an equal amount of courtesy and attention. The men themselves are amazingly decent about the affair. They all know they share the woman's favors, but they are all equally polite and courteous to her and even considerate to one another (one of them produces the smoke that takes them across the river). The amazement in the story is compounded by the fact that although the woman cooks four different kinds of meal together in one pot, she is able to separate them neatly for each lover. The story then ends with the question of which of the parties has acted more remarkably—the woman or the men. Finnegan tells us, "The general verdict after the narration was that they were all equally amazing, and the telling generally caused much amusement."

It is hardly surprising that the performance of this tale gave much pleasure to the audience, as we can see from its measured movement. To start with, the statements are mostly short. This gives a feeling of weightiness, as perhaps befitting a story loaded with expectation: how can she cope with such a complex situation? The steady progression of these short sentences also serves to emphasize the orderliness and decorum with which the various characters, especially the woman, behave in the story. We will also observe the repeated pattern of the statements. On the one hand it helps to establish the ordered sequence of the woman's service to her lovers one after the other. On the other hand—and perhaps more ingeniously—it helps to stir up or sustain an emotional response in the audience to the conduct of the woman: is she an anxious, troubled schemer or a seasoned, methodical flirt? When not properly handled by a narrator, repetition can create a feeling of redundancy. Here, however, the Limba artist has left us in a state of suspended animation to the end of the story.

We have started our examination of fables with a dilemma tale because such a tale almost falls into the category that we have earlier designated as explanatory. It is true that, as in the latter category, the Limba narrator initiates the interpretation of the tale by identifying or dictating the line of discussion. But the question is left entirely to the audience to resolve; and whereas in an explanatory tale the issue is settled once and for all by the exclusive interpretation given by the narrator, in the present tale a great deal of excitement is generated by everyone joining in providing a conclusion to the story. It is this increased involvement of the audience in the performance—of a story that is basically open-ended—that gives tales in the fable category their distinguishing mark.

The greater majority of tales in this category do not even end with a question as in the Limba tale, and this gives each member of the audience ample opportunity to ponder the intended message or simply derive maximum and unconstrained pleasure from the narration. The following is an animal tale which I recorded from James Okoojii at Igbuzo (Ibusa) in the southwestern part of Nigeria.[37]

Narrator:	It (i.e., the tale) went over and captured Cat.
	There was such a famine that year, that if you cooked a meal you could not make the stew.
	It was a tough famine.
	Cat did not know what to do:
	5 Cat here is the pussycat.
Okpewho:	M-hm.
Narrator:	The famine was a tough one.
	He looked all around for what to do, but found none.
	Then he set off, saying, "But I have brothers:
	10 A man's brothers are his guide."
	He set off, went over and called on Earthworm the forager, and he said, "Yes."
	He said, "My children and I are dying of hunger.
	I don't know what to do.
	Whatever you have, do give me,
	14 For we are just about dying from hunger."
	Earthworm the forager cried and said, "Brother Cat," and he replied, "Yes."
	"Don't worry," he said. "How much do you want?"
	He said he wanted two naira.
	(Five-second pause)
	Earthworm the forager went into the house and brought him two naira, saying, "Go feed yourself and your children."
	20 Cat set off.
	Went on and came to Fowl—Fowl that rustles with head and hand—
	And called, "Brother Fowl."
	"Yes," Fowl said.
	He said, "My children and I are dying of hunger.
	25 I don't know what to do."
	"What!" he said.
	"Brother Cat." He said, "Yes". "Did you say hunger?" "Yes," Cat replied. "You will not die of hunger," Fowl told him,
	"You and your children, before my very eyes."
	Went into the house and brought him four naira,
	30 Saying, "Take this and feed yourselves."
	Cat said, "A week from tomorrow, come and take . . . take your money."
	That was what he had told . . . Earthworm the rustler,
	Asking them to come a week from tomorrow to take their money, in the evening.
Mr. Arinze:	Was the money being given on loan?
Narrator:	35 The money was being given on loan.
	He set off.
	WENT ON and came to Fox,
	Calling, "Friend Fox," and Fox replied, "Yes."
	He said, "My children and I are dying of hunger.
	40 I don't know what to do."

Fox said to him, "My dear Pussy Cat," and he said, "Yes." Fox said,
"Can you and your children be dying of hunger while I am alive?
Don't worry."
Went into his house and brought out six naira,
And slipped it into the hand of Cat.
45 Cat set off, SAYING "A WEEK FROM TOMORROW, come and
take your money."

Mr. Arinze:	That makes twelve naira.
Narrator:	That makes twelve naira.
Okpewho:	Hm.
Narrator:	Cat took off.

50 WENT ON and saw Python,
Python, son of Iyele.
KNOCKED AT HIS HOME,
Saying, "Brother Python," and Python replied, "Yes."
"I'm done for," said Cat. "My children and I are dead."
55 "Don't say that," Python told him.
"While I am alive?"
Cat said, "We're dying of hunger."
"Don't say that, I tell you," said Python.
"How much would it be?"
He brought out twelve naira and slipped it into Cat's hand,

Okpewho:	60	Hm—
Narrator:		Telling him, "Go and feed yourself and your children."
Okpewho:		—getting quite rich!
Narrator:		"You will not die of hunger."

Cat said to him, "A week from tomorrow, come and take your money."

Mr. Okeze:	65	That's the way he said it.
Narrator:		He left.

WENT ON,
Behold Hunter the blaster
As he sat.
70 "Hunter my friend," said Cat, and Hunter said, "Yes."
He said, "Please,
My children and I are dying of hunger."
Hunter replied, "What, while I am alive?
What am I doing with all this game I kill: Isn't it money I'm mak-
ing?"
75 Brought out twenty-four naira, saying, "Go and buy . . . feed your-
selves."
Cat said, "You've given me the money I need. A week from tomorrow,
come and take your money.
(*Arinze chuckles*)
Hunter agreed. The same day—all those debts will be settled.

Mr. Arinze:		Forty-eight naira?
Narrator:		*Forty-eight naira.*

80 He set off.
Not long after, he came to Lion, or Tiger.[38]
Getting there, he knocked at Lion's home.

Saying, "Lion who wrestles at the neck!" "Yes," he said.
Cat said, "Your brother Cat is dying of hunger.
85 My children and I have eaten nothing for . . . for several days now."
Lion said to him, "Impossible!
While I am alive?
Would I be alive while you and your children die of hunger?
Don't say it." Rushed into his house,
90 Brought out forty naira,
Saying, "I am Lion.
You go and eat."
Cat hailed him, "Lion who wrestles at the neck!" "Yes!" he answered.
"A week from tomorrow," said Cat, "come and take your money.
95 I am a man (of my word)."
Cat left.
        (Five-second pause, with musical flourish)
When it came to the third . . . to the eve,
Cat went to the market,
And bought himself a mortar of no great size.
100 Brought it out.
Purchased twelve naira's worth of okra,
Brought it out and started slicing it.
He sliced the okra until it filled up the mortar,
Waiting for his creditors to arrive.
        (Three-second pause)
105 Began to cut it up.
Just as he thrust the pestle into . . . into the okra,
Earthworm the forager knocked:
        Alas, Brother Cat!
        A man without money seeks rescue.
110   Alas, Cat, please finish cutting okra and give me my money.
Cat called him, "Brother Earthworm the forager."
        Alas, Earthworm the forager, please come.
        Please, come in and sit down, and eat whatever you find in the
                house, while I finish cutting okra and give you your money.
He was lashing away—kpola, kpola, kpoe, kpololo-kpo, kpololo-kpo,
                kpololo-kpo.
115 Cat laid aside his cutting.
Earthworm turned around and huddled up in one corner of the house,
                hanging up his satchel.
Not long after, Fowl flut . . . fluttered up.
Alas, Earthworm the forager, come—[39]
Oh, he called Cat:
120   Alas, Brother Cat,
        Please finish cutting okra and give me my money, brother.
What! Cat cried:
        Alas, Fowl that rustles with head and hand, come!
        Please, come, eat whatever you find in the house, while I finish
                cutting okra and give you your money, my brother.

125 Fowl dashed into the house kakalala.

WHILE HE WAS ABOUT TO SIT DOWN, HE TURNED TO THE CORNER AND FOUND EARTHWORM CRAWLING:

Let go her mouth on him and snapped him up.

(Low exclamation)

Swallowed up Earthworm,

(Arinze exclaims)

Then went somewhere and sat down.

Mr. Arinze: 130 That's the end of that money, of course *(laughs)*

Narrator: SHORTLY AFTER, PYTHON SON OF IYELE ROLLED IN.

Alas, Cat, please come!

Alas, Cat, my brother!

Please cut the okra and give me my money.

135 [Cat replied!] Alas, Python son of Iyele. Do come, into the house, eat whatever you find in the house, while I finish cutting the okra and give you your money, my brother.

HE WAS ALREADY LASHING OUT THE PESTLE—kpolele, kpolele, kpolele, kololo, kpolele, kpolele, kpolele, kololo—that he was using in pounding the okra.

Python had now come round. On entering the house to sit down, he turned round to find . . .

Mr. Arinze: Fowl.

Narrator: 140 To find Fowl

Sitting down.

What!

Python heaved up, and open his mouth.

Grabbed Fowl,

145 Swallowed him up at once,

Then curled himself over and settled down.

Mr. Arinze: That's the end of Fowl's money.

(Laughter)

Mr. Okeze: Don't you see that Fowl was gone?

Narrator: SHORTLY AFTER, BEHOLD FOX:

150 Alas, Cat, please come!

[Cat replied:] Behold, Fox my brother is here!

Please sit down, Fox, while I cut up the okra and give you your money.

Eat whatever you find in the house.

Fox agreed fully with him,

(Side comments)

155 Then came into the house and sat down,

Laying his tail aside.

As Python turned around,

Fox's tail got in his mouth,

And he immediately snapped at . . . at his leg,

160 And swallowed him up.

Hunched up his stomach where he rested,

And made himself into a dais.
(Arinze utters a low exclamation)
He yelled,
And Cat agreed fully with him.

165   Not long after, Hunter the blaster knocked at the door.
Cat asked, "Who are you?"
   "It's Hunter your brother," he said.
   Alas, Cat please!
   Please, please, please, please, please, grind up your okra and give
      me my money.

170   [Cat replied:] Please, Hunter!
   You and I are brothers!
   Eat whatever you find in the house, while I grind up the okra
      and give you your money, my brother.
Hunter jumped into the house so he could sit down,
Only to find some, massive object by the dais,

175   Then set his bottom on it katii.

Mr. Arinze: E-hen!
Narrator: That was Py . . . the top of Python he was sitting on.
                 HE HAD BEEN SITTING FOR A WHILE WHEN THE OBJECT
                    HEAVED KPUUUUU.
                 (Arinze laughs)
                 Hunter got off.

180   He said, "What can this thing . . . what kind of cushion have they
         got here?
      Cat has really got something going."
BEFORE HE COULD SIT A THIRD TIME,
He said, "Well . . . what's happening here?"
AS HE BARED HIS EYES DOWN—
It was python he'd been sitting with!

185   Hunter turned around,
Got out his hunting knife,
Grabbed Python by the jaws,
Split him right into two halves,
Brought out the carcasses of Fox and Fowl and laid them aside:

190   Put Python in the bag, put Fox in the Bag, put Fowl in the bag.

Mr. Arinze: All that money was gone.
Narrator: All that was gone.
                 HUNTER LICKED HIS MOUTH, saying this visit of his might be a
                    tough one,
                 And set himself up squarely on the dais.

195   Shortly after, Lion That Wrestles at the
         Throat landed:
      Alas, Cat, please come!
      Alas, Cat, please come!
      Alas, Cat, my brother,
      Please, (I know) you are grinding okra, but please grind up the
         okra and give me the money.

200 Cat called out to him:
  Alas, my brother, please come!
  Lion That Wrestles at the Throat.
  Please come, for the doctor has done a good job.
  Eat whatever you find in the house
205   While I grind up the okra and give you your money.
  Lion said, "Really!
  What's the meaning of 'The doctor has done a good job'?"
  Leaped into the house kapiala,
  Sat facing the doorway
210 And waited for the Cat,
  Asking him to grind up the okra and let him have his money.
  Cat said, "Uh . . . what's the matter?
  Take a good look down, man."
   (Three-second pause)
  On turning round,
215 Hunter saw the eyes of Lion rolling,
  Then licked his mouth
  And set his gun properly,
  Saying he had known that this was quite a visit.
  He raised the nozzle of his gun;
220 When Lion appeared to be lowering his eyes,
  Hunter pulled back.
  On further thought, Lion directed his eyes properly to see what was there, and Hunter let him have it:
  GBAIIIII—FASTER THAN I CAN TELL, LION SPRANG OFF AND GRABBED HUNTER, PULLED HIM OUT TO THE OPEN SQUARE,
  AND TORE OUT HIS GULLET.
225 Lion landed over there tem, Hunter landed over here tem.

Mr. Arinze: That was death?
Narrator: That was death.
Mr. Arinze: And the end of their money?
Narrator: And the end of their money.
230   Thanks to God! Thanks to God!
  Thanks to God, my creditors are all gone!
  Thanks to God! Thanks to God!
  (Chorus) Thanks to God, my creditors are all gone!
   Thanks to God! Thanks to God!
235 *(Chorus)* Thanks to God, my creditors are all gone!
   Thanks to God! Thanks to God!
  (Chorus) Thanks to God, my creditors are all gone!
  I ran off from there and left them.
   (General laughter and acclamation)

Here indeed is a tale whose principal aim is to entertain. No explanations proposed, no questions asked. In fact there was hardly any discussion after the performance; most of us were content to have been regaled by the tale, although we may each have had our individual reactions about the behaviors of its characters.

Let us dwell briefly on the beauties of this performance. Okoojii, the narrator, has a clear, beautiful tenor voice, and this was no doubt part of the appeal of his narration to the audience; I had no difficulty at all in making out his words during my transcription of the tale from the tape. Even more impressive is his control of the techniques of storytelling. This is particularly revealed in his manipulation of the behaviors of a mostly animal cast in the drama of a tale characterized basically by human instincts and emotions. For instance, the animal world is seen as united by a bond of brotherhood (line 9); this bond is extended to the hunter (line 171), perhaps because he is occupationally closest to that world. It is this feeling of brotherhood that Cat exploits in his hour of severe need. But he goes on to abuse the bond, and the amity which unites this man-animal society is corrupted by self-interest so that all the natural hostilities between its respective members dominate the latter part of the story: the fowl eats the earthworm, the fox eats the fowl, the python swallows the fox, and so on.

Notice that the characteristic behaviors of the animals here are vividly captured. The fowl is the one that rustles (in refuse, for instance) with head and hand; the lion is the wrestler at the throat, which is what he goes for when he fights to the death with the hunter; and so on. Notice also the role of ideophones in the narration. On one hand they are employed to portray the behaviors of the animals as graphically as possible: thus the disorderly entrance of the rustler Fowl into Cat's house is conveyed by the sound *kakalala* (line 125); and the muscular effort of the agitated python is represented by the sound *kpuuuuu* (line 178). On the other hand, ideophones are used for executing as vividly as possible various other kinds of action in the narrative drama, as in the feverish pounding of pestle on mortar by a Cat pleased to see his schemes working (lines 114, 137), and the heavy thud of Hunter and Lion as they drop dead (*tem,* line 225).

Equally noteworthy is our narrator's handling of repetitions in this story. The musical appeal of the repeated statements and episodes in this story is quite apparent, especially in the chants with which the creditors come to demand their money back. We can also see that the repetitive structure of the story helps to mark off one episode from the next, i.e., repeated statements here serve as formulas that aid the construction of successive episodes in the tale. But the remarkable thing about our narrator is the way he has been able to sneak in a twist, toward the end of the story, that gives an added interest by raising our level of expectation. We know, of course, that when Lion and Hunter finally meet in Cat's house there will be a fight. In such a fight, Hunter will likely have an edge over Lion, since he will have heard Lion coming in and been ready to attack the unsuspecting beast. But the narrator gives them even chances by making Cat hint, deliberately perhaps, how well his schemes have been working ("The doctor has done a good job," line 203); this rather strange statement puts Lion on his guard, and so prepares us for the equal and gripping confrontation between the two characters. A good oral narrator knows how to relieve the possible monotony of repetition by introducing a significant twist or change at the right point in his story. That is what we have here.

This tale is a typical trickster tale—usually, an animal tale in which a smaller animal (e.g., Cat) fools bigger animals (e.g., Lion), often to advantage. Favorite tricksters in African oral narratives are Tortoise, Spider, and Hare. Besides dealing with human beings and animals, fables in the African oral narrative tradition deal with nonnatural figures such as spirits, fairies, ghosts, and monsters. These figures are products or figments of the romantic imagination, sometimes an evidence of man's fear of the unknown or an effort by the human mind to ponder what lies in the darker regions beyond man's habitable world. There is, for instance, a vast body of so-called ogre tales dealing with monsters (part spirit, part animal or man) that confront hunters or travelers at unguarded spots. Here is one such tale from the Maasai of Kenya.

Once upon a time, there lived a young woman who eloped to meet her warrior lover out in the wilderness. The warrior directed the young woman to a place in the forest where he would meet her. He said to her: "If you get to a fork along the path take the right path." Then the warrior went ahead to await her arrival in the forest.

The young woman took off, and when she got to the fork that the warrior had mentioned, she followed the left path, forgetting which path the warrior had instructed her to follow.

As the girl walked on, she came upon an ogre who said to her: "Hey young woman, where are you going; do you have anything to say, now that I'm going to eat you?" The girl answered in song:

Not here my bead
Let us go to the water hole
Where you can eat me
And have a drink
Oh my dear warrior, where was it?[40]

And it so happened that this was very bushy country. The ogre led the young woman on, and when they got to another spot, he said to her: "I am now going to eat you here." The lady again broke into song, urging him not to eat her yet.

They went farther on, and the young woman kept hoping that the warrior would hear her voice. As they walked on, the ogre asked the young lady: "Shall I eat you here?" The girl sang again:

Not here my bead
Let us go to the water hold
Where you can eat me
And have a drink
Oh my dear warrior, where was it?

But the warrior had still not heard her.

When they got to a cave by a river, the ogre collected branches and leaves on which to place the young woman's flesh after he had slaughtered her. When he brought one type of leaf, the girl objected to having her flesh laid on ordinary leaves, preferring the sweet-scented leaves of the *matasia* plant. The ogre brought another type of leaf, but the girl rejected them, until eventually the sweet-smelling leaves of the *matasia* plant were brought. When the ogre asked the girl whether those were the right type of leaves she said: "Yes, these are the ones." The ogre then laid the leaves down on the ground and lit a big fire. All this while, the girl was continuously singing the same song.

Just when the ogre was about to jump on the young woman, the warrior suddenly emerged from the bush. The young woman said to the ogre: "It is now your skinny flesh that will be laid on those leaves." The warrior killed the ogre and placed him on the bed of leaves and took the lady away. And that is the end. (Kipury 1983: 62)

This story reveals once again (as we saw in the preceding story about the debtor Cat) the standard practice in folktales having nonhuman figures, to humanize these figures. Monsters, ogres, fairies, spirits, gods, and goddesses: these are all made to behave in familiarly human ways. So, apart from carrying on a dialogue with a human being, the ogre in our tale is just as liable as human beings are to being fooled. Who would believe, for instance, that a monster, instead of disposing of its victim at once, would permit her to choose not only when to be eaten but on what type of leaf her meat should be spread? This is one of the devices that fables depend on for bringing laughter and delight to the audience.

In this story a conflict is created which is resolved at the end. The conflict arises essentially from the error committed by the young woman in following the left rather than the right path proposed by her warrior lover toward their rendezvous. Thereafter, the story rides on a wave of suspense created in the audience by one delay tactic after another, employed by the girl: first in the matter of the right spot for her to be eaten, then on the kind of leaf on which her flesh should be laid out.

The song repeated in the tale has a significant role in the performance. It is one of the delaying tactics used by the girl to postpone her fate: the ogre is meant to derive some pleasure from the delightful voice of the girl and especially from her flattering reference to him as a lovable jewel ("bead"). The song is also useful (as in our debtor Cat story) in marking the stages of movement of the story. But it is even more useful, from the point of view of the audience, in bringing a melodious relief now and then to the possible monotony of the ordinary speech tones in which the bulk of the story is told. A rather large proportion of tales in Africa is told with this alternation of speech and song, aptly described by the French word *chantefable* (song-story). Very often, too, the song gives the audience an opportunity to participate actively in the narration by joining in the singing.

One more notable point about the above story has to do with the choice of a "warrior" character. Many ogre stories in Africa having women as victims usually set up a confrontation between the ogre and the woman's husband or lover. If a specific occupation is identified for the man in the story, it is often a farmer or a hunter, since these are the kinds of workers traditionally identified with the African forest. The choice of a warrior in this Kenyan story therefore raises two possibilities. Either the narrator considers a warrior qualified to do the most effective physical harm to the monster with his weapons, or else this story (whatever the age of its composition) may have been influenced by the atmosphere of guerrilla warfare (Mau Mau) against the British colonial presence in Kenya: the fighters, like the lover in this story, often used the forest or bush as the base of their operations.

This possibility is not far-fetched: stories, like other aspects of culture, are apt to reflect the political, economic, social, or other environments in which they flourish. There is the interesting case of the old Fang (Cameroon) epic of Akoma Mba in which a chief sends for his secretary and dictates to him a letter summoning all his district heads to a meeting[41]—instead of calling them with traditional means like drum signals or the metal gong!

The above, then, are the basic categories into which I believe the large variety of tales in Africa could be classified. In reviewing them it would be fair to say that each of these categories might usefully be identified with an overriding interest or aim. In the legend the aim is to record, that is to document a historical experience or some stage of a people's cultural growth. The aim of the explanatory tale is to educate by providing the origins or backgrounds to a familiar or accepted phenomenon or habit. And in the fable the narrator basically aims to entertain by exposing the audience to the aesthetic delights of the tale and leaving them free to derive whatever message they see fit.

I say "overriding interest" because one must be careful not to sound so dogmatic, considering that these categories often overlap and many tales reveal characteristics that are not frequently associated with the categories into which they may fall. Even the stories that we have considered above reveal this tendency. For instance, although the Ezemu story told by Simayi is fundamentally a historical record, the narrator sees the events of the Benin-Ubulu war as the background for the boundary between the two powers, thus assuming an explanatory role. And as we have just seen in the Maasai ogre tale, a fable may provide a clue to a historical experience, thus serving as some kind of a veiled record.

But perhaps the most pervasive interest of all is that of entertainment: there is hardly any storyteller who does not welcome an audience's acknowledgement of his or her skill as a performer, however tamely this is expressed. The various incidences of *Laughter* in the performance by Simayi and Okoojii (whose tales belong in different categories) show how seriously these artists take their roles as entertainers. And although the Sierra Leonean tale aims to provide a naturalistic answer to the behavior of dogs toward motorcars, no one can miss the underlying urge to delight. In our study of this subject, we can hardly afford to draw inflexible lines.

Nor is our system of classification intended to ignore habits of categorization recognized by individual communities. Various scholars have stressed the need for us to be guided by these local systems; functionalist scholars such as Bascom (1965) and Ben-Amos (1976) have said so often enough. While this is appreciated, we should perhaps consider that, for us to study the oral literature of Africa across ethnic barriers, the need to work out a valid cross-cultural system should be given equal emphasis.

Storytelling in Africa

We may conclude this chapter by looking briefly at the nature and the essence of storytelling performances in Africa. We have, in chapter 3, tried to cover in considerable detail the various things that happen in the oral performance and how these affect the text of oral literature, especially the oral narrative (from which most of our examples were drawn). While bearing in mind the points made in that chapter, we shall attempt in the present section to give a brief composite portrait of the storytelling session.

In doing so, it is necessary for us to observe, as I have pointed out elsewhere (1979: 34), that there is a slight difference between the storyteller in a familiar communal setting and the one that we find in the published recordings of tales. When they wish to study the African oral narrative, most scholars simply approach a traditional storyteller with such a request, and he or she goes right away to tell a tale. On the contrary, in the traditional setting storytelling is only one of the entertainments provided on an evening of relaxation (for instance), and may come only after other forms of activity, e.g., hide and seek games by children, reminiscences of the day's events by the adults, and perhaps a few songs. Then the tales begin. Even the tales themselves are frequently prefaced with a few riddles and sayings. Take this opening used by the Pokomo of Kenya in their storytelling sessions.

> Generations came and went *(repeated a few times)*
> A chief was born in the North
> A chief was born in the Central
> A chief was born in the South. (Nandwa and Bukenya 1983: 82)

Oyekan Owomoyela has also given us a picture of an evening session among the Yoruba of Nigeria.

> After the evening meal, the members of the family gather on a porch and if there is moonlight, the younger members gather in the courtyard to play games like hide and seek. On the porch, the entertainment begins with riddles. What dines with an *oba* (paramount chief of a community) and leaves him to clear the dishes? A fly. What passes before the *oba's* palace without making obeisance? Rain flood. On its way to Oyo its face is towards Oyo, on its way from Oyo its face is still towards Oyo. What is it? A double-faced drum. After a few riddles, the tales begin. (1977: 214–5)

These are varieties of what is called the opening formula or opening frame for the storytelling event. In some communities, indeed, even before the narrator launches into the story proper, he needs someone from the audience—or, in the case of professional performers, one of his accompanists—to shout some word or phrase (e.g., "Yes" or "It is true") every now and then during the narration as an encouragement to the storyteller. Among the Limba of Sierra Leone, for instance, such an answerer *(bame)* shouts words like *ndo* (yes), *woi* (fancy that!), or *ee* (really!) at appropriate points in the story, and even repeats certain words and names spoken by the narrator as a way of rubbing them in (Finnegan 1967: 67). Among the Mandinka of Mali, the answerer in the *griot* performances is an accompanist called a *naamunaamuna*, or "*naamu*-sayer," since he frequently shouts *naamu* (from Arabic *na'am*, meaning "yes") at the end of several statements made by the narrator. The following is an episode from the Sunjata

story recorded in Mali, describing the capture of the enemy king Sumanguru (Sumamuru) by the hero Sunjata (Son-Jara) and some of his generals.

Tura Magan held him at bladepoint.	
Sura, the Jawara patriarch, held him at bladepoint.	(Indeed)
Fa-Koli came up and held him at bladepoint.	
Son-Jara held him at bladepoint:	(Indeed)
"We have taken you, Colossus!"	(That's the truth)
"We have taken you!"	(Indeed)
Samamuru dried up on the spot: nyɔ̀nyɔ̀wu!	(Indeed)
He has become the sacred fetish of Kulu-Kòrò.	(Indeed)
The Bambara worship that now, my father.	
Susu Mountain Sumamuru,	
He became that sacred fetish.	(That's the truth, indeed, father, yes, yes, yes, yes)

(Johnson 1986: 176).

In other societies, this form of encouragement is not quite so pronounced or formal-
ized; for instance, my narrator Simayi welcomes only judicious inputs from his accompanists and tends to frown at anyone who intrudes into his narration too prominently.
Like most narrators, however, he welcomes and relishes approval of his performance
efforts.

The narration proper begins, in many cases, by the narrator speaking of the tale as
"capturing" his characters—as well as himself, of course, since he has been charged
with the duty to report the events of the story. The idea of capturing is meant as a
symbolic representation of the role of the narrator here: the events of the tale operate
mostly in a fantastic, extraordinary, or extrahuman realm, and the artist and the
characters must be removed from the real world of men to participate in or observe
the events. Hence, at the end of the tale, the narrator talks of himself as having
"returned" from or "left" the scene of the narrative, back to the world of real life.

The idea of "capturing" would be considered part of the opening formula mentioned above, while that of "returning" constitutes the closing formula. *Formula* implies that the device is simply a frame of convenience in a speech-act event like the
oral narrative performance. The fact that the devices have been used in, for instance,
the civil war narrative by Simayi should not be seen to mean that the narrator considers himself as having left the real world. It is true that the experiences of himself
and his people narrated therein surprised or shocked their normal expectations; but
the element of an imaginative flight away from the real world is so thoroughly absent
that the formulas mean no more than, say, "My story begins with . . ." and "That
is the end of my story."

What happens in the main body of the narrative performance we have covered to a
major extent in chapters 3 and 4 above. In chapter 3, we drew attention to various
physical resources and contingencies as they influence the effectiveness of the words of
the performance; that is, the value of things like histrionics, dance, music, remarks
by the narrator's accompanist and by the audience, and even the narrator's consciousness of the tools of recording of the oral text. In chapter 4, we examined various

techniques employed by oral performers to make their works pleasing and effective, e.g., repetition in various forms, digression, ideophones, imagery, and symbolism. Since a large proportion of the examples used in those chapters have to do with oral narratives, the points raised in them are no doubt worth consulting and need no longer be repeated here.

But perhaps we need to emphasize one or two insights that have emerged in recent studies of the oral narrative (with particular reference to Africa), because they help us to understand something of the internal structuring of the story by the performer. One of these has to do with the repetitive movements of episodes in the tale. In our discussion in chapter 4 of repetitive devices—called formular techniques by Albert Lord—in the oral narrative, we saw them as the narrator's way of controlling the movement of his or her imagination by putting successive episodes of the story into convenient frames; such frames, for instance, allow events that have a certain amount of similarity between them to be described in roughly similar terms. More recently, Ronald Rassner has suggested that this periodic repetition of similar symbols and situations (which he calls "images") helps to give the story a certain balance and regularity similar to the structure of rhythmic beats in a musical performance. Because they help to mark off the successive stages of the plot of the story and contain in them the means for manipulating the emotions and responses of the audience— very much like the manipulation of musical beats—he calls these repeated structures "narrative rhythms" (Rassner 1990).

The idea of the narrator's manipulation of the emotions and reactions of the audience is extended by Ropo Sekoni to the successive episodes of the story that may not necessarily be repetitive but nevertheless represent the unfolding of the plot of the story. Sekoni believes that for an oral narrative performance to be successful, the artist needs a good voice and a skillful use of language and body movements. But more than that, he or she should be able to organize the images or situations in such a way as to vary the emotions of the audience and guide them competently to the end. A narrator does this in several ways. First, he or she *activates* their emotions when introducing an event that creates a crisis of expectations, e.g., when a character in a story is set an impossible task. Then the narrator *stabilizes* their emotions when, for instance, events proceed that do not necessarily change the fortunes of that character. Finally, the narrator *depresses* their emotions when the crisis of expectations is resolved. These forms of manipulation of the audience's sensations give to the narrative performance a pattern of beats (upward, downward, etc.) similar to the rhythmic structure which Rassner has found in African oral narratives. By varying them in the right way and at the appropriate intervals, a good narrator is able "to create a complete aesthetic experience" for the audience (Sekoni 1990).

Most previous studies of the African oral narrative have concentrated on examining the qualities evident in the printed text. Some of these studies have discovered the skillful use of idioms and images in the tales. Some scholars, such as Eric ten Raa (1969) and Thomas Beidelman (1961), have been able to show how well the tales employ a system of symbols to reflect deep social and cosmic concerns. The work of scholars such as Sekoni and Rassner represent the latest trend of interest in issues of performance, which is perhaps the most worthwhile trend because oral literature achieves its principal vitality in the context of performance before an audience. The value of the work of these scholars is that it demonstrates more firmly than ever before that contrary to the view of earlier European scholars and thinkers, the African oral narrative reflects a culture of high artistic sophistication.

8. Witticisms

The types of oral literature discussed in this chapter have often been called "shorter" or even "minor" forms. This is in no way intended to underrate their importance within the oral culture of Africa. Take proverbs, for instance. Because they are frequently used in normal, everyday speech situations, native speakers of African languages are far more likely to encounter and to use them than stories or songs. Also, because of their neatness of structure and sharpness of poetic appeal, they might to some extent be seen as a finer form of art than those longer forms. And numerous foreign scholars have found them easier to record and to publish. But they attract far less attention than songs and stories not only because their material is rather small but especially because the scope for (spotlighted) performance is severely limited. And since performance is, as we have frequently stressed, the lifeblood of oral literature, their appeal to traditional audiences and consequently to scholars is that much less. However, let us give these forms their due consideration.

Proverbs

Proverbs are by far the most popular of these shorter forms and have been widely collected and studied by foreign and native African scholars alike. Unfortunately, the value of most of the collections has suffered severely from the poor understanding, especially by the earlier foreign scholars, of the cultural and aesthetic backgrounds of the proverbs. In many cases only a translation into one or the other European language is provided; in many more, we are told nothing of the situations in which the proverbs are used or performed. In more recent times, however, proverb study has been taken a little more seriously and the literary as well as the social significance has become somewhat clearer.[1]

What is a proverb? Put simply, a proverb may be defined as a piece of folk wisdom expressed with terseness and charm. The "terseness" implies a certain economy in the choice of words and a sharpness of focus, while the "charm" conveys the touch of literary or poetic beauty in the expression. We shall dwell on these qualities later. But the element of "folk wisdom" deserves particular attention. Like every other piece of oral literature, every proverb must have started its life as the product of the genius of an individual oral artist. But it becomes appropriated by the people at large (the folk) because it contains a truth about life (whether local or universal) accepted by them and appeals to their imagination by the neatness and beauty in which it has been framed. Again, we shall be expatiating on this issue.

Sources and Themes

Proverbs are the products of intelligent reflection, and careful study has shown that they have three basic sources of origin. One of these is folktales, especially the explanatory kind. In our discussion of such tales in chapter 7, we cited a Swahili story which explores the origin of the metaphor "meat of the tongue." Proverbs are indeed, as one scholar has recently pointed out (Seitel 1976), metaphorical statements, since they reflect a general truth by reference to a specific phenomenon or experience.

In many cases, folktales are used for this same purpose. The Nigerian scholar, E. Ojo Arewa, gives us some interesting examples of how certain proverbs arise from folktales. In 1967 he participated in an agricultural extension project sponsored by the University of Ife (now Obafemi Awolowo University), Nigeria, which involved a socioeconomic survey of the rural community of Moro (near Ife). He visited Moro in the company of an agricultural officer, and there they paid their respects to the *oba* (paramount chief) of Moro and his council of chiefs. After the visitors had declared the purpose of their visit—which was to get the community of Moro to participate in the rural survey project—the *oba* cited a proverb from a folktale (about the tortoise and the leopard) to make the point that the community should first know what the project was all about before agreeing to participate in it, so as not to suffer any untoward consequences. The *oba* then invited one of his junior chiefs to speak to the issue. He too cited a proverb: "The person carrying a burden should know what the burden is." He then went on to narrate the tale from which the proverb originated.

> A thief who stole some goods, which he put in a sack, once looked for somebody to help him carry the stolen goods. The thief asked a passerby to help him carry the goods for some distance. The passerby helped the thief. They got to a gate where a gateman stopped them. The gateman inquired from them the owner of the goods being carried. The thief responded by pointing to his helper. When the helper pleaded that he knew nothing about the goods he was carrying, and that he was just helping the thief to carry them, the gateman who thought that the thief's helper was making a false statement responded by saying, "It is expected of a child carrying a burden to know what the burden is." The helper was consequently found guilty of carrying stolen goods. . . . (Arewa 1970: 432)

Upon inquiry, the junior chief later gave a detailed explanation of the proverb and the tale, which simply reinforced the point earlier made by the *oba:* the project must be fully examined both between the community and the project officials and internally by the citizens themselves, so as to avoid the sort of unfortunate fate that befell the thief's helper. Notice, incidentally, the discretion observed by the chief in his address to the project officials: although the innocent helper in the story is referred to as a "child," the chief avoids such a reference in the proverb he cites to the visitors.

Proverbs can also arise as comments on actual historical experiences. There is the example of a proverbial advice, often expressed as a form of wishful thinking, that is current among the Maasai of Kenya: *Murua rraga mimanya* (stay uninhabited). Kipury (1983: 171) tells us of the origin of this proverb, that it "is very often quoted by the Maasai when they reminisce on the days when they used to be 'Lords of East Africa,' when they see themselves trampled under foot by peoples they once 'ruled.' " Such a proverb is thus used (perhaps unconsciously) for recalling some glorious historical past, however difficult it may be to date such a historical moment.

Alagoa (1968) has, however, been able to trace the actual historical origins of certain proverbs current among the Nembe Ijo of the Niger Delta (southern Nigeria). Having done an extensive study of the oral traditions of the Ijo, Alagoa sees these proverbs as "the pithy sayings of the wise embodying personal and general historical experience." Let us look at three of the proverbs he discusses. The first, *Bila bẹgẹrẹ/ Bila ba* (A Bila spear killed the Bila), refers to an incident that took place in the eighteenth century. The antagonism between two royal cousins, King Ikata of Nembe and King Jike of Bile (Nembe *Bila*) in the Kalabari area, culminated in a battle in which Ikata killed Jike. Although in the actual confrontation the kings fought with cannons and guns lashed to their war canoes, the word *spear* in the proverb is used as a symbol, and the proverb is used today to symbolize hostility between blood relations.

A second proverb, *Kọbaị enel/bekenowei bagha* (Tomorrow, tomorrow did not kill the white man), refers to an incident which took place in November 1830. Two British explorers, the brothers John and Richard Lander, who had been captured and detained by the *obi* (king) of Aboh, were eventually ransomed by King Forday Kulo of Ogbol-omabiri. Apparently, one of these brothers was slated to be killed for some reason but was saved by the dillydallying of one of the kings. The proverb is thus used today to illustrate the effect of delay on decisions.

Our third example is a proverb depicting intergroup relations: *Ado bibi nagha bọl ịkịọ ịkịọ ẹkị Ado bibi na* (One ignorant of the Benin language may yet understand it by common sense). This proverb, Alagoa tells us, "may be an indication of contact with Edo-speaking peoples or merely knowledge of the Benin empire. Several questions relating to this proverb cannot be answered fully. It is unlikely that there was anything like regular direct contact between Edo-speakers from Benin and Nembe because of the great distances separating the two places. There is, of course, the tradition at Nembe of 'Benin' migrants from Warri at, perhaps, the close of the 15th century. The speech of such migrants could have inspired the proverb."

Besides folktales and actual historical events, perhaps the most common source of proverbs may be found in a well-considered observation of various aspects of the natural environment as well as general human affairs and conduct. Some of these proverbs relate to the world of animals, such as the Zulu saying that "no polecat ever smelt its own stink" (Mayr 1912: 958), commenting on the tendency of people to be blind to their own defects. Some are observations of the habits of men or the situations in which they live, such as the Hausa remark (Whitting 1940: 121) that "the want of work to do makes a man get up early to salute his enemy." Other proverbs are observations on the elements and the landscape. A Limba (Sierra Leone) proverb, obviously reflecting the luxuriance of rivers and streams in the West African region, says that "water will not dry up"; it is used for expressing the certainty that money and goods will never cease to be paid in bridewealth, since marriages will never cease to be contracted (Finnegan 1967: 337). Among the Ovimbundu of southwestern Africa, the proverb-name *Mbundu* comes from a proverb which says that "the mist of the coast is the rain of the uplands," implying that customs differ from place to place (Ennis 1945: 3). Whatever the source of these proverbs—whether they are taken from the world of animals or of people, or from the weather and the physical landscape—they ultimately reflect on people's lives and fate in the world.

Who are the authors of proverbs? We have described the proverb as "a piece of folk wisdom," and various scholars have spoken even more pointedly of proverbs as "the wisdom of many and the wit of none" (Browne 1968). The element of communal ownership—and thus of anonymity—which these statements suggest or stress must be carefully qualified. Although scholars of the proverb have devoted much attention to its meaning and its philosophical content, little interest has been shown in studying actual proverb use to discover the variety of twists brought to any one of them by individual users and the circumstances and impacts of such twists. For if the proverb is a result of the skillful use of language, we should be able to monitor the art of the usage as well as the philosophical point that is made. Unfortunately, scholars have not quite come round to giving proverb users the same level of recognition accorded to narrators and singers.

But Schapera, in his discussion of proverbs used by the Tswana of southern Africa in traditional legal settlements (1966), does draw a distinction between old sayings of a more or less anonymous kind and the more recent ones whose creators could be traced. "Almost all the sayings so far quoted," he tells us toward the end of his article, "belong to the cultural heritage of the Tswana. Their origin is not known, but the fact that many occur widely, and among other Sotho peoples too, suggests that they are fairly old. In contrast, certain other sayings are both localized in distribution and specifically attributed to a particular chief of the tribe concerned." These chiefs, chosen no doubt for their age and experience as well as the tested reverence of the line from which they have descended, enjoy the utmost regard among their people: "The chief's word is law," goes one of the Tswana "legal maxims" cited by Schapera. It is thus in these sessions of litigation that we may find the origins of proverbs freshly created. As Shapera suggests, "one of the ways in which 'maxims' may have originated was when a chief, in the course of a judgment or in proclaiming a new law, coined a memorable phrase epitomizing the point involved."

Performance and Purpose

There are three main situations in which proverbs are used in Africa. The first may be broadly classified as a speech-act situation, meaning roughly a situation in which two or more people are holding discourse or exchanging statements on a formal or informal basis.[2] A second situation is a formal performance, such as a storytelling event, in which proverbs are employed for a variety of purposes. A third situation of proverb use is in the performance of chants of a somewhat ritual kind. Some people would add a fourth situation, verbal contests, in which proverbs are bandied by two people; but this situation is not as prominent as the other three and may be more justly discussed along with riddling contests (to be treated below).

When people make speeches or hold discourse with one another, they frequently use proverbs to add some wit or spice to their statements and to make their points more firmly. Before we take a closer look at proverb use in speech situations, however, it may be well to mention some of the traditional etiquette that goes with that use. In many traditional African societies, older people (especially men) are considered better qualified to use proverbs than other members of the society, mainly because it is assumed that their age and experience put them in a better position to understand the full implications of the wisdom and truth contained in the proverbs and so to impart these to the younger members. Younger members may use proverbs freely among themselves, but they are not expected to use proverbs in the presence of elders without prefacing such use with a courtesy like "As you, our fathers, have said . . ."

In normal speech situations, then, older and experienced men may use proverbs freely before any audience. In 1981 I had a general and informal discussion with the artist Charles Simayi in his village, Ubulu-Uno. Our discussion covered several aspects of his life, including his various skills as a builder (he was roofing a school building when we met him), barber, doctor, farmer, and so on. I had pointed out to him that whereas on other occasions I had recorded stories and cultural information from him, on this day I was interested in learning general wisdom of life from him, and I urged him to speak without fear of being misrepresented. In this excerpt from our chat, I have identified his uses of proverbs in italics.

> *Simayi:* Am I a child?
>
> *Okpewho:* Of course not.
>
> *Simayi:* When you were talking about this house (i.e., school building), I said that . . . *a man who decides to stab himself with a dagger just like that—he must have been feeling something within him:* he didn't just think about it one day. He had been thinking *(another proverb, not quite audible).*
>
> *Okpewho:* M-hm.
>
> *Simayi:* Now you bring up this matter. Yes, I've thought about it. I've never been witness to a murder. I've never participated in a useless discussion. Well, what I had thought you were interested in learning was something like customs or storytelling—
>
> *Okpewho:* Precisely.
>
> *Simayi:* Now, I myself have been in the business of telling stories, as the entire Enuani[3] knows. So, this type of thing, if I set myself to it, and it pleases you, I get down to it. That's what . . . But I wouldn't see—because I'm a musician, and the music I play, I know myself how I play it—I wouldn't see a man coming to hear my music, and say I wouldn't let him hear it. Don't you know—as they say, *if a man stole a drum, where would he play it?* Ehn? No. So you can't steal a drum, for where would you play it? No one steals music.
>
> *Okpewho:* *(Laughing)* Wouldn't people hear you?
>
> *Simayi:* No—no one steals music. And *I wouldn't do a tune I wasn't familiar with.* How would it come to my taste? *Would you dream about a trip overseas if you'd never been there?* Do you know a kinsman or anyone else there? So, if you carry on your discussion a little further, and you get carried away by your learning—well, *my face is turned only one way.* Now, what I usually do is this: it's true you wrote to say you were coming, but *you didn't know in which thicket a snake might be lurking.* You didn't know the nature of the business I had in hand. You've come when things are hard with me, when things are generally tight. Those are my workers—you met me in the midst of work. M-hm. But you know that, since I've brought these men to work—*the arm that moves about stems from the body.*

Okpewho: Yes.

Simayi: Take the food we eat: I cook it. I know it's difficult for me, but I cook it, happy that they are assisting me in the work.

Okpewho: Oh, yes.

Simayi: But, *when a man laughs, his thought is within his breast.* So, I've had the intention, and it prevents me from exerting myself too actively. . . .

As this discussion abundantly demonstrates, proverbs used in conversation mainly serve to spice up the talk. The direct relevance of the proverbs to the issue under discussion is often not very clear; sometimes the two are only vaguely associated. The proverbs, as Achebe has pointed out, are simply the "palm-oil" used for eating the "yam" that is the main dish—they are not the main point. However, in this discussion, Simayi has used his proverbs mainly to emphasize two points: that he has nothing to fear because the matters he is going to talk upon are issues that he has thought about for a long time (the "dagger" proverb) and on which he is very competent (the "tune" proverb) and experienced (the "dream" proverb); and that although I (Okpewho) did not know what to expect (the "snake" proverb) when I indicated my desire to come to him, he is a straightforward man (the "face" proverb) and has absolutely nothing to hide (the "drum" proverb).

Proverbs are also frequently used when making speeches in public or for presenting cases in traditional legal disputes. The latter use of proverbs in Africa has been given serious attention by Schapera (1966) and Messenger (1965). Messenger's study of the judicial use of proverbs by the Anang is perhaps better known, because he has cited some quite interesting examples to demonstrate that, when aptly used, proverbs have the capacity to win sympathy for a case that is not so good and may even swing the decision in favor of the guilty party. However, in a more recent study of the situation among the Akan of Ghana, Kwesi Yankah (1986a) has warned against this rather dangerous impression that judges in traditional African disputes are so weak and so easily influenced by proverbs. As Yankah points out,

> the proverb reinforces or foregrounds the argument . . . , enhancing its attention value. My personal observation of traditional courts and my interviews of jury members indicate that a proverb well used by a litigant will not turn a bad case around, even though it may help in clarifying his viewpoint. Issues deliberated upon during judicial proceedings are often too grave for judgment to be based exclusively on competence in proverb use. . . . Generally, litigants employ the proverb in the hope of soliciting sympathy for their cause. But their proverb eloquence is best rewarded when it is matched by a comparable control of evidence in terms of the Akan notion of evidential validity, requiring the provision of witnesses as well as compliance with customary law.

Whatever their differences of opinion, however, these scholars are agreed that proverbs used in speech situations have the tendency to attract the imagination of the listeners by the poetic effectiveness of their expression and to lend authority and weight to argument because they are generally recognized as eternal truths.

The use of proverbs in oral narratives is to some extent related to their use in conversational and judicial situations, since the narrator wishes to lend clarity and charm to his statements as well as authority to his points. The incidence of proverbs in oral narratives will depend partly on the narrator's skill in the use of language: a person may be able to tell a good story but may not have the wit to spice it up now and then with appropriate proverbs. Partly also, we have to depend on the loyalty of the collector of the tale: many tales recorded from African narrators are devoid of proverbs sometimes because their collectors may have considered them irrelevant to the main plot and point of the story and so discarded them (very much as they have often treated other oral techniques such as repetition) from the main body of the story.

However, that proverbs can be used to add spice to the oral narrative is aptly demonstrated by Simayi in his two narratives appearing in chapter 7. For instance, in the civil war story he tells us at one point how he was entertained by the formidable federal soldiers and how he fell heartily to the feast: the proverb "the chameleon is never beset by ants" (line 162) is used both to establish the point that he is equal to any situation in which he finds himself (like the chameleon that adapts its color to any surrounding) and that the soldiers are too small ("ants") to subdue him. Similarly, in the Ezemu story the proverb "the man who dines with the tiger must be left-handed" (line 123) emphasizes the fact that if the Ezomo wishes to confront Ezemu, he should be ready to fortify himself with as much magical power as Ezemu has. In practically every story that I have recorded from him, Simayi uses proverbs to enliven the tale and to reinforce the significance of the points he makes.

Proverbs are also used in some African oral narrative traditions as preludes and interludes. This implies that in between episodes or even before the actual narration begins, the narrator can chant strings of proverbial statements which sometimes have a rather tenuous link either between themselves or with the content of the story itself. Such a device serves various purposes for the narrator: to gather momentum before launching into the act of narrative performance, to recover energy or stability before moving from one episode to another, to recollect a detail that may have been forgotten, or—perhaps more relevantly—to put the content of the story within the larger philosophical and cultural outlook that proverbs generally define.

This practice has been recorded among Mandinka storytellers especially in Mali. For instance, in Seydou Camara's heroic hunter's tale *Kambili* (Bird 1974), we have numerous passages of what the editor (Charles Bird) has called "praise-proverbs." These are series of lines in which the narrator steps a bit outside the main line of story to praise various personalities (the hero Kambili, the narrator's hunter patron, even his accompanists) and especially to chant some proverbial statements relating to life, to the hunting profession, to destiny, to death, and to various other subjects. As a matter of fact, the entire story of 2,727 lines starts off with about 115 lines of such praise-proverbs which set the pace for the performance; it is then interspersed from time to time, between episodes, with other bundles of such lines dealing with various subjects. The story is basically about a hero-child (Kambili) who is born and grows up under unusual circumstances; his mission is to overcome and destroy a lionman (Cekura) who has been ravaging his community (Jimini) and to marry Cekura's wife, Kumba. One passage tells how an old woman goes out to pluck leaves (against all warning) and is devoured by Cekura, who is himself lured away by Kumba into a trap that she and her lover, Kambili ("Dugo's child"), have set for him (the proverbs are in italics).

The old woman went to pick the leaves,
2525 And was leaning over, picking the leaves.
Coming back from a meeting with someone,
He grabbed her by the jaw,
Surprising the little old woman,
And broke her into two pieces,
2530 Giving one to Faberekoro,
Grabbing the other by the bottom,
Making her his toothpick.
Ah! The little old woman was the last meal he would make of people.
Dugo's child came.
2535 And sat in the hamac of the blind.
He climbed with his trace-erasing stick (i.e., rifle)
And so climbed up in the nere-tree.
Born for a reason and learning are not the same.
A man doesn't become a hunter,
2540 *If he can't control his fear.*
The coward doesn't become a hunter,
Or become a man of renown.
Death may end the man; death doesn't end his name.
The omen for staying here is not easy on things with souls.
2545 *A slave spends but a late evening with you;*
A slave doesn't stay long among you.
Look to the rolling stone for the pebble crusher.
Look to the deathless for the sightless.
Kambili the Hunter, Kambili Sananfila.
2550 Kumba has gone off with Cekura.
Kumba herself was a lionwoman.
Cekura was a young lionman.
He followed Kumba, tengwe, tengwe!

We will notice that the praise-proverb lines in this passage appear between two distinct episodes, or at least between two distinct situations. After Cekura has committed what turns out to be the last act of rampage, Kambili climbs a tree and lies in wait for him; then, after the praise-proverb lines, we are introduced to Kumba's effort to lure Cekura to the waiting Kambili. The praise-proverb lines here could thus be taken as performing either or perhaps both of two functions: providing a transition from one event to the next; commenting on the fearless and heroic stature of the hunters' hero Kambili who has been born into the world with the destiny ("Born for a reason," "The omen for staying here") to destroy Cekura and save the community.

Particularly noteworthy is the way that various proverbs here have been used to project the image of Kambili. The first proverb line (2538) emphasizes the superiority of destiny over learning; Kambili is here favorably compared with the learned imams of the society who are mocked in several parts of the story. In line 2543 the narrator seems to imply that Kambili, like a good hunter, does not fear death because he knows that his reputation or renown will survive him after the event. The last three lines of praise-proverb (2547–49) are a salute to the fierce heroism of Kambili. However, whatever role we see in these proverbial lines, they clearly serve as an interlude which, on one hand, brings periodic relief to the narrative performance and, on the other hand, lends to the performance some of that wit and depth that characterize proverbs.

Proverbs also play a prominent part in certain ritual or cultic chants. Perhaps because of the depth and (sometimes) secrecy of the spiritual business conducted on such occasions, proverbs function as a way of establishing a certain aura of mysticism and transcendent truth to the proceedings. A good example is seen in the narrative chants *(ese)* of *ifa* divination among the Yoruba. Many chants in the *ifa* corpus begin with a proverb or series of proverbs, followed by the story which constitutes the main body of text recited or chanted by the diviner to the consulting client. In some of these proverbial preludes, part of the poetic charm consists in a certain amount of word play achieved through tonal changes. In the following preludes to one of the divination chants, the word play is between scarcity *(ọwọn)* and an antecedent client "Ọwọn" for whom the divination was performed.

> It is scarcity of iron which makes the blacksmith to melt needles in his fire.
> It is scarcity of water that leads to the loss of calabash water container.
> It is scarcity of children that makes people of Ido to overlook stealing on the part of a
>   child,
> With the excuse that the stealing was caused by hunger.
> People who are many but are unwise
> Are comparable only to *yun-un-yun* weeds in the farm.
> Ifa divination was performed for Owon
> Who would be installed as a chief in his father's household. (Abimbola 1976: 76)

The parallelism of the first four lines of this proverbial prelude also adds some poetic effect to the chant. The proverbs themselves put the experience of Owon—which constitutes the rest of the chant—into the larger philosophical context of human conditions and behavior.

The Igbo of eastern Nigeria also use proverbs copiously in divination and other rites. Sometimes the proverbs are injected at intervals into the text of the ceremony; but an expert chanter can in fact carry on for so long in proverbs that the main subject of the chant is infinitely postponed.

> If a man taps palmwine and cooks food,
> One or the other is fated to be badly done;
> The man who stands firm by his falsehood
> Is more dignified than he who deserts his truth;
> 5 Frequenting the fortune-teller's shrine
> Does not always bring one wisdom;
> A dog is deep in thought
> And is thought to be asleep;
> A tortoise is advised to be ready for a foe,
> 10 But he is already lying in ambush;
> One who pursues a den to its end
> Often ends up losing his fingers;

> The pursuer after the innocent fowl
> Is doomed to fall down;
> 15 The stick used for removing a millipede
> Is often thrown away with it;
> One who has not eaten the udala fruit
> Never suffers from the disease caused by it;
> For one who holds on to *ọwhọ*
> 20 Is never lost in a journey. (Egudu and Nwoga 1971: 61)

The *ọwhọ* of line 19 is a staff with a protective, talismanic force, but it is also the staff held by the ritual officiant. Although passages like the above are frequently done by divining priests, they also feature prominently in various ritual performances such as the celebrations at the New Yam festival, the conferment of an *ọzọ* (chieftaincy) title, and similar situations where they are chanted by masquerades and other officiants. The overall philosophical message in the above passage seems to be the need for caution, moderation, and steadfastness in human conduct, but the beauty of it lies less in the message than in the skill with which the chanter weaves various insights together in an associative thread and the steadiness with which he sustains a proverbial chant without mixing it with ordinary kinds of statement. In the performance of these proverbial chants, the chanters frequently adopt a vibrato voice style which makes a quite powerful impression on the audience. This practice of proverb chanting is so attractive that nowadays, in an effort to promote traditional culture, various performing groups among the eastern Igbo devote some of their schedule to spinning out extensive passages of proverbial lines, sometimes in a competitive format.

Proverb chanting is also done by drums among some communities in Ghana, especially the Akan, during certain ceremonies. We shall be discussing this phenomenon in our treatment of drum literature below.

From what we have thus said of the various contexts of proverb use, we may briefly summarize what their recognizable functions are. One of these is that, from their use in conversations at least, they help to provide a certain pointedness and clarity of focus to speech. Second, proverbs do have an entertainment value to them; whether we are referring to the way they are used in spicing up statements or making them more exciting to listeners, or we are referring to their preludial or interludial use in narrative performance or even to songs made up entirely of proverbial lines, there is clearly a sense of beauty attached to them that appeals to the ears and to the imagination of their audience. A third and no doubt overriding value of proverbs is that they may be considered the storehouse of the wisdom of the society. Most proverbs have a philosophical depth which is the result of a careful and sensitive observation of human conduct and experience and of the surrounding nature. It is this vast knowledge that proverb users draw from both when they hold informal conversation and when they engage in formal discourse, e.g., in legal disputes and in the meetings of elders. Proverbs in such contexts are treated with authority and respect because they are regarded as truth tested by time, and are often used for resolving conflicts and other problems between citizens.

Internal Qualities

Looking closely at the nature of African proverbs, we can usefully discuss them in terms of their outlook and of certain features of form and style.

In outlook, these proverbs could generally be said to present a philosophical view of human existence or the world by means of an intimate observation of human experience and of the surrounding nature. How else but by intimate observation does one discover, as the Thonga have, that "the centipede's legs are strengthened by a hundred rings" (Finnegan 1970: 405), or with the Gisu that "your heart tells you better than your mother who brought you forth" (Liyong 1972: 152)? The idea of all this is to derive certain fundamental truths and to frame them in language that can both delight and instruct.

In terms of form or structure, we find that proverbs are composed in a variety of ways. For instance, while some proverbs are expressed as a direct statement, others are put in the form of a question, as in these two examples from the Asaba Igbo of southwestern Nigeria: "The palmwine tapper does not reveal what he sees from the top of the palm tree," and "If the squirrel did not go to the dance, then who was it held the whisk?" (in reference to the rodent's bushy tail). Yet other proverbs come in the form of a command, like the Maasai "Do not follow the vanquished into the bush" (Kipury 1983: 178)—suggesting that one should not press one's victory over an opponent too far—or the warning quoted from a Swahili play in which a monkey tells a crocodile, "If you don't believe my words, well, just go on sitting, and you will see what made the guinea fowl lose his feathers" (Eastman 1972: 206), implying that one will surely get what one deserves.

We can also distinguish between the simple and the complex structure in proverb composition. The Ngoni (Malawi) lament "The earth does not get fat" (Read 1937)— i.e., it has a limitless capacity for receiving the dead—and the Yoruba saying "The wearer of a white dress does not sit in a palm oil stall" (Olatunji 1984: 174) may be considered examples of the simple structure in proverb composition, because the statement is a straightforward claim.

The complex structure, on the other hand, reveals a variety of forms. Perhaps the least of these is the kind that has a subordinate clause, like the squirrel proverb cited above, or the Ganda saying, "If you are thanked by many people, then you know that you have cultivated a large patch" (Liyong 1972: 152), implying that the opinion of many people should be considered convincing. Many proverbs are also framed as opposing or parallel statements. For instance, the Fulani say that "an old man does what men don't like, but he does not do what men don't know" (Arnott 1957: 389)—i.e., no one's actions escape unnoticed—while the Yoruba say that "the hands of a child do not reach the high shelf, those of an elderly person do not enter a gourd" (Olatunji 1984: 172), implying that every person has peculiar characteristics.

An even more complex form of the proverb is the kind that is self-explanatory, and this is fairly widespread. For instance, the Lamba say, "One morsel of food does not break a company, what breaks a company is the mouth" (Doke 1947: 150). The Maasai say, "Which of the two would you rather be, the father of the mischievous one or the father of no one? The father of the mischievous" (Kipury 1983: 183), indicating the high premium placed on having children. But perhaps the form is best known among the Yoruba, whose maxim about the value of proverbs deserves to be quoted in full.

Owe l'ẹsin ọrọ—
Bi ọrọ ba sọ nu,
Owe l'aa fii waa.

Proverbs are the horses of speech—
When the truth is elusive,
It is proverbs that we use to discover it. (Olatunji 1984: 170)

A final type of complex structure is the kind that is usually called a "wellerism," a somewhat dramatic form in which a statement is put in the mouth of a fictional person or thing. For instance, among the Asaba Igbo (Nigeria) there is the proverb, "The madman says, 'I have set my own fire; the one raging behind me is not my doing,' " used when a man wishes to disown responsibility for the unintended consequences of an action he has taken. The Ganda also have the saying, " 'I'll die for a big thing,' says the biting ant on the big toe" (Doke 1947: 110). And there is the Swahili maxim which cautions against a reckless discrimination between relatives: "The loose-tongued one says, 'It's not my father, but my father's brother' " (Nandwa and Bukenya 1983: 104). But the full dramatic force of the wellerism comes out in dialogue between two characters. For instance, among the Asaba Igbo, when someone is taking leave of another person or group of persons, the following (playful) exchange is likely to occur: " 'Little bird, are you leaving then?' 'Was I living in your home before?' " This proverbial exchange derives from a fable in which a captive bird maneuvers her escape, but it is employed more or less humorously in the general situation of leave-taking to convey the spirit of absolute freedom.

In terms of style, the proverb could also be examined from a number of perspectives. No doubt the most widely acknowledged stylistic quality of the proverb is its economy of expression. Now this does not mean that every proverb is expressed in few words. Many are, but a couple of the proverbs in Simayi's conversational statements above are somewhat extended in scope, and so are the wellerisms we have just examined. Economy of expression simply indicates that in one statement or so, the proverb captures a large situation or an experience; in a brief, metaphorical way the proverb says what it would have taken many more words to say in direct language. For instance, a Luo (Kenya) proverb, "Giving birth has helped the vegetable," is explained thus: "The young shoot from an old vegetable freed it from the people who plucked its leaves because they now pluck the new plant's"; the message of this statement is further given as "Parents will be helped by their children" (Liyong 1972: 1534)—i.e., the responsibilities of parents will eventually be taken over by their children. One can see how far we have had to go to explain the neat metaphorical or symbolic statement of the proverb.

Linked with this brevity or economy is the metaphorical quality of proverbs. It is sometimes referred to as a figurative or symbolic quality; however, whatever name we give it, we simply mean that in a proverb, one set of images (or items) describing a situation or experience is frequently used for reflecting another situation or experience. For instance, nearly all proverbs are intended to carry messages about the world or the human condition, but they are frequently expressed or framed with images taken from the world of plants or animals. An example is the Luo proverb about vegetables just cited, which carries a message about the relationship between parents and children. We may also cite a saying from the Tswana of southern Africa, "A monkey doesn't see its own hollow eyes" (Doke 1934: 360), implying that some people are quick to notice the faults in others but not in themselves. Proverbs taken from human experience also partake of this metaphorical quality of style; a good example is the historical proverb of the "Bila spear" from Alagoa quoted above. Whatever the case may be, in these metaphorical usages one image or element (e.g., vegetable from the Luo proverb) is seen as comparably representing another element (parent) or one single experience (e.g., the eighteenth-century war between the two Bila blood relations) is comparably seen in the light of the more universal human conflict between relations. By thus referring obliquely to a variety of similar events, the proverb is able to impart an objective message or lesson to us in one situation or the other.

Besides being economical and metaphorical, African proverbs have several other stylistic qualities which mark them out as literary statements. But perhaps they show their oral literary character best of all in the appeal which they make to our ears. Part of this appeal is achieved through the repetition of sounds in successive words or lines; we are referring here to the devices of alliteration, assonance, and rhyme. We may, for instance, refer once again to the Ijo proverb cited above from Alagoa, *Bila begere, Bila ba* (A Bila spear killed the Bila). Besides the terseness and the emotional touch of this proverb, the alliterative charm of *b*-sounds no doubt ensures the durability of the statement. Doke and Knappert have recorded several such proverbs from the Bantu and Swahili-speaking peoples. The following effectively combine the two techniques of alliteration and assonance.

> *Haraka, haraka, haina baraka*
> (Hurry, hurry, has no blessing). (Doke 1947: 110)

> *Kushinda Kupendwa*
> *Kupenda Kushindwa*
> (Victory makes a man popular, and to fall in love means to be conquered). (Knappert 1966: 86)

The latter proverb is particularly notable not only for its alliteration, assonance, and rhymed endings but also for the parallel (chiasmic) structure of the arrangement.

Such sound effects contribute to the poetic flavor of proverbs. Equally effective in this regard is the use of the tonal resources of various African languages. Although, as we have seen in our general discussion of tonality, this device is used in various forms of oral literature, it particularly lends itself to a type such as the proverb which is marked by an economical use of words. In the following lines the tonal variation is on different words.

> *Kòkòrò jowójowó ńnú owó ní í gbe*
> *Kòkòrò jobìjobì ńnú obì ní í wà*

The money-eating worm dwells with the money
The kolanut-eating worm dwells with the kolanut. (Olatunji 1984: 35–36)

Here the shift from high to low tone is on the second, fourth, and last words of the two lines. In the following example, from one of the tales I recorded from Simayi, the tonal change is on the same word.

Mkpikpa wa ji kp' esù n' esú yi elu mmoo
The stick used in ridding the millipede joins him in damnation (i.e., is thrown away with him).

The tonal change on *esu* (millipede) is simply a poetic touch meant to lend the proverb more gravity and pith as well as ensure a more affecting performance before the audience.

Riddles

In discussing the functions of proverbs we saw that, in addition to their entertainment or aesthetic value, they are taken quite seriously in society as a storehouse of deeper philosophical truth and are thus used for such serious purposes as resolving conflict among citizens. The other witticisms which we shall treat in the rest of this chapter are not often accorded that level of seriousness in African society. Although they have attained some status of excellence through long use and bear the same mark of sensitive observation of life and nature as the proverb, they are used primarily for entertainment, or play. We shall, therefore, spend less time on them than we have done on proverbs.

What is a riddle? Many definitions have been propounded by scholars; some are more complex than others, but all essentially recognize the riddle as a word game in which the elements of intellectual exercise and verbal skill are combined to varying degrees. There are, however, two basic assumptions about riddles which we must tackle before we can attempt anything like a dependable definition. The first is that in a riddle there is always an attempt to match the "answer" with the "question" or proposition in terms of content or meaning; in other words, there is always a tendency toward a "semantic fit" between the problem posed and the solution offered. This may be true of the majority of cases, but, as we shall see later, it is certainly not true of "tone riddles" as found, for example, among communities in Nigeria and Mozambique. The second assumption is that there are always two parties involved in a riddling performance, with the one party proposing and the other responding. Again, this is true of most riddles, but it does not take into account the practice of song-riddles among, say, the Makua of Tanzania, wherein the lead singer both proposes and answers riddles largely made up by the singer. When all these and other peculiarities are considered, we may offer the following definition as fundamentally true of this genre of oral literature: a riddle is a verbal puzzle in which a statement is posed in challenge and another statement is offered in response either to the hidden meaning or the form of the challenge.[4]

There are at least three advantages to this definition. First, the challenge–response component emphasizes the performance frame of this genre of oral literature as well as the "play" element in it, and may be considered just as good for the performer who answers his or her own proposition as for the usual two-party situation. Second, the idea of "hidden meaning" recognizes a certain level of seriousness in the verbal play of riddles and thus acknowledges that metaphorical quality as well as the factor of ambiguity which many scholars have seen as underlining the intellectual content of riddles. And third, the separation of "form" from "meaning" in our definition takes account of such traditions as the tone **rid**dle where the interest is far more in the structure or aesthetics of the text than in **its** message.

Sources and Themes

The sources of the riddle are far more limited than we have been able to find of the proverb. In fact, all indications are that riddles arise basically from an intelligent observation of aspects of human life and the environment in which people find themselves: the household, the world of animals and plants, the heavens, the landscape of mountains and rivers, and so on.

We may take a few sample themes. Some riddles relating to human life describe parts of the human body in figurative language. For instance, a Luo riddle goes: "A lake with reeds all round. *Answer:* The eye" (Liyong 1972: 155); here the eyelashes are seen as reeds surrounding the clear, fluid white of the eye. An even more interesting one along these lines comes from the Venda of southern Africa: "A mountain here and a mountain there and in between there is ululation—The buttocks" (Blacking 1961: 26), where the "ululation" obviously refers to noises of friction and farting. Other person-centered riddles deal with activities and occupations, like a Dahomean (Benin Republic) one which goes, "My father eats with his anus and defecates through his mouth"—*Answer:* gun (Herskovits 1958: 13).

For riddles referring to plant and animal life, we may cite a few. The Makua of Tanzania have one which goes, "Water standing up—sugar-cane" (Harries 1942b: 282), capturing the juiciness of the plant. We also have this riddle from the Maasai of Kenya: "I have many warriors all of whom stand on one leg—The candelabra tree," for which we are given the following explanation: "Maasai warriors are often seen standing on one leg. The candelabra tree has a long stem with branches growing only at the upper part" (Kipury 1983: 139).

A still large number of riddles have to do with animals both big and small, domestic and wild. A Karanga riddle goes, "A flame in the hill—A leopard" (Hunt 1952: 94), representing no doubt the fiery eyes and the flashing movement of this predator. A Tlokwa riddle, "Black cattle which stay in a forest—Lice" (Nakene 1943: 136), obviously aims to represent the large numbers of the insect hiding in the dark hair. For aquatic life, the Fulani have a riddle about the "fish" which is framed in a parallel structure (chiasmus): "Always cooked before it's scraped, Always scraped before it's eaten" (Arnott 1957: 382).

For environmental riddles, we have two beautiful examples from the Venda. In "A big red snuff box on Mount Luonde—The setting sun," there is an effort to paint a picturesque image of the sun as it sits on this prominent landmark of the Venda landscape. And the riddle "I wandered around from one village to another with my winnowing basket, saying, Where shall I lie down?—A river" (Blacking 1961: 3) captures two important aspects of this element: one is the restless, endless flowing of the waters; the second, represented by the figure of the "winnowing basket," refers either to the clumps of grass frequently uprooted or eroded by the flowing river or to the network of reeds lining the banks of the river's course.

Observation of life and nature is thus the chief source of riddles. However, from the way a good many riddles are framed, it seems clear that they arise from a skillful contraction of existing proverbs. If we take the example of a Sotho riddle cited by Hamnett (1967), "A tree on which all birds sit?—The chief," we can quite easily see how this could be a transmutation of a proverb such as "A chief is a tree on which all birds sit." This transmutation is possible because riddles are, like proverbs, mostly a concise representation of an obversable phenomenon or a transcendent truth through the medium of metaphor. The Sotho example is a metaphorical way of stating how the chief, from his high and privileged position of authority, offers shelter and protection to everyone. Finnegan also tells us (1970: 431): "Among some of the Central Bantu, for instance, a common riddle that occurs in various forms—'Something I threw over to the other side of the river—Eyes'—recalls the equally common proverb 'The eye crosses a full river,' metaphorically signifying that desire goes beyond the possible."

We can therefore understand why, in some African communities, riddles and proverbs are closely intertwined in a phenomenon that scholars have called "proverb-riddles," in which either or both parts of the riddle are proverbs. An example recorded from Zaire states, "The earth turns—(Today) you have, (tomorrow) you will lose." Proverb-riddles are particularly well known among the Anang of southeastern Nigeria, where the riddle "Who can enter the shed and steal the rifle?—Who can run fast enough to escape the fly?" is employed to "stress the impossibility of accomplishing certain ends and . . . cited to emphasize the impossibility of escaping god's justice" (Messenger 1960: 231).

Who are the creators of riddles? Like proverbs, riddles are rather concise expressions, which makes them particularly easy to reproduce again and again in almost word-perfect form or order. But perhaps we should stress the same need which we expressed in our discussion of proverbs, which is for a careful monitoring of the variety of contexts of riddle performance so as to observe whatever kinds of variation can and do occur. Although riddles are time-honored expressions and although the situations of usage are similar in many cases, every individual performance is a recreation and is in many ways unique. "Every time a riddle is posed," Harries tells us (1976: 319), "it is posed as if for the first time."

A longstanding debate in riddle study concerns the role of the riddle in exercising the intellect as well as the riddle's potential for originality. Some scholars do not credit the riddle with any creative or intellectual quality (Blacking 1961; Haring 1974), while others concede that riddles are a training for the mind and allow room for some originality both in the choice of alternative answers to propositions and even in the creation of new riddles (Schapera 1932; Bascom 1949; Harries 1976; Hamnett

1967; Kallen and Eastman 1979). Even among those who take a negative view, there is some tacit concession to a potential for originality. For instance, Blacking tells us of such a potential in his discussion of riddling contests among the Venda: "If, however, you give an alternative answer that is rarely used, or if you ask a new riddle which nobody knows, you may be asked to explain it before it is accepted as a point in your favour" (Blacking 1961: 2–3).

This potential of people actually having their own riddles, so to speak, is highlighted by Harries in a study of song-riddles among the Makua of Tanzania, traditionally performed during the initiation of youngsters. Harries tells us (1942: 27) of the performance: "These song-riddles *(ikano)* differ in function from the ordinary Bantu spoken riddle. . . . An expert improvisor leads the singing and the solution of some of the song-riddles is known only to himself. Each expert has his own stock of riddles, but a large proportion of these are well-known to other experts and differ only in grammatical forms." Surely the emphasis here seems to be on improvisation or formulation of riddles unknown to a majority of people.

Performance and Purpose

In an often-cited article, "Bantu Wisdom-Lore" (1947), C. M. Doke distinguishes between three kinds of riddles: the simple riddle, the problem, and the song-riddle. Although numerous scholars have recorded findings which make Doke's work seem rather elementary, we may still adopt his division as a fundamental step in discussing the variety of situations in which riddles are performed.

By the simple riddle Doke means the type in which one person throws a question or challenge and another person offers an answer or solution. There are roughly two kinds of situation in which these simple riddles are told. First, they may form part of the prelude to a storytelling session. Owomoyela has reported such a situation among the Yoruba of Nigeria, in which a few riddles are posed and answered before the actual storytelling begins (1977: 264f). In the majority of cases across Africa, however, riddling contests do constitute a specific entertainment by themselves, practiced mostly by children (but sometimes with adults contributing) in the evening after meals.

The standard procedure is for one person in the group to offer himself or herself as a challenger, or proponent, and for another person to come out as the respondent; in some cases, as John Blacking has observed (1961: 3) among the Venda, the game is played more often between two teams than between two individuals. One party says something like "A riddle!" and the other responds, "Yes—bring it" or "Go ahead." The contest then begins, and here we may follow Doke for the rest of the general procedure: "If the accepter is able to solve the riddle, the first must put forth another until he baffles the second. If the second is then unable to answer, he puts forth a counter-riddle, until he in turn baffles the first, when the first has to answer his obscure riddle and the second likewise. They are then quits, and start over again" (Doke 1947: 117).

In some communities, the bafflement between riddlers is resolved in a more exciting way. In an interesting study of the situation among various Fulani groups in

West Africa, Arnott (1957: 379–96) tells us that when a respondent is unable to solve a riddle posed to him, he must "surrender" a town, as in the conclusion of a riddling contest from the Fulani of Pankshin (Nigeria).

Poser: Give me a town.
Victim: Very well, I give you one.
Poser: Which one? Give me a big one.
Victim: I give you Jos.
Poser: I thank you for giving me a big town; I've eaten it; all the shrivelled little bits are yours, and all the lovely little bits are mine. (P. 382n)

A similar but even more interesting use of the town element has been reported for the Swahili by Kallen and Eastman (1979: 418–44). The structure of the riddling performance is roughly as follows. A riddler makes an offer by announcing *Kitendawili!* (A riddle!), and someone answers *Tega!* (Go on, set it!). The proponent then poses his riddle. The respondent is baffled, and after a while says, "Shall I give you a town?" "Okay," says the proponent, "give me a town." The respondent offers Lagos. The proponent then proceeds to tell an impromptu and often completely fictional town story about an experience he once had on visiting Lagos. This town-story component of the riddle simply "allows the riddler, who has successfully baffled an audience with a riddle they could not answer, to further show off creative virtuosity by weaving a story 'on the spot,' based on a town supplied by the audience, and developed by the riddler so that it will embed the riddle's answer" (p. 422).

Another form of the simple riddle—with one side throwing a challenge and the other responding—is what has been called the tone riddle. The practice of this type of riddle has been reported by Donald Simmons for the Efik and Ibibio of southeastern Nigeria and John Kaemmer for the Tshwa of Mozambique. As Kaemmer reports (1977: 204–19), the Tshwa tell riddles for entertainment or relaxation; "in the evening, after the meal and before bed, a group gathers around a fire," without any "distinction of sex, age or kinship," to amuse one another with competition in riddles. In these riddling contests, the emphasis is far more on "tonal correspondence between the query and response" than on semantic fit, as in one of the many examples cited by Kaemmer.

(Query)   *hlókó yáhwàrí kúnonóhá*
             head of partridge is hard
(Response) *wúswá gámùmú kúnanzíhá*
             corn mush of noonday is tasty

The Efik-Ibibio situation is much the same. Simmons reports (1956: 79–82; 1958: 123–38) that a group of young men may be seen gathered to amuse themselves with an exchange of riddles, and that in these riddles the challenge is mostly to match the tones of the response with those of the query. But Simmons also mentions other situations in which these tone riddles are spoken and in what ways.

Among the Ibibio, the tone riddle serves as a form of amusement, greeting, explanation for an action, indirect method of cursing, and erotic *double entendre*. . . . When two friends meet they sometimes use tone riddles to replace the prosaic customary greetings; one says the question of a tone riddle and the other replies with the correct answer. Since cursing frequently results in a suit for slander before the Native Court the tone riddle may be used to express disregard and contempt for an enemy without actually cursing him; a person simply says the query of a tone riddle that possesses an answer which denotes a derogatory meaning and thus obviates any accusation of cursing since the query may be construed as a direct utterance rather than an indirect curse. Occasionally the tone riddle serves as a periphrastic method of explanation; if asked the reason for doing some particular action an individual may reply with the query of a tone riddle and thus intimate the reason, since the answer to the riddle supplies the explanation. . . . Men cite erotic tone riddles for amusement, and to embarrass or insult women. (1956: 79–80).[5]

Although Simmons admits that there are a good number of cases of tonal dissimilarity between the proposition of a riddle and its response, it does seem from the many examples that he cites that the ideal in these riddling situations is to match the tones of the one with those of the other on a one-to-one basis. The Efik-Ibibio do, of course, tell ordinary riddles that follow the common challenge-and-response pattern and do not put much emphasis on tone. But the tonal riddle seems to be a special form which lends itself to creative originality in the manipulation of tone. Here is one of the rather innocuous tone riddles cited by Simmons (1958: 132).

> *(Query)*   afák ókot ké éták úton
>   (placer of chew-stick under ear)
> *(Response)*   esín ényin ké ńkpó ówo
>   (putter of eye in thing of person, i.e., busybody)

The following are two of those "erotic" tone riddles that young men enjoy greeting each other or taunting women with (Simmons 1956: 81–82).

> *(Query)*   ikpó rísung íkang (big ships)
> *(Response)*   okpón ékpong ítit (big clitoris)
> *(Query)*   wún naínti trì (one ninety-three)
> *(Response)*   ítít ádat étubè (vagina is red like palm-nut)

Notice the slight difference in tonal quantities in the latter example. More interesting, however, is the humor achieved in the appropriation of a foreign language in the first line *(wun nainti tri)*, demonstrating rather convincingly that the essence of the riddling is more in the play of sounds than in the sense of the statement.

Song riddles, a slightly different phenomenon, come from the Makua of Tanzania. Not many such traditions have been recorded. "These song-riddles *(ikano),*" Lyndon Harries tells us (1942: 27), "differ in function from the ordinary Bantu spoken riddle. They are either action-songs accompanying a dance or else have a didactic purpose. The meaning of the riddle is not always explained to the children in the rites, but in the case of the didactic riddles the explanation is generally provided with much exhortation from the adults. An expert improvisor leads the singing and the solution of some of the song-riddles is known only to himself. Each expert has his own stock of riddles, but a large proportion of these are well-known to other experts and differ only in grammatical forms. . . . It is tabu for an initiated person to tell these song-riddles to an uninitiated child. An initiated male person must not reveal them to a woman, nor an initiated female person to a man."

The lyrical force of the riddles in these song-and-dance rites certainly comes through in the following example (p. 31)

(Riddle:) *Ndrindima, ndrindima* (Rumble, rumble!)
(Answer:) *Ukukutu* (the sound of thunder)

where the appeal is in the ideophones, and in this one (p. 39):

(Riddle:) The tattooers, O mother, like that; O girl, the tattooers
(Answer:) Monitor lizard

For a riddle that combines poetic pith with the didactic aims of the initiation rites, the following example has a considerable satiric effect (p. 45):

(Riddle:) Gadding about, the pot is burnt.
(Answer:) Adulterous woman

What Doke calls the "problem" is really the same as the so-called dilemma tale—a tale which ends with a question or a problem that the audience is supposed to argue over or discuss. Such a form lacks the pith and brevity usually associated with the riddle, although it shares with the latter the element of intellectual play involved in working out an answer. However, since we have already discussed the dilemma tale under the "fable" category in chapter 7, there will be no need to speak any further about it here.

What is the value of riddles in traditional African society? Obviously the first function of riddles is amusement and entertainment. A respondent derives some pleasure, for instance, in being able to solve the puzzle set by the proponent of a riddle. Even in bafflement there is a certain amount of amused delight. As Jansen has rightly pointed out (1968: 233), "If one could not answer the riddle . . . , or if he were merely the witness of someone else's inability to answer that riddle, I contend that once he heard the answer given he would still be pleased and flattered by his consequent ability to comprehend both the ambiguity and the metaphorical aspect of the riddle."

This delight and satisfaction is felt mostly by the younger elements of society who are more frequently engaged in riddling. In particular the rather concise, almost coded idiom of the riddle allows children to amuse themselves with some of those phrases and references to aspects of the human anatomy that are generally taboo in daily speech. There is a large number of sexual and excremental riddles in various African traditions, and these are the kinds more frequently told especially by the youngsters. We have referred above to the Efik-Ibibio erotic riddles studied by Simmons. For excremental riddles we may cite a Sotho one which says, "We Basotho just throw it away, but the Europeans just hoard it—Snot, slime from the nose" (Hamnett 1967: 392), referring to the European habit of collecting catarrh in a handkerchief. In these ways, the youngsters have an opportunity to speak about things which are not considered decent in ordinary circumstances, and this is one way of releasing social tension.

A further function of riddles is to provide social education, very much in the same way that proverbs do. In his study of the Makuan song-riddle, Harries points to its usefulness in teaching the youths undergoing the initiation rites certain aspects of social conduct. One of these song-riddles goes as follows:

> *(Riddle:)* They came and drew apart
> *(Answer:)* A puddle

The reference here, we are told, is to "abstaining from social intercourse at the time of the menses," the puddle being a metaphor for the blood that prevents the meeting of the man and woman in intercourse (Harries 1942: 29). Another song-riddle

> *(Riddle:)* The sweet stalk of millet within the boundary however sweet I shan't break it
> *(Answer:)* Blood relationship

is said to be a warning to the initiates against incest (p. 44). Messenger also identifies this didactic function in "proverb-riddles" told among the Anang of southeastern Nigeria. One such riddle, about stealing the rifle and escaping the fly, has been given above.

Yet another function of riddles is seen as that of sharpening the intellect, although this claim has been questioned by a number of scholars. Messenger (1960), Blacking (1961), and Haring (1974) think that the principal stimulation received in riddle contests is in the excitement that the participants get in parrying with one another; since the answer is fixed by tradition, the point in riddling is in "knowing the answer" rather than in rationalizing the problem posed. Other scholars, however, give more credit to the riddle for intellectual stimulation. "The problem," contends Harries (1976: 325), "is not so much in knowing the answer, but in knowing the reasons for the answer." In their study of Swahili riddling contests, Kallen and Eastman analyze the relationships between the problem posed ("precedent") and the answer given ("sequent"), and point out that the contest "may involve the supplying of many sequents in response to only one stated precedent" (1979: 437); besides, the practice of the riddler telling a "town story" that will incorporate the solution to a riddle no one can solve does involve a good deal of on-the-spot imaginative effort.

But perhaps the strongest defense of the intellectual quality of African riddles, of their value in exercising the mind, has come from Ian Hamnett. In his study of Sotho (southern Africa) riddles, he finds that the majority of them are of the "oppositional" type in which two different categories of things (in the problem posed) are brought together or reconciled by a third category (in the answer given).

A Sotho example is: "Since you are a Bushman, where did you get that water from?—A water-melon." . . . The quality of being a desert Bushman recalls dryness and conflicts with the possession of water; but the solution depends on the metonymy [i.e., association] whereby a "Bushman" and "redness" are equated (the Sotho call Bushmen "red"). It is as though a secondary riddle ("Why is a Bushman like a water-melon?—They are both red") underlay and was presuposed by the actual riddle under discussion. (Hamnett 1967: 386)

Hamnett also points out that even when a respondent does not know the answer and the proponent provides it, the former makes an intellectual effort to "see the point" or the logic of the answer provided (p. 385). What Hamnett is saying in all this is that for the Sotho, riddles are a traditional way of sharpening the wit and equipping the mind with the techniques for finding the right classificatory relationships between the varieties of objects—e.g., between human beings as in Bushman and plants as in watermelon—which they encounter in their daily lives.

Internal Qualities

Riddles, like proverbs, have been the subject of much recent scholarly attention. Perhaps because of their size, some attention has been given to a study of their structure, although much of this analysis has tended to be unduly "scientific" in posture and so not very rewarding in real terms.

We may begin our brief treatment by looking at the variety of forms in which riddles come. Earlier definitions of the riddle tended mostly to see it as a "question" to which an "answer" had to be given; in many cases, in fact, scholars managed to represent riddles that they collected as questions even when they were not originally framed as such. It is true that some riddles come as questions, like the popular Yoruba one which goes, "What dines with an *oba* and leaves him to clear the dishes?— A fly." But a vast number of riddles in Africa are framed not as questions but as statements (however short) thrown as a challenge or a proposition to be countered or solved. In the tone riddle, for instance, what we have in most cases is a statement framed in one pattern of tones, to be matched with a second statement in a corresponding pattern of tones and often unrelated to the first in terms of meaning or message; in fact, when a question is posed in a tonal riddle, it is often to be matched with another question in a corresponding tonal pattern. It is issues like these that have brought scholars in recent times to speak of the two parts of a riddle as "proposition" and "answer" (Scott 1965), or as "precedent" and "sequent" (Harries 1971). Where two parties are involved in the riddling, we could thus speak of the one as the "proponent" and the other as the "respondent."

The structure of the riddle varies from the exceedingly simple or short to the compound or complex. A Venda example quoted by Hamnett (1967: 26)—"A coal-mine—The anus"—is clearly a riddle with a simple structure. So too are some of the ideophonic riddles recorded from various communities, like the Makuan riddle about the "rumble, rumble" of thunder cited above or another recorded by Arnott (1957: 381) from the Fulani of the "French Sudan":

(Riddle:)   kerbu kerbu njolla
(Answer:) (The sound of) goat's feet on hard ground.

Even full-length statements can be considered of relatively simple structure, like this
riddle from the Kamba of Kenya, which reveals an ancient understanding by the
people of the sphericality of the globe: "The gourd shells of our father are equal—
Heaven and earth" (Liyong 1972: 154).

The structure becomes complicated when a single image or reference is expanded
with qualifications or attributes. Taban lo Liyong also cites (p. 156) a Ganda (Uganda)
example, which says, "I've got a wife; everybody she bears has a beard—Maise cob."
Another Fulani example cited by Arnott (1957: 381) has an interesting parallel (chiasmic)
structure:

(Riddle:)   Always cooked before it's scraped,
             Always scraped before it's eaten
(Answer:) A fish.

However, a large number of African riddles in this class contain some twist which
carries a certain amount of contradiction in terms. In their classic study of riddle
structure, Georges and Dundes (1963) draw a distinction between the "oppositional"
and "nonoppositional" types of riddle. In the nonoppositional structure, the statement
is straightforward and uncontentious, like Liyong's "heaven and earth" riddle from
the Kamba just cited or Hamnett's "A tree on which all birds sit?—The chief" from
the Sotho.

In the oppositional type, however, the statement either carries within it an element of self-contradiction or is so framed that one part of it stands in obvious contrast
to the other. An interesting example from the Yoruba, cited by Olatunji (1984: 186)
and revealing not only the compound structure but the sense of poetic appeal characteristic of Yoruba oral performance generally, goes like this:

Ancient ditch of my father
Ancient ditch of my father
If a small young person enters it, it reaches his neck
If an elderly person enters it, it reaches his neck.

The self-contradiction here is in a "ditch" which reaches to the neck of anyone, old
or young—and, by implication, big or small. The answer to this riddle is "garment,"
which will rest on the shoulders and so reach the neck of whoever wears it.

The riddle structure perhaps attains its most complex level when it is framed in
the dramatic form of a speech, corresponding in a sense to what has been called the
wellerism in proverb study. The Venda example cited from Blacking above is of this
type: "I wandered around from one village to another with my winnowing basket,
saying, Where shall I lie down?—A river." Here the river is represented as speaking.
The following riddle from the Makua, cited by Harries (1942b: 282), is framed as a
reflection with a speech in the middle of it: "To get a child, to try to drive him away

without succeeding, let me beat him, and you beat yourself—Shadow." In these various shades of structure, African riddles achieve a far greater warmth and aesthetic appeal than is possible with the rather formal and staid question-and-answer form.

In terms of style, we can speak first of a distinction between the simple or direct language and the figurative or metaphorical language of the riddle. The simple diction comes quite often with the interrogative structure, as in this example from the Maasai: "What moves across the world but leaves no trace?—The butterfly" (Kipury 1983: 143). It is also found often enough in simple noninterrogative puzzles such as the Venda "It goes plop-plop in the water—Small frog" (Blacking 1961: 16).

But much of the mystery or depth which characterizes riddles comes from their frequently metaphorical language—their tendency, that is, to conceive of one order of reality in terms of another but parallel order. Although a good many of the riddles recorded from Africa are of the simple or direct diction, a safe majority are of the metaphorical diction. Take this one from the Kikuyu: "A man who never sleeps hungry—Fire, which is always lit at night" (Liyong 1972: 155).

The Kikuyu example, in fact, demonstrates a general trait in the metaphorical language of riddles in Africa: a tendency toward personification or at least some anthropocentric outlook, whereby various objects or scenes in the observable world are humanized. This tendency can be seen in riddles dealing with animal life, as in a Kamba example that bears a touch of playful insolence in it, "A small woman who cooks better than your mother—It is a bee" (Nandwa and Bukenya 1983: 105), in reference to honey that is considered sweeter than any food a woman can cook; in riddles dealing with rural activity, as in the Fulani "My short grandfather overthrew my tall grandfather—An axe felled a tree" (Arnott 1957: 380); and in riddles relating to heavenly bodies as also in the Fulani "A beautiful woman who is never married— The moon" (ibid.).

Correspondingly, riddles having to do with parts of the human body are frequently conceived in terms of the surrounding ecology or of objects connected with human activity. A Kgatla riddle, "Tell me: two civet cats which when they fight are not to be separated—It is a married couple" (Schapera 1932: 227), refers no doubt to the ferocity of marital fights, while the Luo say "A lake with reeds all round—The eye" (Liyong 1972: 155). Such instances reveal an underlying feeling for warmth and humor in a primarily recreative activity like riddling.

It is interesting to observe a slight difference between riddles and proverbs in the use of language. In proverbs, the metaphorical language helps achieve a certain economy of expression by squeezing an entire area of human experience within a few well-chosen words. In riddles, on the contrary, the technique works the other way, for here all that large figurative buildup refers only to one object. For instance, the Igbo proverb "A deaf man need not be told that war is raging" can be interpreted to cover a whole range of experiences in which issues are so glaring that no one needs to be guided by explanations provided by someone else. But take the following Yoruba riddle cited by Olatunji (1984: 188):

The great packer of loads, king among divinities
He packs two hundred yams with a groundnut shell

He sends people to tell those in his house,
That he is just learning how to pack loads.

The answer is "termite." Here a tiny ant is adorned with highly metaphorical references, aided in no small way by the hyperbolic quality of the descriptive attribute (*oriki*) in Yoruba praise poetry.

There are, of course, riddle traditions in Africa in which neither the proposition nor the answer is much longer than one word, as in the Nyanja "Invisible—Wind" (Gray 1939: 258). In some cases of ideophonic riddles the proposition simply gives the sound. But the general run of African riddles of the metaphoric style involves a reasonably detailed proposition that is simply answered by one object. Perhaps that goes to stress the point recognized by many scholars of these forms, that while the proverb is art used for broaching larger philosophical issues, the riddle is fundamentally (though not solely) an exercise in imaginative play.

In some traditions, this play element is aided to a considerable degree by devices which are intended to please the ear. These include the use of repetition and parallelism, as in the Yoruba riddle about "garment" and the Fulani riddle about "fish." The tonal counterpoint in Efik-Ibibio and Tshwa tone riddles as discussed above also reflects this phonaesthetic interest in African riddles, as does the use of ideophones in the examples from the Makua and the Fulani.

Puns and Tongue-Twisters

Other witticisms in Africa may not have the same level of literary form or interest as the proverb and the riddle, but they are just as notable for the opportunity they provide for an exercise of the imagination. Like the riddle, they function mainly as forms of lighthearted entertainment by way of a quick-witted play on words and sounds. Again like the riddle, they are games played mostly by children, and they may be played either casually or as a prelude to a storytelling session on an evening.

Puns may come in the form of a double entendre on a word—a word which sounds one way but is capable of more than one meaning or interpretation. Two of the Luhya (Kenya) puns cited by Liyong (1972: 157) have a pornographic touch that is peculiar to verbal games played by youngsters: *Hamba ombeleke* (Come and escort me, or Come and make me conceive); *Umkana wovo atatsa?* (Your girl has not arrived yet? or Your girl is bleeding?).

An equally popular form of the pun is a linking game by two players in which a word mentioned by one player is drawn by the other into association with another word, and the linking goes on until an accepted conclusion has been reached. We said something of this phenomenon in our discussion, in chapter 4, of "piling and association" as a stylistic resource in African oral literature. The passages quoted there provide ample illustrations of this kind of punning and are worth consulting again.

A pun is a play on a word, but a tongue-twister is a play on sounds whereby the syllables of a word are subjected to a variety of tonal changes to produce different meanings. In tongue-twisters, the idea is to see who can rattle off the words with the greatest speed and accuracy. Here is a Luganda example.

Akawala akaawa Kaawa kaawa akaawa ka wa?
The girl who gave Kaawa bitter coffee, where is she from? (Nandwa and Bukenya 1983: 106).

This one is from the Kikuyu.

Kaana ka Nikora kona kora kora, nako kora kona
kaana ka Nikora kora
Nikora's child saw a tadpole and the former ran away;
when the tadpole saw the child, it ran away too. (Liyong 1972: 157–58)

The most interesting study of tongue-twisters I have read is Ayodele Ogundipe's "Yoruba Tongue Twisters" (1972). It is particularly useful because, although we have often spoken of such witticisms as mostly a matter of fun and games, Ogundipe demonstrates one situation in which they serve as a rather grim test of cultural identity. Ogundipe tells us of tests she conducted among schoolchildren and other informants in Lagos (Nigeria) on tongue-twisters, and goes into an interesting analysis of this form of oral literature among the Yoruba, from a largely sociolinguistic point of view. The more remarkable part of this article is the introduction, where she tells us how she came into studying tongue-twisters in the first place.

In October 1966 I returned to Nigeria from Indiana University to accept a lecturership in African Studies at the University of Lagos, Nigeria, and also to do fieldwork for my doctoral dissertation on some aspect of Yoruba mythology. I could not have chosen a more inauspicious time to return home, because soon Nigeria found herself in the throes of a civil war. It became quite hazardous to roam around the countryside because of the many soldiers at innumerable checkpoints. Early in the war the soldiers were very jittery and nervous, especially towards women drivers, whom they suspected of servicing the insurgents. Every traveller was suspect, and I was constantly asked what ethnic group I belonged to. Ordinarily, to give one's name or show an identity card of some sort was sufficient, but on one occasion, while I was on my way to Ibadan from Lagos, the soldiers would accept none of my many identification cards. Instead, they asked me to recite a Yoruba tongue-twister:

Mo ra dòdò ní Ìddó;
Mo je dòdò ní Ìddó;
Mo fi ọwọ dòdò r'ọmọ ònídòdò ní idodo ní Ìddó.
("I bought fried plantains at Iddo;
I ate fried plantains at Iddo;
I wiped my hands on the navel of the fried-plantain seller at Iddo.")

After this scary experience, I thought it best not to venture out of Lagos until the tension at the checkpoints had relaxed a little, but the incident did give me the idea of collecting tongue twisters within Lagos, a sizeable Yoruba-speaking area, now famous in the novels of Chinua Achebe and Cyprian Ekwensi. (Ogundipe 1972: 211–12)

Ogundipe's recitation of that tongue-twister was hardly a matter of entertainment. It marked a possible line between, if not life and death, at least freedom and detention by the military authorities in those grim days of the Nigerian civil war, when it was risky to be identified as a rebel or a rebel collaborator, i.e. as an Igbo (the seceding ethnic group) or one sympathetic to the secessionist cause.

9. Musical and Dramatic Forms

There are two reasons why a separate chapter on music and drama is called for. In the first place, these are the traditional art forms most closely connected with the oral performance as ancillary resources. In chapter 3, we saw how, on one hand, the stability of a performance depended on a proper fit between the pace of the music and that of the words, and on the other, how a singer or a narrator would frequently reinforce a point or the message of the text by an apt dramatic gesture or movement. It so happens, however, that music and drama represent distinct forms with peculiarities of their own that nevertheless reflect certain characteristics we have identified in the oral literature and give us a further understanding of the qualities of the oral culture.

A second reason has to do specifically with the subject of drama: here we have an opportunity to see how the oral culture is both reinforced and modified by present-day conditions and resources. In chapter 10 we shall examine in some detail how oral literature has fared in the culture of the written word. The present chapter gives us our first opportunity to test the strengths of the oral culture in the face of the modifications imposed upon it both by the contemporary socioeconomic climate and by the altered conditions and modes of public entertainment.

The Poetry of Tone Instruments

A tone instrument is a musical instrument that makes sounds similar to the tones of human speech. Three main types of tone instruments are used in traditional African societies: horns, flutes, and drums.

Some horns are made from the long neck of a calabash (gourd). This is hollowed out and dried; a hole is made at the tip for the (left) thumb, and another hole notched a little further down for the blower's lips. Other horns are made from the horns of animals (such as the buffalo and large antelope) and from elephant tusks. Such horns are known among the Bini and Igbo of Nigeria, the Mende of Sierra Leone (Henngeler 1981), and the Lokele of Zaire (Carrington 1949), among others. Carrington tells us of these horns: "There are always two holes pierced in horns transmitting the signal language; one hole at the tip and the other on the side near the tip of the horn. The horn is blown from the side, and the thumb, by stopping or leaving open the end hole, serves to modulate two tones, these being adequate for sending out the tonal melodies of the phrases making up the signal language" (1949: 77).

Flutes are made mostly from wood—bamboo or solid wood—and are usually short. They are common among the Igbo and Ibibio of Nigeria, the Bambole of Zaire, and in northern Ghana. Carrington (1949: 76) also reports that the Bambole "make a small whistle [i.e., flute] out of the spherical fruit of a forest tree"; a tale which he cites at the end of his book (pp. 87–88) suggests that part of an animal's thigh bone may have been used also. In these flutes, held vertically downward from the mouth, there is a hole at the tip for the blower's lips; a little below this there is a notch on either side against which the thumb is placed for modulating the sound to varying tones.

The most distinguished of these tone instruments are the drums. There are two broad classes of drums: slit-drums and skin-covered drums. Slit-drums are known among the Igbo and Ibibio of Nigeria and the Basongye (Merriam 1973: 254–56) and the Lokele of Zaire, to mention a few peoples. Carrington (1949: 21) describes the Lokele slit-drum as being "made from a solid log of reddish wood (*Pterocarpus soyauxii*), hollowed out through a long narrow slit cut in the length of the log so that it looks like a gigantic cylindrical money-box." The player holds a stick in either hand and strikes the "lips" of the log on the two sides of the slit to produce varying tones of sound.

Even more sophisticated than this—and perhaps more highly favored—is the skin-covered drum, known widely across Africa but reported mostly among the Akan of Ghana, the Yoruba of Nigeria, and the Lokele of Zaire. From a study of the traditions of the Akan of Ghana, Nketia (1963b: 4) divides these drums broadly into two kinds, open (single-headed drums with an opening at one end) and closed (single- or double-headed drums without an open end). The drum heads are covered with animal skins, the most favored being the skin of the duyker or (better still) the ear of an elephant.[1]

Various drums are used for signaling and for dance music, but among the Akan and the Yoruba the star of the collection is the talking drum, called *atumpan* by the Akan and *dundun* by the Yoruba. This drum is carved from solid wood and shaped like an hourglass, with a neck at the middle. The two ends are covered with leather sheets, which are connected to each other in varying degrees of tautness by strings stretched all round the drum. A stick curved at the head is used for striking the drum. For the tones of sound thus produced, Nketia says,

> the variation is achieved by increasing or decreasing the tautness of the drum head. This is done by applying pressure to the strings that join the drum heads together. When no pressure has been applied to these strings, the membranes are lax and produce the lowest note of the drum. As pressure is applied, the drum heads increase in tautness yielding higher notes. Gradations of pitch are thus possible between the lowest note or the position of minimum tension and the highest note or the position of maximum tension. (1963a: 98)

Playing these tone instruments is not an easy job. In almost every sense the preparation for the art is similar to what we have seen of the oral artist (chapter 2); in many cases, in fact, the same artist can be proficient as a singer or narrator and as a musician—like my friend Simayi. Although many scholars report that apprenticeship in the art may be informal or may start as a matter of play, they invariably agree that "it takes years of practice and experience to attain the expertise demanded" (Jones 1959: 71) of the more sophisticated forms like drumming. Nketia (1963b: 154–56) indeed paints an elaborate portrait of the Akan master drummer who performs on the talking drums at the royal courts. His training took several years, during which he was constantly in attendance when past masters played, imbibing the rhythms and gaining the experience. A detailed knowledge of tribal history was required of him, for this was going to form much of the basis of his drum salutes to the king. In the old days he enjoyed so much prestige that he was given the title of "Creator's Drummer" (*Odomankoma Kyerema*) and even enjoyed the privilege of being mildly critical of the king without suffering any consequences.

The drums themselves are similarly highly honored. Basden even tells (1938: 360) of one incident among the Igbo involving a slit-drum in which the people were so happy to have the largest drum of all the villages around that they sacrificed the carver and sprinkled his blood on the drum so that he could never make a larger drum for a rival community.

How are these tone instruments made to "talk" like people? The communities where they are found speak basically tone languages, and the idea is for the instrument to reproduce the tones of a statement almost exactly the way it would sound in normal speech. Since most tonal languages operate basically on a two-tone structure (high and low), imitating them is not difficult on these tone instruments. But there is one problem, usefully brought out by Carrington in his study of the language of Lokele slit-drums (1949: 47–54). Since in tone languages many words may have identical syllable tones, the challenge is to play the drum text in such a way that one word is not confused with another. Drum language gets round this problem by providing a peculiar qualification or epithet to go along with the word every time it is played. In this way, every object or person acquires what is called a "drum name."

Two examples used by Carrington[2] for illustration are the words for moon (*sóngé*) and fowl (*kókó*), both of them two-syllable words with the same tone pattern (high-high). The drum name for the moon is *sóngé li tángé là mángá* ("the moon looks down at the earth"), while that for fowl is *kókó òlóngó là bòkiókió* ("the fowl, the little one which says 'kiokio' "); each time these objects are mentioned in a drum message, they are played complete with these stereotyped epithets or formulas. Other drum names commonly used in this context are *girl*, "the girl will never go to the fishing net" (among the Lokele, fishing is a man's occupation); *money*, "the pieces of metal which arrange palavers" (especially because they are used in settling legal fines); *war*, "war watches for opportunities" (reflecting the element of surprise attacks in warfare); *corpse*, "the corpse lying on its back on the clods of earth"; and the *drum* itself, "the log of the bolondo tree" (indicating the source of its wood).

The highly figurative quality of many of these epithets and references is undeniable and "shows the rather poetical nature of the drum phrases" (Carrington 1949: 37). Apart from the use of formulas, drum messages are also marked by the frequent use of repetition both to rub in the point and to enhance the rhythmic texture of the text. The result of using these resources is that a simple message in spoken language will translate into a considerably longer statement in drum language, largely because the message is treated as a statement in poetic music. Carrington tells (1949: 54) how a message of a visit by him—"The missionary is coming up river to our village tomorrow. Bring water and firewood to his house"—was played on the slit-drum.

> White man spirit of the forest
> of the leaf used for roofs
> comes up-river, comes up-river
> when tomorrow has risen
> 5 on high in the sky
> to the town and the village
> of us
> come, come, come, come
> bring water of *lokoila* vine
> 10 bring sticks of firewood
> to the house with shingles high up above
> of the white man spirit of the forest
> of the leaf used for roofs.

The first line is the standard drum name for a white man, while the second makes reference to the leaves of the missionary's Bible. Note also the drum names for "village" and "water" in lines 6 and 9 and for "house" in line 11. The epithets for Reverend Carrington (lines 1–2, 12–13) simply mean "European missionary."

This use of standard formulas and of repetitions would seem to characterize the language even of the skin-covered drums. In the body of drum salutes recorded by Nketia there are certainly standard ways, for instance, of concluding a piece. In the prefatory invocations to divinities and to the (spirits of the) drum parts, the drummer seems invariably to end with the words, "I am learning, let me succeed." The repetitive line *"Firampon, condolences, condolences, condolences"* also features prominently both in the invocations and in actual salutes to chiefs and distinguished persons even when there is no element of funeral lament involved. And Nketia tells us (1963b: 159), with regard to personal names, that any time the drum salutes a person named Osei on any of the festive or social occasions, one of the epithets used for him would be "The watery shrub that thrives on hard ground," even though this epithet was originally attributed to a historical ruler of Kokofu in Ashanti. However, the phraseology of the Akan drum poetry (as in many ways the Yoruba) shows greater control than that of the Lokele, perhaps because the drum language on the west coast is a more intimate element of the cultural life. No wonder that Ellis observed (1887: 326–27) of the Akan that "the native ear and mind, trained to detect and interpret each beat, is never at fault. The language of the drums is as well understood as that which they use in their daily life."

The poetry of these tone instruments has a place in various facets of the social life of the communities where they are found. Horns and flutes, for instance, are used for hailing personalities on certain occasions. Among the Asaba Igbo of midwestern Nigeria, a chief would salute another chief with the soprano-pitched horn *(otulaka)* of a young elephant as he passed by his premises, especially on his way to or from a meeting or ceremonial occasion. The Igbo flute *(oja)* is frequently used to accompany a dancer or other performer (masked or unmasked) during a festivity; as the flutist plays praises and other statements to the performer, the latter often responds by saying "Yes?" or "I hear you!" or "Tell me again!" Armstrong recorded a salute played by a flutist to a chief of Igumale among the Idoma of Nigeria.

> Akpa killed those who have horses *coza loga.*
> The leopard in power is no toy!
> The mouth of him who goes wrongly and pays a fine is what is guilty!
> *Ogo tikpa logwu gokpaawaga!*
> 5 When the land is dry ("strong") they will wait for the rains!
> When the leopard is on the way, the animals fear.
> When the kite calls, it is noon.
> The locusts swarm!
> Big, powerful man *cuna zegba*
> 10 When there is a lion, there is a leopard!
> The Chief, a full-blooded leopard in the hole!
> The horses, here they are!
> When the Chief did this, did that, they said it is not fitting. The Chieftaincy is not a plaything!
> When the girls have no husbands, they say they belong to the Chief!
> 15 The girl from the corner with shame in her head, let her take shame from her head, for dancing is no plaything!
> The leopard and the Chief have claws, have claws; the leopard and the Chief are coming today.
> When the good thing is coming into public, what will the singer do today?
> He who sits on the (royal) stool, Lion of lions, Chief, it is of him that I worry; the leopard and the Chief are no plaything!
> He who is fitted for the kingship, let him be King!
> It is God who makes the King! (See Finnegan 1970: 490–91)

Lines 1, 5, and 7 are said to be salutes to certain persons present at the gathering; other lines are metaphors recognizing the presence of the gathering. But the majority of the lines are heightened praises of a king recognized for his valor (leopard, lion) and his divine right.[3]

Extensive use is made of the slit-drum on a variety of occasions. Carrington reports that among the Lokele it is used for communicating the news of birth, as in this message announcing the birth of twins.

> Ho twins, *kelele* [a greeting word]
> poison ordeal, ho twins
> if you throw your old bit of a net into the river you will catch fish
> many many. (Carrington 1949: 55)

A drum message announcing preparations for a marriage goes like this:

> [drum name of addressee]
> Come in the morning

let us sit down together
let us look into the palaver
let us look into the affair
of my daughter
who is to take the journey of a wife tomorrow. (P. 57)

And then there are messages announcing death, whether in general terms,

you will cry [repeated thrice]
tears in the eyes
wailing in the mouth. (P. 58)

or specifically the death of a warrior:

he has finished in the body of
war of the metal of the spear
and the shield. (Ibid.)

The imagery of these set phrases is striking.

The best documented drum poetry is that of the skin-covered talking drums. Among the Yoruba of Nigeria, the *dundun* is used in a variety of contexts ranging from the royal palaces, where it salutes the king with his appropriate phrases early in the morning and on ceremonial occasions, to ordinary festive occasions where free-lance musicians use it for saluting guests with phrases of praise and eliciting gifts from them. Among the Akan of Ghana, however, the *atumpan* is not so freely used and seems to be traditionally geared mainly to ceremonies involving the royalty. In the grand ceremonies featuring the Ashanti chiefs, for instance, a standard procedure for the drumming seems to have been evolved. Early in the morning, the drummer beats a body of statements generally referred to as "The Awakening," evidently because it ushers in the day of festivities. It takes the form of an invocation to the protective divinities and to certain "early birds" who, like the drummer, have to be awake while others sleep. Here is one such invocation to the "clock-bird."

Kokokyinaka Asamoa, the Clock-bird,
How do we greet you?
We greet you with "Anyaado,"
We hail you as the Drummer's child,
The Drummer's child sleeps and awakes with the dawn.
I am learning, let me succeed. (Nketia 1963b: 44)

These preliminary appeals would also include salutes to various parts of the drum itself.

Drum stick of *ofema* wood,
Curved drum stick,
Drum stick of *ofema* wood,

If you have been away,
I am calling you; they say come.
I am learning, let me succeed. (P. 13)

The principal use of the talking drums, however, is for playing the eulogies of
kings and distinguished ancestors on ceremonial occasions "when their origins, par-
entage and noble deeds are recalled against a background of tribal history." Nketia
gives an example of historical eulogies from a performance recorded at Kokofu in
Ashanti.

Slowly and patiently I get on my feet.
Slowly and patiently I get on my feet.
Osee Asibe, noble ruler
Firampon, condolences, condolences, condolences!

5 Osee Asibe throws away, throws away, throws away,
Throws away to the remotest corner.
Osee Asibe,
Child of Adu Gyamfi Twere,
Tweneboa Adu Ampafrako,
10 Child of the Ancient God,
Dress up and let us go,
Dress up and let us go.

Child of noble Adwoa Seewaa,
Ruler of Kokofu Adu Ampoforo Antwi
15 Child of the Ancient God,
Lifter of towns, noble ruler and last born,
Osee Asibe,
Osee Asibe, the noble ruler says
He hails from Kotoko; he is truly Kotoko.

20 Korobea Yirefi Anwoma Sante Kotoko,
When we are about to mention your name,
We give you a gun and a sword.
You are the valiant man that fights with gun and sword.
If you were to decide, you would decide for war.
25 You hail from Kotoko, you are truly Kotoko.

Osee Asibe, you are a man,
You are a brave man.
You have always been a man of valour.
The watery shrub that thrives on stony ground,
30 You are the large *odadee* tree,
The tree with buttress that stands at Donkoronkwanta,
A man feared by men.
Osee Asibe,
You hail from Kokofu and later you belonged to Kokofu.
35 Also you hail from Kumase "Adu Ampoforo Antwi."
Your ancestry is from Akyeremade Nitibanso,

Where the drinking water is obtained from Suben.
Osee the last born,
Later your home has been Kokofu.

40 The coiling branch that coils round trees,
The *ofuntum* wood that breaks the axe,
Osee Asibe, you are in part the wood of *odum*,
In part the wood of *odan*, in part the wood of the silk cotton,
In part the wood of *ofetefre*, in part *akakapempen*.

45 The hunter that provides for all,
That gives the vulture its carrion,
The vulture says it thanks you:
Give it its carrion.
It thanks you, mighty one.
50 It thanks you, gracious one.
Firampon, condolences, condolences, condolences. (Nketia 1963b: 45–46)

No doubt the most striking element here is the feudalistic outlook of these drum praises of royalty, with the figure of the overlord glorified with the most hyperbolic imagery and the proletarian poet humbly craving largess from him (see especially the last stanza). But there is no denying the poetic force of this drum chant, fired to a large degree by a sense of pride in the noble ancestry of the ruler. As is characteristic of these talking drums, there is ample use of formular drum-titles and of repetition.

Proverbs are also commonly played on these talking drums. They may be played independently, as part of an invocation to a god or distinguished figure, or else as part of the performance in the "Akantam dance." Here is a particularly cryptic piece from the dance.

Duyker Adawurampon Kwamena
Who told the Duyker to get hold of his sword?
The tail of the Duyker is short,
But he is able to brush himself with it.
5 "I am bearing fruit," says Pot Herb.
"I am bearing fruit," says Garden Egg.
Logs of firewood are lying on the farm,
But it is the faggot that makes the fire flare.
Duyker Adawurampon Kwamena
10 *Who told the Duyker to get hold of his sword?*
The tail of the Duyker is short,
"Pluck the feathers off this tortoise."
Tortoise: "Fowl, do you hear that?" (Nketia 1979: 32)

It is true that we have encountered pieces such as the ones discussed in our examination of songs and chants in chapter 6. But our discussion here has given us an opportunity to look at the peculiar musical environments in which such poetry is found and the unique styles of expression utilized by the tone instruments in their statements. The imitation of the tones of human speech is itself a feat, but in addition to that these instruments impress us by the poetic dexterity with which they bend the human resource that they have borrowed. These include the figurative color of names given to objects and actions, the emphatic and rhythmic use of repetition, and the tremendous sense of structural balance thereby achieved, as in the Akantam dance piece just quoted.

Ritual Drama

Our discussion has tried to examine the performance of oral literature through a musical medium—i.e., by means of notes struck by musical instruments simulating human speech. In the rest of this chapter we shall examine another medium through which oral literature is realized but which has manifested such a variety of forms that it commands detailed attention. This is the medium of traditional African drama.

In discussing African drama, it would be useful to draw a line between drama that is based in a ritual or religious environment or context and drama that has a broad popular appeal or setting. In making this distinction, however, we must bear two things in mind. The first is that there has been a controversy among scholars as to whether we could rightly describe the various forms of theatrical activity found in traditional African society as drama. The controversy was perhaps first kindled by Ruth Finnegan, who in *Oral Literature in Africa* states that besides "certain dramatic and quasi-dramatic phenomena" such as may be found in traditional festivals, there is little in Africa that may be described as drama (in the European sense, that is), largely because of the absence of sustained and coherent dialogue, plot, and interaction between characters (1970: 500–517). Her views are shared by a few other scholars, including Rotimi (1981), Echeruo (1973), and Horn (1981), with particular reference to the affecting dramatic spectacles found in Nigerian rituals and festivals. Echeruo in particular seems to have caused some offense by decrying the absence of a coherent story line *(mythos)* in Igbo ritual celebrations and recommending that the Igbo abandon the "dead end" of ritual and borrow a leaf from the growth of Greek drama from antecedent ritual observances: "The Igbo should do what the Greeks did: expand ritual into life and give that life a secular base" (1973: 30).

Some Igbo scholars have, understandably, rejected this assessment. Central to this rejection is the observation that in Africa generally, drama as conventionally understood is only one aspect of a larger spectacle—involving music, dance, and other activities—which may best be described as theatre. Such a position quite often bears a nationalistic tone, best captured perhaps in Ossie Enekwe's rejoinder to Echeruo, that

> myth is not the essence of drama, that the structure of drama is determined by the function that theatre serves in a particular culture, and that, far from being a dead end, ritual can easily be transformed into drama. Because Igbo theatre has a different function and a dissimilar method from that of the Greek theatre, for example, it is wrong to demand that the Igbo should develop a form similar to the Greek's. What the Igbo used they have developed based on their own tastes, outlook, and the resources available to them. There is no need for us to keep talking of evolving Igbo drama when it is already flourishing all over Igboland. (Enekwe 1981: 162)

The second point worth noting is that whatever line we draw between ritual drama and popular drama cannot pretend to be a firm one. This is because many performances may spring from ritual ceremonies or be conventionally consecrated to some religious figure and yet engage in deeply mundane and profane matters in an effort to appeal to popular audiences. Conversely, some traditions of popular theatre endeavor once in a while to pay homage to their ritual origins or to recreate theological or religious issues with paraphernalia and effects characteristic of a ritual environment. Once these possibilities and qualifications are borne in mind, we may safely discuss traditional African drama under the broad subdivisions of the *ritual* and the *popular*, with the guiding understanding of drama as *an entertainment conveyed basically through suggestive or symbolic action and movement and defining an experience.*

One of the most rudimentary kinds of ritual drama is the kind performed in the periodic worship of a local divinity or a family's protective god in the god's shrine. The relevant sequence of movements is repeated in the same order as often as the worship is done. Usually this consists in the recitation of certain words of praise, thanks, and appeal; movements to this side and that; the sacrifice of an animal such as a chicken or goat; the sprinkling of the blood and certain food items on the shrine; and the recitation of further words. The celebrant is often dressed in white handwoven cloth and has white chalk smeared around her eyes, and at intervals may execute a few perfunctory dance steps.

This is ritual drama of a rather private kind, with a minimal audience and often no audience at all. A slightly more elaborate ritual drama—but based nonetheless on a set pattern of movements and recitations—is the kind performed at cult shrines by a priest and before an audience of auxiliaries (or acolytes) and other cult members. Such a performance was reported by a former student of mine, Yomi Akeremale, from his research on the cult of the goddess Aiyelala among the Ilaje of Okitipupa, Ondo State of Nigeria.

Ilaje oral tradition claims that the cult originated from an ancient confrontation between the Ilaje and the Ijo Apoi, a settler branch of the Ijo of the Niger Delta and a neighbor of the Ilaje. An Ilaje man had committed adultery and, on his escape, was hotly pursued. The Ijo offered him protection, and this nearly caused a war between the Ijo and the Ilaje. But good counsel prevailed, and the two communities convened a peace meeting to seal the terms of permanent good-neighborliness between them. A slave was required for a sacrifice to consecrate the peace treaty, and when neither side would make the offer, a certain "beautiful woman from Igomola presented herself." She was put in a boat and consigned to the waves along with a number of food items. "She advanced her boat on the river and retreated," we are told, "advanced her boat and retreated three times. The third time she moved off finally" (Akeremale 1980: 28), but not before laying down for these communities the bases for peaceful coexistence and assurances of protection from her as goddess.

This myth of Aiyelala provides the basis for the ritual ceremonies performed in her honor by the officiants (the priest, two acolytes, some drummers) and other cult members. The performance, which is in two stages, takes place on an appointed day known as *uta* ("the day for ritual enactment and reconsecration of ritual items"). As the people assemble in an "open arena," the priest as "protagonist" leads the proceedings, with a horsetail fly whisk in one hand and a "dome-like gong" in the other. He opens the ceremony with a chanted appeal to Aiyelala, to the rhythm of drums. "As the chief priest renders this song, he is joined by two acolytes; the three of them dance towards the ritual setting or shrine. The protagonist is in the middle holding a horse-tail. On getting to the ritual setting, the chief priest moves forward, raises one of his feet and stretches forward his hands. He does this three times" (Akeremale 1980: 40). After this, he and his acolytes engage in an exchange of chants praising Aiyelala and confirming the ancient pact of peace; they then dance a recessional back to their seats, as the cult members chant a salute to "Ogun Onire . . . the black-smith of heaven." There is more dancing until the second stage of the celebrations, which is the sacrifice. Here the priest and his men settle down to consecrate various items—fowls, cloths, kola, etc.—to the goddess. Then they slaughter a goat and sprinkle its blood on the shrine, break kola to ascertain the favor of the divinity, and chant further appeals for protection.

This may be considered drama of a most elementary kind, going by the standard European conception of the term. But those who dismiss this tradition by saying that there are here only "certain dramatic or quasi-dramatic phenomena" or who argue with Echeruo that the mythos or original story line has been "subsumed in the ritual" (1973: 22) are apt to overlook the sublime mimesis involved in the sequence of events in the Aiyelala performances. First the exchange of songs plays much the same role as the dialogue in a play, for though it does not lead to a conflict of wills between characters it certainly yields an emotional counterpoint which brings the performance to a charged climax. The language of the songs and the dramatic movements contribute to the sublimity of the representation in the performance. These are some of the verses with which Aiyelala is venerated.

    10 Great mother
        Possessor of a mighty vagina
        Possessor of six vaginas
        She gave two to the Ilaje
        She gave two to the Ijo
    15 She keeps the remaining two to herself
        With these two she promised to let loose her wrath
        With these two
        She impregnates a man
        With these two she impregnates a woman
    20 That there may be neither jealousy nor envy
        She makes equal distribution. (Akeremale 1980: 43–44)

The apotheosis of Aiyelala raises her above the level of ordinary femininity and thus encourages the sublime imagery of a superwoman with a sextuple vagina. This sexual symbol is useful not only for portraying the supreme motherly munificence and fair-ness with which the goddess brings the two communities together under her fold, but indeed for rousing the sensations of the worshipers into the appropriate level of ecstasy at the celebration. Ritual drama fully recognizes the value of affect in perfor-mances aimed at eliciting communal response, and the image of Aiyelala here certainly achieves the effectiveness recognized by Victor Turner in all ritual symbols, which is the capacity to "condense many references, uniting them in a single cognitive and affective field" (Turner 1974: 55).

Equally effective in mimetic terms is the action of the priest-protagonist in raising his leg three times, a reenactment of Aiyelala's act in thrusting her boat back and forth three times before finally disappearing from the shore. It is important to note that the priest does not make any boating movements; he raises his leg instead in a gesture of dance, a strategy designed not only to achieve a symbolic effect but also to instill a musical feeling into the audience.

The Aiyelala ritual may thus be seen as a spectacle combining the elements of mimesis and celebration. Akeremale acknowledges the seriousness of the ritual's sequence of actions, but gives more recognition to the sheer spectacular and aesthetic appeal of the event.

> However, the action of the chief priest is not a mere imitation of the goddess' movement. While it is true that lurking behind the action is the belief that the goddess did it this way, which gives the action its seriousness, the chief priest's reenactment is quite different. The animated spirit with which the priest performs this action, spreading his arm as he hails the third time, is a product of his artistic skill. In addition, the swift roundabout turn of the chief priest and the two acolytes in order to dance back to their seats, their graceful movements left and right of the arena, with the chief priest rolling the horse tail, are artistic displays which contribute to the beauty of the occasion. When the chief priest and the two [acolytes] have taken their seats music continues and the repeated verses of the song allow the audience to prolong the music and give members the opportunity to dance. . . . [Although] the participants in this ritual cannot be said to have forgotten the religious basis of the occasions, they can be said to have relegated it to the background and thereby rendered it subsidiary to the aesthetic aspect of the ritual. (1980: 51–52)

A second shade of ritual drama may be seen in spirit possession and mediumship. Raymond Firth has defined these shades of experience.

> *Spirit possession* is a form of trance in which behaviour actions of a person are interpreted as evidence of a control of his behaviour by a spirit normally external to him. *Spirit mediumship* is normally a form of possession in which the person is conceived as serving as an intermediary between spirits and men. (1959: 141)

This distinction implies that whereas in possession a person is simply overcome by the power of the spirit to which he or she has surrendered his or her personality, in mediumship the person interacts with others under the influence and prompting of the spirit. Clearly, the potential for drama—insofar, that is, as this involves a relationship between actor and audience—is greater in mediumship than in possession. It is convenient, however, to speak of both shades of experience as simply possession.

We see something of the drama of possession in John Beattie's study of mediumship among the Banyoro of Uganda (1969: 159–70). Nyoro religion recognizes two classes of spiritual beings in daily life: the *mbandwa,* or protective spirits (ancestral spirits, household spirits, spirits of the farm and jungle, etc.) and *mizimu* (sing. *mu-*

zimu), or ghosts of dead people who haunt the living. These forces are considered benevolent especially where things go well for the people and the forces are continually consulted by periodic rituals and appeals. When these consultations are not held and the spirits feel neglected, it is believed they are liable to visit the people with all sorts of misfortunes, such as sickness and the death of children, poor harvests, miscarriage, loss of fortunes, or jobs, and so on. The solution to these is to undergo a possession ceremony in an *mbandwa* cult, supervised by a priest and under the influence of music, hallucinogenic herbs, and other agents. In the ensuing state, the patient (or representative, if it is a mother doing this for her sick baby) begins to act in a way that reveals which spirit or ghost (spirit of lion, ghost of a departed neighbor, etc.) is responsible for the misfortune. If it is a minor *muzimu*, it can be easily expelled from the patient, imprisoned in a pot, and summarily destroyed in a raging fire. If, however, it is a powerful spirit, especially an ancestral *mbandwa* or the *muzimu* of a close relative, it will speak through the patient and declare its wishes. In such a case, the patient must enter into "a lasting mediumistic relationship" with the spirit by being initiated into its cult.

The stages of the initiation cover several days and are quite rigorous. Of the various stages enumerated by Beattie, two are of particularly dramatic relevance.

> First, there is the *rite de passage* aspect; the initiate's acquisition of a new status is marked by the dramatic enactment of death and rebirth, by his being given a new name, and by his being presented with a special headdress and other cult objects. Secondly, and associated with the foregoing, the ritual has a didactic or "learning" aspect. The initiated has to acquire an unfamiliar vocabulary, different from ordinary Runyoro, which is said to be used by ghosts and *mbandwa* spirits. Also, and most important, he receives detailed instructions on how to simulate possession by the spirit whose medium he is to be. (P. 165)

The ritual of possession can be theatre of a most affecting kind, especially when set in "the fire-lit darkness of the hut, the noise and steady rhythm of the rattles and drums, the singing, and (sometimes) the use of inhalants such as tobacco and other herbs" (p. 166). Under such a state, the individual—who may be a rather sick patient—performs the most unbelievable feats of strength as in running, dancing, or climbing, or else puts on amazing dramas as of an authoritarian chief, a meek and beggarly old hag, or a raging lion. When the trance is over, the patient usually slumps to the ground from sheer fatigue; some have been known to die from exhaustion.

These sessions of mediumship are tremendously popular, especially in rural communities where life may be ordinarily uneventful and such occasional performances are a welcome relief. The idea that mediumship can be simulated does indeed suggest that these rituals are in some sense conducted as deliberate theatre and should therefore be dismissed as fraud. Beattie, who warns against such an oversimplification of the rituals, nevertheless concedes the dramatic element in them.

> A Nyoro ex-medium informant perhaps provided the clue. She knew, she said, that *kubandwa* [i.e., the ritual] was deception. "But," she went on, "I thought that all the same

it would be good for the patient if I did what I was required to do" (she was being initiated on behalf of her small child who was ill); What she saw herself as performing was, it might be said, a religious ritual or drama, and such a rite may be thought to be pleasing to the spirits and an effective means of influencing them, even when it is recognized . . . to be a dramatic performance, and not taken to be literally "true." This at any rate appears to be the way in which the matter is regarded in twentieth-century Bunyoro. Perhaps the first beginnings of drama in ancient Greece were not dissimilar. (P. 167)

A similar use of trance as theatre is seen in the *bori* spirit-medium cults among the Hausa of northern Nigeria. Like the *mbandwa* performances, their rituals are held to exorcise illness and other forms of misfortune, are accompanied by the patient's use of unfamiliar language, and are subject to simulation. These performances, done mostly by women to the accompaniment of music provided by men, are extremely popular with both rural and urban audiences. A description by Onwuejeogwu reveals not only the theatrical appeal of the act but the element of communication with the attending audience.

> In order to illustrate its dramatic and expressive character, I shall briefly describe a typical Bori dance. The woman puts on the colour appropriate to the spirit and in some cases carries the miniature symbolic object, bow or spear, etc., in her hand. She is now the spirit and acts as the spirit. If, for example, she is possessed by the spirit called Mallam Alhaji, she walks around bent and coughing weakly like an old learned mallam and reads an imaginary Koran. If she is possessed by Dan Galadima, the prince, she acts like a nobleman wearing kingly robes. She sits on a mat hearing cases, and people around make obeisance. If she is possessed by *Mai-gangaddi*, "The nodding one," who causes sleeping sickness, she dances and suddenly dozes off in the middle of some act and wakes up and sleeps again and wakes, etc. If possessed by *Ja-ba-Fari*, "neither red nor white," a spirit that causes people to go mad, she eats filth and simulates copulation. . . . In some cases she leaps into the air, and lands on her buttocks with feet astride—thrice. She falls exhausted and is covered with a cloth. During this state she may foretell the future. Spectators wishing to obtain a favour from or appease the spirit that has mounted her place their gifts and alms on the mat. Then she sneezes, the spirit quits her, and she becomes normal. During this period she is never referred to as herself but as the spirit. (Onwuejeogwu 1969: 286–87)

Simulation is a common feature in *bori* trances, especially those displays held in public *(borin jama'u)* and backed by a full orchestra of drummers, rattlers, and horn players. Although by its very nature possession is an unconscious experience, the role playing is often so elaborate and the music and singing so affecting that there is no doubt the cult members have a full sense of their act as both ritual and theatre.[4]

A third shade of ritual drama may be seen in masquerade performances. With masquerades, ritual realizes its full potential as theatre, and we begin to witness some dissolution of the line between ritual drama and popular drama.

In traditional African societies, masquerades are generally treated as manifestations or representatives of the spiritual world: spirits of ancestors, spirits protecting the home and the environment, spirits of the newly dead, even the superior divinities of the clan. They are often covered all over, partly to achieve the effect of the eerie and the colorful and partly because at the time they died (as people) they were wrapped up in a shroud, but generally also because as spirits their physical identities should not be exposed. The head mask—"through which the spirit breathes," as Leopold Senghor says in his poem "Prayer to Masks"—is designed for this protection of identity (especially, of the human wearer) but often also as an emblem of the figure being venerated or the rite being performed; this is the case, for instance, with the *chi wara* (antelope) masks worn by dancers among the Bambara of Mali, an emblem of the spirit of fertility and plenty in the natural environment. Masquerades also often speak through voice modifiers—pieces of metal, bamboo, or bone made in the form of a whistle, with a porous tissue placed across the opening, which are held in the mouth to further enhance the nonnatural, eerie character of the masquerades' spiritual essence. In many cases it is taboo for women, children, and those not initiated into the cult of the particular spirit to be around, let alone touch, the masquerade when it is out and about.

Despite their eerieness, masquerades are often quite colorfully clad and, by means of their looks and their movement, present an affecting spectacle. As representatives of the protective spirits of the community, these masquerades appear in ritual ceremonies and festivals either to enact roles characteristic of particular spirits or to superintend the activities conducted at the occasion. However, because each community has its own peculiar traditions and pantheon of protective spirits, its masquerades perform within the community's boundaries and hardly ever cross over to communities where the spirits represented are not recognized. Masquerade performances are therefore almost invariably ritual theatre of a localized sort, restricted either to cult precincts or to recognized public places within a community.

Let us examine a tradition of masquerade performance from a community in Zambia reported by Kafungulwa Mubitana (1971: 58–62) so as to see the theatrical quality of a ritual event. In the Wiko community living in the suburbs of the industrial city of Livingstone, masquerades appear regularly during initiation ceremonies for youths. The appearances are more prominent toward the end of the initiation period, when the masquerades (called *makishi*) provide a wide variety of entertainment, such as dancing and acrobatics, as well as the policing of the lodges where the final rites are held. Their costumes and especially their masks (representing specific beasts and spirits) are quite colorful, and they give their fullest display a week before the initiates are released from their long seclusion, "when the resurrection of the ancestors and nature spirits occurs."

The height of this spectacle occurs on the actual day of release of the youths. On this day, the *makishi* do not appear; their place is now taken by the initiates ("novices") themselves, who "wear helmets made of straw, twigs and grass. Around their loins they wear skirts made from strips of bark or palm leaves. Their bodies are painted with white chalk and the patterns resemble those on *makishi* costumes." These surrogate masquerades leave their lodge of confinement, which is immediately burned down, and give a spirited entertainment which includes singing and dancing to drum music and recitation of "time-honoured ballads and riddles." Then comes a brief dramatic display.

As the morning progresses on this day of emerging, the dancing arena assumes more the spirit of an open-air theatre. A dialogue involving a novice and the Leading Drummer starts. The novice has shot a pig, but his quarry gets away. The novice tracks it, and the trail leads him to the spot where the Leading Drummer is teaching the novices to sing and dance. Immediately, the frustrated novice accuses the Leading Drummer of concealing his pig. A quarrel ensues that ends in the novice being proved wrong and charged. (P. 61)

The novice approaches his relatives (who have come to witness the rites of release) and is given the means to pay the fine. About midday, all the initiates are led to a stream, where they are given the final ritual meal and washed.

The dramatic sketch is mock-serious, intended as a lesson in proper conduct to these newly weaned citizens: do not rush to conclusions and precipitate decisions. But the sketch is significant because it points to the secular, temporal outlook of much masquerade theatre. Although the spectacle is performed in ritual circumstances and under the superintending eye of protective spirits, it endeavors frequently to reflect the concerns of daily life—the dilemmas of family and social relations, the burdens of political authority, the morality of the youth, etc.—as well as general problems of human existence. Such concerns are reflected in the performances of the *odo* masquerades of the Anambra Igbo of eastern Nigeria, a phenomenon that Ossie Enekwe has characterized as "ritual drama" (1981: 158).

The arena for the performance follows roughly the pattern outlined by Nnabuenyi Ugonna in his analysis of *mmonwu* (masquerade) performances (1984). There is a central square called *obom oshaka*. At one end of it two huts are erected for the *odo* masquerade "family," serving both as home and as dressing room or prop room; ranged around the arena are sheds for the audience. The masquerade family consists of the father, called Ezembo, costumed as a dignified elder and leader; the mother, Ogolimaluihe (or Ogoli, for short), beautifully costumed as a model of feminine charm and respectable womanhood; the son Akawo, a truant, decked out with knives and whips and looking every inch the troublesome youth of today that he represents; two teenage sons, also dressed to reflect youth; and Ada Odo, a maiden, costumed to reflect delicate femininity and beauty. The drama enacted by such a group, complemented by music, singing, and dancing as well as occasional exchanges with the audience, necessarily mirrors the problems of family life. Enekwe gives us this sketch of one episode.

A flutist blows his flute in praise of Ezembo who, together with the rest of his family, is in the hut at the rear of the playing area. Ezembo steps out from the hut and moves round the arena slowly and majestically, surveying the ground to be sure that the environment is safe for his family. He returns to the hut, and comes out with his shy and beautiful wife whom he fans. As they take their seats, Akawo the rough son dashes out of the hut and charges at the spectators who run back in fear. Ezembo chases his son, catches him, and drags him to a seat. There is an interlude of music during which Ezembo persuades his wife, Ogoli, to dance. She dances with slow steps, shaking her body and waving her hands sideways. Next, Ezembo asks her to sing for his guests (the spectators), but she declines, feigning headache. But, after a while, she gets up, kneels before her husband, who wipes her face with a cloth. She then stands up and sings in praise of him. As the audience sings the chorus, she starts dancing, and Ezembo, impressed and thrilled, pastes coins on her face, according to custom. The *Odo* escorts and the audience follow his example. Afterwards, Ezembo and Ogoli embrace each other, and the music stops. This scene shows how a father should control his family and how couples should live and love one another. (1981: 159–60)

Other episodes show the taming of Akawo's truancy and Ogoli's exhortations of the wives to respect and obey their husbands.

The appeal and popularity of African masquerade theatre is supported by the sheer sense of spectacle inspired by the physical form of the masquerades and the feats they perform. Apart from being colorfully decked out and dressed, masquerades are often adorned with features that inspire terror as befitting the beings of the spirit world whom they represent. For example, Onuora Nzekwu cites among Igbo masquerades "those wearing two-faced masks, those that carry swarms of bees or smoke-belching fires in their masks" (1981: 135). Other forms of stylization show the influence of foreign cultures on the traditional arts of the masquerade. Nzekwu also talks of masks with a long pointed nose representing a European, and Seigmann and Perani, in their study of masquerades in Sierra Leone and Liberia, mention the "use of Arabic script on the costumes . . . as well as the practice of tying strips of paper with passages from the Koran inside the masks" (1976: 47). Whatever the aims of these elements of costumery, it is clear that the performers wish to invest their act with an affecting presence and aura and that to a large extent the urge for popular appeal has invaded if not overtaken the more serious purposes of the ritual.

"A ritual," says Enekwe, "becomes entertainment once it is outside its original context" (1981: 155). We observed above that African masquerades frequently move out of the cult precincts to perform in public places around the town. But perhaps no tradition has done more to break the territorial sanctions ritually observed by masquerades, and thus to attenuate the line between ritual drama and popular drama, than the Alarinjo traveling theatre of the Yoruba.

Joel Adedeji, the authority on this subject, has given us a quite readable account (1981) of the history and career of this theatre tradition. According to Adedeji, the Alarinjo theatre has its roots in the *egungun* (masquerade) tradition of "ancestor worship" but was first established as court entertainment by Alaafin Ogbolu, the last Alaafin (king) of the old Oyo kingdom in exile. Ogbolu was resolved to move the seat of the kingdom from exile in Igboho to the ancestral capital of Katunga. Many of his subjects and followers, especially the king's council (Oyo-Mesi), opposed the move; when the king would not be persuaded, some council members conceived a strategy to thwart him. They formed a group of masked actors (ghost-mummers) who went ahead to Katunga and frightened off the emissaries sent by the Alaafin to inspect the old sites and make propitiatory sacrifices to the gods. Their scheme was, however, later revealed by the king's Ologbo (or Ologbin), himself a member of the *egungun* cult that had cooked up the scheme. The mummers were rounded up, but in lieu of the condign punishment, Alaafin Ogbolu kept them in a special building within the palace as a troupe of court entertainers under the management of Ologbin. The *egun-*

gun cult never forgave Ologbin for his betrayal of their sworn resolve. They tried to thwart the performances of the troupe, and when they failed, secretly contrived the death of Ologbin by poison.

Ologbin Ologbojo[5] was thus the acknowledged founder of the Alarinjo theatre. Upon his death the troupe came under Esa Ogbin, "a maternal relation to whom professionalism in masque-dramaturgy has been traced" (Adedeji 1981: 224). Esa Ogbin, for instance, moved the performances from the court and the governing classes to the masses beyond the palace and inspired the formation of similar troupes by other lineages in the Oyo kingdom. Each lineage has, however, its own closely guarded cult and performance secrets as well as its own area of specialization—poetry *(iwi)*, acrobatics and dance, dramatic sketches, or *tableaux vivants*. The standard material resources of the troupe are the mask, the costume, and the *bata* drums, which provide the rhythmic accompaniment to the chants and the displays of dance and acrobatics.

The basic revolution in this tradition consists in the movement of the cult performance from the narrow and hallowed precincts of the court to the populace in the town. There was also another significant advance. The *egungun* performance was traditionally an act of ancestor worship with the due glorification and supplication of ancestral spirits and divinities. But the professionalization of these performances led to the introduction of profane topics from low life into the satirical sketches (e.g., the wayward wife, the adulterer, etc.) put on by the troupes. In addition, as a result of the conflict within the court that gave rise to the Alarinjo troupe, there arose the element of condemnation of the authorities as part of the dramatic sketches performed by the mummers. "In the past," says Adedeji of the masked performer, "he had lived by flattering the elite, that is, the court and the nobility, for their amusement; now he could include them in his satirical sketches if he desired" (1981: 225).

In the history of the Alarinjo theatre, then, we have evidence of the growth of popular drama away from the constraints of ritual. The emphasis was on popular appeal—so much so that even the cherished divinities were often ridiculed in the revues—and an exploration of the problems of daily life. The performances were operatic in nature, each consisting of a series of brief dramatic sketches and acrobatic displays linked together by *bata* drum music and choral chanting, with little dialogue or storytelling within sketches.

Despite the professionalism and the popular appeal of the Alarinjo masquerades, the theatre never really took full leave of its ritual roots. In the first place, the patronage provided for their performances as they moved from one town to another came from the leader *(alagbaa)* of the *egungun* cult in the host community; from whatever source the invitation to mount a performance came, the affair was in the final analysis conducted under the superintending eye of the *alagbaa* (Adedeji 1981: 234).

Second, although the subjects created in the main body of the performances were profane, each performance nevertheless invariably started with an "opening glee," which was essentially a salute *(ijuba)* to a variety of cult figures. Here is a sample of the *ijuba* by a masqued company (the Agbegijo troupe) recorded in 1965.

> I submit my pledge, may my pledge be fulfilled.
> It is the pledge I will first submit, my performance comes at the end.

I behold a pledge, the pledge is to my father, Ajankoro Dugbe.

He is the masque-actor, with a concealed knot at the hem of his garment.

5 The scrupulously neat masque-histrione who is a threat to the existence of other masquerades.

My father, hearken to my voice,

Behold the pledge,

Let me become worthy of this outing.

I pledge to you my open hand,

10 I pledge to you my flat foot,

I pledge to you the underfoot that grows no hair, even as far as knee-high.

To you who have passed before me, I humbly bow.

From you my companion, I beg for courage.

The pledge is to you,

15 Iyami Osoronga,

A "bird" with divers hands,

A "bird" with divers legs,

The scrupulously neat "bird" whose stories are at midnight.

I hereby submit my pledge;

20 Let me become worthy of today's outing.

My pledge is also to you Esu Laalu who patrols the road,

Who slashes and inflicts wounds.

Esu Laalu, behold my pledge,

I submit the pledge,

25 Let me become worthy of this outing. (Adedeji 1977: 190)

Whatever the level of profanity treated in the various sketches, therefore, the license employed is in the end protected by the ancestors and divinities invoked in the opening glee; the entire performance is indeed part of the general package of reverence and celebration of these hallowed figures.[6]

A third and no doubt most conspicuous index of the ritual character of these masked performances is the separation between players and audience. As in most traditional dramatic performances, masquerade drama is organized as theatre-in-the-round, with the performers surrounded by, and enjoying occasional impromptu verbal communication with, the crowd of spectators. But the latter are constantly reminded that the masquerades are spirits whose identities are concealed behind mask and costume. The divide between spirits and humans is therefore maintained by the respectful distance between the crowd and the masquerades; if the crowd gets too close, one or the other of the masquerades restores the distance by chasing the spectators back with a whip or a playfully threatening move.[7] Ebun Clark clinches the point when she draws a line between these traveling masques and the unmasked players of the concert party.

In the theatre of the Alarinjo, audience participation is at one level, and a barrier exists between the actor and his audience. The barrier is not caused through the use of the proscenium stage but by the religious taboo that surrounds the actor. In the Alarinjo theatre the audience can hear the actors but cannot see them because they are masked. Again, they can look but not touch. The religious barrier therefore renders complete rapport between the Alarinjo and the audience impossible. The audience does participate in the show by cheering the actors along, and by keeping up a running commentary on their performance, but to us this type of participation, however involved it is, is limited. (Clark 1979: 121–22)

Popular Drama

Popular drama is distinguished from ritual drama by a total disengagement from the environment of, and obligations to, cult or ritual and by the enactment of themes of essentially popular concern. It is true that once in a while the religious backgrounds of drama echo when a troupe reenacts a religious theme, but this is often no more than an effort to diversify its repertoire; in many cases, in fact, the religious figures are treated with a touch of satire or ridicule. The basic thrust of popular drama is to explore the concerns of social life, whether lofty or lowly, in a lighthearted style that offers entertainment and relaxation to a sufficiently large cross section of the people. In this sense, David Mayer is right when he defines popular drama as "that drama produced by, and offered for the enjoyment of, the largest combinations or groupings [of people] possible within a society" (quoted in Jeyifo 1984: 3).

A principal mark of this disengagement from ritual is that characters in popular drama appear not in any protective covering that conceals a spiritual essence but as themselves in proper and conspicuous habit. In some cases, as in some concert parties, colors are painted over the face, but these are no more than caricatures that identify specific character types, e.g., the old grouch, the clown, the happy-go-lucky playboy. We shall now discuss three different traditions of popular drama: puppet theatre, rural revues, and the traveling theatre.

Puppetry is a worldwide form of theatrical entertainment in which sculpted or stuffed figurines, manipulated from behind the scenes with strings, fingers, or rods, are made to perform a variety of social or mythical roles for the amusement and edification of the audience. The amusement is achieved mostly by the grotesque roles which these miniature figures are made to perform and by the jerky, irregular movements which the manipulation imposes on them. This effect is sometimes complemented in no small way by the use of voice modifiers—little objects shaped like whistles, with tissue or membrane stretched across the opening, which are inserted by manipulators into their mouth so that their voice sounds squeaky or hoarse, depending on the character being projected.[8] In some cases, especially in Africa, puppets are complemented by masquerades when spiritual or mythical figures feature in the episodes under display, and by drum music and song. Because of these caricatural devices and the emphasis on amusement, children constitute the major audience of puppet performances; but adults also attend in large numbers because the caricatures frequently carry a more serious social or political message.

Puppet theatre has been reported in various communities of West Africa: among Bambara and other groups in Mali and the Hausa of Niger Republic (Labouret and Travélé 1928, Chesnais 1965), the Kanuri of Borno State (Ellison 1935), the Tiv of Benue State (Kyaagba 1978, Hagher 1980), and the Ibibio of Akwa Ibom State (Messenger 1971) in Nigeria. Chesnais tells us that puppetry in the region around Bamako (in Mali) is fundamentally geared toward moralizing goals: extolling virtues such as generosity, wisdom, courage, and respect for the older generation as well as condemning evil and particularly those in power, including "the chiefs, the notabilities, the ancestors, even the gods if their presumed intervention is not commensurate with the sacrifices offered" (1965: 448). His description of a Hausa puppet show he watched in Zinder (Niger Republic) is fuller. The puppets, called *dabo dabo* ("soulless beings with whom one plays"), were accompanied by the puppeteer *(dabola)*, an interpreter, a master of ceremonies, and three drummers, one of whom was a child. Chesnais's description of the show gives a representative picture of the phenomenon in much of the western Sudan.

> The puppeteer chooses his site with extreme care. After making a barrier of sand 20 centimeters high and about a metre long, he drives a stick into the ground, to the height of a man in a squatting position, roughly one metre to the rear of the barrier; having placed the bags containing the puppets in their prescribed position, he sits down tailor-wise beside the stick; he then envelopes both himself and his material in a large "boubou" with a hole at its centre. The puppets later make their appearance through this hole which is situated just above [the] puppeteer's head; the "interpreter" stands close by, the drummers occupy a position slightly to the rear while the master of ceremonies remains aloof with his eyes fixed compellingly on the spectators and only intervenes during the intervals when he plays the dual role of conjuror and fakir. During the whole performance, the puppeteer speaks—if it can really be called speaking—with the traditional "Punch and Judy" show "squeaker" in his mouth: the succession of nasal sounds emitted thanks to the "squeaker"—two silver disks fastened loosely together and fixed to the palate—constitute the puppet's language; what they say is rendered perfectly intelligible by the "interpreter" who not only answers but frequently repeats their remarks!
>
> When everything is in place, the drummers get to work and out of the hole in the "boubou" rises a series of obscene effigies that the "interpreter" arranges in a row at the top of the specially prepared embankment: finally, the actual puppets make their appearance: glove-type puppets made out of printed cotton. Some are extremely life-like and have undoubtedly been inherited; the others, on the contrary, verge on the abstract and are very certainly the puppeteer's own handiwork. The face, notably, is merely suggested by a section of the printed pattern, the general outline is stylized and conventional, attributes indicative of sex are unmistakable.
>
> The repertory is largely satirical. We were shown: *The Maidens, The Peddler, The Witch Doctor, The Domestic Scene,* etc. . . . which were all performed with considerable verve. (Chesnais 1965: 450–51)

Perhaps the most detailed study of African puppet theatre is Iyorwuese Hagher's doctoral thesis (1980) of the *kwagh-hir* of the Tiv. The interesting thing about this tradition is that it is of recent origin. Although it borrows heavily from traditional storytelling performances among the Tiv, the *kwagh-hir* puppet theatre "was conceived and born in the Tiv revolt against an oppressive political party, the N.P.C. (Northern People's Congress), which erupted in the riots of 1960 and 1964" (p. 10). This party was dominated by the Hausa-Fulani group of northern Nigeria which, under the leadership of Sir Ahmadu Bello, the Sardauna of Sokoto, had a great deal of trouble bringing its allegedly feudalistic style of governance upon the traditionally republican Tiv. Adikpo Songo, generally acknowledged as the founder or "father" of the *kwagh-hir* art, formed his group in 1960.

The puppets, made mostly from wood, are frequently adorned with raffia leaves, cloth, and other cosmetic materials. They are manipulated from behind a portable wooden booth *(dagbera)* with strings or wooden rods. A typical performance consists essentially of brief sketches on the sitcom model, although somewhat longer narrative sequences often form part of the fare. This puppet theatre does give some of its time to extolling certain fundamental virtues and upholding Tiv national values against foreign life-styles; however, considering its origins in political revolt, it is no surprise that a far larger proportion of the time is given to satirical attacks not only on social vices but also on various shades of traditional and contemporary authority—political, religious, etc.

Kwagh-hir is today a flourishing art form among the Tiv, practiced by a considerable number of professional groups. It is also a well-organized affair, and Hagher has listed the "component units" of this organization. First, the occasion *(mir kwagh-hir)* has to be identified or agreed upon. These performances are frequently done in the dry season—after harvesting, when there is ample time for relaxation. In addition to this, a sponsor or promoter seeks out special occasions like title-taking or marriage ceremonies and organizes a competition between various *kwagh-hir* groups to determine which one should put up the show at the chosen occasion. That done, rehearsals *(iyor karen)* are held for the group: the puppets and masquerades are dusted and rehearsed, and the group practices its songs and dances rigorously to ensure that tune and movement are properly synchronized. Then comes the setting of the stage *(due akyav)*, in which an appropriate location is chosen, the props are duly arranged thereat, the use of the space is rehearsed so that the performers are thoroughly at home there, and music and song are rehearsed once more to ensure that the acoustics of the setting are right.

In addition to the puppeteers, two principal components of the group are the narrator *(shuwa)*, who introduces the show by telling the audience what the performance is going to be about (i.e., providing a coherent summary of the puppet play) and engages in a good-humored banter with the audience, and the orchestra, made up of the drummers *(mbaagbandev)* and singers *(mbaamoov)* who provide a rhythmic background and play the theme songs linking one episode or sketch with the next. When the stage is finally set, the *kwagh-hir* performance kicks off with an opening glee *(kwan yaran)*.

The performance itself is total theatre, involving puppetry, narrative summaries, song, dance, and dialogue between the prompter/narrator and the audience. The following outline of a performance by the group led by Leo Agatsa gives us a good picture of what a *kwagh-hir* event is like. The "opening glee" itself is a full package. The orchestra leads off with music and song (often extolling the excellence of the *kwagh-hir* group), the narrator introduces the performance, and, while the orchestra is still performing, a most hilarious tug-of-war comes on: thirty men in a file are straining vigorously to pull in an object, which turns out to be a tiny slit-gong. This is followed by another hilarious scene. A player with a huge gourd tied between his legs and sticking out like scrotal elephantiasis (just under his raffia skirt) jumps on-stage; he does a wild dance (despite his "disease") and plays frenetic beats on the little slit-gong. The entire group then files out for the real show to begin.

The first piece after this opening sequence is the *fefa nyam*, in which a puppet masquerade dressed as a wild beast comes out of the wooden booth to do a fast, wild dance to music and song. He clears the stage for the main sequence: a series of puppet plays. The wooden booth is now moved from "backstage" to the center of the arena, and it is on top of it that the various puppets will be manipulated. The first show is that of the "grinding woman" (*ioravaa*), in which a woman grinds grain dutifully while her middle-aged husband with a pipe and a fly whisk smokes and nods contentedly: a purely domestic scene with a male-chauvinistic touch. Next comes a symbolistic scene, with three puppet toads shaking rattles (*akpom asoho*) to the accompaniment of music and a song taunting the rivals or enemies of the Leo Agatsa group.

The third puppet show is the *shawon* (spinning), a nationalistic episode upholding traditional Tiv industry. An old man in Tiv national dress (*anger*) is shown spinning cotton while his wife, facing him, weaves on the loom. In introducing this scene, the narrator proudly reminds the audience that the Tiv have never depended on factory-made clothes or on the white man for clothing needs; the accompanying song lauds the art of Tiv clothmaking and ends with further jabs at rival performing groups. The fourth puppet show is etiological. It is a divination scene (*ishor ikpehen*) based on a folktale in which, according to the narrator, a quarrel between the leopard and the dog is settled by the gorilla as diviner; the scene is aimed at tracing the origin of the art of divination. The final puppet show is the rampage of the *ajikoko*, reputedly the fiercest beast in Tiv mythology; this episode is also said to be a favorite staple of all *kwagh-hir* performances in Tivland. As the huge animal masquerade appears, the narrator changes roles and becomes a hunter; the accompanying song warns the audience against the menace of certain forces (*adzov*) recognized by the Tiv and here represented by the *ajikoko*. The show is a sample of a group of puppet performances described as "antispiritual."

Puppet theatre is stylized popular drama: the little wooden figures are in essence designed to expose and undercut the over-exertions of men by reducing them to the dimensions of stiff-jointed caricatures subject to easy manipulation. The principal aim is to make the audience laugh by ridiculing a variety of social vices and habits. In addition to the sort of scenes described above, there are others that explore more topical events. Sample favorites are the *Mohammed Ali*, which shows "the greatest" flooring his opponents after only a few jabs, and the *Doctor Anageende*, which caricatures quacks engaging in drug salesmanship. Even the serious purposes of the establishment are frequently satirized. Hagher reports on a 1978 performance by the Leo Agatsa group of the *Operation Feed the Nation* theme. This agricultural program promoted by the federal government was presented by the group ostensibly in support of the government's campaign for a green revolution. But there was a jab at the unevenness of the project.

> The narrator told the audience the show they were about to see was a man who excelled the Operation Feed the Nation in the whole land. When the puppet farmer arrived on a platform he was a tall thin man who appeared to be struggling with the oversize hoe in

his hands. While it was clear the puppet show was in support of the government policy, it was difficult to ignore the underlying irony of starting a green revolution with archaic and primitive tools. (Hagher 1980: 194–95)

In some African communities such caricaturing is done not by puppets but by real, unmasked men operating nevertheless within the same structure of brief sketches as we have seen in the *kwagh-hir*. Perhaps the best-known tradition is of the rural revues performed mostly in the Bamana (Bambara) communities of Mali. Unlike puppets whose actions have to be explained by the interpreter, the characters in these revues engage in dialogue between themselves, though they depend mostly for their humorous effect on their grotesque miming acts as well as props used in the episodes.

These dramatic productions of the Bamana—known as *kote-tlon*, or *kote koma nyaga* in some communities—are usually put on by youths from several age-grade associations *(ton)* most especially during the dry season (November to May) when the youths are free from work in the farms. During this period, a wide variety of special occasions require the standard forms of entertainment in the community: marriage, the visit of an official delegation, the death of a village elder, or just the need to provide fun and excitement. Dramatic displays combine with other shows (music and song, acrobatics, etc.) to constitute the total theatre known as *koteba*. The *kote-tlon* more specifically refers to the dramatic performances.

There are usually three parts to a *koteba* evening. The entertainment begins at about 8:00 P.M. with the *bamoukou*, which is a dance performance by young boys and young girls. Four drummers are positioned in the middle of the village square, providing a variety of dance beats; immediately around them there is a circle of girls, then around these a circle of boys, both executing various dance routines in a counterclockwise movement and singing several tunes to the drum beats. After some two hours of this comes the next performance, the *badoukou*, or acrobatic dancing by youths, again to drum music and in a more or less competitive spirit. At about 11:30 P.M., the *badoukou* displays come to an end and *kote-tlon* takes over for the rest of the night. The drummers move from the center to the edge of the arena; young girls with the best voices spread a cloth and sit near the drummers; little boys run around carrying various props and costume parts for the actors' use; older men move around to bring some order to the excitement generated by the expectation of the dramatic shows; and suddenly, without warning, an opening glee—in the form of a short dance known as *kaka*—gives the signal that *kote-tlon* is about to begin.

This dramatic tradition is organized as a series of brief sketches caricaturing a whole variety of social evils and propensities, with the principal aim of amusing the audience as much as possible but also of driving home certain lessons of social conduct. James Brink, who studied Bamana folk drama with admirable insight, has described *kote-tlon*.

As dramatic material, *kote-tlon* represents a tradition of farcical comedy in which kernels of truth and personal experience are selected and spotlighted for the audience's enjoyment. Universal human qualities such as avarice, greed, infidelity, stupidity, unfaithfulness and disrespect are projected as caricatures of daily life. The caricature is completed by casting the main characters of the theatre as immoral, sick, insane, broken, or aged persons. (1977: 61)

So many dramatic sketches are presented on any *kote-tlon* program—from eight to about thirty—that each is necessarily short, with some lasting only twenty seconds and the longest no more than about fifteen minutes. There is frequently no thematic continuity between one play and another; the gaps are filled in with drum music and singing (which also feature within sketches), and the effect of the speed of productions is to keep the excitement of the entire entertainment at a persistently high level for the two or three hours that it lasts.

There is an even deeper aesthetic basis for the fast pace of the sketches. The Bamana apparently believe that the various acts of stupidity and immorality portrayed in the sketches are a result of hasty and unreflective judgment; the challenge is thus on the actors to capture the ridicule in these social misdemeanors by the appropriate pace of representation. "It is in the fast tempo," says Brink, "that an actor's dramatic skill is truly tested, and it is by means of the fast tempo that a play's humor is brought to its entertaining climax. Underlying these facts is the theory that comic experience in general is mainly attributable to fast tempo perception. . . . The motivation behind Bamana comedy generally, and *kote-tlon* drama specifically, is to organize states of outwardly directed ecstasy, states that are not deeply reflective but spontaneously amusing and exhilarating" (1982: 429).

A brief sampling of these *kote-tlon* plays gives us an insight into the combined aims of amusement and edification which characterize this dramatic tradition. In "The Unfaithful Wife," a blind man sings about the misfortunes of blindness as he is being led around by his wife; shortly after, he discovers that his wife has absconded to have a rendezvous now with one lover, now with another. The play ends with the blind man beating his wife as they run off the arena. In "The Drunkard and His Wife," the drunken husband does not realize that the object underneath his wife's waistcloth is not a drum, as she tells him, but her boyfriend; he allows himself to dance wildly to the music provided by the woman and the drum, and when he belatedly discovers the trick played on him he chases the boy from the arena. Such plays are intended to satirize various shades of social stupidity such as adultery and drunkenness.[9]

In "The Woman Who Lost Her Vagina in the River," however, the criticism comes in the form of a subtle protest. A woman goes to the river to wash clothes. While there, her vagina accidentally drops off and gets lost in the water. Her husband cries rather disconsolately, and his two sons undertake to go and find the lost organ. Having found it, they contend with their father over the right to put the vagina back where it came from, arguing that after all the organ was their former home. The old man eventually gives in, and the play ends with the two boys thrusting their hands under their mother's waistcloth. This may sound like an expensive joke, but it is really intended as a large social metaphor. Respect for the elders is a cardinal element—one, indeed, often obsessively enforced—in traditional African cultural behavior; theatre of the *kote-tlon* type thus provides the youths with the sort of liberal atmosphere within which they can gleefully violate behavioral taboos and revolt against their subjugation without necessarily seeking to overthrow the system. "The drama, in other words," says Brink, "offers the youths a nondurational play context in which their challenge to the elders is conducted within a joke framework defined and controlled by the aesthetic and performance-determined criteria of the drama" (1982: 420).

Kote-tlon theatre is such a well-established tradition that there is now a set of recognized conventions for everything from the props used to the gestures made by the actors. For instance, a stick with a wad of cloth rolled up at one end of it represents a penis. A character who wears an oversize shirt, bulges his unblinking eyes, and walks off-rhythm to the drum music is no other than a blind man. And when, in "The Drunkard and His Wife," the husband leaves the woman and goes to sit near the audience, it is easily understood that he has gone to drink millet beer even though he does not make any obvious gestures of drinking. Despite these set conventions, *kote-tlon* shares with much of African oral art the creative quality of spontaneity and a controlled fluidity that responds to the demands of variable audiences. Each *kote-tlon* play is a "scripted performance" [10] in the sense of operating within a recognized system of audience expectations as well as structure of episodes; but there is ample room nevertheless for the actors to demonstrate their ingenuity and mature control of the cultural idioms that constitute part of their learning process. Brink articulates the creativity of *kote-tlon* quite pointedly.

> *Kote-tlon* is exclusively an oral form of theatre that encourages spontaneity and individual creativity. Actors strive to put their stamp on plays by inventing new dialogue and emphasizing different aspects of characters. For this reason any play's contents vary with each performance and with the actors involved. Instead of actors learning a body of standardized dramatic material, then, it is more appropriate to say they learn basic thematic patterns or ideas from which they generate their own interpretations. (1977: 65)

This element of controlled fluidity is clearly in tune with the African spirit. It is certainly characteristic of the African concept of drama, as is amply demonstrated by a somewhat similar kind of popular drama which has developed in response to the peculiar character of urban life and the facilities yielded by the modern industrial economy.

The urban counterpart of rural revues of the *kote-tlon* type is the "concert party." But there is a slight difference. The rural revue takes place mostly in the dry season after the period of sustained farm work and is organized primarily by youths who will themselves have done that work; it is therefore very much integrated with the cycle of work and relaxation that constitutes the rural economy. The members of the concert party, however, are often dropouts who have no other work and are participating in the plays only because there is nothing else to do. However, in more recent times, the concert party groups have begun to achieve a certain amount of professional self-assurance, traveling around with their productions so as to provide themselves with steady economic support.

The concert party in West Africa had its roots in the activities of foreign missions that operated in this part of Africa toward the end of the nineteenth century and in the first few decades of the twentieth century. In major cities such as Lagos in Nigeria and Accra in Ghana, these missions used their churches and schools as venues for the production of plays with biblical themes, partly as a way of spreading Christian morality among the populations and partly as a strategy for raising funds for running their institutions. These plays, or "cantatas," were invariably written and chanted to the accompaniment of Christian music. But in time it became clear that the music was alien to the ears of the Africans who wrote and performed the morality plays, and they consequently pressed for the introduction of peculiarly African styles of singing and instrumentation (e.g., drum music) into the plays. The agitation was resisted by some of the foreign missions and this resulted in the splitting away of some groups to form indigenous African churches where they could conduct Christian worship in a peculiarly African style and with peculiarly African music. These African churches also put on plays that were then called "native air operas," very much like the original cantatas (i.e., sung plays) but this time against the background of African songs and music. Such developments were particularly evident in Nigeria.

The concert party is an extension of this movement away from the Western European style of dramatic production as practiced by the foreign missions. But whereas in the cantatas the parts were sung to musical accompaniment and the themes were religious, in the concert party the parts are spoken and music is used only for linking one theme or episode with another; also, the subjects of the plays are taken from the daily social and political life of the community.

The first such concert party was started by a schoolteacher named Yallay in southern Ghana; he was followed by Ishmael ("Bob") Johnson, Charles B. Hutton, and J. B. Ansah. These men organized their shows under a combination of influences from church plays, folklore, and the early cinema acts of stars such as Charlie Chaplin. In 1930 Johnson, Hutton, and Ansah combined to form a group known as the Two Bobs. Charles Angmor gives us an idea of the beginnings and the characteristics of the comedies of the concert party in Ghana.

> The comic play combines spontaneous dialogue with music and action to dramatize simple themes drawn from everyday social experiences, and its characteristic vein is comic even in presenting sad or pathetic experiences. . . . This style of acting real life stories in speech and song embellished with the art of character disguise through facial make-up and also female impersonation was the tradition of the comic play that has been preserved to this day by Ghanaian comedians. (1978: 56)

The interest of this type of drama for oral literature is that, like *kote-tlon*, it is in a large sense spontaneous, unwritten, improvised. Although many of the leaders and players in the concert parties have some Western education and know the conventions of written drama of the European tradition, these urban players have maintained their uniqueness (while adjusting their techniques) to such an extent that they are now a force to be reckoned with in the social and cultural lives of their communities. Today in Ghana, the most prominent troupe is the Happy Star of Accra. The company has been long in existence, and has in many ways influenced the formation of the Happy Star of Lome in neighboring Togo. Let us take a brief look at the latter company so as to understand this form of theatre a little better.

The Happy Star of Lome was founded in 1965 by Pascal d'Almeida and a few of his friends. Pascal had worked for a short time at the commercial firm of SCOA and later as a guitarist in a dance band; but after observing some concert parties at Aflao (a border town between Ghana and Togo and a suburb of Lome), he decided to form his own group. Some members of this group have links with Ghana and have in fact played in the Happy Star of Accra.

The group plays mostly in the large patios of night clubs; they also perform in the level courtyards of community centers, but because of the obtrusiveness of audiences they prefer being mounted on a raised stage from where they can hold a safer intercourse with the crowd. They hold their performances mostly in the evenings after working hours to ensure maximum patronage from the large working population. An evening program usually begins at about 7:00 P.M. with a sustained prelude of "highlife" music from the group's orchestra, a strategy which goes on until enough people have gathered at the club; after about two hours, the theatre begins.

The actors are all male and, as in *kote-tlon,* some of them play female roles. From this we can already see that the principal business of this concert party troupe is caricaturing. This is clear enough from the general get-up. Apart from those of them who play the roles of women or the urban playboy, the actors usually mask their dark faces with white shoe polish painted round their eyes and mouths to indicate a variety of character types. The costumes also help in this typecasting; for instance, the "gentleman" or dandy regularly appears in a coat, long trousers, hat, dark glasses and with a cigarette; the old father usually has a lamp hanging round his neck and a pipe in his mouth, and leans shakily on a cane; a steward or rustic fellow comes on in rags and a cloche hat, and with a rag thrown over one shoulder; and so on.

The comedies played by the Happy Star center mostly on family or marital problems. For instance, John, an apprentice driver, is injured in a train accident. One of his two wives, Marie, runs off with Francis the "Parisian" whom she finds fanning himself with a wad of bank notes; but Elise sticks with John. Later, things go better for John; he gets well, finds a new job, and lives a decent and comfortable life with Elise. The reverse goes for Marie and Francis. The latter is exposed for the "fake" that he is: little by little his clothes are stripped off his back by the people he borrowed them from; even Marie loses her clothes in payment for the food she had bought on credit. Francis and Marie beg for forgiveness from John and Elise, and are eventually taken in as servants. But they begin to plot against their benefactors, are caught in the act, and chased out.

In addition to such marital dramas, other skits are put up to fill out the evening's fare. The performances are on the whole episodic, one show linked to the next rather tenuously and musical interludes filling the space between the end of one show and the beginning of the next. The audiences are heavily involved in these performances: not only do they engage the players with occasional dialogue and comments, but every once in a while someone jumps on the stage and pastes a coin on the forehead of an actor who has impressed him. It is all a communal celebration very much as in a traditional oral performance.

The Happy Star of Lome have today achieved a considerable measure of success, with a large number of plays in their repertoire. The following portrait of this group gives us an insight into the sources of their materials and the basis of their appeal.

> Plays are not written: each text is the collective creation of the group which improvises around a storyline presented by one of its members. Plays are drawn from folktales heard in the village, from plays copied from other Concert Parties (usually Ghanaian), from newspapers and popular novels. The text is theatrical in that it calls for participation of the public; it is open-ended and permits the actor to insist on a comic episode or to draw out a sad scene. The text produced by the troupe is in the language of Lome: this vernacular language is at the meeting point of two languages, Ewe and Mina, which for certain linguists are merely dialectal variants of the same language complex. It is highly probable that a homogenization of the different dialectal variants is occurring, to the advantage of the variant spoken in Lome. The radius of performance of the "Happy Star" troupe furnishes striking evidence of this process. Their area covers all of southern Togo, that is, a region including at least four dialectal variants. The troupe is understood everywhere. (Ricard 1977: 230)

The strength of the concert party, then, lies essentially in the fact that it is a communal dramatic celebration which, by combining folk traditions with elements of contemporary life, provides amusement and relaxation to the urban masses in an idiom they can easily relate to. It is also evident from the career of the Happy Star that to survive economically the concert party has to be frequently on the road. Perhaps no theatre tradition illustrates this truth, or demonstrates the peculiar strengths of this popular art form, better than the Yoruba traveling theatre of Nigeria. We begin a portrait of this tradition with a review of the career of its most celebrated practitioner, Hubert Ogunde.

Ogunde came into the Nigerian dramatic scene in the 1940s when, as we noted earlier, separatist movements within the Christian missions had formed their own sects and had evolved the native air opera as a replacement for the predominantly European-flavored cantatas of the missions. The forties was also the period of fervid Nigerian nationalism, when men such as Herbert Macaulay and Nnamdi Azikiwe were firing the minds of Nigerians with the zeal for self-rule (the Richards Constitution of 1946 was to prepare the way for this) and Nigerian workers, under the leadership of labor leaders such as Michael Imoudu, were protesting the unjust conditions of work and pay imposed upon them by the colonial authorities. These various influences were to mold the career of Ogunde. There was also another formative influence. The theatre of itinerant masked mummers, the Alarinjo already discussed, was very much alive at this time. As a young boy, Ogunde had run away with one such company until his angry father forced him back home (see Jeyifo 1984: 39); throughout his career, he never abandoned the deep feeling for Yoruba traditions which this early attachment inspired in him.

Ogunde's dramatic career began in 1943–44 when he produced a play entitled *The Garden of Eden and the Throne of God*, a native air opera by which his church (the Church of the Lord, Ebute-Metta, Lagos) hoped to raise funds for its building. "The Opera is in Yoruba," announced the program notes, "and Mr. Ogunde has ably blended church music with jazz music in order to interpret his thoughts more effectively to his audience" (see Clark 1979: 6). The next few plays done by Ogunde show a certain advance in his artistic consciousness. These plays—notably *Africa and God* (1944) and *Israel in Egypt* (1945)—were still native air operas produced under church patronage, but now Ogunde was beginning to infuse elements of Yoruba history and folklore as well as black nationalism into his material. *Africa and God* dealt with the confrontation between a traditional Yoruba ruler (King Labode) and the colonial administration, resulting in the defeat of the king and his submission to British rule and Christianity. *Israel in Egypt* explored the fortunes of a subjugated people, an appropriate metaphor for the Nigerian colonial situation. The program notes to the latter advertised it as "a wonderful combination of slavery scenes, songs and dances in the deepest Yoruba music" (see Clark 1979: 13).

The growing nationalist zeal in Ogunde was to find its first firm articulation in *Worse Than Crime* and *Strike and Hunger.* By this time (1945) he had resigned his job as a policeman and, after initial difficulties posed mainly by the prevailing antitheatrical prejudice,[11] formed his own professional company under the name African Music Research Party. Ogunde was now growing gradually away from the religious themes that enjoyed the patronage of the churches and looking more in the direction of contemporary nationalist concerns as well as traditional themes and styles of artistic expression. *Worse Than Crime* was, according to the advertisement for the performance, designed to show that "Slavery in any shape or form is WORSE THAN CRIME," but the real butt of the attack was, as Ogunde's coproducer Kuyinu told Ebun Clark (1979: 11), the colonialism of the day. The play was particularly moving for its folk music and folk dancing, especially by a troupe of masquerades, and a reviewer praised Ogunde for livening the story with "ancient folk songs and community airs." Significantly, the premier production was chaired by the nationalist leader Nnamdi Azikiwe. But it was *Strike and Hunger* that put Ogunde in true nationalist limelight. For a 1946 production in Jos of this play, which dramatized the plight of Nigerian workers in the general strike of 1945, Ogunde was prosecuted and fined by the colonial authorities; the Yoruba community in Jos rallied round him and paid not only the one hundred pounds required "to fight the case as a national one" but also the 125 pounds imposed on him as fine.

Other nationalist plays followed. But all these were still operas. And although Ogunde had infused in them some dialogue confrontation between actors, he nevertheless retained the basic operatic format of statements being performed in song to the accompaniment of instrumental music (African and foreign). By this time, however, other things were happening to theatre life especially in Ogunde's base, Lagos. Some amateur music societies were staging variety shows featuring impromptu dialogue interspersed with music (especially jazz, which was the fad in urban entertainment at the time). Some Ghana (then Gold Coast) concert parties were coming on tour to Nigeria and making an impression on the public; indeed, in 1948 Ogunde himself led a brief sojourn in Ghana and did a few productions along the lines of the variety shows made famous by Bob Johnson's Two Bobs concert party.

When he returned to Nigeria later that year, Ogunde discovered that another Nigerian, Bobby Benson, who had studied music in America and Britain and whom

Ogunde had met during a foreign tour in 1947, had started Nigeria's first professional variety theatre company. Run under the joint management of Bobby and his Brazilian wife, Cassandra, the company produced a mixed bag of entertainment featuring mostly improvised dialogue (on the model of the Black and White Minstrel Show of America) and American-style music (jazz, boogie-woogie, ragtime, etc.). Bobby and his group also thrilled the fashion-conscious Lagos public by dressing themselves up—mostly on-stage but often also off—in trendy American-style outfits such as the zoot suit and pointed shoes to match.

Ogunde realized he simply had to jazz up his own performances to survive, and produced concert varieties such as *Gold Coast Melodies* (1949). But his forte was drama; so, rather than giving himself over to musical varieties, he now produced what may be called concert operas, such as *Bread and Bullet* (1950) and *Highway Eagle* (1953). However, the most enduring element that he took from this period was the improvised dialogue of the concert party. From 1954, when he produced *Princess Jaja*, Ogunde gave a good deal more of his time to this style than to the operatic mode. "In the theatre of improvization begun by Ogunde," says Ebun Clark, "because the actor could now extemporize his dialogue, he was free to engage his audience in conversation, and this he still does throughout the play" (1979: 122). The result was that Ogunde began to recover much of the public patronage that Bobby Benson had gradually taken away from him.

Perhaps we could safely say that, with the concert party, Ogunde finally came home to the oral mode (as against the carefully scripted opera) which was his first encounter with theatre in that luckless adventure with the *Alarinjo* early in his youth. Ogunde has gone on to produce memorable operas in the Yoruba language [12] and with supporting traditional music. No doubt the most memorable is *Yoruba Ronu* (1964), which laments the effects of the prevailing political turmoil and exhorts Yorubas to "think" *(ronu)* hard about the destiny of the race. So provocative was the play that it was banned by the unpopular civilian government of the Western Region at the time. But the concert party remains the favorite idiom, especially in the use of improvised dialogue and the treatment of social misdemeanors to comic satire. Among the most notable plays in this mode is *Onimoto* (1971), a play in four acts that exposes the pretenses of urban types—smart business operators, ruthless lorry touts, streetwise vegetable sellers, money-conscious Lagos girls.

Two other elements reveal Ogunde's attachment to the Alarinjo theatre. One is his use of the traditional frame of the opening glee and the closing glee, that is, tunes that introduce and end the performance. The former is something of an *ijuba* (a pledge or salute), such as the masquerades use in paying homage to protective forces (e.g., Osoronga) and the patrons or founders of the masque-dramaturgy (e.g., Esa Ogbin); the latter is simply a closing call that serves the role of the final curtain. Ogunde has used the format frequently in his career. In his early native air opera days he used both the opening and the closing glee to give praise to God (as in *Africa and God*), and the more recent *Onimoto* ends with a tune which simply serves "as an opportunity to make general social or philosophical comments, and . . . . is also used as a device to exhort the audience to pay heed to the moral lessons dealt with in the play" (Clark 1979: 140). The second element is the traveling routine of the theatre, which not only ensures the economic viability of the enterprise but helps to bring the theatre to the grassroots. Ogunde's itinerary has taken him not only across the length and breadth of Nigeria but also to other West African countries such as the Republic of Benin, Togo, Ghana, and Ivory Coast.

With his treatment of the fortunes of King Labode in *Africa and God* (1944) and his use of several aspects of the Yoruba folk tradition, Ogunde inspired the growth of several theatre companies with a special interest in dramatizing Yoruba history and folklore. The most notable of these were the troupes led by Kola Ogunmola and Duro Ladipo. The significant thing about these two men is that, unlike Ogunde, they enjoyed the attention of the intellectual circles which recognized the potentials of their dramatic talents. The University of Ibadan hosted each of them as artists in residence and so encouraged the development of their art along somewhat "serious" lines.

Although Ogunmola produced a number of biblical themes, he is best known for his folk opera *Omuti*—his adaptation of Amos Tutuola's *Palm Wine Drinkard*—which tells the story of a man visiting the land of the dead in search of his palmwine tapster. Tutuola's story is a storehouse of motifs from the Yoruba oral narrative tradition, and Ogunmola's adaptation is essentially a homage to that tradition. However, Ogunmola found he did not have much luck with serious themes and so gave more of his time to comedies on social life. "Ogunmola's *forte* is his acting—his mime in particular," Ulli Beier tells us. "He is most successful when he attempts social satire and in this field *Love of Money* is probably his greatest play" (1979: 273). The play tells the story of a foolish man who allows himself to be attracted by a pretty girl into bringing her in as his second wife; the new wife eventually destroys the entire marital home and abandons the man to loneliness. Although the theme is serious, the treatment is extremely hilarious; this, as Ogunmola discovered, was more to his audiences' taste than the tragic themes. [13]

Duro Ladipo had much better luck with his treatment of serious themes. He is perhaps best remembered for three myth-historical plays in his repertoire: *Oba Koso*, *Oba Waja*, and *Moremi*. It was *Oba Koso* that gave him the greatest prominence and won him acclaim with audiences in Africa, Europe, and the United States. The play is an euhemeristic reconstruction of the career of Sango, the Yoruba god of thunder and lightning. As a king of Oyo, he was anxious to swell his kingdom and so urged his generals on endless campaigns. Eventually his subjects got tired of war and wanted peace, but he was unable to check the war-mongering zeal of his generals. In desperation, Sango took his life by hanging, but zealous supporters denied the news of the suicide—"Oba Koso" means "The King did not hang"—and declared him a god, who is worshipped to this day. *Oba Waja* deals with a historical event of 1946. The king of Oyo dies, and his master of the horse (Elesin) must commit suicide (as custom dictates) so as to accompany the king to the grave; in his final farewell dance through the town, Elesin is arrested on the orders of the colonial district officer, who cannot stand this "barbaric custom"; meanwhile Elesin's son returns from abroad to give his father (who he knows must die) a fitting burial, but on finding that the man is still (shamefully) alive, takes his own life; the people of Oyo declare the act of the district officer, now reduced to a confused and tragic figure, as the will of the unpredictable god of fate (Eshu). *Moremi* recreates the career of a tragic heroine in the war between the Ife people and an autochthonous group for the settlement of Ife; Moremi plays a prominent role in the Ife military strategy and offers her own son Oluorogbo to seal the cause of settlement. A praise chant from *Oba Waja*, in which the Oyo citizens address the bewildered British district officer, gives us an insight into the high seriousness of Ladipo's tragic theatre.

> White man, bringer of new laws,
> White man, bringer of new times,
> Your work was confounded by Eshu,
>   confuser of men.
> Nobody can succeed against the will of Eshu
> The god of fate;
> Having thrown a stone today—he kills
>   a bird yesterday.
> Lying down, his head hits the roof—
> Standing up he cannot look into the cooking pot.
> With Eshu
> Wisdom counts for more than good intentions,
> And understanding is greater than justice. (Beier 1979: 279–80)

The texts of these folk operas are a combination of carefully scripted canto and dialogue aptly improvised, the latter of which gives an opportunity for some audience involvement. In the latter part of his career, however, Ladipo found he was losing audiences to the up-and-coming theatre companies whose province was entirely comedy. He used to be furious, for instance, that the public was abandoning the serious cultural business of his plays for the lowlife stuff of groups such as Moses Olaiya's Alawada International. To join the game, therefore, and recover his thinning patronage, Ladipo devoted a good proportion of his schedule to social satires of the concert party type, all based entirely on improvised dialogue. The comedy series produced by the Duro Ladipo Theatre, under the title *Bode Wasimi*, was easily one of the favorites on the Oyo State television circuit (BCOS).

If Nigerian theatre audiences today show a preference for comic over tragic theatre, it is not because they have no regard for the serious issues of life or the deeper concerns of cultural history. It is simply that in the increasingly depressed condition of the Nigerian economy, the convenient concerns of "high culture" are becoming steadily marginalized.

And yet it was the economic situation which fostered the growth of the modern theatre companies. In the 1950s there was only a handful of them, including Ogunde's, and even then Ogunde was the only one who had anything like a nationwide itinerary and popularity. By the 1970s, when Nigeria enjoyed an oil boom, there was a good deal of money available to spend on entertainment. A pattern had been set, a habit bred; so that, even today when economic activity has slowed down, the currency severely devalued, and there is far less money in people's hands, there is still an illusion of wealth and so a reasonably high inclination to attend the comic theatre. Although no one has measured the statistical toll that the present economic slump is taking on various forms of enterprise (artistic and otherwise), by 1984 Biodun Jeyifo could state that there were about 120 Yoruba traveling theatre troupes, two of them led by women. Of those still on circuit, perhaps the most prominent are the troupes led by Hubert Ogunde, Moses Olaiya, Oyin Adejobi, Isola Ogunsola, Akin Ogungbe, Lere Paimo, Ola Omonitan, and Jimoh Aliu. Ogunde continues to occupy his revered position as the greatest largely because he has been around the longest and has attained both national and international acclaim. But in terms of mastery of the comic tastes of audiences and of the theatrical skills suited to these, most Yoruba theatre-goers would unequivocally swear by the name of Moses Olaiya.

Although Ogunde inspired the emergence of these traveling theatre groups, they have put far more emphasis on low-life comedies than he has ever done. Ogunde himself once drew a distinction between the serious cultural plays and what he called the *jeun-jeun* or "bread and butter" kind (Beier 1979: 272). These more recent groups concentrate their interest on the latter kind: slapstick comedies and uproarious satires of contemporary manners, very much along the lines of *kote-tlon* fare, simply to earn a good laugh and a good patronage. Every once in a while, of course, they explore serious themes. Some are taken from the vast storehouse of Yoruba folklore; in addition to Kola Ogunmola's *Omuti* (an adaptation of the quest motif in Tutuola's *Palm-Wine Drinkard*), we have Oyin Adejobi's *Fowo Raku* (Buying death), in which a rich man goes off in search of death so he could buy him off and enjoy eternal life, and Jimoh Aliu's *Agba Aarin,* which plumbs the rich proverbial lore of Yoruba divination poetry *(ifa)* to explore the contest between good and evil. In more recent times, some groups have turned works of modern Yoruba fiction into successful dramatic productions. Most notable perhaps are the dramatization by the Isola Ogunsola group of Dejo Okediji's *Aja lo le'eru* (which was serialized on television), Akinwunmi Isola's *Efunsetan Aniwura* (which has been made into a big-screen movie), and Jimoh Aliu's adaptation for stage of D. O. Fagunwa's *Ogboju Ode Ninu Igbo Irunmale* (translated by Wole Soyinka as *The Forest of a Thousand Daemons*). The emphasis, however, remains on social comedies, and that in the largely disconnected format of variety entertainment.

The premium placed on entertainment should be stressed, because it reinforces once again the point made by recent scholars of African dramatic arts (e.g., Ogunba, Enekwe), that in this genre of art we are dealing more with a concern for a fulfilling spectacle (theatre) which goes beyond but embraces a mere reenactment of a story (mythos) or representation of action and event. In our discussion of Bamana rural revues, we saw dramatic sketches sharing an evening's bill with music, song, dance, and wrestling matches. The same goes for these troupes of the Yoruba traveling theatre. Jeyifo has usefully pointed out (1984: 54–55) that this concern for spectacle spans the entire history of the tradition from Ogunde to his present-day colleagues. As part of his opening glee, Ogunde frequently lets his "lightly dressed girls go wild on saxophones" (Beier 1979: 272) and presents various forms of floor show to complement the dramatic production for the evening. Akin Ogungbe and his company have performed acrobatic and fire-eating acts, while Moses Olaiya has on occasion done some magical displays as part of the evening's fare. The principal aim in all this is to satisfy the audience's craving for fulfilling spectacle and entertainment.

For traditional African theatre is, in the final analysis, an "audience's theatre" in a deeper sense than is conventionally understood. In the Yoruba traveling theatre, it does happen that an actor so impresses himself or herself on the audience by the excellence with which he or she acts a particular role that he or she becomes regularly identified with the role. For instance, the image of Duro Ladipo as Sango, which is the role he played in his most memorable play *Oba Koso,* stuck with him till his death. In the variety format of the concert party—in which there is a variety of plays not necessarily united by any thematic link—one role could be featured in as many plays as possible so that the player emerges as a recognizable "star." Thus Moses Olaiya regularly appears as "Lamidi Sanni Oropo, alias Baba Sala" in just about every one of his productions either on circuit or on television, and his leading lady Aduke George as "Iya Sala"; in the Isola Ogunsola theatre, Ogunsola himself regularly plays the lead role of "I-Sho Pepper"; and so on. It may also happen that an actor gets so inspired by his role that he or she stretches the text beyond regular proportions—as in the delivery of a chant. These are the reasons why Biodun Jeyifo has concluded that "what we have in this theatre is an actor's theatre, not a playwright's: the necessities and inner consistencies of plot construction and characterisation such as we 'normally' expect in literary drama, are manifestly subordinated to the known and expected specialities of a given troupe's 'star' performers" (1984: 95).

The fact remains, however, that in the performances even the stars are subject to the whims and preferences of the audience. Because the plays are unwritten and in many cases thoroughly improvised, the fate of the text and individual episodes and productions depends very much on the demands made by the audience involved; for instance, audience members frequently hold dialogue with the actors and actually influence the expansions, curtailment, or even total elimination of details and moves in the sequence of events. Jeyifo is therefore much more to the point when he says (p. 97):

> Values and structures that are normally sacrosanct in the literary drama, such as motivated plot development or consistency and economy of structural logistics, are casually sacrificed to achieve either improvised, momentary effects or extended displays in gratification of an audience's request. This feature is of course at its most pronounced, most self-indulgent in the farces and comedies which now predominate in the dramatic fare of many companies; in these plays, only the thinnest thread of a general synopsis connects the episodes and situations which make up the play. Within such a thin synoptic line is then packed every conceivable and permissible detail or routine which a performer's inspired enthusiasm may produce or the audience's voluble solicitude may generate.

It is in this quality of looseness of structure, which allows for the audience's whimsical intervention, that the productions of the Yoruba traveling theatre best reflect their indebtedness to the tradition of the oral performance.

Despite its indebtedness to the oral tradition, the modern Yoruba traveling theatre reveals a certain progressiveness of outlook and a considerable level of enterprise which disposes it to avail itself of the benefits of the technological culture. The progressiveness can be seen at least in the presence of females in the performing troupes. In traditional society, there are certain kinds of oral performance that women feature prominently in, as in the chanting of dirges or the song and dance routines of choral groups, or even in certain ritual performances. But playing dramatic roles of the secular sort is traditionally not considered proper for women, and in this regard the Yoruba traveling theatre is at least one step ahead of rural revues like *kote-tlon* or even urban concert parties like the Happy Star of Lome, in which men play female roles. To be sure, there is considerable comic effect in having a man play a woman's role: it is a caricature that will draw an easy laugh. But having a real woman do a woman's business is even better; not only is it more realistic, but there is a much higher potential for sexual appeal which enhances the quality of the play as spectacle or entertainment.

Ogunde was the first to realize this. At first he had trouble recruiting women when he formed his professional group (the African Music Research Party) largely because it was unusual and almost taboo for a woman to be acting on stage, like the "rogues, vagabounds and sturdy beggars" that the *alarinjo* players were judged to be. But once he recruited his women he dignified them—and thus ensured their lasting commitment to his enterprise—by marrying every one of them.[14] The same is true of Ladipo's and Ogunmola's troupes, in which at least the leading lady is the proprietor's wife. Such women hardly flinch from playing certain alluring roles if they have to. Ogunde's leading wives—the late Adeshewa and Ibisomi—frequently played the types of the citified lady, ogling their eyes and swaying their hips to the riotous titillation of the audience; and, as we observed above, a whole line of lightly clad ladies often usher in his shows by playing wild riffs on the saxophone.

A second evidence of the progressive outlook in the modern Yoruba traveling theatre is the way the troupes have exploited modern advances in sound and screen. In the first place, the troupes have revolutionized their sound equipment. The old native air operas used Yoruba drums in their musical accompaniment, and for a while Ogunde did that too when he went professional. But from his concert party days, he has adopted European musical instruments (e.g., guitars and saxophones) in his musical acts and has recorded numerous albums not only of tunes played by his troupes but even of dramas (e.g., *Yoruba Ronu*) performed by them. The Institute of African Studies of the University of Ibadan has produced an album of Duro Ladipo's *Oba Koso* and of Kola Ogunmola's *Omuti*. These and other groups have also recorded Yoruba music (mostly from their plays) as a way of advertising their productions and swelling their earnings. Several groups have produced plays for radio, but they have frequently complained of poor payment for their pains and have lately not shown much enthusiasm for that medium; the radio houses, however, give them patronage by playing their albums and tapes.

Perhaps the biggest rewards—in terms, that is, of exposure and even money—come from television and big screen. The productions of the troupes are now a regular feature on program schedules of the TV stations in the Yoruba-speaking states of Nigeria. There have been serialized productions of major works of modern Yoruba literature. For instance, the Duro Ladipo group did a somewhat masterly series of D. O. Fagunwa's *Igbo Olodumare* for the Oyo State television service (BCOS). The Isola Ogunsola troupe has also done Akinwunmi Isola's historical novel *Efunsetan Aniwura* and Oladejo Okediji's detective novel *Aja lo l'eru* for television, while the Oyin Ade-jobi company produced *Ekuro Oloja* also for TV. In a lighter vein, Adejobi himself has done a courtroom series titled *Kootu Asipa*. The Duro Ladipo group's *Bode Wasimi* is also a series based on life in a fictional Yoruba community of the 1920s, somewhat along the lines of Nigerian national television's *Village Headmaster* and with just as much comic effect. Finally, there is a regular weekly slot on BCOS called *Tiata Yoruba*, which gives a variety of troupes an opportunity to display their dramatic art.

The more recent and no doubt more lucrative venture is, however, in big-screen filming. Ogunde was the first to go into this with *Aiye, Jaiyesimi*, and other films; in these he has frequently exploited "special effect" techniques most suited to the bizarre mythical content of the tales. Other theatre companies have followed suit. The Ade Afolayan company has joined with the Duro Ladipo and Oyin Adejobi groups in the production of *Ija Ominira*, an adaptation for screen of Adebayo Faleti's novel *Omo Olokun Esin;* Isola Ogunsola has adopted his stage version of *Efunsetan Aniwura* for the big screen; and Moses Olaiya has teamed with Ajimajasan and others in Ola Balogun's production of *Owo l'Agba* (Money Power).[15]

In their television and big-screen productions, the "star" performers do get an occasional chance to recreate their acclaimed roles, as Moses Olaiya has done in his role of Baba Sala. But these screen productions have put a harder test on the dramatic art of the traveling theatre troupes than they are accustomed to in their itinerant routines. In the latter, they could entertain their audiences with short comic skits (some lasting no more than ten minutes) and intersperse these with other types of "floor show." But a thirty- to sixty-minute slot on television, or a two-hour span on the big screen, would require the group to produce a play with a far more coherent plot, and a greater intercourse between character and action, than it has time to develop when it takes to the road. In this regard, needless to say, the actors have shown that they can intuit the art as deeply as their counterparts in the European literary tradition.

This point leads us to conclude our discussion of African drama with the question that we broached at the beginning of it: is there such a thing as drama in traditional African society? There certainly is, and our discussion so far demonstrates convincingly enough the presence of all those elements that Finnegan, in *Oral Literature in Africa* (p. 501), recognized as the determining criteria: "the idea of enactment, of representation through actors who represent persons and events . . . linguistic content; plot; the represented interaction of several characters; specialized scenery, etc.; often music; and—of particular importance in most African performances—dance." Although there are situations in which all these elements are not fully combined in one performance—for example, in the often informal and hurried productions of some troupes—there are numerous cases in which they all cohere in the same work. This is true of all types and phases of traditional African drama that we have examined: e.g., the festival drama of Igbo masquerades; the rural revues of the Bamana; and the concert operas of various troupes of the Yoruba traveling theatre. The point should be stressed, however, that African drama is more than just the representation of action, that in Africa, drama is treated as the representation of action in the spirit and context of a communal celebration, often with music and dance, in which the audience members see themselves as participant observers of the efforts of the actors. Drama is a universal concept whose realization is, nevertheless, culture-bound; the trouble with dramatic criticism is to assume that the Aristotelian definition represents a universal model or is even right.[16]

Part Three

The Survival of Oral Literature

10. Oral Literature and Modern African Literature

What we have just seen in chapter 9—of modern concert parties incorporating stories from the oral tradition into their repertoire of oral theatre and transforming materials from contemporary written fiction into their peculiar format of oral dramatic performance—goes to show that oral literature has a continued vitality for modern-day society. No group of people have tried to promote this vitality more than the creative writers—poets, novelists, and playwrights. One major reason that the concert party troupes have found it worthwhile to transform some modern fiction (especially by Yoruba writers) into their peculiar oral styles is that the works themselves show a certain attachment to modes of behavior and of expression characteristic of oral culture.

There has, indeed, been an increasing tendency on the part of modern African writers to identify with the literary traditions of their people in terms both of content and of technique. The reason is not far to seek. For a long time before African nations won political independence from their European colonizers, African culture was misunderstood and misrepresented. Words such as *savage* and *primitive* were used in describing it and, as we saw in chapter 1, the literary or artistic quality of the oral literature was underplayed and undermined by foreign scholars who had little or no feeling for the languages and the attitudes in which that literature was expressed. It was only inevitable that, when these African nations won their independence from foreign domination, they undertook to reexamine and overhaul not only the institutions by which they had been governed but also the image of their culture that had long been advertised by outsiders. The aim was to demonstrate that Africa has had, since time immemorial, traditions that should be respected and a culture to be proud of.

As far as the creative writers are concerned, the main offshoots of this program have been to collect and publish texts of the oral literature of their people as practiced by them over time and to use that literature as a basis for writing original works that reflect, from a more or less modern perspective, some of the major concerns of today so as to demonstrate that traditional African culture is not obsolete but relevant for the articulation of contemporary needs and goals. In this chapter, we shall examine the various ways in which modern African writers have made their contribution toward this vindication of traditional African culture.

Translation

As we have often stressed, many Europeans who studied African oral literature and culture from the mid-nineteenth to the mid-twentieth century were laboring under a prejudice as well as a misconception. Often, this is reflected in the rather cavalier ways in which they translated the pieces of oral literature or sought to give them a respectability which, it was thought, they lacked. Burton reported one of the old prejudices about African oral literature prevalent in his time: "Poetry there is none. . . . There is no meter, no rhyme, nothing that interests or soothes the feelings, or arrests the passions" (1865: xii). The result of this was that some European collectors, in their translation of the songs that they encountered in African communities, tried to force them into schemes of versification that made music to European ears but were characteristically un-African.

When African writers and scholars started doing their own translations, they saw it as their primary duty to dress African oral literature in a European language in such a way as to bring out the poetic quality, the charm, of the original. Unfortunately, some of them tried to be so "fashionable" that in the end their translations sounded just as un-African as the ones the Europeans did. Although the following rendition by the Ghanaian poet G. Adali-Mortty of a traditional Ewe dirge endeavors to capture the depth of sentiment of the original, his recourse to the idiom of Elizabethan poetry leads us to question the authenticity of the translation.

> Methinks it's been a dream:
> But the dream has come to life!
> Atangba's son, Drofenu, says:
>> Believe them not:
>> A dream's a dream.
>>> No more!
> Truly, had dreams been real,
> Death, I'd have fathomed death. (Adali-Mortty 1979: 4)

In defending his technique, Adali-Mortty makes a claim which many translators have frequently advanced in support of the liberties they have taken, that in African poetry "the thoughts are condensed in terse language, making their translation into English a hazardous venture!" This is certainly true, and I do not mean to trivialize or underestimate the depth of sentiment in much traditional African poetry. But the point is that it is not necessary to try to capture this depth by straining after archaic idioms and techniques that have an all too foreign flavor. One of the characteristic qualities of traditional African song is repetition, either of single lines or groups of lines. It is significant that in the original Ewe version of this dirge, Adali-Mortty indicates in parenthesis that the first two lines of the song are sung twice—"(bis)"—but omits that indication from the English version, as if to suggest that such a repetition has no place in the English poetic sensibility. This may well be so. But the song being translated is an African song, and the repetition does help, as we saw in chapter 4 above, to invest a piece of oral performance with an intensity or depth by way of emphasis.

Those African writers who appreciate this fact have consequently aimed to strike a compromise between a due regard for the European idiom and a firm loyalty to the peculiarly African character of the material at their disposal. In this dirge translated from the Acoli, Okot p'Bitek does not tamper with the repetitive structure and diction of the original, and the result is poetry that captures the vibrancy and sauciness of the oral performance and yet manages to affirm, by the sheer force of the repetition, the tragic fate of the poor.

Ee, my aunt,
The death of the poor is sudden;
My aunt, was she strangled?
What death has killed my aunt?
The poor woman died on the roadside;
The poor thing died suddenly;
Who has strangled my aunt?
The death of the poor is sudden.

Oh, mother,
I heard her by her smell oh,
The death of the poor is sudden;
I heard her by her smell on the roadside;
What snake bit my aunt?
The poor woman died on the roadside;
The poor thing died suddenly;
Was she killed by a lion?
The death of the poor is sudden.

Ee, harlot;
The death of the poor is sudden;
Ee, harlot, somebody slept with her,
Perhaps a bull syphilis killed my aunt?
My aunt has died a foolish death;
The poor thing died suddenly;
Who killed her?
The death of the poor is sudden. (p'Bitek 1974: 137)

Here, truly, is an African writer who has a feeling for the peculiar lyricism of his people's poetic traditions, and I do not think the lucidity of the English compromises the poetic intensity of the original.

There has been an equally large number of translations of African oral narratives. The first known "translation" of African tales was the Frenchman J-F. ("Le Bon") Roger's *Fables Senegalaises recueillies dans l'Ouolof* (1828), which is really a retelling or recapitulation. In the later nineteenth and much of this century, in fact, there have been volumes of translations of uneven quality. Some of them are little more than summaries of tales collected by anthropologists interested more in the ideas (of culture and social life) than in the literary merits of the tales.

African writers and scholars have, however, sought to correct the picture and to demonstrate that their narrative traditions can boast as much charm as anything found

in modern narrative. One of the most notable nationalist ideologies of this century
has been the philosophy of negritude, especially as propagated by the Senegalese Leopold Sedar Senghor in his poetry and essays. The aim of negritude was to project
everything African—the color black, the physical features of the African and his environment, the humane quality of African culture, etc.—as beautiful and salutary.
This movement, designed to put Africa in a good light at a time (in the 1940s and
1950s) when African nations were agitating for independence from European powers,
was advertised mostly in the verse of the period—by Francophone African poets such
as Senghor, Birago Diop, David Diop, and Bernard Dadie as well as the Caribbean
poets Leon Damas and Aime Cesaire—but there were also works of prose narrative.

One of the most outstanding of these prose works is the historian Djibril T. Niane's edition of the legend of Sunjata, the thirteenth-century Malian king and emperor, under the title *Soundjata ou l'épopée mandingue* (1960), translated into English
by G. D. Pickett as *Sundiata: An Epic of Old Mali* (1965). In this evocation of the
great historical tradition of the Mandinka, Niane was obviously influenced by Thomas
Mofolo's narration of the life and career of the legendary Zulu leader Chaka. Although
the story of Chaka's exploits has traditionally been told by *imbongi* (bards) who render
their subject in highly metaphorical praise chants, Mofolo—then working on the staff
of a missionary publishing house—chose to render his *Chaka* as a historical novel
presented "as a study of human passion, of an uncontrolled and then uncontrollable
ambition leading to the moral destruction of the character and the inevitable punishment."[1] Niane also casts his own story of Sunjata as a historical novel, although it is
traditionally told in poetic chants by *griots* (bards) to the accompaniment of a chor-
dophone called *kora*. However, in place of Mofolo's moral didacticism, Niane retains
the element of glorification by portraying Sunjata as an insuperable champion of a
just cause and the architect of an eternal imperial glory.

More recent editions of the Sunjata story observe the linear order—determined by
a combination of the narrator's breath stops and the rhythm of the musical accompaniment—of the *griot*'s narration. In rendering his edition in prose, however, Niane
has unavoidably sacrificed the characteristic flavor of the oral performance to the peculiar aims of nationalist history. Let us take the episode, for instance, in which
Sunjata's sister tricks the usurper king Sumanguru (Soumaoro) into telling her the
secret of his magical powers and invincibility in war. Niane makes the girl, Nana
Triban, a pawn by whom one of Sunjata's rival brothers seeks to secure Sumanguru's
support against Sunjata. In the following passage, she has been reunited with her
half-brother Sunjata from captivity by Sumanguru and relates to Sunjata her mode of
discovery of Sumanguru's secret.

When you left Mali, my brother sent me by force to Sosso to be the wife of Soumaoro,
whom he greatly feared. I wept a great deal at the beginning but when I saw that perhaps
all was not lost I resigned myself for the time being. I was nice to Soumaoro and was the
chosen one among his numerous wives. I had my chamber in the great tower where he
himself lived. I knew how to flatter him and make him jealous. . . . One night I took
the bull by the horns and said to Soumaoro: "Tell me, oh you whom kings mention with
trembling, tell me Soumaoro, are you a man like others or are you the same as the jinn

who protects humans? No one can bear the glare of your eyes, your arm has the strength of ten arms. Tell me, king of kings, tell me what jinn protects you so that I can worship him also." These words filled him with pride and he himself boasted to me of the might of his Tana. That very night he took me into his magic chamber and told me all. (1965: 57–58)

Now compare this passage with the same episode as recorded from the Malian *griot* Fa-Digi Sisoko by John William Johnson (1986: 171–73). Here Sunjata's sister (Su-gulun Kulunkan) undertakes to go to Sumanguru (Sumamuru) to find out his secret so as to turn the tables against him in his war with Sunjata (Son-Jara). Notice the bravado of her appearance.

2676	Sugulun Kulunkan arose,	(Indeed)
	And went up to the gates of Sumamuru's fortress. . . .	(Indeed)
	"Come open the gates, Susu Mountain Sumamuru!	(Indeed)
2690	Come make me your bed companion!"	(Indeed)
	Sumamuru came to the gates:	(Indeed)
	"What manner of person are you?"	(Indeed)
	"It is I Sugulun Kulunkan!"	(Indeed)
	"Well, now, Sugulun Kulunkan,	(Indeed)
2695	If you have come to trap me,	(Indeed)
	To turn me over to some person,	(Indeed)
	Know that none can ever vanquish me.	(Indeed)
	I have found the Manden secret,	(Indeed)
	And made the Manden sacrifice,	(Indeed)
2700	And in five score millet stalks placed it,	(Indeed)
	And buried them here in the earth.	(Indeed)
	'Tis I who found the Manden secret	(Indeed)
	And made the Manden sacrifice,	(Indeed)
	And in a red piebald bull did place it,	(Indeed)
2705	And buried it here in the earth.	(Indeed)
	Know that none can vanquish me.	(Indeed)
	'Tis I who found the Manden secret,	(Indeed)
	And made a sacrifice to it,	(Indeed)
	And in a pure white cock did place it.	(Indeed)
2710	Were you to kill it,	(Indeed)
	And uproot some barren groundnut plants,	(Indeed)
	And strip them of their leaves,	
	And spread them round the fortress,	(Indeed)
	And uproot more barren peanut plants	(Indeed)
2715	And fling them into the fortress,	(Indeed)
	Only then can I be vanquished."	(Indeed)
	His mother sprang forward at that:	(Indeed)
	"Heh! Susu Mountain Sumamuru!	(Indeed)
	Never tell all to a woman,	
2720	To a one-night woman!	(Indeed)
	The woman is not safe, Sumamuru."	(Indeed)
	Sumamuru sprang towards his mother	(Indeed)

And came and seized his mother;   (Indeed)
And slashed off her breast with a knife, magasi!   (Indeed)
2725 She went and got the old menstrual cloth.   (Indeed)
"Ah! Sumamuru!" she swore.   (Indeed)
"If your birth was ever a fact,
I have cut your old menstrual cloth!"
O Kalajula Sangoyi Mamunaka![2]   (Indeed)
2730 He lay Sugulun Kulunkan down on the bed.   (Indeed)
After one week had gone by,
Sugulun Kulunkan spoke up: (Indeed)
"Ah, my husband,   (Indeed)
Will you not let me go to the Manden,   (Indeed)
2735 That I may get my bowls and spoons,
For me to build my household here?" . . .   (Indeed)
2742 Sugulun returned to reveal those secrets
To her flesh-and-blood-brother, Son-Jara.   (Indeed)

This passage clearly shows what an oral performance is like and what we lose in the version presented by Niane. The repetitive device has a certain lyrical beauty about it, and the continual concurrence ("Indeed") by the accompanist reveals the warm, collaborative act of storytelling in this tradition. Although this technique may not be a factor in the performance of the *griot* (Djeli Mamoudou Kouyate) from whom Niane recorded his version, it is nevertheless clear that the latter's interest as a historian, driven by a desire to set down the most cherished historical monument of his people, has led him to edit the material rather severely.

For instance, most available versions of the Sunjata story dwell at some length on Sumanguru's dialogue with Sunjata's sister in this scene, and indeed (as in the passage just quoted) treat the audience to the sexual appeal of the liaison between Sumanguru and the woman. Some of these elements may have seemed of peripheral interest to our historian. However, since the Sunjata story can hardly be told without a good dose of the fantastic—as in the combatant's use of magic and sorcery to accomplish the most amazing feats—Niane, in his edition of the story, has had to settle for a historical romance similar to Mofolo's *Chaka*. We may thus conclude that although Niane has made an invaluable contribution to our awareness of Africa's rich heritage of oral literature and history, in his translation of the Sunjata story he has allowed his interest as a historian to attenuate the peculiar virtues of the oral performance.

Taban lo Liyong is another African writer who has undertaken to translate the oral narrative traditions of his people, and here we see a slightly different shade of interest. His story, "The Old Man of Usumbura and His Misery," from his collection *Fixions* (1969b), tells the tragic tale of a wealthy man who is so struck by the misery of his friend that he decides to seek out the meaning of misery. The very first paragraph of Liyong's translation of this tale gives us a good taste of the traditional flavor of the narrative.

There was an old man of Usumbura who was very rich. *This old man of Usumbura.* He was so rich he had eight thousand cows. *The rich old man of Usumbura.* With these cows he married for himself sixty-five wives. *The old man of Usumbura.* He was so healthy that he had three hundred children from these wives. *Our healthy man of Usumbura.* He was so happy and successful that with industry his wealth increased manifoldly. *This happy successful and industrious man of Usumbura.* He and all the members of his family were so lucky none of them ever felt sick. *These lucky people of Usumbura.* All his life he had never known the pangs of sorrow or grief. *This lucky Usumburan.* (P. 2)[3]

The peculiar element lies in those heavy, reflective comments that punctuate the narrative statements alternately. This seems to represent the tradition of storytelling performance in many societies across Africa. We have seen something of this nature in the passage from Fa-Digi Sisoko's version of the Sunjata story above. Finnegan, in her study of storytelling among the Limba of Sierra Leone, tells us of the practice whereby a storyteller, about to begin a performance, chooses an "answerer" whose job is to interject comments like "fancy that" and "really!" at appropriate moments and who "often repeats the important points or proper names of the characters in an undertone to emphasize them" (1967: 67–68). So important, indeed, are these comments and asides for the storyteller's morale that, as Herskovits tells us in *Dahomean Narrative,* "where the interjection is too long delayed, the narrator himself pauses to exclaim 'Good' " (1958: 52). Liyong's translation may therefore be seen to reflect such a tradition.

A closer look at those comments shows, however, that there is something mannered in their style. Liyong happens to be a quite sensitive poet, and it is arguable that it is the poetic possibilities in those traditional responses that drew him to record a story such as this. The following passage comes much later in the same story. At this point, the rich man's search for misery has brought him untold woe: his children quarrel over a gift and kill one another, and he and his factious wives are forced to go looking for them.

On the way the smell of new blood tickled their noses. *Smell that travels in the wind.* They became wild. *These good people.* Soon they stepped on cadaver instead of earth. *Oh, organic flesh and earth.* They kissed their lifeless sons because there was nothing else to do. *These virtuous sons and wives.* They had no more stomach for misery. *These misery-filled parents.* (Pp. 9–10)

This is a truly tragic moment in the story. There is no doubt that the respondent or commentator in the audience would, in his contributions, show some disdain for the insane ambition of the rich man and his family. But anyone familiar with the poetry and prose of Liyong will have noted one characteristic ingredient in it—the biting, saucy irony—and recognize a touch of it in this passage. In comments like "These good people" and "These virtuous sons and wives," Liyong would seem to have pushed the disdain of the traditional commentator to the point of biting mockery; the measured brevity of the statements of both narrator and commentator would also indicate that some cosmetic editorial hand has been laid on the traditional narrative which Liyong has tried to set down here. Perhaps we should say that Liyong's translation of this Ugandan story is one notable example of an African writer imposing his own stylistic idiosyncracies on the text of the traditional narrative, no doubt in his desire to present the narrative in a way that would be as attractive to the contemporary reader as possible.[4]

That is what makes the poet-playwright J. P. Clark's translation of *The Ozidi Saga* such a landmark in the preservation of the oral narrative traditions of Africa. As we have noted, the story is a heroic narrative or epic relating the exploits of a posthumously born hero (Ozidi) who undertakes to eliminate all the assassins of his father (Ozidi Senior) and who can hardly control his urge for killing until he has destroyed every menace and monster in his community that stood in his way. Only then does he lay down his sword.

What Clark has done in his transcription and translation of this story (the original Ijo text and the English translation are published on facing pages throughout) is to reproduce, with a degree of faithfulness unknown in previous editions of the African oral narrative, the peculiar circumstances of a performance of the tale. For one thing, the tale was tape recorded in Ibadan (then regional and now state capital) in 1963, in the heat of the political turbulence that led to the collapse of Nigeria's First Republic. In his edition of the text, Clark has wisely retained his narrator's exploitation of the geographical setting of the place as well as the political idiom of the time. For instance, at one point in the gruesome fight between Ozidi and Odogu, we are told that "the other would drive his opponent before him as far as this market inland, Mokola market" (1977: 299)—a market in Ibadan, although the story is set in Orua, hundreds of kilometers away in the Niger Delta southeast of Ibadan. Also, in the interminable contest between Ozidi and Azeza, we learn that the latter on crushing a medicinal gourd underfoot fully recovers his flagging power: the loan word *pawa*, which the narrator uses in the Ijo (p. 94), echoes a well-known political slogan of that turbulent period ("Power!") and draws an appropriate response *(Laughter)* from the audience.

An earlier generation of editors would have shown far less awareness of these nuances and would have been inclined to expunge or edit the references as not being particularly relevant to the essence of the tale. In preserving those references, Clark has helped to establish a fact that scholars and students of oral literature have only lately begun to grasp: that every narrative text is the product of the genius of an artist or artists working within a particular context, irrespective of the essence of the tradition it seeks to retail.

A second and equally commendable aspect of Clark's faithfulness to the oral narrative tradition is his effort throughout the text to reproduce the intercourse between the artist and some Ijo persons attending the performance. In chapter 3 we saw how these people maintained a running commentary throughout the performance, sometimes aiding the narrative imagination of the artist but at other times constituting a menace to the integrity of his genius. Whatever the case may be, Clark's edition makes it abundantly clear that the traditional African narrative performance is a collaborative act in which audience members see themselves as participant observers free to make occasional inputs into the unfolding drama. This approach is clearly an advance on earlier editions of African tales that presented them as dry monologues, sometimes even in bare summaries. A few lines from Ozidi's contest with Fingrifin, portraying the final triumph of the hero and Oreame over their opponent, bring out adequately the dramatic interchange between the narrator and members of his audience.

> So brake out the cry of slaughter, and all the trees in the forest trembled and splintered.
> *Spectator:* Has he cut him down?
> Oh, he had cut through him and carried him off,
> the fruits overhead showering all over the place.
> Next, Oreame brought out a bag, a big bag, and into that sack she threw it.
> *Spectator:* Deep down it . . .
> This woman, throwing the head into the bag, she slung the bag over her shoulders. "My son, on with it to the house."
> *Spectator:* Terrible!
> "Let's be off. Let's continue with our walk," she said . . .
> *Spectator:* Your child is off again!
> *(Laughter)*
> That's right. (P. 189)

Clark is able to bring out the full dramatic impact of the intercourse between performer and audience because he is himself a dramatist sensitive to the nuances of the performance situation. His edition of this Ijo story is a watershed in oral literary scholarship and in invaluable credit to Africa's rich cultural heritage. Of course, his edition is not without its flaws, for Clark takes a few liberties with his translation and interpretation.[5] Despite all this, *The Ozidi Saga* shows how much writers have done to establish the African oral narrative tradition as a proud heritage and a source of inspiration for modern creativity. One thing, however, stands out most clearly from our discussion of the various translations of African oral literature by contemporary writers whether in scholarship (e.g., Niane) or in creative literature: although these translators are all motivated by an honest desire to preserve the best in their indigenous traditions, they cannot help but reflect in their translations elements of their own styles and outlooks.

Adaptation

It must be emphasized—and we shall examine the issue a little further in the next chapter—that translation is by no means an easy task. Indeed, we shall go further and say that there is hardly any translation that does not show some element of stylization, however close the translator may have tried to stay to the original text. The reason for this is not hard to understand. However deeply attached the translator is to the proud heritage of a people, he or she is equally aware that some of the outlook revealed by the text no longer prevails. Things have changed somewhat, and although there is a continuing need to translate the old classic tales and songs so as to save them from extinction, it is equally inevitable that they will be presented in ways that reflect the changed styles of living and perception in contemporary society.

Translating the old texts in stylized language and techniques is one way of adapting to the changed outlook; finding new subjects and new contexts for the old forms is

another. A good example of this form of adaptation is the Sotho writer B. M. Khaketla's description of a train (Kunene 1970: 150–51). The author's closeness to the
traditions of his people may be seen in the fact that he has chosen the language of
praise (as in the *lithoko*) to describe this object, especially in reflecting the beastly
fierceness of the train's movement. Take the opening lines of the poem:

> *Tjhutjhumakgala,*[6] beautiful thing of the White man,
> There's a steel rope tethering this black bovine,
> As for a woven rope, he would break it!
>
> It is, indeed, the mother-of-smoke-that-trails behind,
> A Madman, Wearer-of-a-*towane*-grass-hat,
> Creator-of-fog even while the skies are clear,
> Churner-of-clouds even while the winds are still,
> Leaving us covered with blackness;
> Smoke billows up, and sparks fly,
> As when a bonfire is fed with dry reeds.

Like the praise poet of the oral tradition, Khaketla tries to mix this heroic portrait of
the train with a tone of subtle protest or disclaimer:

> The train is spiteful, Little-Black-One,
> It took away my brother and he was lost forever,
> My heart was sore, tears welled in my eyes,
> And flowed like rivers down my cheeks,
> And there I stood crying aloud with grief!

The significant thing here, however, is the treatment of an object of modern technology—the train. Although Khaketla writes in his own native tongue (Sotho) and remains attached to the Sotho tradition of poetic eulogy, he has chosen to treat a
modern subject as a way of demonstrating the adaptability and the continuing relevance of that tradition.

A similar achievement has been recorded by the Ugandan poet Okot p'Bitek in his
songs, most notably the *Song of Lawino*. To his death in 1982, Okot remained a
staunch believer in the vitality of the oral traditions. When some of his colleagues,
including Taban lo Liyong, complained that compared with West Africa, East Africa
was a kind of "literary desert," Okot replied that critics like Taban were suffering
from some form of "literary deafness" (p'Bitek 1974: v). Although he went to some
of the best universities in Britain (Bristol, Oxford, etc.), he had a firm attachment to
the traditions of his native Acoli, devoting himself to a study of its indigenous belief
systems and translation of the oral literature. Even when he wrote his own poetry in
English he tried to stay as close as possible to the forms of his native Acoli, mainly
to demonstrate that there were enough resources in his indigenous traditions for him
to use in the treatment of any topic whatsoever.

Song of Lawino was the first such effort that Okot made. Like Khaketla perhaps,
Okot had written the poem in Acoli under the title *Wer pa Lawino;* but he soon

translated it into English to give it larger circulation.[7] The poem, a work of social criticism, follows closely on the Acoli tradition of the poetry of abuse. A young woman (Lawino), aggrieved that her educated husband (Ocol) has ignored her in favor of a sophisticated urban mistress (Clementina), pours complaint and abuse not only on her husband and his mistress but also on the ways of Western civilization which have drawn him away from the traditions in which he was raised. Although the English translation of this poem fails to capture much of the lyrical appeal of the Acoli original, as Heron has shown (1984: 6), Okot manages to stay as close as possible to the tone and imagery of the tradition. Notice, for instance, the sauciness and contempt with which Lawino describes the act of kissing between Ocol and Clementina.

> You kiss her on the cheek
> As white people do,
> You kiss her open-sore lips
> As white people do
> You suck the slimy saliva
> From each other's mouths
> As white people do. (p'Bitek 1984: 44)

We can see here the repetitive structure of the traditional African song. Heron has pointed out (1984: 7) how closely the poem borrows from the imagery of specific Acoli traditional songs. For example, take this image of a spear from one of the traditional songs recorded by Okot in his collection *Horn of My Love:*

> The spear with the hard point
> Let it split the granite rock
> The spear that I trust
> Let it split the granite rock
> The hunter has slept in the wilderness
> I am dying, oh. (p'Bitek 1974: 69)

It reoccurs in *Song of Lawino,* with rather strong echoes, toward the end of the poem where Lawino urges her husband to be reconciled with the sustaining forces of his native traditions.

> Beg forgiveness from them
> And ask them to give you
> A new spear
> A new spear with a sharp and hard point
> A spear that will crack the rock
> Ask for a spear that you will trust. (1984: 119)

As a protest against the shortcomings of contemporary African society, Lawino's complaint is just as notable for the images of Western civilization that it derides as for those of the tradition that it upholds. The satirical tone is very effective; Okot has convincingly demonstrated that the local idiom is up to the task of representing the new ideas and habits from the chosen perspective of the protagonist. In the following passage, Lawino ridicules the experience in catechism classes where youths like her are taught the Apostles' Creed and the Christian concept of creation.

We recited
The Faith of the Messengers
Like the yellow birds
In the *lajanawara* grass

The teacher shouted
As if half-mad
And we shouted back:

> *I accept the Hunchback*
> *The Padre who is very strong*
> *Moulder of Skyland and*
> *Earth . . .*

My mother
Was a well-known potter,
She moulded large pots,
Vegetable pots
And beautiful long-necked jars.
She made water pots
And smoking pipes
And vegetable dishes
And large earthen vessels for bath.
She dug the clay
From the mouth of the Oyitino River [. . .]

Where did the Hunchback
Dig the clay for moulding things,
The clay for moulding Skyland
The clay for moulding Earth
The clay for moulding Moon
The clay for moulding the Stars?
Where is the spot
Where it was dug,
On the mouth of which River? (Pp. 86–87)

Christians will, of course, dismiss Lawino's view of creation as simpleminded; Liyong indeed has charged that her argument "is conducted in a low key" and leaves "little to be felt with the intellect" (1969a: 141). But Okot's method has been based on the conviction that Western scholars have for long debased and misrepresented African culture with the most simpleminded lies and gossip. In using Lawino as spokesman, therefore, the author is putting the West on the level of its own logic. Here we have a modern African writer adapting the traditional song of abuse to the needs of his revolutionary treatment of a contemporary problem. The tone, the idioms, and even the technique (e.g., of repeated phrases) are the same as may be found in the old Acoli poetry of social comment; only the subject is new.

Modern African writers have also made an effort to adapt the oral narrative tradition to more or less contemporary needs and outlook. Perhaps the most notable examples in this regard come from the Yoruba of western Nigeria. Two Yoruba writers in particular have shown a unique skill in using the novel form for recreating tales of the fantastic with which their people's oral narrative tradition is replete.

One is Daniel O. Fagunwa, who, although a Western-educated man, chose to write all his novels in Yoruba as his contribution to the promotion of the language and culture of his people. A notable subclass in the Yoruba oral narrative tradition, as we have seen, is made up of hunters' tales—tales told by hunters of extraordinary confrontations with supernatural creatures and spirits in the eerie bush. It is this body of tales that Fagunwa plumbed for the bulk of his writing. Beginning with *Ogboju Ode ninu Igbo Irunmale* (1938), Fagunwa produced five such works of the fantastic which have remained classics of contemporary Yoruba fiction.[8] In them a brave hunter tells of his harrowing experiences with these beings of the charmed bush, with the declared aim of instructing his fellowmen, through these tales, in the ways of wisdom, virtue, and good conduct. Although the tales are fundamentally indebted to the oral tradition in both matter and manner of narration, Fagunwa has nevertheless borrowed enough elements not only from the tradition of the classic and modern European fiction but also from the wealth of allegorical material in Christian literature to make his works enormously attractive to the contemporary reader.

A second Yoruba writer equally indebted to the oral tradition and obviously influenced by Fagunwa is Amos Tutuola, who has chosen to write in English. Like Fagunwa, Tutuola has produced many stories based on the oral tradition, but there is a fundamental difference between the two writers. As noted, Fagunwa was an educated man. Living and working in colonial Nigeria at a time (mostly in the 1940s and 1950s) when nationalists were striving for the political and cultural liberation of the country, he felt perhaps that he had to make his own contribution to the growing cultural awareness. He therefore wrote his stories in the Yoruba language and filled them with moral lessons because he wanted his fellow Yoruba to feel a strong pride in their language and culture and at the same time have a healthy sense of values.

But Tutuola has no such serious purpose. To start with, he never completed elementary school. When he wrote his first novel, *The Palm-Wine Drinkard,* in 1950, he was a messenger in the Labor Department in Lagos. Bored with sitting down most of the time and simply watching the clock, he picked up a pencil and set down the story in two days. "To compose the thing is not hard for me," he told a journalist in 1954. "Even at work I compose, for I cannot be pleased to do nothing, and messenger does not always have work to do in the office." He had in fact written out a story earlier titled *The Wild Hunter in the Bush of Ghosts* and was to confess later, "I was just playing at it. My intention was not to send it to anywhere" (see Lindfors 1975: 25–26). Tutuola's stories—at least the earlier ones—were thus just the easy pieces of an idle hand. He simply recalled the stories he had learned from older men at the farm and from the abundant oral narrative stock available to every child who listened well, and he set them down. He had not the least clue what purpose they would serve to anyone; he simply used them to fill his idle hours. Not long after the publication of *The Palm-Wine Drinkard,* he was interviewed by an American. "When I asked him," said the latter, "what his future writing plans were, he said that possibly there were more stories down on the farm and that if I liked he might be able to get some" (Larrabee 1975: 38).

The Palm-Wine Drinkard (1952) was the first of a long line of stories of adventure that Tutuola has continued to bring from "the farm." The plot is familiar. A young man, long wedded to a life of idleness and drink, discovers one day that his palmwine tapster has fallen from the palm tree and died. Unable to adjust to this loss of his vital source of contentment, the "drinkard" decides to journey to the land of the dead in the hope of finding his tapster and bringing him back. He is confident that his abundant mystical powers—all through the story he lets it be known that he is "Father of gods who could do anything in this world"—will see him through the worst encounters.

One of his early encounters is with an old man who sets him the task of rescuing his daughter from an infernal monster who has decked himself out as a "complete gentleman" from parts of body and clothes borrowed from various sources. On completing this task, the drinkard is rewarded with the lady as his wife, and together they set out in search of the palmwine tapster. They finally find him in the "Deads Town," but not before surviving the most frightening experiences: a half-child ("ZURRJIR") is born through the drinkard's wife's thumb and nearly harrasses his parents to death until they are able to get rid of him; the couple encounter a hideous monster (Red-Fish) but eventually kill it and rescue a whole community from annual sacrifices of their citizens to the monster; after an idyllic interlude with a "Faithful-Mother" in a White Tree, the drinkard and his wife encounter various other horrors. When they eventually find the tapster in the Deads Town, he regrets that, being dead, he can no longer return to the land of the living; but he sends them home with a gift of a magic egg which can perform any command given to it. On their way home, there are yet more dangers. The couple are swallowed by an insatiably hungry monster and escape only when the drinkard shoots it in the womb and cuts their way out with a cutlass. The last encounter is with a frightful horde of Mountain Creatures, from whom the drinkard escapes by transforming himself into a pebble that hurls itself across the river separating the land of the living from the realm of the dead.

The drinkard returns to find his people in the throes of a famine: the Sky and the Earth are quarreling over seniority, and the Sky reacts by withdrawing rain from the Earth, thus causing severe scarcity and death. At first the magic egg satisfies the craving for food; but inordinate greed and wantonness cause disorderly behavior among the citizens, and the egg falls and splits in pieces. When it is glued back, it can only produce whips, which beat these unruly citizens and send them fleeing. The famine continues to take its toll; the quarrel between Sky and Earth is finally settled when a slave is sent to the former with a sacrifice to appease it. The result is rain which falls for three months, putting an end to the suffering of the people.

Gerald Moore has observed (1975: 34) that the experiences of the drinkard reflect "one variant or another of the cycle of the heroic monomyth, Departure–Initiation–Return." It is only remotely possible that Tutuola, given his extremely limited exposure to literate education, imbibed these universal ideas in any conscious way. What is certain is that he has borrowed consciously from the stock of tales available within the Yoruba oral narrative tradition, and we can see this indebtedness in the content, structure, and style of the story.

For content, it is not an overstatement to say that most of the incidents in *The Palm-Wine Drinkard*—of a strongman or medicine man who journeys to and from the land of the dead, of transvestites or spirit figures with borrowed human parts, of miraculous all-providing gifts which bring weal to wise users and woe to the foolish or wicked, and many more—are familiar motifs not only in Yoruba oral tradition but indeed in the traditions of numerous peoples along the west coast of Africa. Afolayan particularly identifies three episodes in the story—("Complete Gentleman," "Not too small," and "Cause of the Famine")—as peculiarly Yoruba. "These three stories," he says, "respectively represent the common stories *Oloko sin lehin mi* (Hoe-seller get back), *Obalaran be we* (Obalaran asked for help), and *Ile ja oun Olorun* (Land and Sky-dweller fought). Besides there is perhaps little doubt that the entire plot of the novel—the journey of the drinkard to heaven to see his palm-wine tapster, and his return to his town—is itself built round the common story of an aggrieved person going to heaven to seek the help of a beloved dead relation and returning with a valuable possession" (Afolayan 1975: 157–58). It is no doubt such heavy indebtedness that forced Omolara Ogundipe-Leslie to declare Tutuola "a borrower. Tutuola did not invent much in *The Palm-Wine Drinkard*" (1975: 109).[9]

In structure the story is equally indebted to the oral tradition. It is true that the numerous episodes are united by the personality of the drinkard and that, in particular, the persistent image of abundant palmwine preserves the unity of purpose throughout the tale. But these are all we have for the organic unity of the tale; otherwise, it is a thoroughly episodic account of the picaresque kind. The protagonist goes through one adventure after another, each one thoroughly different from the last. "Like boxcars on a freight train," says Bernth Lindfors, "they are independent units joined with a minimum of apparatus and set in a seemingly random and interchangeable order. There is no foreshadowing of events, no dramatic irony, no evidence of any kind that the sequence of events was carefully thought out" (1975: 232).

There are several proofs of the random, episodic nature of the plot of *The Palm-Wine Drinkard*. To start with, most characters are encountered once and never appear again. Would there, for instance, not have been some logic in a recall, however tenuous, of the old man who gave the drinkard his daughter as wife and faithful companion? Second, the interlude with the Faithful-Mother in the White Tree (pp. 65–72) provides a relief from the toll of horrid experiences, but it has no discernible logic within the context of the drinkard's career. Perhaps the strongest evidence of the episodicity of the story is in the appearance every now and then of etiological conclusions. "This was how I got a wife," the drinkard says (p. 31), as he is rewarded with the lady he has rescued from the Complete Gentleman. "That was how we were saved from the Unknown creatures of the 'Unreturnable-Heaven's town' " (p. 63). "That was how our life went in the Red-town with the Red-people and the Red-king and how we saw the end of them in their new town" (p. 91). Of his victory over Death early in the story the drinkard says, "So that since the day that I had brought

Death out from his house, he has no permanent place to dwell or stay, and we are hearing his name about in the world" (p. 16). What makes the encounter with Death particularly interesting is that the abstract condition of death (in which the tapster lives) is treated as distinct from the personified figure that the drinkard here overcomes.

Finally, in between these disconnected episodes, Tutuola has room for a few subplots, such as the stories of the two cases the drinkard is called upon to judge in the "Mixed-Town" (pp. 110–15). Even the story of the seniority fight between Sky and Earth (pp. 118–19) is set "in the olden days," presumably long before the experiences of the drinkard, although we do not hear of this problem at the beginning of the book. The plot of the story is so disconnected, indeed so arbitrary, that there is little evidence of careful craftsmanship even in the assemblage of familiar motifs from the oral tradition. No wonder Obiechina concludes that "the quest-tale plot is more structurally akin to the Spanish picaresque than to the 18th century English imitations with their more coordinated plots" (1975: 95).

In style, too, *The Palm-Wine Drinkard* sounds like a narrative of the oral tradition. Perhaps we should first look at Tutuola's relationship with his "audience." Although he is aware that he has written a story to be read rather than performed before a crowd of listeners, he nevertheless tries in at least one place to establish the sort of rapport with his readers that an oral narrator would have felt with a listening audience. When the drinkard finds he cannot decide either of the problematic cases referred to him by the people of the mixed town, he tells us: "So I shall be very much grateful if anyone who reads this story-book can judge one or both cases and send the judgement to me as early as possible, because the whole people in the 'mixed town' want me very urgently to come and judge the two cases" (p. 115).

Tutuola must have conceived this story in terms of a stupendous performance. In this regard, he was no doubt influenced by the surrounding culture, which is to a large degree marked by music and dancing on a high scale. Despite the limitations of print to which this story has been reduced, we now and then find scenes in which the representation of a musical performance is so strong that we can almost perceive it with our physical senses. A striking example is the description of the merrymaking—led by the three figures of Drum, Song, and Dance—that follows the liberation of the citizens of Red-town from their bondage to the Red-Fish and their resettlement in a new town.

> But when the day that they appointed for this special occasion was reached, these fellows came and when "Drum" started to beat himself, all the people who had been dead for hundreds of years, rose up and came to witness "Drum" when beating; and when "Song" began to sing all domestic animals of that new town, bush animals with snakes etc., came out to see "Song" personally, but when "Dance" (that lady) started to dance the whole bush creatures, spirits, mountain creatures and also all the river creatures came to the town to see who was dancing. When these three fellows started at the same time, the whole people of the new town, the whole people that rose up from the grave, animals, snakes, spirits and other nameless creatures, were dancing together with these three fellows and it was that day that I saw that snakes were dancing more than human-beings or

other creatures. When the whole people of that town and bush creatures started dancing together none of them could stop for two days. (P. 84)

Music and dance—or, as we saw in the last chapter, the folk opera—is a significant feature of Yoruba culture. That is one reason why this scene has been raised to such a stupendous level, and why, in the dramatization of *The Palm-Wine Drinkard* by Kola Ogunmola's concert party, this scene was treated as a major climax.

The imagery in this story has also been raised to the stupendous level of the folk fantasy. The figures of Tutuola's folktale world and the horrors they evoke are described in such vivid hyperboles that we recoil as if we could actually see them. When the young lady attempts to escape from the "Complete Gentleman" now reduced to a skull, all the skulls of the neighbourhood roll after her in pursuit as noisily "as if a thousand petrol drums were pushing along a hard road" (p. 22). The half-bodied child ("ZURRJIR"—his name is printed in loud capitals) forces his "mother" to carry him on her head, from where he whistles "as if he was forty persons" (p. 36). The white, one-eyed ghostly giant whom the drinkard and his wife encounter in a bush at night "was long about ¼ of a mile and his diameter was about six feet" (p. 42). A palm tree laughs "so loudly that as if a person was five miles away would hear" (p. 52); another tree standing by a river bank "was about one thousand and fifty feet in length and about two hundred feet in diameter" (p. 65). For sheer horror, perhaps the masterpiece of the entire tale is the bizarre figure of the red fish to which citizens of Red-town are annually sacrificed.

At the same time that the red fish appeared out, its head was just like a tortoise's head, but it was as big as an elephant's head and it had over 30 horns and large eyes which surrounded the head. All these horns were spread out as an umbrella. It could not walk but was only gliding on the ground like a snake and its body was just like a bat's body and covered with long red hair like strings. It could only fly to a short distance, and if it shouted a person who was four miles away would hear. All the eyes which surrounded its head were closing and opening at the same time as if a man was pressing a switch on and off. (Pp. 79–80)

The language of *The Palm-Wine Drinkard* is one more indicator of the oral sources of the story. Owing to Tutuola's limited schooling, it was inevitable that when he came to compose the story he should adopt structures of expression familiar to him from his mother tongue. In an early review of the book in the British newspaper *Observer* (July 6, 1952), the poet Dylan Thomas erroneously described the language of Tutuola as "Young English" (Thomas 1975: 2). But Afolayan, being better informed of the backgrounds to Tutuola's language, identifies "elementary grammatical mistakes in his English which a sounder education in English would have removed. . . . Tutuola's English is 'Yoruba English' in the sense that it is representative of the English of the Yoruba users at a point on the scale of bilingualism" (1975: 153). If we set aside the numerous cases of sheer bad English, we will find several expressions which a Yoruba speaker will easily recognize as straightforward transliterations—e.g., "Even you have never seen anything yet" (p. 20), "Then I thought over that how could I escape from this fearful animal" (pp. 47–48); and several other cases which Afolayan (1975: 148–55) and Ogundipe-Leslie (1975: 111–13) have pointed out.

But perhaps the more striking aspect of Tutuola's recourse to Yoruba oral arts is his evocation of the rhetorical ring of Yoruba speech. Writing in Yoruba, Fagunwa is able to put this resource to good use, especially that rhetorical trick whereby a sound is repeated several times but in such permutations as to produce different meanings or effects. But English, which Tutuola has chosen to write in, does not quite work that way. Still, he manages to turn repetition to good account for an approximate effect. The following passage, about an experience with the people of Red-town, shows Tutuola working permutations with the word *red* very much in the spirit of Yoruba puns and tongue-twisters.

> My wife had said of the woman we met: "She was not a human-being and she was not a spirit, but what was she?" She was the Red-smaller-tree who was at the front of the bigger Red-tree, and the bigger Red-tree was the Red-king of the Red-people of Red-town and the Red-bush and also the Red-leaves on the bigger Red-tree were the Red-people of the Red-town in the Red-bush." (P. 83)[10]

In *The Palm-Wine Drinkard*, therefore, Tutuola has shown that the oral narrative form can be transferred almost in its entirety to the literate medium with little loss of appeal. Some peculiarities of the oral style may suffer, but this is part of the price the tradition must pay in the process of adjustment or adaptation to a new culture.

Tutuola's concessions to the new culture are indeed many, and are due partly to his limited grasp of the medium in which he has chosen to express himself but partly also to a genuine desire to make a connection with a wider world. His limitations show easily enough in those forms of officialese which Tutuola the "civil servant" may have gleaned from government files. For instance, we are told of the "Complete Gentleman" in his borrowed finery: "As this gentleman came to the market on that day, if he had been an article or animal for sale, he would be sold at least for £2000 (two thousand pounds)" (p. 18). But some of Tutuola's images conjure the contemporary scene in a rather effective way. The following tableau from the abode of the Faithful-Mother in the White Tree certainly enhances the idyllic image of this benevolent figure in an otherwise fearful world.

> The hall was decorated with about one million pounds (£) and there were many images and our own too were in the centre of the hall. But our own images that we saw there resembled us too much and were also white colour. . . . This beautiful hall was full of all kinds of food and drinks, over twenty stages were in that hall with uncountable orchestras, musicians, dancers and tappers. The orchestras were always busy. The children of seven to eight years, etc. of age were always dancing, tapping on the stage with melodious songs and they were also singing with warm tones with non-stop dance till morning. There we saw that all the lights in this hall were in technicolours and they were changing colours at five minutes intervals. (Pp. 68–69)[11]

One more notable adjustment to modern culture is Tutuola's use of the first-person mode of narration. Tales of the oral narrative tradition are generally told in the third person; the present method, which Tutuola may have borrowed from the European novel though Fagunwa, no doubt supports the heroic claims and scale of endeavor of the hero of Tutuola's story. But Tutuola has achieved something more in this regard. It seems obvious that his choice of a narrative persona has been influenced by his own peculiar circumstances. As he was sitting all day in the Labor Department and doing virtually nothing, it is perhaps inevitable that, in writing down his story in those idle hours, he should choose for his protagonist a character given over to a life of leisure. This combination—a self-mirroring persona, weaving a variety of motifs randomly picked from the oral tradition with scenes and effects chosen from contemporary life, and telling his story in a language that is part "Yoruba English" and part officialese and in a bold idiosyncratic voice—is clearly a departure even from the Fagunwa that everyone agrees is Tutuola's closest model.

What, then, do we make of Tutuola's adaptation of the oral tradition to contemporary modes? We started our discussion of him by observing that he could not be credited with that seriousness of cultural purpose that is evident in Fagunwa. However, as Tutuola has published more of these tall tales and his popularity has grown, so has his own awareness of the contribution made by his works. In a letter to Lindfors in 1968, he stated: "I wrote *The Palm-Wine Drinkard* for the people of other countries to read the Yoruba folk-lores. . . . My purpose of writing is to make other people to understand more about Yoruba people and in fact they have already understood more than ever before" (Lindfors 1975: 229). It is doubtful that Tutuola had such a mission when he started out.

Let us consider one more adaptation of the oral tradition, this time in the area of drama. Modern drama is essentially a form that enacts a story on a stage within certain conventions and constraints of time and space. In an effort to recreate the traditional culture, some modern African dramatists have found it convenient to turn to stories from the oral narrative stock. Two of the most significant efforts in this direction are J. P. Clark's play *Ozidi* (1966) and Efua T. Sutherland's *The Marriage of Anansewa* (1975). These two plays, products of the cultural revivalism that followed the political independence of several African countries (e.g., Ghana 1957, Nigeria 1960), share many elements and techniques of the traditional narrative drama. Since I discussed Clark's play at length in *Myth in Africa* (1983: 163–74), I will dwell here only on Sutherland's as an adaptation of the oral narrative performance.

The Marriage of Anansewa follows the familiar plot line of *ananse* (spider) stories, a tradition of trickster tales among the Akan-speaking people of Ghana. Anansewa (Ananse's daughter), cannot continue her studies at E. P.'s Secretarial School because her father can no longer pay her fees. Ananse seems sad enough about his daughter's plight to want to do something about it, but it is really his inordinate greed for material wealth that drives him to weave a scheme aimed at rescuing the family from its misery. So he makes a secret arrangement promising four different chiefs the hand of Anansewa in marriage, even getting the poor girl to type the letters that seal the contracts. In time Anansewa discovers, to her alarm, the scheme her father has woven around her, but she is coaxed by her cunning father into cooperating in a scheme designed to assure their material well-being. The scheme works rather well, as huge gifts of money roll in from the suitors.

The real climax of events comes when the four chiefs arrive independently to offer the "head-drink" that will legally establish their marriage to Anansewa. Ananse convinces his daughter to act dead and sends out messages to the four chiefs announcing his daughter's death. The idea is to determine, from their various responses, which of them is best qualified to marry his daughter. Two of them reveal how they were hoping to use the poor girl to settle personal scores and problems in their kingdoms; one brings no gifts but has come to offer condolences; the last considers himself already married to Anansewa and so accepts full responsibility for her funeral. It is this last chief who ultimately wins the hand of Anansewa. On receiving the chief's offer, Ananse pretends to go into a deep trance and spiritual consultation that ends with his daughter awakening from her "death" and claiming to have heard the chief calling her. The chorus of players conclude the performance with a rousing epithalamion celebrating the power of "true love."

Although the play is structured, like modern drama, into "acts" (four in all) within the format of the modern African folk theatre, the author leaves us in no doubt about her indebtedness to the tradition of the oral narrative performance. Perhaps we should begin our analysis of the play by acknowledging a few of the modern elements that give it a contemporary appeal. The studentship of Anansewa in a secretarial school was a standard training favored by West African girls in those days (the 1960s) when Efua Sutherland was working out themes for plays like *The Marriage of Anansewa* in the Ghana Experimental Theatre; nowadays, of course, the vogue is a university education. Ananse's eagerness to go to church with his newly acquired wealth and "deposit with the best of the spenders" (p. 24) is no doubt a jibe at so many ostentatious *nouveaux riches* in West Africa with their ill-gotten gains. The modernization of the spider Ananse is indeed a key aspect of the contemporary appeal in the play. Notice, for instance, that he is called "George" (sometimes "Georgie") Kweku Ananse by his mistress Christie, and that he avails himself of secretarial services in addressing his messages to chiefs. Also, it is possible that in the image of the "chief whose name is whispered in the ear" (p. 14)—one of Anansewa's suitors—Sutherland is suggesting the military leadership which had long been a factor of Ghanaian life before the play was published. All these contemporary elements promote the comic effect in a play built around the celebrated trickster figure Ananse.

The play, however, comes straight out of the tradition of the oral narrative performance. In her foreword to the printed version of the play, Sutherland tells clearly the source of her inspiration and the framework within which she has tried to work.

> There is in Ghana a story-telling art called *Anansesem* by Akan-speaking people. The name, which literally means Ananse stories, is used both for the body of stories told and for the story-telling performance itself. Although this story-telling is usually a domestic activity, there are in existence some specialist groups who have given it a full theatrical expression with established conventions. It is this system of traditional theatre which I have developed and classified as *Anansegoro*. (P. v.)

Sutherland further tells us about the tradition, that "the stories are composed with performance demands in mind and in a number of different forms and styles. Most are in a combination of narrative prose and a poetry which is meant to be sung or rhythmically recited on the basis of solo and choral response." Perhaps in response to those who see the tradition as static or fossilized, she states that "stories in the tradition are under constant revision for renewal and development. Also, contemporary interest inspires the composition of completely new stories to replenish the repertoire" (pp. v–vi).

No doubt the most significant element in the relocation of the oral narrative tradition in the dramatic format of the *Anansegoro* is the Storyteller. He is central to the action in Clark's *Ozidi,* and just as central in *The Marriage of Anansewa.* Sutherland sees him as "the owner of the story with a conventional right to know everything" (p. vi). He certainly exercises a proprietary control over the entire spectrum of events in the drama—preparing us for successive scenes, explaining the significant events and commenting on the behaviors of characters, even participating in the action and engaging both actors and members of the audience in occasional repartee. In exercising his proprietorship over the action, for instance, he abbreviates time by recalling an event that took place in the past and now influences the present situation. Thus the Storyteller, who tells us that "Anansegoro doesn't take long to grow," [12] stops the wailing over the "dead" Anansewa to demonstrate how the "tragedy" came to pass.

> STORYTELLER: (*addressing the audience*) Last night, everybody was asleep by the time the Methodist Church clock struck twelve o'clock.
>
> [PROPERTY MAN *strikes this hour while* STORYTELLER *counts, leaping numbers to reach twelve o'clock quickly.*]
>
> The town deserted, with nobody coming or going, suddenly there was Mr. George K. Ananse's voice, screaming.
>
> VOICE OF ANANSE: Come, somebody! Come to my aid! Ah, my one and only possession! I'm about to see disaster!
>
> STORYTELLER: You hear that?
>
> VOICE OF ANANSE: Alas! Anansewa! She has fainted! Something has descended on her! Where is everybody? Alas! Help! People! People!
>
> STORYTELLER: By the time people who heard the call arrived on the scene, there was Anansewa, lying as though she were dead. And then, you should have seen Ananse here.
>
> VOICE OF ANANSE: Where are the doctors? Oh! Dispenser Hammond! Call in Dispenser Hammond! Ah! Ah! Ah!
>
> STORYTELLER: Thereupon, one tears off this way, another that way. And as for Mr. Ananse, he was by this time rolling on the ground, and striking his head violently against the wall, pum, pum, pum.
>
> [PROPERTY MAN *produces the "pum, pum" sound to help* STORYTELLER.]
>
> Believe me, had there not been tough-muscled men present to restrain him, he would have done violence to himself and died instead. Friends, Anansegoro doesn't take long to grow! (Pp. 60–61)

Next in significance in this oral dramatic performance is the audience. In the extract just quoted, it is to the audience that the Storyteller addresses his recreation, for it is important that he should carry them with him in the unfolding performance. Ananse himself tries to involve the audience in his schemes early in the play; as he ponders a way of overcoming his misery, he asks (p. 2): "Won't somebody who thinks he has discovered the simple solution for living this life kindly step forward and help out the rest of us? [To the audience:] Brother, could it be you? Mother, how about you? Nobody?" We may recall, from our discussion of the oral performance in chapter 3, how deeply involved the audience frequently becomes in the process of the performance. The whole enterprise is a collaborative activity from which the audience expects to derive as much benefit and delight as the performer. For instance, the audience joins in singing the occasional song that crops up in the narrative and to make contributions in the form of comments or, as Sutherland tells us (p. vi) of the practice in Anansesem, "halt the narration of a story" to make contributions of songs, sometimes "merely from a high-spirited desire to show off!" We may also recall how, in *The Ozidi Saga*, there is an occasional call-and-response with the audience aimed principally at sustaining the high level of attention and excitement in the performance. Sutherland herself remarks on this urge for excitement or delight as a principal incentive to the audience's involvement in the performance (p. vii).

One more aspect of Sutherland's adaptation of the Anansesem to the needs of her dramatic composition is the use of songs (*mboguo*). In *The Marriage of Anansewa* the songs play a variety of roles. They give an opportunity for members of the audience to participate periodically in the unfolding performance, as so often in the oral narrative tradition. Even more significant is their structuring of the performance. "Many of the Mboguo," Sutherland tells us (p. vi), "are part and parcel of the stories themselves" in the sense that, as again in the oral narrative, they contain the central ideas of an episode or of the action of the entire narrative drama. [13] Sutherland uses these songs at successive segments to punctuate the action and thus invest the drama with the same quality of episodicity and the same ventilation that we find in the oral narrative. "A typical story-telling session," she further tells us, "opens with a series of rousing Mboguo songs led by a specialist group's signature tune." Therefore, songs appear periodically as a way of "serialising the story by breaking up the narration at various points with different kinds of Mboguo. . . . Mboguo in its traditional concept and usage has been inherited wholesale by Anansegoro" (pp. vi–vii).

Exploitation

The line between adaptation and exploitation of the oral literary tradition is not a sharp one, but it is nevertheless noteworthy. In adaptation, both the matter and the manner of the tradition are quite recognizable. For instance, the fantasy world of Tutuola's works appears much as it is in the tales of the oral tradition. In *The Marriage of Anansewa* the trickster is still called Ananse, and the occasional introduction of the spider's web into the setting serves to enhance the theme of entanglement by his cunning. In exploitation, however, the modern writer makes only a selective use of elements of the oral tradition. The form of presentation bears a limited relationship to the oral tradition, and even when familiar characters are used, they are deployed in an unfamiliar setting and in a somewhat altered order of relationships. What appeals to the writer in his or her recourse to the oral tradition is not so much the physical factors of performance as the essential concepts and ideas contained in it which are seen as having an enduring relevance.

Naturally, there are various levels of subtlety in African writers' exploitation of the material of the oral tradition. One level may be seen in the fiction of Chinua Achebe. Although his novels deal with the realistic world largely of Igbo society (whether past or present) and although there is no noticeable effort on his part to structure them on any known folktale pattern, he nevertheless sprinkles them with elements of content and technique taken from the oral literary tradition. One of these is proverbs. In *Things Fall Apart* Achebe tells us: "Among the Ibo the art of conversation is regarded very highly, and proverbs are the palm-oil with which words are eaten" (1962: 6). Consequently, when characters (especially adult males) converse in Achebe's Igbo-set novels, they season (or oil) their speech quite liberally with these well-chosen witticisms.

The art of conversation or public speaking is marked not only by the copious use of proverbs but also by the selective use of stories. Stories and songs are found once in a while in Achebe's *Arrow of God*, especially in interludes of relaxation when women and children sit in the yard in the evenings to amuse themselves; such moments bring needed relief to the tragic tension in the story of the confrontation between the traditional culture and the European presence. In the following passage Ezeulu harangues two bellicose clansmen with both proverbs and a story told, in a manner characteristic of the explanatory tale, to drive home a moral lesson about the fate of a headstrong son of the clan.

Ezeulu did not speak until the last. He saluted Umuaro quietly and with great sadness.

"Umuaro kwenu!"

"Hem!"

"Umuaro obodonesi kwenu!"

"Hem!"

"Kwezuenu!"

"Hem!"

"The reed we were blowing is now crushed. When I spoke two markets ago in this very place I used one proverb. I said that when an adult is in the house the she-goat is not left to bear its young from the tether. I was then talking to Ogbuefi Egonwanne who was the adult in the house. I told him that he should have spoken up against what we were planning, instead of which he put a piece of live coal into a child's palm and asked him to carry it with care. We have all seen with what care he carried it. I was not then talking to Egonwanne alone but to all the elders here who left what they should have done and did another. They were in the house and yet the she-goat suffered in her parturition.

"Once there was a great wrestler whose back had never known the ground. He wrestled from village to village until he had thrown every man in the world. Then he decided that he must go and wrestle in the land of spirits, and become champion there as well. He went, and beat every spirit that came forward. Some had seven heads, some ten; but he beat them all. His companion who sang his praise on the flute begged him to come away, but he would not. He pleaded with him but his ear was nailed up. Rather than go home he gave a challenge to the spirits to bring out their best and strongest wrestler. So they sent him his personal god, a little, wiry spirit who seized him with one hand and smashed him on the stony earth.

"Men of Umuaro, why do you think our fathers told us this story? They told us because they wanted to tell us that no matter how strong or great a man was he should never challenge his *chi*. This is what our kinsman did—he challenged his *chi*. We were his flute player, but we did not plead with him to come away from death. Where is he today? The fly that has no one to advise it follows the corpse into the grave. But let us leave Akukalia aside; he has gone the way his *chi* ordained. . . ." (Pp. 31–32)

Although Achebe makes a selective use of resources from his people's oral literary art, as the above example demonstrates, we can still see the physical factors of performance exactly as they appear in the tradition from which he has borrowed. On a more subtle level of exploitation, however, these factors are not so readily evident. In fact, the basis of exploitation of the oral literary tradition by modern African writers lies in the understanding that times have changed. Although they are driven by cultural pride to identify with the legacies of their people, the painful facts of contemporary life require that they reorder these cultural legacies in a way that represents sometimes a slight, sometimes a radical, departure from the tradition, especially if the tradition itself presents an outlook with which the writer does not necessarily agree. At any rate, at this level the oral tradition is turned to metaphorical or symbolic use rather than slavishly mirrored.

Something of this radical exploitation of the oral tradition may be seen in the works of the writers Sembene Ousmane, Wole Soyinka, and Ayi Kwei Armah. Ousmane is a committed writer of a Marxist-socialist persuasion, a novelist who in his works portrays and exposes the indignities suffered by the underprivileged classes of citizens at the hands of the corrupt and ruthless middle and upper classes who manipulate the system to their own advantage. A good example of Ousmane's radical use of the oral tradition is revealed in his short novel *The Money Order* (1977).

It may be useful, for a start, to draw a basic comparison between this work and Sutherland's *Marriage of Anansewa*, already discussed. Sutherland's play follows the regular trickster tale pattern whereby the trickster (Ananse) finds himself beset by a whole series of problems but surmounts every one of them and exploits the system to his own advantage. *The Money Order*, on the other hand, is fundamentally based on the trickster tale pattern but subverts the pattern: its protagonist is made the victim of a whole series of "tricksters" who exploit him from the beginning to the end and leave him a thoroughly disoriented man.

In *The Money Order*, a postman brings Ibrahima Dieng a letter from his nephew Abdou in Paris, and with it a money order for 25,000 francs: 2,000 for Dieng, 3,000 for Abdou's mother, the rest to be saved up for Abdou. Overjoyed, Dieng hurries to the post office to cash the money order; but he is frustrated when he is rudely told there that to cash the money order he needs an identity card, to be obtained at the police station. At the police station, he is again rudely turned away with the news that to get an identity card he needs a birth certificate (with three photographs and stamps), to be obtained from the town hall. At the town hall Dieng is further humiliated by a rude clerk who tells him that to get a birth certificate, Dieng must tell him his exact date and place of birth; but Dieng does not know the exact date. Advised by a bystander to "find someone with influence" to help him, Dieng resorts to a relative, Amath, who gives him a check for 1,000 francs and fixes him up with a friend of his at town hall who could give him a birth certificate. Dieng then goes to the bank to cash the check, and there he is duped by someone who claims 300 of the 1,000 francs for "services" rendered. Dieng goes to have his photograph taken; when he returns to claim the pictures he is told by the photographer's assistant that they have been burned. The two men fight, and Dieng goes home with a bloody nose.

Dieng next seeks credit for goods from a neighborhood shop owner, Mbarka, and Mbarka advises Dieng to sell his house to redeem the credit; this infuriates Dieng, and they scuffle. Mbaye, a slick political activist, restores calm and takes Dieng away in his car. Dieng then makes the mistake of giving Mbaye power of attorney to cash the money order. Mbaye later reports to him that he cashed the 25,000 francs but lost it to thieves, and sends Dieng away with a bag of rice and 5,000 francs. The story ends with the postman revisiting a thoroughly frustrated Dieng, who vows that from now on he is "going to put on the skin of the hyena."

While Sutherland's Ananse is a trickster who thrives by triumphing over a whole string of innocent "dupes," Ousmane's Ibrahima Dieng is a pitiable dupe who is thoroughly frustrated and impoverished by a whole string of tricksters. All through the story Ousmane draws a sharp contrast between the simplicity and naiveté of the poor as represented by Dieng (along with beggars and hangers-on) on one hand and, on the other, the corruption and insensitivity of the bourgeoisie (as represented by Mbarka and Mbaye) as well as the arrogance and insolence of the bureaucracy. Although there is sometimes a touch of irrationality in the ease with which Dieng dispenses money and food to less fortunate people, the author clearly wishes to celebrate what he calls "the feeling of solidarity that binds the needy" (p. 119), to denounce the inhumanity of the rich and powerful, and to expose the threats that they pose to the well-being of society.

The film critic Mbaye Cham (1990) has compared the film version *(Mandabi)* of *The Money Order* with two trickster tales—"How Spider [Ananse] Obtained the Sky-God's Stories," an Ashanti tale, and "The Feats of Leuk the Hare," a Wolof tale from Birago Diop's *Tales of Amadou Koumba*—which narrate the successes of the two little animals in performing seemingly impossible tasks. In the Ashanti tale, Ananse the spider demands to buy the Sky-God's stories from him. As his price, the Sky-God demands that spider bring him a python, a leopard, a fairy, and hornets; spider agrees, and even throws his own mother into the bargain. With the help of his wife, spider tricks every one of these figures into his snares and takes them, one after the other, to Sky-God, who surrenders his stories to spider with ample praises. In the Wolof story, Leuk the hare gets Boar the king's daughter heavy with child, against the king's orders. He is arrested and as a price for his own life the king demands a leopard's skin, two elephant tusks, a lion's skin, and the hair of Kouss the goblin. One by one, Leuk tricks all these animals in a most humiliating way and makes away with each of the objects demanded by Boar, thus regaining his freedom.

Cham sees in the three stories (i.e., of the film and the two folktales) a "common thematic thread . . . of greed and corruption within a social framework 'where only scoundrels live well,' " as well as an "artistic and highly effective use of repetition as a device for structuring." His analysis also leads him to conclude that "in spite of differences in detail, as far as setting, character and story are concerned, . . . one is dealing here with one basic structural pattern. In this pattern, a protagonist sets out to obtain an ultimate objective, but in order to achieve this goal, a number of tasks and conditions (seemingly impossible ones, too) have to be accomplished and fulfilled."

The pattern is the same in all three stories, says Cham, although the results are not: Ananse the spider and Leuk the hare succeed gloriously, while Dieng fails woefully. Indeed, Cham allows that despite the depravity of their ways, Ananse and Leuk may "inspire a mild sense of admiration" in us for their wit; but this is only because of "the distance that exists between our real world and that of Ananse and Leuk. . . . This gap becomes a kind of protective shield that provides us a safe shelter from the potentially catastrophic and humiliating machinations" of those figures. In his story, however, Ousmane does not allow his tricksters any such redeeming qualities. "These modern day tricksters," says Cham, "are the very incarnation of greed, evil, corruption and reaction, and there can be nothing worthy of admiration in such individuals who, according to Sembene, constitute the greatest real threat not only to the moral fiber of the masses of society but also to their material viability. Sembene's tricksters are too close to everyday reality and too adept at their trade to merit any light or favorable treatment."

From Cham's careful analysis of Ousmane's story against the background of the two oral narratives, one is inclined to suggest that the novelist had the oral narrative tradition in mind as he composed his work. Cham puts Ousmane in the company of those African writers—Wole Soyinka, Amadou Kourouma, Okot p'Bitek, and others—for whom "African oral narrative traditions have always constituted a seemingly inexhaustible source of inspiration." However, according to Cham, "Ousmane has carefully avoided the efforts of some African artists in modeling their works on specific oral narratives. The film *Mandabi* is not based on any particular oral narrative. Its affinities with African oral narrative are to be found in theme and structure, and more specifically, in the skill with which Sembene utilizes repetition"—in the same way as the tales of Ananse and Leuk—"to structure his film for maximum impact of his message to his fellow compatriots about the state and direction of their society."

As a revolutionary writer, therefore, Ousmane is not about to condone the manipulation (however skillful) of innocent victims that the oral narratives frequently glorify. In *The Money Order,* he has subverted the outlook revealed in so many trickster narratives while using the same theme of exploitation and the same structure of repeated confrontations underlying them, in his radical aim to show how many evils threaten the moral and material well-being of society. Rather than adapt the oral narrative tradition by making modest adjustments to its content, he has simply exploited those aspects of it that he needs for advertising an entirely different outlook on society.

The exploitation of the African oral literary tradition attains perhaps its most intense and skillful level in the work of Wole Soyinka. In a number of his plays and in some of his poems, and definitely in both his novels, he has borrowed heavily from traditional mythology for the construction of characters and situations. He is principally indebted to Yoruba mythology, especially that aspect of it that narrates the relationships between the divinities and so contains for Soyinka the basic elements of the Yoruba outlook on life.

Soyinka's favorite god is Ogun, and the guiding story about him is as follows. In the beginning, a huge gulf existed between the gods and mankind, and the gods had constantly failed to make any contact. But Ogun rose in council and volunteered to end the separation. With a metal staff made from iron ores buried in the earth, he cleared a path through the intervening jungle to the world of men; in gratitude the gods tried to crown him king of the gods, but he declined the offer and withdrew into solitude. After several appeals from the people of Ire (in Ondo State, Nigeria), he finally agreed to lead them to war against their marauding enemies. Unfortunately, this wine-loving and temperamental god got so blood-drunk in the killing that he mowed down friend and foe alike. When he finally realized his mistake, he withdrew again to the hills around Ire. But with the war won, the people pleaded with him to descend and be their king. He finally agreed. Although he nearly scared them to death when he came down in his blood-soaked looks, he later reappeared in palm fronds and was crowned king of Ire amid much rejoicing.

Traditionally, the Yoruba recognize Ogun as the god of war; for his feat in fashioning a metal staff from iron ores, he is conceived as god not only of war but also of various other occupations carried out with metalware—smithery, hunting, driving of motor vehicles, wood cutting and carving, and so on. Soyinka has added further dimensions to these readings. For his bold establishment of a connection between divinity and mankind, Ogun stands as the first "explorer"; for his championship of the cause of the people of Ire, Ogun is "restorer of rights"; for his solitary withdrawal from both gods and men so as to reflect on his acts, Ogun represents for Soyinka the ideal of the meditative intellectual as well as the artist; and for the ease with which Ogun both creates (e.g., the metal staff) and destroys (e.g., the people of Ire), Soyinka sees the god as a symbol for mediating the contradictions of human existence, not least of which is that between life and death. Let us now see how Soyinka has used this symbolic reading of the Ogun myth in at least one poem and one play.

In 1976 Samora Machel, president of Mozambique, announced that his nation had placed itself in a state of war with white-ruled Rhodesia (now Zimbabwe). To celebrate this "primary detonation of a people's collective will," this "summation of the continent's liberation struggle against the bastion of inhumanity—apartheid South Africa," Soyinka published a long poem, *Ogun Abibiman* (1976b), which is essentially a symbolic tribute to Machel as a (military) champion of the black cause.[14] In this poem, Soyinka brings the mythical figure of Ogun together with the historical figure of Shaka—the nineteenth-century leader of the Zulu nation—and sets them squarely within the volatile political arena of present-day southern Africa, poised for one final confrontation with the persecutors and tormentors of the black race. It is significant that in this meeting of legendary warmongers, it is Ogun who rouses Shaka from his long sleep. In an early essay (1966) in which he reviews Leopold Sedar Senghor's somewhat sentimental portrait of the Zulu leader in a verse play titled *Chaka,* Soyinka proposes Ogun as the proper inspiration for Africans in their search for a solution to the African problem.

Soyinka does not, of course, underestimate Shaka's significance—which is why, in that essay, he criticizes Senghor's emasculation of the dying Zulu leader by celebrating his black beauty over his love of action. Thus, when in *Ogun Abibiman* (pp. 1–3) Ogun reawakens to forge his war weapons anew at Idanre and tramples the "hills and forests / pulses and habitations of men" across the continent to reach Shaka, the latter gradually awakes from his dreams and recognizes a kindred spirit.

> Lost in dreams of Noliwe, I, Shaka
> Dread that takes bull elephants by storm
> Voice that breaks upon their mad stampede
> And brings them low on trembling knees,
> Trumpets raised in worship, I, Shaka
> Sunk in gossamer memories of she
> Whose naming was Breeze-that-cools-Bayete's-blood
> Felt the rain of sand as nerve-ends
> On my hairless head, and knew this tread—
> Of wooded rockhills, shredded mists of Idanre,
> The heart of furnaces, and pulsing ore,
> Clang of anvils, fearsome rites of passage
> Harvests in and out of season, hermit feet
> Perfumed in earth and dung of all Abibiman—
> Shape of dread whose silence frames the awesome
> Act of origin—I feel, and know your tread
> As mine. (P. 10)

In this poem, then, Soyinka summons the forces of myth (Ogun) and history (Shaka) to Machel's declaration of war against whites in southern Africa. The basis for this union is the feeling that there has been too much diplomatic talking done on the southern African situation; much of it has been dishonest, and has at any rate been of no avail.

> For Dialogue
> Dried up in the home of Protestations [15]
> Sanctions
> Fell to seductive ploys of Interests
> Twin to dry-eyed arts of Expediency.
> Diplomacy
> Ran aground on Southern Reefs. . . .
>
> Pleas are ended in the Court of Rights. Hope
> Has fled the Cape miscalled—Good Hope. (P. 6)

In the first section of the poem ("Induction"), Ogun awakes from the rocky hills of Idanre, forges a new set of weapons suited to contemporary warfare ("this novel form, this dread / conversion of the slumbering ore," p. 3), and marches across the

continent in dreadful pace, driven by his contempt for the farce of diplomatic nego-
tiations over the fate of the black man in southern Africa. In the second section
("Retrospect for Marchers: Shaka"), the Zulu king awakes from his long sleep under
the pressure of Ogun's powerful steps. He is filled both with the memory of his past
greatness ("Where I paused, Ogun, the bladegrass reddened") and the prospect of the
unification of the black race under a common geopolitical cause.

> Our histories meet, the forests merge
> With the savannah. (P. 11)

In this section, Shaka laments his weaknesses, which made him easy prey for the
traitors within his ranks who took his life and delivered the nation to the foreign
intruder. He is confident that the salvation of the black race lies in the restorative
force of Ogun, and urges him with particular reference to the southern African situation:

> Reclaim my seeds. Restore my manhood.
> Their cries are trumpeted in the dead above,
> Image swarms of that first incompletion,
> Lives usurped, Shaka's pride of nation
> Robbed of being. O Silent one, my tap-roots
> Wait your filling draught to swell
> To buttresses. Restore my seeds. Reclaim
> The manhood of a founder-king. (P. 13)

The last section of the poem is titled "Sigidi!"—glossed by Soyinka as "Shaka's
war-cry." Here the poet issues the final clarion call for war, but not without reviewing
the reasons why the black race has deemed it time to take up arms. European technology is indicted for its destructive tendencies—"processes that strip / Millennial
trees of grandeur, ingenuities / Beamed to atomise the creative palm of man." With
reference to the inhuman policies of apartheid South Africa, the poet particularly
reminds those who preach peace and love that their pleas are pointless in the face of
the toll of horrors for which that government is notorious: "the lash, contempt, / The
silenced screams in blood-lit streets"; the death-cells of South African jails; a determined policy to eliminate the black man *("Another Kaffir gone, saves us the sweat")*;
"the random bullet" shot across the street by the white police to destroy the poor,
helpless black; and so on. The poet also reminds these pacifists of various horrors
across time—the bombing of Guernica (1937), the World War II massacre in Lidice
(1942), but especially the shooting of black people in Sharpeville (1960)—and declares that his song is intended not to inspire hate or vengeance but to celebrate the
resolve of a race which is determined to put an end to a long history of persecution
and despair. That song, performed to cheer the hearts of the millions of black warriors
now assembled under the leadership of Ogun in this blessed hour of black rebirth, is
a refrain of the proverbial chant at the end of section I.

In time of race, no beauty slights the duiker's
In time of strength, the elephant stands alone
In time of hunt, the lion's grace is holy
In time of flight, the egret mocks the envious
In time of strife, none vies with Him
Of seven paths, Ogun, who to right a wrong
Emptied reservoirs of blood in heaven
Yet raged with thirst—I read
His savage beauty on black brows,
In depths of molten bronze aflame
Beyond their eyes' fixated distances—
And tremble!

Soyinka's exploitation of the oral tradition here consists essentially in reordering its facts in the service of his radical vision of the contemporary African struggle. In the poem, Ogun and Shaka are recognizable enough in the terms in which they are portrayed in their respective accounts. Ogun, the "silent one" who withdrew into solitude from all divine and human company, does not say a single word in the entire poem; he is here called the "Prince of Restitutions" (p. 20) for coming to the rescue of the brutalized blacks of southern Africa, very much as he did for the beleaguered citizens of Ire; the pathfinder who cleared the impassable thickets separating the abodes of men from contact with the gods now tramples the hills and forests of the continent to reach the black kinfolk of southern Africa; and, more especially, the poet, who recognizes the bloodthirsty terror of Ogun on the brows of the assembled black warriors, no doubt trembles at the memory of what the god is fabled to have done in the battle of Ire.

Shaka in his long statement recalls various details of his own legend: his ill-fated love affair with Noliwe; the terror he spread across the land with his rampaging army; the treachery of his most trusted counsellors and kin; and his defiant last words to his murderers: *"The whites have come, / And though you seize my throne, you will never / Rule this land."* [16] But in the poem these two figures come together as they never did in the oral tradition and are set within a conflict which transcends their known careers (though Shaka is in somewhat familiar terrain). Here the unification of Ogun and Shaka is Soyinka's symbolic portrait of the prospects for the southern African situation of Samora Machel's declaration of a state of war against white-ruled Rhodesia. The rest, indeed, is history.

Soyinka's exploitation of the Ogun myth is more intense in his play *The Road* (1965). It was published in the period, early in his literary career, when Soyinka had recognized the relevance of the god for the contemporary sociopolitical situation and was testing his fabled qualities on certain protagonists in his works and the situations in which they find themselves. In the play *A Dance of the Forests* (1963), Demoke projects that duality of the creative and the destructive temperaments inherent in Ogun. In *The Interpreters*, a novel published in the same year as *The Road*, Egbo reflects the impetuous and revolutionary temper of the god, the urge to do something about the moral degeneracy of his society.

The connection between Ogun and these characters is not merely apparent but openly acknowledged. In *A Dance of the Forests* Ogun, as one of the spiritual figures superintending the judicial "gathering of the tribes," declares openly of Demoke, "In all that he did he followed my bidding. I will speak for him" (p. 66). In *The Interpreters* Egbo complains to Joe Golder of the artist Kola's representation of him in his painting of the Yoruba pantheon: "Our friend has very uneven talents. Look at that thing he has made of me for instance, a damned bloodthirsty maniac from some maximum security zoo. Is that supposed to be me? Or even Ogun, which I presume it represents?" (p. 233). In both works we feel a certain restless energy which fully becomes the god. This restless energy is equally present in *The Road*. Here, however, the fabled image of the god is subverted by Soyinka in his radical criticism of the contemporary leadership.

The play is built around the personality of Professor, a Sunday school teacher and lay preacher who has been dismissed from the church for misrepresenting the Christian doctrine (one sense of "the Word" in the play) as well as misappropriation of church funds, and has now set up a palmwine bar and motor parts store in the vicinity of the church. This double enterprise is housed in a broken-down mammy-wagon named the "AKSIDENT STORE"—so named because the goods sold there are motor parts recovered from road accidents (before the police have arrived at the scene)—and serves as a nesting place for lorry drivers and touts and various hangers-on of dubious character.

The principal characters here are all men of "the road." Prominent among them are Kotonu, a lorry driver who has decided to retire from the numerous deaths on the road he has both seen and caused; Samson, his tout, who recalls their heroic days on the road and so desperately urges him to revoke his retirement; Salubi, the driver-trainee, anxious to get a driver's job with forged documents; and Say Tokyo Kid, a driver of timber-loaded trailers who affects a vulgar American diction and is attended by a cache of motor-park thugs. Other characters include Particulars Joe, a corrupt policeman who is very much privy to the shady dealings in motor parts and forged documents which are Professor's source of livelihood, and Chief-in-Town, a local politician whose rallies are powered by thugs supplied by Say Tokyo Kid.

And then there is Murano. Although he is speechless throughout the play, he is just as central to its design as Professor, to whom he is a "personal servant." Before the action of the play, he had been knocked down and critically wounded by Kotonu's lorry while performing as a masquerade in an orgiastic festival of motor drivers in honor of Ogun, their patron divinity. He has subsequently been nursed back to partial life—living in a kind of suspended death—by Professor who has now employed him as his palmwine tapster. As soon as the accident occurred, Kotonu had hurriedly hidden Murano's body in the lorry and donned his blood-clogged mask, to evade the wrath of Murano's fellow revelers who had started searching for their masquerade.

This mask narrowly eludes discovery at one point in the play. In the final moments of the play, it reemerges with tragic consequences. At the height of drunken conviviality between Professor and the others, who have been helping themselves liberally to the palmwine served by Murano, the mute rediscovers the mask, and his addled memory is slowly tickled back to life, to the utter consternation of the others. Professor prevents the group from recognizing the long-concealed identity of Murano by pushing him and the mask behind the curtain. The conviviality resumes, but the atmosphere has become charged. Shortly after, Murano reappears as an *agemo* masquerade, resuming the activity from which he had been plucked by Kotonu in the motor accident. Music from the revelers grows, becoming mixed with sounds from the church organ; the masquerade dances with increasing delirium; the emotional charge builds up to a confrontation; and Professor and Say Tokyo Kid kill each other in the process.

The mystical charge here and the confrontation between Professor and Say Tokyo Kid have been carefully built up in the play, arising largely from Professor's manipulation of the so-called Word. The reader is almost as mystified as Professor's friends are by the various senses he attaches to this concept, but the Word which the Professor claims to be searching for is really the meaning of life in its relationship to death. This mystical project has earned him an expulsion from the church, and he now turns it to something of a necromantic concern: for he not only visits graveyards but also dresses himself in black, like a magician, and continues to bemuse his friends with the mumbo jumbo of his high-flown language. He has concealed the identity of Murano, suspended between life and death in the midst of his act as a god-medium, and pressed him into service to tap the palmwine favored by the god Ogun: "for it came to the same thing," says Professor (p. 90), "that I held a god captive." In seeking to control the god he is, as Say Tokyo Kid warns him (p. 93), "fooling around where you ain't got no business."

Say Tokyo is thus one man who has seen through the Professor's game, but this is partly because he is equally guilty not only of grandiloquence—with his big-stuff Americanisms—but also of toying with divinity. When he taunts Kotonu with carrying filthy people and "all kinda rubbish" in his lorry, the other retorts that Say Tokyo as timber driver is merely "carrying dead load . . . from one end of the world to another." This hurts Say Tokyo's pride, and he lets Kotonu know what a tough job it is to drive those logs, for there are dangerous spirits trapped in them who are angry that their abode has been cut down. He tells Kotonu:

> You wanna sit and feel that dead load trying to take the steering from your hand. You kidding? There is a hundred spirits in every guy of timber trying to do you down cause you've trapped them in, see? There is a spirit in hell for every guy of timber. *{Feels around his neck and brings out a talisman on a string.}* (P. 26)

Say Tokyo has thus, like Professor, held divinity captive and is himself fooling around where he "ain't got no business." Killing one another in a drunken orgy, under the mystical gaze of Ogun in the form of the *agemo* masquerade Murano, is thus the god's punishment on Professor and Say Tokyo for engaging in a reckless, irreverent gamble.

The role of Ogun here brings us to Soyinka's manipulation or exploitation of the oral tradition in his treatment of familiar social life. It may be well to start by observing the various ways in which the Ogun essence superintends the action of the play both as spirit and as metaphor. Sharply represented in the physical setting of the play are a road and a broken-down motor vehicle, symbols of the deadly trade of drivers who manipulate Ogun's metal and must therefore pay him due obeisance: Kotonu looms as a tragic failure in this career chiefly because, as Samson reminds him now and again (Pp. 18–19 and 59), he has shirked his duty by refusing to kill a dog on the road as the due sacrifice to Ogun. The wine fetched by Murano, the delirium and excitement which it causes, and the charged emotional atmosphere which ends in the shedding of blood, are no doubt symbols of the presence of the temperamental god in the midst of these men: we will recall that Ogun slaughtered his own men in battle at Ire under the influence of palmwine which he had liberally imbibed. And perhaps most significantly, scattered throughout the play are references to the inter-relatedness of life and death, the most obvious of which is the fact that the road, which provides a livelihood for these men—drivers, touts, even Professor himself, the trader in motor parts—also leads them to their death.

Although Murano the silent one acts the god-medium in this play, it seems equally obvious that Professor takes upon himself the greater burden of the Ogun essence in its various manifestations. Like the god, he is frequently given to fits of temper, losing patience with his colleagues, as when *("in mounting rage")* he orders Salubi out of his sight for threatening to commit suicide before him (p. 41) or abandons them to pore over his papers *"with ferocious concentration"* (p. 46) or berates Samson and Kotonu for not bringing in motor parts from the accident at the bridge (pp. 55–56). Like Ogun the sulking ponderer, Professor is the quintessential intellectual—often sulking and aloof—who engages in abstruse reflection on a Word whose meaning is lost to the ordinary men around him. More significant, however, is the Ogun-derived patronage which Professor assumes here in a number of ways. As proprietor of the "Aksident Store" he provides a livelihood as well as a refuge for the various drivers, touts, and motor-park layabouts who seem to be out of luck with the road. As pro-prietor of the palmwine bar, he provides the resource most favored by Ogun, fetched for him by the god-medium Murano. Most prominent of all, he acts the mediator between life and death not only by nursing Murano to a limbo of existence but also by exploring a mystical Word which, from all appearances, reflects the dualities of human existence.

All these, however, are mere appearances, for in this play Soyinka has treated the personality of Professor to a stupendous absurdist joke—and herein lies his overturn-ing of the material of the oral tradition for a radical purpose. "I do not believe," says Eldred Jones (1973: 71), "that the playwright expects anyone to derive eternal wis-dom from Professor," and I agree entirely. Rather than being a true Ogun surrogate, the great mystic-pundit is simply an impostor who in many ways negates everything the god stands for.

To start with, whereas Ogun is revered as the patron of artists, Professors' skill is turned toward forgery and misrepresentation, especially in forging vehicle papers and driver's licenses. Even the grandiose quest for the Word is a hollow mask. All that high-blown grammar is simply a posture for covering up his petty mercenary interest (notice how he hustles for cheap change, pp. 41–43 and 61–62); his criminal will in fomenting accidents to support his trade ("The man is a menace," sneers Salubi. "Pulling up road signs and talking all that mumbo-jumbo," p. 32); and indeed his woeful ignorance, for the great lay preacher and philosopher does not know basic spelling and grammar ("AKSIDENT STORE—ALL PART AVAILEBUL") and the great pundit does not recognize that the strange signs in the paper he is studying are only pools in a football coupon (pp. 65–66). Also, although Ogun passionately cherishes sex (no doubt as a token of the regeneration of life after destruction), Professor "indignantly" disavows any relationship with women (p. 48).[17] As a further joke on the impostor, this high-class consultant on vehicle matters descends so low as to order roasted corn and groundnuts (p. 62).

I have said that the play is a tragicomedy, and indeed there is a greater emphasis on the comic element as a way of deflating the lofty pretenses in the play especially inherent in the postures of Professor. Of the numerous comic touches in this play we shall mention just two key ones. The first is the mimicry by Samson of various personalities and situations. One of his early spoofs is on Professor in his days as a lay preacher: spreading out before himself on the pew a hundred handkerchiefs (none of which he ever used twice) and engaging the bishop in a resounding battle of words that brought down a wall nearby. "Politics," comments Samson in conclusion, "no get dramatic pass am" (pp. 15–18). Several such spoofs by Samson throughout the play serve to portray the behaviors of Professor and the more lowly figures as a perverse joke.

The other prominent comic touch in the play is in the use of language. This may be seen from two angles, each no doubt revealing the playwright's reduction of Professor's image. First, there is a motley of languages and registers in the play. Yoruba is used in the chants and sometimes in the speeches (as in the spoof by Samson and Salubi of the preacher's funeral oration, p. 58). Samson and Salubi in turn frequently mix pidgin with standard English, and in a sense they give an honest reflection of the linguistic situation in Nigeria. But the real joke is on Professor and Say Tokyo Kid, who speak throughout in affected, pretentious diction; again, their death may be Soyinka's verdict on their falsification of the social vision.

A second aspect of the use of language may be seen in telling echoes of certain texts. For instance, Professor's obsession with the Word is characteristically reflected in an echo of the Christian text. When he spreads out the pools coupon and tries to decipher the intricate "signs" printed on it, he says, "say the Word in our time, O Lord, utter the hidden Word" (p. 65). These words, which recall part of the text of the Offertory, are here spoken in the manner of a fortune-teller or a magician trying to decipher the symbols before him. Soyinka even lets his Professor parody the drivers' prayer. It is he who, reflecting on the dangers of the road, enunciates an equivalence between a rock, a woman, and the road: "They know how to lie and wait" (p. 58). This image of Ogun as the hungry, "gluttonous god" is soon after echoed by Samson in obeisance to the god: "May we never walk when the road waits, famished" (p. 60).[18]

What, then, is Soyinka's radical message in this tragicomedy? There have been several interpretations of *The Road* by scholars of varied persuasion. Most immediately see the play as a metaphorical comment on the dangers of the Nigerian highways, a topic with which Soyinka has shown a longstanding concern in his life and writing.[19] Others, like Eldred Jones, see the play as a satire on corruption within the fabric of the Nigerian social and political life and even on organized religion (Jones 1973: 71–72). Ideologically oriented critics such as Biodun Jeyifo (1985: 11–22) seem to endorse Soyinka's radical vision by seeing the signs of a class conflict in the relationships between the pretentious bourgeoisie (Professor, Chief-in-Town) and the dispossessed urban proletariat (Say Tokyo, the drivers and touts, and the thugs).

All these are valid interpretations in their own ways. But Soyinka has chosen to project these social problems against the background of the traditional literature (the Ogun myth and attending chants) and belief, and I think that any interpretation that ignores this element misses the point somewhat. Central to Soyinka's conception are the two characters Professor and Say Tokyo Kid (representing, as it were, the higher and lower orders of society) who exercise two different but parallel forms of control on the other characters in the play: Professor on the drivers and touts, Say Tokyo on the thugs and layabouts. This control, this power, is symbolically reflected in their "holding captive" divinities of varying orders—Ogun on one hand, and on the other the spirits of timber, no doubt among the divinities resulting from the god Obatala's fragmentation, by the slave Atunda's boulder, into myriad particles.[20] Professor's and Say Tokyo's crime, for which they are punished by death, is that they have arrogated to themselves certain powers and a false cultural outlook (Professor British, Say Tokyo American) for toying with the destinies of their less fortunate fellows.

Seen in this light, *The Road* is Soyinka's critique of the sort of leadership that has been emerging in various African countries (especially Nigeria) since their attainment of independence from foreign political control. In his earlier plays *The Swamp Dwellers* and *A Dance of the Forests* (both 1963), Soyinka expressed his misgivings about the emerging leadership both spiritual and temporal, "his severely circumscribed hopes for what African independence might achieve" (Moore 1971: 29). These misgivings have since been justified, and Soyinka has continued to decry the abuse of power in play after play: *Kongi's Harvest* (1967), *Madmen and Specialists* (1971), *Before the Blackout* (1971), *Opera Wonyosi* (1981), and *A Play of Giants* (1984). The original title of *The Road* is *The Road of Life* (Ogunba 1975: 84), and perhaps the shortening has achieved the wider advantage of stretching the metaphor of the play from the social to the metaphysical domain. When Professor says that the Word—the elusive essence which he pretends to be pursuing throughout the play—"may be found companion not to life, but death" (p. 11), he is telling the truth albeit through his distorted vision. He means—or, rather, Soyinka is saying through him—that the ultimate wisdom and well-being of society lie not in the survival but in the death of charlatans and impostors like him (and, of course, Say Tokyo Kid) who toy with the destinies of their people. In this play, then, Soyinka has employed the myth of Ogun—which provides the metaphor of the complementarity of life and death—to offer a radical critique of the African social and political experience.

11. Preserving Oral Literature: Fieldwork and After

This chapter offers a guide on how to do fieldwork and what to do with the material collected from the field. It can be no more than a modest guide. The methods and approaches used in doing fieldwork in various disciplines—anthropology, social work, psychology, history, and especially folklore—have been the subject of scholarly study for so long that any of the relevant publications may be consulted with much profit.[1]

There are, of course, differences of interest and therefore of approach between disciplines. For instance, the student of oral *history* is basically anxious to elicit the *facts* of a community's origins or experiences from the storyteller's account and has little interest in much of the accompanying apparatus of performance and style that we discussed in chapters 3 and 4. Consequently, the student is much happier isolating the informant in a room where the latter may be guided along the path of "sober" recollection, away from all those influences (audience, music, etc.) which encourage a considerable degree of artistic self-consciousness and thus an embellishment of the facts of an account. The student of oral *literature,* on the other hand, is interested precisely in that *embellishment.* The storyteller is recognized in the community primarily for the skill with which he or she tells tales whether of animals or of people. The collector of these tales is anxious to put the narrator in an atmosphere which inspires the utmost display of skills. Consequently, the collector is much happier recording the narrator in the presence of an audience and (if possible) against the background of musical accompaniment which encourage the narrator's artistic self-consciousness and bring out the best of that aesthetic skill for which he or she is widely acknowledged.

Despite these disciplinary biases, the student of oral literature will have much to gain from reading fieldwork guides and accounts by scholars in other areas, mainly because they shed useful light on how to relate to other persons—which is what fieldwork entails to a large degree. This, indeed, is the basic problem in fieldwork and the main reason why most of the published literature on the subject has to be taken with a great deal of caution. Let us deal with that problem first.

Attitudes

In earlier chapters of this book, we had occasion to observe the inadequacies of earlier studies of African oral literature especially by foreign scholars. The point needs to be made at least once more that many of those inadequacies were engendered by wrong attitudes on the part of the scholars. Someone who believes that people are "primitive" or "savage" and have no capacity for imaginative or sophisticated forms of expression surely will have no respect for anything they say or the way in which they say it and will consequently represent it in a somewhat cavalier or reckless manner.

It was inevitable, therefore, that with the emergence of native African scholars the attitude to the study of the subject should change, even if the quality of the work done does not always match the zeal of the inquiry. The change in attitude could in fact be radical. A colleague once told me he didn't like the word *fieldwork;* he said it reminded him of some outfit which the British call a "bush shirt" and was simply a reflection of white people's contempt for the rural communities of the "Third World" into which they ventured now and then. That may be taking things a bit too far. Kenneth Goldstein wrote his *Guide for Field Workers in Folklore* (1964) on the basis of his researches among communities in Scotland. Fieldwork need mean no more, of course, than investigation and data collection in a specific area of study, and the context of the investigation may be the enlightened or middle-class folk as well as the underprivileged masses of town or country. But the reaction simply goes to show how suspicious many African scholars have become on discovering how much the indigenous culture was shortchanged.

This book is addressed to anyone anywhere interested in the subject of African oral literature. But as an African I cannot help hoping that it will be more valuable to Africans in gaining a better understanding of and respect for their literary traditions than anything else previously published may have done. It is also a token of my gratitude to my students, with whom I have explored these issues of our culture for more than a dozen years, that I have written the book primarily with their interests in mind. And my first piece of advice to my students or for that matter to all students wishing to do fieldwork in oral literature is to go to their hometown or at least a community where they feel at home—a community whose language they understand and can speak, whose customs won't be that much different from those of their own place, and where they won't have much trouble communicating with their informants.

There are of course situations in which researchers find themselves outside their familiar culture—for instance, if they take it upon themselves to collect prison songs—but nothing can compare with that feeling of intimacy and welcome that you get when you research among your own people. There is no greater feeling than that of knowing that you are helping to keep the cherished traditions of your people alive, and you cannot help feeling a great deal of respect rather than contempt or condescension when you come to appreciate the level of skill and sophistication in these time-honored ways of expression. And you will be amazed how much cooperation you will get from folk who find how much their way of life, improverished though it may be, means to such as you.

I say this because most guides for fieldwork available today have been written for those who will be stepping out—as it were—from their familiar middle-class or foreign environments to underprivileged communities which to all intents and purposes are "alien" to them. There are usually problems of adjustment when informants don't regard you as one of their own. You may give them money and try in many ways to put them at ease; but they will never treat you as a native, and if there is anything like a communication gap or any kind of gulf between you and them, they will hardly be inclined to trust you with intimate aspects of their traditions.

Let me illustrate from personal experience with one of my favorite artists, Charles Simayi. The Bendel Igbo dialect of his native Ubulu-Uno is somewhat different from that of my maternal hometown, Asaba, which I speak very well. But after a few days of my getting acquainted with Simayi and his town and people (in the company of my friend and guide, Ignatius Osadebe), I was no longer such a "foreign body" and felt very much at home. On the last night of Simayi's performances for my benefit, during the parting courtesies between us, he finally came to understand that my father was Urhobo, an entirely different ethnic group. His initial reaction was an instinctive twitch of withdrawal, as though realizing he had all along opened up his secrets to an outsider. He soon relaxed again, however, either because we had struck an irreversible friendship or because he reflected that my mother at least was his ethnic kin and spoke his tongue; and he has been no less hospitable to me since than he was before. But the experience does reveal that in the relationship between researcher and informant, a lot depends on the attitude that either party brings to the enterprise.

Another bit of advice I have frequently given my students is this: never assume you are going out there to teach anybody anything; on the contrary, you are going there to learn. The point is worth stressing because it is easy to misconstrue the humility and the homely civility with which the folk (especially the rural ones) treat the researcher as a dumb docility. Many of them (but by no means all) listen to you intently and are intrigued by your technical equipment, the likes of which they may never have seen. But they hardly lose their bearings, for after all they are in their own territory and you are the outsider.

Indeed it is amazing to find, during fieldwork, how much our education and consequent removal to the urban setting have alienated many of us Africans from the indigenous culture. When the time comes to observe the traditional courtesies and protocol, we find ourselves fumbling for the right cues and making all kinds of apologies. Under such circumstances we are hardly justified in adopting a superior posture. I believe the best attitude to adopt in a fieldwork situation is one of good-natured or friendly reciprocity. Informants have the skill or wisdom which you have come to consult for your own good. They should also be made to feel that you are all partners in the business of promoting the traditional culture and to realize that they do stand to gain something from your advertisement of their reputation. Informants may be your uncles or aunts or someone whom you have never met before. But it is only fair that you should give them some friendly reassurance and consider their interests very much as you hope they will serve yours.

This brings me to another issue in the matter of attitudes, and that is the spirit or disposition with which the research should be pursued. Fieldwork is arguably the last enterprise that anyone should pretend to do with an "objective" mind. Of course, the aim of it all is to go out there and gather the available information and report it as fully and honestly as you can. But there are principally two things involved in the effort. First, you do have a vested interest, which is either professional or political or a combination of these. Professionally, you may be a student undertaking the research toward the presentation of a course paper or the writing of a thesis, or a scholar working on a book in an area for which your curiosity has been aroused. You are determined to consummate the project, and you will allow nothing to impede your resolve or frustrate your effort. Many a professional, for this reason, has been driven to "trade off" certain things in order to get the job done, and this includes favoring certain kinds of evidence against others, especially if the latter threaten to demand more time, energy, and money than the researcher can afford. Many researchers have, in fact, been known to close their eyes to or suppress evidence that contradicts the preconceptions which they brought to the investigation. This is wrong, but the temptation is ever present.

The political interest frequently manifests itself as a pious mission or a subtle prejudice. We have constantly drawn attention to prejudice as one of the major weaknesses of European scholars who studied African oral literature in the colonial period, when they showed little regard for the cultures of subjugated peoples. Prejudice may also take the form of hostility toward the views of a previous scholar. You may so dislike the scholar as a person, or else be so filled with the iconoclastic zeal to establish your scholarly authority above the other person's, that you tend to dismiss everything that scholar says and bend every evidence you find to his or her discredit, even when there is no real need to do so. The pious mission is all too evident in the work of many a "Third World" scholar. Some of us African scholars are so filled with the urge to defend African culture against the disservice of foreign scholars that we sometimes descend to the level of undiscerning analysis if not inelegant romance. Such political piety may draw a good deal of applause in a public forum but is often incapable of providing a dependable heuristic guide through the territory of African culture that we, as native children who are much closer to the evidence, are that much better placed to explore.

In the final analysis, however, fieldwork brings us face to face with people—the men and women from whom we hope to gather the material that will form the basis of our analysis and judgment. Whether you are an African or an American, there is something about you that sooner or later brings you to like or dislike the informant or brings him or her to feel the same way about you. As a foreigner you may come to be treated so well by the whole family that your negative complexes are transformed into a superfluous zeal. In time familiarity may breed such a measure either of attachment or of disdain that the investigation suffers from the growing emotional disposition. Or you may find, as frequently happens, that certain persons or elements constitute such a distraction or impediment to your relationship with the informant that aspects of your research are inevitably modified if not shelved. Fieldwork does impose on our feelings and our perspectives. "Folklore fieldwork is personal work," says Bruce Jackson. "It isn't neutral and it isn't objective. It's too much subject to such factors as the unique chemistry between people at a specific moment in time, by the presence or absence of indigestion that day, by a slight memory of someone who had exactly that color eyes, by the response to the fabric and hue of the shirt one of

you happens to be wearing, to a faint odor there below the edge of consciousness"
(1987: 57).

The fallacy of objectivity in fieldwork is perhaps best illustrated by the diverse
portraits of an African community presented by two researchers—both female, white,
and North American and studying the community within six months of one another
in the early 1960s.[2] The people under study were the Nyiha (or Nyika) of southwest
Tanzania. The researchers were Beverley Gattrell (formerly Beverley Brock), a journalist, and Mariam Slater, an anthropologist. Although the two women agreed on a
number of issues about Nyiha culture, they reached some fundamentally opposing
conclusions about the character of the people and their culture that are in many ways
traceable to the dispositions they brought to the research as well as the peculiar
conditions under which they worked. Gattrell came to the Nyiha first. Slater came
later.

To start with, the one was a journalist while the other was an anthropologist;
clearly certain disciplinary biases and approaches separated the two scholars which
were bound to condition the nature of the reports presented. Then there was the
element of social image. Gattrell was married to Patrick Brock, a geologist who had
endeared himself to the local leaders by mixing freely with them and giving them
practical help in many ways. To this fund of goodwill Gattrell added her own liberal
and free-spirited approach to the Nyiha, becoming friendly with the women and
teaching them self-help skills; besides, in this rather male-centred culture, she cut a
good image by letting her husband (who spoke better Swahili than she) take the
initiative in their contacts and general socializing among the Nyiha. Slater, on the
contrary, came to the Nyiha alone and apparently left a poor impression by arguing
with men "on subjects women were not supposed to know about." Worst of all, while
Gattrell and her husband generally avoided the white settler community and got
closer to the Africans, Slater maintained a somewhat superior distance by not only
living with an unpopular white family but also frequenting the European club. The
result of these differing social attitudes was that while the Nyiha hardly invited Slater
to a meal in their homes, Gattrell was invited many times; obviously the one researcher was better placed to understand the Nyiha than the other.

But perhaps the most fundamental divergences between the two scholars were inspired by the political circumstances in which they carried out their researches. Tanzania at that time was looking toward political independence, and although the basic
antagonism was between the African activists and the white settlers, equally strong
conflicts arose between the local chiefs and the educated Africans who were poised to
wrest from these chiefs the authority and control of affairs traditionally vested in
them. As Europeans, both Slater and Gattrell stood suspect to the two groups of
Africans, but the Africans' responses to the researchers were in a large measure determined by the attitudes the researchers adopted. Slater spoiled her chances by playing
the superior European, mixing freely with the white settlers at the European club,
and especially by first living "as guest of a settler couple with a general reputation
for hostility to independence." Gattrell, on the other hand, "was militantly egalitarian," "developed friendly contacts with the young African leaders," and "felt great
sympathy towards the coming of independence"; besides, her participation in their

lives, especially by offering free knitting lessons to the women, endeared her to the people as one who had a positive stake in their fortunes.

We may well imagine, then, the differing ethnographies of the Nyiha emerging from a researcher who was treated as an outsider and one who enjoyed considerable welcome in their homes. To Slater Nyiha culture was thin; the people "seemed like zombies" and "lived in what seemed to me a kind of suspended animation"; the society was marked by a certain "diminution of individuality" and "endemic hostility"; and she found she "was unable to participate in silence and the inaction of formalism." Gattrell, on the contrary, recalled feeling among the Nyiha "a sense of strong, intense, highly varied personalities"; she "was impressed by their warmth, hospitality and generosity and the speed with which it was possible to overcome their suspicion of an enquiring European." She continues:

> I observed traits absent from Slater's account: cheerfulness, vitality, and in certain situa-
> tions, openness to other Nyiha. As for "silence and the inaction of formalism," I was
> impressed with the grave dignity shown on formal occasions, but in more relaxed inter-
> actions at people's homesteads, silence was so rare that I developed a craving for it; there
> was so much action I despaired of ever keeping up. . . . Slater left when she could not
> bear to spend one more night amongst the Nyiha . . . ; I left in tears, frustrated because
> I had no time left to explore the new veins of data opening up to me, and sad to leave
> individuals I had come to value as friends.[3]

The insights revealed by these conflicts in ethnography are significant for fieldwork in oral literature and folklore. Whatever kind of oral literature we may be investigating, we ultimately have to equip ourselves with a dependable understanding of the society or culture from which that literature comes in order to properly appreciate the images and messages contained in the text and its performance. To that extent, the tools of field investigation available in a discipline such as anthropology (or oral history) are just as valuable for the oral literary scholar, and the insights just as enlightening, so long as the scholar is careful not to be unduly influenced by the biases of those disciplines.

But an even deeper insight is revealed by this controversy between two white scholars investigating the same African society. It is clear that the divergences between them are due far less to racial factors than to their personal dispositions. While Slater came to Africa with the old colonial posture and encountered hostility, Gattrell "went with positive expectations" of an egalitarian nature and enjoyed the friendship of the people. The position may not be significantly different with two native African scholars investigating an oral artist even in their own hometown; the results they get will depend to a good degree on the attitudes they adopt and the responses they get. What this means is that although each investigator will, like Slater and Gattrell, report her findings as honestly as she can, what she is giving us is her own personal, subjective portrait of the situation, not an objective one in the sense that every detail of it is replicable by anyone else working in the same setting.

Gattrell titles her review of Slater's book with the question "Is ethnography possible?" Neither her question nor the points I have raised above are meant to discourage honest investigation and report; far from it. They are simply aimed at drawing attention to the fundamentally personal or human character of fieldwork and to caution the fieldworker, especially the native Africans among us, against making unrealistic claims for the value of their findings.

Preparations

I am not concerned here with some of the advice usually given to non-African scholars intending to do research in Africa—such as the need to undergo basic language training or to be loaded with an adequate armory of drugs against Third World diseases (as in Henige 1982: 28–30). Enough advice of that nature is available in other fieldwork guides, so the reader will excuse me if I address myself only to the basic needs of African students working in familiar environments.

If you are a student working on a term paper, an honors essay, or a thesis, you will have to do some preliminary planning in the form of conceptualizing your topic, i.e., having a clear idea of the area of oral literature you wish to investigate and how much of it you can cover. For instance, if you are working on the heroic poetry of your people, you may want to limit yourself to war songs or initiation songs or hunters' songs or epics having to do with conquest and settlement. When you have made up your mind, it will be useful to work out a preliminary scheme of headings with the help of your supervisor; this will be modified or expanded as the research progresses. I am assuming, of course, that in choosing to investigate heroic poetry you already know that that kind of oral literature exists in a viable quantity in the community you wish to investigate. If you know your people (and perhaps grew up among them), that sort of information will already be at your disposal; if not, finding out would be the first step to take.

The next stage, after the tentative scheme, is reading for the project. Basically two kinds of reading need to be done. The first is a general reading in the genre of your interest, across and beyond the culture you are researching. Folktales are perhaps the most widely studied class of oral literature; if you are working in that area, it would be a shame to ignore classic works covering other cultures such as Stith Thompson's *The Folktale* (1946), as well as a few tale collections. If you are investigating epics, you should not only explore the growing literature on the African epic but also read in the vast body of work on the subject from other parts of the world, such as Albert Lord's *Singer of Tales* (1960), Felix Oinas's *Heroic Epic and Saga,* and C. M. Bowra's *Heroic Poetry* (despite Bowra's prejudices). If your subject is funeral poetry, you will do well to read not only J. H. Kwabena Nketia's studies of it among the Akan (see the bibliography in this volume) but also as much on the subject of elegiac poetry generally as you can. And whatever part of Africa you come from, if you are working on hunters' poetry, S. A. Babalola's *Content and Form of Yoruba Ijala* (1966) is a respectable starting point. Such general reading will indeed broaden your conceptualization of your project and enhance the draft scheme of headings. But you should resist the temptation to go on reading until your conception of the topic becomes woefully diffuse.

The second kind of reading to be done is a more targeted one on the community you will be working in. There is a temptation among some of us to think that just because we grew up in a town, speak the local language perfectly, and have participated in the social and cultural life, we know all we need to know about the place. That temptation should be fought vigorously; for while we were doing all that growing and participating, somebody else (possibly from outside) was busy exploring, as scrupulously as possible, the sources, the interrelations, and the import of the various facets of that culture, some of which may never indeed have been accessible to us. So we should find out what has been discovered and documented about the community and absorb it as much as possible. Some communities in Africa have had a better chance of being covered by various disciplines (history, archaeology, ethnology, the physical sciences, and even colonial and missionary reports) than others. The rest have only recently begun to feature in the reports of amateur researchers and journalists or in official documents. Whatever you can lay your hands on, read it, for the chemistry between those mostly well-considered comments and your own personal instincts is a better guarantee of the validity of your investigations; two heads, they say, are better than one. Here again, the material gathered from these sources will make a further input into the designing of your scheme of contents.

The next stage of the preparations is finding out who the local experts are in the kind of oral literature you wish to investigate. If you already know who they are, fine; if not, relatives or friends should be able to help you. You must, however, not assume that these "experts" are the only ones who can sing or narrate all you want. Other performers not so well known or forthcoming may not be significantly inferior to those "experts"; they have simply never had a chance or been inclined to show how good they can be. "There may be nothing 'folksy' about the best informants," says Donald MacDonald (1972: 414).

When I was busy recording the ingenious Ojiudu Okeze in Ibusa in 1977, my brother-in-law Patrick Arinze hinted that the retired schoolteacher S. O. Aniemeka also lived in the town and had been known to spin a tale or two. My eyes lit up with the memory of my old headmaster. Aniemeka, whom we youngsters had dreaded for his dangerously eloquent indictments, was delighted to have the opportunity of turning those well-chosen words to good account for his former pupil; at the recording session which we held on his front porch on Christmas night, I gathered some of my best Ibusa collection, not only from him but also from other members of the attending crowd (especially neighborhood women).[4] At Ubulu-Uno in 1980, Simayi introduced his second percussionist, a young man rather well dressed for the sort of company he was in, as a teacher in the local primary school. Toward the end of the evening the young man, Dennis Amamfueme, revealed that he had won prizes in two state-organized storytelling competitions, and he regaled us with one of his tales. The researcher should, therefore, keep an open mind for sources other than the best known or accredited.

Having put your mind in the appropriate disposition—with the right attitude and adequate information—you must now ensure that you assemble the right material tools for your fieldwork. Basically two kinds of tools are needed: writing materials, i.e., notebook and pencil or pen, and audiovisual apparatus such as camera, tape recorder, and (for maximum fidelity) filming equipment (usually video). Since you will find everything you always wanted to know about all this audiovisual tackle in Polunin (1970), Ives (1980), and Jackson (1987)—the most readable being Jackson— I will speak only briefly about them.

Anyone who cannot acquire the most basic piece of equipment, a portable cassette recorder, is simply not qualified to venture into fieldwork. The days when researchers recorded songs and stories with notebooks, whether during performance or in an isolated dictation, have long since passed. Notebooks should be reserved for recording the little impressions you form as your artist is speaking into the tape recorder or for noting down subtle movements occurring at the scene of an interview or performance if you don't use a video recorder to capture them. Any texts of songs or tales recorded by notebooks whether now or in the past should be adjudged somewhat less than accurate or reliable.

Let us now run through the various kinds of technical apparatus that may be used for fieldwork.

Cameras. There is no need discussing the more expensive types of camera, since most African researchers (especially students) are not going to be able to afford them. In any case, if you have enough money to make a respectable visual record of your subject both at interview and in performance, you may as well get yourself a video recorder, about which we shall speak later. So you need no more than an instamatic camera for your purposes. The advantages are twofold. One, you can record a few scenes in the town or village as supporting ethnographic material for your subsequent writeup. Two, it helps you to establish good relations with your artist and the general audience; many people are thrilled to see an instant image of themselves and would be even more beholden to you if you let them have it for keeps. But make sure you carry a small plastic bag for dumping the disposable materials from your camera (film strips, flash bulbs, etc.), or the curious children there might snatch them up for play. Some of this disposable stuff is treated with chemical preservatives that might create health problems for the children long after you have gone.

Audio recorders. There are basically two types of tape recorders at present: open-reel (or reel-to-reel) recorders and cassette recorders. Either of these will give you a good recording if properly handled, but there are a few notable differences between them. Cassette recorders are far cheaper than open-reel and are steadily driving the latter out of the market (most open-reel parts, even the tapes, are hard to find in Nigeria today). However, although the quality of cassette manufacture is steadily improving, open-reel tapes preserve recorded material much longer than cassette tapes. Second, the cassette player is automatically set and compact; but if anything goes wrong with the tape during the recording (say it cuts or tangles), there is very little you can do about it. If an open-reel tape tangles, you can straighten it up manually even if there is a slight loss of material in the interval. If an open-reel tape cuts, you can "splice" it (i.e., join the two parts) with a splicing tape. But make sure to splice on the non-magnetic (i.e., shining) surface of the recording tape; otherwise you will peel off the magnetic deposit on which the sound is recorded. And avoid splicing with cellotape.

A third and more important difference between open-reel and cassette recorders concerns the setting of the speeds. An open-reel recorder is calibrated for four recording speeds, measured in inches per second (i.p.s.) or centimeters per second (c.p.s.):

$15/16$ i.p.s. (= 2.4 c.p.s.), $1\frac{7}{8}$ i.p.s. (= 4.7 c.p.s.), $3\frac{3}{4}$ i.p.s. (= 9.5 c.p.s.), and $7\frac{1}{2}$ i.p.s. (= 19 c.p.s.). As a rule, the higher the tape speed, the greater the fidelity of the recording (the higher speeds are particularly good for musical performances). Cassette tapes, on the other hand, are automatically set at one speed only, $1\frac{7}{8}$ i.p.s., or 4.7 c.p.s. Although this is all right for interviews, it may not be adequate for certain chanted or sung performances—as I found to my cost in some of my recordings of Odogwu Okwuashi Nwaniani of Onicha Ugbo (southwestern Nigeria), who constantly switched between the three modes of speech, song, and chant in his narratives. For such performances you need the higher speeds provided for in an open-reel recorder. However, make sure that you don't switch the setting from one speed to another in the course of the same recording. Stay with one speed all the way through or you might create problems for yourself when you come to transcribe the recorded text.

Tapes (whether cassette or open-reel) come in different sizes or thicknesses which bear a relation to their duration of play. "Standard play" tapes are 1.5 mil thick and are often designated C-60; they are 600 feet long and play for 60 minutes altogether (i.e., 30 minutes each side). "Long play" tapes are about 1.25 mil thick and are marked C-90, i.e., they are 900 feet long and play for 90 minutes (45 minutes each side). "Extended play" tapes are 1.0 mil thick and are marked C-120; they are 1200 feet long and play 120 minutes altogether (60 minutes each side). And so on. As a rule, the longer the tape, the thinner it is and consequently the greater the risk of "printthrough," i.e., the magnetic deposit rubs off from one layer of the tape to the next, so that when you play back you may occasionally hear one sound echoing within another. That is why it is always best to use the standard play tapes (C-60). You spend a bit more money that way, but the quality of recording is the best of the lot.

Every tape recorder is designed to use either electrical current or batteries. Electricity is excellent if your informant's (or host's) house is wired, he or she doesn't mind your running up the bill, and the power is steady (it's somewhat erratic in Nigeria). But electricity may not help much if for any reason (especially during an interview) your informant takes you out of the room where the recording has been going on, e.g., to show you where in the far backyard he carves his musical instruments; and electricity may not be available for open-air performances that attract sizable audiences. For such situations, you may need to use your set of batteries.

Batteries. There are several kinds of batteries, varying in quality and thus cost. The most common and the cheapest is the "carbon–zinc oxide," used in torchlights (flashlights); some of them are designated "heavy duty," but the difference is not much. Then there are others: the "alkaline" (manganese dioxide) batteries are far more expensive than the torchlight batteries but are rather hard to find, at least in Nigeria. The least available—which are also the highest quality—are the "mercury" batteries and the "nickel-cadmium" (or "rechargeable") batteries; but these two are not really made to fit into the kinds of tape recorders available.

In any case, whatever the advantages of batteries, they (and I am thinking mostly of the carbon–zinc oxide, which is the most easily available type) have a comparatively limited life. For one thing, no one knows how long they have been on the seller's shelf. Some people will tell you to buy from an air-conditioned chemist or supermarket rather than an open-air kiosk. Fair enough, except that there is no way of knowing how long the batteries were in the warehouse before they moved to the air-conditioned shop; and for the battery cells, every minute of life counts. For another thing, these carbon-zinc batteries should be treated with care because they are both weak and dangerous. Try to observe the following rule. If you are going to record for several hours in one day, take along several packs of batteries. Never use a set for more than 90 minutes at a time, then leave them to recuperate for the rest of the day; do not use each set for more than four or five hours on the whole. When a battery is overused, the quality of sound recorded suffers (you can hear eerie sounds on replay). And never leave the batteries in the tape recorder for a long period (like weeks), because the chemicals inside them might leak; the liquid stuff is an awful mess and may damage the tape recorder.

Microphones. One more important component of the recording apparatus that needs to be discussed is microphones. Basically two types of microphones are used for recording. The first—which most people, especially students, use—is the kind that is built into the chassis of the tape recorder; it picks up as much of the sound around it as possible. Such a microphone is usually good enough, but it does not make for proper concentration on the principal artist in a performance situation. To get better concentration of sound, you need to use the second type of microphone, i.e., the "external," or what is sometimes called the "plug-in,"microphone, i.e., plugged in to the recorder.

Several kinds of external microphones are manufactured today, some of them quite compact and fanciful. Some—especially those used in espionage—may be shaped like pens or brooches, so that you can clip them to your shirt or dress. They are not connected to the tape recorder (which may be far away from the recording scene) by a cord but by powerful magnetic waves. For our noncovert type of work, however, you need the plug-in microphone.

Such microphones also come in two main types. One is the "cardioid" (i.e., heart-shaped) type, which is particularly useful for interviewing in a noisy setting. The more common type is called omnidirectional. As the name implies, it is designed to pick up sounds from all directions, though the greatest concentration of sound is from the source immediately in front of the microphone. These omnidirectional microphones are, I think, ideal for recording the artist either in an interview or in performance. When I started fieldwork several years ago, I used to take along a "muffler" and fit it around the mike just before recording, the idea being to filter out any extraneous, or "ambient," noise. But I don't do that any more. Some of these other sounds may be asides thrown in by members of the audience either in an interview or in performance; they may be occasional coughs from a child or a cup dropping, or even the sustained croaking of frogs or screeching of insects or distant buzzing of a machine. To the extent that these noises condition the reaction or response of the artist, they are part of the emotional context of the activity at hand and should be welcomed or (if you receive them and can't help them) condoned.

So where should you place the mike? At a point sufficiently central for all involved in the recording, but especially facing the artist, since he or she is the major focus of the performance or (in an interview) of the information. If the scene gets a little rowdy (especially in an interview), do not hesitate to pick up the mike and train it closer now to your mouth, now to the mouth of the informant. But don't stick it so close as to be a nuisance.

Video recorders. Reporting the performances of Ila-speaking narrators in 1920, two British colonial scholars lamented the reduction of so much fervid activity into cold print in a foreign idiom, and recommended that "it would need a combination of phonograph and kinematograph to reproduce a tale as it is told" (Smith and Dale 1920: 336). That was in the days of the silent screen. In 1963 a native African researcher, the poet-playwright J. P. Clark, in his early recording of the Ozidi epic of his Ijo homeland in the Niger Delta, had this to say of the performance: "not just the tape recorder or bound volume which records the sound alone, but perhaps a full-length colour film appears to be the one medium that can catch and convey something of the complete, complex and magnificent texture that is the . . . epic" (1963: 9). And in 1968 Donald MacDonald lamented that the School of Scottish Studies at the University of Edinburgh, which sponsored his fieldwork, could not film the extraordinary performances of "waulking" songs earlier recorded by him and the Knudsens from women in Earsary, Barra (1968: 428).

There is no longer need for such laments. Film is here to stay, and it should be the ideal of every scholar who takes the job seriously to capture significant moments of a subject on sound film. J. P. Clark did finally make a 16-mm color film of a dramatized performance of the Ozidi story which has been shown to mostly professional audiences. However, these recordings for large screens are rather expensive and offer limited possibilities for reproduction and circulation—which is partly why they have now been considerably replaced by video recordings, at least for fieldwork purposes. The other reason for preferring video is that the equipment is more compact and can be operated by fewer people than 16-mm equipment. I am not by any means pretending that video is cheap; far from it. The cost of both recorder and tape is prohibitive in Nigeria, and from my general knowledge of our profession, few scholars go to the field with that tackle. However, if we hope to reduce to a minimum all that circuitous act of describing the histrionic and other movements that accompany the performance of a tale or a song, we should aim seriously at taking along a video-tape recorder (VTR).

Much of what I have said about audio recorders also goes for video recorders, as far as the recording of sound is concerned; the only added dimension in the latter is the recording of vision. Video recorders come in three basic formats or systems: VHS (vertical-helical scanning), Betamax (or "Betacord," according to some manufacturers), and U-matic. These terms reflect the methods by which the machines process the sound and vision signals they receive, a technicality we need not go into here. Each system can be carried in a compact, portable case with a shoulder strap. The VHS and Beta sets can load videocassettes that run for as long as two or three hours; the 4800-range recorders available in Nigeria carry U-matic cassettes of only twenty minutes' duration (e.g., the Sony KCS-20). But these U-matic recorders are professionally preferable to the VHS or Beta formats. The U-matic tapes are shorter than the others because they are appreciably wider; and because they are wider, they provide a larger field for the recording of images and give a better response to the impressions captured by the camera.

If you are recording a narrative performance that lasts as long as, say, two hours, you can do it all conveniently with just one VHS or Beta recorder. To capture such a recording on a U-matic format, you would need at least two recorders. One of them could be a desk recorder that can load a 60-minute U-matic videotape (the Sony KCA-60, for instance), alternating with the portable type that carries the KCS-20, or else two portable recorders alternating with each other for the duration of the performance; this may look like a nuisance, but you compensate for it in the quality of the recording.

Each of these various recorders is accompanied by three basic components: a power source, a microphone, and a camera. (Whatever we have said about microphones above goes also for these video recorders.) Every recorder is packed with a battery for situations where there is no electric power supply; if, as frequently happens in Nigeria, that pack cannot be replaced, you can make do with a 12-volt battery of the type that scooters use. Whatever kind of battery you use, make sure it is periodically charged, especially the night before you set out for the field recording.

The cameras are mostly portable and can be either carried on the shoulder with a C-shaped metal bar at the base or hitched to the top of a tripod. It is much better to set the camera on a tripod (preferably the "fluid-head" ones), because unless you are an absolute expert at maneuvering the camera on your shoulder, your body movements may cause awkward bobbings and image displacements that would be difficult to correct at the final editing of the film. With the camera comfortably hitched to the head of the tripod, you will find it much easier to pan (i.e., move the lens to the left or right of the range under focus), zoom (narrow or widen the focus depending on how small or large you want the object recorded), or tilt (follow the object as it moves along a vertical plane). With the camera on your shoulder, you may feel so uncomfortable after a while that you will find it difficult to combine these delicate maneuvers with the basic job of focusing on your object clearly.

Cameras operate with light. If you are filming in the open air in bright daylight, you need no added gadgets. If you are in a faintly lit room, however, you would need to connect at least two halogen (i.e., gas-filled) lamps to your power source (electric current or battery) and position them so as to illuminate the scene or object adequately. It is true, of course, that there are cameras these days that can produce excellent color images in ordinary room light, but it will take a long time before these are available in Africa at affordable prices.

Most oral performances by average-size groups can be captured with these portable recorders. For a truly professional job, however, you may want to hire the services of an outside broadcast van with a full team of technicians. The ordinary portable sets can be handled by one or two men, with camera and recorder all at the scene of performance. With the van, however, you can conveniently separate the camera from the recorder. In a full professional set, two separate cameras are located at two different points at the scene of performance, each relaying its images through a camera control unit. These gadgets are connected by a long cord to the van, which may be fifty meters away. In the van, a vision controller relays instructions to the camera operators, telling them what maneuvers to make (pan, zoom, etc.) and whether or not to take any images at all. These images are passed through a mixer (manned by the vision controller), and ultimately selectively transmitted to the recorder.

One value of the outside broadcast van in such a setup is that it saves much of the complex and delicate recording machinery from the sometimes destructive curiosity of a thronging crowd in a performance. Another is that it provides a kind of mini-editing of the images recorded, by helping the camera operators in their often difficult job of selecting the right exposures to capture. But it is a machinery you can use only if you have a lot of research money in your pocket.

Final checks. Before you take out any of these sophisticated recording gadgets (camera, audio recorder, video recorder, etc.), make sure everything is working well. Two things in particular need special attention, the first being batteries. If you are working in an area where the electricity is rather unstable, you are probably better off relying on batteries for your recordings; you should at least carry a good quantity with you just in case, and make sure that there is sufficient life in those batteries; recharge the relevant ones the night before you set out.

The second final check is on the recorder heads—the cylindrical knobs round which the magnetic surface of the tape passes as it receives the signals from the object being recorded (sound on an audiotape, sound and image on a videotape). If the recorder heads are dirty with dust or grease, you will get poor results; the pictures in the videotape, for instance, will appear blotchy on replay. The heads could also be "dirty" from having received too much magnetic substance (iron oxide) from the magnetic surface of the tape. A clear recording requires direct contact between the tape and the recorder heads, so no form of dirt should be allowed on the latter. Before you set out, clean the heads gently with cotton or cloth dipped in alcohol. Standard solutions—methylated spirit, ethyl alcohol, carbon tetrachloride—are usually available in sufficient quantities; but if all you have is local gin (which is usually strong), you should "denature" it by mixing in the ratio of one part gin to five parts water. Remember, rub the heads gently.

Meeting the Artist

You either know your artists and go to them directly, or you are introduced to them by someone else. If you work in your hometown, as I suggested earlier, then you have relatively few problems. You won't need an introduction to your uncles and aunts—it was such a relative, by the way, who told me the Nwakadimkpolo story (Okpewho 1983: 79–80). Even the artist you don't know may turn out to be a distant relative; parents and uncles and aunts are usually good at tracing family ties and, if need be, taking you to a relative for the proper introduction. Of course, there may be the odd problem or two. The artist you really want may be an enemy of the family; too bad—go and look for someone else, or choose another topic. On the other hand, who knows?—your approach to that person may be the key to a reconciliation between families. Such an effort would surely make a better person of you.

If you go to villages outside your own, as I have often done, you need a guide who is either a citizen or sufficiently well known in the place. At Ibusa I met Ojiudu Okeze through my brother-in-law Patrick Arinze, who was a teacher there, though he hailed from Asaba. At Ubulu-Uno it was Ignatius Osadebe, an indigene, who took me to Charles Simayi. Osadebe had previously taught at Onicha-Ugbo and was also responsible for my contact with Odogwu Okwuashi there. But whether you are working in or outside your hometown, you will find that artists are generally so sympathetic to your efforts to record their time-honored arts that only the minimal introduction of yourself and your subject is required (unless, of course, the informant has had a bad previous experience, a matter I shall discuss later).

When you do meet the artist, try to observe the proper courtesies (traditional and otherwise) and generally "behave yourself." If the artist is titled, be sure to give him or her the greeting proper to the title. In any case, it would help to know the generally accepted modes of greeting in the place. In 1988 I did a videotaped interview with the Etsu Nupe (though not for an oral literature project), and I recall what an appreciative response I got from him after I greeted him with the customary *Kubelaji*. Such gestures help to smooth the path of contact. At this point, too, remember you are a guest, not the host. Some students are apt to overdo their courtesies. They have been told they must treat their artists well and so, on settling down with an artist, are in a hurry to offer him a bottle of gin or a carton of beer. I have never yet met an artist so poor as to have lost pride or decorum; however hard things are, he or she will insist on splitting a kola nut with you—and you must accept.

After the initial courtesies, you must let the artist know why you have come. Tell him or her what kinds of material you will be collecting and to what use it will be put. Less professional artists may be a little embarrassed to be asked to tell stories and sing songs at their age, and usually chuckle shyly at the prospect. A good many are so preoccupied with earning their meager keep from farm or factory that they rub their heads more to put their memories right than out of any embarrassment. But once you let them know how important it is to record these traditions (e.g., "so as to save them from extinction"), and once they realize you have come to them out of sincere recognition of their talents in that regard, these artists are generally quite welcoming and cooperative.

The subject of your recordings should not be allowed to dominate this initial meeting. Talk about other things—the artist's house or work, your schooling or career, the state of affairs in the town and in the country at large, and so on. But be careful of one thing. Let your statements be more inquisitive or exploratory than assertive. Charles Simayi once told me a proverb: "If you too readily declare who your friends are, soon enough you'll end up in someone's list of enemies." In other words, do not be too outspoken, do not take extreme positions, and do not show off your knowledge. You are there to learn, not to teach, so be careful not to offend your informant's ego, or the artist will have no trouble finding an excuse for terminating the project at this initial stage.

Once the proper note has been struck and you have spent a reasonable amount of time for a guest, you may then make an appointment for a recording. It should be clear from the above that the first meeting with the artist should be as informal and relaxed as possible. This means you should not take any recording hardware with you.

You may keep a pencil and small notepad in your pocket to jot down significant names the artist may drop now and then, and you may take a Polaroid snapshot of the artist's little child and let the child have it. That should help consolidate the positive impression you've made. But avoid bringing things like tape recorders this first time. Save that for the next visit, when you really get down to business.

Recording the Artist

When you finally bring your equipment to the appointed place, do one more check on the various components to be sure everything is working properly ("Testing, testing, testing; one, two, three," etc.). Once you are set for the recording, announce the details of the occasion into the recorder: "Today is Friday the 27th of May, 1987. I am in the home of . . . , and I am here to record him and his group of performers. The time now is . . . and, besides . . . , his group of four men, and myself, there are twenty-two people in the audience—men, women, and children. All right." That is for future reference.

What do you record first, interview or performance? That will depend on the kind of oral literature you are investigating. If you are studying proverbs or riddles, which are usually set within the context of a conversation or discussion, then surely one cannot easily draw the line between interview and performance.

Songs and stories are, however, slightly different in that they are marked by a higher level of performance and require a different tuning of the personality. Of course, there will be a brief discussion, with the tape switched on. You have previously told the artist what kinds of tales or songs you are collecting. So the artist will tell you what piece he or she is going to perform and perhaps make a few other introductory remarks. After that, let the artist go ahead and do the performance. The value of doing the performance first is that it helps to relax the atmosphere and keep everyone in sufficiently good spirits. There may be a tune or two in which the audience joins; the artist may discover that after so many years he or she can still tell a good tale; the old woman at the corner is delighted to be part of it all and welcomes the chance that she will be allowed to tell stories she used to tell her children by the fireside; and so on. Everyone is excited, and there is fun and laughter at the end of the story or the song. Now, thank the artist and the others, but don't go straight into an interview. Ask for one more performance. This time you will discover how much more involved the general audience becomes. That level of excitement and involvement is very much in the interest of your study.

Some performers will demand certain courtesies albeit politely, and it will be in your interest to oblige them. After I discovered that Charles Simayi liked Guinness stout, I made sure I brought a carton along for every performance session. Odogwu Okwuashi and his group are happy with Star lager beer. When I asked Odogwu if he thought he and his men could survive the nightlong wake-keeping at my mother's funeral rites in 1984, they all laughed, and he said, "It's our patron we're usually sorry for," meaning that my resources might not cope with their demands. But none of these performers is a drunken fool. The alcohol keeps up their spirits and their stamina, but they remain in control of themselves during their performances. You cannot but comply with their preferences.

What role do you play in all this exciting experience of stories and songs? Do you maintain an objective neutrality, believing that you are there to do a job and are not supposed to influence the performance one way or the other, or do you rather participate as actively as you can in what is going on? The latter attitude is known as participant observation, and there have been various debates about its merits and shortcomings. Personally speaking, I think it's the better approach; in all my field-work I have never been anything but a participant observer. It helps to break the barriers and make the atmosphere thoroughly relaxed and communal. The rural folk are usually flattered to see that their life-style means something to city folk. The old ones are pleased that your education has not alienated you from the traditional culture, and there is a general desire to give their child a good "welcome home." And if you speak the language well and remember the songs, why not have yourself a good time?

You may—but you should also remember you are there to work, not play. Indeed, if you take your work seriously enough you will discover that a good deal of your attention will be occupied by your recording apparatus. If you are recording on au-diotape, you will have to jot down the occasional movement or impression, as well as details of audience participation, in your notebook. You must also watch the tape so that it doesn't run out at a climactic moment. If you are recording on videotape, you want to watch the camera operator and ensure that the significant effects are recorded at the proper angles. If you are doing the recording yourself, participant observation is out of the question, because half the time you are looking through the lenses and the other half you are watching the tape rolling in the recorder. These are the burdens of the job. Occasionally you may get some help. Being the subject of several previous recordings, my friend Odogwu Okwuashi was particularly helpful in observing the tape and throwing in a song just before the tape ran out and had to be turned over; in that way, the sequence of his tale was not rudely broken by the snapping sound of the recorder. But mostly you are the one who must worry about whether everything is working properly, and that takes a considerable toll on the joys of participant observation.

Now let's discuss recording interviews. Two kinds of interviews are involved. One is a discussion of points and issues arising from a tale or a song just performed; the other is a more comprehensive inquiry into the society, the life, and the art of your artist. Although certain differences in emphasis exist between the two kinds of interview, a few basic attitudes and approaches are common to both. To start with, in this part of your fieldwork, you as a student of oral literature are not much different from the student of oral history or of anthropology: your main aim is to elicit facts or information that will help you understand the artist and the art better. So the more deeply you probe, the better for your aim; don't be afraid of being thought too inquisitive, but be sensible enough to know when a line of questioning is not welcome to the informant.

Also, in either form of interview there are usually two recognized styles: directive and nondirective. The directive style asks specific questions and gets specific answers

Interviewer: What kind of work did your mother do?
Informant: She was a cloth weaver.
Interviewer: Did she do anything else?
Informant: I don't think so; no.

The nondirective style is much freer: the interviewer simply gives a lead or a prompting, and the informant is free to say all he or she wants. In psychology this is called free association.

Interviewer: Tell me about your mother—her life, her work, her interests.
Informant: Well, my mother—she was a remarkable woman. A very tough woman. She never allowed us to fool around with our work. If your job in the morning was to sweep the kitchen, and she caught you leaning on the wall with your broom, she gave you one on the backside. Tough woman—we were a little uncomfortable then, but looking back I owe her everything I am today as a man. She herself worked hard. She wove cloth. You know, in those days woven calico was the fashion among . . .

Some scholars feel that the nondirective approach can be time-consuming and that informants should be discouraged from going too far beyond the needs of the questions asked. This may be true, but the interviewer should take care not to be rude to the artist by cutting him or her short. In speaking so freely the informant is telling you a lot about his or her personality, and you will need this for understanding the informant's peculiarities as an artist.[5]

What kinds of questions should you ask the artist? For questions arising from tales or songs performed, much will depend on what the performance contains. Even then, you are likely to get a bit more information if you ask "why" or "how come" questions than "what" ones. In other words, the nondirective style is not out of place even when you are looking for specific kinds of information. The more general type of interview is slightly different. Here there is more room for the nondirective approach. However, since even the nondirective style depends on initial questions asked, we can do no more here than give the kinds of general information you, as a student or scholar of oral literature, should be seeking about your artist's life and art.

Life and backgrounds. When was the artist born? Who were the parents, and what positions did they hold in the society? How many wives did the father have? How many children were there altogether, and how many by the artist's mother in particular? What was the atmosphere like in the family among the wives and the children? What was the father like in relation to the children and in general as the head of the household? Who is the artist's favorite relative and what is it that binds them together? Any illness in the family? Any tragedies or traumas in the family? When and how did the parents die (if they did)? What is the artist's major occupation, and what has been the major preoccupation in the artist's life? What religion or form of worship is followed? What is the artist's role in it? How much traveling has the artist done, and to what places? What impressions have been formed of the places visited? How long was the stay in each place, and what was done there? How much Western education does the artist have? What were the artist's impressions of school? Is the artist married? If not, why not? If married, what is the size of the family? What has family life been like? How much education have the artist's children had? How far have the children gone in life? How much support does the artist get from them? What is the artist's relationship with in-laws and grandchildren? What is the artist's present status in society—titled person, councillor, etc.? What cult or club does the artist belong to, and what are the qualifications for membership? What is the artist's role in it? What does the artist consider his or her basic qualities as a person and what are the artist's shortcomings? What personal experiences (both happy and sad) stand out sharply in his or her memory? What are the artist's goals in life?

Society and times. What (briefly) are the traditions of origin of the artist's people? What have been the major upheavals in the life of the community—wars (civil and foreign), epidemics, famine, rampage of wild beasts, etc.? What has been the relationship between these people and neighboring communities? Has the community ever been under the control of powerful kingdoms and movements—e.g., Benin, Sunjata and his generals, Arochukwu, Shaka, Moshoeshoe, Sheihu Umar, Uthman dan Fodio, other jihads? What was the relationship with that power like? In what ways did that power affect the customs, traditions, and other systems of the society? What was life like under colonial rule? What foreign missionary influences were there, and what were the results of the coming of the missionaries? What are the major occupations of the people—e.g., farming, hunting, trading? What are the major divinities of the people, and how are they worshiped? What are the major festivals of the community? What are the main forms of oral literature practiced by the people? What have been the effects of urbanization and industrialization on these cultural practices?

Art. What forms of oral art is the artist proficient in? How did the artist develop an interest in those forms? How long has the artist been practicing the art? What kind of training or preparation was undergone for the purpose? What does the artist consider as sources of inspiration (e.g., spiritual)? Are there any constraints on the performance of his or her form or oral literature—e.g., occasion (work, ceremony, etc.), time of year, ownership of the text (cult or otherwise), sex of the performer? What are the origins of the art in the artist's society—was it borrowed or indigenous? If borrowed, what changes had to be made, and for what reasons? Where or before what audiences or patrons has the artist usually performed? Are they any organized artistic competitions in the local community or at state and national levels in which the artist has participated? Who else in the community performs the same kind of oral literature? What does the artist think of them? How do people compare the artist with the other performers? Does the artist have a group of accompanists and apprentices? How long have they been together? How is the artist related to them—family, friend, or just job relationship? What are their specific duties on and off the job? Does the artist play any musical instruments to accompany his or her words? How does the artist manage the relationship between the music and the text? How does the artist's style differ (if at all) from the traditional modes of performance, and why have changes been made? What does the artist think about audience participation? What kind of preparations does the artist make before a performance? Does the artist find it necessary to adjust the material of the performance to suit particular audiences?

Is there any specific diction or dialect employed for the specific forms practiced or for any parts of the text? Is the art seen as a solid source of sustenance? Does the artist charge any specific rates or dues to patrons and apprentices? If a more lucrative form of existence was offered, would the artist abandon the art for it?

These are only sample questions. Others may be added or preferred to them. And considering that a few amplifications will surely be made by you to your questions and by the artist to the answers—avoid asking too many questions that demand a simple "yes" or "no"—do not try to elicit all the information too quickly. These interview sessions should indeed be interspersed with recorded performances to relieve both you and the artist of the drudgery of the discussion.

Let the interviews cover a few days. And make sure that they take place at the artist's convenience, not at times dictated by you when the artist might rather be more gainfully employed. If you are going to be asking questions at times when the artist would normally be at work, it is only fair that you take account of the interruption in your remuneration (we shall speak about remuneration later in this chapter). But remember one final thing: while the interview is going on, check on the tape recorder every once in a while to avoid having wasted the artist's time and your own.

Transcription and Translation

David Henige has advised students of oral history never to "leave for the field without a typewriter" (1982: 38), no doubt for doing preliminary transcriptions and other related jobs with the material collected for the day. I can hardly think of a more cheerless advice to give to fieldworkers, after all the burdens already placed on them. Of course, Henige's book is addressed primarily—from all indications—to foreign scholars (mostly from Europe and America) who don't have a long time to stay in the community they are visiting and must therefore get everything cleared before their patience or their money runs out. I also admit that some on-the-spot clarifications have to be made. That is why the tapes should be replayed soon after the recording of performances (more on this later), and questions asked during the interview that follows. But my honest advice to a fieldworker after all this is: collect your materials together (both the recorders and the things recorded), lay them aside for a while, and give yourself a good sigh of relief. It has been a lot of hard work.

Transcribing the recorded material later from the tape is equally hard work and has to be taken seriously, not only for the needs of the project in hand but indeed for the sake of future generations who may depend on your findings. It involves sitting and listening to the tape for many hours (sometimes with your ear close to the speaker) so as to get the words—not only the artist's but also the accompanists' and by-standers'—accurately down on paper. If there are any words or statements you don't understand, make a note to check with the artist afterward. That doesn't guarantee your problems will be solved; the artist may be as baffled as you are. But there's no harm in trying.

Before you actually start transcribing the text, listen to the recording a couple of times just to recreate the experience and have the occasion before your mind's eye. If you are then set to write, the first thing you should take down is the information you announced into the tape: date, time, name of artist, context, audience, etc. That piece of information will be useful for later analysis, among other things. It would also be helpful to time the recording so as to know how long it took, and to indicate this at the end of the introductory material just mentioned, somewhat like this: "This interview (or tale performance) lasted 1 hour 15 minutes."

Now for the actual text. First of all, what linguistic medium are you going to use? There has been some debate as to whether African oral literature should be set down in the dialect in which it was performed or in the standardized form of the language used by the performer. Those who support the latter position argue that for the treasure to be enjoyed by the wider readership, it should be presented in a form that transcends the peculiar speech habits of a limited group. Among those who hold such a view are champions of one culture or the other who are looking for all possible tools—language, art, music, dress, food—for projecting the unified outlook of the various subdivisions of the culture in question.

That is no doubt a valid effort. But standardization is a form of transliteration (almost a translation, in fact) and should really be somebody else's job, not immediately that of the person who collected the material in the first place. If the collector has any respect for the material recorded, his or her first duty is to transcribe it in the exact form in which it was captured. Indeed, if the example of Igbo (in which I have mostly worked) is anything to go by, the standardized medium is a language that you find only in books written for conscious instruction (e.g., the Igbo Bible and primers); nobody speaks it. Oral literature is a living speech act, not a compromise decided upon by a committee juggling with the alphabet or an orthography. In transcription, therefore, it should be accorded all the integrity and respect it enjoys in the familiar context of its expression. If I were to turn the texts of Charles Simayi into standard Igbo, he would hardly recognize his own stories.[6]

The next question to ask yourself is what to transcribe. Is it just the words said by your informant or artist, or do you include questions, comments, and even exclamations by the others around, including yourself? The more acceptable practice today, encouraged in no small way by Clark's edition of the Ozidi story, is to set down whatever the audiotape has captured that may be regarded as related in one way or another to the performance or to have affected the performers likewise. No comment should be considered trivial or treated as an "aside"; the artist may have heard it and been influenced by it in the development of the performance. Innes's documentation of the comments made to a *griot* by his accompanist and Clark's recording of the various interpolations of members of the audience of the Ozidi story amply demonstrate how valuable such an editorial effort is, not only for our understanding of the full dimensions of an oral performance (as distinct from written literature) but also for the business of literary and other analysis which follows that understanding. When we see the annotation *Laughter* or *Exclamation,* we are forced to reexamine the value of or the force behind the text that immediately precedes or succeeds it, as the case may be. And when we find a statement by a bystander, we try to examine what the statement forces the performer to do in terms not only of the size of the ensuing text but also of the direction in which the performance develops.

Indeed the study of oral literature has become a more exciting and rewarding affair because of these developments in its documentation. The subject was previously ignored or underrated because earlier collectors and editors treated contextual factors such as audience participation as of no consequence to the matter of the performance and so systematically threw them out of their documentation. It is true that to some extent those earlier scholars were deterred by the size of the text that would materialize if everything was left as observed or recorded. But we paid for the choice they made in the unfortunate judgment about the nature and quality of the oral culture which they and their contemporaries reached.

The size of material resulting from full documentation—which may ultimately determine whether a work of research gets published—nevertheless remains a problem for us today and forces us to make certain compromises. A case in point is the transcription of songs. Once the music is good and the mood happy, some performers have a tendency to indulge the happy feeling and sing the same lines over and over and over, hoping perhaps to impress the researcher and the recording machine thereby. So what do you do when a song goes on endlessly, and hardly any changes are made to the verbal text: set down the entire thing? Daniel Avorgbedor tells us, in his discussion of Ghanaian song performances (1990), that even though the verbal text is the same, the mode of performance by the singer and of reception by successive listeners is not quite the same. That may be true. But few publishers will accept a text of perhaps sixty lines made up of four lines repeated fifteen times over. For all his loyalty, even Clark, in his transcription of songs within the Ozidi narrative, frequently just sets down the basic text and then indicates how many times the tune is sung by the bard and his group. Publication of *The Ozidi Saga* was held up for several years, partly because publishers complained that the text was too long.

An equally illuminating effort has been made in recent times in connection with the linear form of the transcription: do we transcribe in prose or in verse lines? With songs and chants there is fairly general agreement that the transcription should be done in verse lines, since these are treated as musical forms of one level or another. With narratives, however, the matter is not quite so simple, and some of the more recent developments have not met with general acceptability.

Earlier collections of African oral narratives were published invariably in prose (translations mostly). The logic of prose has been that since the tales are told mostly in the everyday speech form (some with a few songs thrown in here and there, these being transcribed in verse lines), they should be set down in the running prose form that fits the medium. Even *The Ozidi Saga* was transcribed fundamentally in prose. During Clark's sabbatical leave at Ibadan in 1979–80, Chukwuma Azuonye (then of the University of Ibadan's Department of Linguistics and Nigerian Languages) and I asked him one day if he had ever considered transcribing the story in verse, considering the strong musical presence in the performance. Clark replied emphatically that the story had been told in everyday speech, so he had to use prose for his transcription. Although Clark's text has greatly helped our understanding of the nature of the oral performance, the same can hardly be said for most prose renditions; for in them the peculiarities of orality (repetition, audience input, etc.) are severely edited, and the text ends up looking like a chicken with plucked feathers. Even D. T. Niane's

Sundiata: An Epic of Old Mali (1965; original French edition, 1961), for all its classic status, leaves the serious student of oral literature with certain doubts about the authenticity of the presentation: it looks more like a well-edited historical novel than the record of an oral performance.

A more recent option has been to use verse lines in transcribing narratives. Many acknowledged narrators tell their stories against a musical accompaniment of some kind, and it is recognized that whether or not this is consciously intended, the music does play a modulating role on the verbal expression. For this reason, some editors are inclined to transcribe such a narrative text in lines separated either on the basis of what can be established as the beat structure of the music or, perhaps more commonly, on the basis of the artist's breath stops—i.e., each line represents what the artist has chosen or been able to say in one breath. The lines of text are thus said to have been divided on the basis of breath groups. The principle has long been applied in the treatment of such traditions of poetic chant as the Zulu *izibongo* and the Yoruba *ijala* (which frequently contain narrative portions). Some editors of the highly poetic narrative traditions of the Western Sudan after Niane—including Gordon Innes on Sunjata and other Gambian Mandinka traditions, Charles Bird on the Malian legend of Kambili, and John William Johnson also on some Malian versions of the Sunjata legend—have regularly used the system also.

But the real revolution in this regard was initiated by Dennis Tedlock in his transcription of Zuni (Native American) oral narratives. In an epoch-making paper, "On the Translation of Style in Oral Literature" (1971), he points out the shortcomings of earlier editions and translations of oral narratives by mostly American scholars, arguing that the main reason these earlier scholars had such a defective understanding of the so-called "primitives" was that they had such a poor record of their speech behavior. They gave mostly cavalier translations of the narratives they collected, in the belief that what mattered was not so much the style as the content of the narrative.[7]

Tedlock reverses the emphasis. He objects to the use of prose in recording these narratives on the grounds that, considering the emotionally charged atmosphere of the narration and the complex of moods within the narrator (and between the narrator and the audience), it would be a mistake to represent the statements in the cheerless and undifferentiated landscape of prose. He stresses that "prose (as we now understand it) has no existence outside the printed page" and "spoken narratives are better understood as 'dramatic poetry' than as an analogue of our own written prose fiction" (1977: 513). In several publications since his 1971 paper, he presses the case for an "oral poetics." With reference to the business of transcription and translation, he warns his colleagues (with the appropriate speech breaks): "If anthropologists, folklorists, linguists, and oral historians are / interested in the full meaning / of the spoken word / then they must stop treating oral narratives as if they were reading prose / when in fact they are listening to dramatic poetry" (1975: 123).

Perhaps the most striking element in Tedlock's system is that he transcribes all forms of spoken account in broken verse lines, whether or not these accounts are accompanied by musical instrumentation. The idea is that when people speak they observe periodic breaks, and these breaks are determined not only by breath but especially by the emotional rhythm of what they are saying. Consequently, some statements are long while others are short; at some points speakers speak fast, at other points slow; at some points they raise their voice high, at other points they bring it down so low it is barely audible. These changes are emotionally determined, and if we are to do justice to the statements, we must observe the appropriate differentiations between them not only by means of line breaks but also by the use of appropriate forms of typography. Accordingly, in a Tedlock text of an oral narrative we have the following cardinal elements that project a sense of "dramatic poetry":

1. Line breaks, as in verse
2. Various typographic devices for indicating pause
3. Boldface or capital type for words said in a high tone
4. Italics for words said in a low tone
5. Ordinary roman type for normal or ordinary voice
6. Stage directions to indicate mood, histrionics, etc.[8]

Tedlock's arguments have influenced a few scholars. Harold Scheub, in his collection of Xhosa *ntsomi* (1975), uses slash marks and numbering to differentiate the various statements that make up a story. In a collection of tales from the Haya of Tanzania, Peter Seitel (1980) adheres strictly to the Tedlock system. In my own edition of Igbo heroic narratives, I have used that system with slight modifications. I have found the system particularly useful for understanding what goes on during the performance, with both the narrative and the narrator. Take, for instance, the typographic differentiation of tonal levels, which I have accounted for elsewhere in the following way.

> I have noticed that when my narrator speaks in a high voice, it is either because he wishes to indicate a new turn in the development of the story, which helps us to understand something of the organisation of the oral narrative; or because he wishes to underscore the heroism of a character by endowing his statements with a due touch of menace, which helps us to understand something of the narrator's conception or development of character; or because he wishes to emphasize the significance of a particular event or act in the story. It may even have something to do with the personality of the narrator. Mr. Simayi, from our various general discussions, has struck me as a man with considerable personal pride and self-assuredness; he once told me that he had trained his children and made something of them, and that modern civilization therefore held no surprises for him! A man of such inclinations is therefore unwilling to be superseded or preempted; thus every once in a while, whether during the narration of a tale or in the course of our general discussions (in which other members of his group participated), he raised his voice whenever he felt an interpolator was, as it were, trying to get the better of him. By putting such high-toned words or statements in bold print or capitals (which eliminates the need for further "stage directions"), we certainly will be providing some aids towards analysis from various perspectives. (Okpewho 1990a).[9]

The discussion so far will have shown that the fortunes of transcription and translation are closely intertwined, especially because—whether we are dealing with a reduction of the recorded text to print or a rendition of the text from an African to a

European language—we are essentially dealing with (in Tedlock's words) the "translation of style." However, there are certain salient issues in the translation from an African to a non-African language that we must give some attention to.

The first of these brings us back to the vexed issue of repetition. It has become fashionable—and rightly, too—for scholars to publish the indigenous texts along with an English (or French) translation, usually on facing pages. Now, the editor who undertakes such a task is duty bound to fulfill the task all the way: translate everything found there. It will not do for the editor to put all diligence into producing an excellent indigenous text only to treat the translation somewhat cavalierly; the translation should be able to stand on its own as a document almost equal to the original in its reflection of the performance. Besides, even though many of us will not understand the indigenous text, we are sufficiently curious to want to take a peep every now and again, especially when we come to a passage whose content is particularly affecting. It will not, therefore, leave a good impression of the editor if we come upon what looks like a disalignment. Take the following passage from Wande Abimbola's *Sixteen Great Poems of Ifa* (1975).

> *Títíítí lorí ogbó*
> *Bìirìpe bìirìpe lomi okoo dà.*
> *Omi oko kii yi.*
> The soul of elders is everlasting.
> The water inside a moving canoe splashes
>   about persistently.
> The water inside a canoe splashes about.
> It does not spill away. (P. 110)

There are at least two things wrong with the English translation, and they both stem from the effort the editor seems to be making to reduce the "din" of the repetitions. The first is that in the English we do not at all feel the music (and so the force) of the ideophones *Títíítí, Biripe biripe* in the Yoruba. There is a feeble attempt to represent the repeated ideophone in the second line with "persistently," but that's not good enough. Ideally, the translation should match the effectiveness of the original one to one. Two approaches have been used to tackle such a task. One is to leave such ideophones exactly as they are, since English does not normally use that device in the way African languages do. The other approach is to find in English an effect as poetically forceful as the ideophone has in the indigenous text. Whatever the approach used, the key to the task is effectiveness; and if you don't trust your poetic talents, please save us the trouble which the indigenous text never gave in its original context.

The second error in Abimbola's translation is in the last line, where the *omi oko* ("water inside a canoe") has been reduced to the pronoun "it," apparently because the translator feels that one repetition is good enough for the phrase. Again, if the extract was to be used elsewhere only in the English translation, such a translation as we have above is obviously not quite so useful as it should be; it certainly does not achieve the effectiveness that we feel in the indigenous text.

I have harped on the idea of effectiveness because I do not believe that we should descend to insipidity all in the name of fidelity. A tasteless translation is just as offensive as one that is visibly disaligned with the original. If we insist that the translation should be able to stand in the stead of the original under certain circumstances, then it should be able to read just as well as the original sounded when it was performed.

This issue is such a touchy one as to lead so distinguished an editor as Gordon Innes to doubt the efficacy of the "faithful" translation. In translating the Sunjata and other epics from the Gambian Mandinka, he has come to feel that something is wanting. He has observed that the performances (and texts) of these epics attain their affective peaks at those points where the narrators recite the standard (formularized) salutes to the heroes—for Sunjata, "Cats on the shoulder," etc.; for Sumanguru, "Cut and sirimang," etc.; and yet he feels that the literal way in which he has tried to render these lines in English does not do justice to the poetic appeal of the original. He compares his effort to that of Niane, who, for all his transformation of the text he collected into some kind of historical novel, has nevertheless become tremendously popular, his translation attaining the status of a classic. Innes therefore ends up wondering if Niane's method, despite the liberties that it takes, is not the one that does full justice to the poetic character of the tradition and thus the most fitting way "to secure for the best in the oral literature of African its rightful place in world literature" (1990).

Although I think that Innes has greatly underestimated the quality of his own work, and especially its value for oral literary study, there is nevertheless some wisdom in the issue that he raises. It will be hard for an African scholar who takes indigenous tradition seriously and feels empathy at the scene of a moving performance not to endeavor in translation to recall and record the effect that the performance had. It is precisely because they remember how much the traditional masters moved them in their youth that poets such as J. P. Clark and Kofi Awoonor undertook the labors that yielded *The Ozidi Saga* and *Guardians of the Sacred Word*. There really is nothing wrong in a scholar's wishing to make a poetic English translation out of an equally poetic oral performance so long, as I said above, as he or she has sufficient faith in his or her own poetic skill and does not inflict upon readers a dose of bombast.

If translators do have any claims to poetic talent, they should try not to press them too hard. The sort of effort which Adally-Mortty makes in the piece cited in chapter 10 should be avoided; so too the propensities of John William Johnson toward a rather stilted diction in his translations of the Sunjata story.

> What seek you here?
> Have you not heard that none e'er come to us? (1979: 117)

> 'Tis I who found the Manden secret,
> And made the Manden sacrifice,
> And in a red piebald bull did place it,
> And buried it here in the earth. (1986: 172)

Poetry, as I have argued elsewhere (1985: 7; 1988: 78), consists far less in a fanciful manipulation of the physical form of language than in the evocation of a depth of sentiment. On the whole, I would urge that in the translation of traditional African texts to foreign languages, we should locate our attitudes somewhere between two extremes. On one end is the delusion of Lévi-Strauss: "The mythical value of a myth remains preserved, even through the worst translation. . . . Its substance does not lie in its style, its original music, or its syntax, but in the *story* which it tells" (1968: 210). On the other end is the overzealous poeticity of those who are determined to match the indigenous text with a flawlessly lofty translation, forgetting that even the best of the traditional masters are themselves prone to the occasional "nod" if not outright bathos.

Storage

The moment you make that announcement into your tape recorder about the occasion of the recording, you have taken the first step in the storage process. And don't first mark up a tape case (whether audio or video), because you never know how much sound or vision (or both) you are going to capture. It looks like a point too obvious to make, but I have actually seen someone indicate on a cassette the name of the artist he was going to record; even if you are sure he'll be there, how do you know how much tape he will take? I prefer to make the record only when the taping session is over or as each tape is completed.

Some people also look at their watch at the beginning and the end of a recording, so as to write down on the slip or case how long it took. There is nothing technically wrong with that, except that too much time consciousness makes the whole business of fieldwork (not excluding your relationship with the artist or informant) that much more mechanical and impersonal. Besides, there is so much to cope with at the scene of the recording that there is some chance you will forget exactly when the recording started, and may thus end up giving the wrong information. This is why I would rather indicate the duration of the recording as part of the headpiece to a transcription.

The real storage I am concerned with in this section is what happens to the tape and the transcript after you have taken what you want out of them and you don't need them anymore (at least for the moment). As a student, you have completed your project or your thesis; as a scholar, you have written your paper or your book. Ideally, these materials should be properly stored away so that you can check with them again if any problems arise or further clarification is needed later. They should also be available for someone else to consult who happens to be working in the same area (place or subject) that you have explored.

Every institution or establishment has its own archiving system, and so I am simply going to state what operates at Ibadan University's English Department. In recent years we have begun to give a special classification to materials produced by our students as their original work (honors essays, theses). Since the student projects are produced on a yearly basis, we index each project according to year, name of student (abbreviated), and number in the log: 1978/Bal/5. For the oral literature thesis and tapes, we provide additional classification. An entry that goes thus—78/Yor/KW/S/ Bal—indicates the following facts: it was recorded in 1978; it is from the Yoruba of

Kwara State; the material taped is a song or songs; the material was collected by Balogun.

The first classification mark is fleshed out in the general logbook entry, which gives the full name of the student and the title of the project. There is, however, a separate oral literature logbook which provides fuller information on the material recorded. "Song" is a general classification which covers both songs and chants; in this second logbook we state more specifically whether we have a masquerade chant, a hunters' chant, a bridal song, or a satirical song. The classification 80/Igb/BD/T/Okp simply tells us that this is a recording of a tale from the Igbo of Bendel State made by Okpewho in 1980. The oral literature logbook will indicate what type of tale it is, and other relevant information.

Bruce Jackson says in *Fieldwork* (1987: 91) that "tape is cheap." In Nigeria it isn't, and for that reason few Nigerian fieldworkers do what they should professionally do. Ideally, researchers should make at least two copies of each tape, so that they can keep one while the other is deposited with the archives available to them. But in the increasingly inflationary economy of Nigeria and many other African countries, this is a counsel that I would give with some heaviness of heart.

It would also help if transcripts from the tapes could be stored in the same library or archives; it would be so much nicer if the results of fieldwork—tape and transcript—were preserved in the same building. At Ibadan, however, transcription as an independent activity has not been practiced very much. In our department, students systematically include transcriptions and translations as appendices to the project or thesis, e.g., at the end of the ethnographic and analytical work that forms the main body of the document. Now, projects at the bachelor's and master's levels are kept in the departmental library and the head of department's office. Doctoral theses, because of the relative fewness of the output across the university each year, are deposited in both the postgraduate school and the university library; a copy is also kept at the head of department's office.

What Do They Get for Their Pains?

For a long time, since European scholars started recording them in the nineteenth century, African oral artists have been treated at best as fragile repositories to be delicately cuddled till they have given all their possible service, at worst as disposable vessels serving an impersonal professional end. It is only in more recent times, with both the refinement of method in the discipline and the growth of social sensitivity against all forms of exploitation, that serious questions have begun to be raised about the lot of informants in the research enterprise. It is clearly a healthy development. Early in our discussion of fieldwork procedures in this chapter, we drew attention to a few issues concerning decorum in our dealings with the artist. These ethical issues will engage the researcher from the beginning to the end of a project; hence we shall devote a section of this chapter to a consideration of them.

We have already mentioned that on meeting artists for the first time, you should greet them in a manner befitting persons of their social standing. We have also advised that artists should be allowed the privilege of entertaining you in their home on this informal visit. And we have suggested that should artists and their groups ask to be regaled with drink in the course of their performance, you should do the best you can to oblige. We should also add that everything possible should be done to make the recording work succeed. It may happen, for instance, that an artist does not have the money for procuring one of the tools (e.g., a musical instrument) needed for the performance. If you really need the artist's skill, you should do all you can to help get the instrument. The first time I was to record Ojiudu Okeze at Ibusa, he had lost his *opanda* (box-harp). He had not performed for anyone in a long time, and could not account for the whereabouts of the instrument, and had no money to buy one; things are hard in the village. So I gave him money to buy the pieces of wire and metal to be tacked to the wood; in no time he had his *opanda* again, and had no trouble at all fetching back the old musical feeling.

The fieldwork enterprise should also be seen as a mutual learning process. You have come to tap the reserves of traditional art and wisdom which artists possess; you should also make the fruits of your own wisdom available to them. Goldstein (1964: 130–131) thinks it is a good idea for the researcher to have a few tales and songs to tell at intervals, as informants are often just as curious to learn about things they don't know as they are willing to impart wisdom they have. On the whole this is good advice, as long as the researcher doesn't take too much of the center stage and set up as a rival to the artist. If properly offered, the unfamiliar pieces could in fact increase your artists' repertoire of oral literature. Ruth Finnegan found this out when she told the story of the temptation of Adam and Eve to her Limba (Sierra Leone) narrator; two years later, she returned to discover that the narrator had reformulated the story in a peculiarly Limba way and had been telling it happily to his people (Finnegan 1967: 267–70).

If you cannot perform stories or songs yourself but have been recording them from other artists in cognate communities, you may want to play them to your artists. You would still achieve the same effect of firing their curiosity. I remember with what eagerness and glee my uncle at Asaba would listen every morning to stories I had been recording from raconteurs in neighboring villages the evening before. The material you play from the tape should include, as I mentioned earlier, playbacks of the texts collected from the artist on the same or previous occasions. Country folk (if such are your subjects) are always amused to hear their own voices on the tape; you yourself will get a chance thereby to ask questions about things you did not understand. And if you have recorded on videotape and can play this back to your audience, you can imagine how deeply you will be entertaining them with a view of their own images in action. You have also opened up a new vista of knowledge for them.

They should indeed be opportuned to keep a piece of the technological benefits you have brought. Again, as I said earlier, if you carry a Polaroid camera with you to the field, do your best to take shots of the artists, their family, and fellows, and let them keep a copy. If they desire to know how the machines operate, explain it to them to the best of your ability. Everyone has a right to learn something new and make their lives richer thereby.

One of the most sensitive aspects of fieldwork relations is the issue of material rewards, especially in terms of payment of money. Some scholars have reported that in the areas where they have worked, it would be considered an insult to offer money to informants and even awkward to raise the issue. They are lucky people. "Country hard," as we say in the local patois, and it is a particularly painful truth in the rural areas. To be sure, however poor these folk are, they generally manage to keep their pride and decency in these matters. Some of my students have, it is true, reported encountering subjects who refuse to tell or perform anything unless an acceptable sum is guaranteed. But my own experience has been that artists wait until the affair is over and see how you reciprocate. And you should give what you think is fair, especially considering the amount of the artist's time you have taken and how rewarding you think the whole experience has been. They may even make you feel the money doesn't matter very much. One of my students was told by the group she recorded in her hometown: "Even if you did not give us any money at all, we are happy that you are going to tell the world about us" (Okogbo 1988: 18). Such courteous and touching disclaimers should nevertheless not deter you from offering what your heart tells you is a fair recompense.

Payment may not end with the immediate occasion of performance. Suppose you publish a collection of tales or songs from your artist's repertoire and make considerable money from it in royalties; should you not share some of that money with the artist? Or let's take another example. Some of us have become professors partly (at least) on the basis of research and publications emanating from fieldwork; how do we show our gratitude to those who helped us up the ladder?

These are not easy questions to resolve, and have been known to generate all sorts of emotional and irrational responses. On one hand, there are those who argue that oral literature is communal property and no one has any copyright on it, so the question of monetary obligations is superfluous. The argument about communal ownership of authorship is, however, nonsensical, not only on aesthetic (as I think we have demonstrated in chapter 2) but also on moral grounds. It would be fair, I think, to counter by saying that if the material is truly communal, then the distribution of any benefits accruing from it should be communally determined. Besides, if it was so publicly owned, why didn't you consider recording a performance by yourself and sell it—and see how much you are really worth?

On the other hand, those who are eager to prise the scholar's earnings from him or her should endeavor to find out how much money, really, comes from all this and weigh it against the expenses entailed in the work. If my experience and that of my colleagues is anything to go by, many scholars deserve a good pat on the back for their exertions. In the last several years, with university budgets being severely slashed by successive state and federal governments, research grants have become something of a distant memory, although scholars are still expected to research and publish if they hope to be promoted. Those of us who are "crazy" enough to carry on working with no help from anyone find that we simply have to pay our own expenses. So we buy our own tapes and other materials, wear down our cars and repair them, pay the artists, fall ill from the fatigue of the fieldwork routine, and pay the medical expenses—all from our meager salaries. When you do publish a book, you may earn a laughable amount because the publisher says it's an academic book and academic books don't sell. How can any self-righteous judge seriously defend the claim that you have exploited the oral artist, when what you paid the artist after the performances may be more than you will earn in two or more years' royalties? Even when you do get promoted (assuming it was only the artist's songs or tales that earned you the elevation), how do you reckon how much of your new salary to give the artist after what you already paid?

As I said, these are not easy issues to resolve. But I believe that the answer lies fundamentally in acknowledging that artists are people like ourselves and are entitled to the same decent treatment we expect others to give us. There are really other ways besides payment in which this decency can be guaranteed. One of these is to recognize that your relationship with the artist does not end the moment the field trip winds up. Circumstances have brought you together to share happy moments and indeed confidences (some informants tell the most intimate secrets of their lives), and you are now friends. As you visit home once in a while, or happen to pass through the vicinity of artists' villages, drop in on them and exchange courtesies. If you have some money to spare, you may brighten the day for them if you give them something before you leave.

But look what happened to me once. A few years ago, I went home to the village with my wife and children. On one of the few days we spent, I took time off to pay one of my old artists a call in a nearby village. He received me very well, and I thanked him for being so welcoming when I visited him on fieldwork a few years earlier. Before I left his house, I gave him something. He was extremely grateful, but I could also see he felt a little awkward. As I was about to enter the car, he came out with the business I suspected was on his mind: if I was at all ready, he could still tell me those stories I always wanted—he had, in fact, some I'd never heard before. I said no, I simply came to pay him a friendly visit, and would call again some other time for those tales. He may well have said what he did out of an honest feeling that, if I took the trouble to give him money, he should give me something in return. Or he may have been genuinely broke and thought there was a chance he could earn some money. Whatever his reason, it was unfortunate that he should readily see our relationship in terms of payment for services rendered. I thought I was being friendly. But money can get in the way of true friendship—something that those who insist on material compensations seldom consider.

Another way of guaranteeing decency comes with the work you publish. What image do you give an artist in the publication, and what share of the credit does the artist get? The question of image is a serious one. You may have asked artists some very intimate questions, and they may have revealed to you aspects of their life and background they would never have told a stranger (which you may be): illness in the family, a crime here or a tragedy there, and other delicate details. How do you think they would feel if they knew you were going to expose them to the world in that light? Would you like it if the same was done to you? In some societies, these ethical issues are resolved by getting the artist to sign a "release"—a document that says you are free to use the material you have collected in any way you want. This is particularly done in the United States.[10] But Americans have an uncommon propensity to go to court at the slightest provocation, and scholars there have found the release a safe way of protecting themselves against possible lawsuits from aggrieved informants.

The idea of a release may be somewhat out of place in Africa, at least for the moment; the people from whom we collect folklore are mostly not literate enough to sign releases or to be persuaded of the absolute need of them. In any case, people are not so litigious here as to be easily driven to court by a negative image in a book. But we should not exploit the situation nevertheless. As always, conscience should be the guide. Bruce Jackson has recommended the golden rule: "When you're in doubt about whether an action on your part is ethical or not, a good starting place is to put yourself in the subject's position and consider how you would feel if you learned what that friendly person was really up to" (1987: 278–79). I for my part don't think any information is so crucial that we must reveal the name of the person with which it has to do. If it is really crucial, skip the name of the subject; you haven't told the whole truth, but you haven't told a lie either. For instance, I haven't told you which of my artists I mentioned a short while ago in connection with giving money.

Finally, what credit does the artist—who told you those tales and sang you those songs that made your research so much worth the while—get when you finally publish your project or your book? You must make sure you give the artist adequate prominence by highlighting the artist's name and if possible reproducing the artist's photograph. For instance, it is grossly unfair, if not outright dishonest, to publish a collection of an artist's text as though they were your own work. The cover and title page of such a collection should not indicate that the book is "by" you; at best you should claim to have edited and translated the book, and the name of the artist who gave you your material should be printed in both places, with equal prominence. The credits for *The Ozidi Saga* read as follows: "Collected and Translated from the Ijo of Okabou Ojobolo by J. P. Clark." That's honest. The credits on *The Epic of Son-Jara* go thus: "Analytical Study and Translation by John William Johnson. Text by Fa-Digi Sisoko." That's also honest. Although both D. T. Niane and Gordon Innes have given full attention inside their editions of the Sunjata story to the *griots* from whom they collected their texts, I think they have not been fair in having only their own names mentioned as authors on the cover and title pages.

The aim of these arguments is to stress the human factor in our research. Besides, you should remember that if you don't treat your artists decently, you are making it difficult for anyone else to get from them the kind of cooperation and goodwill they will seem to have wasted on you. If we honestly mean in our research to promote knowledge and truth, we must learn to treat those from whom we gather our material with decency and respect. They don't have to tell us what we have asked them to tell us, but if they have taken the trouble to tell us, then we have a duty to respect that integrity which they have chosen to oblige us with. Fieldwork and all that goes with it should, as Joan Cassell reminds us, be rooted in "respect for individual autonomy based on the fundamental principle that persons always be treated as ends in themselves, never merely as means" (1980: 32).

12. Suggested Further Work

This book has tried to demonstrate that African oral literature is not just a gathering of old tales and songs or of wisecracks that the old folk delight in seasoning their chat with. It is these and more. It is a reflection of those customs, ideals, and outlooks whereby Africans have traditionally identified themselves and constantly sought reassurance in the face of severe cultural and other challenges. But above all this, it provides evidence of a fundamental creative spirit whereby, in the oral culture, cherished traditions are subjected to continual reconstruction and recreation and thus increased by new material; in contemporary writing, artists feel a certain urge to nourish their genius with ideas and modes of expression sanctioned by the time-honored habits of their people. In the preceding pages, therefore, we have tried to explore African oral literature far less as an anthropological curiosity than as a subject of serious scholarly interest. To ensure that the subject continues to enjoy the respectability and relevance it has achieved, it seems necessary that research be pursued along certain lines in which scholars have shown a certain amount of interest in recent times.

Fieldwork and Documentation

There are two main reasons why we must continue to collect and preserve African oral literature with renewed vigor. One, there are numerous communities across the continent whose traditions have hardly been discovered or sufficiently documented; every once in a while we read of one community or the other recently discovered in a census drive. There is therefore a wealth of oral traditions in Africa waiting—like the vast reservoir of mineral resources—to be unearthed.

Two, if we agree that a large number of the published texts of African oral literature (in original and translation) have been improperly represented, then we need to revisit the field again and again to correct the record. This will mean more work in recording and documentation along the lines recommended in the last chapter. Of course, I have heard it said now and again (especially in conferences) by critics of these new techniques that they are an exercise in futility because we cannot hope to capture an oral performance in print, since they are two basically distinct mediums; if we have to bring the oral text to print, we must reduce it to the level of unadorned linearity in which both the eye and the mind—to borrow a thought from Marshall McLuhan (1962)—have been trained to read the message. This would seem to me to be a counsel of despair: so long as our principal aim remains an understanding of oral culture, then we should at least make an effort to represent it in its proper dimensions.

How do we proceed? The days of "ragbag" or "dragnet" collecting, when one went into the field and collected everything one could find—songs, tales, proverbs, riddles, etc.—and published the entire thing under a catch-all title like *Ashanti Folklore*, must be judged pretty well over. Individuals should be encouraged to be more discriminating in their interests and make up their minds what specific type of oral literature from what specific community they want to investigate. It might even help, for intensive analysis, to concentrate on one group of performers or one artist. We shall be speaking shortly about the need for the latter kind of study.

This task of recording and documentation would seem to me to belong first to the educational institutions in Africa, especially university departments (of literature, folklore, linguistics and languages, etc.) and research institutes. The job of keeping our traditions alive seems also urgent enough for the subject of oral literature to be given full recognition (at Ibadan we have compulsory courses in oral literature at both the undergraduate and graduate levels) as a prerequisite to an organized program of collection and documentation. The research institutes are a little better placed for the job because, for the most part, the staff have a lesser burden of classroom teaching and supervision; they can thus spend longer periods in the field and make fuller use of whatever research grants may be attracted by the institute.

The task is also urgent enough for governments to take an active interest and part in it. It is sad to observe that most governments in Africa take only a superficial interest in matters of culture. Culture is more often treated as the subject of tourist displays and periodic jamborees than as a matter of serious national value. A government that cares enough about culture should have a properly formulated cultural policy and set up the right sort of machinery for promoting and supporting the kind of activities that we have said university departments and research institutes should be engaged in: a properly organized program of collection and documentation of the oral literature practiced in various regions; sufficient funds for supporting those involved in the work; and a suitable archival system for storing the materials collected. Ireland took a giant stride in 1935 by constituting the Irish Folklore Commission to coordinate the various collecting efforts of scholars dating from the previous decade, and today that country has enviable archives of all forms of oral literature and folklore and an equally enviable library of works recording the results of those labors. Similar successes have been recorded in Europe and America. It is about time African governments took the business a little more seriously.

The Urban Scene

The earliest studies in African oral literature and folklore were done among mostly illiterate folk in rural communities. By and large, in fact, the tendency among scholars even today is to think of them first. The bias is evident enough in the pages of this book. Although two of the informants I have mentioned are literate—my ex-teacher S. O. Aniemeka of Ibusa and Odogwu Okwuashi of Onicha-Ugbo, a former railways clerk with whom I have exchanged correspondence—the majority of them have been men and women who had not systematically learned to read and write. I go back to the village for my fieldwork because it is the culture I was raised in and because I feel committed enough to it to want to understand it better from my now adult, well-informed perspective. And I can still speak the language of the place.

But things have changed, and fieldwork need no longer be done only in rural communities. I am saying this for two main reasons, each of which urges that we devote some of our attention to the verbal arts of urban centers. The first is that, unlike the monoethnic culture that we find in the rural community, the culture of most big towns and cities in Africa is generally polyethnic and multilingual, entailing the use of a European language (of the erstwhile colonial power)—or a resultant patois like pidgin or Swahili—as some kind of lingua franca. This situation has an implication for both researchers and subjects. Many children who grow up and go to school in cities are unable to speak the indigenous language of their parents with adequate fluency, and it would be unfortunate—indeed wrong—to discourage them from doing their fieldwork in the city in a language in which they communicate effectively with people they might wish to study. These subjects provide the second justification for doing fieldwork in the city: there are pockets and aspects of life in the city which reflect very much the same sorts of outlook and behavior that we find among the traditional folk of the village and are in many ways a carryover from traditional life.

In recent times, in fact, urban fieldwork has become fashionable in disciplines which normally went to rural communities in search of their material—such as anthropology and folklore. This turn of events has been in large measure influenced by a rethinking of the concept *folk*. The term, as we saw in chapter 1, was traditionally used to identify the illiterate citizens of rural communities especially in the so-called Third World or—to borrow a phrase from standard nineteenth-century European prejudice—the members of a "primitive society." But one of the most radical breaks from that usage has been recorded by Alan Dundes in an epoch-making statement on the subject. Rejecting the prejudices of the nineteenth-century scholars on one hand and on the other the mid-twentieth century typology of Robert Redfield which saw "folk" as antithetical to "urban," Dundes offers the following definition:

> The term "folk" can refer to *any group of people whatsoever* who share at least one common factor. It does not matter what the linking factor is—it could be a common occupation, language, or religion—but what is important is that a group formed for whatever reason will have some traditions which it calls its own. In theory a group must consist of at least two persons, but generally most groups consists of many individuals. A member of the group may not know all other members, but he will probably know the common core of traditions belonging to the group, traditions which help a group have a sense of group identity. (1977a: 22).

Although this conception of folk has been questioned, there certainly is to it a coherent logic whereby we can speak of the fishing folk, the factory folk, the academic folk, etc. And if we can speak of the rural folk, we can certainly speak of the urban folk. Says Dundes: "For the modern folklorist, there is no paradox whatsoever in speaking of an urban folk. There are urban folk just as there are rural folk" (1977a: 31).

Such a reorientation in thinking has influenced several studies in the United States and Europe of the folklore of several urban groups. For instance, Roger Abrahams has done an incisive study of the "narrative folklore" among streetwise black Americans in Philadelphia (1970), and more recently Richard Dorson has done an excellent job on the folklore and folklife of factory workers in the industrial towns of northwest Indiana (1979). In both works these scholars have set out to study the life-styles of, and especially the stories told by, their subjects as instances of carryovers from traditional patterns. For instance, Dorson asked himself questions which sought to relate the verbal arts of the folk in these urban communities to those of their counterparts in more rural settings: "Did steelworkers possess a body of traditions comparable to that shared by men who herded cattle, cut timber, mined ore, and drilled for oil?" and—in his examination of stories told about crime in the rather temperamental lives of these people—"Did talk about muggings fall into narrative patterns that might be classed as modern folktales?" (1979: 3). He got positive answers to these questions.

I believe the study of African oral literature can benefit from similar investigations. So far, most studies of the urban scene have concentrated on exploring direct carryovers from rural life, such as we have seen in chapter 9 of masquerades in Zambia and Sierra Leone; even here, seldom have there been detailed studies that incorporate an investigation of the effect of technology on these basically rural phenomena, such as Jeyifo has done to a good extent in his study of the Yoruba folk theatre (1984). There are other lines of inquiry that could yield fruitful results. What about popular music groups like Sunny Ade in Nigeria or Manu Dibango in Cameroon—what are the elements of orality in their performances as well as their texts? What about the songs and stories of prisoners? If we may follow a lead from Wole Soyinka's play *The Road*, what stories do lorry drivers and touts tell about their dangerous profession—what sorts of heroes do they project? What about night guards—what stories do they tell? What about the songs composed for political campaigns? What relations do these bear to recognized traditional models? Such lines of investigation would yield fruitful insights not only about the adjustments of oral literature to the imperatives of urban life but also about the stresses we undergo in adjusting both to the pluralistic structure of our societies and from a traditional rural to a technological existence. Our business is literature, but it is also ultimately life.

Biocritical Studies

Evolutionist scholars—and not a few other theorists as well—believed that oral traditions were verbal lore handed down from one generation to another and contained essentially the surviving elements of a pristine outlook. Mostly, the people who told the traditions had no clear understanding of the original import of their texts and simply transmitted them rather passively. There was therefore very little sense in which we could speak of the creative skill of these transmitters beyond the physical efforts (e.g., histrionic movements) that they made to hold the attention of their audience. Even functionalist scholars who emphasize the relevance and significance of these traditions for contemporary society have given little more credit to the creativity of their performers and the sheer energy of their exertions. As William Bascom tells us,

> Many folklorists have given us far less information than Malinowski about the context and performance of the texts that they have published, but on both topics even his discussions are general and leave many questions unanswered. With regard to performance and enactment where, in particular stories, does the Trobriand audience laugh? Where do exchanges between the audience and narrator occur, and what [is] the nature of these rejoinders, interruptions, and other exchanges? Where does the narrator change his voice, and how? Where does he gesticulate, and what are his gestures? (1977: 14).

This neglect of the creative personality of the oral artist—in terms at least of the control exerted over the material whatever its derivation—has, as we saw in the last chapter, resulted in the collectivist approach to the study of a people's oral literature and the inevitable nonacknowledgment of the authorship of collected texts. In more recent times, scholars have sought to correct the imbalance by publishing the names of the performers on the cover and title pages of their works (as Clark 1977), and even giving us a biographical sketch of the artists (as Innes 1974, 1976, 1978).

But this is hardly enough. It is true that some of these biographical sketches provide insights into analysis (see chapter 2), but they are often not detailed enough to afford more than cautious propositions, however plausible. We need more detailed studies of the life and art of the oral artist to enable us to make firmer and fuller judgments of the nature of oral art and culture. MacEdward Leach has done invaluable service by drawing attention to the creative personality of oral artists, arguing that "literary artists exist in every preliterate community," that "new songs and stories" are composed, and urging that the scholar should not only "collect folk literature as oral literature and in its cultural context, but he must go beyond that and collect the singer of the songs and the teller of the tales" (Leach 1962: 338).

Leach's point about new compositions should be taken seriously, for we need to erase the false impression that oral artists transmit only texts they received from other persons and generations, an impression that many of us have aided by asking the artists to perform for us "those old-time" stories and songs.[1] Leach goes on to stress the need for us to explore what he calls "the folk esthetic": by presenting "all the data from texts and from the general culture of the folk," we will have laid the foundation for discovering an expressive style which "cuts across language and geographical barriers and, more importantly, also cuts across genres. A common thread runs through folk song, story, dance, ritual, painting, sculpture" (1962: 139).

Again, this aestheticist argument is sound talk. But I suggest that we must concentrate our energies now on exploring the personal aesthetic of these oral artists so as to restore them to their proper artistic integrity. Modern literature is studied principally through the works of acknowledged authors, and I don't see any reason why we should not do the same with oral literature. Despite the old-fashioned arguments about the collective outlook of traditional African societies, anyone who has done serious fieldwork will have observed how jealously artists guard their integrity; there is just as much emphasis on individuality as on communality, a point stressed by

Abrahams in his recognition of "apart-playing" and the "polymetric" character of African oral narratives and other art forms (Abrahams 1983: 18–20).[2]

There have been very few detailed studies of oral artists comparable to the work of Albert Lord (1956) on the Yugoslav *guslar* Avdo Mededovic or, even better, of Edward Ives (1964, 1986) on songmakers in Maine in the American Northeast. In Africa the record is even scantier. In Ghana, Kofi Anyidoho (1977) has done some work on the Ewe *anlo* poet Domegbe, and in Nigeria Chukwuma Azuonye (1983, 1990) has turned out some incisive analyses of the Ohaffia oral poet Kaalu Igirigiri. Several of my students have carried out field projects on the life and art of one artist or the other in their respective communities.[3] We need many more studies along these lines. There is no point in continuing to call these performers artists if we cannot demonstrate in what senses they qualify to be described as such. Besides, considering that these oral artists (like their literate counterparts) so readily reflect in their texts the progressive stages of culture change, they surely deserve all possible attention as the harbingers of our cultural history.

Other Specialized Investigations

There are at least three other pressing areas where I believe further intensive study of African oral literature may be pushed to profit. The first of these is the analysis of smaller forms such as proverbs, riddles, jokes, and puns. Several collections of these forms have existed for some time, but far less effort has gone into understanding them than has been devoted to the major types such as tales and songs. There is a lot of art locked within these brief statements, and we might even derive from them further insights on the relationship between art and the specific experience which art invariably endeavors to reflect or refract.

A second area—closely related to the point just made—is the interaction between oral literature and other forms of folk culture. Take music. A good deal of oral literature is performed against the background of musical accompaniment. But few collectors and editors have any competence beyond recognizing where the music occurs or is stressed and unstressed between the oral text. Yet, to properly understand the nature of the total performance, we have to understand the music; so important indeed is this factor that one scholar has suggested that "the student of African Oral Literature (and the student of any oral literature for that matter) should acquire literacy in musical notation and use it" (Okafor 1979: 90).

If the music blends with the words, then this may be because there is something in the structure or texture of the music that corresponds to that of the oral performance. Here I am ultimately agreeing with MacEdward Leach's recognition of a "folk esthetic" as a thread of expressive style running through various forms of folk art, although I stress that we have to begin by studying those who create these forms. There is surely room for investigating the "structure of feeling"—to borrow a phrase from Raymond Williams (1961)—uniting the artistic life of a community: in painting, sculpture, dance, architecture, cloth-making as well as in songs and tales. Although there is an ever-present danger of impressionism such as we find in the analyses of Robert Farris Thompson (1983) and especially Claude Lévi-Strauss in the four volumes of his *Mythologique* (1964, 1966, 1968, 1971), the "folk esthetic" can be gainfully explored in careful stages, such as in the comparative analyses of various traditions of African poetry and weaving by Jeanette Harries (1977) and Femi Ayewoh (1979).

Thompson at least endeavors to take into consideration the aesthetic views of the African and African-derived peoples whose cultures he analyzes. This brings us to the third area of oral literary study that needs to be explored: in what ways can we benefit, in our literate analysis of African oral art, from the critical judgment practiced by the folk under study? Functionalist scholars have, of course, frequently urged that we base our classification of oral literature on the systems recognized by the people who own the literature—see Bascom (1965) and Ben-Amos (1971, 1976, 1977)—though they themselves have not always convincingly demonstrated how this may be done. One way to explore the convergence of oral criticism and literate analysis is surely to ask a number of searching questions of the artist after a performance, as I have suggested in my discussion of interviewing in the last chapter. Another is to carefully probe the ethnography of a people to see if it validates the sort of conclusions which the artist draws at the end of a performance—such an effort as I have made, for instance, in my structural analysis of an Ijo creation tale (Okpewho 1983: 134–54). Whatever the case may be, when people make judgments about their own art and culture, we may be certain that some amount of thought has gone into their formulation, and we can at least try to probe the basis of such formulation. No one perhaps has better articulated the need for this effort in our oral literary study than Arewa and Dundes in their discussion of the ethnography of Yoruba proverbs:

> If there is oral literature, then there is oral literary criticism, that is, native, as opposed to exogenous, literary criticism. The shelves of folklorists are filled with explanations of what folklore means and what its value is, but few of these explanations and valuations come from the folk. Native literary criticism, which could be considered as an aspect of "ethnoliterature," . . . does not eliminate the need for analytical literary criticism, but it certainly should be recorded as part of the ethnographic context of folklore, both for its own interest, and because undoubtedly native interpretations and valuations of proverbs influence the decisions to employ a particular one in a particular situation. (1964: 73)[4]

From an investigation of indigenous aesthetic and critical thought, we move finally to an inquiry into indigenous rational systems. We began in chapter 1 with a discussion of the work of evolutionist anthropologists such as J. G. Frazer who credited traditional culture with a capacity only for "rude philosphy"; others, such as Lucien Lévy-Bruhl, spoke even less charitably of the incapacity of the "primitive mentality" for rational thought. In more recent times, a number of Western scholars have revisited these cultural dichotomies with a view partly to restating them in more polite terms and partly even to revising them. On one hand, there are those who restate the dichotomies differently; while a scholar such as Robin Horton (1970) separates "traditional thought" with its tendency toward a metaphysical view of reality and "Western science" with its empirical analysis of it, Lévi-Strauss (1966) believes that every human society is marked by an antithesis (or coexistence) between a "science of the concrete" and a "science of the abstract." On the other hand, scholars such as Jack Goody (1968, 1977, 1987), and Walter Ong (especially 1982), while taking the views of Lévi-Strauss, Horton, and others into account, believe that these cultural dissimilarities are in large measure bound up with technological innovations (e.g., the advent of the alphabetic script) and the attendant changes in modes of communication. At least one recent line of investigation (Scribner and Cole 1982), however, has endeavored to demonstrate, on the basis of fieldwork done in Liberia, that literacy has made no appreciable difference in the modes of oral thinking in a traditional society.[5]

Many of these insights in cognition have been derived from an examination of the oral literature of various African peoples. Undoubtedly the investigation will continue to be carried out from the related fields of philosophy and psychology. But the classic works of Marcel Griaule among the Dogon (1965) and Wande Abimbola among the Yoruba (1975, 1976) show clearly that mythological literature provides the most enduring base for such inquiries. At any rate, cognitive analysis is one area in which oral literary scholars can demonstrate the larger relevance and significance of their exciting subject.

Notes

1. The Study of African Oral Literature

1. The term *oral tradition* is used more fashionably in historical studies for stories or accounts narrated by word of mouth, with an emphasis on their being passed on from one source or generation to another. We shall use the term in this book a number of times to denote the literature, but without any of the prejudice attaching to the word *tradition*. Incidentally, it seems a waste of time to contend that *oral literature* is a contradiction in terms on the ground that it confuses the two concepts of orality and literacy (see Ong 1982: 10–15). Whatever the archival etymology of the term *literature*, the concept of oral literature is now widely accepted and is far from losing ground. See also Finnegan 1988: 124–26.

2. See, for example, Bascom 1955, Crowley 1969, and Herskovits 1961; cf. Berry 1961.

3. For an equally illuminating use of photography in the study of African artistic expression, see Charles Keil's representations of the energetic song and dance routines of the Tiv of Nigeria as well as of the vitality attending their storytelling session (Keil 1979). See also Opland 1982 and Cosentino 1982.

2. The Oral Artist

1. Cf. Innes 1976: 72.

3. The Oral Performance

1. The attention which we have given here to the background music is quite important for a proper understanding of the creative process in an oral performance. If writers are disoriented by something happening in the room where they are writing, they may drop their pen and stop work, to return to it much later. When they do resume the work, there will most likely be nothing to indicate the interruption (such as a break in the logic of the story or play). But oral performers cannot afford to suspend the performance, for they would lose the respect or the support of their audience if they did. In their attempt to correct a disorientation caused by, say, imbalance in the music, there is likely to be a slight wavering in the flow of thought or a slight disruption in the logic of the text; for instance, the narration is made to drag on until the musical accompaniment is stabilized. Such indeed is what happens in *Kambili*, lines 333–34, 2002–3, 2104–6, etc.

2. Cf. the extracts from Johnson (1986) in chapters 7 and 10.

3. The entry is obviously a distraction, a nuisance which must be disposed of so that the performance can continue smoothly. Simayi faced such a situation in a performance I recorded in 1980. A little boy had come in while Simayi was telling a story and took a fairly long time settling down. Simayi digressed briefly to ask the boy in a slightly impatient voice to sit down.

4. Stylistic Qualities

1. *Gbawaa* also means "blow up," which is of course the fate of the gun.

2. The root *verb* of this ideophone is *tulu-*, "to peck or pick up (with the beak)," and *-nzam* may be a subtle suggestion of the bird *nza* (finch).

3. Babalola also cites Beier and Gbadamosi 1959: 10: "Much of Yoruba poetry speaks in very brief allusions which are not understood by people who grew up outside the culture."

5. Social Relevance

1. We shall not here be discussing oral literature as a source of livelihood, since that role is obvious enough and we have, in any case, accounted for it in the final section of chap. 2.

2. See Okpewho 1987 for a fuller treatment of the Simayi and Egharevba versions of this account.

3. See Beier 1966: 23–41.

6. Songs and Chants

1. A good example of this differentiation may be seen in Finnegan 1970.

2. See chap. 4.

3. Even here we must be careful. There are many instances of tales told entirely in song.

4. Ogunmodede's knees are "bald" from scars of the sores he had on them. As a hunter, he had to kneel frequently to take aim at animals.

5. See Darah 1982: 299, 438–41.

6. The self-praise is emphasized by the appearance of the first-person pronoun at the beginning of virtually every line of this chant. The sense of action is equally marked by the preference for attributive phrases or epithets not only for the poet himself (e.g., "I Who Am Not Reluctant in Battle") but also for his companions (e.g., "The One Who Draws Tight His Bow," line 13) over actual names. Even more noteworthy, perhaps, is the metaphorical quality of some of these epithets (e.g., "The Bringer of Sorrow," line 19) and the sense of urgency conveyed by the succession of one epithet by another denoting ceaseless and tireless action.

7. See, for instance, Okpewho 1985: 188. Moshoeshoe is pronounced *Mshweshwe,* an ideophone for the slashing sound of a razor. His praise-name "Thesele" (line 3) means "The Beater" or "The Thumper," the image of a rampaging warrior.

8. The Mau Mau forces, led by General Kariba, fought the British on Tumu Tumu Hill, near Kirimukuyu.

9. The Kapmorosek are a clan of the Kipsigis of Kenya.

7. Oral Narratives

1. See, for instance, Turner 1969 and Okpewho 1983: 134–54.

2. As, for instance, Bascom 1965.

3. For a detailed consideration of myth as an imaginative element or quality in narrative rather than a type, see Okpewho 1983, chaps. 2 and 5.

4. The hesitation is due to the fact that I had just started off the tape recorder, and Simayi was trying to take control of the narration. For the methods of transcription used in this translation of the story, see chap. 11.

5. The titled elders of the community.

6. The proverbs in lines 30 and 35 are spells designed to ensure the efficacy of these articles (buzzard and fowl) in the charm being prepared, to protect the emissary against any obstacles to his mission (to rescue the cows).

7. That is, fetch the articles (e.g., cows) for the coming ceremony.

8. That is, the Second World War.

9. Meaning there was a total impasse.

10. Repetition emphasizing the multitude of soldiers with camouflage helmets.

11. The original words translate literally as "up palm" and "down palm," in the sense that the one sort of wine is tapped from a live, upright palm, the other from a felled palm.

12. This proverb implies that Simayi is equal to any situation he finds himself in. Note his self-assurance throughout this story.

13. An ideophone for the stampede of Simayi's cow (named Akuamaka, i.e., "Wealth Is a Good Thing") toward him.

14. These were soldiers observing the installation rites.

15. The sergeant here speaks in pidgin, ordering Simayi out of his sight ever so rudely.

16. This was addressed to me and my brother-in-law Patrick Arinze, a teacher at a college in Ibusa (Igbuzo) who was on vacation from his studies at Ibadan University.

17. Ideophones for gunshots.

18. The shrine where the rites were being performed.

19. Ubulu-Ukwu, a sister village to Ubulu-Uno, the setting of the events of the story.

20. See chap. 5 for summary.

21. Ezemu was of Ubulu-Ukwu.

22. In his last two statements, Enyi is warning the narrator to be careful what he reveals in his story; the information about medicines and the intimate facts of history should not be readily divulged to outsiders like myself. The artist is impatient and asks Enyi to mind his business, on the ground that he is sensible enough to handle the situation appropriately.

23. This proverb is a spell to arm Ezemu with forevision in any eventuality during his journey.

24. In an earlier tale that evening, the narrator had talked about *ikoma* as a ruler's privy council.

25. The narrator's tone at this point is low and tremulous, and his mien timorous, effectively dramatizing Ezemu's brief moment of diffidence and terror. It is this histrionic effort that makes the audience laugh.

26. I think this is wrong for "sword."

27. This proverb comments on the flawless efficacy of the charm Ezemu had come to Benin with.

28. The Ezomo (or Ozoma among the Igbo) is a kind of chief of staff of the imperial army and director-general of palace affairs.

29. Proverb meaning that a man should not be long separated from his business or his belongings.

30. The Ekumeku war was a war of colonial resistance fought in this area, in which the citizens were equipped with charms, among other weapons.

31. Ideophone for the cumbrous movement of these aged women.

32. Code name for the charm, boiled in a pot *(ite),* to hold those witches down.

33. That is, one good turn deserves another; the diviner explains in lines 248ff.

34. Abudu and Ugonoba are villages between Ubulu-Ukwu and Benin, the latter much closer to Benin.

35. Although the narrator is less than accurate about the administrative delimitations in this area, the Ika tongue spoken there is somewhat a mixture of Bini and Igbo elements.

36. During the Nigerian civil war, many of the Igbo of the (then) Midwest State suffered the fate of their kith and kin in secessionist Biafra with particular severity because they were said to have facilitated the movement of the Biafrans from the east. The federal army included many Bini, and the narrator apparently implies that the Bini had a hand in the killing of Ubulu soldiers during the war. Oba Akenzua II of Benin died a few years after the war.

37. Okoojii came as accompanist to Ojiudu Okeze (see Okpewho 1983: 58–59). They are close friends and have long performed together. The recording was done in the yard of my brother-in-law Patrick Ibe Arinze at St. Thomas's College, Ibusa, on the night of October 3, 1980. There was an audience of about twelve.

38. The narrator can't seem to decide, or doesn't think it matters.

39. An obvious slip of the tongue.

40. The ogre does not, of course, understand that the girl is trying to call her lover's attention; he probably takes "dear warrior" as a praise of him.

41. See Okpewho 1979: 74.

8. Witticisms

1. For general studies of the proverb, see esp. Abrahams 1972, Browne 1968, Mieder 1985, Taylor 1985 (1931). For recent area studies see esp. Penfield 1983, Seitel 1976, Yankah 1986b, Zholkovsky 1984.

2. Chinua Achebe tells us in his novel *Things Fall Apart* (1962: 6) that in Igbo conversations, "proverbs are the palm-oil with which words are eaten." The Fon of Benin Republic (as well as the Yoruba of Nigeria) describe proverbs as the "horses of speech" (Olatunji 1984: 170).

3. That is, communities in the Aniocha local government area of Nigeria.

4. On the problem of riddle definition, see esp. Georges and Dundes 1963 and Scott 1976.

5. Cf. Messenger 1960: 232.

9. Musical and Dramatic Forms

1. See the hunter's chant in chapter 5.

2. We shall use forward (´) and backward (`) strokes for high and low tones as against Carrington's system.

3. The horn player is also a familiar figure in many a folktale, where his strains serve especially to warn a hero of coming danger. See, for instance, *The Ozidi Saga* (Clark 1977), p. 312. With regard to flute praises, we will recall how, in Chinua Achebe's *Things Fall Apart*, Okonkwo's father fires him to victory in a wrestling match by blowing his praises on a flute.

4. Money is routinely collected from the audiences at these *bori* displays.

5. On Ologbojo, see further Adedeji 1977: 188.

6. Cf. Olajubu 1977 for Alarinjo as masquerades representing ancestors.

7. Cf. Ugonna 1984: 70.

8. For a detailed discussion of the function and significance of voice modifiers, see Proschan 1981.

9. For further examples of the rather popular theme of adultery in Bamana folk theatre, see Delafosse 1916 and Labouret and Travélé 1928.

10. The phrase is borrowed from Thomas Green (1981), who sees the stock themes and episodes as the guiding "text" of the performances. Any association of "script" here with writing should, however, be avoided.

11. See Adedeji 1981: 244–45.

12. Slangy English has been used in the variety shows, just to be modish.

13. See the interview with Ogunmola in Jeyifo 1984: 138.

14. See Jeyifo 1984: 89 for an interesting interview with Ogunde on the family-business character of his troupes.

15. Moses Olaiya has taken a further innovative step: film clips feature in some of his stage shows.

16. See further Ogunba 1978: 25.

10. Oral Literature and Modern African Literature

1. Mofolo's *Chaka* was published first in the Sesotho language in 1925, then in an English translation by F. H. Dutton (1930). A more authoritative translation by fellow Sotho Daniel Kunene was published in 1981.

2. This is an invocation to a legendary *griot* of Old Mali, said to be Sunjata's hunting companion and originator of the Sunjata epic.

3. I have added the italics in this passage and the next one quoted to identify the reflective comments from the audience as recorded by Liyong.

4. Birago Diop's *Tales of Amadou Koumba* is another translation—perhaps *retelling* is a better word—which stylizes the nuances of the oral narrative tradition.

5. For a detailed critique of these liberties, see Okpewho 1983: 166–74.

6. This is an ideophone for the chug-chug movement (or choo-choo sound) of the train.

7. We also learn from Heron, in his introduction to the *Songs* (p'Bitek 1984: 3), that Okot had written a novel in Acoli in 1953.

8. Wole Soyinka has translated *Ogboju Ode ninu Igbo Irunmale* as *The Forest of a Thousand Daemons* (1968). The four other Fagunwa novels are *Igbo Olodumare* (1949), *Ireke Onibudo* (1949), *Irinkerinto ninu Igbo Elegbeje* (1954), and *Adiitu Olodumare* (1961).

9. Ogundipe-Leslie says that sixteen of the book's twenty-four episodes are "unoriginal." See Lindfors 1975: 235–37 for a detailed discussion of Tutuola's sources and analogues.

10. See chap. 8 on puns and tongue-twisters.

11. Growing up in the 1940s and 1950s, when the rising Western technology of sight and sound—the cinema and concert music—was infiltrating Nigerian cultural life and entertainment, Tutuola was obviously open to the same influences that we saw operating in the arts of Hubert Ogunde and Bobby Benson in chap. 9.

12. My oral informants frequently use the same abbreviation device in their stories in the form of the proverb "a tale is born on the same day that it is conceived."

13. For more discussion of the role of songs in the oral narrative performance, see Okpewho 1983: 94–95.

14. Soyinka translates *Abibiman* (an Akan word) as meaning "the Black Nation; the land of the Black Peoples; the Black World; that which pertains to, the matter, the affair of, Black peoples" (1976b: 23).

15. I.e., the United Nations, where sanctions had been urged against the South African government and the government of Rhodesia.

16. For these last words, see Daniel Kunene's translation (1981: 167) of Thomas Mofolo's *Chaka*.

17. Although Professor dryly compares the road to a woman (p. 58), Ogunba has aptly noted the absence of women in the play (1975: 162).

18. This is Soyinka's translation of a Yoruba prayer popular among drivers: *Aa ni rin ni'jo t'ebi np'ona*. For further discussion on the use of language in this play, see Izevbaye 1976.

19. See various poems in the collection *Idanre and Other Poems* (1967), and compare the novel *The Interpreters* (1965). Soyinka holds a government position as chairman of the Federal Road Safety Commission.

20. Accounts of this incident are contained in Soyinka 1967b: 82–83 and 1976a: 27–28.

11. Preserving Oral Literature

1. Of the numerous fieldwork guides, the following are particularly recommended for oral literature: Goldstein 1964, Ives 1980, Jackson 1987, Leach 1962, MacDonald 1972, and Okafor 1979. For ethical issues involved in fieldwork generally, see esp. Cassell 1980, Gattrell 1979, and Georges and Jones 1980.

2. The controversy reported here is contained in Gattrell 1979, which is a detailed critique of Slater 1976.

3. For an even more celebrated case of disagreement between two scholars working on the same society, though at widely different times, see Freeman's critique (1983) of Margaret Mead's ethnography of Samoa.

4. For Aniemeka's contributions see Okpewho 1983: 62–63.

5. The artist Simayi tells an incredible number of proverbs and anecdotes during interviews, and it would be a shame to discourage this, since he does the same thing in the tales.

6. Says Ives (1980: 98): "Dialect is important, but a transcription should not be made to bear the burden of it." This view is clearly not good enough for the transcription of non-English texts. Even for English texts, would it make sense to transcribe African American street toasts in "standard" English?

7. These scholars were among the earliest anthropologists. The classic anthropological position on translation is contained in the statement by Claude Lévi-Strauss on myth (1968: 210).

8. These techniques are best illustrated in Tedlock's classic translation of Zuni mythology, *Finding the Center* (1972).

9. I have treated other issues of textual representation of oral literature in an earlier paper (Okpewho 1977).

10. See Ives 1980: 111–14 and Jackson 1987: 269–74.

12. Suggested Further Work

1. For examples of new compositions, see Azuonye 1990 and Simayi's civil war story in chap. 7. Cf. Ise 1986.

2. See also Okpewho 1990b.

3. Examples are Ude 1981, Oruobu 1978, Gbenoba 1987, Ijaduolu 1985, Okoiruele 1982, Otiono 1989.

4. Cf. Yai 1989.

5. Cf. also Finnegan 1988.

Bibliography

Abimbola, W. 1975. *Sixteen Great Poems of Ifa*. Paris: UNESCO.

———. 1976. *Ifa: An Exposition of Ifa Literary Corpus*. Ibadan: Oxford University Press.

Abrahams. R. D. 1970. *Deep Down in the Jungle . . . : Negro Narrative Folklore from the Streets of Philadelphia*. Chicago: Aldine (1964).

———. 1972. Proverbs and Proverbial Expressions. In *Folklore and Folklife*, ed. R. M. Dorson. Chicago: University of Chicago Press.

———. 1983. *African Folktales*. New York: Pantheon.

Achebe, C. 1962. *Things Fall Apart*. London: Heinemann (1958).

———, and Iroaganchi, J. 1972. *How the Leopard Got Its Claws*. Enugu: Nwankwo-Ifejika.

Adali-Mortty, G. 1979. Ewe Poetry. In *Introduction to African Literature*, ed. U. Beier. London: Longman.

Adedeji, J. A. 1977. Trends in the Content and Form of the Opening Glee in Yoruba Drama. In *Forms of Folklore in Africa*, ed. B. Lindfors. Austin: University of Texas Press.

———. 1981. Alarinjo: The Traditional Yoruba Traveling Theatre. In *Drama and Theatre in Nigeria*, ed. Y. Ogunbiyi. Lagos: Nigeria Magazine.

Afolayan, A. 1975. Language and Sources of Amos Tutuola. In *Critical Perspectives on Amos Tutuola*, ed. B. Lindfors. London: Heinemann.

Akeremale, Y. 1980. Function and Aesthetics in Folklore. Ritual Poetry: A Case Study of Aiyelala from Okitipupa. B.A. honors essay, Department of English, University of Ibadan.

Alagoa, E. J. 1968. The Use of Oral Literary Data for History: Examples from Niger Delta Proverbs. *Journal of American Folklore*, 81: 235–42.

Andrzjewski, B. W., and Lewis, I. M. 1964. *Somali Poetry*. Oxford: Clarendon Press.

Angmor, C. 1978. Drama in Ghana. In *Drama in Africa*, ed. O. Ogunba and A. Irele. Ibadan: Ibadan University Press.

Anyidoho, K. 1977. The Anlo Dirge Poet, Domegbe. Paper presented at the Conference on Oral Poetry in Africa, University of Ibadan.

Arewa, R. O. 1970. Proverb Usage in Natural Context and Oral Literary Criticism. *Journal of American Folklore*, 83: 430–37.

———, and Dundes, A. 1964. Proverbs and the Ethnography of Speaking Folklore. *American Anthropologist*, 66.6 (part 2): 70–86.

Armstrong, R. G. 1983. Idoma Origin Myth. In Okpewho 1983: 82.

Arnott, D. W. 1957. Proverbial Lore and Word-Play of the Fulani. *Africa*, 27: 379–96.

Avorgbedor, D. 1990. The Preservation, Transmission and Realization of Song-texts: A Psycho-musical Approach. In Okpewho, ed. 1990.

Awona, S. 1965–66. La Guerre d'Akoma Mba contre Abo Mama. *Abbia*, 9–10: 180–214; 12–13: 109–209.

Awoonor, K. 1974. *Guardians of the Sacred Word*. New York: Nok Press.

Ayewoh, M. E. 1979. Tradition and Originality in Ishan Poetry and Weaving. B.A. honors essay, Department of English, University of Ibadan.

Azuonye, C. 1983. Stability and Change in the Performance of Ohafia Igbo Singers of Tales. *Research in African Literatures*, 14: 332–80.

———. 1990. Kaalu Igirigiri: An Ohafia Igbo Singer of Tales. In Okpewho, ed. 1990.

Babalola, S. A. 1966. *The Content and Form of Yoruba Ijala*. Oxford: Clarendon Press.

Bascom, W. R. 1949. Literary Style in Yoruba Riddles. *Journal of American Folklore*, 62: 2–15.

———. 1955. Verbal Art. *Journal of American Folklore*, 68: 245–52.

———. 1959. *Ifa Divination*. Bloomington: Indiana University Press.

———. 1965. Four Functions of Folklore. In Dundes, ed. 1965.

———. 1977a. Oba's Ear: A Yoruba Myth in Cuba and Brazil. In *African Folklore in the New World*, ed. D. J. Crowley. Austin: University of Texas Press.

———. 1977b. Introduction. In *Frontiers of Folklore*, ed. W. R. Bascom. Boulder: Westview Press.

Basden, G. T. 1938. *Niger Ibos*. London: Seely Service.

Beattie, J. 1969. Spirit Mediumship in Bunyoro. In *Spirit Mediumship and Society in Africa*, ed. J. Beattie and J. Middleton. London: Routledge and Kegan Paul.

Beidelman, T. O. 1961. Hyena and Rabbit: A Kaguru Representation of Matrilineal Relations. *Africa*, 31: 61–74.

Beier, U., ed. 1966a. *African Poetry*. Cambridge: Cambridge University Press.

———. 1966b. *The Origin of Life and Death: African Creation Myths*. London: Heinemann.

———. 1979. Yoruba Theatre. In *Introduction to African Literature*, ed. U. Beier. London: Longman (1967).

———, and B. Gbadamosi, eds. 1959. *Yoruba Poetry*. Ibadan: Government Printer.

Belinga, E. 1965. *Littérature et musique populaire en Afrique Noire*. Paris: Cujas.

Ben-Amos, D. 1971. *Sweet Words: Storytelling Events in Benin*. Philadelphia: Institute for the Study of Human Issues.

———. 1972. Two Benin Storytellers: In *African Folklore*, ed. R. Dorson. Bloomington: Indiana University Press.

———. 1976. Analytical Categories and Ethnic Genres. In *Folklore Genres*, ed. D. Ben-Amos. Austin: University of Texas Press.

———. 1977. Introduction: Folklore in African Society. In *Forms of Folklore in Africa*, ed. B. Lindfors. Austin: University of Texas Press.

Berry, J. 1961. *Spoken Art in West Africa*. London: School of Oriental and African Studies.

Beuchat, P. D. 1965. Riddles in Bantu. In Dundes, ed. 1965.

Biebuyck, D. 1978. *Hero and Chief: Epic Literature of the Banyanga*. Berkeley: University of California Press.

———, and Mateene, K. C. 1969. *The Mwindo Epic from the Banyanga*. Berkeley: University of California Press.

Bird, C., et al., eds. 1974. *The Songs of Seydou Camara I: Kambili*. Bloomington: African Studies Center, Indiana University.

p'Bitek, O. 1974. *Horn of My Love*. London: Heinemann.

———. 1978. *Hare and Hornbill*. London: Heinemann.

———. 1984. *Song of Lawino and Song of Ocol*, ed. G. Heron. London: Heinemann (1966, 1967).

Blacking, J. 1961. The Social Value of Venda Riddles. *African Studies*, 20: 1–32.

Brill, A. A., ed. 1938. *The Basic Writings of Sigmund Freud*. New York: Random House.

Brink. J. T. 1977. Bamana Kote-tlon Theatre. *African Arts*, 10: 36, 61–65, 87.

———. 1982. Time Consciousness and Growing up in Bamana Folk Drama. *Journal of American Folklore*, 95: 415–34.

Browne, R. B. 1968. "The Wisdom of Many": Proverbs and Proverbial Genres. In *American Folklore*, ed. Tristram Coffin III. Washington: Voice of America Forum Lectures.

Burton, R. F. 1865. *Wit and Wisdom from West Africa*. London: Tinsley Brothers.

Carrington, J. 1949. *Talking Drums of Africa*. London: Carey Kingsgate Press.

Cassell, J. 1980. Ethical Principles for Conducting Fieldwork. *American Anthropologist*, 82: 28–41.

Cham, M. B. 1990. Art and Society in Oral Narrative and Film. In Okpewho, ed. 1990.

Chesnais, J. 1965. African Puppets. *World Theatre*, 14: 448–51.

Christensen, J. B. 1958. The Role of Proverbs in Fante Culture. *Africa*, 28: 232–43.

Clark, E. 1979. *Hubert Ogunde: The Making of Nigerian Theatre*. Ibadan: Oxford University Press.

Clark, J. P. 1963. The Azudu Saga. *African Notes*, 1: 8–9.

———. 1966. *Ozidi: A Play*. London: Oxford University Press.

———. 1977. *The Ozidi Saga*. Ibadan: Ibadan University Press/Oxford University Press.

Cope, T. 1968. *Izibongo: Zulu Praise Poems*. Oxford: Clarendon Press.

Cosentino, D. 1982. *Defiant Maids and Stubborn Farmers*. Cambridge: Cambridge University Press.

Coupez, A., and Kamanzi, Th. 1970. *Littérature de cour au Rwanda*. Oxford: Clarendon Press.

Crowley, D. J., ed. 1977. *African Folklore in the New World*. Austin: University of Texas Press.

Daaku, K. Y. 1971. History in the Oral Traditions of the Akan. *Journal of the Folklore Institute*, 8: 114–26.

Damane, M., and Sanders, P. B. 1974. *Lithoko: Sotho Praise-Poems*. Oxford: Clarendon Press.

Darah, G. G. 1982. Battles of Songs: A Study of Satire in the *Udje* Dance-Songs of the Urhobo of Nigeria. Ph.D. thesis, Department of English, University of Ibadan.

Delafosse, M. 1916. Contribution a l'étude du théâtre chez les noirs. *Annuaire et Mémoires du Comité d'Etudes Historiques et Scientifiques de l'Afrique Occidentale Française*, 352–55.

Deng, F. M. 1973. *The Dinka and Their Songs*. Oxford: Clarendon Press.

Dennet, R. E. 1898. *Notes on the Folklore of the Fjort, French Congo*. London: David Nutt.

Diop, B. 1985. *Tales of Amadou Koumba*, trans. D. S. Blair. London: Longman (1966).

Doke, C. M. 1934. Lamba Literature. *Africa*, 7: 351–70.

———. 1947. Bantu Wisdom-Lore. *African Studies*, 6: 101–20.

Dorson, R. M. 1975. *American Negro Folktales*. Greenwich: Fawcett.

———. 1979. *Land of the Millrats*. Cambridge, Mass: Harvard University Press.

Dundes, A. 1971. The Making and Breaking of Friendship as a Structural Frame in African Folktales. In *Structural Analysis of Oral Tradition*, ed. P. and E. Maranda. Philadelphia: University of Pennsylvania Press.

———. 1977a. Who Are the Folk? In *Frontiers of Folklore*, ed. W. R. Bascom. Boulder: Westview Press.

———. 1977b African and Afro-American Tales. In *African Folklore in the New World*, ed. D. J. Crowley. Austin: University of Texas Press.

———, ed. 1965. *The Study of Folklore*. Englewood Cliffs: Prentice-Hall.

Eastman, C. M. 1972. The Proverb in Modern Written Swahili Literature: An Aid to Proverb Elicitation. In *African Folklore*, ed. R. M. Dorson. Bloomington: Indiana University Press.

Echeruo, M. J. C. 1973. The Dramatic Limits of Igbo Ritual. *Research in African Literatures*, 4: 21–31.

Edemode, J. 1979. The Hero in Uzairue Heroic Narratives. B.A. honors essay, Department of English, University of Ibadan.

Egharevba, J. U. 1960. *A Short History of Benin*. Ibadan: Ibadan University Press.

Egudu, R. N. 1975. The Forms of Igbo Traditional Poetry. *African Studies*, 34: 203–10.

———, and Nwoga, D. I., eds. 1971. *Poetic Heritage: Igbo Traditional Verse*. Enugu: Nwankwo-Ifejika.

Ellis, A. B. 1887. *The Tshi-speaking Peoples of the Gold Coast of West Africa*. London: Chapman and Hall.

Ellison, R. E. 1935. A Bornu Puppet Show. *Nigerian Field*, 4: 89–91.

Enekwe, O. 1981. Myth, Ritual and Drama in Igboland. In *Drama and Theatre in Nigeria*, ed. Y. Ogunbiyi. Lagos: Nigeria Magazine.

Ennis, E. L. 1945. Women's Names Among the Ovimbundu of Angola. *African Studies*, 4: 3–15.

Finnegan, R. 1967. *Limba Stories and Storytelling*. Oxford: Clarendon Press.

———. 1970. *Oral Literature in Africa*. Oxford: Clarendon Press.

———. 1988. *Literacy and Orality*. Oxford: Blackwell.

Firth, R. 1959. Problems and Assumptions in an Anthropological Study of Religion. *Journal of the Royal Anthropological Institute*. 89: 129–48.

Frazer, J. G. 1911–36. *The Golden Bough: A Study in Magic and Religion*. London: Macmillan.

Freeman, D. 1983. *Margaret Mead and Samoa: The Making and Unmaking of an Anthropological Myth*. Cambridge, Mass.: Harvard University Press.

Gattrell, B. 1979. Is Ethnography Possible? *Journal of Anthropological Research*, 35: 426–46.

Gbenoba, F. E. 1987. When a Performer Changes His Audience and Patronage. M. A. project, Department of English, University of Ibadan.

Georges, R. A., and Dundes, A. 1963. Toward a Structural Definition of the Riddle. *Journal of American Folklore,* 76: 111–18.

———, and Jones, M. O. 1980. *People Studying People: The Human Element in Fieldwork.* Berkeley: University of California Press.

Goldstein, K. S. 1964. *A Guide for Field Workers in Folklore.* Hatboro: Folklore Associates.

Goody, J. 1972. *The Myth of the Bagre.* Oxford: Clarendon Press.

———. 1977. *The Domestication of the Savage Mind.* Cambridge: Cambridge University Press.

———. 1987. *The Interface between the Written and the Oral.* Cambridge: Cambridge University Press.

———. ed. 1968. *Literacy in Traditional Societies.* Cambridge: Cambridge University Press.

Green, T. A. 1981. Introduction to special issue on Folk Drama. *Journal of American Folklore,* 94: 431–32.

Grenfell-Williams, G. ed. N.d. *BBC Network Africa: Myths and Legends.* London: British Broadcasting Corporation.

Griaule, M. 1965. *Conversations with Ogotemmeli.* London: Oxford University Press.

Hagher, I. 1980. The Kwagh-hir: An Analysis of a Contemporary Indigenous Puppet Theatre and Its Social and Cultural Significance in Tivland in the 1960s and 1970s. Ph.D. thesis, Ahmadu Bello University, Zaria.

Hamnett, I. 1967. Ambiguity, Classification and Change: The Function of Riddles. *Man,* 2: 379–92.

Haring, I. 1974. On Knowing the Answer. *Journal of American Folklore,* 87: 197–207.

Harries, J. 1977. Pattern and Choice in Berber Weaving and Poetry. In *Forms of Folklore in Africa,* ed. B. Lindfors. Austin: University of Texas Press.

Harries, L. 1942a. Makua Song-Riddles from the Initiation Rites. *African Studies,* 1: 27–46.

———. 1942b. Some Riddles of the Makua People. *African Studies,* 1: 275–91.

———. 1971. The Riddle in Africa. *Journal of American Folklore,* 84: 377–93.

———. 1976. Semantic Fit in Riddles. *Journal of American Folklore,* 89: 319–25.

Henige, D. 1982. *Oral Historiography.* London: Longman.

Henngeler, J. 1981. Ivory Trumpets of the Mende. *African Arts,* 14, no. 2: 59–63.

Heron, G. 1984. Introduction to p'Bitek 1984.

Herskovits, M. and F. 1958. *Dahomean Narrative: A Cross-Cultural Analysis.* Evanston: Northwestern University Press.

Horn, A. 1981. Ritual Drama and the Theatrical: The Case of *Bori* Spirit Mediumship. In *Drama and Theatre in Nigeria: A Critical Source Book,* ed. Y. Ogunbiyi. Lagos: Nigeria Magazine.

Horton, R. 1970. African Traditional Thought and Western Science. In *Rationality,* ed. B. R. Wilson. Oxford: Blackwell.

Hunt, N. A. 1952. Some Karanga Riddles. *Nada,* 29: 90–98.

Ijaduolu, O. E. 1985. Potrait of an Oral Artist: Oyekunle Agbegende Alufagejo of Abeokuta, Ogun State. B.A. honors essay, Department of English, University of Ibadan.

Innes, G. 1974. *Sunjata: Three Mandinka Versions.* London: School of Oriental and African Studies.

———. 1976. *Kaabu and Fuladu: Historical Narratives of the Gambian Mandinka.* London: School of Oriental and African Studies.

———. 1978. *Kelefa Saane: His Career Recounted by Two Mandinka Bards.* London: School of Oriental and African Studies.

———. 1990. Formulae in Mandinka Epic: The Problem of Translation. In Okpewho, ed. 1990.

Ipinmisho, B. 1980. Art as a Mirror of Life: The Case Study of a Folktale in Ogidi-Ijumu, Kwara State. B.A. honors essay, Department of English, University of Ibadan.

Ise, J. I. 1986. Once There Was a War: Personal Narratives from the Nigerian Civil War. B.A. honors essay, Department of English, University of Ibadan.

Ives, E. D. 1964. *Larry Gorman: The Man Who Made the Songs*. Bloomington: Indiana University Press.

———. 1980. *The Tape Recorded Interview*. Knoxville: University of Tennessee Press.

———. 1986. *Joe Scott: The Woodsman-Songmaker*. Urbana: University of Illinois Press.

Izevbaye, D. S. 1976. Language and Meaning in Soyinka's *The Road*. *African Literature Today*, 8: 52–65.

Jackson, B. 1987. *Fieldwork*. Urbana: University of Illinois Press.

Jackson, M. 1982. *Allegories of the Wilderness: Ethics and Ambiguity in Kuranko Narratives*. Bloomington: Indiana University Press.

Jansen, H. 1968. Riddles: "Do-It-Yourself Oracles." In *American Folklore*, ed. T. P. Coffin. Washington: Voice of America Forum Lectures.

Jeyifo, B. 1984. *The Yoruba Popular Travelling Theatre of Nigeria*. Lagos: Nigeria Magazine.

———. 1985. *The Truthful Lie: Essays in a Sociology of African Drama*. London: New Beacon.

Johnson, J. W. 1986. *The Epic of Son-Jara: A West African Tradition*. Bloomington: Indiana University Press.

Jones, A. M. 1959. *Studies in African Music*, Vol. 1. London: Oxford University Press.

Jones, E. D. 1973. *The Writing of Wole Soyinka*. London: Heinemann.

Junod, H. 1912–13. *The Life of a South African Tribe*. 2 vols. Neuchatel: Attinger Frères.

Kaemmer, J. E. 1977. Tone Riddles from Southern Mozambique: *Titekatekani* of the Tshwa. In *Forms of Folklore in Africa*, ed. B. Lindfors. Austin: University of Texas Press.

Kallen, J. L., and Eastman, C. M. 1979. "I Went to Mombasa / There I Met an Old Man": Structure and Meaning in Swahili Riddles. *Journal of American Folklore*, 92: 418–44.

Keil, C. 1979. *Tiv Song*. Chicago: University of Chicago Press.

Kilson, M. 1976. *Royal Antelope and Spider: West African Mende Tales*. Cambridge, Mass.: Langdon Associates.

King, A. 1974. Music. In Innes 1974.

Kipury, N. 1983. *Oral Literature of the Maasai*. Nairobi: Heinemann.

Knappert, J. 1966. Swahili Rhyming Proverbs. *Afrika and Ubersee*, 59: 59–88.

———. 1970. *Myths and Legends of the Swahili*. London: Heinemann.

Kunene, D. P. 1970. *Heroic Poetry of the Basotho*. Oxford: Clarendon Press.

———, trans. 1981. *Thomas Mofolo: Chaka*. London: Heinemann.

Kunene, M. 1979. *Emperor Shaka the Great*. London: Heinemann.

Kyaagba, A. H. 1978. Kwagh-hir: The Musico-Dramatic Art of the Tiv as Oral Literature. B.A. honors essay, Department of English, University of Ibadan.

Labouret, H., and Travélé, M. 1928. Le Théâtre Mandingue (Soudan Francaise). *Africa*, 1: 73–97.

Larrabee, E. 1975. Palm-Wine Drinkard Searches for a Tapster (review). In *Critical Perspectives on Amos Tutuola*, ed. B. Lindfors. London: Heinemann.

Lasebikan, E. L. 1955. Tone in Yoruba Poetry. *Odu*, 2: 35–36.

Leach, E. 1969. *Genesis as Myth and Other Essays*. London: Jonathan Cape.

Leach, MacE. 1962. Problems of Collecting Oral Literature. *Publications of the Modern Language Association*, 77: 335–40.

Lestrade, G. P. 1937. Traditional Literature. In *The Bantu-speaking Tribes of South Africa*, ed. I. Schapera. London: Routledge.

Lévi-Strauss, C. 1958. The Structural Study of Myth. In *Myth: A Symposium*, ed. T. A. Sebeok. Bloomington: Indiana University Press.

———. 1966. *The Savage Mind*. London: Weidenfeld and Nicolson.

———. 1964. *Le Cru et le cuit*. Paris: Plon. Trans. J. and D. Weightman as *The Raw and the Cooked* (New York: Harper and Row, 1970). Vol. 1 of *Mythologiques*.

———. 1966. *Du Miel au cendres*. Paris: Plon. Trans. J. and D. Weightman as *From Honey to Ashes* (New York: Harper and Row, 1972). Vol. 2 of *Mythologiques*.

———. 1968. *L'Origine des maniéres de table*. Paris: Plon. Trans. J. and D. Weightman as *The Origin of Table Manners* (New York: Harper and Row, 1979). Vol. 3 of *Mythologiques*.

———. 1971. *L'Homme nu*. Paris: Plon. Vol. 4 of *Mythologiques*.

————. 1977. The Story of Asdiwal. In *Structural Anthropology*, vol. 2. London: Allen Lane.

Lindfors, B. 1975. Amos Tutuola: Debts and Assets. In *Critical Perspectives on Amos Tutuola*, ed. B. Lindfors. London: Heinemann.

Liyong, T. lo. 1969a. *The Last Word*. Nairobi: East African Publishing House.

————. 1969b. *Fixions and Other Stories*. London: Heinemann.

————, ed. 1972. *Popular Culture of East Africa*. Nairobi: Longman Kenya.

Lord, A. B. 1960. *The Singer of Tales*. Cambridge, Mass.: Harvard University Press.

————, ed. 1956. *Slavic Folklore: A Symposium*. Philadelphia: American Folklore Society.

MacDonald, D. A. 1972. Fieldwork: Collecting Oral Literature. In *Folklore and Folklife*, ed. R. M. Dorson. Chicago: University of Chicago Press.

McLuhan, M. 1962. *The Gutenberg Galaxy: The Making of Typographic Man*. Toronto: University of Toronto Press.

Mafeje, A. 1963. A Chief Visits Town. *Journal of Local Administration Overseas*, 2: 88–99.

Malinowski, B. 1922. *Argonauts of the Western Pacific*. London: Routledge.

————. 1926. *Myth in Primitive Psychology*. New York: Norton.

Mapanje, J., and White, L., eds. 1983. *Oral Poetry from Africa*. London: Longman.

Mayr, F. 1912. Zulu Proverbs. *Anthropos*, 7: 952–65.

Merriam, A. P. 1973. The Bala Musician. In *The Traditional Artist in African Societies*, ed. W. L. d'Azevedo. Bloomington: Indiana University Press.

Messenger, J. C. 1960. Anang Proverb-Riddles. *Journal of American Folklore*, 73: 225–35.

————. 1965. The Role of Proverbs in a Nigerian Judicial System. In *The Study of Folklore*, ed. A. Dundes. Englewood Cliffs: Prentice-Hall.

————. 1971. Ibibio Drama. *Africa*, 41: 207–22.

Mieder, W. 1985. Popular Views of the Proverb. *Proverbium*, 2: 109–43.

Moore, G. 1971. *Wole Soyinka*. London: Evans Brothers.

————. 1975. Amos Tutuola: A Nigerian Visionary. In *Critical Perspectives on Amos Tutuola*, ed. B. Lindfors. London: Heinemann.

Morris, H. F. 1964. *The Heroic Recitations of the Bahima of Ankole*. Oxford: Clarendon Press.

Mubitana, K. 1971. Wiko Masquerades. *African Arts*, 4, no. 3: 58–62.

Mvula, E. S. T. 1982a. Chewa Folk Narrative Performance. *Kalulu*, 3: 32–45.

————. 1982b. Four Songs from Malawi. *Kalulu*, 3: 62–64.

————. 1990. The Performance of *Gule Wamkulu*. In Okpewho, ed. 1990.

Mwangi, R. 1982. *Kikuyu Folktales*. Nairobi: Kenya Literature Bureau.

Nakene, G. 1943. Tlokwa Riddles. *African Studies*, 2: 125–38.

Nandwa, J., and Bukenya, A. 1983. *African Oral Literature for Schools*. Nairobi: Longman Kenya.

Nettl, B. 1956. *Music in Primitive Culture*. Cambridge, Mass.: Harvard University Press.

Niane, D. T. 1965. *Sundiata: An Epic of Old Mali*, trans. G. D. Pickett. London: Longman.

Nketia, J. H. K. 1955. *Funeral Dirges of the Akan Peoples*. Achimota: Ghana Universities Press.

————. 1963a. *African Music in Ghana*. Evanston: Northwestern University Press.

————. 1963b. *Drumming in Akan Communities of Ghana*. Edinburgh: Thomas Nelson.

————. 1973. The Musician in Akan Society. In *The Traditional Artist in African Societies*, ed. W. L. d'Azevedo. Bloomington: Indiana University Press.

————. 1979. Akan Poetry. In *Introduction to African Literature*, ed. U. Beier. London: Longman.

Nwoga, D. I. 1981. The Igbo Poet and Satire. In *Oral Poetry in Nigeria*, ed. U. N. Abalogu, G. Ashiwaju, and R. Amadi-Tshiwala. Lagos: Nigeria Magazine.

Nzekwu, O. 1981. Masquerade. In *Drama and Theatre in Nigeria*, ed. Y. Ogunbiyi. Lagos: Nigeria Magazine.

Obiechina, E. N. 1975. Amos Tutuola and Oral Tradition. In *Critical Perspectives on Amos Tutuola*, ed. B. Lindfors. London: Heinemann.

Ogbalu, F. C. 1974. *Igbo Poems and Songs*. Onitsha: University Publishing Company.

Ogunba, O. 1975. *The Movement of Transition*. Ibadan: Ibadan University Press.

———. 1978. Traditional African Festival Drama. In *Drama in Africa*, ed. O. Ogunba and A. Irele. Ibadan: Ibadan University Press.

Ogundipe, A. 1972. Yoruba Tongue Twisters. In *African Folklore*, ed. R. M. Dorson. Bloomington: Indiana University Press.

Ogundipe-Leslie, O. 1975. *The Palm-Wine Drinkard:* A Reassessment of Amos Tutuola. In *Critical Perspectives on Amos Tutuola*, ed. B. Lindfors. London: Heinemann.

Okafor, C. A. 1979. Research Methodology in African Oral Literature. *Okike*, 16: 83–97.

Okogbo, M. M. 1988. The Glory of the Game: A Study of Isiko, The Hunters' Performance in Auchi. B.A. honors essay, Department of English, University of Ibadan.

Okoiruele, I. E. 1982. The Oral Artist and His Society: A Portrait of Chief Umobuarie Igberaese. B.A. honors essay, Department of English, University of Ibadan.

Okpewho, I. 1977. Oral Narratives: How Healthy Are Our Texts? Paper delivered at the Conference on Oral Poetry in Africa, University of Ibadan.

———. 1979. *The Epic in Africa: Toward a Poetics of the Oral Performance*. New York: Columbia University Press.

———. 1983. *Myth in Africa: A Study of Its Aesthetic and Cultural Relevance*. Cambridge: Cambridge University Press.

———. 1987. "Once Upon a Kingdom . . .": Benin in the Heroic Traditions of Bendel State, Nigeria. In *The Heroic Process*, ed. B. Almqvist, S. O'Cathain, and P. O'Healai. Dublin: Glendale Press.

———. 1988. African Poetry: The Modern Writer and the Oral Tradition. *African Literature Today*, 16: 3–25.

———. 1990a. Towards a Faithful Record: On Transcribing and Translating the Oral Narrative Performance. In Okpewho, ed. 1990.

———. 1990b. The Oral Performer and His Audience: A Case Study of *The Ozidi Saga*. In Okpewho, ed. 1990.

———, ed. 1985. *The Heritage of African Poetry*. London: Longman.

———, ed. 1990. *The Oral Performance in Africa*. Ibadan: Spectrum.

Olajubu, O. 1977a. Oriki: The Essence of Yoruba Oral Poetry. Paper delivered at the Conference on Oral Poetry in Africa, University of Ibadan.

———. 1977b. Iwi Egungun Chants: An Introduction. In *Forms of Folklore in Africa*, ed. B. Lindfors. Austin: University of Texas Press.

Olatunji, O. 1984. *Features of Yoruba Oral Poetry*. Ibadan: University Press Ltd.

Ong, W. J. 1982. *Orality and Literacy: The Technologizing of the Word*. London: Methuen.

Onwuejeogwu, M. 1969. The Cult of the Bori Spirits among the Hausa. In *Spirit Mediumship and Society in Africa*, ed. J. Beattie and J. Middleton. London: Oxford University Press.

Opland, J. 1983. *Xhosa Oral Poetry*. Cambridge: Cambridge University Press.

Oruobu, D. K. J. 1978. Rex Jim Lawson and the Tradition of Kalabari Folk Song. B.A. honors essay, Department of English, University of Ibadan.

Otiono, A. N. 1989. Eke Momah: A Portrait of an Oral Artist. M.A. thesis, Department of English, University of Ibadan.

Ousmane, S. 1972. *The Money-Order*, trans. C. Wake. London: Heinemann.

Parry, M. 1971. *The Making of Homeric Verse*, ed. A. Parry. Oxford: Clarendon Press.

Penfield, J. A. 1983. *Communicating with Quotes: The Igbo Case*. Westport: Greenwood Press.

Polunin, I. 1970. Visual and Sound Recording Apparatus in Ethnographic Fieldwork. *Current Anthropology*, 11: 3–22.

Propp, V. 1968. *The Morphology of the Folktale*, trans. L. Scott. Austin: University of Texas Press.

Proschan, F. 1981. Puppet Voices and Interlocutors. *Journal of American Folklore*, 94: 527–55.

Raa, E. ten. 1969. The Moon as a Symbol of Life and Fertility in Sandawe Thought. *Africa*, 39: 24–53.

Rassner, R. 1990. Narrative Rhythms in Agiryama *Ngano:* Oral Patterns and Musical Structures. In Okpewho, ed. 1990.

Read, M. 1937. Songs of the Ngoni People. *Bantu Studies*, 11: 14–20.

Ricard, A. 1977. The Concert Party as a Genre: The Happy Stars of Lome. In *Forms of Folklore in Africa*, ed. B. Lindfors. Austin: University of Texas Press.

Roscoe, J. 1965. *The Baganda: An Account of Their Native Customs and Beliefs*. London: Frank Cass (1911).

Rotimi, O. 1981. The Drama in African Ritual Display. In *Drama and Theatre in Nigeria*, ed. Y. Ogunbiyi. Lagos: Nigeria Magazine.

Schapera, I. 1932. Kgatla Riddles and Their Significance. *Bantu Studies*, 6: 215–31.

———. 1965. *Praise Poems of Tswana Chiefs*. Oxford: Clarendon Press.

———. 1966. Tswana Legal Maxims. *Africa*, 36: 121–34.

Scheub, H. 1972. The Art of Nongenile Mazithathu Zenani, a Gcaleka Ntsomi Performer. In *African Folklore*, ed. R. M. Dorson. Bloomington: Indiana University Press.

———. 1975. *The Xhosa Ntsomi*. Oxford: Clarendon Press.

———. 1977a. Performance of Oral Narrative. In *Frontiers of Folklore*, ed. W. R. Bascom. Boulder: Westview Press.

———. 1977b. The Technique of the Expansible Image in Xhosa *Ntsomi*-Performances. In *Forms of Folklore in Africa*, ed. B. Lindfors. Austin: University of Texas Press.

Scott, C. T. 1965. *Persian and Arabic Riddles: A Language-Centred Approach to Genre Definition*. The Hague: Mouton.

———. 1976. On Defining the Riddle. In *Folklore Genres*, ed. D. Ben-Amos. Austin: University of Texas Press.

Scribner, S., and Cole, M. 1982. *The Psychology of Literacy*. Cambridge, Mass.: Harvard University Press.

Seigmann, W., and Perani, J. 1976. Men's Masquerades of Sierra Leone and Liberia. *African Arts*, 9, no. 3: 42–47.

Seitel, P. 1976. Proverbs: The Social Use of Metaphor. In *Folklore Genres*, ed. D. Ben-Amos. Austin: University of Texas Press.

———. 1980. *See So That We May See: Performances and Interpretations of Traditional Tales from Tanzania*. Bloomington: Indiana University Press.

Sekoni, R. 1990. The Narrator, Narrative-Pattern, and Audience Experience of Oral Narrative Performance. In Okpewho, ed. 1990.

Shorter, A. 1969. Religious Values in Kimbu Historical Charters. *Africa*, 39: 227–37.

Simmons, D. 1956. Erotic Ibibio Tone Riddles. *Man*, 56: 79–82.

———. 1958. Cultural Functions of the Efik Tone Riddle. *Journal of American Folklore*, 71: 123–38.

Slater, M. 1976. *African Odyssey: An Anthropological Adventure*. Garden City: Anchor.

Smith, E. W., and Dale, A. M. 1920. *The Ila-Speaking Peoples of Northern Rhodesia*. London: Macmillan.

Soyinka, W. 1963. *Five Plays*. London: Oxford University Press.

———. 1965. *The Road*. London: Oxford University Press.

———. 1966. And After the Narcissist? *African Forum*, 1: 53–64.

———. 1967a. *Kongi's Harvest*. London: Oxford University Press.

———. 1967b. *Idanre and Other Poems*. London: Andre Deutsch.

———. 1971a. *Before the Blackout*. Ibadan: Orisun Acting Editions.

———. 1971b. *Madmen and Specialists*. London: Methuen.

———. 1976a. *Myth, Literature and the African World*. Cambridge: Cambridge University Press.

———. 1976b. *Ogun Abibiman*. London: Rex Collings.

———. 1981. *Opera Wonyosi*. London: Rex Collings.

———. 1984. *A Play of Giants*. London: Methuen.

———, and Fagunwa, D. O. 1968. *The Forest of a Thousand Daemons*. Edinburgh: Thomas Nelson.

Sutherland, E. 1975. *The Marriage of Anansewa*. London: Longman.

Talbot, P. A. 1912. *In the Shadow of the Bush*. London: Heinemann.

Taylor, A. 1985. *The Proverb*. Bern: Peter Lang (1931).

Tedlock, D. 1971. On the Translation of Style in Oral Literature. *Journal of American Folklore.* 84: 114–33.

———. 1972. *Finding the Center: Narrative Poetry of the Zuni Indians.* New York: Dial Press.

———. 1975. Learning to Listen: Oral History as Poetry. In *Envelopes of Sound,* ed. R. J Grele. Chicago: Precedent Publishing.

———. 1977. Toward an Oral Poetics. *New Literary History,* 8: 507–19.

———. 1983. *The Spoken Word and the Work of Interpretation.* Philadelphia: University of Pennsylvania Press.

Thomas, D. 1975 (1952). Blithe Spirits (Review of Amos Tutuola's *The Palm-Wine Drinkard*). In *Critical Perspectives on Amos Tutuola,* ed. B. Lindfors. London: Heinemann.

Thompson, R. F. 1983. *Flash of the Spirit.* New York: Random House.

Thompson, S. 1946. *The Folktale.* New York: Dryden Press.

———. 1955–58. *Motif-Index of Folk Literature.* 6 vols. Bloomington: Indiana University Press.

Turner, T. S. 1969. Oedipus: Time and Structure in Narrative Form. In *Forms of Symbolic Action,* ed. R. F. Spencer. Seattle: University of Washington Press.

Turner, V. W. 1974. *Dramas, Fields and Metaphors.* Ithaca: Cornell University Press.

Tutuola, A. 1952. *The Palm-Wine Drinkard.* London: Faber.

Ude, K. A. 1981. Ukwa Ufiem: The Oral Artist and His Environment. M.A. thesis, Department of English, University of Ibadan.

Ugonna, N. 1984. *Mmonwu: A Dramatic Tradition of the Igbo.* Lagos: Lagos University Press.

Vansina, J. 1965. *Oral Tradition: A Study in Historical Methodology,* trans. H. M. Wright. Harmondsworth: Penguin.

———. 1985. *Oral Tradition as History.* London: James Curry.

Whitting, C. E. T. 1940. *Hausa and Fulani Proverbs.* Lagos: Government Printer.

Williams, R. 1961. *Culture and Society 1780–1950.* Harmondsworth: Penguin.

Willis, R. G. 1964. Traditional History and Social Structure in Ufipa. *Africa,* 34: 340–52.

Yai, O. 1989. Issues in Oral Poetry: Criticism, Teaching and Translation. In *Discourse and Its Disguises: The Interpretation of African Oral Texts,* ed. K. Barber and P. de M. Farias. Birmingham: Centre for West African Studies.

Yankah, K. 1986a. Proverb Rhetoric and African Judicial Processes: The Untold Story. *Journal of American Folklore,* 99: 280–303.

———. 1986b. Proverb Speaking as a Creative Process: The Akan of Ghana. *Proverbium,* 3: 195–230.

Zahan, D. 1969. Essai sur les mythes africains d'origins de la morte. *L'Homme,* 9: 41–50.

Zemp, H. 1964. Musiciens autochtones et griots malinké chez les Dan de Côte d'Ivoire. *Cahiers d'Etudes Africaines,* 4: 371–82.

Zholkovsky, A. 1984. *Themes and Texts: Toward a Poetics of Expressiveness.* Ithaca: Cornell University Press.

Index

ISIDORE OKPEWHO, who was for many years Professor of English at the University of Ibadan and more recently Visiting Professor of English at Harvard University, is currently Chair of Afro-American and African Studies at the State University of New York, Binghamton. He is the author of *The Epic in Africa* and *Myth in Africa* and the editor of *The Heritage of African Poetry* and *The Oral Performance in Africa*. He has also published two novels, *The Victims* and *The Last Duty*.